Preventing Bluetooth and Wireless Attacks in IoMT Healthcare Systems is a comprehensive companion for anyone in healthcare. The insights you gain here will enhance your understanding and help drive the mission to create a safer, more secure healthcare environment for everyone.

—Tom Brays
Cybersecurity Analyst and Technical Editor

Preventing Bluetooth and Wireless Attacks in IoMT Healthcare Systems is a masterful guide for navigating the challenges of securing healthcare environments, from physical spaces to digital systems. It empowers leaders to protect what matters most. Worth a read for anyone committed to advancing the safety and integrity of our healthcare institutions.

—Robert Blake
President, E1

I've worked in healthcare for over 30 years and *Preventing Bluetooth and Wireless Attacks in IoMT Healthcare Systems* is necessary reading.

—Jean Dwyer
RN and Clinical Educator in Labor & Delivery

Preventing Bluetooth and Wireless Attacks in IoMT Healthcare Systems is vital for anyone navigating the intersection of healthcare and cybersecurity. With real-world insight and practical strategies, I can confidently say it belongs on every security leader's shelf.

—T. Mills
Chief Information Security Officer and Author

I highly recommend reading as it illustrates the importance of cybersecurity in healthcare, ethical concerns, and how devastating life can be without it.

—Deb Martin
Privacy and Security Advisor

Preventing Bluetooth and Wireless Attacks in IoMT Healthcare Systems unpacks the complexities of technologies in healthcare with a playbook of security strategies.

—Renee Vogley
Director, Business Operations at Cardinal Health

Preventing Bluetooth and Wireless Attacks in IoMT Healthcare Systems tackles Bluetooth and wireless communication vulnerabilities within connected medical device infrastructures. Moreover, it offers practical mitigation strategies such as encryption, secure device pairing, continuous network monitoring, and multifactor authentication—solutions that align with modern cybersecurity best practices. Its clear structure makes it accessible to both technical professionals and nontechnical audiences.

—Pam Kennedy
Security Compliance Auditor and Technical Editor

Whether you're fortifying infrastructure or ensuring compliance in 2025's stricter regulatory requirements, *Preventing Bluetooth and Wireless Attacks in IoMT Healthcare Systems* is an indispensable tool.

—Kevin Knapp
Sr. Cybersecurity Engineer

John has done a phenomenal job creating a comprehensive treatise on IoMT threat management. This is worth a read for anyone dealing with the deployment and operational use of technology in healthcare. He adeptly covers the technical security challenges but does not stop there. Healthcare administrators, clinical staff, support, and even patients will find this book invaluable. Join John on the journey as he digs into the overall threat landscape, enumerating indicators of threat and attack while offering crucial guidance on best practices, security testing, policy, and response.

—Steve Nardone
Division Chief and Head of the Trusted Product
Evaluation Program at the NSA
Sr. Dir. Security and Compliance, Ret.

Preventing Bluetooth and Wireless Attacks in IoMT Healthcare Systems

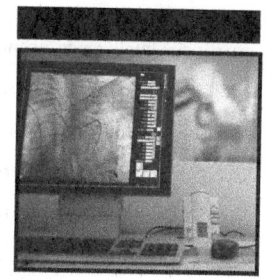

Preventing Bluetooth and Wireless Attacks in IoMT Healthcare Systems

John Chirillo

WILEY

Copyright © 2025 by John Wiley & Sons, Inc. All rights reserved, including rights for text and data mining and training of artificial intelligence technologies or similar technologies.

Published by John Wiley & Sons, Inc., Hoboken, New Jersey.

Published simultaneously in Canada and the United Kingdom.

ISBNs: 9781394349418 (Paperback), 9781394349432 (ePDF), 9781394349425 (ePub)

No part of this publication may be reproduced, stored in a retrieval system, or transmitted in any form or by any means, electronic, mechanical, photocopying, recording, scanning, or otherwise, except as permitted under Section 107 or 108 of the 1976 United States Copyright Act, without either the prior written permission of the Publisher, or authorization through payment of the appropriate per-copy fee to the Copyright Clearance Center, Inc., 222 Rosewood Drive, Danvers, MA 01923, (978) 750-8400, fax (978) 750-4470, or on the web at www.copyright.com. Requests to the Publisher for permission should be addressed to the Permissions Department, John Wiley & Sons, Inc., 111 River Street, Hoboken, NJ 07030, (201) 748-6011, fax (201) 748-6008, or online at http://www.wiley.com/go/permission.

The manufacturer's authorized representative according to the EU General Product Safety Regulation is Wiley-VCH GmbH, Boschstr. 12, 69469 Weinheim, Germany, e-mail: Product_Safety@wiley.com.

Trademarks: Wiley and the Wiley logo are trademarks or registered trademarks of John Wiley & Sons, Inc. and/or its affiliates in the United States and other countries and may not be used without written permission. Bluetooth is registered trademark of Bluetooth Sig, Inc. All other trademarks are the property of their respective owners. John Wiley & Sons, Inc. is not associated with any product or vendor mentioned in this book.

Limit of Liability/Disclaimer of Warranty: While the publisher and author have used their best efforts in preparing this book, they make no representations or warranties with respect to the accuracy or completeness of the contents of this book and specifically disclaim any implied warranties of merchantability or fitness for a particular purpose. No warranty may be created or extended by sales representatives or written sales materials. The advice and strategies contained herein may not be suitable for your situation. You should consult with a professional where appropriate. Further, readers should be aware that websites listed in this work may have changed or disappeared between when this work was written and when it is read. Neither the publisher nor author shall be liable for any loss of profit or any other commercial damages, including but not limited to special, incidental, consequential, or other damages.

For general information on our other products and services or for technical support, please contact our Customer Care Department within the United States at (800) 762-2974, outside the United States at (317) 572-3993 or fax (317) 572-4002. For product technical support, you can find answers to frequently asked questions or reach us via live chat at https://support.wiley.com.

If you believe you've found a mistake in this book, please bring it to our attention by emailing our reader support team at wileysupport@wiley.com with the subject line "Possible Book Errata Submission."

Wiley also publishes its books in a variety of electronic formats. Some content that appears in print may not be available in electronic formats. For more information about Wiley products, visit our web site at www.wiley.com.

Library of Congress Control Number: 2025934397

Cover image: © sudok1/Getty Images
Cover design: Wiley

SKY10105696_051625

About the Author

John Chirillo, an accomplished and published programmer and author, has written numerous influential books on cybersecurity, ethical hacking, and IT compliance. His writings are celebrated for their ability to demystify intricate technical concepts, making them accessible to professionals and enthusiasts alike. With decades of hands-on experience, John has built a career that seamlessly integrates the art of ethical hacking with the science of IT governance. His work ensures that businesses stay ahead in an ever-evolving threat landscape.

About the Technical Editors

Stephen Nardone has been involved in almost every aspect of information security for over 40 years. This includes systems security, operations security, telecommunications security, testing, evaluation, and program security. He began his career at the National Security Agency, where he spent 15 years supporting the NSA's mission in various challenging roles. He was division chief and head of the Trusted Product Evaluation Program at the NSA, responsible for executing security evaluations against DoD Standard 5200.28 and the "Rainbow" series of documents (Orange, Red, and Lavender Books). The Orange Book, *DOD 5200.28-STD, The Department of Defense Trusted Computer System Evaluation Criteria*, published in December 1985, set the standard for computer systems security evaluations.

Stephen became the chief technology and security officer for the Commonwealth of Massachusetts, eventually leading to his role as senior director of the Security Center of Excellence at Connection. He is now enjoying retirement while staying engaged in the evolving world of cybersecurity.

Pamela Kennedy has over 20 years of experience in IT service management (ITSM), cybersecurity, compliance, and IT audit. She has developed deep expertise in government, healthcare, and financial services. Pamela specializes in cybersecurity, auditing, and regulatory compliance, providing assurance and advisory services to organizations looking to strengthen or expand their internal controls to meet regulatory requirements. Her experience spans cyber policy and risk analysis, including information security, protection of critical national infrastructure, IT operations, government regulatory assessments, control design, IT compliance, governance, and incident response. She has led initiatives to help organizations align their IT policies, security protocols, and operational strategies with industry best practices and regulatory mandates.

Acknowledgments

First and foremost, I want to express my heartfelt thanks to my family and friends for their unwavering support and patience throughout the writing process. This is especially true for my wife, Kristi, and son, Conner. Your understanding during long nights and busy weekends has been invaluable.

I am profoundly grateful to my cybersecurity and healthcare IT colleagues, who have shared their knowledge and experiences.

I want to acknowledge the contributions of the ethical hacking community, whose responsible disclosure of vulnerabilities has been crucial in advancing IoMT security. Your work continues to be a driving force in improving the safety of medical devices.

My gratitude extends to the legal and ethics experts who provided invaluable insights into the complex regulatory landscape of healthcare technology. Your guidance has been essential in addressing this field's critical legal and ethical considerations.

I am grateful to my publisher, Wiley, for believing in the importance of this project and providing the platform to share this critical information with the broader community. A special note of thanks goes to the managing editor, Navin Vijayakumar; acquisitions editor, James Minatel; editorial assistant, Annie Melnick; and project manager, Brad Jones, whose keen eyes and insightful suggestions have greatly improved the clarity and structure of this book. Also, to my technical editors and reviewers, Stephen Nardone and Pamela Kennedy, your expertise has been instrumental in making complex topics accessible to a diverse readership.

Lastly, I want to thank my readers—the cybersecurity professionals, healthcare leadership, IT specialists, and experts who protect our medical systems. Your dedication to securing the Internet of Medical Things inspired me to write this book. I hope the knowledge shared here will support your crucial work.

I sincerely thank everyone who has contributed, directly or indirectly, to the realization of this book. This work is a testament to the collaborative spirit of the cybersecurity and healthcare communities, which are united to create a safer digital healthcare environment for all.

Contents at a Glance

Preface		xxvii
Foreword		xxix
Part I	**Foundation**	**1**
Chapter 1	Introduction to IoMT in Healthcare	3
Chapter 2	The Evolving Landscape of Wireless Technologies in Medical Devices	23
Chapter 3	Introduction to Bluetooth and Wi-Fi in Healthcare	46
Part II	**Attack Vectors**	**65**
Chapter 4	Bluetooth Vulnerabilities, Tools, and Mitigation Planning	67
Chapter 5	Wi-Fi and Other Wireless Protocol Vulnerabilities	104
Chapter 6	Man-in-the-Middle Attacks on Medical Devices	161
Chapter 7	Replay and Spoofing Attacks in IoMT	196
Chapter 8	Denial of Service in Wireless Medical Networks	208
Part III	**Case Studies and Real-World Scenarios**	**227**
Chapter 9	Pacemaker Hacking	229
Chapter 10	Insulin Pump Vulnerabilities and Exploits	247
Chapter 11	Attack Vector Trends and Hospital Network Breaches with IoMT Devices	263

Chapter 12	Wearable Medical Device Security Challenges	282
Part IV	Detection and Prevention	295
Chapter 13	Intrusion Detection and Prevention for IoMT Networks	297
Chapter 14	Machine Learning Approaches to Wireless Attack Detection	338
Chapter 15	Secure Communication Protocols for Medical Devices	366
Chapter 16	Best Practices for IoMT Device Security	391
Part V	Future Trends and Emerging Threats	441
Chapter 17	5G and Beyond and Implications for IoMT Security	443
Chapter 18	Quantum Computing in Medical Device Security	459
Chapter 19	AI-Driven Attacks and Defenses in Healthcare	476
Part VI	Legal and Ethical Considerations	491
Chapter 20	Regulatory Frameworks for IoMT Security	493
Chapter 21	Guidelines for Ethical Hacking in Healthcare	510
Conclusion		525
Index		527

Contents

Preface		xxvii
Foreword		xxix
Part I	**Foundation**	**1**
Chapter 1	**Introduction to IoMT in Healthcare**	**3**
	What Is IoMT in Healthcare?	4
	Impact of IoMT on Healthcare	5
	Continuous Patient Monitoring	5
	Remote Medical Support	7
	Seamless Healthcare System Integration	10
	Data-Driven Insights	12
	Early Disease Detection	14
	Resource Optimization	14
	How IoMT Works in Healthcare and Its Applications	16
	Challenges and Considerations in IoMT Adoption	17
	Best Practices for IoMT Security	18
	Future Trends in IoMT	20
	Key Takeaways of IoMT in Healthcare	22
Chapter 2	**The Evolving Landscape of Wireless Technologies in Medical Devices**	**23**
	Overview of Wireless Technologies in Medical Devices	24
	Bluetooth	25
	Wi-Fi	26
	Zigbee	26
	LoRaWAN	27
	Cellular	27
	RFID	28
	Near Field Communication	28

Contents

Benefits of Wireless Technologies in Medical Devices	29
Introduction to Risks in the Applications of Wireless Technologies in Medical Devices	31
Wireless Remote Patient Monitoring Risks	31
Security Risks in Telemedicine	33
Implantable Medical Device Security Concerns	35
Targeted RFID in Hospital Equipment Management	35
Vulnerable Smart Pill Bottles and Dispensers	36
Threats to Surgical and Imaging Systems	37
Wireless Integration Challenges and Considerations	38
Emerging Wireless Trends and Future Directions	40
Regulatory Landscape for Wireless Medical Devices	41
Best Practices for Wireless Technology Implementation	43
Key Takeaways of Wireless Technologies in Healthcare	44

Chapter 3 Introduction to Bluetooth and Wi-Fi in Healthcare — 46

Bluetooth Communication in Healthcare	47
Understanding Bluetooth Technology	48
Bluetooth Classic	48
Bluetooth LE	49
Understanding BLE Profiles and Services	51
Applications and Advantages of Bluetooth in Healthcare	52
Wi-Fi Communication in Healthcare	52
Understanding Wi-Fi Technology in Healthcare	53
Applications and Advantages of Wi-Fi in Healthcare	56
Overview of Bluetooth and Wi-Fi Security Risks	58
Mitigation Concepts	60
Overview of AI in Detecting and Protecting Against Bluetooth and Wi-Fi Attacks	61
Key Takeaways of Bluetooth and Wi-Fi	64

Part II Attack Vectors — 65

Chapter 4 Bluetooth Vulnerabilities, Tools, and Mitigation Planning — 67

Introduction to Bluetooth Security	68
Pairing and Authentication	70
Encryption	70
Privacy Features	70
Challenges of Bluetooth Security	71
Common Bluetooth Vulnerabilities	71
Data Interception	71
Impersonation Attacks	72
Man-in-the-Middle Attacks	75
BLUFFS	76
Bluesnarfing	79
Denial of Service	80
Bluejacking	81
Bluetooth Remote Code Execution	81

	Bluetooth Hacking Tools	82
	Overview of Popular Linux Distributions	83
	Flipper Zero	87
	BlueZ	88
	Bluelog	90
	btCrawler	92
	BTScanner	93
	Ubertooth One	94
	BtleJack	95
	GATTacker	96
	BlueMaho	98
	HCIDump	98
	PyBluez	99
	Mitigating Bluetooth Vulnerabilities	101
	Example Case Studies and Lessons Learned	102
	Key Takeaways of Bluetooth Vulnerabilities and Exploits	103
Chapter 5	**Wi-Fi and Other Wireless Protocol Vulnerabilities**	**104**
	Introduction to Wi-Fi Security	105
	WPA: The Gold Standard in Wi-Fi Security	105
	Opportunistic Wireless Encryption	105
	Protected Management Frames	107
	Building a Resilient Network Architecture with Segmentation	107
	Why Network Segmentation Matters	108
	Key Technologies Enabling Segmentation	108
	Strong Authentication and Access Control	108
	Wi-Fi 6/6E Security Solutions	110
	Secure IoMT Device Management	110
	Challenges for Device Management	110
	Common Wi-Fi Vulnerabilities with Examples and Case Studies	111
	Unencrypted Data Transmission	111
	Weak Authentication Protocols	112
	Rogue Access Points and Evil Twin Attacks	112
	Lack of Network Segmentation	113
	Outdated Firmware and Insecure IoMT Devices	113
	Deauthentication and Disassociation Attacks	114
	Phishing Through Wi-Fi Networks	114
	Captive Portal Attack	115
	How to Mitigate Captive Portal Attacks	116
	PEAP Exchange Vulnerabilities and Attacks	117
	Understanding PEAP Exchange Vulnerabilities	117
	How to Mitigate PEAP Vulnerabilities	119
	Wi-Fi Hacking Tools	120
	Aircrack-ng	120

Bettercap	122
Strengths of Bettercap	124
Limitations of Bettercap	124
Key Takeaways Regarding Bettercap	124
coWPAtty	125
Example Penetration Test on a WPA2 Wi-Fi Network	126
Strengths of coWPAtty	127
Limitations of coWPAtty	127
Key Takeaways Regarding coWPAtty	127
Fern Wi-Fi Cracker	128
Example of Fern Wi-Fi Cracker in Action	129
Strengths of Fern Wi-Fi Cracker	130
Limitations of Fern Wi-Fi Cracker	130
Key Takeaways Regarding Fern Wi-Fi Cracker	130
Hashcat	131
Cracking a WPA2 Wi-Fi Password Example	132
Strengths of Hashcat	133
Limitations of Hashcat	133
Hashcat Key Takeaways	133
Wifite	134
Strengths of Wifite	137
Limitations of Wifite	138
Wifite Key Takeaways	138
Kismet	138
Strengths of Kismet	140
Limitations of Kismet	141
Kismet Key Takeaways	141
Reaver	141
Strengths of Reaver	144
Limitations of Reaver	144
Reaver Key Takeaways	145
STORM	145
WiFi Pineapple	146
Strengths of WiFi Pineapple	148
Limitations of WiFi Pineapple	148
WiFi Pineapple Key Takeaways	148
WiFi-Pumpkin	149
Steps During a Clinic Coffee Shop Wi-Fi Network Attack	149
WiFi-Pumpkin Key Takeaways	150
Wifiphisher	151
Steps During a Corporate Wi-Fi Network Attack	151
Strengths of Wifiphisher	152
Limitations of Wifiphisher	153
Wifiphisher Key Takeaways	153
Wireshark	153
Strengths of Wireshark	155
Limitations of Wireshark	155

	Wireshark Key Takeaways	156
	The Evolution of Tools	156
	Modern Wireless Operational Guide for Healthcare Compliance	156
	Defining the Sensitive Data Environment	157
	Key Challenges in Securing Healthcare Wireless Networks	157
	Modern Solutions for Wireless Security and Compliance	157
	Operational Best Practices	158
	Additional Compliance Recommendations	159
	Key Takeaways for Healthcare Compliance	159
	Key Takeaways of Wi-Fi Vulnerabilities and Exploits	159
Chapter 6	**Man-in-the-Middle Attacks on Medical Devices**	**161**
	Understanding Medical Device Man-in-the-Middle Attacks	162
	Types of MITM Attacks	162
	Real-World Implications of MITM Attacks on Medical Devices	163
	Key Vulnerabilities Enabling MITM Attacks	164
	Exploits and Other Potential Impacts of MITM Attacks on Medical Devices	167
	Data Theft and Privacy Violations	167
	Device Manipulation and Patient Safety Risks	167
	System Downtime and Operational Disruption	168
	Challenges in Securing Medical Devices	168
	Mitigation Strategies for Healthcare Organizations	169
	Leverage Strong Encryption for Healthcare Communications	169
	Strengthen Wireless Network Encryption	169
	Secure Communication for Medical Devices	170
	Encrypt Data in Transit Across All Systems	170
	Implement Robust Device Authentication	171
	Secure Pairing with Strong Authentication Mechanisms	171
	Mutual Authentication for Devices and Central Systems	172
	Enforce Multifactor Authentication for Administrative Access	172
	Integrate Role-Based Access Control	173
	Continuous Monitoring and Authentication Validation	173
	Deploy Network Segmentation and Isolation	174
	Ensure Regular Updates and Patching	176
	Establish a Comprehensive Patch Management Program	176
	Collaborate Closely with Medical Device Vendors	177
	Implement Proactive Vulnerability Management	177
	Overcome Challenges with Legacy Systems	178
	Audit and Monitor Patch Compliance	178
	Deploy Advanced Monitoring and Intrusion Detection	179
	Using Artificial Intelligence to Analyze MITM Attacks	180
	Integrated Monitoring for IoT and Connected Medical Devices	181

	Conduct Training and Awareness Programs	182
	Collaborate with Vendors to Enhance Device Security	186
	Use Case for AI-Driven Detection	189
	Key Benefits of a Comprehensive Mitigation Strategy	190
	Case Study of a MITM Attack on Infusion Pumps	190
	The Role of Vendors and Regulators	192
	Key Takeaways of Man-in-the-Middle Attacks on Medical Devices	194
Chapter 7	**Replay and Spoofing Attacks in IoMT**	**196**
	Understanding Replay Attacks in IoMT	197
	How Replay Attacks Work in IoMT Systems	197
	Implications of Replay Attacks in Healthcare	198
	Use Case of a Replay Attack on an Infusion Pump	199
	Other Examples of Replay Attacks in IoMT	200
	Strategies for Mitigation of Replay Attacks	200
	What Is a Spoofing Attack in IoMT?	202
	How Spoofing Attacks Exploit IoMT Vulnerabilities	202
	Weak Authentication	202
	Lack of Secure Communication Protocols	203
	Insecure Device Pairing	203
	Insufficient Device Hardening	204
	Lack of Network Segmentation	204
	Real-World Implications of Spoofing Attacks	204
	Mitigation Strategies for Spoofing Attacks in IoMT	205
	Key Takeaways of Replay and Spoofing Attacks in IoMT	206
Chapter 8	**Denial of Service in Wireless Medical Networks**	**208**
	Understanding DoS Attacks	208
	Common Types of DoS Attacks, Targets, and Device Impact	209
	Flooding Attacks	209
	Jamming Attacks	210
	Battery Drain Attacks	211
	Deauthentication Attacks	211
	Amplification Attacks	212
	Distributed Denial-of-Service Attacks	213
	Impact of DoS Attacks on Healthcare Operations	213
	Common Vulnerabilities That Enable DoS Attacks in Wireless Medical Networks	214
	Insecure Wireless Communication Protocols	214
	Lack of Device Authentication and Authorization	214
	Limited Resource Capacity	215
	Legacy Systems and Outdated Software	215
	Overloaded Wireless Networks	216
	More on the Impact of These Vulnerabilities	216
	Mitigation Strategies for Denial of Service Attacks	217
	Implement Strong Network Segmentation and Isolation	217

	Deploy Intrusion Detection and Prevention Systems	217
	Prioritize Strong Device Authentication and Authorization	218
	Upgrade to Resilient Wireless Infrastructure	219
	Monitor for Anomalies and Implement Rate Limiting	219
	Consider DDoS Protection Services	219
	Comparison Between DoS and DDoS Attacks in Healthcare	222
	Ensure Regular Updates and Patch Management	223
	Conduct Security Training and Awareness Programs	223
	Perform Regular Network Audits and Penetration Testing	224
	Key Takeaways from DoS in Wireless Medical Networks	224
Part III	**Case Studies and Real-World Scenarios**	**227**
Chapter 9	**Pacemaker Hacking**	**229**
	Understanding Pacemaker Technology and Its Risks and Limitations	230
	How Does the Heart Normally Function?	230
	What Is a Pacemaker?	230
	Components of a Pacemaker	231
	How a Pacemaker Works	231
	How Is a Pacemaker Implanted?	232
	Risks and Limitations	233
	Pacemakers and Patient Quality of Life	233
	Understanding Vulnerabilities in Pacemakers in Today's Connected World	233
	Real-World Case Studies and Impact	235
	Ethical Hacking Demonstration	236
	ICD Study	238
	Barnaby Jack's Ethical Hacking Demonstration	239
	MedSec and St. Jude Medical Controversy	239
	FDA Pacemaker Recall	240
	Academic Demonstrations: 2018 Onward	240
	Medtronic's Paceart Optima System Risks: 2023	241
	The Impact of Pacemaker Vulnerabilities	241
	Strategies and Technologies to Mitigate Pacemaker Cybersecurity Risks	242
	Securing Wireless Communication with Strong Encryption	242
	Implementing Strong Authentication and Access Controls	242
	Regular Firmware Updates and Patch Management	243
	Monitoring for Intrusions and Anomalies	243
	Physical Security and Access Controls	243
	Vendor Accountability and Regulatory Compliance	244
	Raising Awareness and Training Healthcare Staff	244
	Building a Resilient Future for Pacemakers	244
	More on Consequences of Pacemaker Hacking	244
	Breaches of Patient Privacy	245
	Reputation Damage to Healthcare Providers	245
	Key Takeaways from Pacemaker Hacking	245

Chapter 10	**Insulin Pump Vulnerabilities and Exploits**	**247**
	Understanding Insulin Pumps and Their Vulnerabilities	249
	Current Vulnerabilities in Insulin Pumps	250
	Vulnerability Testing	251
	Implications and Real-World Scenarios of Insulin Pump Exploits	258
	Security Research	259
	FDA Warning on Insulin Pumps	259
	Ransomware Attack on a Hospital Network Impacting Insulin Pumps	260
	Mitigation Strategies for Insulin Pump Security	260
	Education and Training for Patients and Healthcare Providers	261
	Key Takeaways from Insulin Pump Vulnerabilities and Exploits	261
Chapter 11	**Attack Vector Trends and Hospital Network Breaches with IoMT Devices**	**263**
	Understanding the IoMT Risk Landscape	264
	Key Vulnerabilities of IoMT and Healthcare Network Breaches	264
	Anatomy of a Healthcare Cyber Attack	265
	Attack Vector Trends and Landscape	268
	Attack Vector Trends Takeaways	271
	Malware Analysis for Digital Forensics Investigations	272
	Key Tools and Challenges	273
	Findings of a Healthcare Security Event	274
	Technical Analysis	275
	Post-Event Lessons Learned	280
	Key Takeaways from Hospital Network Breaches with IoMT Devices	280
Chapter 12	**Wearable Medical Device Security Challenges**	**282**
	The Rise of Wearable Medical Devices	282
	Key Benefits of Wearable Devices	283
	Security Challenges of Wearable Medical Devices	283
	Key Vulnerabilities in Wearable Medical Devices	284
	Data Privacy Risks	285
	Regulatory and Compliance Challenges	286
	New Trends and Threats in Wearable Device Security	289
	AI-Powered Attacks	289
	IoMT Botnets	289
	Data Poisoning	290
	Supply Chain Exploits	290
	Proactive Measures for Mitigating Wearable Device Threats	290
	How AI Can Help	291
	Key Takeaways from Security Challenges of Wearable Medical Devices	294

Part IV	**Detection and Prevention**	**295**
Chapter 13	**Intrusion Detection and Prevention for IoMT Networks**	**297**
	Introduction to Intrusion Detection and Prevention Systems for IoMT	297
	Understanding IoMT Ecosystems	299
	What Is Intrusion Detection and Prevention in IoMT Environments?	299
	Case Study: Implementing IDPS in a Healthcare Environment	302
	IDPS Solutions	304
	Cisco Secure IPS	306
	Trend Micro TippingPoint	309
	Check Point IPS	312
	Palo Alto Networks Threat Prevention	315
	OSSEC HIDS	319
	Snort	323
	Suricata	327
	Best Practices for IoMT IDPS Deployment	331
	Modern Innovations in IoMT IDS	333
	AI-Powered Detection	333
	Behavioral Analytics	333
	Edge-Based IDSs	334
	Threat Intelligence Integration	334
	Deception Technology	334
	Emerging Trends in IoMT IDS	336
	Future Directions in IoMT IDS	336
	Key Takeaways from IDPS for IoMT Networks	336
Chapter 14	**Machine Learning Approaches to Wireless Attack Detection**	**338**
	Introduction to Machine Learning for Wireless Attack Detection	339
	Why ML Is Critical for Wireless Attack Detection	339
	How Machine Learning Enhances Wireless Attack Detection	341
	Anomaly Detection	341
	Feature Extraction and Classification	341
	Real-Time Analysis	342
	Attack Prediction	342
	Machine Learning Feature Engineering for Wireless Attack Detection	342
	Types of Machine Learning Techniques	344
	Machine Learning Applications in Healthcare and IoMT	350
	Securing Wearable Devices	350
	Rogue Access Point Detection	351
	Preventing Denial-of-Service Attacks	351
	Bluetooth and Zigbee Security	352
	Enhanced Network Segmentation	352
	Challenges in Applying ML to Wireless Security in IoMT	352

Future Directions of Machine Learning for Attack Detection
   in Healthcare 356
    Federated Learning 356
    Explainable AI 356
    Edge AI 357
    Machine Learning Integration with Existing Security
      Infrastructure 357
    Integration with Zero Trust Architectures 359
    Future Research Directions for Machine Learning in
      Wireless Security 359
Ethical and Legal Considerations for Machine Learning
   in Wireless Security 361
Machine Learning Case Studies in Healthcare 362
Key Takeaways from Machine Learning Approaches
   to Wireless Attack Detection 364

Chapter 15 **Secure Communication Protocols for Medical Devices** **366**
Importance of Secure Communication in Medical Devices 366
Key Security Requirements for Medical Device
   Communication 368
Secure Communication Protocols for Medical Devices 371
Encryption Algorithms and Key Management 373
    Authentication Mechanisms 375
    Multifactor Authentication 375
    Biometric Authentication 375
    Digital Certificates 376
    OAuth 2.0 and OpenID Connect for Authorization 376
    RADIUS and TACACS+ for Network Device Authentication 376
Secure Device Pairing and Onboarding 377
    Out-of-Band Authentication Methods 377
    QR Code-Based Pairing 377
    Near Field Communication for Secure Setup 378
    Bluetooth Low Energy Secure Connections 378
    The Importance of Secure Pairing and Onboarding 379
Regulatory Compliance and Standards 379
    FDA Guidance on Cybersecurity for Medical Devices 379
    HIPAA Security Rule Requirements 380
    EU Medical Device Regulation (MDR) 380
    ISO/IEC 27001 Information Security Management 380
    IEC 62304 Medical Device Software Life Cycle Processes 381
    Key Points Regarding Regulatory Compliance 381
Challenges in Implementing Secure Communication Protocols 381
Best Practices for Secure Medical Device Communication 383
Emerging Technologies and Future Trends 384
Secure Communication Strategies 386
Ethical Considerations 387
Key Takeaways from Secure Communication Protocols
   for Medical Devices 389

Chapter 16	**Best Practices for IoMT Device Security**	**391**
	Endpoint Security Best Practices	392
	Network Security Best Practices	393
	Perimeter Security Best Practices	394
	Cloud Security Best Practices	395
	Network Segmentation	396
	Strong Authentication and Access Controls	397
	Regular Updates and Patching	401
	AI-Powered Monitoring and Analytics	403
	Zero Trust Security Model	405
	Encryption and Data Protection	407
	Asset Inventory and Management	409
	Vendor Management and Third-Party Risk Assessment	411
	Compliance with Regulatory Standards	414
	Continuous Monitoring and Incident Response	417
	Employee Training and Awareness	420
	Secure Device Onboarding and Decommissioning	422
	Physical Security Measures	425
	Backup and Recovery	428
	Secure Communication Protocols	430
	Data Minimization and Retention Policies	433
	Cybersecurity Insurance	435
	Regular Security Audits	436
	Key Takeaways of Best Practices for IoMT Device Security	438
Part V	**Future Trends and Emerging Threats**	**441**
Chapter 17	**5G and Beyond and Implications for IoMT Security**	**443**
	Introduction to 5G and Beyond Technologies	443
	Impact of 5G on IoMT	445
	Security Implications for IoMT	447
	Regulatory Considerations	450
	Future Research Directions	455
	Industry Collaboration and Knowledge Sharing	456
	Key Takeaways of 5G and Beyond and Implications for IoMT Security	458
Chapter 18	**Quantum Computing in Medical Device Security**	**459**
	Fundamentals of Quantum Computing	459
	Potential Applications in Medical Device Security	461
	Challenges Posed by Quantum Computing	462
	Quantum Attack on IoMT Firmware	463
	Stage 1: Interception	464
	Stage 2: Decryption	464
	Stage 3: Modification	465
	Stage 4: Re-signing	465
	Stage 5: Installation and Damage Assessment	465
	Quantum-Resistant Cryptography for Medical Devices	466
	Quantum Sensing and Metrology in Medical Devices	467

	Quantum-Safe Network Protocols for Medical Devices	468
	Regulatory and Standardization Efforts	469
	Ethical and Privacy Considerations	470
	Future Research Directions	472
	Preparing the Healthcare Industry for the Quantum Era	473
	Key Takeaways from Quantum Computing in Medical Device Security	475
Chapter 19	**AI-Driven Attacks and Defenses in Healthcare**	**476**
	Types of AI-Driven Attacks in Healthcare	476
	Impact of AI-Driven Attacks on Healthcare	478
	AI-Driven Defenses in Healthcare	480
	Challenges in Implementing AI-Driven Defenses	484
	Future Trends in AI-Driven Healthcare Cybersecurity	486
	Best Practices for Healthcare Organizations	488
	Key Takeaways from AI-Driven Attacks and Defenses in Healthcare	489
Part VI	**Legal and Ethical Considerations**	**491**
Chapter 20	**Regulatory Frameworks for IoMT Security**	**493**
	Key Regulatory Bodies and Frameworks	493
	Legal Considerations	495
	Ethical Considerations	498
	Challenges in Regulatory Framework Development	500
	Best Practices for Regulatory Compliance	502
	Future Trends in IoMT Security Regulation	504
	Examples of Benefits from Regulation Implementation	505
	Recommendations for Stakeholders	507
	Key Takeaways from Regulatory Frameworks for IoMT Security	509
Chapter 21	**Guidelines for Ethical Hacking in Healthcare**	**510**
	Importance of Ethical Hacking in Healthcare	510
	Scope of Ethical Hacking in Healthcare	512
	Legal and Regulatory Considerations	513
	Ethical Boundaries and Guidelines	515
	Best Practices for Ethical Hacking in Healthcare	516
	Challenges in Healthcare Ethical Hacking	519
	Emerging Trends and Future Considerations	520
	Training and Certification for Healthcare Ethical Hackers	521
	Specialized Certifications	521
	Continuous Education	522
	Case Studies	523
	Successful Ethical Hacking Engagements	523
	Key Takeaways from Ethical Hacking in Healthcare	524
Conclusion		**525**
Index		**527**

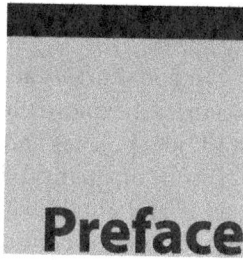

Preface

In today's world, healthcare and technology are deeply intertwined, transforming how we diagnose, treat, and care for patients. At the center of this transformation are connected medical devices—smart tools that collect, share, and analyze health data in real time. These devices improve daily lives, from wearable heart monitors to robotic surgical systems. But with this progress comes a growing challenge: ensuring the security of the technology we increasingly rely on. The Internet of Medical Things (IoMT) has introduced new risks as cyber threats targeting healthcare systems become more sophisticated. This book was born from the need to understand these evolving risks and offer practical solutions to protect the devices that keep us healthy. I hope to shed light on cybersecurity's critical role in our connected health systems through this book's use cases and case studies and make complex topics accessible.

Part I explores the rapid rise of connected medical devices and the technologies behind them. It explains why securing these devices is essential—not just for technical reasons but also for the safety and well-being of patients and healthcare providers.

Part II examines the attack vectors that threaten IoMT systems. I analyze how malicious actors exploit vulnerabilities in Bluetooth and other wireless protocols standard in healthcare, equipping defenders with a deeper understanding of these threats.

Part III brings theory to life with case studies that show how security breaches have impacted healthcare institutions and patients. These examples underscore why cybersecurity must be a top priority.

Part IV focuses on solutions and best practices for securing IoMT devices and preventing attacks. I highlight the latest advancements in safeguarding healthcare technology, from artificial intelligence to advanced encryption methods.

Part V looks ahead to emerging trends in IoMT security, including 5G/6G and quantum computing. These technologies offer new opportunities for innovation—but also create new risks. I discuss what they mean for the future of secure healthcare systems.

To end, Part VI addresses the legal, ethical, and regulatory landscape of IoMT security. I explore the responsibilities of healthcare providers and manufacturers and how policies and privacy laws are evolving to protect patient data.

Securing medical devices is not just a technical challenge; it's a matter of patient safety and public health. I hope this book sparks greater awareness, better security practices, and continued innovation in protecting healthcare environments. As healthcare technology evolves, so too will the threats it faces. This book is just the beginning of an ongoing conversation. I encourage you to keep exploring, asking questions, and staying informed. Together, we can build a future where connected healthcare delivers its full potential—securely and safely.

Finally, I transformed several attack vectors into a story to help readers visualize the impact. Suppose you're interested in a fast-paced fictional depiction of the latest in healthcare attack vectors. In that case, you can find my novel, *Silent Intrusions*, in various marketplaces online or scan the following QR code:

John Chirillo

Who Should Read This Book

This book is for anyone interested in the intersection of the Internet of Things (IoT), healthcare, and security threats. It is especially relevant to cybersecurity professionals, healthcare leadership, IT specialists, and experts protecting our medical systems, as it suggests exploring attack techniques, their impact, and mitigation strategies.

Foreword

This book is a vital resource for anyone involved in the healthcare ecosystem. With clarity and depth, John begins by laying out the foundational elements of healthcare technologies and then guides readers through the complex landscape of cyber threats that put these systems at risk. Along the way, he demystifies how attacks unfold and, more importantly, how they can be prevented.

What makes this work stand out is its practical relevance. John doesn't just talk about the "how"; he talks about the "why" through real-world case studies that ground the concepts in reality. Whether you're a healthcare executive, IT professional, or security practitioner, you'll find the content accessible, actionable, and thought-provoking.

The book also looks ahead, equipping readers with an understanding of emerging innovations poised to shape the future of healthcare delivery and security. John addresses not just technical challenges but also the pressing legal and ethical questions that must be considered as our systems grow more interconnected and intelligent.

This is a timely and essential read, and it reflects John's deep commitment to creating a safer, more resilient healthcare environment. His insights are a call to action. Kudos to John for delivering a work that is both influential and inspiring.

—Tom Brays, cybersecurity analyst and technical editor

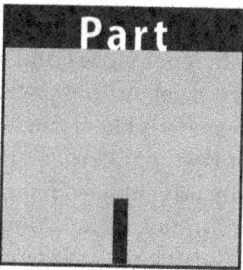

Part I

Foundation

The introduction of the Internet of Medical Things and the integration of wireless technologies have ushered in a new era in healthcare. These innovations promise to enhance patient care, improve operational efficiency, and enable seamless connectivity between medical devices, healthcare providers, and patients. Part I lays the groundwork by exploring the core concepts of IoMT and wireless technologies—their current capabilities, impact on healthcare delivery, and challenges.

Chapter 1 introduces IoMT and examines how connected medical devices are reshaping healthcare. From continuous patient monitoring to data-driven insights, it highlights how IoMT enhances patient outcomes, enables real-time care, and optimizes resource allocation. This chapter also traces the historical evolution of IoMT technologies and their growing role in building an interconnected healthcare ecosystem. Chapter 2 focuses on the wireless technologies that support IoMT, including Bluetooth, Wi-Fi, Zigbee, and LoRaWAN. These technologies enable efficient data exchange and continuous patient monitoring, introducing security risks and interoperability issues. This chapter explores wireless technologies' critical role in advancing healthcare while examining the vulnerabilities that healthcare organizations must address. Chapter 3 deeply explores the risks and security challenges of IoMT and wireless systems. As healthcare increasingly relies on connectivity, protecting sensitive patient data and ensuring device reliability are vital concerns. This chapter outlines how vulnerabilities can be exploited and emphasizes the need for robust security frameworks.

These chapters provide the foundation for understanding the complexities and risks inherent in IoMT and wireless healthcare technologies. Establishing this foundation is crucial. Addressing security risks without a solid understanding of the underlying systems is like trying to repair an engine without knowing how it works—ineffective at best, dangerous at worst. A clear understanding of these systems offers three key advantages. First, it provides context for identifying risks. IoMT and wireless technologies are complex, involving layers of devices, protocols, and data flows. It's difficult to pinpoint potential vulnerabilities that attackers may exploit without knowing how these components interact—how a Bluetooth-connected heart monitor communicates with hospital databases or how Wi-Fi enables real-time patient monitoring. Second, it allows for more effective risk mitigation. Not all threats carry the same weight; some may pose minor inconveniences, while others can jeopardize patient safety or expose sensitive healthcare data. A strong foundation helps prioritize these risks, ensuring resources are directed where needed rather than wasted on low-priority issues. Third, it builds adaptability to evolving threats. Cybersecurity is never static, and attackers are constantly developing new techniques. Understanding how systems operate makes it easier to anticipate vulnerabilities as technologies evolve. For example, recognizing how a wireless protocol handles authentication can help predict where attackers may focus their efforts in the future.

Finally, a firm grasp of foundational concepts bridges the gap between theory and practice. It's one thing to know what risks exist; it's another to apply that knowledge in a real-world healthcare setting. This foundational understanding ensures that security strategies are proactive and aligned with the specific needs and challenges of connected healthcare environments. As I move forward into discussions about identifying, exploiting, and mitigating risks, it's important to remember that the effectiveness of any strategy depends on how well we understand the systems we're working to protect. A solid foundation isn't just the starting point—it's the core that keeps our efforts grounded, focused, and effective.

CHAPTER 1

Introduction to IoMT in Healthcare

One of the most impactful changes in healthcare today is the rise of the Internet of Medical Things (IoMT). This chapter sets the stage for understanding how IoMT redefines patient care, operational efficiency, and healthcare innovation.

At its core, IoMT is about creating a connected ecosystem where smart devices like wearable fitness trackers, intelligent heart monitors, or even connected surgical equipment communicate seamlessly. These devices collect, share, and analyze data in real time, enabling healthcare providers to make informed, timely decisions. This isn't just technology for convenience; it's technology with the power to save lives and reduce costs.

This chapter begins by tracing IoMT's roots back to the 1990s. Simple remote monitoring and limited telehealth services have evolved into an ecosystem powered by wearables, smart sensors, and advanced data analytics. Today, IoMT is central to healthcare systems' innovation, offering solutions for real-time patient monitoring, personalized care plans, seamless sharing of patient information, and system integration.

One key impact of IoMT is continuous patient monitoring. Imagine tracking a patient's heart rate, blood pressure, or glucose levels 24/7. IoMT devices alert healthcare providers or caregivers when these metrics deviate from safe ranges, allowing immediate intervention. This capability is a game changer for chronic disease management and elderly care, where early detection can mean the difference between a minor adjustment and a major medical emergency.

Another transformative aspect of IoMT is its ability to support remote medical care. Patients in rural areas or those with mobility issues can now consult with specialists or manage chronic conditions without leaving their homes. Connected medical devices transmit critical health data directly to healthcare providers, enabling telemedicine services that are both effective and accessible.

This technology's impact isn't limited to patient care; it's also increasing the efficiency of healthcare systems. By integrating devices with electronic health records and hospital management systems, IoMT reduces redundancy, prevents errors, and accelerates diagnoses. For example, a wearable electrocardiogram (ECG) monitor can send real-time data to a cardiologist, enabling quicker and more accurate treatment decisions.

Data is another primary focus of IoMT. The devices don't just collect data; they generate insights. By analyzing patterns, they can detect early warning signs of illnesses or help personalize treatments. This data-driven approach opens new doors in precision medicine, where care is tailored to the individual rather than just the condition.

Of course, as this technology grows, so do its challenges. Data security and interoperability are key concerns, as are the ethical implications of who controls and benefits from this information. Addressing these challenges is vital to unlocking the full potential.

This chapter shows how IoMT is reshaping healthcare at every level, from patient monitoring and remote support to operational efficiency and groundbreaking insights. It's not just a trend; it's the future of connected care, empowering providers to deliver more innovative, safer, and personalized healthcare solutions.

What Is IoMT in Healthcare?

IoMT is paving the way for a new network of connected care that promises to improve patient outcomes, streamline healthcare delivery, and reduce costs. This network allows devices, like smart heart monitors or wearable fitness trackers, to communicate with each other, share data, and provide real-time insights into a patient's health. By making it easier to collect, analyze, and act on health information, these connected medical devices are helping doctors and healthcare providers make informed decisions and deliver more personalized care.

Based on my research, the idea behind the technology began in the 1990s, with early technologies that allowed for remote patient monitoring and basic telehealth services. Over time, as technology advanced, so did the possibilities (see Figure 1-1). Smaller, smarter devices and more powerful data tools emerged, leading to the rise of wearable health monitors and intelligent medical equipment. Today, IoMT is at the heart of healthcare innovation, offering new ways to monitor patients remotely, tailor treatments to individual needs, and make faster, data-driven decisions that improve patient outcomes.

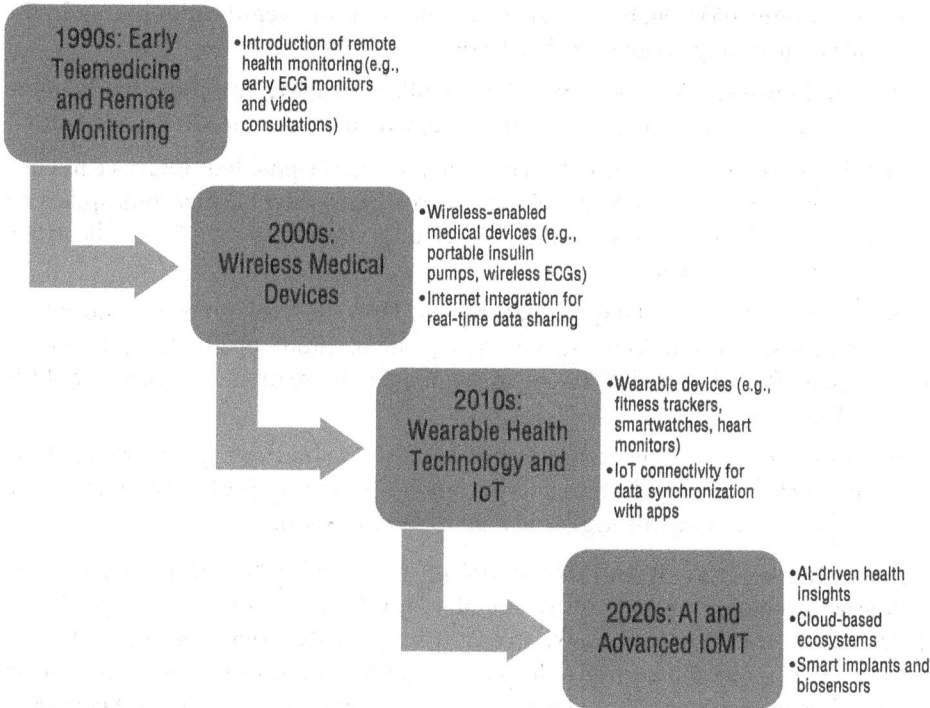

Figure 1-1: Evolution of IoMT in healthcare

Impact of IoMT on Healthcare

Integrating the IoMT in healthcare has far-reaching implications for patients, healthcare providers, and the healthcare system. Many examples of today's use cases are available. This section reviews some positive impacts on healthcare, including continuous patient monitoring, remote medical support, seamless healthcare system integration, data-driven insights, early disease detection, and resource optimization.

Continuous Patient Monitoring

IoMT devices allow for ongoing tracking of patients' vital signs and health parameters. Smart sensors can monitor various metrics such as blood pressure, glucose levels, and heart rate. The technology automatically alerts consumers, caregivers, or medical professionals of any irregularities, enabling prompt action and helping to reduce the risk of serious health complications.

Traditional healthcare models often rely on periodic check-ups or hospital visits to assess a patient's health. Still, IoMT modernizes this by providing real-time and ongoing vital signs and health parameters. This continuous monitoring is possible using smart sensors embedded in various devices, such as wearables, patches, and other connected medical equipment. The most consumed real-time vital sign monitoring includes the following health metrics:

- **Heart rate:** IoMT-enabled devices can monitor for irregularities like arrhythmias, indicating serious cardiac issues.
- **Blood pressure:** IoMT-enabled devices allow for early detection of hypertension or sudden drops in blood pressure, which can lead to stroke or fainting.
- **Glucose levels:** For patients with diabetes, IoMT-enabled devices can continuously track blood sugar levels, helping to prevent dangerous spikes or drops in glucose, and enabling timely intervention to avoid complications like a diabetic coma.
- **Respiratory rate and oxygen saturation:** These metrics can be monitored for patients with respiratory issues, such as asthma, chronic obstructive pulmonary disease (COPD), or COVID-19, to ensure timely treatment if breathing difficulties arise.
- **Temperature and hydration levels:** Monitoring body temperature for signs of infection or dehydration is especially important in post-surgery recovery or for elderly patients at risk of health deterioration.

One of the key benefits of this technology is its ability to automatically alert healthcare providers or caregivers when vital signs fall outside of safe ranges. These alerts are triggered in real time as soon as any irregularity is detected, whether it's a sudden spike in blood pressure, a drop in oxygen saturation, or an abnormal heart rhythm. Timely intervention is key as these alerts can be sent directly to healthcare professionals' mobile devices or monitoring stations, enabling them to act immediately without waiting for the next scheduled visit or a patient to report symptoms. According to some doctors, it's common for patients to misreport or misunderstand symptoms, whereas the technology is typically more accurate.

This capability is particularly valuable for high-risk patients, such as those with chronic conditions (e.g., heart disease, diabetes, hypertension) or the elderly who may not have the ability to self-report changes in their health status. Because issues are detected early, emergencies can be avoided or mitigated, potentially preventing hospital readmissions, strokes, heart attacks, or diabetic complications. For example, if a patient's glucose level becomes dangerously high, an alert can prompt a caregiver to intervene before the patient experiences a hypoglycemic crisis. This also helps decrease emergency room delays by reducing the number of physical visits and congestion of people in the waiting room.

Continuous monitoring enables a proactive approach to healthcare instead of a reactive one. Healthcare providers can adjust medications or treatments in real time by detecting issues before they escalate into serious complications based on continuous data. For example, insulin dosages for a diabetic patient can be adjusted based on real-time blood glucose levels, minimizing the risks associated with over- or under-dosing. This contributes to avoiding hospital readmissions by keeping track of patients' health remotely. Continuous monitoring allows healthcare providers to manage chronic conditions outside the hospital, reducing the need for frequent hospital visits and lowering the chances of readmission for complications that could have been detected and addressed earlier.

For patients, continuous monitoring via IoMT devices provides real-time contiguous access to their health data, which they can review and share with their healthcare providers. This helps patients feel more in control of their health and fosters a sense of empowerment and engagement in their care. For instance, wearable fitness trackers or smartwatches allow patients to observe trends in their physical activity, heart rate, sleep patterns, and more, all of which can be shared with their doctor to help guide treatment decisions. Data from IoMT devices can be analyzed to provide patients with insights about their health trends, identifying areas that may need attention and encouraging healthier behaviors, such as improving diet, increasing physical activity, getting better sleep, or managing stress.

Again, continuous monitoring through IoMT devices is especially critical for high-risk patients, such as the elderly, individuals with multiple chronic conditions, or those recovering from surgery. Early detection of health issues enables timely interventions that can prevent the deterioration of a patient's condition, reducing the likelihood of emergency hospitalizations, and in some cases, life-threatening events. For instance, an elderly patient living alone with a heart condition could wear a heart rate monitor that alerts a caregiver if irregularities are detected, allowing for early intervention before a more severe episode occurs.

IoMT devices enhance the integration of telehealth services, especially in underserved or rural areas. In case of abnormal readings, doctors can initiate virtual consultations, analyze real-time data, and adjust treatments without the patient needing to travel. For example, a patient with COPD can wear a smart device that monitors oxygen saturation and alerts their healthcare team if oxygen levels drop. This leads to an immediate telemedicine consultation to discuss the next steps. For patients in remote areas or those with mobility issues, connected medical devices allow healthcare providers to deliver timely and meaningful recommendations even when patients are not physically present, dramatically improving access to healthcare and reducing healthcare disparities.

In summary, continuous patient monitoring through IoMT, albeit an exposed high-risk target I'll discuss later, is a game-changer in healthcare. By providing real-time, day-and-night tracking of vital health parameters, these devices enhance patient outcomes and empower patients to be more active in managing their health. With automatic alerts, real-time access to health data, and the ability to intervene proactively, this technology is a powerful tool for reducing healthcare costs, preventing medical emergencies, improving the quality of care, and potentially saving lives.

Remote Medical Support

Connected medical technology facilitates remote consultations and communications with equipment. This capability is beneficial for individuals with mobility issues or, as mentioned prior, those living in rural areas, as it allows doctors and patients to connect and consult on healthcare issues without in-person meetings.

One of the most compelling advantages is its ability to facilitate remote medical support. This capability enables real-time consultations, data sharing, and communication between healthcare providers and patients, regardless of physical location. By connecting patients with remote healthcare professionals via IoMT-enabled devices, the technology overcomes geographical and physical barriers, improving access to medical care and expanding the scope of healthcare delivery.

There are many ways remote medical support powered by IoMT is transforming healthcare. Remote consultations with healthcare providers are one of the most popular. IoMT devices enable patients and doctors to engage in virtual consultations, often called telemedicine or telehealth. Through video conferencing, secure messaging, and integrated monitoring tools, patients can have face-to-face consultations with doctors or specialists without the need to travel to a clinic or hospital. Patients can discuss their symptoms, receive advice, or even get diagnoses based on real-time health data transmitted from their connected medical devices using video calls or secure messaging platforms. For example, a patient with asthma can use a smart inhaler to report their medication usage, lung function, and breathing patterns, allowing the doctor to assess their condition and provide guidance remotely. This also applies to patients with sleep apnea, where data from their CPAP machine is sent directly to their pulmonologist. Remote consultations also open up access to specialists that may not be locally available. The technology can connect patients to expert care without needing long-distance travel, reducing time and financial barriers to accessing specialized medical advice.

For patients with mobility issues, whether due to age, disability, or chronic conditions, remote care can be a lifeline. Traveling to a medical facility can be a significant challenge, sometimes even dangerous, for these individuals. IoMT allows these patients to stay in the comfort of their own homes while still receiving quality healthcare. Through remote monitoring, healthcare providers can track vital signs, medication adherence, and other health parameters in real time, ensuring the patient's condition is carefully managed. IoMT devices can track daily health data for patients with chronic conditions, such as blood pressure, blood glucose levels, heart rate, or oxygen levels, and automatically transmit it to healthcare professionals. Based on this data, healthcare providers can adjust treatment plans and offer recommendations for self-care, ensuring continuous, personalized management of chronic diseases. It's been reported to me that some patients who would have put off a doctor visit or check-ins have been willing to use IoMT devices instead, reducing the likelihood of medical emergencies.

Rural communities often face challenges when it comes to access to healthcare. Hospitals, clinics, and specialists may be far away, leading to delayed diagnoses, long travel times, and increased patient costs. Long and difficult travel also impacts the well-being of patients via mood alteration, as many patients arrive unhappy. IoMT dramatically improves healthcare accessibility for these individuals by eliminating the need for travel and enabling care to be delivered directly to their homes. For example, a smart blood pressure cuff can send readings to a doctor in real time, allowing for timely medication. After an initial consultation, patients in rural areas can also use IoMT devices for follow-up care, such as checking on the progress of wound healing or monitoring the effectiveness of prescribed treatments. With IoMT's real-time capabilities, patients don't have to wait weeks for an in-person follow-up appointment, improving outcomes and patient satisfaction.

The elderly often face various health issues requiring constant monitoring and medical intervention. However, many elderly individuals experience difficulty traveling to healthcare facilities or may have limited access to transportation. IoMT-enabled wearables such as smartwatches, fall detection sensors, and activity trackers are particularly beneficial for elderly patients. These devices can monitor physical activity and sleep patterns and detect falls, sudden changes in vital signs, or early signs of health deterioration (e.g., elevated heart rate, low oxygen levels). In an emergency, such as a fall, many devices are equipped with automatic emergency alerts, which can immediately notify healthcare providers or caregivers. For instance, if an elderly patient falls and cannot reach their phone, their device can alert emergency contacts and initiate a response without the patient needing to take any action.

Chronic conditions such as diabetes, heart disease, hypertension, and COPD require ongoing care and regular check-ins with healthcare providers. IoMT devices like continuous glucose monitors (CGMs), smart blood pressure cuffs, and wearable ECG monitors collect and transmit data to healthcare providers over time. For example, a diabetic patient using a CGM can send real-time glucose readings to their healthcare provider, enabling the doctor to adjust insulin dosages or make dietary recommendations based on the patient's real-time data. With constant monitoring, healthcare providers can intervene early when there are signs of complications, such as a sudden rise in blood pressure or irregular heart rhythms, preventing the condition's progression and avoiding emergency interventions.

IoMT enables seamless communication between patients and their healthcare providers via interconnected devices using protocols I'll discuss later. This connected ecosystem creates a holistic view of the patient's health, with data from multiple sources, including wearables, home monitoring devices, and mobile health apps. Information from various IoMT devices can be integrated into a single system, allowing healthcare providers to gain a comprehensive understanding of the patient's health status. This integration helps doctors track a patient's progress over time, spot potential issues earlier, and make data-driven decisions about treatment adjustments. Remote medical support becomes even more effective when doctors have immediate access to up-to-date information about a patient's condition. IoMT technologies allow for instantaneous sharing of diagnostic results, lab reports, and imaging data, eliminating delays that could compromise care.

Remote medical support, enabled by IoMT, also helps reduce overall healthcare costs. By leveraging remote consultations and monitoring, patients can avoid unnecessary hospital admissions and emergency room visits, which can be costly. For example, patients with stable chronic conditions can manage their health remotely, reducing the number of in-person visits to doctors or specialists. Healthcare professionals can then focus their time and resources on patients who need immediate or intensive care, rather than spending time on routine follow-ups. This streamlines care delivery, allowing healthcare providers to optimize their time and manage larger patient volumes efficiently.

Integrating IoMT for remote medical support is fundamentally changing how healthcare is delivered. For individuals with mobility issues, patients living in remote or rural areas, and the elderly who face challenges accessing traditional healthcare, IoMT provides an essential tool for maintaining continuous, quality care. By enabling real-time health monitoring, virtual consultations, and remote diagnostics, IoMT reduces barriers to care, improves patient outcomes, and makes healthcare more accessible, efficient, and personalized.

Seamless Healthcare System Integration

As mentioned, IoMT enables automatic communication of patient data between hospitals, doctors' offices, and intelligent medical devices. This integration enhances the speed and accuracy of diagnosis, treatment, and patient monitoring while reducing errors, eliminating duplicate data entries, and improving healthcare worker efficiency.

One of the most profound impacts is IoMT's ability to integrate various healthcare systems, devices, and platforms seamlessly. By enabling automatic communication of patient data across hospitals, doctors' offices, and intelligent medical devices, IoMT facilitates the efficient flow of critical health information. This integration not only enhances the quality of care but also contributes to significant improvements in diagnosis, treatment, patient monitoring, and overall operational efficiency.

Seamless healthcare integration has many impacts. One core feature is the real-time transmission of patient data from various connected devices to healthcare providers' systems, including electronic health records (EHRs), hospital information systems, and other clinical platforms. This integration streamlines the communication of patient data. It ensures that healthcare teams have immediate access to up-to-date information, regardless of location or role in the healthcare process.

When patients visit a hospital, doctor's office, or specialist, their health data is directly transmitted from IoMT-enabled devices (such as smart glucose monitors, ECG devices, or wearable health trackers) into the provider's EHR system. Healthcare professionals don't have to manually input data as they did years before, saving valuable time and reducing the risk of transcription errors. For example, a remote ECG monitor worn by a heart patient can send heart rhythm data directly to the cardiologist's office in real time, allowing the doctor to monitor the patient's condition continuously and intervene if necessary. Healthcare providers have a more comprehensive and holistic view of a patient's health when they can access all relevant data from across the healthcare ecosystem in one unified platform. This ensures faster, more informed decisions, such as adjusting medications based on real-time glucose readings or monitoring the effectiveness of a treatment regimen. The ability to access real-time data from multiple devices and systems improves clinical decision-making, reduces diagnostic errors, and facilitates a more personalized approach to treatment.

Integrating IoMT with healthcare systems allows for rapid data aggregation from multiple sources. As patient data is automatically uploaded into an integrated system, advanced data analytics tools can immediately begin processing the information to detect patterns, trends, and anomalies. For instance, a smart MRI scanner might send imaging data to a radiologist's workstation, where artificial intelligence (AI) algorithms automatically analyze it to detect early signs of cancer or structural abnormalities. The system can then flag these findings for review, significantly reducing the time it takes for the radiologist to provide an initial assessment. These integrated systems share data and provide real-time decision support based on that data. For example, if a patient's blood pressure spikes, the system can automatically alert, suggest possible diagnoses or treatments, and even recommend follow-up actions based on medical guidelines. This reduces the chances of human error and improves diagnostic accuracy, ensuring patients receive the proper treatment more quickly.

Data collected from wearable devices, home health sensors, and connected medical equipment can be immediately integrated into the patient's EHR, enabling healthcare professionals to track progress, detect early signs of complications, and make treatment adjustments as needed. One of the most significant challenges in traditional healthcare systems is the risk of data entry errors. Manual transcription of patient data can lead to inaccuracies that negatively impact treatment decisions, delay diagnoses, or lead to unnecessary procedures. With IoMT-enabled systems, automated data transmission removes the need for manual data entry, ensuring patient information is transferred accurately from devices to healthcare systems. At times, even documenting details from the patients can incur inaccuracies, especially in older patients whose memories might be fading. IoMT devices automatically upload data directly into EHRs or other healthcare systems, reducing the likelihood of misinformation and errors arising when data is manually inputted by administrative or clinical staff.

Another common problem is duplicate data entry. When patients visit different specialists or healthcare facilities, their data is often re-entered into multiple systems, leading to duplication, inefficiency, and sometimes even conflicting information. IoMT integration ensures that patient data is consistent across all platforms, eliminating redundancy and improving the accuracy of medical records. This reduces administrative burden, enhances data integrity, and ensures a more coordinated approach to patient care.

Seamless integration between IoMT devices and healthcare systems significantly improves the efficiency of healthcare workers by reducing the time spent on administrative tasks. Healthcare workers no longer need to spend time manually collecting, transcribing, or verifying patient data. Instead, the system automatically updates patient records with real-time health data, reducing administrative workload. As mentioned, this is especially beneficial for patients in remote areas as doctors can intervene as soon as abnormalities are detected. This efficiency gain reduces the burden on healthcare providers and optimizes the allocation of medical resources, improving overall system performance.

IoMT's seamless integration also enhances the patient experience. For instance, a CT scan result can be instantly available to both the radiologist and the patient's primary care physician, speeding up diagnosis and treatment decisions. Integrated healthcare systems allow multiple providers to access the same patient data, helping ensure coordinated care.

To sum up, seamless integration of healthcare systems represents a significant advancement in modern healthcare. By enabling automatic communication between medical devices, healthcare facilities, and clinical systems, IoMT enhances patient care's speed, accuracy, and efficiency. This integration not only helps reduce human error, eliminate redundancy, and improve operational workflows but also leads to faster diagnoses, more personalized treatment plans, and ultimately better patient outcomes.

Data-Driven Insights

The automated data collection from IoMT devices provides valuable information for medical professionals. By analyzing this data, healthcare providers can identify trends and correlations between various health markers, leading to more precise treatment decisions and disease management strategies. These insights also contribute to developing innovative healthcare approaches and even more meaningful medical research.

One of the most transformative aspects is the ability to generate data-driven insights that inform clinical decision-making, personalized treatment plans, and disease management strategies. Among those is automated and continuous data collection. Connected medical devices enable real-time data collection from patients. This constant data stream includes various health markers, including blood pressure, heart rate, glucose levels, oxygen saturation, physical activity, sleep patterns, and more. Unlike traditional methods where data is collected in isolated, periodic visits to healthcare providers, this enables constant, noninvasive monitoring in the background of a patient's daily life.

For patients with chronic conditions, this automated data collection allows healthcare providers to monitor patient conditions between in-person visits, detect changes early, and intervene before small issues escalate into larger health problems. For healthy individuals or those with specific health goals, this allows continuous monitoring of activity levels, sleep quality, and other factors that contribute to overall health that they are interested in tracking. I see this use case in nearly every family I know of. This personalized tracking for folks who are into health and wellness enables them to take control of their health and make informed decisions about their lifestyle, fitness, and care.

The wealth of data generated by IoMT devices can be analyzed to uncover trends, patterns, and correlations that may not be immediately obvious to healthcare providers or even a patient. This ability to detect subtle changes or irregularities over time enables providers to make more informed decisions. By leveraging machine learning (ML) and AI algorithms, healthcare providers can analyze the large volumes of data collected by IoMT devices to identify predictive patterns. For example, a gradual increase in a patient's heart rate or a spike in blood glucose levels over time can signal an early onset of a condition like hypertension or diabetic ketoacidosis. Detecting these trends early allows healthcare providers to adjust treatment plans proactively, rather than waiting for symptoms to become severe. Based on these insights, the provider can customize prevention plans or change medications to reduce that patient's risk.

Another benefit from this data is the ability to offer precision medicine, which is treatment that is tailored specifically to the individual based on their unique health data. The insights derived from these devices help healthcare providers make decisions that are not just informed by symptoms but by personalized health data. With IoMT, healthcare providers can continuously track the effectiveness of a unique treatment plan. This ensures that treatment plans are dynamic and adaptive, continually evolving based on the patient's real-world data rather than static assumptions.

Data from IoMT devices also plays a crucial role in medication adherence. For patients on complex drug regimens, IoMT devices like smart pill dispensers or connected inhalers can ensure that medications are taken on time and in the correct dosage. Data from these devices can also be used to adjust treatment based on how well the patient is responding.

The aggregated data from IoMT devices also helps advance medical research. The continuous and wide-scale collection of health data offers researchers insights into disease progression, treatment efficacy, and public health trends. By analyzing the large datasets collected from IoMT devices, researchers can gain a better understanding of how diseases progress in real-world populations. For example, longitudinal data on heart disease can help researchers understand how lifestyle factors, genetics, and environmental factors contribute to heart health, leading to better prevention and treatment strategies.

IoMT data can also enhance the design and conduct of clinical trials. Continuous data from connected devices can be used to track participants' health in real time, offering more granular insights into the effects of new treatments. This can also improve patient retention in trials, as data can be gathered remotely, reducing the burden of in-person visits. The insights from large datasets enable healthcare companies and startups to develop new medical technologies and improve existing ones. For example, AI-powered diagnostic tools that use IoMT data to interpret ECG readings, MRI scans, or blood work can become more accurate as they are trained on real-world data from a wide range of patients, leading to more innovative healthcare solutions and better patient outcomes.

On a broader scale, IoMT data can play a role in population health management. By analyzing aggregated health data across large populations, healthcare providers and public health agencies can identify patterns and trends that inform public health initiatives, disease prevention campaigns, and policy decisions. For instance, during an outbreak of infectious disease, IoMT devices can help track symptoms in real time, allowing for quicker identification of new cases and better containment strategies. By analyzing health data from wearables, public health authorities can see emerging trends in symptoms or exposure and respond quickly. By analyzing patterns in healthcare usage (e.g., hospital admissions, chronic condition exacerbations), healthcare providers can identify underserved populations and adjust resource allocation to ensure equitable healthcare delivery. IoMT data can reveal gaps in care and help optimize the distribution of medical resources.

In conclusion, the data-driven insights derived from IoMT devices are transforming healthcare by enabling personalized, precision medicine, enhancing chronic disease management, improving clinical decision-making, and fostering medical research. The continuous flow of real-time data allows healthcare providers to make more accurate, informed decisions; detect conditions earlier; and optimize treatment plans for individual patients. In addition, the vast datasets generated by IoMT devices hold significant potential to advance public health initiatives, improve clinical trials, and contribute to innovative healthcare solutions.

Early Disease Detection

Everything I discussed about IoMT use cases points to identifying early warning signs of illnesses and issuing timely notifications. This capability allows patients and caregivers to take early action against disease progression, potentially improving overall quality of life. One of the takeaways and most promising capabilities is its potential to identify early warning signs of illness, allowing for proactive intervention that can significantly improve patient outcomes.

IoMT devices, with their continuous and real-time data collection, enable healthcare providers to detect abnormalities or trends in a patient's health that may signal the onset of a disease or the worsening of an existing condition. Early detection of health issues is critical because it can lead to timely interventions, reducing the risk of complications, improving treatment effectiveness, and in some cases, preventing the progression of the disease altogether.

Resource Optimization

IoMT applications can streamline healthcare processes and optimize resource utilization. By managing inventory, tracking assets, and optimizing patient flow, they can facilitate efficiencies and save time in healthcare settings. This is not only transforming the clinical aspects of healthcare but also playing a crucial role in optimizing operational efficiency. By automating and improving the management of critical assets, optimizing patient flow, and enhancing inventory control, they can reduce operational costs, eliminate inefficiencies, and free up healthcare staff to focus more on patient care rather than administrative tasks. That said, IoMT-specific applications are helping healthcare organizations get the most out of their available resources.

Effective management of medical inventory and assets is a challenge for healthcare facilities. With more medical devices, medications, and equipment being used daily, the risk of stockouts, overstocking, or equipment misplacement is a significant concern. This technology addresses these issues by real-time asset and inventory tracking through connected sensors and RFID tags. These systems can track medical equipment's location, condition, and usage history. In addition, these systems can monitor device traffic, looking for anomalies with IoMT device communication and identifying data traffic issues. Later in this book, I'll discuss how these technologies and assets can also be vulnerable to attack.

Regarding inventory and leveraging smart systems, these can automatically track the stock levels of medications, personal protective equipment, and disposables, sending alerts when supplies are running low or when items are nearing their expiration dates. This helps hospitals ensure they always have critical supplies on hand, avoiding shortages that could delay treatment or patient care.

These systems can also prevent over-ordering, reducing waste and cutting down on unnecessary costs associated with storing and maintaining excess supplies. In addition to tracking consumables, connected medical devices can enhance the management of high-value equipment. Medical devices like MRI machines, CT scanners, and patient monitoring systems are expensive and often have long wait times for usage. By tracking the usage patterns of such equipment, these can help hospitals optimize their deployment, ensuring that equipment is being used efficiently. It can also aid in predicting maintenance needs, thus avoiding costly breakdowns and extending the lifespan of expensive medical devices.

Efficient patient flow is essential to the smooth functioning of healthcare facilities, particularly in busy hospitals and outpatient clinics. Delays in patient intake, long wait times, and overcrowded waiting areas are common problems that can affect patient satisfaction and the quality of care. IoMT technologies can play a role in optimizing these processes by tracking patient progress through various stages of care. For example, patient tracking systems using wearables or RFID tags previously mentioned can provide real-time data about a patient's location within the hospital. This data can be used to monitor the progress of a patient's care, from admission to discharge, and help staff anticipate bottlenecks or delays in care delivery. If a patient is waiting for an MRI or lab test, these systems can flag potential delays, allowing staff to adjust schedules or communicate more effectively with patients about waiting times.

By integrating electronic health records with patient tracking systems, healthcare providers can monitor how long patients have been waiting for tests, surgeries, or consultations, and prioritize care based on urgency. This can also streamline the coordination between departments, ensuring that resources (like nurses, technicians, or equipment) are assigned in the most effective way possible. This leads to a more predictable, efficient flow of patients through the hospital, reducing unnecessary wait times, minimizing delays, and improving the overall patient experience.

Based on my interviews and research, staffing is an area where IoMT can have a significant impact. Healthcare facilities often face challenges related to staff shortages, and not just for medical doctors but also veterinarians, as well as understaffing during peak hours and the misallocation of staff. IoMT can help optimize staffing levels by providing real-time data on patient volume, the severity of cases, and the overall workload. This data can be used to make data-driven decisions about when to increase staff presence in certain areas, ensuring that resources are allocated where they are most needed. For instance, wearable health devices worn by healthcare staff can track their location and activity levels, providing insight into how much time staff spend on tasks like patient care, paperwork, or waiting for equipment. By analyzing this data, administrators can identify inefficiencies or gaps in staffing, adjust schedules, or delegate tasks more effectively to improve overall staff productivity. Additionally, the automation of administrative tasks like patient check-in and patient data entry reduces the administrative burden on staff, allowing them to focus more on patient care.

By improving asset management, optimizing patient flow, and automating administrative tasks, healthcare organizations can significantly reduce operational costs. For example, by ensuring that medical equipment is maintained properly and used efficiently, hospitals can avoid costly repairs, reduce the need for renting equipment, and extend the lifespan of their assets.

By streamlining these processes, healthcare organizations can reduce these indirect costs and increase revenue by enabling the hospital or clinic to accommodate more patients without sacrificing the quality of care. For instance, IoMT can predict high patient demand periods based on historical data, allowing healthcare facilities to prepare in advance with the appropriate number of staff, equipment, and beds. By anticipating demand, healthcare organizations can prevent overcrowding and avoid the unnecessary costs associated with emergency interventions or extended hospital stays. All that said, resource optimization is one of the most significant and immediate benefits of this technology integration in healthcare. By leveraging real-time data to track assets, streamline patient flow, optimize staffing, and reduce waste, IoMT enables healthcare facilities to function more efficiently and cost-effectively.

How IoMT Works in Healthcare and Its Applications

For patients, connected medical devices empower them to take a more active role in managing their health. Wearable IoMT devices continuously collect vital signs and activity data, which patients can access in real time through mobile apps. This advancement allows individuals to monitor their health status and make informed decisions about their own well-being. For patients with chronic conditions like diabetes or hypertension, connected glucose monitors and blood pressure cuffs enable regular health monitoring, contributing to better disease management. Connected pill dispensers and smart pill bottles can improve medication adherence by reminding patients to take their medications on time, leading to better treatment outcomes.

For healthcare providers, this technology creates a connected healthcare network that facilitates the continuous flow of patient data. As mentioned, the range of interconnected medical devices collects health data from patients via sensors, including vitals, medication usage, sleep patterns, and activity levels. This data is securely transmitted to the cloud through network technologies that I'll talk about in more detail later, such as Wi-Fi, ZigBee, Bluetooth Low Energy, or local area networks (LANs). Advanced data analytics can then be applied to uncover valuable insights and patterns, enabling healthcare providers to offer higher quality care. The applications of IoMT in healthcare are diverse and continually expanding. Some of the key areas I highlighted include the following:

- **Remote patient monitoring:** IoMT devices offer value with patient monitoring, especially for those with chronic conditions or recovering from surgery.

Wearable ECG monitors, pulse oximeters, and other connected devices allow healthcare providers to monitor patients' vital signs remotely, reducing the need for frequent hospital visits and enabling early detection of potential complications.

- **Medication management:** Smart pill bottles and dispensers can track medication adherence and send reminders to patients, improving treatment efficacy and reducing the risk of medication errors.
- **Asset management:** IoMT can be used to track and manage medical equipment and supplies within healthcare facilities, improving efficiency and reducing costs.
- **Environmental monitoring:** IoT sensors can monitor environmental conditions in healthcare facilities, ensuring optimal conditions for patient care and equipment operation.
- **Telemedicine:** IoMT enables remote consultations and diagnoses, improving access to healthcare services, especially in rural or underserved areas.
- **Personal health tracking:** Consumer-grade wearables and health apps allow individuals to monitor their own health metrics, promoting preventive care and early intervention.
- **Advanced diagnostics:** IoMT-enabled diagnostic devices, such as smart MRI and CT scanners, allow for remote monitoring, control, and maintenance, providing healthcare professionals with real-time data access and settings adjustment.

Challenges and Considerations in IoMT Adoption

While the potential benefits of the IoMT are exciting, several important challenges need to be addressed to make sure these technologies are safely and effectively integrated into healthcare. One of the biggest concerns is the security and privacy of the sensitive health data that these devices generate. These devices collect vast amounts of personal health information, making them attractive targets for cyberattacks. To protect this data, strong security measures like encryption, secure data-sharing methods, and compliance with privacy laws, such as the Health Insurance Portability and Accountability Act (HIPAA), are essential to ensure patient confidentiality.

Another challenge comes from the complex web of regulations that govern healthcare technologies. Connected medical devices must meet a range of standards that can vary by region, which can be difficult to navigate. In the United States, the Food and Drug Administration (FDA) ensures these devices meet safety and accuracy standards, while in the European Union (EU) and the Medical Device Regulation (MDR) sets guidelines for their use. Staying up-to-date with constantly evolving regulations is a significant hurdle for both device developers and healthcare providers.

IoMT devices also need to work seamlessly with one another, but this can be tricky. With so many different devices and technologies in play, ensuring they communicate smoothly and securely can be challenging, and not without exposing themselves to cyberattacks. Without standardized protocols, devices can face compatibility issues, potentially creating gaps in security or making it harder to share data between systems.

Managing the massive amounts of data generated by IoMT devices is another key issue. The volume of data can be overwhelming, making it difficult to store, process, and analyze effectively, let alone safeguarding. Ensuring that the data is accurate and reliable is crucial, as poor-quality data could lead to mistakes in diagnoses or treatment decisions.

As healthcare organizations increasingly adopt IoMT devices, scalability becomes an important challenge. These systems must be able to handle growing numbers of devices and larger data volumes without compromising security or performance. Let's not dismiss the hurdle of user adoption. Both healthcare professionals and patients need training to understand how to use IoMT devices properly and interpret the data they generate. For these technologies to reach their full potential, it's vital that users feel confident in using them effectively.

Finally, the rise of IoMT brings up important ethical questions, such as who owns the data and how to ensure that everyone, including underserved communities, has equal access to these technologies. It's essential to address these concerns to ensure that this technology benefits everyone and not just a select few.

Best Practices for IoMT Security

To address the security challenges associated with IoMT, healthcare organizations and device manufacturers should implement best practices. Throughout this book, I'll review in much more detail the strategies for implementing best practices, including principles of Zero Trust (covered in Chapters 14 and 16). Some of the most recommended standards (shown in Figure 1-2) include solutions that I'll introduce here:

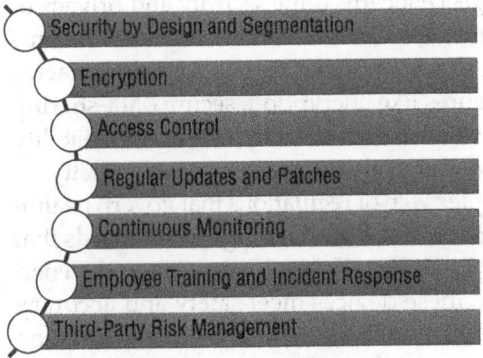

Figure 1-2: Common security best practices

- **Encryption:** Implement strong encryption protocols, such as a minimum of AES-256, for data at rest and TLS 1.3 for data in transit to protect sensitive patient information from unauthorized access. Use end-to-end encryption for all communications between IoMT devices and servers. Implement secure key management practices, including regular key rotation and secure storage of encryption keys.

- **Access control:** Implement robust access control measures, including multi-factor authentication (MFA), to ensure that only authorized personnel can access IoMT devices and data. Utilize biometric authentication where appropriate, such as fingerprint or facial recognition. Implement role-based access control (RBAC) to limit user privileges based on job functions. Regularly audit and review access logs to detect any unauthorized access attempts.

- **Network segmentation:** Divide IoMT networks into smaller, isolated segments to contain potential security breaches and prevent lateral movement by attackers. Implement virtual LANs (VLANs) and firewalls between segments. Use network access control (NAC) solutions to ensure only authorized devices can connect to the IoMT network. Monitor network traffic for anomalies.

- **Regular updates and patches:** Maintain a rigorous schedule for updating IoMT device firmware and software to address known vulnerabilities and enhance security features. Implement an automated patch management system to ensure timely updates, while coordinating updates with healthcare providers to minimize disruption to patient care. Conduct thorough testing of patches in a staging environment before deployment to production systems.

- **Security by design:** Incorporate security considerations into the design and development process of IoMT devices, rather than treating security as an afterthought. Conduct threat modeling during the design phase to identify potential vulnerabilities. Implement secure coding practices and perform regular code reviews. Utilize static and dynamic application security testing (SAST and DAST) tools throughout the development lifecycle.

- **Continuous monitoring:** Implement real-time monitoring systems to detect and respond to potential security threats promptly. Utilize security information and event management (SIEM) solutions to aggregate and analyze logs from multiple sources. Implement behavioral analytics to detect anomalous devices or user behavior. Set up automated alerts for suspicious activities.

- **Employee training:** Provide comprehensive cybersecurity training to healthcare staff to raise awareness about potential threats and best practices for device usage. Conduct regular phishing simulations to test and improve staff awareness. Develop and distribute clear, easy-to-follow security guidelines for IoMT device usage. Implement a security champion program to foster a culture of security awareness. Ensure security is embraced from the C-suite to the loading dock staff.

- **Third-party risk management:** Carefully vet and monitor third-party vendors and service providers to ensure they adhere to stringent security standards. Conduct regular security assessments of third-party systems that interact with IoMT devices. Include security requirements in vendor contracts and service level agreements (SLAs). Implement a vendor risk management program to continuously monitor and assess third-party security postures.

- **Incident response planning:** Develop and regularly test incident response plans to ensure rapid and effective action in the event of a security breach. Create detailed playbooks for different types of IoMT security incidents. Conduct tabletop exercises and full-scale simulations to test the effectiveness of the incident response plan. Establish clear communication channels and protocols for incident reporting and escalation. Regularly update the incident response plan based on lessons learned from exercises and actual incidents.

Securing the IoMT is a complex but crucial task that requires a multilayered approach to mitigate risks and protect sensitive healthcare data. By implementing best practices such as robust encryption, strict access controls, segmentation, and regular updates, healthcare organizations can safeguard against the growing array of cyber threats.

Furthermore, integrating security by design into the development of connected medical devices, continuously monitoring networks for anomalies, and providing ongoing employee training all play essential roles in building a resilient cybersecurity framework. A proactive approach to third-party risk management and a well-prepared incident response plan ensure that organizations can respond swiftly and effectively to any potential breach. As IoMT continues to expand and evolve, adhering to these best practices will help maintain the trust of patients and ensure the integrity of critical healthcare systems.

Future Trends in IoMT

Several emerging trends are shaping the future of the IoMT. One of the most exciting developments is the integration of artificial intelligence and machine learning, mentioned earlier in this chapter, with IoMT devices. These technologies will enable more sophisticated analysis of health data, allowing for faster and more accurate diagnostics, as well as personalized treatment plans. AI and ML will help healthcare providers make predictions about patient health and even detect potential issues before they become critical, offering a new level of proactive care.

Another game-changer on the horizon is the further evolution of 5G and beyond (some people are calling this 6G) networks. With much faster and more reliable connections, 5G enhances the capabilities of IoMT devices, enabling real-time data transmission. This allows for more advanced applications, such as remote surgeries or real-time monitoring of critical patients, with minimal lag or delays. The speed and reliability of 5G opens up new possibilities for how healthcare is delivered, making care more responsive and efficient.

Edge computing is also poised to continue to play a key role in the future of IoMT. By processing data closer to where it's generated, rather than relying on distant cloud servers, edge computing will reduce latency and speed up data analysis. This is particularly important for time-sensitive medical applications, such as monitoring heart rates or responding to medical emergencies, where every second counts. Faster processing will lead to quicker decisions and better outcomes for patients.

Blockchain technology is an innovation that could greatly enhance the security and efficiency of IoMT systems. By providing a secure, transparent way to store and share medical data, blockchain can protect patient privacy while improving interoperability between different healthcare systems. This would make it easier for doctors, hospitals, and patients to access and exchange medical records, all while ensuring that the data remains secure and tamper-proof. I'll talk more about this in later chapters.

Augmented reality (AR) and virtual reality (VR) are also making their way into healthcare through IoMT. These technologies have the potential to revolutionize medical training, surgical planning, and patient education. For example, AR and VR can provide immersive simulations for medical students to practice procedures or help surgeons visualize complex operations before they begin. Patients can also use these technologies to better understand their conditions and treatment options, making them feel more engaged in their care. They are great tools for learning about the human anatomy.

Nanotechnology is pushing the boundaries of what IoMT can achieve by developing ultra-small devices that can operate at the cellular level. These nanoscale devices could allow for more precise diagnostics and targeted treatments, such as delivering medication directly to affected cells. Nanotechnology holds the promise of making medical care even more precise and effective, particularly in fields like cancer treatment or genetic disorders.

Finally, the vast amount of data generated by IoMT devices is paving the way for the future of personalized medicine. With this wealth of information, doctors will be able to tailor treatments to individual patients based on their unique health profiles. This means that treatments can be more precise, with fewer side effects and better outcomes, as each patient receives care that is specifically designed for their needs. Together, these trends point to a future where IoMT not only improves how we monitor and treat diseases but also personalizes healthcare, making it more effective, efficient, and accessible for everyone.

The IoMT represents a paradigm shift in healthcare delivery, offering unprecedented opportunities to improve patient care, enhance operational efficiency, and drive medical innovation. As this continues to evolve, it promises to make healthcare more proactive, personalized, and accessible. However, realizing the full potential of IoMT requires addressing significant challenges, particularly in the areas of data security, privacy, and regulatory compliance. I will dive into those aspects in detail throughout the remainder of this book. By implementing robust security measures, adhering to best practices, and fostering collaboration between healthcare providers, technology companies, and regulatory bodies, the healthcare industry can harness the power of IoMT to create a more connected, efficient, and patient-centric healthcare ecosystem.

As we look to the future, the continued integration of IoMT with emerging technologies like AI, beyond 5G, and blockchain will unlock new possibilities in healthcare delivery and medical research. By staying informed about these developments and embracing the opportunities presented by connected medical devices, healthcare organizations can position themselves at the forefront of this digital healthcare revolution, ultimately leading to better health outcomes and improved quality of life for patients worldwide.

Key Takeaways of IoMT in Healthcare

The IoMT has introduced smart, connected medical devices that enhance patient care, improve system efficiency, and drive innovation. This technology evolved from simple remote monitoring in the 1990s to advanced wearables and intelligent medical equipment that enable real-time monitoring and data sharing. IoMT offers numerous benefits, including continuous monitoring of vital signs, remote patient support, seamless system integration, data-driven insights, early detection of health issues, and resource optimization.

In real-world applications, IoMT empowers patients with wearables and connected devices for health tracking and medication management while providing doctors with tools for remote patient monitoring and personalized care. Hospitals benefit from improved resource management and streamlined patient flow. However, implementing IoMT faces challenges such as data security, regulatory compliance, device compatibility, data management, and user adoption.

To address these challenges, healthcare organizations should implement best practices for IoMT security, including encryption, access controls, secure networks, regular software updates, and comprehensive staff training. Looking ahead, the future of IoMT is promising, with advancements in AI and machine learning, 5G networks, edge computing, blockchain, and emerging technologies like AR/VR and nanotechnology poised to transform healthcare delivery further. By proactively addressing challenges and embracing these emerging trends, IoMT has the potential to create a more innovative and connected healthcare ecosystem that benefits everyone.

CHAPTER 2

The Evolving Landscape of Wireless Technologies in Medical Devices

Imagine a world where your health is monitored in real time, with data seamlessly transmitted from your wearable devices to your doctor, no matter where you are. Well, this is the reality of wireless technologies in healthcare today. This chapter explores how wireless technologies have moved us from stand-alone medical devices to a web of interconnected systems, creating an ecosystem of continuous care, real-time monitoring, and advanced data-driven decision-making.

First, let's break down some of the major players in this space:

- **Bluetooth:** This is the workhorse of wearable health tech. Think of fitness trackers or glucose monitors that communicate with your smartphone. These devices balance power efficiency and functionality with Bluetooth Low Energy (BLE).
- **Wi-Fi:** This is the high-speed network backbone in hospitals, enabling central monitoring systems to manage data from infusion pumps, heart monitors, and more. It's like a superfast highway for critical patient information.
- **Zigbee:** Zigbee is often overlooked but suitable for some home healthcare setups. Zigbee's low power needs make it ideal for devices that must last for years without constant maintenance.
- **Cellular and LoRaWAN:** These are for long-distance, real-time remote patient monitoring. These technologies bring care to rural areas or hard-to-reach places, eliminating distance as a barrier.

- **RFID and NFC:** These are the watchers in hospital asset tracking and patient identification, ensuring the right equipment is always in the right place.

Each of these technologies offers unique benefits, but they also present challenges, particularly in security, privacy, and interoperability. Wireless devices have certainly improved patient care, and they allow outcomes such as the following:

- **Freedom of movement:** Patients can stay mobile while under continuous monitoring, improving recovery and quality of life.
- **Data-driven decisions:** With advanced analytics on real-time data, healthcare providers (with the help of AI and ML) can predict health issues and intervene before emergencies arise.
- **Efficiency gains:** Automated data entry reduces errors and frees up staff for direct patient care.

For example, wearable ECG monitors can instantly alert a doctor about abnormal heart activity, potentially saving lives. I recall the classic line "With great power comes great responsibility," originally coined by French author, Voltaire, and then commercialized by Marvel's Spider-Man franchise. In that context, the connectivity that empowers healthcare also exposes it to vulnerabilities and other challenges that should be addressed, including the following:

- **Security risks:** Weak encryption and outdated or unpatched systems can lead to cyberattacks. Imagine the implications of someone remotely tampering with a pacemaker.
- **Interoperability hurdles:** Different devices need to speak the same language to work together seamlessly, which is easier said than done.
- **Battery limitations:** Power efficiency is critical for implantable devices, as battery replacements often require invasive procedures.

The future is even more exciting. As mentioned in the previous chapter, technologies like 5G provide faster, more reliable connections, enabling remote surgeries and ultra-responsive care. AI and edge computing are making wireless devices smarter, helping to detect health issues before symptoms appear. Let's not forget blockchain, which could revolutionize securing and sharing sensitive health data. I'll discuss all of these technologies later in this book.

Overview of Wireless Technologies in Medical Devices

According to Precedence Research, the global wireless health market is worth around $239 billion and expected to reach $1.3 trillion by 2034 (illustrated in Figure 2-1). These wireless technologies, especially in medical devices, encompass many communication protocols and standards that enable data transmission without physical connections. The technologies have transformed devices from stand-alone units to interconnected systems that communicate with each other, healthcare providers, and patients. The standard wireless technologies used in medical devices will be dissected in more detail throughout this book, so I'll start with a high-level summary of the key points of these technologies.

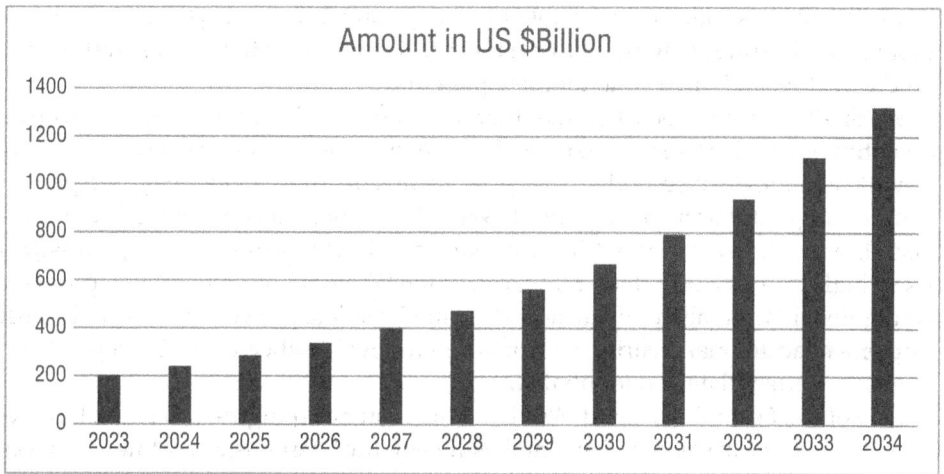

Figure 2-1: Wireless health market size and forecast 2023 to 2034

Bluetooth

Bluetooth is like a wireless language that lets devices talk to each other over short distances without much power. It's become a favorite for medical devices, especially those you wear to allow healthcare providers to monitor patients. BLE is a special type of Bluetooth that is even better at saving power. It works on a specific radio frequency and can send information if there's little to no interference and at times, with the help of extenders or in version 5 or later, up to about the length of a football field. The newer versions of Bluetooth can reach farther, send data faster, and share information with more devices simultaneously. This makes it great for medical tools.

As discussed in Chapter 1, you'll find Bluetooth in the following:

- Devices that check blood sugar and send the results to your phone.
- Heart monitors you wear that can send your heart's activity to your doctor.
- Hearing aids that connect to your phone or TV.

In Chapters 3 and 4, I'll discuss in detail why it's essential to understand the risks associated with Bluetooth. If not set up safely, someone could potentially listen in on the information being sent or even try to change it, so it's crucial to ensure that these devices are adequately secured.

Wi-Fi

Wi-Fi is commonly used in hospital settings to connect medical devices to central monitoring systems and offers higher data rates and more extended range than Bluetooth. Imagine a hospital where all the medical devices can talk to each other and share information instantly. That's what Wi-Fi does in modern healthcare settings. It's like a super-fast, invisible highway connecting everything from heart monitors to infusion pumps, allowing them to send information to a central system where doctors and nurses can monitor patients.

Wi-Fi is faster and reaches farther than Bluetooth, making it perfect for covering an entire hospital. The latest version, Wi-Fi 6, is so quick in some tests that it can download a movie in seconds. This speed means doctors can get real-time patient condition updates immediately. While Wi-Fi is excellent at connecting devices, it's also designed to keep patient information safe. It uses strong security measures like a high-tech lock on a door. However, while Wi-Fi can be secure when properly configured, it's not inherently designed for medical data protection. Hospitals must implement additional security measures and follow healthcare-specific regulations to ensure patient data confidentiality.

One of the best things about Wi-Fi is that it can be configured to extend everywhere in the infrastructure. This makes it easy for hospitals to add new devices to their network without installing a whole new system. It's like plugging into a universal power outlet where everything could work together seamlessly. Chapter 5 discusses Wi-Fi risks, exploitation, and security best practices.

Zigbee

Zigbee is a low-data-rate wireless technology often used in home healthcare applications and sensor networks. Imagine a network of tiny, energy-efficient communicators working together to monitor your health at home. That's what Zigbee does in the world of healthcare technology. It's like a soft-spoken friend who doesn't need much energy to communicate their message. It's a wireless technology perfect for devices that don't need to send large amounts of information but do need to keep working for a long time without changing batteries.

In your home, Zigbee can connect various health gadgets, like a blood pressure monitor in your bedroom, a weight scale in your bathroom, and a medication reminder system in your kitchen. These devices form a team, passing information to each other and ultimately to your healthcare provider. One of Zigbee's superpowers is its ability to create a mesh network. This means each device can act like a mini-relay station, passing data from one to another. So, even if your bedroom monitor is far from your central hub, it can still get its message through by passing it to other devices.

While Zigbee isn't built for sending large files or streaming video, it excels at regularly sending small bits of essential health data. This makes it ideal for tracking vital signs or daily health routines without quickly draining device batteries.

In essence, Zigbee is the quiet, efficient worker in the background of home healthcare, helping to keep you connected to your care team without fuss or complexity. It's also potentially vulnerable to attacks, which I'll review in Chapter 5.

LoRaWAN

Long Range Wide Area Network (LoRaWAN) is a low-power, wide-area network (LPWAN) technology for long-range communication. LoRaWAN's key strength is its ability to transmit data over very long distances (up to several kilometers) while consuming very little power, making it especially useful in areas where traditional cellular networks might not reach. It's particularly valuable for healthcare applications such as remote patient monitoring in rural areas. It is also used for tracking medical devices, monitoring environmental conditions, and sending health-related data back to healthcare providers from remote locations.

Since LoRaWAN covers wide areas with low power usage, it's suitable for devices that run on batteries, like sensors placed in outdoor or remote areas. However, it has some limitations, such as handling only small amounts of data at a time, so it's best for simple tasks like sending basic sensor readings. Additionally, setting up and using LoRaWAN requires specialized equipment and infrastructure, which isn't as common or easy to access as technologies like Wi-Fi or Bluetooth.

Cellular

Cellular technologies enable long-range communication, making them suitable for remote patient monitoring and telemedicine applications. 3G offers data rates up to 2 Mbps, 4G can reach 100 Mbps, while 5G gives speeds up to 20 Gbps with ultra-low latency. Imagine checking on a patient's health from miles away or having a video call with your doctor as clear as if you were in the same room. That's what cellular technology brings to healthcare.

Cellular networks, the same ones that power our smartphones, are being used to connect medical devices and patients to their healthcare providers over long distances. As discussed in Chapter 1, this is especially useful for keeping an eye on patients at home or in remote areas. As cellular technology has evolved, it's gotten faster and more reliable. The latest version, 5G, is so quick and responsive that doctors can even perform surgeries remotely. It's like upgrading from a dirt road to a paved superhighway for medical data.

Cellular-connected medical devices can send health information directly to doctors or hospitals, allowing instant analysis and quick responses if something goes wrong. It's like having a personal health assistant who's always on duty. However, there are a couple of drawbacks. Cellular-connected devices use more battery power than other wireless devices, so they might need charging more often. Also, just like with cell phone plans, costs might be associated with all that data being sent back and forth.

Despite these challenges, cellular technology is opening up exciting new possibilities in healthcare, making it easier for patients to get the care they need, no matter where they are. This flexibility, of course, lends itself to attack vectors, which I'll explore throughout Part II.

RFID

Radio-Frequency Identification (RFID) is commonly used to track medical equipment, supplies, staff, and even patients within healthcare facilities. Imagine a busy hospital where doctors, nurses, and staff need to quickly find equipment, manage supplies, and keep track of patients. That's where RFID comes in as a high-tech version of those beeping key finders, but for healthcare. It uses tiny tags attached to things (or even people) and special readers that can detect these tags. These tags come in different types, some working only when the reader is nearby (called *passive tags*) and others with their power source that can be detected farther away (called *active tags*).

In hospitals, RFID helps in many ways, but the most popular are as follows:

- **Finding equipment:** Doctors can quickly locate critical medical devices when needed.
- **Managing supplies:** Keeping track of medicines and other supplies is easier, ensuring nothing runs out unexpectedly.
- **Patient safety:** RFID wristbands can help prevent mix-ups and ensure patients receive proper care.

While RFID is beneficial, it's important to use it carefully. If not set up correctly, there's a risk that someone could potentially scan or copy the information without permission. That's why hospitals need to make sure their RFID systems are secure. Overall, it's like a silent helper in hospitals, ensuring everyone is where and when they should be.

Near Field Communication

Picture a technology that works only when two devices are almost touching. That's Near Field Communication (NFC). It's like a secret handshake between devices that happens only when they're close together, usually about as far apart as the width of your hand. In healthcare, NFC is becoming a handy tool for securely sharing important information (given it occurs nearby). Here are some ways it's making a difference:

- **Smart pill bottles:** They can tell your doctor if you've taken your medicine on time.
- **Hospital wristbands:** They help patients get the proper care by storing their information.

- **Smartphones:** You can use your phone to access your medical records or even pay for healthcare services.
- **Hearing aids:** NFC makes it easy to connect hearing aids to smartphones without fuss.

The best part about NFC is that it's tough for anyone to snoop in on shared information because the devices must be so close together. It's like whispering a secret where you must be next to someone to hear it.

While NFC is generally very secure, it's not perfect. Clever hackers still find ways to trick the system, so extra security measures are often used to keep everything safe and sound. In a nutshell, NFC is bringing a touch of high-tech convenience to healthcare, making it easier and safer to share important medical information.

Benefits of Wireless Technologies in Medical Devices

In Chapter 1, I discussed the impact and benefits of IoMT in healthcare. If you skipped it, I'll reiterate some of these benefits and address them from different perspectives. The adoption of wireless technologies in medical devices was a catalyst for those advantages. Wireless capabilities' most popular benefits include improved patient mobility, enhanced data collection and analysis, increased efficiency, cost reduction, better patient engagement, improved accessibility, and real-time alerting.

Wireless devices are evolving patient care by allowing freedom of movement. Unlike traditional monitoring equipment that required patients to be physically connected to stationary machines, wireless devices enable continuous monitoring without restricting mobility. This is beneficial, for example, in post-operative recovery, where early mobilization is crucial for preventing complications like deep vein thrombosis or pneumonia.

In long-term care settings, wireless monitoring allows patients to engage in physical therapy or daily activities while still under constant observation. For patients with chronic conditions, such as those requiring continuous glucose monitoring or cardiac telemetry, wireless devices enable them to maintain a more normal lifestyle while ensuring their health status is continuously monitored. This increased mobility not only improves physical recovery but also significantly improves patients' mental well-being and overall quality of life during treatment.

The continuous data transmission capabilities of wireless medical devices can collect an array of health metrics, from vital signs like heart rate, blood pressure, and oxygen saturation, to more complex data such as gait analysis, sleep patterns, and even biochemical markers, all in real time. When combined with advanced analytics and machine learning algorithms, this data enables healthcare providers to gain insights into patients' health trends and patterns. For instance, subtle changes in patient condition can be detected early, allowing for proactive interventions before a situation becomes critical. In chronic disease management, this continuous data stream helps fine-tune treatment plans, predict worsening conditions, and understand the impact of various factors (like diet, exercise, or medication) on the patient's condition. Furthermore, the aggregation of data from multiple patients can contribute to population health management and medical research, potentially leading to new insights and treatment strategies.

Wireless technologies have also streamlined workflows in healthcare settings, leading to marked improvements in operational efficiency. Automated data collection and transmission eliminate the need for manual data entry. In hospital settings, wireless-enabled equipment can automatically update EHRs, ensuring that patient information is always current and accessible to all care team members. This real-time data sharing facilitates faster decision-making and improves coordination among different departments. In outpatient care, wireless technologies enable seamless sharing of patient data between various healthcare providers, reducing redundant tests and enhancing continuity of care. The efficiency gains also extend to administrative tasks, with wireless systems facilitating smoother patient flow, inventory management, and resource allocation.

Implementing wireless technology in healthcare can reduce costs across various aspects of patient care. Remote monitoring capabilities enabled by wireless devices can substantially reduce the need for hospital readmissions. By allowing healthcare providers to detect and address issues early, many complications that typically require hospitalization can be managed on an outpatient basis. Telemedicine, facilitated by wireless communication, cuts down on unnecessary visits. Moreover, the efficiency gains from wireless technologies can lead to shorter hospital stays, optimized use of healthcare resources, and reduced administrative overhead.

Wireless, in the form of wearable devices and mobile health apps, has increased patient engagement in healthcare. These tools give patients real-time access to their health data, fostering that sense of ownership and active participation in their health management. Mobile health apps also provide personalized health tips, offer medication reminders, and facilitate provider communication. This constant engagement and feedback loop can lead to improved adherence to treatment plans and better health outcomes. Furthermore, the gamification elements often incorporated in these technologies can make health management more fun for patients. Studies have shown that wireless technologies are shifting the paradigm from reactive to proactive healthcare by providing patients with tools to understand and actively manage their health.

Wireless technologies have dramatically improved access to healthcare services. As mentioned, telemedicine, which is enabled by high-speed wireless Internet, allows patients to consult with specialists who might be hundreds of miles away, reducing the need for travel and improving access to expert care. In emergencies, for example, wireless technologies enable paramedics to transmit patient data to hospitals while en route, allowing for better preparation and faster treatment upon arrival. Mobile health initiatives leveraging wireless technologies in developing regions have expanded access to basic healthcare services, health education, and disease prevention programs. Additionally, wireless technologies facilitate the rapid dissemination of public health information, crucial during disease outbreaks or public health emergencies.

Introduction to Risks in the Applications of Wireless Technologies in Medical Devices

The integration of wireless technologies has expanded the reach of healthcare services beyond traditional clinical settings, enabling more personalized, efficient, and accessible medical care. These innovations have not only improved patient outcomes but also enhanced the efficiency of healthcare delivery systems. By leveraging wireless capabilities, healthcare providers can offer continuous care, make better decisions based on meaningful data, and intervene proactively in patient health issues. This shift toward connected healthcare has the potential to reduce hospitalizations, improve chronic disease management, and empower patients to take a more active role in their health.

In Chapter 1, IoMT applications in healthcare were introduced. This section explores the diverse applications of wireless technologies in healthcare and introduces some security risks. Figure 2-2 summarizes risk distribution by top category. These estimates reflect how interconnected medical devices are exposed to various risks. The exact distribution may vary depending on device type, network configuration, and the organization's security posture. To mitigate these risks, healthcare providers must invest in strong encryption, regular patch management, and compliance auditing.

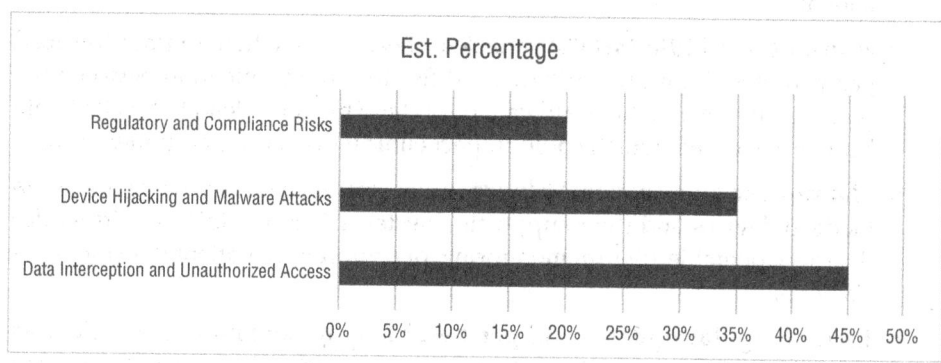

Figure 2-2: Summary of risk distribution

Wireless Remote Patient Monitoring Risks

Wireless-enabled devices such as wearable sensors, implantable monitors, and smart home systems monitor critical metrics like heart rate, blood pressure, glucose levels, respiratory patterns, and even falls, providing unprecedented access to patient health data. These devices communicate over wireless networks, allowing seamless and secure data transmission to healthcare providers' systems.

However, while wireless technologies have significantly enhanced patient care, they also introduce security risks at the hospital and home. The same wireless connectivity that enables seamless monitoring can expose patient data to potential vulnerabilities. Without robust security measures, sensitive health information can be intercepted by unauthorized parties, leading to privacy breaches or even manipulation of critical health data. These risks highlight the urgent need to address security concerns in parallel with technological advancements.

In Part II, I will dive deeper into the applications of wireless technologies in healthcare and the security challenges they pose. As an introduction to wireless security risks, specifically for patient safety and data integrity, I'll introduce the top 10 here:

- **Data interception and eavesdropping:** Wireless communication channels can be vulnerable to interception. Without strong encryption, unauthorized individuals can access sensitive health data such as vital signs, medication schedules, or diagnostic results during transmission.

- **Unauthorized access to devices:** Devices used for remote monitoring may lack strong authentication protocols, making them susceptible to unauthorized access. Malicious actors could exploit weak or default passwords to manipulate device settings or access private data.

- **Device hijacking:** Cybercriminals may gain control of wireless medical devices, potentially altering their functionality. For example, a pacemaker or insulin pump could be tampered with, leading to life-threatening outcomes for the patient.

- **Man-in-the-middle (MITM) attacks:** These occur when an unauthorized party intercepts and potentially modifies the communication between the patient's device and the healthcare provider. This could lead to falsified data being transmitted, which could impact clinical decisions and patient care.

- **Malware and ransomware:** Malware or ransomware attacks can target wireless medical devices and their supporting systems. These attacks could render devices inoperable, disrupt monitoring, or compromise patient data for financial gain.

- **Lack of regular updates and patches:** Many remote monitoring devices operate on proprietary software that may not be updated regularly. Unpatched vulnerabilities can become entry points for attackers seeking to exploit outdated systems.

- **Interference with network availability:** Wireless systems depend on reliable network connections. Denial-of-service (DoS) attacks or network disruptions could prevent timely transmission of critical health data, delaying care and increasing risk to patients.

- **Insider threats:** Employees with access to monitoring systems may inadvertently or maliciously compromise patient data. Poor access controls and lack of auditing can exacerbate this risk.

- **Third-party integrations:** Remote patient monitoring often involves third-party platforms and cloud services for data storage and analytics. If these third parties do not adhere to stringent security standards, they can become weak links in the security chain.

- **Privacy concerns and regulatory noncompliance:** The collection and transmission of sensitive health information must comply with regulations like HIPAA (in the United States) or GDPR (from the European Union). Security lapses can result in significant legal and financial penalties, along with loss of patient trust.

By examining both the benefits and risks, we can develop a comprehensive understanding of how these technologies are shaping modern healthcare while emphasizing the importance of safeguarding patient safety and data integrity. Some of the mitigation strategies that I'll discuss in detail throughout Parts II through IV include enhancing security in interconnected systems by adopting a multilayered approach.

Encryption should be implemented to ensure end-to-end protection for all data transmissions, safeguarding sensitive information from unauthorized interception. Authentication measures, such as multifactor authentication (MFA), are essential to secure device access and prevent unauthorized logins. Regular firmware updates must be prioritized to address known vulnerabilities and keep devices protected against emerging threats.

Network security should be fortified using firewalls, virtual private networks (VPNs), segmentation, and intrusion detection and prevention systems to monitor and defend communication channels. Strict access controls must be enforced, limiting permissions to authorized personnel only and conducting regular audits of access logs to detect anomalies. Additionally, third-party vetting is crucial to ensure that all external providers meet rigorous security and compliance standards, minimizing supply chain risks. Finally, a good incident response plan should be developed and tested regularly, enabling organizations to swiftly address potential breaches and mitigate damage in the event of an attack.

Security Risks in Telemedicine

Telemedicine enables remote consultations, diagnostics, and treatment through digital platforms. While it increases accessibility, reduces costs, and improves convenience, it also introduces security risks. These risks, if not properly mitigated, can compromise patient privacy, data integrity, and overall trust in the healthcare system.

As mentioned in wireless remote patient monitoring risks, unauthorized access, MITM, ransomware/malware, third-party, and compliance risks also correlate with telemedicine use cases. However, the following are some additional concerns, as well as some from a different viewpoint, which I'll cover later in detail:

- **Data transmission vulnerabilities:** Sensitive patient information, including medical histories, prescriptions, and diagnostic reports, is transmitted over the Internet. Without adequate encryption, this data can be intercepted by attackers during transit.

- **Platform and software exploits:** Telemedicine platforms may contain vulnerabilities in their software, which attackers can exploit to gain access to patient data or disrupt services.
- **Privacy breaches:** Inadequate data storage practices or misconfigured cloud services can lead to unintentional exposure of patient data to unauthorized parties.
- **Unsecured devices:** Both patients and providers may use personal devices that lack robust security measures. Unsecured devices are prime targets for attackers seeking access to telemedicine sessions or stored medical data.
- **Phishing and social engineering attacks:** Cybercriminals may use phishing emails or social engineering techniques to trick patients or healthcare providers into disclosing login credentials or sensitive information.

To address the security risks associated with telemedicine, healthcare providers and platform developers must adopt a comprehensive set of strategies to protect sensitive data and ensure secure operations. Encryption, strong authentication, and maintaining secure software development practices are crucial. Regularly updating telemedicine software to patch vulnerabilities and adhering to security best practices during development can help mitigate potential exploits.

Ensuring hardy network security is equally important. Telemedicine platforms should be protected using firewalls (including those with web application protection features), VPNs, and intrusion detection systems to safeguard data transmission from cyber threats. Complementing network security is device security, which involves encouraging both patients and providers to use secure, up-to-date devices for telemedicine sessions. Basic security measures, such as using antivirus software, multifactor authentication, and strong passwords, can further reduce vulnerabilities.

Another key principle is data minimization, which entails collecting only the essential patient information necessary for telemedicine sessions. This data should then be stored securely with proper access controls to limit potential exposure. Alongside this, training and awareness initiatives are vital. Educating healthcare staff and patients about identifying phishing attempts, maintaining strong password hygiene, and ensuring secure device usage can significantly improve overall security posture.

Evaluating third-party services through third-party audits is also critical. Ensuring that these services adhere to stringent security and compliance standards can help prevent vulnerabilities introduced by external vendors. Regular risk assessments should be conducted to identify and address potential weaknesses in telemedicine platforms, keeping security measures up-to-date with evolving threats.

Finally, having a well-prepared incident response plan is essential for mitigating the impact of security breaches. Developing and regularly testing the response plan ensures that healthcare organizations can quickly address and recover from any incidents that occur. That could also correlate with disaster recovery (DR) and business continuity planning (BCP).

By proactively addressing the risks associated with telemedicine through comprehensive security measures and ongoing vigilance, healthcare organizations can ensure the safe and effective delivery of telemedicine services. This not only protects sensitive patient data but also fosters trust and confidence in the evolving landscape of digital healthcare.

Implantable Medical Device Security Concerns

The integration of wireless capabilities in implantable medical devices (IMDs) has transformed the management of various chronic conditions. Modern pacemakers and implantable cardioverter-defibrillators (ICDs) can wirelessly transmit data on heart rhythm and device function to physicians, allowing for remote monitoring and adjustment without the need for invasive procedures. Implantable insulin pumps can now be programmed and adjusted wirelessly, improving diabetes management. Neurostimulators for conditions like Parkinson's disease or chronic pain can be fine-tuned remotely. These wireless capabilities not only improve patient comfort and reduce the need for frequent clinic visits but also enable more responsive and personalized treatment adjustments.

IMDs, such as pacemakers, insulin pumps, and neurostimulators, rely on wireless communication and embedded software that introduce some security concerns. One major issue is the potential for unauthorized access to these devices. IMDs often use wireless protocols to enable monitoring, programming, or data transmission, but insufficient encryption or authentication measures are common and leave them vulnerable to hacking. If an attacker gains access, they could interfere with the device's functionality, potentially delivering harmful commands or disrupting essential medical treatments.

Another concern is the lack of regular software updates for many IMDs. These devices are often deployed for long periods without routine maintenance, leaving them susceptible to exploitation through outdated firmware. Cybercriminals could exploit known vulnerabilities to compromise the device, jeopardizing patient safety. Furthermore, as IMDs rely on wireless communication, they can be exposed to threats such as eavesdropping or man-in-the-middle attacks, where attackers intercept and manipulate data transmissions. This poses a risk to patient privacy and the integrity of critical medical information.

Targeted RFID in Hospital Equipment Management

RFID and Wi-Fi technologies have significantly improved the efficiency of hospital operations and asset management. RFID tags attached to medical equipment allow for real-time tracking of location and usage. This system can prevent loss or theft of expensive equipment, ensure timely maintenance, and optimize utilization rates. In emergency situations, staff can quickly locate critical equipment. These technologies also facilitate inventory management, ensuring that supplies are restocked efficiently. Advanced systems can even track the movement of patients and staff, improving workflow and reducing wait times.

However, the use of RFID also introduces unique security concerns that can pose risks to hospital operations and patient safety. RFID systems operate by transmitting data wirelessly between tags and readers, which makes them vulnerable to interception, unauthorized access, and manipulation. If an attacker exploits these vulnerabilities, they could potentially disrupt hospital workflows by misdirecting or falsifying critical asset location data. For example, tampering with RFID systems could result in essential medical equipment, such as ventilators or infusion pumps, being marked as unavailable or misplaced during emergencies.

A form of interception risk associated with RFID technology is eavesdropping, where attackers intercept the communication between RFID tags and readers to gain access to sensitive data. Depending on the system, this data could include equipment identification, usage logs, or even patient-related information tied to the asset. Additionally, RFID systems are susceptible to cloning and spoofing attacks, where an attacker duplicates legitimate RFID tags or introduces fake ones to manipulate the system. This can lead to equipment theft, tampering, or mismanagement, potentially jeopardizing patient care and hospital efficiency.

Another concern is the lack of encryption in many older RFID implementations, particularly in legacy systems. Without proper encryption protocols, data transmitted by RFID tags can be easily intercepted and exploited. Furthermore, hospitals often rely on third-party vendors to implement and manage RFID systems, which can introduce additional vulnerabilities. Weak vendor security practices, insufficient oversight, or inadequate system updates can open the door to cyber threats targeting RFID infrastructure.

To mitigate these risks, hospitals must adopt a multilayered approach to RFID security. Implementing strong encryption protocols, segmentation, and strict access controls can help ensure that only authorized personnel can interact with RFID systems, and activity logs should be monitored for any suspicious behavior. Regular security assessments and updates are critical to addressing vulnerabilities and ensuring that both RFID tags and readers are secure. Additionally, hospitals should establish clear policies for RFID use and train staff to recognize potential risks, such as unauthorized devices or anomalies in equipment tracking.

By addressing these challenges, hospitals can better secure their RFID systems and ensure that the benefits of this technology, such as improved efficiency and asset visibility, are not overshadowed by potential security threats. Safeguarding RFID infrastructure is an essential step toward maintaining operational integrity, protecting sensitive data, and ensuring high-quality patient care.

Vulnerable Smart Pill Bottles and Dispensers

Smart pill bottles and dispensers have evolved medication management by improving adherence through automated reminders, tracking usage, and alerting healthcare providers or caregivers about missed doses. However, these devices also introduce security concerns when they are not adequately protected against cyber threats.

As they often rely on wireless communication technologies like Bluetooth or Wi-Fi to transmit data, they are susceptible to interception, unauthorized access, and manipulation as with other healthcare applications I discussed. Attackers could exploit these vulnerabilities to tamper with medication schedules, disrupt alerts, or even gain access to sensitive patient data, such as health conditions and prescribed medications.

One of the primary risks associated with these devices is the lack of encryption in data transmission due to older technologies still being used today. If the communication between the smart dispenser and a connected application is not encrypted, attackers can intercept this data, potentially exposing sensitive health information or altering instructions. Another concern is the risk of unauthorized access to the device itself. Weak authentication measures, such as default or easily guessable passwords, can allow attackers to gain control of the dispenser, enabling them to modify dosage schedules or disable alerts, potentially causing harm to patients. In healthcare facilities around the globe, cybersecurity experts have witnessed weak authentication risks in many areas. I'll explain the attack vector in more detail in Chapter 11.

Additionally, smart pill bottles and dispensers often rely on cloud-based systems to store and manage data, introducing risks related to cloud security. If the backend servers or applications associated with these devices are not adequately secured, they can become a target for breaches, exposing patient records on a larger scale. Furthermore, many of these devices are developed by third-party manufacturers who may not follow rigorous security standards, leaving vulnerabilities unaddressed. This risk is heightened by the use of outdated firmware or a lack of regular security updates, making devices more susceptible to emerging threats.

By prioritizing the theme of security in the design, deployment, and use of smart pill bottles and dispensers, healthcare organizations can mitigate risks and ensure that these devices fulfill their intended purpose, which is enhancing medication adherence and improving patient outcomes without compromising safety or privacy.

Threats to Surgical and Imaging Systems

Surgical and imaging systems, including robotic surgical platforms, MRI machines, CT scanners, and X-ray equipment, are integral to modern healthcare. However, they present unique security concerns due to their complexity and critical role in patient care. These systems often rely on sophisticated software and network connectivity for their operation, making them potential targets for cyberattacks. A compromise of these systems can result in significant harm, ranging from patient safety risks during procedures to disruptions in diagnosis and treatment.

One concern is the potential for malware or ransomware attacks. Surgical and imaging systems often operate on older or specialized operating systems that may not be regularly updated due to compatibility concerns, leaving them vulnerable to known exploits. A ransomware attack could encrypt the data or disable these devices, leading to delayed or canceled procedures and creating a backlog in patient care. Additionally, unauthorized access to these systems could allow an attacker to tamper with settings, manipulate imaging data, or interfere with surgical procedures, potentially causing physical harm to patients.

Another unique risk is the interception of sensitive patient data during transmission. Imaging systems often transmit diagnostic images and patient information to EHRs or remote specialists for analysis. If these communications are not encrypted or adequately secured, attackers could intercept and exfiltrate this data, leading to privacy violations and potential compliance breaches under regulations like HIPAA.

Furthermore, the integration of surgical and imaging systems into hospital networks introduces a potential attack vector for lateral movement. Once inside the network, attackers could use vulnerabilities in these systems as entry points to access other critical systems, including EHRs or administrative tools. This risk is heightened by the use of third-party software or components that may not adhere to stringent security standards, increasing the attack surface.

In Part IV, I'll address these challenges and the best practices that healthcare organizations must implement to ensure robust security measures tailored to these systems. By addressing the unique vulnerabilities of surgical and imaging systems, healthcare providers can protect patient safety, maintain the integrity of critical medical devices, and safeguard sensitive diagnostic and procedural data from emerging cybersecurity threats.

Wireless Integration Challenges and Considerations

While wireless technologies have enabled better monitoring and care for medical devices, they come with challenges. These include security, privacy, regulatory compliance, interference, power management, interoperability, reliability, and user acceptance. Each of these areas presents unique risks that must be addressed to ensure patient safety and the effectiveness of these technologies.

Protecting sensitive patient data from cyber threats is a top priority. Wireless medical devices transmit highly personal health information, making them interesting targets for cybercriminals. Implementing encryption ensures that data remains secure during transmission and storage, but this must be balanced with the need for quick access in emergencies. Authentication protocols, such as multifactor authentication, can restrict access to authorized personnel, while regular updates and vulnerability management are essential to address emerging security threats. Additionally, protecting data integrity against man-in-the-middle attacks and adhering to privacy regulations like HIPAA or GDPR add layers of complexity. Even physical security, such as preventing device theft or tampering, is an important consideration.

Meeting regulatory requirements is complex for wireless medical devices, as they must adhere to local and international standards. In the United States, devices must comply with HIPAA and the Health Information Technology for Economic and Clinical Health (HITECH) Act (that strengthens HIPAA) for patient data protection and FDA guidelines for cybersecurity in medical devices. Many organizations have a Chief Compliance Officer to address these challenges. Internationally, standards like the EU's Medical Device Regulation further complicate compliance, especially for devices used across multiple jurisdictions. Keeping up with evolving regulations requires constant updates to software, processes, and documentation while balancing the need for innovation and global market compatibility.

In environments crowded with wireless devices, interference is a challenge. Electromagnetic interference (EMI) from other equipment or crowded frequency bands can disrupt device communication, leading to malfunctions or data errors. Reliable spectrum management and coexistence strategies are necessary to ensure seamless operation. Protocols must prioritize critical medical devices, and systems for detecting and mitigating interference in real time are essential to maintaining functionality in busy healthcare settings.

Wireless medical devices, especially implantable ones, rely on battery power, making efficient energy use crucial. Prolonging battery life is vital for devices like pacemakers, where replacements require surgery. Energy-efficient protocols like BLE and innovative solutions like energy harvesting can reduce dependency on traditional power sources. Additionally, user-friendly charging methods and sophisticated power management algorithms help ensure that devices remain operational without compromising performance or patient safety.

Ensuring that wireless medical devices communicate effectively with healthcare systems is a persistent issue. Devices must follow standardized data formats and exchange protocols, such as HL7 Fast Healthcare Interoperability Resources (FHIR), to integrate seamlessly with electronic health records. HL7 FHIR is a standard for exchanging healthcare information electronically. It combines the best features of HL7 v2, HL7 v3, and CDA, while using modern web technologies like RESTful APIs, JSON, and XML. FHIR enables seamless data sharing between healthcare systems, improving interoperability, accessibility, and patient care. Cross-vendor compatibility and scalability are necessary as healthcare systems expand and evolve. Integrating modern devices with older legacy systems adds complexity, making interoperability crucial for coordinated care and streamlined workflows.

The critical nature of medical devices demands unwavering reliability. Systems must be designed to tolerate faults and maintain functionality even during network disruptions. Consistent signal quality, data integrity, and low latency are particularly important for real-time monitoring and emergency alerts. Backup communication channels and predictive maintenance systems help ensure continuous operation, while fail-safe modes provide essential fallback options in case of failures.

For wireless medical devices to be effective, healthcare providers and patients must trust and feel comfortable using them. Intuitive designs, comprehensive training for healthcare staff, and patient education ensure proper usage and build confidence in the technology. Addressing concerns about privacy, reliability, and cultural sensitivity is key to fostering acceptance. Accessibility features and efforts to reduce technophobia, particularly among older patients, also play a significant role in adoption. Demonstrating the tangible benefits of these technologies in improving healthcare outcomes and efficiency helps build trust and widespread acceptance.

While wireless medical technologies offer transformative benefits, addressing their associated challenges is critical. By focusing on security, compliance, reliability, and user adoption, the healthcare industry can ensure that these advancements deliver on their promise while safeguarding patient well-being and data integrity.

Emerging Wireless Trends and Future Directions

The landscape of wireless technologies in medical devices is rapidly evolving, with several exciting trends. One of the most significant advancements is the integration of 5G networks. The rollout of 5G provides faster data speeds, lower latency, and the ability to connect an exponentially larger number of devices simultaneously. This enables more real-time, high-bandwidth medical applications, such as high-definition remote surgeries, seamless remote patient monitoring, and the integration of multiple medical devices in a connected ecosystem.

Another promising trend is the incorporation of artificial intelligence and machine learning in wireless medical devices. By combining AI with data collected from connected medical devices, healthcare systems can unlock new possibilities in predictive healthcare. AI and ML algorithms can analyze vast amounts of patient data to identify patterns and predict potential health issues before they occur, enabling preventative care.

Edge computing is the trend that is set to transform the functionality of wireless medical devices. By processing data closer to the source, on the device itself, rather than sending it to a centralized cloud or server, edge computing can significantly reduce latency and improve the responsiveness of medical systems. This is particularly important in time-sensitive applications, such as remote surgeries or real-time patient monitoring, where delays in data transmission could have serious consequences. Additionally, edge computing can enhance patient privacy by ensuring that sensitive health data is processed locally and shared only when necessary, reducing the risk of data breaches or unauthorized access.

Advancements in sensors are also playing a role in the evolution of wireless medical technologies. As sensor technology continues to improve, devices will become smaller, more accurate, and more capable of monitoring a wider range of health parameters. The miniaturization of sensors will allow for more discreet devices that patients can wear, or in some cases have implanted, comfortably throughout the day, improving adherence to treatment plans and fostering proactive health management.

In parallel, implantable and ingestible sensors are becoming increasingly advanced, thanks to innovations in miniaturization and biocompatible materials. These sensors, which can be implanted under the skin or ingested, offer the potential for continuous, real-time monitoring of vital health metrics such as blood glucose levels, organ function, or drug delivery. They can transmit data wirelessly to healthcare providers, reducing the need for frequent hospital visits and enabling more personalized, patient-centered care. These devices hold great promise for managing chronic conditions and improving the quality of life for patients who require constant monitoring.

Another groundbreaking development is wireless power transfer technology. This innovation could eliminate the need for battery replacement surgeries in patients with implanted medical devices, such as pacemakers or neurostimulators. Wireless power transfer allows these devices to be charged remotely without the need for invasive procedures, offering patients greater convenience and reducing healthcare costs. As this technology improves, it could also pave the way for smaller, longer-lasting implantable devices that can operate autonomously for extended periods, further enhancing patient care.

Lastly, I mentioned blockchain technology in Chapter 1, and it's gaining attention for its potential to secure and enhance the integrity of medical data transmitted wirelessly. Blockchain, known for its decentralized and immutable ledger system, could provide a more secure way to store and share sensitive patient data, ensuring that it cannot be tampered with or altered during transmission. By integrating blockchain into wireless medical devices, healthcare providers can create more transparent, secure, and tamper-resistant data exchange systems, fostering greater trust among patients and clinicians and ensuring compliance with strict data protection regulations like HIPAA.

These emerging trends highlight the exciting potential for wireless technologies in medical devices to not only improve patient outcomes but also reshape the healthcare landscape by enhancing efficiency, security, and accessibility. As these innovations continue to evolve, they will undoubtedly open up new possibilities for the future of healthcare.

Regulatory Landscape for Wireless Medical Devices

The regulatory environment for wireless medical devices is both complex and continuously evolving, as the adoption of new technologies brings unique challenges to patient safety, device performance, and data security. In the United States, the Food and Drug Administration plays a pivotal role in overseeing the approval and regulation of wireless medical devices. The FDA provides detailed guidance for manufacturers on a range of factors, including the devices' safety, effectiveness, and compliance with various standards. In particular, the FDA emphasizes the importance of cybersecurity measures, ensuring that wireless devices are protected from unauthorized access or tampering that could compromise patient safety. Additionally, the FDA addresses electromagnetic compatibility, requiring manufacturers to ensure that devices operate reliably without causing harmful interference to other electronic equipment in medical environments. These regulations are critical for maintaining the integrity of wireless medical devices and ensuring they function as intended in complex healthcare settings.

In the European Union, the Medical Device Regulation (EU MDR) provides a comprehensive regulatory framework for medical devices, including those that are wireless enabled. The EU MDR includes specific requirements for wireless medical devices in areas such as risk management and post-market surveillance. Manufacturers must implement risk management processes to identify, assess, and mitigate any potential hazards associated with wireless technologies. Furthermore, the regulation mandates ongoing post-market surveillance, ensuring that devices are monitored after they enter the market to identify any emerging safety concerns or performance issues. These measures are designed to ensure that wireless medical devices not only meet safety standards at the time of approval but continue to meet these standards throughout their lifecycle.

In addition to national and regional regulations, several international standards govern the development and deployment of wireless medical devices. Among them, organizations such as the Institute of Electrical and Electronics Engineers (IEEE) and the International Organization for Standardization (ISO) create and maintain standards that focus on the safety, reliability, and interoperability of wireless technologies in medical applications. These standards are crucial for ensuring that devices can communicate effectively with one another and integrate seamlessly into healthcare systems. For example, wireless medical devices must meet interoperability standards to ensure they can exchange data reliably with other devices, electronic health records, and hospital monitoring systems. Compliance with these international standards helps manufacturers ensure that their products meet global safety and performance expectations, reducing the risk of device failure or malfunction in diverse clinical environments.

As wireless medical devices become increasingly prevalent, cybersecurity has emerged as a primary concern for regulatory bodies worldwide. Given the sensitive nature of the data these devices collect and transmit, protecting patient information and device integrity is critical. Regulatory bodies, including the FDA, European Medicines Agency (EMA), and other international agencies, have introduced updated (stricter) cybersecurity guidelines to ensure that medical devices are resilient to cyberattacks. These guidelines require manufacturers to implement strong encryption, access control, and vulnerability management practices to safeguard against potential data breaches, hacking attempts, and unauthorized access. Furthermore, manufacturers are encouraged to conduct regular security assessments and implement robust incident response protocols to quickly address any security vulnerabilities. As the number of connected devices in healthcare continues to grow, the importance of maintaining secure communication channels for patient data cannot be overstated.

The takeaway here is that the regulatory landscape for wireless medical devices is multifaceted and evolving. It requires manufacturers to navigate complex guidelines from local, regional, and international bodies, each of which emphasizes safety, cybersecurity, interoperability, and ongoing monitoring. As the use of wireless technologies in healthcare expands, regulatory agencies will continue to adapt and refine their standards to ensure that these devices are both effective and secure, ultimately safeguarding patient health and promoting the responsible use of innovative medical technologies.

Best Practices for Wireless Technology Implementation

Successfully implementing wireless technologies in medical devices requires a thoughtful and structured approach to ensure functionality and safety. One of the first and most critical considerations I talked about is security by design. Integrating security measures from the earliest stages of device development is essential. This proactive approach helps mitigate potential cybersecurity risks, such as data breaches or unauthorized access, which could compromise patient safety or device integrity. Security features should include data encryption, secure communication protocols, and strong user authentication mechanisms. By addressing security concerns at the design phase, manufacturers can build trust with users and healthcare providers, ensuring that the devices meet high patient privacy and protection standards.

Thorough testing is a theme in this book and a cornerstone of successfully implementing wireless medical devices. Before devices are brought to market, they must undergo extensive testing to ensure they meet safety, performance, and regulatory standards. This includes testing for EMC to ensure that wireless devices do not interfere with other medical equipment or cause harmful electromagnetic emissions. Additionally, testing for electromagnetic interference is crucial to verify that the devices can function reliably in the complex environments of hospitals, clinics, or home healthcare settings. Beyond EMC and EMI, reliability testing is also critical, particularly for devices that will be used continuously or in life-threatening situations, such as pacemakers or insulin pumps. These tests should simulate a range of real-world conditions to ensure that the device performs consistently and safely under various environmental factors, including temperature fluctuations, humidity, and physical impact.

In designing wireless medical devices, it is essential to adopt a user-centric design approach. The wireless features of a device should enhance the user experience, not complicate it. For healthcare providers, the device should be intuitive and easy to integrate into existing workflows without adding unnecessary complexity. For patients, the wireless technology should be seamless and unobtrusive, ensuring that it doesn't interfere with daily activities while providing the necessary monitoring and feedback. A user-friendly interface, clear instructions, and accessible support are all important factors in improving adherence to device use, particularly for chronic condition management. A well-designed wireless device ensures that both healthcare professionals and patients can effectively leverage its capabilities without encountering technical difficulties or confusion.

Let's also consider scalability. As healthcare technologies continue to evolve, it is important to design wireless medical devices with future growth in mind. This includes anticipating increases in data volume, new features, and the potential for software updates or upgrades. Devices should be built with flexible architectures that can accommodate future advancements, whether that means handling larger amounts of patient data, integrating with new platforms, or incorporating additional sensors or capabilities. Scalability also involves designing systems that can easily interface with other medical devices or healthcare systems, supporting future interoperability needs as new technologies are introduced.

Battery optimization is also important, given the reliance of many wireless medical devices on battery power. Efficient power management strategies should be incorporated to extend the battery life of devices, ensuring that they can operate effectively without frequent recharging or battery replacement. This is especially critical for implantable devices, where battery life can directly impact the need for invasive surgeries to replace the device. Power-saving features such as energy-efficient sensors, low-power communication protocols, and sleep modes for non-active periods can significantly reduce energy consumption, while also improving the patient experience by minimizing the need for maintenance or device downtime.

Lastly, ensuring regulatory compliance is essential for the successful implementation of wireless technologies in medical devices. Medical devices are subject to stringent regulatory standards, and it is crucial for manufacturers to stay up to date with the latest requirements, whether they are set by the FDA, the EMA, or international bodies like the ISO. Compliance with regulatory standards ensures that the device is safe, effective, and trustworthy for use in clinical settings. Manufacturers must also consider specific regulations related to wireless communication, such as the need for devices to comply with electromagnetic emission standards, cybersecurity requirements, and data privacy laws. Adhering to these regulations not only ensures patient safety but also helps manufacturers avoid costly fines, recalls, or legal liabilities.

By adhering to best practices, manufacturers can create wireless medical devices that are not only technologically advanced but also reliable, secure, and user-friendly, meeting the needs of healthcare providers and patients while complying with strict safety and regulatory standards.

The landscape of wireless technologies in medical devices is evolving, offering opportunities to improve patient care, enhance healthcare delivery, and empower individuals. However, this evolution also brings challenges in areas of security, privacy, and regulatory compliance. As the field continues to advance, it will be crucial for device manufacturers, healthcare providers, and regulatory bodies to work collaboratively, as opposed to on islands, to ensure that these technologies are implemented safely, effectively, and ethically.

The future of wireless medical devices holds immense potential, with emerging technologies like 5G and beyond, AI, and advanced sensors promising to unlock new capabilities and applications. As we move forward, the focus must remain on leveraging these technologies to improve patient outcomes, increase healthcare accessibility, and drive innovation in medical care.

By understanding the current landscape, addressing challenges head-on, and embracing emerging trends, the medical device industry can harness the full potential of wireless technologies to create a more connected, efficient, and patient-centric healthcare ecosystem.

Key Takeaways of Wireless Technologies in Healthcare

Wireless medical devices offer significant benefits to healthcare, including improved patient mobility, enhanced data collection and analysis, increased efficiency, cost reduction, and real-time alerts. These advantages improve patient care, early interventions, and chronic disease management. However, integrating wireless technology in medical devices also presents notable security challenges, such as data interception, unauthorized access, and device hijacking, necessitating stringent adherence to regulatory standards like HIPAA and GDPR.

Implementing wireless medical devices faces additional hurdles, including electromagnetic interference, power management, and interoperability issues. Addressing these challenges requires stronger security protocols, innovative energy solutions, and adherence to healthcare integration standards. The landscape of wireless medical devices is rapidly evolving, with emerging trends such as 5G networks, AI integration, edge computing, and advanced sensors promising to revolutionize healthcare delivery and patient outcomes.

Navigating the complex regulatory landscape is crucial for manufacturers. The compliance requirements set by the FDA and EU MDR emphasize cybersecurity, risk management, and ongoing monitoring. Adherence to international standards ensures interoperability and safety across diverse clinical environments. To effectively implement wireless medical technologies, best practices include security-by-design approaches, thorough testing, user-centric design, and scalability and battery optimization.

Ultimately, the successful integration of wireless medical devices requires a delicate balance between innovation and safety. Collaborative efforts among manufacturers, healthcare providers, and regulators are essential to harness these technological advancements responsibly while maintaining patient trust and ensuring safe, effective device performance.

CHAPTER 3

Introduction to Bluetooth and Wi-Fi in Healthcare

I talked about a world where doctors can monitor a patient's vitals in real time, even from miles away, and a wearable device can detect early warning signs of a health condition and immediately alert medical professionals. This is not the future; it's our present, made possible by wireless technologies like Bluetooth and Wi-Fi. In Chapter 2, I started with a high-level summary of the key points of wireless communication technologies. They have made a profound impact on the healthcare industry. These technologies enable seamless data exchange, remote monitoring, and enhanced patient care, all while reducing the burden on healthcare providers and improving patient outcomes. This chapter investigates how Bluetooth and Wi-Fi are further evolving modern healthcare. They're enabling smarter, more efficient systems for patient care, real-time monitoring, and seamless data integration across devices.

Bluetooth has emerged as a cornerstone for many healthcare innovations. Its ability to connect devices wirelessly over short distances with minimal power consumption makes it ideal for medical applications. Take, for instance, Bluetooth Low Energy, which powers wearables like fitness trackers and heart monitors. These devices transmit small bursts of data efficiently, ensuring long battery life, which is critical for continuous monitoring.

While Bluetooth handles short-range communication, Wi-Fi connects the broader ecosystem. Hospitals today rely heavily on extensive Wi-Fi networks to ensure smooth operation. From enabling telemedicine consultations to integrating imaging devices like MRIs with centralized systems, Wi-Fi supports critical, high-bandwidth tasks. Wi-Fi also powers real-time communication between devices. An example would be a heart monitor sending continuous data to a nurse's station. It's a force behind EHR systems, wearable tech, and even hospital management software that schedules appointments and allocates resources efficiently.

That said, this comes with challenges. Wi-Fi networks in healthcare must balance high-speed performance with rigorous security and reliability. A misstep could compromise sensitive patient data or disrupt life-saving services. Recall that with great power comes great responsibility, and wireless technologies are no exception. Bluetooth and Wi-Fi are not immune to risks, not by a long shot. Bluetooth vulnerabilities can include eavesdropping or rogue device impersonation, while Wi-Fi threats often involve rogue access points or outdated encryption and authentication protocols.

These risks underscore the importance of mitigation strategies. Regular updates, advanced security measures, and encryption standards like WPA3 for Wi-Fi or secure pairing for Bluetooth are vital. The stakes couldn't be higher when it comes to healthcare. Then there's artificial intelligence, a newer game changer for securing wireless networks. AI systems now detect anomalies, predict vulnerabilities, and automate threat mitigation for Bluetooth and Wi-Fi. For example, AI can identify rogue devices attempting to infiltrate a hospital's network or block suspicious pairing requests on Bluetooth-enabled devices.

Through real-world examples, we see how AI tools quickly pinpoint the root causes of complex issues. AI's ability to connect the dots in vast datasets is essential in ensuring the safety and efficiency of wireless healthcare environments.

Bluetooth Communication in Healthcare

Traditional wired systems are often cumbersome, inflexible, and prone to interference, while wireless solutions offer greater mobility, scalability, and ease of integration. Wireless protocols enable devices to exchange data without physical connections, especially in hospitals, clinics, and home care settings.

In healthcare, wireless technologies facilitate a wide range of applications discussed in Chapter 1, from wearable medical devices that track vital signs to complex systems for real-time patient monitoring and management. Bluetooth has emerged as one of the most prominent wireless communication technologies due to its low energy consumption, widespread adoption, and strong device support.

Understanding Bluetooth Technology

Bluetooth is a widely used wireless technology that allows devices to connect and share data over short distances. It's known for its efficiency and low energy use, making it a popular choice for many healthcare applications. Bluetooth operates on a specific radio frequency (2.4 GHz), part of the Industrial, Scientific, and Medical (ISM) band. This means it uses a frequency range that is free to use globally, making it practical and versatile. Initially developed in the 1990s for simple tasks like connecting mobile phones to wireless headsets, Bluetooth has advanced significantly and has become a key technology in modern healthcare.

Bluetooth is used in medical devices like health monitors, sensors, and fitness wearables today. It's also commonly found in devices that help transmit patient data, such as heart rate monitors or blood sugar sensors, from one location to another. Two primary types of Bluetooth are essential in healthcare:

- **Bluetooth Classic:** This version was designed to transfer larger amounts of data, such as music or files, between devices. However, it uses much more power, making it less ideal for battery-powered medical devices. It's still useful when power consumption, such as stationary medical equipment, isn't a significant concern.

- **Bluetooth Low Energy (BLE):** Introduced with Bluetooth 4.0, BLE is a more advanced version optimized for devices that need to send small bits of data without using as much energy. For example, a fitness tracker or a wearable heart monitor doesn't need to send large files; it sends only tiny pieces of data, like steps taken or heart rate readings, at regular intervals. BLE is perfect for these applications because it saves battery life, allowing devices to operate longer without recharging.

Think of Bluetooth Classic as a heavy-duty delivery truck. It can carry a lot of data but uses more fuel (or power). BLE, on the other hand, is like a lightweight scooter. It's perfect for quick trips (or small data exchanges) and uses much less energy, which is why it's ideal for devices that run on small batteries, like fitness bands or health monitors.

In healthcare, Bluetooth, particularly BLE, has become crucial for enabling wearable devices and remote patient monitoring systems, ensuring reliable and energy-efficient data transfer to improve patient care.

Bluetooth Classic

Bluetooth Classic, or Bluetooth Basic Rate/Enhanced Data Rate (BR/EDR), is a short-range wireless technology for direct communication between two devices. Operating within the globally available 2.4 GHz ISM frequency band, it uses 79 distinct channels and a frequency hopping spread spectrum (FHSS) technique to ensure stable and reliable connections while minimizing interference from other devices in crowded environments.

This technology supports direct communication between devices, making it ideal for applications that require consistent and reliable data streaming. Its Basic Rate (BR) mode offers data rates up to 1 Mbit/s, while the Enhanced Data Rate (EDR) mode provides faster transmission speeds of 2–3 Mbit/s. Its EDR mode employs advanced modulation techniques, which reduce latency and power consumption while accommodating larger data loads.

One primary use of Bluetooth Classic is wireless audio streaming, which powers technologies like wireless speakers, headphones, and in-car entertainment systems. It has become the standard for transmitting high-quality audio, facilitating seamless music playback, hands-free calls, and multimedia experiences. Additionally, Bluetooth Classic supports general data transfer applications such as mobile printing and file sharing, enabling devices like smartphones, tablets, and laptops to communicate directly with compatible peripherals without relying on Internet connectivity. This versatility makes it useful in both consumer and industrial contexts.

Despite its capabilities, Bluetooth Classic consumes more power than newer technologies like BLE. However, its power efficiency has improved significantly, balancing data transfer capabilities and energy consumption. This makes it suitable for devices with reliable power sources, such as headphones and car systems.

Bluetooth Classic is also widely compatible, and decades of development have ensured its adoption across consumer electronics, including keyboards, mice, and game controllers. Thanks to operating in an unlicensed spectrum, its global usability adds to its appeal. However, it is better suited for one-to-one communication rather than managing multiple simultaneous connections, and it may face interference in environments dense with other 2.4 GHz devices, such as Wi-Fi routers.

In simpler terms, Bluetooth Classic is a reliable and efficient technology that enables devices to communicate wirelessly. It excels at tasks like streaming music to speakers, facilitating hands-free car calls, and printing directly from a smartphone. While it uses more power than newer Bluetooth versions, it is still the backbone of many modern devices and plays a vital role in wireless communication.

Bluetooth LE

BLE, a cornerstone of modern wireless communication, is designed to enable devices to exchange small amounts of data efficiently, with minimal power consumption. This capability makes BLE indispensable in applications such as wearable health devices, smart home gadgets, fitness trackers, and industrial IoT solutions. That said, I'll spend a bit more time in an overview. To fully grasp BLE, however, you need to dive into its architecture, procedures, and protocols, which are meticulously defined in the Bluetooth Core Specification you can find at www.bluetooth.com. Additionally, how BLE-enabled products achieve interoperability hinges on specialized profiles and services, which are collections of specifications that standardize their interactions.

Here's my concise summary of the primary specification. This comprehensive document defines every facet of BLE technology. The BLE stack is illustrated in Figure 3-1.

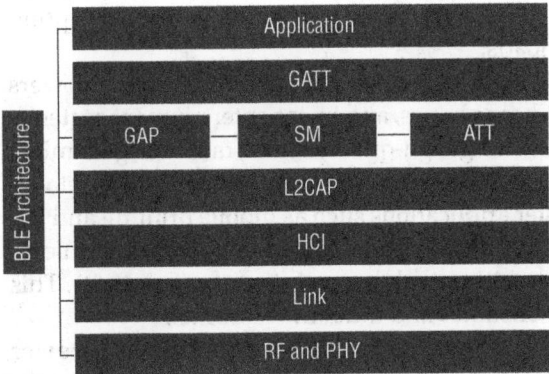

Figure 3-1: BLE architecture: layers and distribution across the host and controller components

BLE uses a structured layering system to enable efficient communication between devices. I'll run through a more technical overview, but feel free to skip ahead to the next section if this is not of interest. A simple way to look at BLE's architecture is modular, enabling seamless integration of various components and protocols such as the following:

- **Physical:** Controls radio transmission/receiving.
- **Link:** Defines packet structure, includes the state machine and radio control, and provides link layer-level encryption.
- **HCI:** A host-to-controller interface that standardizes communication between the controller and the host.
- **L2CAP:** The Logical Link Control and Adaptation Protocol, which acts as a protocol multiplexer and handles segmentation and reassembly of packets.
- **ATT:** Attribute protocol for data transmission between Bluetooth low energy devices.
- **SM:** Security Manager for bonding devices, encrypting and decrypting data, and enabling device privacy.
- **GAP:** Generic Access Profile layer for Bluetooth low energy devices to advertise themselves or other devices, make device discovery, open and manage connections, and broadcast data.
- **GATT:** Used to group individual attributes into logical services and provide information about the attributes, such as how they can be accessed and security level.

BLE also incorporates features, including secure pairing, where two devices exchange information to establish a secure encrypted connection; secure bonding, where shared secret keys generated during the pairing phase are stored; and encryption to safeguard data integrity and privacy.

Understanding BLE Profiles and Services

BLE technology uses a specific set of rules that ensure devices can communicate effectively. At the heart of this communication system are profiles and services, which work together to create seamless interaction between BLE-enabled devices. Here's what these terms mean and their roles in making devices talk to each other.

Profiles act as blueprints that define how BLE devices interact for specific tasks. Think of a profile as a set of instructions that outline how two devices, such as a fitness tracker and a smartphone, should behave to share data effectively. Here are two example use cases:

- The HRP specifies how heart rate monitors send data to devices like phones or fitness apps.
- The Proximity Profile is commonly used in devices like key finders to alert users when an item moves out of range.

Profiles are critical because they ensure that devices from different manufacturers can work together. They define which services and features a device must support to fulfill a particular function.

Services break down device functionality into smaller, modular components. Each service is like a mini application within the device, designed to perform a specific task. A service consists of one or more data points that can be shared, written to, or updated. Three common examples of services are as follows:

- **Battery service:** Shares the battery status of a device.
- **Device information service:** Provides metadata such as the manufacturer's name or device model.
- **Health thermometer service:** Transmits temperature data from a sensor to a connected device.

Services can be standardized (for universal compatibility) or customized (for proprietary use cases). Standardized services are widely supported across devices, enhancing interoperability.

Profiles and services are meticulously defined to ensure seamless communication between BLE devices. For example, a smartwatch made by one company can easily interact with a heart rate monitor made by another if both follow the Heart Rate Profile and use its defined services.

When your phone tells your fitness tracker to share heart rate data, the Heart Rate Profile ensures they understand each other, and the Battery Service ensures they can also share the device's battery level. BLE ensures that devices work together by adhering to these standardized systems, creating a connected ecosystem that simplifies everyday life.

Applications and Advantages of Bluetooth in Healthcare

Bluetooth's efficiency and ease of integration have made it an essential technology in healthcare, powering a wide range of applications. Smartwatches, fitness trackers, and wearable ECG monitors use Bluetooth to send vital health data to smartphones, tablets, or cloud-based platforms. This allows for continuous monitoring and timely health interventions. In remote patient monitoring, Bluetooth-enabled devices transmit health data from patients at home directly to healthcare providers, making it easier to manage chronic conditions like diabetes, hypertension, or COPD while reducing the need for frequent hospital visits and improving patient outcomes.

Bluetooth is also pivotal in point-of-care devices such as thermometers, blood pressure cuffs, glucose meters, and pulse oximeters. It enables fast and seamless data transfer from these devices to EHR systems or mobile apps, streamlining diagnostics and patient care. BLE beacons are used for asset tracking in hospitals, providing real-time location data for medical equipment, staff, and patients. This reduces equipment misplacement, improves operational efficiency, and enhances workflow management. Additionally, Bluetooth plays a critical role in in-hospital patient monitoring by enabling real-time data transmission of vital signs, such as ECG, heart rate, temperature, and oxygen saturation. This allows healthcare providers to respond swiftly to changes in a patient's condition, ensuring better care and timely interventions.

One key advantage of Bluetooth, especially BLE, is its low power consumption. Devices can operate for extended periods without frequent charging or battery replacement, making them ideal for wearables and other healthcare devices. Bluetooth devices are generally interoperable, meaning they can work with various devices, from smartphones to hospital-grade medical equipment. This facilitates integration into existing healthcare infrastructures.

Bluetooth is relatively inexpensive in terms of hardware and implementation costs compared to other wireless communication protocols, making it an attractive choice for healthcare providers and device manufacturers. Bluetooth also offers several layers of security to ensure that data remains confidential and protected from unauthorized access. With encryption, authentication, and secure pairing features, Bluetooth ensures that sensitive health data is kept private.

Finally, Bluetooth technology is widely recognized and user-friendly, requiring minimal setup for connecting devices. This ease of use is crucial in healthcare settings, where both patients and healthcare providers need intuitive and quick solutions for connecting devices.

Wi-Fi Communication in Healthcare

Wireless connectivity has modernized healthcare, enabling efficient patient care, improved resource management, and real-time monitoring. Wi-Fi stands out as a basis among the many wireless technologies powering this transformation.

By providing reliable, high-speed communication over local networks, Wi-Fi facilitates the seamless transfer of data between devices, bridging gaps in connectivity and fostering innovation in patient care.

Wi-Fi is ubiquitous in healthcare settings, serving as the backbone for various applications, from connecting EHR systems to enabling smart medical devices and wearables. Its ability to support high-bandwidth tasks like video consultations, image transfers, and real-time monitoring makes it a crucial tool in hospitals, clinics, and home care environments.

Understanding Wi-Fi Technology in Healthcare

Wireless Fidelity (Wi-Fi) allows devices to connect to a network without physical cables. Wi-Fi operates on radio frequencies (primarily 2.4 GHz and 5 GHz) and provides a multipurpose platform for transmitting data. Its widespread adoption and adaptability make it the go-to wireless technology for consumer and professional applications, including healthcare.

Key components of Wi-Fi technology include the following:

- **Frequency bands and channels:** Wi-Fi operates in unlicensed frequency bands. Each band is divided into multiple channels, allowing multiple devices to communicate without interference. The 2.4 GHz band offers more extended range but lower speeds and is ideal for larger facilities where coverage is key. The 5 GHz band delivers faster speeds but shorter range, making it suitable for high-density environments like operating rooms or data hubs.

- **Access points (APs) and routers:** Access points are hardware devices that create Wi-Fi networks, allowing devices to connect wirelessly. Routers act as intermediaries, directing traffic between devices on the network and external systems like the internet. Healthcare facilities often use enterprise-grade APs to ensure more robust and secure connectivity.

- **Wi-Fi standards:** Wi-Fi protocols are governed by IEEE 802.11 standards, with advancements bringing increased speed, range, and reliability. These standards are a set of technical specifications for wireless local area networks (WLANs). These include the following:

    - **802.11n:** Widely used, supports both 2.4 GHz and 5 GHz frequencies, offering balanced performance.

    - **802.11ac:** Optimized for high-speed data transfers over the 5 GHz band, commonly used in environments requiring fast communication, such as diagnostic imaging.

    - **802.11ax (e.g. Wi-Fi 6):** The latest standard, designed to handle dense device environments with improved speed and efficiency, making it ideal for IoMT-heavy hospitals.

As wireless connectivity continues to be the backbone of modern communication, securing Wi-Fi networks has become more critical than ever. With the rapid proliferation of connected devices and increasingly sophisticated cyberattacks, older, traditional Wi-Fi security protocols like WEP (hopefully no one uses it anymore) and WPA2 are no longer sufficient to protect sensitive data. Newer protocols like Wi-Fi Protected Access 3 (WPA3) and Opportunistic Wireless Encryption (OWE) have been introduced to address these challenges and set a new standard for wireless security.

Several factors drive the need for new Wi-Fi security protocols. First, the evolving threat landscape has exposed vulnerabilities in WPA2, such as the Key Reinstallation Attack (KRACK) exploit, which highlights its limitations. Second, the rise of IoT devices, billions of which are now connected to networks and often lack robust security features, necessitates stronger protocols. Finally, the sensitive data transmitted over Wi-Fi in applications like smart homes, healthcare, and financial systems demands enhanced protection to prevent breaches and ensure privacy.

WPA3 is the latest Wi-Fi security protocol, developed by the Wi-Fi Alliance, and designed to address the shortcomings of WPA2 and provide stronger security. Key features of WPA3 include enhanced encryption, which, for example, supports 192-bit encryption in Enterprise mode and 128-bit encryption in Personal mode to provide a higher protection standard. It also implements Simultaneous Authentication of Equals (SAE), replacing the Pre-Shared Key (PSK) authentication used in WPA2, which reduces the risk of brute-force attacks. Additionally, WPA3 provides individualized data encryption, ensuring that each device on the network has its traffic encrypted independently, preventing eavesdropping. Forward secrecy, another important feature, ensures that even if an encryption key is compromised, past sessions cannot be decrypted, as keys are regenerated for each session. These improvements protect against common attacks like dictionary attacks and eavesdropping while offering better security for connected medical IoT devices with simplified configuration options.

Opportunistic Wireless Encryption (OWE) enhances security for open Wi-Fi networks, which traditionally lack encryption. When a device connects to an open network, OWE automatically encrypts the traffic between the device and the access point using Diffie-Hellman (DH) key exchange. Using DH, OWE establishes a shared secret key without directly exchanging the key itself, ensures privacy for open networks, and mitigates the risks of eavesdropping. OWE requires no passwords, making it particularly useful in coffee shops, airports, and hotels. OWE, often implemented alongside WPA3, enhances overall network security by securing open Wi-Fi environments.

Despite their benefits, these protocols face challenges in adoption. Compatibility issues arise because not all older devices support WPA3 or OWE, making it difficult for network administrators to manage mixed environments. Additionally, a lack of awareness and hesitancy to invest in infrastructure upgrades hinder widespread implementation. However, the importance of these protocols is evident, particularly in sensitive environments like healthcare and enterprises. In healthcare, WPA3 secures the transmission of patient data, helping to ensure compliance with regulations like HIPAA, while OWE secures public networks in areas such as hospital lobbies. For enterprises, WPA3's robust encryption and resistance to credential theft safeguard critical operations and sensitive data.

As cyber threats continue to evolve, so must our defenses. WPA3 and OWE represent some of the latest Wi-Fi security, providing the protection needed for personal and enterprise environments. Whether managing a healthcare facility, running an IoT-powered smart home, or simply browsing at a coffee shop, these protocols ensure data remains private and secure. Investing in next-generation security protocols is critical to safeguarding the increasingly connected world.

Securing Wi-Fi networks is critical in healthcare environments to protect sensitive patient data and ensure the integrity of medical devices. Key security considerations, as mentioned, include WPA3 and its implementation of SAE. With SAE, even if an attacker captures the initial handshake, they cannot perform offline guessing attacks to determine the password. This is particularly important in healthcare settings where complex passwords may not consistently be enforced due to practical constraints.

While healthcare facilities should avoid open networks, OWE provides an additional layer of security for scenarios where open networks are necessary, such as guest Wi-Fi in waiting areas. OWE automatically encrypts traffic between devices and access points without requiring a password. This encryption by default approach helps protect against eavesdropping in public areas of healthcare facilities.

Network segmentation is another critical aspect of Wi-Fi security in healthcare. By separating medical devices, guest access, and administrative networks, healthcare organizations can contain potential breaches and limit unauthorized access to sensitive systems. Implementing virtual LANs (VLANs) or virtual wireless LANs (WLANs) effectively achieves this segmentation, isolating different types of traffic and applying appropriate security policies to each segment.

For example, medical devices should be on a separate, highly secured network segment with strict access controls. Guest Wi-Fi should be completely isolated from internal networks, preventing any potential access to sensitive systems or data. Administrative networks, which may handle billing information or electronic health records, should have their own secure segment with strong authentication measures.

Regular security audits are essential to maintain the integrity of Wi-Fi networks in healthcare environments. These audits should include comprehensive penetration testing and vulnerability assessments. Penetration testing helps identify weaknesses in the network that could be exploited by attackers, while vulnerability assessments help discover and address known security flaws in systems and software.

Finally, healthcare IT teams must stay updated on the latest Wi-Fi security threats and patches. The threat landscape constantly evolves, with new vulnerabilities and attack vectors emerging regularly. Subscribing to security bulletins, participating in healthcare IT security forums, and maintaining relationships with vendors for timely updates are all essential practices. Chapter 16 provides a more detailed list of best practices.

Applications and Advantages of Wi-Fi in Healthcare

Wi-Fi's versatility plays a critical role in enabling a variety of essential healthcare functions. It connects smart medical devices to centralized systems, allowing healthcare providers to monitor patient vitals in real time and respond quickly to emergencies. High-speed Wi-Fi also supports telemedicine, facilitating video consultations that enable remote diagnosis and patient care. Wearable devices, like fitness trackers and health monitors, rely on Wi-Fi to upload data to cloud platforms, where healthcare professionals can access it for ongoing monitoring. Hospital management systems benefit from Wi-Fi by integrating EHRs, appointment scheduling, and resource allocation, streamlining operations, and reducing errors. Additionally, imaging devices, such as MRIs and CT scanners, utilize Wi-Fi to transfer high-resolution images to specialists in real time, ensuring faster and more effective diagnoses.

In healthcare, Wi-Fi's high bandwidth allows for the seamless transmission of large files, such as medical imaging data, and supports high-speed video consultations. The interoperability of this ensures compatibility across a wide range of devices and systems, making it a handy solution for healthcare facilities. Wi-Fi networks are also scalable, capable of accommodating an increasing number of connected devices, which is ideal for expanding healthcare infrastructures. Moreover, Wi-Fi provides mobility, allowing healthcare professionals to access critical data from anywhere within the facility, unlike wired connections that restrict movement.

However, Wi-Fi in healthcare faces challenges such as signals that can be disrupted by other devices operating on the same frequency bands. These could be Bluetooth or microwaves, leading to potential connectivity issues. Security concerns arise due to the open nature of Wi-Fi networks, which makes them susceptible to cyberattacks, necessitating better encryption and strict access control measures. Ensuring consistent Wi-Fi coverage in large or complex facilities can be difficult without a carefully designed network infrastructure. Finally, as the number of connected devices increases, the bandwidth demands on the network grow, often requiring upgrades to maintain optimal performance. Despite these challenges, Wi-Fi still remains a cornerstone of modern healthcare, offering unmatched flexibility and efficiency.

Wi-Fi is like a wireless bridge that connects your devices to the internet or to each other. In a hospital, it's what allows your doctor to pull up your health records on a tablet to send your vitals to a central system, or even your smartwatch to share your heartbeat data with a health app. It's fast, flexible, and everywhere, but it also needs strong passwords and careful planning to keep it safe and reliable.

Maintaining robust security and infrastructure is essential to ensure Wi-Fi's continued success in critical medical applications. WPA3 significantly enhances healthcare security by addressing some vulnerabilities in earlier Wi-Fi protocols and providing better protection for the sensitive data that healthcare organizations handle daily. Here's a summary of how WPA3 improves security in healthcare environments:

- **Stronger encryption for data confidentiality:** WPA3 uses 192-bit encryption in Enterprise mode and 128-bit encryption in Personal mode, offering higher levels of protection than WPA2. This ensures that sensitive patient data, such as electronic health records, lab results, and imaging files, remain confidential during transmission across wireless networks. Even in the event of intercepted traffic, the advanced encryption makes it hard for attackers to decrypt the data.

- **Simultaneous authentication of equals:** SAE replaces WPA2's Pre-Shared Key authentication, which is more vulnerable to brute-force and dictionary attacks. SAE helps resist password-guessing attempts and can maintain a secure connection even with weak passwords. This protects critical systems like medical devices, wireless monitoring tools, and hospital networks from unauthorized access. Healthcare facilities can safely connect IoT medical devices, such as infusion pumps and patient monitors, without compromising security.

- **Individualized data encryption:** WPA3 encrypts data traffic for each device individually on a shared network, preventing one device from eavesdropping on another's communication. In hospital environments where multiple devices connect to the same network, such as smartphones, tablets, and medical equipment, individualized encryption ensures that data remains private between authorized devices.

- **Forward secrecy:** Forward secrecy ensures that even if an attacker compromises the encryption key, they cannot decrypt past sessions. Keys are generated anew for each session. This provides additional protection for healthcare organizations storing or transmitting long-term patient data, ensuring that past communications cannot be accessed even if a breach occurs.

- **Improved security for IoT devices:** WPA3 simplifies the connection process while enhancing security, making it ideal for IoT devices, which are often limited in processing power and prone to weak security configurations. Many modern healthcare devices rely on IoT technology for functions such as remote monitoring and real-time diagnostics. WPA3 helps ensure these devices are securely connected without sacrificing usability.

- **Protection for public networks:** WPA3's companion protocol, Opportunistic Wireless Encryption, adds encryption to open networks, providing a baseline level of security without requiring passwords. Hospital lobbies and public Wi-Fi zones where visitors and patients connect to open networks gain an added layer of privacy, protecting users from casual eavesdropping and other potential attacks.

- **Compliance with regulatory standards:** WPA3 aligns with stringent data protection regulations by enhancing wireless network security. Secure data transmission helps healthcare organizations comply with regulatory requirements like HIPAA and GDPR, avoiding penalties and maintaining patient trust.

- **Resilience against attacks:** WPA3 mitigates some common attack methods such as dictionary attacks, session hijacking, and KRACK, which were weaknesses in WPA2. This resilience ensures that networks supporting critical operations, such as surgery scheduling, patient monitoring, and telemedicine, remain protected against disruptions.

By adopting WPA3, healthcare organizations can build a more secure, resilient, and privacy-compliant wireless network infrastructure. This protocol not only helps safeguard sensitive patient data but also provides peace of mind to both healthcare providers and patients, reinforcing trust in the digital systems that underpin modern medical care.

Overview of Bluetooth and Wi-Fi Security Risks

Bluetooth and Wi-Fi are two of the most commonly used wireless communication technologies in the modern world. Their widespread adoption in consumer devices, healthcare, industrial IoT, and other sectors has also made them prime targets for malicious actors. Understanding the security risks associated with these technologies and how hackers exploit them is critical for implementing more robust security measures.

If you didn't glean from earlier in this chapter, Bluetooth is a short-range wireless technology used to connect devices like smartphones, fitness trackers, and headphones. While it's convenient, it comes with its own set of vulnerabilities that hackers often exploit. If Bluetooth communication is not properly encrypted, hackers can intercept and decode sensitive data exchanged between devices, such as passwords or personal information. They often use specialized tools called *sniffers* to capture these transmissions. I will review some of those technologies later in this book.

During the pairing process, attackers can intercept or modify the communication between two devices if encryption and authentication are weak. Older devices or those with outdated pairing mechanisms are especially vulnerable. Other attack types, that I'll also get into the weeds in later chapters, include the following:

- Bluejacking involves sending unsolicited messages to nearby devices, which can be annoying or used for phishing.
- Bluesnarfing allows hackers to access a device's data, like contacts or messages, without permission.
- Bluetooth impersonation attacks (BIASs) is accomplished by exploiting flaws in Bluetooth authentication. Hackers can impersonate trusted devices, gaining unauthorized access to a target.
- In a form of DoS attack, hackers can flood a device with Bluetooth connection requests, overwhelming it and draining its battery or disrupting normal functions.
- Exploits like the Key Negotiation of Bluetooth (KNOB) attack are capable against many Bluetooth-enabled devices that don't receive regular updates.

Common Bluetooth attack methods, which you can read about in Chapter 4, include several techniques that exploit vulnerabilities in wireless communication. One such method is sniffing, discussed previously. Another approach is the replay attack, where attackers record a communication session and replay it later to gain unauthorized access or disrupt the connection. Exploiting pairing mechanisms is another prevalent tactic, targeting devices that use outdated or insecure methods, such as simple personal identification numbers (PINs), which are easier to compromise. Additionally, hackers may use rogue device injection, where malicious devices disguise themselves as legitimate peripherals to connect with a target device, stealing data or installing malware under the guise of normal functionality. These methods underscore the importance of robust Bluetooth security measures.

A summary of common Wi-Fi security risks and attack methods include the following:

- **EAP Tunneling (Sycophant):** Extensible Authentication Protocol (EAP) is widely used in enterprise Wi-Fi networks to provide secure authentication. Sycophant is a novel attack exploiting vulnerabilities in EAP tunneling implementations. By establishing malicious inner tunnels within EAP sessions, attackers can bypass authentication mechanisms. The attacker sets up a rogue access point that mimics a legitimate network. Users unknowingly connect to the rogue AP, and the attacker exploits misconfigurations in the tunneling process to extract sensitive data like authentication credentials.

- **Eavesdropping:** Unencrypted Wi-Fi traffic can be intercepted by hackers to steal sensitive information, such as passwords or financial data. Public Wi-Fi networks are especially vulnerable to this risk.

- **LootyBooty (EAP-GTC Downgrade):** LootyBooty leverages a downgrade attack on EAP-GTC (Generic Token Card), an older and less secure authentication method. By tricking networks into using this weaker protocol, attackers can intercept and potentially compromise authentication credentials. Attackers interfere with the authentication negotiation phase, forcing the access point or client to revert to EAP-GTC, which does not encrypt credentials. Once the protocol is downgraded, attackers capture and exploit plaintext authentication data.

- **MITM attacks:** Hackers place themselves between a user and the Wi-Fi network, intercepting and potentially altering transmitted data.

- **PMKID Cracking:** Pairwise Master Key Identifier (PMKID) cracking is an evolution of traditional Wi-Fi handshake attacks. It targets WPA2 and WPA3 networks to extract the pre-shared key without needing a full handshake capture. Attackers capture the PMKID directly from the first EAPOL (EAP over LAN) to establish an encrypted connection sent during a WPA handshake. Using this PMKID, they apply brute-force or dictionary attacks to recover the PSK.

- **Rogue access points:** Attackers set up fake Wi-Fi networks that mimic legitimate ones (also known as *evil twins*). When users connect, hackers can access their data or redirect them to malicious websites.

- **Wi-Fi protected access weaknesses:** Older protocols like WPA2 are vulnerable to attacks like KRACK, which allows hackers to decrypt communications.

- **Brute-force and dictionary attacks:** Hackers systematically guess weak Wi-Fi passwords using automated tools or precompiled wordlists.
- **Packet injection:** Malicious packets are introduced into a network to disrupt communications or execute commands.
- **Unsecured IoT devices:** IoT devices connected to Wi-Fi often lack robust security measures, creating weak points in the network.

Common Wi-Fi attack methods, which you'll read about in Chapter 5, exploit vulnerabilities in wireless networks to gain unauthorized access or disrupt communications. One popular method, evil twin attacks, is where hackers create fake Wi-Fi networks with names similar to legitimate ones, tricking users into connecting and exposing their data. Packet sniffing, using tools like Wireshark, allows attackers to capture and analyze data on unsecured networks, revealing sensitive information. In wardriving, hackers drive through areas searching for vulnerable Wi-Fi networks to exploit. Session hijacking is where attackers take over active sessions on a network to impersonate users or access sensitive resources. Hackers may also target open ports on Wi-Fi routers, exploiting them to gain unauthorized access or install malware. Finally, brute-forcing WPA2 involves systematically cracking weak passwords on WPA2-secured networks using tools like Aircrack-ng. These commonly used methods highlight the critical need for robust Wi-Fi security practices to protect users and data.

Mitigation Concepts

For Bluetooth security, regular software updates are crucial to patch vulnerabilities and protect against known exploits. Modern secure pairing modes, such as Secure Simple Pairing (SSP), should be used, as they incorporate encryption and authentication, making them significantly more secure than legacy modes. It's also advisable to disable Bluetooth when not in use to minimize exposure to attacks and setting devices to nondiscoverable mode further reduces visibility to potential hackers. For devices that require PIN pairing, opting for strong, random PINs enhances security by making it more difficult for attackers to guess access codes.

For Wi-Fi security, transitioning to the WPA3 protocol is a good step, as it offers stronger encryption and better resistance to brute-force attacks compared to older standards like WPA2. Default router usernames and passwords should always be replaced with unique, strong credentials to prevent unauthorized access. Implementing network segmentation is another effective strategy that I mention throughout this book, as it isolates IoT devices on a separate network, limiting their access to sensitive systems. When using public Wi-Fi, employing a VPN is a way to encrypt traffic and prevent eavesdropping or data interception. Lastly, organizations should regularly monitor and secure access points, using specialized security tools to detect and eliminate rogue access points that could be exploited by attackers. By combining these strategies, users and organizations can significantly enhance their security posture, mitigating the risks associated with Bluetooth and Wi-Fi technologies and ensuring safer communication and exchange of data.

Both Bluetooth and Wi-Fi are incredibly convenient but can also be vulnerable. Imagine Bluetooth as a short-range handshake between devices; if someone sneaks in during the handshake, they might steal information or disrupt the connection. Similarly, Wi-Fi is like a highway where data travels; without proper barriers and safeguards, hackers can jump onto the highway and spy on or steal data.

By keeping devices updated, using strong passwords and enabling advanced security features, you can reduce the risks and enjoy the benefits of wireless connectivity without falling prey to cyberattacks.

Overview of AI in Detecting and Protecting Against Bluetooth and Wi-Fi Attacks

I mentioned earlier that I'll talk more about artificial intelligence in this chapter. Reason being, AI is revolutionizing cybersecurity by enabling more advanced detection and protection mechanisms against Bluetooth and Wi-Fi attacks. These wireless communication technologies, while critical for modern connectivity, are vulnerable to various security threats such as eavesdropping, unauthorized access, and malware injection. AI's ability to process vast amounts of data, recognize patterns, and make real-time decisions has made it a cornerstone in combating these threats.

AI is increasingly used to detect and mitigate threats targeting Bluetooth and Wi-Fi networks by leveraging advanced monitoring and analysis techniques. One key application is behavioral anomaly detection, where AI-powered systems monitor the behavior of devices and networks to flag unusual activities that may indicate malicious intent. For instance, irregular Bluetooth pairing attempts, such as unrecognized devices repeatedly trying to connect, or abnormal Wi-Fi traffic spikes involving unexpected data packets or communication with suspicious IP addresses, can signal potential attacks.

Packet analysis is another critical function of AI, where machine learning algorithms examine data packets transmitted over Bluetooth and Wi-Fi networks to identify threats. AI can detect patterns associated with eavesdropping tools, pinpointing unauthorized attempts to intercept communication. Additionally, advanced models can recognize the signatures of malicious payloads embedded within packets, enabling early intervention.

Real-time threat detection allows AI systems to respond instantly to emerging threats, such as MITM attacks or rogue access points. By analyzing communication flows, AI can identify Bluetooth pairing interceptions or impersonation attempts, as well as Wi-Fi access points that mimic legitimate networks to lure users. This immediate recognition helps prevent unauthorized access and data breaches.

Lastly, AI employs device fingerprinting to enhance security by creating unique profiles for each device on a network based on specific behaviors and characteristics. This technique aids in detecting unauthorized devices attempting to masquerade as trusted peripherals and identifying spoofed Bluetooth devices or fake Wi-Fi hotspots. Through these advanced capabilities, AI ensures more robust protection against a wide range of wireless threats.

AI helps protect Bluetooth and Wi-Fi networks by offering predictive, adaptive, and automated security measures. Through predictive security measures, AI analyzes historical attack data and current network activity to forecast potential vulnerabilities. For Bluetooth, it identifies device weaknesses based on past exploits and recommends updates or configuration adjustments, while for Wi-Fi, it highlights weak encryption settings or unpatched router vulnerabilities, suggesting immediate remediation to prevent exploitation.

Automated threat mitigation is a critical advantage of many AI-driven systems I'll explain later, which respond autonomously to threats, significantly reducing response times. For instance, AI can disconnect compromised Bluetooth devices or block suspicious pairing attempts in real time. Similarly, on Wi-Fi networks, AI isolates or quarantines infected devices or disables rogue access points to stop intrusions before they escalate.

AI also improves encryption and authentication protocols, dynamically adapting security measures based on risk assessments. For Bluetooth, it enhances authentication processes to counter impersonation attacks, such as BIASs. For Wi-Fi, AI ensures the consistent implementation of strong encryption protocols like WPA3 and monitors for potential vulnerabilities, proactively strengthening the network.

Lastly, AI's ability for continuous learning and adaptation sets it apart from traditional security solutions. AI models evolve as they learn from new attack patterns, enabling them to counter emerging threats. For Bluetooth, this includes adapting to advanced replay attacks or rogue device injections. For Wi-Fi, AI learns to recognize and neutralize sophisticated attacks such as KRACK or evil twin setups, ensuring robust, up-to-date protection. Through these capabilities, AI offers a dynamic and comprehensive approach to securing wireless networks.

In enterprise Wi-Fi security, AI-powered systems are used to monitor expansive corporate networks, detect anomalies, and neutralize potential threats before they escalate. In the realm of consumer device security, AI has been integrated into modern smartphones and smart home systems to safeguard wireless connections. These systems can alert users about suspicious pairing attempts or untrusted Wi-Fi networks. Additionally, AI can automatically disable discoverability modes or restrict connections to trusted networks, reducing exposure to attacks. In healthcare, AI can detect unauthorized attempts to access medical devices like infusion pumps or patient monitors. Similarly, in industrial IoT environments, AI prevents attacks by segmenting networks and isolating compromised devices, ensuring uninterrupted operations in smart homes and factories.

Despite its advantages, AI-driven security systems face certain challenges. False positives can disrupt operations when legitimate activities are mistakenly flagged as malicious. The effectiveness of AI also hinges on the availability of extensive training data, which is necessary for accurately identifying and countering emerging attack vectors. Moreover, AI-based security solutions can be resource-intensive, requiring robust computational infrastructure to operate efficiently. While these challenges exist, the benefits of AI in wireless security far outweigh its limitations, making it a vital tool in safeguarding modern networks.

By leveraging AI, organizations and individuals can help stay ahead of cybercriminals and ensure safer communication and data exchange in an increasingly connected world.

Here's an overview of a case study that demonstrates how AI tools, in this case Microsoft Copilot for Security, can modernize the approach to cybersecurity problem-solving: A global organization operating with a lean IT infrastructure and strong adherence to cybersecurity frameworks encountered a dual crisis—potential security threats and disruptions to critical business operations. Despite following best practices, the company faced what initially appeared to be a brute force attack, triggering alarms and causing panic. Simultaneously, key financial reports failed to generate, further escalating concerns.

Upon investigation, it was revealed that a third-party software module integrated with their ERP system had been using a hard-coded password, which failed authentication after routine password updates. This oversight created a cascade of issues, resembling a coordinated attack. Leveraging an AI security assistant during the incident enabled the team to rapidly analyze logs and pinpoint the root cause within hours, saving valuable time. Security analysts would have had to manually comb through logs, correlate events, and piece together the sequence of actions that led to the incident. This would have been a time-consuming and potentially error-prone process.

This case study illustrates the power of AI in cybersecurity. It's not about replacing human expertise but about augmenting it. Copilot for Security provided the insights, but it was still up to us, as security professionals, to interpret those insights, verify the findings, and help recommend/implement the solution.

So, what lessons can we take away? Consider these:

- Always be aware of your third-party integrations. Understand how they interact with your systems and what dependencies exist.
- Avoid hard-coded passwords at all costs. They're a security risk and can lead to situations like this one.
- Implement robust change management processes. Before making changes, even routine ones like password updates, consider the potential impacts across all systems.
- Invest in comprehensive logging and analysis tools. The more data you have and the better you can analyze it, the quicker you can identify and resolve issues.
- Consider the potential of AI tools like Microsoft Copilot for Security. They can significantly enhance your ability to detect and respond to security incidents quickly and accurately.
- Embrace Zero Trust. It's one umbrella of IAM, PAM, and monitoring endpoints, etc., that I'll talk about in more detail later in this book.

Key Takeaways of Bluetooth and Wi-Fi

Bluetooth and Wi-Fi are two prominent wireless technologies widely used in healthcare settings, each with unique characteristics and applications. Operating on the 2.4 GHz ISM band, Bluetooth is valued for its efficiency, low energy consumption, and interoperability. It comes in two variants: Bluetooth Classic, suitable for high-data transfer tasks, and Bluetooth Low Energy, optimized for devices that transmit small data bursts with minimal power consumption. Conversely, Wi-Fi operates across 2.4 GHz and 5 GHz bands, supporting high-bandwidth tasks while ensuring mobility and scalability in healthcare environments.

Both technologies, however, face security risks. Bluetooth is vulnerable to eavesdropping, man-in-the-middle attacks, and rogue device impersonation, while Wi-Fi risks include eavesdropping, rogue access points, and brute-force password attacks. To mitigate these risks, various strategies can be employed. Regular updates and secure pairing mechanisms are crucial for Bluetooth, while Wi-Fi security can be enhanced by upgrading to WPA3 and employing network segmentation.

AI plays a significant role in bolstering wireless security. AI systems can detect behavioral anomalies, analyze data packets for threats, and provide real-time responses to attacks. They also predict vulnerabilities, automate threat mitigation, and improve encryption protocols. A case study of a global company demonstrated how AI tools, such as Microsoft Copilot for Security, can quickly identify complex security issues, highlighting the interconnectedness of IT systems and the value of proactive, AI-driven security solutions.

Organizations can learn valuable lessons from these insights. They should ensure visibility into third-party integrations, implement robust change management processes, leverage AI tools for advanced threat detection and resolution, and adopt a Zero Trust framework to enforce strict access controls and comprehensive monitoring. By implementing these measures, healthcare organizations can harness the benefits of wireless technologies while maintaining a strong security posture.

Part II

Attack Vectors

This section reaches the heart of cybersecurity threats facing wireless medical networks and devices. I'm not just talking about surface-level risks; I'm unpacking the complex, evolving tactics attackers use to infiltrate and compromise critical systems in healthcare. From Bluetooth vulnerabilities to replay attacks on IoMT, this part is about understanding the attacker's playbook to better protect patient safety.

Bluetooth, Wi-Fi, and other wireless protocols have changed how hospitals operate. They power everything from heart monitors and infusion pumps to imaging systems and wearable devices. But this connectivity also brings risks. Every connection, every data packet transmitted over the air, is a potential entry point for cybercriminals. The attack vectors I'll review in this part aren't just theoretical; they're real, happening, and evolving.

Bluetooth is everywhere, from wearable health trackers to in-hospital medical devices, making it an identifiable target. Chapter 4 explores vulnerabilities like insecure pairing mechanisms and the infamous Bluetooth Impersonation Attack (BIAS). These exploits allow attackers to intercept or manipulate sensitive health data without leaving a trace. Understanding these vulnerabilities is key to hardening Bluetooth-enabled systems against attacks.

Wi-Fi is the backbone of connectivity in most healthcare environments. Yet, it's also one of the most attacked. Rogue access points, evil twin attacks, and weaknesses in older encryption standards like WPA2 pose significant risks. Chapter 5 unpacks these threats and explores the unique challenges healthcare settings face, such as balancing usability with security.

Imagine an attacker intercepting and altering the communication between a pacemaker and its monitoring system. That's the terrifying potential of man-in-the-middle (MITM) attacks. Chapter 6 explores how these attacks work, why they're so dangerous to healthcare, and what can be done to prevent them.

In Chapter 7, I discuss how replay and spoofing attacks can undermine the integrity of IoMT devices. Attackers can record legitimate data transmissions and replay them later to cause system errors or spoof device identities to gain unauthorized access. These threats highlight the need for better encryption, secure device authentication, and ongoing monitoring.

Finally, Chapter 8 centers on denial-of-service (DoS) and distributed denial-of-service (DDoS) attacks, focusing on their catastrophic impact on wireless medical networks. From flooding networks with malicious traffic to exploiting weak points in medical device protocols, DoS attacks can bring hospital operations to a halt. In healthcare, downtime isn't just inconvenient—it's life-threatening. This chapter explores the mechanics of these attacks and the mitigation strategies that can keep systems online.

Across these chapters, a few recurring themes stand out. First, healthcare systems are uniquely vulnerable because of the high stakes involved, and attackers know that even minor disruptions can cause significant chaos. Second, many medical devices and networks still rely on legacy systems that weren't built with modern cybersecurity threats in mind. Third, the need for proactive, layered defense strategies has never been greater.

Understanding how these advanced attack vectors work can help us better anticipate and counteract them. However, there is no room for complacency. Security in healthcare isn't just about compliance. It's about creating a resilient, trustworthy system that protects patients, staff, and data.

Part II is a wake-up call. It challenges us to think critically about the vulnerabilities in our systems and pushes us to act decisively to address them. Because in healthcare, every second counts, and so does every byte of data.

CHAPTER 4

Bluetooth Vulnerabilities, Tools, and Mitigation Planning

Bluetooth technology is foundational to modern communication, connecting devices from smartphones to medical equipment. It's everywhere, literally, making it a target for cybercriminals seeking to exploit its vulnerabilities for data breaches, device control, and surveillance. I recall a podcast from GreyNoise Storm Watch, aired on September 24, 2024, with statistics in terms of enumerated Bluetooth, albeit mainly consumer Apple products, that are astonishing. Over the years, Remy, who also wrote about some of this in his blog on August 20, 2024, collected data leaked from millions of devices and discussed how Bluetooth vulnerabilities impact everything from insulin pumps to firewalls.

This chapter provides a deeper dive into Bluetooth security, focusing on specific vulnerabilities, their potential impact, and tools used to discover, enumerate, and test for risks. It also introduces practices for reducing the risk of Bluetooth exploitation. In later chapters, I'll discuss using some tools and focus on various attack vectors to identify and exploit vulnerabilities. I'll also explain how to reduce risk and help prevent wireless attacks in healthcare systems.

Some of the software and products covered in this chapter are BlueZ, Bluelog, Ubertooth One, and BtleJack, which are employed for penetration testing and security assessments but can also be misused by attackers to exploit vulnerabilities. Bluetooth vulnerabilities in medical devices do pose a threat, and in some cases, they may be hiding where you least expect them. Weak pairing protocols and unencrypted communication in devices such as infusion pumps and monitors expose sensitive patient data and critical care systems to potential breaches. New attack methods continue to exploit Bluetooth vulnerabilities, underscoring the importance of proactive security measures. Real-world incidents, such as Bluetooth impersonation attacks and forward and future secrecy targets, demonstrate the necessity of regular updates, improved security configurations, and ongoing vigilance.

By understanding the threats and implementing effective security measures, individuals and organizations can maximize Bluetooth's benefits while minimizing risks. This chapter underscores the importance of a proactive approach to securing Bluetooth-enabled devices as a prelude to later content.

Introduction to Bluetooth Security

As discussed in Part I, Bluetooth operates in the 2.4 GHz ISM band and is designed to enable short-range wireless communication between devices. Bluetooth's security framework was initially created to support low-power, high-efficiency connections. Over time, the protocol has evolved, with newer versions (e.g., Bluetooth 4.x, 5.x) adding advanced security features with improvements in encryption, authentication, and privacy.

However, despite these improvements, some Bluetooth is inherently vulnerable to certain types of attacks due to factors like device discovery, low-level communication protocols, and misconfigurations. Some vulnerabilities result from flaws in the Bluetooth specification itself, while others stem from poor implementation, weak cryptographic practices, or insufficient user awareness.

Bluetooth technology incorporates security mechanisms designed to address three primary information security tenets (shown in Figure 4-1): confidentiality, authentication, and integrity. These pillars, introduced in mobile and other smart device security principles, ensure that data transmitted between devices is protected from unauthorized access, tampering, or eavesdropping.

When discussing information security in healthcare, particularly about Bluetooth-enabled medical devices, it's crucial to understand the three tenets. These principles form the foundation of a robust security strategy for protecting sensitive patient data and ensuring the proper functioning of medical devices. Albeit similar, don't confuse the tenets with the other CIA (confidentiality, integrity, and availability), a triad used as a foundation to develop strong information security policies, which I'll discuss later in this book.

In this case, confidentiality means keeping information private and accessible only to authorized parties. In the context of Bluetooth medical devices, this means ensuring unauthorized individuals cannot intercept or read patient data transmitted between devices. For example, when a Bluetooth-enabled glucose monitor sends readings to a patient's smartphone, that data should be encrypted to prevent eavesdropping. Implementing strong encryption protocols and secure pairing methods is essential for maintaining confidentiality.

Authentication is the process of verifying the unique identity of users or devices before granting access to sensitive information or systems. In healthcare, this is critical for ensuring that only authorized personnel can access patient data or control medical devices. For Bluetooth devices, authentication often involves secure pairing processes and the use of unique identifiers. For instance, when a doctor's tablet connects to a patient's heart monitor, both devices should authenticate each other to prevent unauthorized access or potential manipulation.

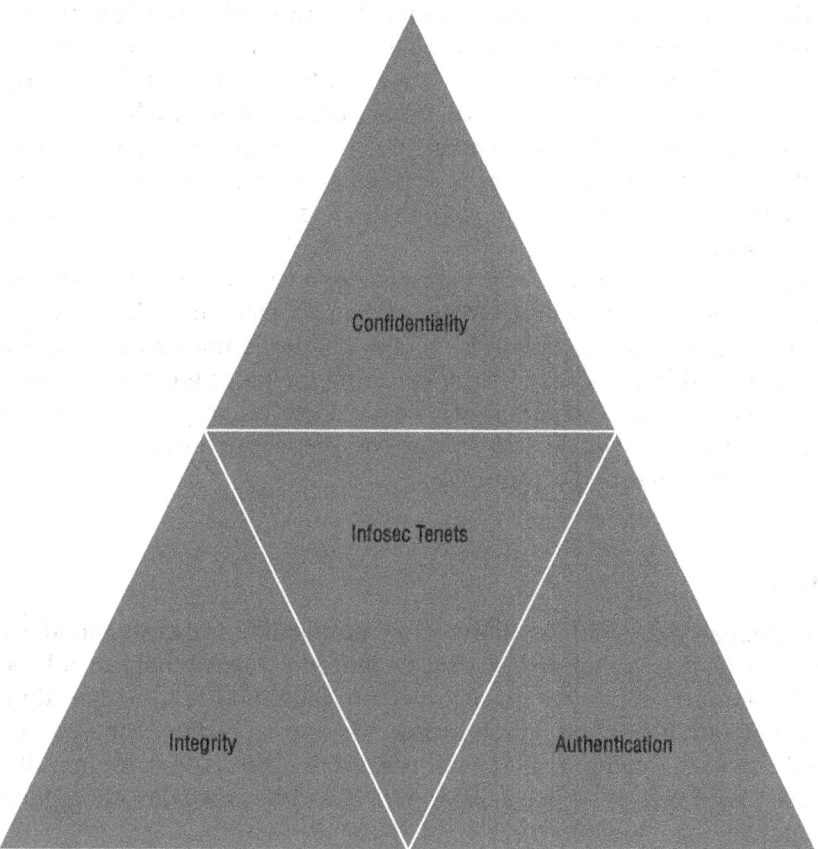

Figure 4-1: 3 Tenets of information security

Integrity refers to maintaining the accuracy and consistency of data throughout its lifecycle. Data integrity is vital for medical devices, as any alteration could lead to incorrect diagnoses or treatments. In Bluetooth communications, integrity checks ensure that the data received is the same as what was sent without any unauthorized modifications. This is typically achieved using checksums or digital signatures that can detect any tampering or corruption of data during transmission.

By focusing on these three tenets, healthcare organizations can significantly enhance the security of their Bluetooth-enabled medical devices and protect patient information. It's important to note that these principles should be applied to the devices themselves and the entire ecosystem in which they operate, including networks, applications, and user practices. To achieve these goals, Bluetooth employs a combination of features and protocols. These include pairing, authentication, encryption, and several privacy features.

Pairing and Authentication

Bluetooth devices establish a trusted relationship through pairing that verifies their identity, forming the foundation for secure communication. Pairing methods have evolved to improve security and address vulnerabilities. Early Bluetooth versions relied on PIN-based authentication, which, while simple, is now considered weak and highly susceptible to brute-force attacks. Newer pairing methods, such as numeric comparison, enhance security by displaying a numeric code that users must confirm on both devices, providing an additional layer of user verification.

Secure simple pairing (SSP) was a significant advancement introduced in Bluetooth 2.1. This method utilizes elliptic curve Diffie-Hellman (ECDH) public key cryptography to securely exchange encryption keys. It dramatically improves resistance to eavesdropping and impersonation attacks during the pairing process. Strong authentication remains a critical component of Bluetooth security. It ensures that only trusted devices can establish connections and prevent unauthorized access, safeguarding sensitive data and communications.

Encryption

Encryption safeguards the confidentiality of data transmitted over Bluetooth by transforming readable information into a secure, encoded format that can only be deciphered by authorized devices. Some Bluetooth relies on the AES algorithm, a widely trusted and robust encryption method that protects data using unique cryptographic keys. The strength of Bluetooth encryption varies depending on the version in use. Older versions, such as Bluetooth 2.0, utilized weaker encryption standards, making them more vulnerable to attacks.

In contrast, newer versions, starting with Bluetooth 4.0 and continuing into version 5, incorporate enhanced encryption capabilities that meet modern security standards. Encryption plays a vital role in secure communication, ensuring that even if data is intercepted, it cannot be decoded without the proper decryption key, thereby maintaining the integrity and privacy of sensitive information.

Privacy Features

Bluetooth also includes features to protect user privacy, particularly against tracking and surveillance attacks. Some of the most interesting features include the following:

- **Address randomization:** With Bluetooth 4.0, devices began using dynamic address randomization. This feature periodically changes the device's Bluetooth address, making it difficult for attackers to track it over time.

- **Mitigating tracking attacks:** Frequently altering identifiers thwarts attackers attempting to identify or follow a device in public spaces.
- **User-controlled visibility:** Devices can also be set to non-discoverable mode, which prevents them from broadcasting their presence to nearby devices unless explicitly paired.

Challenges of Bluetooth Security

While Bluetooth's security mechanisms are improving, the technology's inherent design and implementation mistakes expose devices to specific challenges, such as the following:

- **Legacy weaknesses:** Older pairing methods and weak encryption standards in earlier Bluetooth versions are susceptible to brute-force and replay attacks.
- **Implementation errors:** Variations in how manufacturers implement Bluetooth protocols can introduce security gaps, leaving devices vulnerable to exploits like the key negotiation of Bluetooth (KNOB) attack.
- **Man-in-the-middle (MITM) attacks:** Without proper authentication during pairing, attackers can intercept and manipulate communication between devices.
- **Device discovery and tracking:** Despite privacy features, attackers may exploit weaknesses to identify and track devices over time.
- **Lack of regular updates:** Many Bluetooth-enabled devices, especially low-cost IoT gadgets (and I can attest with a lab full of them), fail to receive regular firmware updates, leaving known vulnerabilities unpatched.

Bluetooth's security mechanisms, pairing and authentication, encryption, and privacy features form a framework to protect wireless communication. However, as Bluetooth becomes even more widespread across personal, healthcare, and industrial devices, attackers continue to exploit weaknesses in outdated protocols, poor implementations, and user practices. Understanding these security features and their limitations is essential for mitigating risks and ensuring safe Bluetooth usage.

Common Bluetooth Vulnerabilities

Following the feature discussion, this section provides an organized overview of the most common Bluetooth vulnerabilities, technical explanations, layperson's terms for the less technical, examples, and some high-level case studies.

Data Interception

As discussed in earlier chapters, Bluetooth communication occurs over radio frequencies. If encryption is weak or improperly implemented, attackers can intercept and decode the transmitted data, including personal information, audio, or medical data. Think of Bluetooth as a private conversation. Anyone nearby can listen in without a secure lock on the door (i.e., encryption).

An example is an attacker using tools like Bluetooth packet sniffers, which can capture communication between two paired devices and extract sensitive data. Research teams have demonstrated how weak encryption in early Bluetooth implementations allowed attackers to eavesdrop on device-to-device communication, leading to breaches of sensitive information in medical devices transmitting patient vitals.

Impersonation Attacks

Bluetooth impersonation attacks (BIAS) represent a significant threat to the security of Bluetooth-enabled devices. These attacks exploit vulnerabilities in the Bluetooth authentication process, allowing attackers to impersonate legitimate devices and establish secure connections without possessing the long-term key shared between the victims.

BIAS attacks target the authentication phase of secure connection establishment, affecting both legacy and newer secure connections. They are particularly concerning because they can bypass Bluetooth's strongest security modes, including secure, simple pairing, and connections.

These attacks are standard-compliant, potentially affecting any Bluetooth device regardless of its version, security mode, manufacturer, or implementation details. The stealthy nature of BIAS attacks is amplified by the Bluetooth standard's lack of requirement to notify end users about the outcome of an authentication procedure or the lack of mutual authentication.

Researchers have successfully demonstrated BIAS attacks against dozens of Bluetooth devices from major hardware and software vendors, representing all major Bluetooth versions. This includes devices from industry giants like Apple, Qualcomm, Intel, Cypress, Broadcom, Samsung, and CSR.

The vulnerabilities exploited by BIAS attacks include the following:

- Lack of mandatory mutual authentication
- Overly permissive role switching
- Authentication procedure downgrade

To protect against BIAS attacks, it's crucial to implement security practices such as these:

- Keeping Bluetooth turned off when not in use
- Using strong passwords and multifactor authentication
- Avoiding pairing devices in public spaces
- Keeping device operating systems up-to-date
- Making devices nondiscoverable when possible

For example, if tasked with evaluating the security of a hospital's IoMT environment, focusing on older Bluetooth-enabled insulin pumps, let's walk through the steps. The goal is to simulate a BIAS to test whether the insulin pump's pairing and encryption mechanisms can be exploited. If interested, and you have proximity to test devices, here are the simplified steps; otherwise, feel free to skip to the next section:

Step 1: Set Up

Tools Utilized:

- **Flipper Zero:** Used for scanning, spoofing, and injecting packets
- **Laptop with Wireshark:** For packet capture and analysis
- **Bluetooth Adapter (e.g., Ubertooth One):** Enhances Bluetooth sniffing capabilities
- **Kali Linux or Pentoo OS:** For additional Bluetooth exploitation tools like Btlejack and GATTacker

Environment Configuration:

- Install Bluetooth penetration testing tools on the laptop, for example:

    ```
    sudo apt-get install bluez
    sudo apt-get install gatttool
    sudo pip install gattacker
    ```

- Update the Flipper Zero and enable developer mode to activate advanced Bluetooth features.

Step 2: Identify Target Bluetooth Device(s)

1. Activate Flipper Zero's Bluetooth Scan Mode and locate nearby BLE devices by selecting Menu ⇨ Bluetooth ⇨ Scan Devices.
2. Record the MAC address and device name of the insulin pump.
3. Use Bluetooth Class of Device (CoD) filtering to isolate medical devices.

    Output Example:

    ```
    Device Found: InsulinPump_01
    MAC Address: 12:34:56:78:9A:BC
    Signal Strength: -45 dBm
    Services: Generic Access, Health Monitor
    ```

Step 3: Pairing Interception and Address Spoofing

The goal is to impersonate the trusted controller previously paired with the insulin pump with the following simple steps:

1. Activate Bluetooth Sniffing Mode to monitor pairing requests and use Flipper Zero to sniff pairing data and capture the Long Term Key (LTK) or session keys.
2. Identify the Temporary Key (TK) exchanged during the pairing process.

3. Emulate the pump's trusted device by spoofing its MAC address:

   ```
   hciconfig hci0 down
   bdaddr -i hci0 12:34:56:78:9A:BC
   hciconfig hci0 up
   ```

4. Replay pairing requests using the captured keys to bypass encryption without requiring re-authentication.

Step 4: Perform the Impersonation Attack

The goal is to establish a trusted connection with the target device in the following steps:

1. Use Flipper Zero to emulate a trusted paired device:
   - Select Menu ⇨ Bluetooth ⇨ Emulate Device.
   - Enter the MAC address and pairing keys obtained earlier.
2. Send spoofed pairing requests to establish a connection without triggering alerts.
3. Test commands using Generic Attribute Profile (GATT) manipulation to interact with the insulin pump once connected.

   ```
   gatttool -b 12:34:56:78:9A:BC --interactive
   connect
   ```

4. Read and write characteristics to simulate attacks like these:
   - Unauthorized insulin dose commands
   - Data injection
   - Firmware downgrade attempts

Step 5: Analyze and Record Findings
- Log the commands sent and their impact using Wireshark to analyze packet exchanges.
- Check if the device alerts the hospital's system about unauthorized connections.
- Document whether encryption keys or pairing processes were bypassed.
- Evaluate vulnerabilities, including unpatched firmware, lack of encryption, or reliance on outdated Bluetooth standards.

Step 6: Report Vulnerabilities and Recommend Fixes

Findings:

- The device accepted impersonated connections without requiring re-authentication.
- Encryption was bypassed due to outdated pairing protocols.
- Insulin doses could be altered remotely.

Recommendations:

1. Enforce Bluetooth Secure Connections (Bluetooth 4.2 or higher) to prevent BIAS attacks, which may require asset updates, upgrades, or replacement.
2. Implement pairing mode restrictions—disallow auto-pairing and require user verification.
3. Regularly update firmware to patch vulnerabilities and enforce stronger encryption keys.
4. Deploy Bluetooth intrusion detection systems to monitor anomalies.

This simulated penetration test of a Bluetooth impersonation attack on a critical medical device demonstrates how attackers could exploit weaknesses in pairing protocols and encryption mechanisms. While no actual harm should be caused, the test could reveal gaps in the device's security posture, highlighting the need for stronger defenses in IoMT environments. The findings could be used to strengthen hospital cybersecurity and safeguard patient safety against potential attacks.

A blacktooth attack is another example that lets an attacker mimic a trusted device, gaining unauthorized access. It's like a stranger pretending to be your friend to join a private party. You let them in, thinking they're someone you trust. Older Bluetooth versions, using legacy pairing methods, are highly vulnerable. Attackers can create fake devices that appear as legitimate peripherals, such as a keyboard or speaker. Penetration testers have revealed how a rogue device imitating a fitness tracker accessed sensitive user data, including step counts and heart rate, leading to a breach of health information.

Man-in-the-Middle Attacks

Bluetooth man-in-the-middle (MITM) attacks are also a security concern. These attacks occur when a malicious actor intercepts communications between two Bluetooth devices without their knowledge. In a typical Bluetooth MITM attack, the attacker positions themselves between two legitimate devices, such as a smartphone and a wireless keyboard. They create two connections, one with each device, effectively inserting themselves into the communication path. This allows the attacker to eavesdrop on the transmitted data and potentially even alter or inject malicious content.

The risks associated with these attacks are substantial. Attackers can intercept sensitive information like passwords, financial data, or personal messages. They may also compromise connected devices, potentially gaining unauthorized access to smart locks or other IoT medical devices. In some cases, attackers can inject malware into the communication stream, compromising device security.

What makes these attacks particularly concerning is their practicality. Despite the Bluetooth specification considering active MITM attacks difficult, they can be executed with relatively simple equipment. An attacker only needs hardware capable of acting as a BLE central and peripheral device, which could be as common as a Linux device or an embedded board. To carry out an attack, the malicious actor might force a disconnection between legitimate devices or wait for a natural break in the connection. Once the devices attempt to reconnect, the attacker can intercept and manipulate the communication.

Bluetooth has implemented several security measures to combat MITM attacks, primarily through pairing protocols. These protocols aim to authenticate devices and establish encrypted connections. However, vulnerabilities still exist. For example, researchers have identified flaws in the pairing process where specific unencrypted messages can be manipulated, leading to method confusion or BIAS attacks, as discussed.

In other words, an attacker intercepts and alters communication between two devices during the pairing process in a MITM attack. Without strong mutual authentication, these attacks can go undetected. Imagine someone secretly listening to your phone call and changing what you say before it reaches the other person.

MITM attacks are common during just works pairing, where minimal user interaction leaves devices vulnerable. Researchers have simulated MITM attacks on smart medical device systems, intercepting real-time patient data and altering vital signs transmitted to healthcare providers.

To reduce the risk of Bluetooth MITM attacks, it's crucial to implement some best practices, such as these:

- Use the latest Bluetooth security standards and keep devices updated.
- Employ strong pairing authentication methods, such as numeric comparison or passkey entry.
- Avoid pairing devices in public spaces where attackers may be present.
- Utilize additional layers of encryption for sensitive data transmission.
- Regularly monitor connected devices for unusual behavior.

BLUFFS

The Bluetooth forward and future secrecy (BLUFFS) attack series represents a sophisticated class of exploits targeting vulnerabilities in Bluetooth communication protocols. These attacks attempt to undermine the confidentiality and integrity of Bluetooth sessions by exploiting weaknesses in encryption key management, session resumption mechanisms, and pairing processes. The primary objective of BLUFFS is to compromise forward secrecy (the ability to keep past communications secure even if encryption keys are exposed) and future secrecy, ensuring that future sessions cannot be decrypted even if session data is captured.

Key features of BLUFFS attacks include the following:

- **Session hijacking:** This exploits vulnerabilities in Bluetooth's session resumption process, allowing attackers to impersonate a previously authenticated device without re-establishing trust. Attackers can inject malicious commands, intercept data, and manipulate device behavior.
- **Key compromise through weak encryption protocols:** BLUFFS leverages flaws in Bluetooth's legacy encryption protocols, which often fail to rotate

session keys securely. Once attackers access the current session key, they can decrypt past and future communications due to poor key derivation mechanisms.

- **Forward secrecy violations:** The attack manipulates the key negotiation process, forcing devices to reuse old keys instead of generating fresh, ephemeral ones. This allows attackers to decrypt past data by capturing old session keys.
- **Future secrecy violations:** BLUFFS introduces the ability to capture and decrypt encrypted data streams later once session keys or device secrets are compromised. Attackers use pre-computed keys to establish control over future communications, breaking the assumption that keys cannot be reused or predicted.
- **Downgrade attacks:** This attack forces devices to fall back to weaker encryption standards or outdated Bluetooth versions (e.g., Bluetooth 4.0 or earlier). Exploits compatibility modes, causing devices to use keys with lower entropy, making them easier to crack.
- **Man-in-the-middle attacks:** This attack intercepts Bluetooth pairing processes to alter key exchanges without detection. It introduces false identities or injects malicious payloads into encrypted sessions, enabling data theft or manipulation.

The stages of a BLUFFS attack are as follows:

1. **Initial Reconnaissance:**
   - Attackers scan for nearby Bluetooth-enabled devices using readily available tools to identify vulnerable targets.
   - They profile devices based on metadata such as supported encryption modes, Bluetooth versions, and pairing status.
2. **Session Hijacking or Pairing Exploitation:**
   - Exploits weaknesses in session resumption protocols or pairing mechanisms to impersonate trusted devices.
   - By leveraging weak key exchange methods, attackers infiltrate ongoing Bluetooth connections.
3. **Key Extraction and Analysis:**
   - Captures encrypted packets during the session to analyze key derivation patterns.
   - It uses brute-force attacks or pre-computed lookup tables to uncover encryption keys, enabling the decryption of past and future sessions.
4. **Session Manipulation and Data Injection:**
   - Manipulates encrypted traffic to alter commands, inject malware, or reroute data streams without detection.
   - Examples include modifying health data from IoMT devices or disrupting medical workflows.

5. **Persistent Control and Monitoring:**
   - Establishes long-term control by embedding malware or backdoors into Bluetooth firmware or paired devices.
   - Enables ongoing surveillance, data exfiltration, or system disruptions even after initial detection.

BLUFFS attacks present security risks across multiple sectors, particularly in healthcare, industrial systems, consumer IoT, and surveillance operations. In healthcare, BLUFFS exploits pose critical threats to IoMT devices, including pacemakers, insulin pumps, and wearable monitors. Attackers can manipulate device readings, alter medication dosages, or disable alerts, risking patient safety.

Bluetooth-connected machinery and inventory management systems are vulnerable to exploitation in industrial and enterprise environments. This could disrupt supply chains or manufacturing processes. Additionally, breaches of confidential communications between devices could expose sensitive intellectual property and trade secrets.

Consumer IoT devices, such as smart locks, security cameras, and voice assistants, are prime targets. These attacks allow attackers to gain unauthorized control, intercept personal data, and facilitate privacy violations or identity theft. Beyond individual devices, these attacks pose a substantial risk in surveillance and espionage, enabling attackers to infiltrate government or corporate networks, intercept encrypted communications, and monitor activities undetected. These wide-ranging threats highlight the urgent need for robust Bluetooth security measures to defend against vulnerabilities exploited by BLUFFS attacks.

To defend against these attacks, organizations and individuals must implement a combination of advanced encryption protocols, authentication mechanisms, and proactive monitoring strategies. Upgrading to a minimum of Bluetooth 5.2, for example, is essential as these offer enhanced encryption algorithms and stronger key management practices. Disabling outdated legacy modes and enforcing the rejection of insecure connection attempts are equally important. Frequent key rotation protocols should be established to minimize the risk of key reuse, utilizing ephemeral keys that ensure past and future communications remain secure even if a session key is compromised. Adding multifactor authentication during pairing and reconnection processes provides an additional layer of security to block unauthorized devices.

For ongoing monitoring, organizations should deploy intrusion detection systems capable of analyzing Bluetooth traffic to detect anomalies, unauthorized connections, and suspicious key exchanges. Regular firmware updates and patching are critical to address known vulnerabilities and protect against downgrade attacks. In high-security environments, signal jamming techniques and establishing Bluetooth-free isolation zones can reduce exposure to attacks by blocking unauthorized traffic. Finally, implementing end-to-end encryption layers on top of Bluetooth communications ensures that sensitive data remains protected, even if the base protocol is compromised. While these strategies are technically accurate, their implementation may vary depending on the specific devices and organizational needs. Additionally, as Bluetooth technology evolves, new vulnerabilities and defense mechanisms may emerge, requiring ongoing vigilance and adaptation of security practices. By integrating these measures, organizations can significantly enhance the security of their Bluetooth-enabled systems and mitigate the risks posed by BLUFFS attacks.

Bluesnarfing

Bluesnarfing is a cyberattack that exploits vulnerabilities in Bluetooth-enabled devices to gain unauthorized access to sensitive information. This technique allows attackers to silently infiltrate smartphones, tablets, laptops, and other Bluetooth-connected devices, potentially compromising personal and corporate data.

Here's how bluesnarfing typically works in four simplified steps:

1. Attackers scan for discoverable Bluetooth devices within range, usually up to 10 meters.
2. The attackers exploit vulnerabilities in the Object Exchange (OBEX) protocol used for Bluetooth communication.
3. Using specialized software like bluediving, hackers bypass security measures and gain access to the target device.
4. Once connected, the attacker can steal a wide range of data, including contacts, emails, text messages, and photos, and even make calls or send messages from the compromised device.

The implications of bluesnarfing are severe. For individuals, it can lead to identity theft and financial fraud. For businesses, it poses risks of corporate espionage, data breaches, and potential lawsuits if employee or customer information is stolen.

To protect against bluesnarfing, there are similar best practices as mentioned with the attack vectors discussed previously:

- Keep Bluetooth turned off when not in use.
- Set devices to nondiscoverable mode.
- Avoid pairing devices in public spaces.
- Regularly update device software and firmware.
- Use strong, unique pairing codes.
- Monitor connected devices and remove unrecognized connections.

Since bluesnarfing is unauthorized access to a device's data, contacts, messages, and files are at risk. Attackers often exploit weak or default Bluetooth profiles. This is similar to unlocking your car, allowing thieves to take anything inside. Devices left in discoverable mode are particularly vulnerable, allowing attackers to exploit known vulnerabilities. For example, a hospital suffered a breach in which attackers accessed unencrypted Bluetooth data from discoverable devices used for patient monitoring.

To safeguard against bluesnarfing, adopting proactive security practices introduced in this chapter is essential. Start by turning off Bluetooth when it is not actively needed to minimize exposure to unauthorized access. Configure devices to operate in nondiscoverable mode, preventing them from being visible to potential attackers. Regularly update software and firmware to patch vulnerabilities and enhance security features. When pairing devices, use strong and unique codes to reinforce protection against unauthorized connections. Avoid pairing devices in public or unsecured areas where attackers may exploit weak signals. Additionally, routinely monitor connected devices and promptly remove unrecognized or suspicious connections to maintain control over your Bluetooth-enabled systems.

Denial of Service

Bluetooth denial-of-service (DoS) attacks pose a significant threat to the security and functionality of Bluetooth-enabled devices, particularly in critical environments like healthcare. These attacks aim to disrupt or disable Bluetooth communications, potentially causing serious consequences. One common form of Bluetooth DoS attack is known as *bluesmacking*. This attack involves bombarding a Bluetooth device with an overwhelming number of data packets or oversized packets that the device cannot handle. The targeted device may crash, stop responding, or malfunction, effectively denying service to legitimate users.

In a healthcare setting, a bluesmacking attack could have severe implications. Imagine a scenario where a critical medical device, such as an insulin pump or heart monitor, is taken offline due to such an attack. The consequences could be life-threatening for patients who rely on these devices for continuous monitoring or treatment. Another concerning aspect of Bluetooth DoS attacks is their potential to mask more dangerous attacks. While a device struggles to handle the flood of malicious packets, an attacker might exploit other vulnerabilities to gain unauthorized access or manipulate the device's functionality.

In DoS attacks, attackers overload a device with excessive connection requests, rendering it unusable or draining its battery. It's like someone constantly ringing your doorbell, so you can't focus on anything else. Overwhelming devices with requests to render them unusable. Attackers can disrupt the functionality of Bluetooth medical devices, such as infusion pumps or monitors, by bombarding them with connection requests. For example, imagine the impact of malicious actors disrupting critical medical devices during surgery by initiating multiple connection attempts.

I read about where a simulated DoS attack on a wearable medical device caused it to stop functioning temporarily, demonstrating the critical need for robust firmware to handle such scenarios. During another cybersecurity simulation, a DoS attack on hospital systems caused disruptions in patient monitoring. You can find articles, research, and more at the Network of the National Library of Medicine (NNLM) at www.nlm.nih.gov.

To protect against Bluetooth DoS attacks, healthcare organizations and device manufacturers must implement robust security measures:

- Performing regular software and firmware updates to patch known vulnerabilities
- Implementing strong authentication and encryption protocols

- Using intrusion detection systems to monitor for unusual Bluetooth traffic patterns
- Educating staff about the risks of leaving Bluetooth enabled on devices when not in use

Bluejacking

Bluejacking is a technique that exploits Bluetooth technology to send unsolicited messages to nearby devices. While often seen as harmless, it raises important security and privacy concerns. Bluejacking typically involves an attacker that scans for discoverable Bluetooth devices within range, usually about 30 feet. They then send a pairing request that includes a message. This message could be anything from a prank to an advertisement or malicious link. The goal is to get the recipient to interact with the message. A bluejacking message can be considered a form of phishing if it contains a link or content designed to trick the recipient into providing personal information or downloading malware, even though bluejacking itself is typically just sending unsolicited messages without actively trying to steal data.

While bluejacking doesn't directly access the victim's device or steal data, it can be a precursor to attacks like bluebugging. Bluebugging is when someone attains access into a device through discoverable Bluetooth connection weaknesses. Through bluebugging, someone could listen to calls, read and send messages, and access contacts. Here are some key points about bluejacking that you should know:

- It works only on devices with Bluetooth enabled and set to discoverable mode.
- Attackers often target crowded public places to find vulnerable devices.
- Messages may contain generic greetings, spelling errors, or a sense of urgency.
- Multiple messages in quick succession are common.

Bluejacking is like receiving spam messages from a stranger in a crowded place. An attacker can send phishing messages via Bluetooth to trick users into clicking malicious links. For example, a retail environment saw attackers bluejacking customers, tricking them into downloading malware targeting their smartphones.

To protect against bluejacking, keep Bluetooth turned off when not in use, set devices to be non-discoverable, be cognizant of pairing requests from unknown devices, and don't click links or download attachments from unsolicited messages. While bluejacking is relatively harmless, it still highlights Bluetooth security's importance.

Bluetooth Remote Code Execution

Bluetooth Remote Code Execution (RCE) is a critical security vulnerability that threatens some devices. This type of attack allows malicious actors to execute arbitrary code on a target device without any user interaction, simply by being in Bluetooth range. Here's what you need to know about Bluetooth RCE:

- Bluetooth RCE exploits vulnerabilities in devices' Bluetooth implementation. Attackers can exploit flaws in the Bluetooth pairing process or other Bluetooth protocols to gain unauthorized access.
- This vulnerability affects many devices, including smartphones, laptops, IoT devices, and vehicles with Bluetooth capabilities. Major operating systems, such as Android, iOS, macOS, and Linux, have all been impacted by Bluetooth RCE vulnerabilities.
- Bluetooth RCE is a critical threat because it can lead to complete device takeover. Attackers can steal data, install malware, or use the compromised device as a gateway to infiltrate networks.
- What makes Bluetooth RCE particularly dangerous is that it requires no user interaction. To execute the attack, an attacker only needs to be within Bluetooth range of the target device.

To protect against Bluetooth RCE, it's crucial to keep devices updated with the latest security patches. Turning off Bluetooth when not in use can also reduce the attack surface. Consider using Bluetooth only when necessary and in controlled environments for critical systems. As Bluetooth technology continues to evolve and be widely adopted, new vulnerabilities will likely emerge. Continuous monitoring and rapid patching are essential to maintaining security against Bluetooth RCE attacks.

RCE vulnerabilities let attackers execute malicious code on a target device without physical access. In 2020, a critical Android Bluetooth bug allowed RCE without user interaction. More recently, researcher Marc Newlin disclosed a vulnerability (CVE-2023-45866) affecting Android, macOS, iOS, and Linux devices. This vulnerability enables attackers to remotely connect and control devices by injecting keystrokes.

Bluetooth Hacking Tools

Because Bluetooth technology has many vulnerabilities, a growing suite of penetration testing and security assessment tools is available. Attackers can also misuse these to exploit weaknesses. Understanding these tools and their capabilities is essential for both defenders and ethical hackers working to protect Bluetooth-enabled devices and networks. This section explores some of my favorite tools used in Bluetooth network discovery, enumeration, and exploitation. In later chapters, I will discuss using some of these tools and provide a good understanding of navigating them to run in your environments.

Overview of Popular Linux Distributions

Before I get into the tools in my arsenal, I want to talk briefly about Linux distributions designed for penetration testing. Cybersecurity professionals widely use these to assess and secure wireless and Bluetooth networks. These specialized distributions come preloaded with tools for reconnaissance, vulnerability scanning, exploitation, and post-exploitation analysis. The following is an overview of the most popular Linux distributions that I have used in Bluetooth and wireless penetration testing:

Kali Linux

- **Developer:** Offensive Security
- **Website:** www.kali.org
- **Key features:**
  - Pre-installed with more than 600 penetration testing tools, including wireless and Bluetooth assessment utilities.
  - Comprehensive hardware support for wireless cards capable of monitor mode and packet injection.
  - Regular updates ensure compatibility with modern exploits and protocols.
  - Compatible with ARM devices, enabling portable testing setups like Raspberry Pi.
- **Popular tools included:**
  - **Aircrack-ng:** Wireless network auditing suite for cracking WEP/WPA/WPA2 keys.
  - **hcxdumptool/hcxtools:** Advanced tools for capturing and analyzing WPA handshakes and PMKID hashes.
  - **Wireshark:** Packet analyzer for real-time traffic monitoring and decryption.
  - **Bettercap:** Framework for wireless attacks, Bluetooth sniffing, and MITM attacks.
  - **Bluesnarfer:** Bluetooth vulnerability exploitation tool.
  - **BluetoothScanner:** Scans and maps Bluetooth devices.
  - **Hcitool and Hciconfig:** Bluetooth device configuration and manipulation tools.
- **Best use case:**
  - Ideal for security professionals performing comprehensive wireless network penetration tests and Bluetooth vulnerability assessments.

Parrot Security OS

- **Developer:** ParrotSec
- **Website:** www.parrotsec.org
- **Key features:**
  - Lightweight and optimized for performance, suitable for older hardware and virtual environments.
  - Includes wireless and Bluetooth penetration testing tools, digital forensics, and programming environments.
  - Ships with AnonSurf for privacy and anonymity.
  - Sandbox environments for safe malware testing and exploit development.
- **Popular tools included:**
  - **Airgeddon:** Wireless network auditing framework for WPA/WPA2 cracking.
  - **Wifite:** Automated Wi-Fi cracking tool with multi-tool integration.
  - **BlueZ:** Suite of tools for Bluetooth configuration and attacks.
  - **Bluelog:** Bluetooth device discovery and logging tool.
  - **Spooftooph:** Tool for Bluetooth device spoofing and identity impersonation.
- **Best use case:**
  - Suitable for privacy-focused testers and those requiring a balance between performance and security tools.

BlackArch Linux

- **Developer:** BlackArch Team
- **Website:** www.blackarch.org
- **Key features:**
  - More than 2,800 pre-installed tools specifically for penetration testing.
  - Supports ARM-based devices and can be installed alongside other Linux distributions.
  - Extensive repository of tools for wireless and Bluetooth exploitation.
  - Advanced configurations for hardware-based attacks and exploitation testing.
- **Popular tools included:**
  - **BlueMaho:** Bluetooth security tool for testing vulnerabilities in Bluetooth devices.
  - **Grimwepa:** GUI-based tool for wireless network cracking.
  - **Reaver:** WPS attack tool for recovering WPA/WPA2 passphrases.

- **Kismet:** Passive wireless network discovery and packet sniffer.
- **Ubertooth:** Tool for Bluetooth sniffing and traffic monitoring with compatible hardware.
- **Best use case:**
  - Ideal for advanced penetration testers who need a vast library of tools and hardware compatibility.

Pentoo

- **Developer:** Pentoo Team
- **Website:** www.pentoo.ch
- **Key features:**
  - Based on Gentoo Linux, optimized for penetration testing and security auditing.
  - Focuses on wireless and radio frequency attacks, including Bluetooth security.
  - Kernel support for packet injection and various hardware drivers.
  - Modular design allows customization based on testing requirements.
- **Popular tools included:**
  - **Bluesnarfer:** Extracts sensitive data from Bluetooth devices.
  - **Bluelog:** Monitors and logs Bluetooth traffic and device presence.
  - **Kismet:** Wireless sniffer and intrusion detection system.
  - **Aircrack-ng Suite:** Wireless network cracking and monitoring tools.
  - **Fern Wi-Fi Cracker:** GUI-based wireless cracking tool for WPA/WPA2.
- **Best use case:**
  - Great for niche penetration testing scenarios that involve radio frequency and Bluetooth vulnerabilities.

BackBox Linux

- **Developer:** BackBox Team
- **Website:** www.backbox.org
- **Key features:**
  - Ubuntu-based lightweight distribution designed for security assessments.
  - Minimalistic interface optimized for speed and efficiency.
  - Pre-installed with essential penetration testing tools, including wireless and Bluetooth utilities.
  - Supports virtualization and cloud-based testing environments.
- **Popular tools included:**
  - **Airgeddon:** Automated wireless penetration testing tool.

- **Reaver and Bully:** WPS exploitation tools for WPA key recovery.
- **Bluesnarfer:** Bluetooth hacking and data extraction.
- **BlueZ Utilities:** Bluetooth analysis and vulnerability testing.
- **Wireshark:** Traffic analyzer for packet inspection.
- Best use case:
  - Suitable for security professionals looking for a fast and resource-friendly platform for wireless and Bluetooth penetration testing.

Fedora Security Spin

- **Developer:** Fedora Project
- **Website:** labs.fedoraproject.org
- Key features:
  - Part of the Fedora Labs project, tailored explicitly for security assessments and penetration testing.
  - Equipped with tools for network analysis, intrusion detection, and wireless exploitation.
  - Strong focus on modularity and customization.
  - Provides reliable support for modern wireless drivers and Bluetooth testing hardware.
- Popular tools included:
  - **Aircrack-ng suite:** Comprehensive wireless cracking tools.
  - **Kismet:** Wireless network monitoring and discovery.
  - **BlueMaho:** Bluetooth vulnerability scanner.
  - **Wireshark:** Packet analysis and decryption utility.
  - **Bettercap:** MITM attacks and Bluetooth manipulation.
- Best use case:
  - Preferred by Red Hat Linux users and those working in environments that require enterprise-grade security testing.

The choice of Linux distribution for Bluetooth and wireless penetration testing depends on the specific needs and expertise of the user:

- **Kali Linux:** Ideal for general-purpose penetration testing with extensive community support.
- **Parrot Security OS:** Balanced performance and security tools focusing on anonymity.
- **BlackArch Linux:** Suitable for advanced users requiring a massive library of tools.
- **Pentoo:** Focused on RF and wireless hacking with kernel optimizations.

- **BackBox Linux:** Lightweight and user-friendly for efficient wireless and Bluetooth testing.
- **Fedora Security Spin:** Modular and enterprise-friendly distribution with reliable wireless driver support.

By leveraging the capabilities of these distributions, security professionals can conduct thorough assessments, identify vulnerabilities, and then fortify wireless and Bluetooth networks against potential threats. In the next section, I'll review my favorite discovery, enumeration, and exploitation tools.

Flipper Zero

Figure 4-2 shows the Flipper Zero (https://flipperzero.one), a compact, versatile, open-source hardware device designed for security research, penetration testing, and debugging. Its Bluetooth capabilities have recently been significantly enhanced, expanding its wireless analysis, device manipulation, and vulnerability testing functionality.

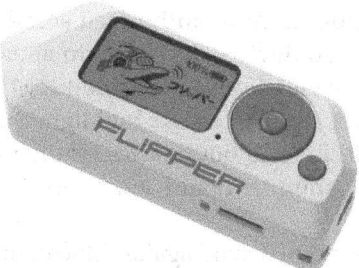

Figure 4-2: Flipper Zero

I've used this tool in various projects, and it was previously mentioned in a penetration testing example. With its compact design, intuitive controls, and multiprotocol support, including RFID, NFC, infrared, GPIOs, and sub-GHz radios, Flipper Zero has become an essential tool for cybersecurity professionals, especially in testing IoT and IoMT systems.

The latest firmware and hardware updates empower Flipper Zero to conduct advanced BLE and Classic Bluetooth operations, enabling researchers to more precisely explore vulnerabilities. These enhancements allow Flipper Zero to sniff and analyze Bluetooth packets, capturing advertising data, pairing requests, and connection attempts between devices. It can also identify MAC addresses, supported services, and encryption weaknesses, providing insights into vulnerabilities in pairing protocols.

The device also supports Bluetooth spoofing and emulation, which involves impersonating trusted devices by mimicking identifiers and services. This is particularly useful for testing susceptibility to spoofing attacks. Flipper Zero can actively and passively scan for Bluetooth devices, monitor advertisements stealthily, and test encryption mechanisms through MITM attacks, intercepting and relaying communications to identify flaws in authentication.

Flipper Zero's recent updates include remote control automation, which enables users to send commands to Bluetooth devices, manipulate IoT systems, and execute pre-programmed attacks. Enhanced scripting tools also make it capable of automating actions, testing defenses, and exploiting devices such as health monitors and fitness trackers. Integration with external tools like Wireshark provides additional packet analysis and supports replay attacks, while open-source Python APIs allow custom script development for advanced simulations and data manipulation.

In practical applications, Flipper Zero is excellent for device testing. It enables researchers to simulate real-world attacks, such as BLE injection and key hijacking, and evaluate compliance with security standards like HIPAA. It is also powerful for wireless security audits, identifying rogue devices and assessing Bluetooth encryption policies. It can simulate spoofing, session hijacking, and eavesdropping scenarios for penetration testing. Additionally, Flipper Zero aids privacy investigations, testing vulnerabilities in tracking devices like Apple AirTags and evaluating anti-tracking systems.

Despite its legitimate uses, Flipper Zero's enhanced capabilities also raise ethical and legal concerns. Malicious actors could misuse it for unauthorized access, identity theft, and data manipulation through spoofed devices. Its ability to intercept and alter Bluetooth traffic may lead to privacy violations and exploit IoMT vulnerabilities in sensitive environments like healthcare. These risks highlight the importance of using Flipper Zero ethically and within legal boundaries, as unauthorized hacking activities violate laws such as the Computer Fraud and Abuse Act (CFAA) in the United States.

Organizations must adopt proactive security measures to defend against Bluetooth-based threats exposed by this product. These measures include secure pairing protocols with numeric comparison and passkey entry, regular firmware updates to address vulnerabilities, and turning off unused Bluetooth services to prevent unauthorized connections. Implementing signal monitoring tools and intrusion detection systems can help detect unusual Bluetooth activity, while enforcing end-to-end encryption ensures intercepted data remains secure.

BlueZ

BlueZ (www.bluez.org) is the official Linux Bluetooth stack. It provides the core protocols and utilities to operate Bluetooth devices on Linux systems. Let me explain some key points about BlueZ and its importance in the Linux ecosystem.

BlueZ was introduced in 2001, and has since become the de facto standard for Bluetooth functionality in Linux. Its modular architecture allows for flexibility and easy integration into various Linux distributions. One of BlueZ's strengths is its comprehensive support for Bluetooth standards. It implements the core Bluetooth layers and protocols, including L2CAP (Logical Link Control and Adaptation

Protocol), RFCOMM (Radio Frequency Communication), and SDP (Service Discovery Protocol). This broad support ensures compatibility with a wide range of Bluetooth devices.

BlueZ operates as a system daemon, typically running as *bluetoothd* for general Bluetooth functionality or *bluetooth-meshd* for Bluetooth mesh networks. Daemons continuously run in the background and perform specific tasks without direct user interaction. This daemon-based approach allows efficient resource management and enables multiple Bluetooth applications to run simultaneously on a single device.

BlueZ provides developers with APIs that can be accessed through D-Bus, a system service that facilitates inter-process communication. This architecture allows applications to interact with Bluetooth functionality without directly calling BlueZ APIs, promoting a more modular and maintainable system design.

BlueZ supports Bluetooth Classic (BR/EDR) and Bluetooth Low Energy (BLE) protocols. This dual support is crucial as the industry shifts toward more energy-efficient IoT devices while maintaining compatibility with older Bluetooth technologies. Security is a key concern in Bluetooth communications, and BlueZ addresses this through regular updates and security patches. For instance, in 2021, BlueZ released updates to mitigate potential vulnerabilities that could lead to information disclosure.

BlueZ enables secure Bluetooth communication for Linux-based IoMT devices in IoT and smart healthcare systems. As these devices become more prevalent, the importance of a robust, secure Bluetooth stack like BlueZ cannot be overstated.

The following are the capabilities of BlueZ:

- Allows interaction with Bluetooth devices.
- Can be used for sniffing, enumerating paired devices, and testing Bluetooth connections.
- Provides command-line tools like `hcitool` and `gatttool` for discovery and communication with Bluetooth devices.

The following are use cases for BlueZ:

- Ethical hackers use BlueZ to test device communication protocols.
- Attackers might exploit BlueZ for reconnaissance, identifying vulnerable devices within range.

For example, BlueZ can identify devices with weak or no encryption during a penetration test and flag them as potential vulnerabilities.

To summarize, BlueZ is a cornerstone of Linux's Bluetooth functionality. Its comprehensive protocol support, modular architecture, and ongoing development make it essential for any Linux system interfacing with Bluetooth devices. As Bluetooth technology continues to evolve, BlueZ may play a crucial role in keeping Linux systems at the forefront of wireless communication capabilities.

Bluelog

Bluelog (see Listing 4.1) is a powerful yet lightweight Bluetooth scanner that detects and tracks Bluetooth devices within range. It benefits security professionals, researchers, and anyone interested in monitoring Bluetooth activity in their environment.

Listing 4.1: Bluelog in the Kali Linux Toolbox

```
root@kali: ~# bluelog -h
Bluelog (v1.1.2) by Tom Nardi "MS3FGX" (MS3FGX@gmail.com)
----------------------------------------------------------------
Bluelog is a Bluetooth site survey tool, designed to tell you how
many discoverable devices there are in an area as quickly as possible.
As the name implies, its primary function is to log discovered devices
to file rather than to be used interactively. Bluelog could run on a
system unattended for long periods of time to collect data.

Bluelog also includes a mode called "Bluelog Live" which creates a
webpage of the results that you can serve up with your HTTP daemon of
choice. See the "README.LIVE" file for details.

For more information, see: www.digifail.com

Basic Options:
   -i <interface>    Sets scanning device, default is "hci0"
   -o <filename>     Sets output filename, default is "devices.log"
   -v                Verbose, prints discovered devices to the terminal
   -q                Quiet, turns off nonessential terminal outout
   -d                Enables daemon mode, Bluelog will run in background
   -k                Kill an already running Bluelog process
   -l                Start "Bluelog Live", default is disabled

Logging Options:
   -n                Write device names to log, default is disabled
   -m                Write device manufacturer to log, default is disabled
   -c                Write device class to log, default is disabled
   -f                Use "friendly" device class, default is disabled
   -t                Write timestamps to log, default is disabled
   -x                Obfuscate discovered MACs, default is disabled
   -e                Encode discovered MACs with CRC32, default disabled
   -b                Enable BlueProPro log format, see README

Advanced Options:
   -r <retries>      Name resolution retries, default is 3
   -a <minutes>      Amnesia, Bluelog will forget device after given time
   -w <seconds>      Scanning window in seconds, see README
   -s                Syslog only mode, no log file. Default is disabled
```

Bluelog continuously scans for discoverable Bluetooth devices in the vicinity. It logs essential information about each detected device, including its name, MAC address, and class. This data is invaluable for understanding the Bluetooth landscape in a given area.

One of Bluelog's key features is its ability to run in the background for extended periods. This makes it ideal for long-term monitoring scenarios, such as tracking foot traffic in retail environments or identifying potential security threats in sensitive areas. The tool also offers various output formats, including plain text and HTML, making analyzing and presenting the collected data easy. It can also generate live web pages, allowing for real-time monitoring of Bluetooth activity.

Bluelog is highly configurable, allowing users to customize scan intervals, output formats, and filtering options. This flexibility makes it suitable for various applications, from casual use to professional security audits. It's important to note that while Bluelog is a powerful tool, it should be used responsibly and in compliance with local laws and regulations regarding privacy and electronic surveillance.

The following are the capabilities of Bluelog:

- Bluelog scans for Bluetooth-enabled devices in the vicinity.
- It identifies devices in discoverable mode, capturing their basic information, such as MAC address, name, and class.
- It captures and logs discovered devices for later analysis.
- It tracks Bluetooth devices over time, helping to monitor their presence or movement within a specific area.
- It recognizes the type of device based on its Bluetooth class, such as smartphones, headphones, laptops, or IoMT devices.
- It provides information about the signal strength of detected devices, helping assess proximity or the strength of the connection.
- Bluelog can be used in automated scripts for continuous monitoring or data collection during a Bluetooth reconnaissance.
- It is commonly used in wardriving scenarios to map the locations of Bluetooth devices in a given geographic area.
- It is designed for efficiency and simplicity, making it suitable for deployment on lightweight systems or single-board computers like Raspberry Pi.

The following are use cases for Bluelog:

- It can be used to map Bluetooth devices in wardriving scenarios in a specific area.
- Attackers use Bluelog for reconnaissance, compiling a list of target devices.

In a simulated attack on a corporate environment, for example, Bluelog could identify employee devices with discoverable Bluetooth settings. Bluelog provides a simple yet effective way to monitor Bluetooth activity, offering valuable insights into the wireless landscape and potential security implications in any given environment.

btCrawler

btCrawler (https://petronius.sourceforge.net/btcrawler and shown in action in Figure 4-3) is a powerful Bluetooth scanning tool designed for penetration testing and ethical hacking purposes. This versatile application offers a comprehensive suite of features for discovering and analyzing Bluetooth devices in the vicinity.

Figure 4-3: btCrawler

The key capabilities of btCrawler include the following:

- Scanning for visible Bluetooth devices, providing detailed information such as device names, MAC addresses, device classes, vendors, and signal strengths
- Querying and enumerating Bluetooth services on discovered devices
- Support for BLE scanning, including the ability to query BLE attributes and characteristics
- Database functionality to store scanned device information, including timestamps for when devices are first and last seen
- The ability to list currently paired devices on the scanning device
- Options to pair or unpair with discovered Bluetooth devices
- Exporting scan results to CSV files for further analysis

btCrawler's user-friendly interface makes it accessible for novice and experienced security professionals. However, it's crucial to note that this tool should be used only for authorized testing, as improper use could violate privacy laws or security policies.

For security teams, btCrawler is key in assessing Bluetooth vulnerabilities within an organization's environment. Providing a detailed view of the Bluetooth landscape enables the identification of unauthorized or potentially malicious devices and the assessment of security configurations on approved devices.

As Bluetooth technology proliferates in consumer and enterprise environments, tools like btCrawler are vital for maintaining robust security postures and identifying potential weaknesses before malicious actors exploit them.

BTScanner

BTScanner (https://salsa.debian.org/pkg-security-team/btscanner) is another tool designed for comprehensive Bluetooth device detection and analysis. It is often utilized in security assessments and penetration testing. This scanner offers a range of capabilities that make it usable for cybersecurity professionals.

At its core, BTScanner allows users to discover and gather detailed information about Bluetooth devices in the vicinity without pairing with them (see Listing 4.2). This nonintrusive approach is crucial for security assessments, as it mimics the initial reconnaissance phase of potential attackers. When deployed, BTScanner can reveal a wealth of information about nearby Bluetooth devices, including the following:

- Device names and MAC addresses
- Manufacturer details
- Device types and capabilities
- Signal strengths and link qualities
- Available services and open channels

Listing 4.2: BTScanner Options in Kali Linux

```
root@kali: ~# btscanner -h
Usage: btscanner [options]
options
    --help              Display help
    --cfg=<file>        Use <file> as the config file
    --no-reset          Do not reset the Bluetooth adapter before scanning
```

BTScanner's key strengths are its ability to extract host controller interface information and service discovery protocol data. This level of detail provides security professionals with critical insights into potential vulnerabilities and attack surfaces.

BTScanner maintains an open connection to monitor received signal strength indication and link quality in real time. This feature allows for more accurate device positioning and can help identify rogue or unauthorized devices within a secure environment.

For penetration testers, BTScanner is an excellent starting point for further exploitation. Identifying open RF channels lays the groundwork for more advanced attacks like bluesnarfing or bluejacking. While BTScanner is a powerful tool for security professionals, it should be used responsibly and ethically. Always obtain proper authorization before scanning devices or networks you don't own or manage.

The following are the capabilities of BTScanner:

- Extracts detailed information about devices, including supported services and signal strength
- Can be used to identify vulnerabilities in Bluetooth pairing mechanisms

The following are examples of use cases for BTScanner:

- Security teams use BTScanner to assess the exposure of Bluetooth devices in public areas.
- Attackers use the tool to facilitate exploitation of unpatched or misconfigured devices.
- For example, a penetration tester may use BTScanner to identify devices susceptible to bluesnarfing or MITM attacks.

BTScanner is a comprehensive and essential tool for Bluetooth security assessments. Its ability to gather detailed device information without pairing makes it invaluable for identifying potential vulnerabilities and strengthening the overall Bluetooth security posture.

Ubertooth One

Ubertooth One (see Figure 4-4) is an open-source hardware platform designed for Bluetooth experimentation and monitoring. I have one at home and at the office. This compact device, developed by Michael Ossmann and Dominic Spill from Great Scott Gadgets, has changed Bluetooth security research and development.

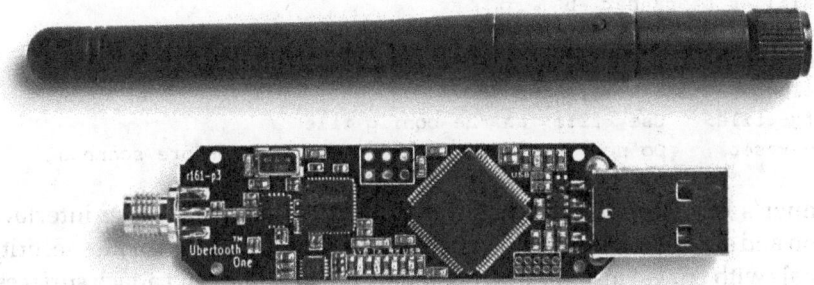

Figure 4-4: Ubertooth One

Source: From Great Scott Gadgets / https://greatscottgadgets.com/ubertoothone / last accessed March 03, 2025.

The Ubertooth One I have is built around the LPC175x ARM Cortex-M3 microcontroller, coupled with a full-speed USB 2.0 interface. This hardware configuration allows for the development of custom Class 1 comparable Bluetooth devices and provides a versatile platform for various BLE hacking activities.

What sets Ubertooth One apart is its dual capability of sending and receiving 2.4 GHz signals. This feature enables real-time Bluetooth traffic monitoring, previously unavailable in affordable consumer devices. The tool can also capture BLE packets, analyze Bluetooth communications, and analyze the 2.4 GHz spectrum.

Priced between $100 and $150, Ubertooth One offers an accessible entry point for novices and experts in wireless development and hacking. Its open-source nature extends to hardware and software, providing a wealth of resources for custom projects and modifications. This openness has fostered a vibrant community of developers and researchers continually expanding the device's capabilities.

Ubertooth One has diverse applications. It can be used to discreetly capture BLE packets, access devices like microphones in headsets, or exploit vulnerabilities in smart home systems. In the hands of ethical hackers and security researchers, it's an invaluable tool for identifying and addressing security flaws in Bluetooth-enabled devices.

However, it's crucial to emphasize that Ubertooth One should be used only with permission in controlled testing scenarios or educational settings. Again, unauthorized use for malicious purposes is illegal and unethical.

The following are the capabilities of Ubertooth One:

- Sniffs and captures Bluetooth communication packets
- Can analyze and decode BLE traffic
- Identifies vulnerabilities in pairing and encryption mechanisms

The following are use cases for Ubertooth One:

- Ethical hackers use Ubertooth One to validate the security of Bluetooth connections.
- Malicious actors can intercept communication to capture sensitive data or credentials.

For example, an attacker with an Ubertooth One device could intercept BLE traffic from a fitness tracker and extract private user information. Ubertooth One represents an advancement in accessible Bluetooth security research tools. Its affordability, versatility, and open-source design make it an essential device for anyone serious about exploring and securing Bluetooth technology.

BtleJack

BtleJack (https://github.com/virtualabs/btlejack) is a powerful and versatile tool for monitoring and interacting with Bluetooth Low Energy devices (BLE). This open-source Swiss Army knife for BLE security testing provides researchers and security professionals comprehensive capabilities for analyzing and manipulating BLE communications.

At its core, BtleJack offers three primary functions: sniffing, jamming, and hijacking BLE connections. Let's break these down:

- **Sniffing:** BtleJack can passively monitor BLE traffic, capturing and decoding packets in real time. This allows security professionals to analyze the communication between BLE devices, identify potential vulnerabilities, and gain insights into how devices interact.
- **Jamming:** The tool can actively disrupt BLE connections by flooding the airwaves with interference. This capability helps test the resilience of BLE devices against denial-of-service attacks or isolating specific devices for further analysis.
- **Hijacking:** Perhaps its most powerful feature is that BtleJack can hijack existing BLE connections. This allows researchers to intercept and modify communications between devices, potentially uncovering security flaws or testing the robustness of BLE implementations.

What sets BtleJack apart is its hardware flexibility. While initially designed to work with BBC Micro:Bit devices, it supports other hardware platforms, such as the Adafruit Bluefruit LE sniffer and nRF51822 Eval Kit. This versatility makes it accessible to many users and adaptable to various testing scenarios.

BtleJack offers comprehensive support for different BLE versions, including 4.x and limited support for 5.x. It can handle various BLE packet types and protocols, making it a valuable tool for analyzing legacy and modern BLE implementations. For security professionals, BtleJack provides a user-friendly command-line interface that allows for quick setup and execution of complex BLE analysis tasks. Its ability to export captured packets to various PCAP formats also facilitates integration with other analysis tools and workflows.

The following are the capabilities of BtlJack:

- Sniffs BLE traffic and reconstructs pairing sessions
- Exploits known vulnerabilities in BLE protocols, such as pairing mechanisms

The following are BtlJack use cases:

- Security researchers use BtleJack to test BLE implementations in IoT devices.
- Attackers exploit BtleJack to hijack connections or extract sensitive data.

An attacker, for example, targeting a BLE-enabled medical device, could use BtleJack to interfere with data transmission. BtleJack stands out as a comprehensive and flexible tool for BLE security analysis. Its combination of sniffing, jamming, and hijacking capabilities, hardware flexibility, and user-friendly interface make it an invaluable asset for anyone in BLE security research or testing.

GATTacker

GATTacker (https://github.com/securing/gattacker) is another open-source tool designed to test the security of BLE devices by exploiting vulnerabilities within the GATT or Generic Attribute Profile protocol, hence the name. As the primary framework for BLE communication, GATT facilitates data exchange through services and characteristics, making it a critical component of BLE device functionality. GATTacker analyzes, emulates, and manipulates these interactions, enabling penetration testers, security researchers, and developers to simulate real-world attacks and evaluate device security.

This tool is particularly effective for scanning and capturing BLE communications, emulating devices, replaying commands, and modifying data packets. It can intercept data between BLE devices to identify vulnerabilities, clone legitimate devices to mimic behaviors and simulate attacks like MITM, data injection, and device spoofing. GATTacker also evaluates encryption strength, pairing mechanisms, and permission settings, exposing weaknesses in device security protocols.

Key features of GATTacker include sniffing and logging BLE traffic to capture service and characteristic data, device emulation to clone BLE profiles for testing authentication vulnerabilities, and MITM attack capabilities to intercept and manipulate communication patterns. It also supports service discovery and enumeration, mapping out BLE profiles to identify exposed attributes that could be exploited. Additionally, GATTacker can replay GATT commands to test the resilience of devices against unauthorized commands or session hijacking attempts. Its custom scripting support (through Node.js) and integration with tools like Wireshark allow for advanced attack simulations and traffic analysis.

GATTacker has wide-ranging applications, including penetration testing of IoT and IoMT devices, device spoofing and cloning to assess pairing vulnerabilities, and MITM simulations to evaluate encryption weaknesses. It is particularly valuable for testing medical devices such as insulin pumps, heart monitors, smart home systems, and fitness trackers. Additionally, it assists in firmware and protocol testing, verifying compliance with Bluetooth security standards and uncovering backdoors or encryption flaws.

Despite its value as a research and testing tool, GATTacker demonstrates several security risks in the hands of an attacker. It can help exploit pairing mechanisms to impersonate trusted devices, manipulate transmitted data to alter behavior, and hijack sessions by replaying pairing keys. It also exposes vulnerabilities to firmware downgrade attacks, forcing devices to revert to older, less secure versions.

To reiterate, mitigating these risks requires organizations to enforce secure pairing mechanisms, update firmware regularly, restrict GATT services and permissions, implement device whitelisting, and deploy intrusion detection systems to monitor BLE traffic for anomalies. These steps help to defend against unauthorized access, spoofing, and data manipulation threats.

GATTacker can be an indispensable tool for identifying vulnerabilities in BLE devices, especially in IoT and IoMT environments. Its ability to emulate, sniff, and manipulate BLE traffic makes it highly effective for penetration testing and cybersecurity research. However, it also underscores the growing need for robust defenses as Bluetooth technologies continue to integrate into critical systems, including healthcare and smart infrastructure.

BlueMaho

BlueMaho (https://github.com/zenware/bluemaho) is a suite of Bluetooth hacking tools bundled into a single application. Designed for security testing of Bluetooth devices, BlueMaho provides a comprehensive set of features for both novice and experienced penetration testers.

Key features of BlueMaho include the following:

- **Device scanning:** BlueMaho can scan for nearby Bluetooth devices and provide detailed information such as device names, MAC addresses, and available services.
- **Device tracking:** The tool allows you to monitor specific devices over time, tracking their presence, name changes, and connection patterns.
- **Vulnerability testing:** BlueMaho includes tools for testing known and unknown vulnerabilities in Bluetooth devices.
- **Customizable alerts:** You can set up alerts to notify you when new devices are discovered in range.
- **Multi-dongle support:** BlueMaho uses separate Bluetooth dongles for scanning and running exploits, enhancing its versatility.
- **File transfer capabilities:** The tool allows you to send files to discovered devices.
- **Device spoofing:** BlueMaho can modify local Bluetooth adapter settings, including device name, class, and MAC address.
- **Statistical analysis:** The suite can generate detailed statistics on discovered devices, including unique devices by time and vendor distribution.

As an open-source project written in Python, BlueMaho offers a user-friendly GUI interface built with wxPython. This makes it accessible to security professionals who may not be comfortable with command-line tools.

The following are the capabilities of BlueMaho:

- Performs device discovery, reconnaissance, and vulnerability scanning
- Includes features for bluesnarfing and bluejacking

The following are the use cases for BlueMaho:

- Penetration testers use BlueMaho to assess the comprehensive security of Bluetooth devices.
- Attackers exploit it to identify and exploit weak Bluetooth implementations.

HCIDump

HCIDump (see usage help at https://helpmanual.io/help/hcidump) is a tool for capturing and analyzing Bluetooth communication. It is handy for developers, security researchers, and network administrators using Bluetooth technology. Let me walk you through its key features and applications.

HCIDump is designed to read and display the raw Bluetooth HCI data packets sent between a Bluetooth host and a Bluetooth controller. This low-level communication provides valuable insights into how Bluetooth devices interact. One primary use of HCIDump is debugging Bluetooth connections. By capturing the HCI packets, developers can identify pairing processes, data transfer, or connection stability issues. This granular view of Bluetooth communication allows for precise troubleshooting that might not be possible through other means.

HCIDump is particularly valuable in security research. It allows security professionals to analyze Bluetooth traffic for potential vulnerabilities or unauthorized access attempts. By examining the raw packet data, researchers can identify unusual patterns or potential exploit attempts in real time. The tool offers various output formats, including raw hexadecimal data and human-readable ASCII. This flexibility allows users to choose the most appropriate format for detailed analysis or a quick overview. HCIDump can be used with Bluetooth tools like hcitool for a comprehensive Bluetooth analysis toolkit. For instance, you can use hcitool to initiate a Bluetooth scan or connection while simultaneously capturing the HCI traffic with HCIDump.

It's worth noting that while HCIDump is a powerful tool, it requires a good understanding of Bluetooth protocols to interpret the data effectively. In Chapter 3, I discussed the Host-to-Controller Interface (HCI), which standardizes communication between the controller and the host. Users need to be familiar with the structure of HCI packets and the Bluetooth specification to make the most of the captured information.

Capabilities of HCIDump include the following:

- Logs raw Bluetooth traffic for in-depth analysis.
- Helps identify anomalies or unencrypted data transmissions.

These are use cases for HCIDump:

- Security analysts use HCIDump to audit Bluetooth network activity.
- Attackers leverage it to capture and display the HCI-level packets from intercepted communication.
- A penetration tester analyzing Bluetooth traffic in a smart home system could identify insecure communication patterns using HCIDump.

PyBluez

PyBluez (https://pybluez.github.io) is a Python library that enables developers to programmatically interface with Bluetooth devices. It provides a high-level abstraction for Bluetooth functionality, making it easier for programmers to use Bluetooth technology in their Python applications.

PyBluez offers a range of features for Bluetooth programming, including the following:

- **Device discovery:** PyBluez allows you to scan for nearby Bluetooth devices, retrieving information such as device names and MAC addresses. This is crucial for identifying and connecting to specific Bluetooth devices.
- **Service discovery:** The library supports the Service Discovery Protocol, enabling applications to find available Bluetooth services. This feature is essential for determining how to interact with a discovered device.
- **RFCOMM communication:** PyBluez supports RFCOMM, or Radio Frequency Communication, which emulates serial port connections over Bluetooth. This is particularly useful for applications that exchange data with Bluetooth-enabled devices.
- **L2CAP communication:** For more advanced use cases, PyBluez supports the Logical Link Control and Adaptation Protocol, or L2CAP, allowing for lower-level Bluetooth communication.
- **Cross-platform compatibility:** Though some features may be platform-specific, PyBluez works on multiple operating systems, including Windows, Linux, and macOS.

One of the key advantages of PyBluez is its simplicity. With just a few lines of code, developers can perform complex Bluetooth operations. For example, scanning for nearby devices can be accomplished with this:

```
import bluetooth
nearby_devices = bluetooth.discover_devices(lookup_names=True)
for addr, name in nearby_devices:
    print(f"Address: {addr}, Name: {name}")
```

PyBluez also allows for creating Bluetooth servers and clients, enabling two-way communication between devices. This makes it ideal for developing wireless file transfer systems, remote control applications, or IoT device management tools.

However, it's important to note that PyBluez has some limitations. It primarily supports Bluetooth Classic and has limited support for BLE. The library's development has also slowed recently, so it may not support the latest Bluetooth features.

The following are the capabilities of PyBluez:

- Enables the creation of custom Bluetooth tools and scripts
- Can automate scanning, pairing, and data exchange tasks

These are use cases for PyBluez:

- Ethical hackers use PyBluez to develop custom tools for specific security assessments.
- Attackers create tailored scripts to exploit unique vulnerabilities in target systems.

- A security team could use PyBluez to simulate a targeted attack, testing the resilience of their Bluetooth-enabled devices.

PyBluez is still an appreciated tool for Python developers working with Bluetooth technology. It offers a balance of simplicity and functionality for various Bluetooth-related tasks.

Mitigating Bluetooth Vulnerabilities

Bluetooth vulnerabilities can expose sensitive data and compromise device functionality. Users, manufacturers, and organizations can mitigate these risks by adopting proactive measures. In this section, I'll summarize seven rules of thumb, why they matter, and a synopsis of their strategies with examples as part of best practices explained later in this book, especially for tackling Bluetooth vulnerabilities.

Regular Updates and Patches   Outdated firmware and Bluetooth stacks are among attackers' most commonly exploited entry points. Vulnerabilities in legacy systems are well-documented, making older devices prime targets. Manufacturers should release regular updates to address newly discovered vulnerabilities, and users must ensure their devices are up-to-date.

For example, the "2017 BlueBorne" attack exploited unpatched Bluetooth devices, allowing attackers to spread malware. Regular updates could have closed these security gaps.

Disable Bluetooth When Not in Use   Leaving Bluetooth enabled unnecessarily increases the attack surface, exposing devices to potential exploits such as bluejacking, bluesnarfing, or unauthorized connections. Users should turn off Bluetooth when not actively using it, particularly in public spaces where attackers are more likely to operate.

For example, a user keeping their smartphone's Bluetooth on in a crowded airport could unknowingly expose it to an attacker attempting to send malicious files or intercept data.

Strong Pairing Methods   Weak pairing mechanisms, like Just Works, which I discussed previously, lack robust authentication, leaving devices vulnerable to MITM attacks. To help reduce risk, use advanced pairing protocols, such as Passkey Entry or Numeric Comparison, which provide stronger mutual authentication.

Manufacturers should default to secure pairing methods and phase out legacy options like simple PIN-based authentication. A medical device, for example, using Just Works pairing in a hospital, could be intercepted, compromising sensitive patient data. Switching to Numeric Comparison would reduce the risk of such attacks.

Enable Strong Encryption   Encryption protects the confidentiality of data transmitted between devices. Without strong encryption, attackers can intercept and decode Bluetooth communication. Therefore, it is essential to implement encryption standards like AES-128 and use secure cryptographic algorithms, such as Elliptic Curve Diffie-Hellman, for key exchange during pairing.

A fitness tracker transmitting unencrypted health data to a smartphone could be intercepted. Using AES-128 encryption ensures that the intercepted data remains unreadable.

Limit Discoverability   Discoverable devices broadcast their presence, making it easier for attackers to identify and target them. As a mitigation strategy, devices should remain in nondiscoverable mode by default. Users should enable discoverability only when pairing with another device and turning it off immediately afterward.

For example, a smart thermostat left in discoverable mode could be identified and targeted for unauthorized control. Restricting discoverability reduces this exposure.

Robust Device Authentication   Weak or absent authentication mechanisms allow unauthorized devices to connect and access sensitive data or control functionality. You should implement strong authentication protocols during pairing, such as:

- Requiring unique PIN codes.
- Leveraging public key cryptography to verify device identities.

For example, a Bluetooth-enabled lock that uses PIN-based authentication can be brute-forced if the PIN is short or predictable. Stronger cryptographic authentication makes such attacks infeasible.

Deploy Security Solutions and Network Controls   This matters because organizations that rely on Bluetooth-enabled devices are particularly vulnerable to large-scale attacks that can compromise critical data and infrastructure. Segmenting Bluetooth-enabled IoT devices from the main network in a smart factory can prevent attackers from accessing critical operational data if a single device is compromised.

Part of your mitigation strategy should include the following:

- Using network segmentation to isolate Bluetooth devices from sensitive systems
- Employing VPNs to secure data transmitted over Bluetooth connections

Example Case Studies and Lessons Learned

The following are case studies and lessons learned regarding Bluetooth and its vulnerabilities:

- **BlueBorne vulnerability (from 2017):** Attackers exploited vulnerabilities in Bluetooth stacks to spread malware and execute remote code. The lesson is that regular firmware updates and stronger encryption would have mitigated this attack.

- **Healthcare IoT devices:** A hospital's Bluetooth-enabled infusion pumps were found to use weak pairing protocols, potentially exposing patient data. Implementing Secure Simple Pairing and encryption could ensure patient data remains secure.
- **Retail environment attack:** Bluetooth point-of-sale systems were targeted to skim payment card information. As a lesson learned, turning off discoverability and requiring strong authentication prevents unauthorized connections.

Mitigating Bluetooth vulnerabilities requires a multilayered approach involving users, manufacturers, and organizations. Regular updates, secure pairing methods, robust encryption, and strict authentication protocols form the foundation of Bluetooth security. To reduce risks, unnecessary features like discoverability can be disabled, and broader security solutions such as VPNs and network segmentation can be employed.

As Bluetooth-enabled devices continue to proliferate, the importance of addressing these vulnerabilities will only grow. By staying informed about emerging exploits, implementing stronger security measures, and adopting best Bluetooth usage practices, consumers and organizations can reduce exposure to Bluetooth-specific threats.

Key Takeaways of Bluetooth Vulnerabilities and Exploits

Bluetooth technology presents security risks in modern devices due to its widespread adoption. The technology's vulnerabilities encompass various attack vectors, including data interception, impersonation attacks, MITM attacks, bluesnarfing, denial of service, bluejacking, and remote code execution. Despite built-in security mechanisms like encryption and authentication, legacy protocols and poor implementation can introduce weaknesses. Tools such as BlueZ and Ubertooth One demonstrate the potential for security testing and the risk of malicious exploitation. In the healthcare sector, Bluetooth-enabled medical devices are particularly vulnerable, with weak pairing methods and unencrypted communication exposing sensitive patient data and critical care systems to potential attacks. Mitigation strategies include regular firmware updates, disabling Bluetooth when not in use, implementing strong pairing methods, limiting device discoverability, and employing robust authentication and encryption protocols. Real-world incidents like the BlueBorne attack underscore the ongoing threat landscape and the critical need for improved security practices and constant vigilance in the face of emerging Bluetooth-related threats.

CHAPTER 5

Wi-Fi and Other Wireless Protocol Vulnerabilities

Today, Wi-Fi and wireless technologies are the backbone of modern healthcare operations. From seamless patient monitoring to ensuring administrative efficiency, these networks drive the critical exchange of data that supports life-saving decisions for you and your loved ones. However, as these systems evolve, so do the risks. Wi-Fi networks and other wireless protocols are prime targets for cybercriminals who exploit vulnerabilities to disrupt operations, steal sensitive data, or compromise patient safety.

This chapter covers the details of Wi-Fi security, laying the foundation with an overview of current standards and best practices. In more detail, I'll explain advancements like Opportunistic Wireless Encryption (OWE) and Protected Management Frames (PMF), which have been reshaping secure wireless communication. Building resilient network architectures with segmentation, using strong authentication, and adopting cutting-edge technologies like Wi-Fi 6/6E are also components of modern healthcare security, which will be examined as well.

To truly understand the scope of risks, I'll highlight common Wi-Fi vulnerabilities, complete with examples and case studies. These include unencrypted data transmissions, weak authentication protocols, and attacks such as rogue access points, phishing, and captive portal exploits. I'll explore the risks posed by outdated firmware, insecure IoT/medical devices, and the lack of network segmentation, which have proven particularly challenging in healthcare settings.

For those looking to strengthen their understanding of wireless attacks, I will introduce a range of Wi-Fi hacking software and products, detailing their capabilities, use cases, and countermeasures. Attackers and security professionals employ tools like Aircrack-ng, Bettercap, Reaver, and Wireshark for testing and defense.

The chapter closes with a wireless operational guide correlating with healthcare compliance and providing actionable insights into defining and securing sensitive data environments. By addressing challenges such as rogue devices, IoT vulnerabilities, and evolving threat landscapes, this guide offers practical solutions, including advanced monitoring tools, network segmentation, and updated encryption standards like WPA3.

This chapter combines technical expertise with practical guidance to help equip healthcare leaders, IT professionals, and security teams with the knowledge to navigate the ever-changing landscape of wireless security. By understanding vulnerabilities and embracing modern solutions, organizations can ensure compliance with stringent regulations and the trust and safety of their patients.

Introduction to Wi-Fi Security

As healthcare systems increasingly rely on wireless networks for seamless connectivity, securing Wi-Fi becomes vital to protecting sensitive patient data, ensuring compliance, and safeguarding critical operations. I'll explore some key Wi-Fi security features and strategies that can fortify healthcare networks against existing and emerging threats.

WPA: The Gold Standard in Wi-Fi Security

WPA3 is still considered the latest stable Wi-Fi security protocol. It was designed to address vulnerabilities present in its predecessor, WPA2. With features like 192-bit encryption in enterprise mode and 128-bit encryption in personal mode, WPA3 raises the bar for data protection. Simultaneous Authentication of Equals (SAE) replaces the older Pre-Shared Key authentication, making brute-force attacks far more challenging.

Additionally, forward secrecy helps ensure that even if an encryption key is compromised, past sessions cannot be decrypted, maintaining the integrity of historical data. Public networks benefit from individualized data encryption, which protects user traffic, even in shared environments like hospital lobbies or waiting areas.

Opportunistic Wireless Encryption

Opportunistic Wireless Encryption (OWE) is a feature designed for open Wi-Fi networks without password authentication. By automatically encrypting traffic between devices and access points, OWE provides encryption by default, making it ideal for public areas in healthcare facilities, such as cafeterias or visitor lounges.

OWE ensures that patient and visitor personal data remains protected against eavesdropping or interception, even in open networks.

Traditionally, open networks lacked encryption, leaving users vulnerable to eavesdropping. With OWE, all traffic between a user's device and the access point is automatically encrypted, ensuring the privacy of visitors, patients, and staff using the network for basic browsing or communication. An example would be a patient in a hospital lobby who connects to the facility's open Wi-Fi to check their medical records via a patient portal or log into other online portals. OWE encrypts the connection, helping to prevent malicious actors nearby from intercepting their login credentials or sensitive health data.

As mentioned in earlier chapters, healthcare facilities often set up temporary Wi-Fi networks during emergencies, mobile clinics, or vaccination drives. OWE helps these networks provide secure connections without password distribution or a complex setup, ensuring rapid deployment while protecting data transmission. During a disaster response, a mobile clinic deploys an open Wi-Fi network for healthcare workers to access patient records. Again, OWE encrypts the communications, ensuring the integrity and confidentiality of patient data despite the temporary nature of the network.

Many IoMT devices in healthcare settings, such as wearables, smart beds, or patient monitoring systems, communicate over open networks. By encrypting all device-to-network communications, OWE ensures that sensitive data is not exposed to eavesdropping or interception, even if no password is required for connectivity. A wearable health monitor, for example, sends real-time patient vitals to a central monitoring system via an open Wi-Fi network in some hospitals. OWE encrypts this data stream and prevents unauthorized access to the patient's medical information.

Most hospitals offer open Wi-Fi for visitors and nonclinical users who may not need access to the main secured network. OWE allows these users to connect to an open network while ensuring their data is encrypted and maintaining privacy without password authentication. Another example would be a visitor who uses the hospital's guest Wi-Fi to communicate with family members about a patient's condition.

Healthcare staff often use mobile devices to access critical systems or communicate within facilities. When staff rely on open Wi-Fi for quick communication, OWE ensures their sessions are encrypted, reducing the risk of intercepting information. Nurses often access an internal scheduling app over the hospital's open Wi-Fi network while on break. This is another example of OWE ensuring the session remains private, preventing unauthorized access to hospital schedules or staffing information.

Hospitals and healthcare organizations that host sizable public health events, such as vaccination drives or community health fairs, benefit from OWE's ability to provide secure open networks. During a vaccination drive in a large public venue, an open Wi-Fi network is usually set up for attendees to register for appointments.

OWE transforms open Wi-Fi networks in healthcare by providing encryption without the need for passwords. This capability is handy in public-facing and temporary healthcare scenarios where quick, secure connectivity is essential. By protecting data transmission in open environments, OWE enhances privacy and security for patients, visitors, staff, and medical IoT devices, reinforcing trust and compliance in healthcare settings.

Protected Management Frames

Protected Management Frames (PMF) represents a leap forward in Wi-Fi security. It safeguards one of the most vulnerable aspects of wireless networks: management frames. These frames are the backbone of how devices and access points communicate, orchestrating everything from network association to disassociation. However, traditional Wi-Fi protocols left these frames unprotected, creating a significant security gap that attackers could exploit.

PMF addresses this by ensuring that management frames are encrypted and authenticated, preventing attackers from intercepting or manipulating them. Imagine a healthcare provider using a tablet to monitor patient vitals in real time. An attacker could exploit unsecured management frames to launch a deauthentication or disassociation attack, disconnecting the tablet from the network. This interruption could jeopardize patient care. With PMF, such attacks are thwarted, helping to ensure uninterrupted connectivity and operational stability.

Management frames also define how devices interact with the network, such as setting up roaming protocols or prioritizing traffic. An attacker manipulating these frames could reroute traffic or disrupt network efficiency. PMF protects these frames, ensuring that network configurations remain secure and reliable.

In hospitals, IoT medical devices such as infusion pumps or monitors rely on stable, secure Wi-Fi connectivity. PMF helps these devices remain connected without interruption from malicious attacks. In enterprise environments, PMF helps prevent attacks that aim to disrupt employee productivity by disconnecting devices or creating rogue access points. Additionally, for environments like cafes, airports, or hospital waiting areas, PMF ensures that malicious actors cannot easily hijack or manipulate network connections to target users or devices even on public Wi-Fi networks.

PMF enhances Wi-Fi networks' overall security posture by protecting these critical network communication components. Whether for healthcare, enterprise, or public Wi-Fi, PMF keeps networks operational, secure, and resilient against emerging threats.

Building a Resilient Network Architecture with Segmentation

Network segmentation is a cornerstone of cybersecurity, particularly in environments like healthcare, where the stakes are high and the attack surface is massive. By dividing a wireless network into distinct, controlled segments, organizations can dramatically reduce risks, control access, and help prevent breaches from escalating into full-scale security incidents. I'll examine why this strategy is critical and how it works.

Why Network Segmentation Matters

First, imagine a scenario where a single medical device is compromised by malware. Without segmentation, that breach could allow attackers to traverse the entire network, accessing sensitive patient data or critical systems. Segmentation contains the breach in its isolated segment, limiting its impact. By separating traffic into distinct segments, such as medical devices, guest access, and administrative systems, IT teams gain clearer visibility into how data flows and where anomalies may arise. This segmentation allows for more precise monitoring and rapid response to threats.

Key Technologies Enabling Segmentation

Virtual LANs (VLANs) act like barriers within a network, grouping devices logically rather than physically. For example, a VLAN for medical devices ensures that infusion pumps, heart monitors, and other critical equipment communicate securely within their own space. A separate VLAN for guests isolates their internet usage from sensitive hospital systems.

Access control lists (ACLs) enforce strict rules about which devices or applications can communicate across network segments. For instance, a heart monitor on a medical VLAN may be allowed to send data to the central monitoring system but not to administrative systems or the Internet. A guest user accessing public Wi-Fi cannot communicate with devices on the medical or administrative VLANs.

Containing threats is a key benefit of segmentation (sometimes called *enclaving*), which helps comply with regulations. Network segmentation prevents lateral movement by isolating traffic, ensuring that a single compromised device doesn't threaten the entire network. Many laws, like HIPAA, mandate strict control over access to sensitive healthcare data. Network segmentation helps meet these requirements by ensuring only authorized devices and users can access protected systems. Segmentation also allows IT teams to quickly identify and contain the affected segment when a security incident occurs, reducing downtime and mitigating risks.

In an increasingly connected healthcare environment, network segmentation is not just a best practice—it's essential. By leveraging VLANs (and/or wireless LANs, which are known as WLANs) with ACLs, healthcare organizations can create a safer, more resilient wireless network infrastructure, protecting patient data and critical systems from ever-evolving cyber threats. Segmentation helps ensure your organization remains secure, operational, and compliant despite an attack.

Strong Authentication and Access Control

Strong authentication and access control are essential to protecting Wi-Fi networks in healthcare environments. These measures safeguard sensitive patient data, ensure the seamless operation of life-saving medical devices, and maintain reliable connectivity for administrative functions. Weak authentication systems can allow unauthorized access, exposing networks to data breaches, ransomware, or system interruptions, making strong security protocols non-negotiable.

A key strategy for securing healthcare networks begins with unique, complex passwords. Each network segment, such as those supporting medical devices, guest access, or administrative systems, should use long, randomized passwords comprising a mix of letters, numbers, and symbols. These passwords must be distinct and updated regularly to minimize the risk of exploitation by attackers. For example, a guest Wi-Fi network should never share passwords with a segment supporting sensitive medical devices.

Multifactor authentication (MFA) adds a vital layer of security by requiring users to verify their identity using two or more factors, such as a password, a fingerprint, or a one-time passcode. Even if a password is compromised, MFA provides a secondary defense. Healthcare environments should mandate MFA for administrative access to critical systems like electronic health records and network management tools. For instance, a hospital administrator logging in using their laptop might need to provide a secure password and a code sent to their phone.

Enterprise-grade 802.1X authentication is another cornerstone of strong access control, particularly in healthcare settings. This framework validates user or device credentials before granting network access. Medical devices like infusion pumps or heart monitors should be authenticated using 802.1X to ensure only trusted devices can connect. Similarly, staff devices such as laptops or tablets can be validated to create a secure and accountable network environment. I'll discuss this more when I discuss Zero Trust later in this book.

Centralized authentication management via Remote Authentication Dial-In User Service (RADIUS) servers simplifies and strengthens network security. A RADIUS server enforces consistent security policies, verifying user credentials against a centralized database to ensure only authorized staff or devices gain access. It also streamlines operations by allowing IT teams to modify permissions or revoke access from a single control point. This approach supports logging and monitoring, which is critical for compliance with laws, regulations, and incident investigations.

Strong authentication and access control deliver several critical benefits for healthcare networks. They enhance security by ensuring only authorized users and devices access the network, reducing the risk of breaches and unauthorized data access. These measures also help healthcare organizations comply with regulations like HIPAA, which demand rigorous controls to protect patient health information. Additionally, these protocols improve network resilience by defending against phishing, credential theft, or brute-force attacks. Centralized management further streamlines operations, reducing administrative overhead while maintaining a secure and compliant environment.

As healthcare increasingly depends on digital systems, strong authentication, and access control are no longer optional but crucial. Strategies like unique passwords, MFA, enterprise-grade 802.1X, and centralized RADIUS management enable healthcare organizations to protect their networks from evolving cyber threats.

Wi-Fi 6/6E Security Solutions

Deploying enterprise-grade access points is essential for building a reliable and scalable foundation for secure Wi-Fi in modern environments, particularly in industries like healthcare. These advanced access points should support the latest Wi-Fi 6 or 6E standards, which offer improved performance, greater capacity for connected devices, and enhanced security features.

Incorporating WPA3-Enterprise, these access points also ensure stronger encryption and authentication protocols, significantly reducing some vulnerabilities to cyber threats. Additionally, enterprise-grade access points provide centralized management and monitoring capabilities, allowing administrators to oversee and control the network efficiently. With these features, organizations can simplify network administration while maintaining the high level of security and performance required for critical operations.

Secure IoMT Device Management

Comprehensive Wi-Fi security management platforms have become indispensable for safeguarding networks against evolving threats. These platforms provide real-time threat detection and response, enabling IT teams to swiftly identify and neutralize risks before they escalate. With automated policy enforcement, organizations can ensure a consistent application of security rules, minimizing human error while maintaining compliance. Centralized visibility across the entire network further empowers IT teams to monitor activity, manage configurations, and address vulnerabilities proactively, all while preserving optimal network performance.

These platforms are even more critical in healthcare, where IoT medical devices present unique security challenges. Medical IoT devices like infusion pumps and patient monitors often lack built-in security features, making them vulnerable entry points for attackers. Implementing IoT-specific security solutions is essential to address this complexity. These solutions can identify and classify connected devices, monitor their behavior for anomalies, and enforce device-specific security policies. Regular updates and patches for IoMT device firmware are vital to minimizing vulnerabilities and maintaining a strong security posture. By integrating these advanced tools and strategies, healthcare organizations can create a secure wireless ecosystem that protects sensitive patient data, ensures operational continuity, and complies with regulatory requirements.

Challenges for Device Management

While Wi-Fi's security features and solutions are getting more robust, the technology's inherent design and implementation mistakes expose devices to challenges, including the following:

- **Unencrypted data transmission:** Unencrypted or poorly encrypted Wi-Fi networks can expose sensitive patient data to attackers' interception. This includes medical records, diagnostic images, and billing information.

- **Weak authentication protocols:** Networks using outdated authentication methods, such as WPA2-PSK, are susceptible to brute-force attacks or credential theft. These vulnerabilities are exacerbated in healthcare settings where multiple devices share the same credentials.
- **Rogue access points and evil twin attacks:** Rogue access points mimic legitimate Wi-Fi networks, tricking users into connecting and exposing sensitive data. Attackers can also use evil twin networks to intercept communication and steal login credentials.
- **Lack of network segmentation:** Failing to segment networks allows attackers who breach one part of the network to move laterally and compromise sensitive systems, such as medical device networks or EHR databases.
- **Outdated firmware and insecure IoT devices:** Many medical IoT devices, such as infusion pumps or patient monitors, lack robust security features and are often left running obsolete firmware. These vulnerabilities can be exploited to gain unauthorized access or launch more significant attacks.
- **Deauthentication and disassociation attacks:** Attackers can use deauthentication or disassociation attacks to disrupt Wi-Fi connectivity, causing delays in accessing critical patient data or medical systems.
- **Phishing through Wi-Fi networks:** Phishing attacks can be carried over Wi-Fi by redirecting users to malicious login pages, often mimicking legitimate hospital systems.

Common Wi-Fi Vulnerabilities with Examples and Case Studies

Wi-Fi networks are the backbone of modern healthcare operations, supporting everything from patient monitoring systems to EHRs. The reliance on wireless connectivity makes it a prime target for cyberattacks. Understanding common vulnerabilities and their real-world implications is essential for strengthening Wi-Fi security in environments, especially healthcare. I'll look at the most common types in more detail in this section, including unencrypted data transmission, weak authentication protocols, rogue access points, evil twin attacks, lack of segmentation, outdated firmware, deauthentication and disassociation attacks, phishing through Wi-Fi networks, captive portal attack, and PEAP exchange attacks.

Unencrypted Data Transmission

Unencrypted data transmission poses a risk to healthcare organizations, leaving sensitive patient information vulnerable to cyberattacks. When Wi-Fi networks lack proper encryption or rely on outdated encryption standards, malicious actors can access critical data such as medical records, diagnostic images, and billing information. This exposure can lead to data breaches, regulatory noncompliance, and severe reputational damage to healthcare institutions.

For example, an attacker using basic packet-sniffing tools on an unsecured network could capture unencrypted patient data transmitted between a doctor's tablet and the hospital's electronic health record system. To mitigate this risk, healthcare organizations adopt modern encryption protocols like WPA3, ensuring encryption standards protect all data transmitted over Wi-Fi networks. This approach safeguards sensitive information, reinforces patient trust, and complies with stringent regulatory requirements like HIPAA.

I have read about many hospital settings with unsecured guest Wi-Fi networks that staff use for quick access to EHRs. These networks allow attackers to capture login credentials or patient data through packet sniffing. A regional hospital in California suffered a data breach when attackers intercepted unencrypted Wi-Fi traffic from a nurse's tablet, exposing the personal health information of more than 20,000 patients. The incident led to significant fines and reputational damage.

Weak Authentication Protocols

Weak authentication protocols, such as the outdated WPA2 pre-shared key, present a critical vulnerability for healthcare networks. These methods rely on shared credentials across multiple devices, making them susceptible to brute-force attacks. Attackers can systematically guess passwords to be granted unauthorized access. In a healthcare setting, the risks are magnified due to the high number of connected devices, including medical equipment, administrative systems, and personal devices.

For instance, an attacker who gains access to shared credentials could infiltrate the network, potentially accessing sensitive patient data or disrupting critical medical systems. To address these vulnerabilities, healthcare organizations implement WPA3, with SAE, to defend against brute-force attacks. Additionally, deploying enterprise-grade authentication frameworks such as 802.1X with unique credentials for each user or device ensures a higher level of security. Strengthening authentication protects against unauthorized access and preserves the integrity of sensitive healthcare operations and patient data.

An example would be a medical clinic using a shared Wi-Fi password for staff and guests who unknowingly provided an entry point for attackers who used a brute-force attack to gain network access.

Rogue Access Points and Evil Twin Attacks

Rogue access points and evil twin attacks can pose significant threats to healthcare Wi-Fi networks, exploiting users' inherent trust in legitimate connections. Rogue access points are unauthorized devices that mimic the appearance of legitimate networks, tricking users and devices into connecting. Once connected, attackers can intercept sensitive data such as patient records, login credentials, or financial details. Similarly, an evil twin attack involves creating a fake Wi-Fi network that replicates the name and appearance of a trusted network. Users unknowingly connect to this malicious network, allowing attackers to monitor traffic, steal credentials, or inject malware. For example, in a hospital setting, an attacker could set up an evil twin in a waiting room, targeting patients, visitors, or staff accessing the network.

These attacks are particularly dangerous because they often go unnoticed until significant damage has been done. To combat this threat, healthcare organizations implement measures such as enabling WPA3 encryption, deploying network monitoring tools to detect unauthorized access points, and educating users about verifying the authenticity of Wi-Fi networks before connecting. Vigorous defenses against rogue access points and evil twins are essential to protecting sensitive data and maintaining trust in healthcare environments.

For example, an attacker could set up a fake Wi-Fi network in a hospital waiting area named "Hospital_Guest_Free." Patients and staff may unknowingly connect, exposing their devices to credential theft and malware. A security assessment at a large hospital revealed multiple rogue access points near the facility. Attackers used these access points to intercept communications between medical devices, creating vulnerabilities in the patient monitoring system.

Lack of Network Segmentation

A lack of network segmentation is a critical vulnerability in healthcare environments, where sensitive systems like medical devices, electronic health record databases, and administrative networks often coexist on the same network. Without segmentation, an attacker who breaches one part of the network, such as a guest Wi-Fi or a less secure IoMT device, can move laterally to access critical systems, escalating the scope of the attack. For example, if a cybercriminal gains access to a network through a compromised smart thermostat or infusion pump, they could exploit that access to infiltrate EHR systems, steal sensitive patient data, or disrupt life-saving medical devices.

As mentioned earlier, proper segmentation isolates these systems using solutions like VLANs, WLANs, and ACLs. This limits communication between segments and reduces the risk of lateral movement. By creating distinct zones for guest access, medical devices, and administrative operations, healthcare organizations can contain potential breaches and protect their most critical assets.

For example, a compromised tablet on the hospital's guest Wi-Fi could allow attackers to access the main administrative network. In news and security wires, I hear about ransomware attacks on hospitals that were traced back to a single compromised device on a poorly segmented network. The attackers encrypted patient records, forcing the hospital to divert emergency services for days.

Outdated Firmware and Insecure IoMT Devices

Outdated firmware and insecure IoMT devices present a significant security challenge in healthcare environments. Medical IoT devices, such as infusion pumps, patient monitors, and wearable sensors, are often designed with functionality and ease of use in mind, but security features are frequently an afterthought. Many of these devices operate on outdated firmware that lacks protection against cyber threats developed after the original device was created. Thus, the device needs updated protection.

Attackers can exploit these weaknesses to gain unauthorized access, disrupt device functionality, or use the compromised devices as entry points to infiltrate the broader network. The consequences of these attacks are not just financial or reputational, as they can directly impact patient health. To mitigate these risks, healthcare organizations prioritize regular firmware updates, implement patch management processes, and enforce strong security protocols for IoMT devices. Additionally, network segmentation and device-specific security policies can limit exposure and protect these devices within a secure network environment.

An example is an unpatched Wi-Fi-enabled infusion pump in an ICU that an attacker exploits to inject malware into the network. In a security demonstration, researchers gained control of an unpatched insulin pump via a hospital's Wi-Fi network, showcasing the potential for life-threatening attacks if device vulnerabilities are not addressed.

Deauthentication and Disassociation Attacks

Deauthentication and disassociation attacks risk the reliability and functionality of Wi-Fi networks. These attacks involve sending fraudulent signals to disconnect devices from the network, effectively disrupting communication and causing service interruptions. In a healthcare setting, such disruptions can have serious consequences, as they may delay access to critical patient data, hinder real-time monitoring of vital signs, or disrupt the operation of medical systems reliant on continuous connectivity.

For example, during an attack, devices like infusion pumps or patient monitoring systems might lose connection to centralized systems, delaying alerts or critical interventions. Attackers often exploit this tactic as a precursor to more invasive breaches, such as launching rogue access points or eavesdropping on reconnecting devices. Another example would be an attacker that launches a deauthentication attack on the hospital's Wi-Fi, disconnecting nurses' tablets and delaying access to patient vitals in the ICU.

To mitigate these risks, healthcare organizations implement PMF, a feature in modern Wi-Fi protocols like WPA3 that protects against deauthentication and disassociation attempts. Additionally, continuous network activity monitoring and rapid incident response protocols can help detect and neutralize such attacks before they escalate into more significant security events.

Phishing Through Wi-Fi Networks

Phishing through Wi-Fi networks is a growing threat. Attackers exploit users' trust in familiar networks to redirect them to malicious login pages. They set up fake portals that mimic legitimate hospital systems, such as electronic health record platforms or employee dashboards, tricking users into entering their credentials. Once credentials are stolen, attackers can gain unauthorized access to sensitive systems, compromising patient data, operational workflows, and financial records.

These attacks are particularly concerning in healthcare, where timely access to systems is critical. Organizations enforce secure Wi-Fi configurations, including encrypted connections and multifactor authentication, to combat this risk and provide ongoing phishing awareness training for all staff. Deploying automated security tools to detect and block suspicious redirection attempts can strengthen defenses against phishing over Wi-Fi networks.

For example, a staff member connecting to the hospital's Wi-Fi is redirected to a fake login page for the EHR system, unknowingly providing attackers with their credentials. In a notable incident, phishing over Wi-Fi compromised the login credentials of administrative staff, allowing attackers to exfiltrate sensitive billing information from a healthcare network.

Healthcare organizations must prioritize Wi-Fi security by adopting next-generation protocols like WPA3, implementing network segmentation, and ensuring robust device management. Regular security audits, firmware updates, and staff training can significantly reduce the risk of these vulnerabilities.

Captive Portal Attack

Captive portals are standard in public Wi-Fi networks, such as airports, cafes, and healthcare facilities. They serve as a gateway page that users must interact with, usually by entering login credentials, agreeing to terms, or providing personal information before gaining access to the network. While they are intended to enhance user experience and control, attackers can exploit captive portals to execute phishing attacks, harvest credentials, or inject malware.

A captive portal attack is a Wi-Fi hacking method where attackers set up a rogue access point that mimics a legitimate Wi-Fi network with a fake captive portal. Unsuspecting users connect to the network and interact with the fraudulent portal, believing it to be genuine. Through this, attackers can do the following:

- **Harvest credentials:** Users may enter usernames, passwords, or personal information on a fake login page.
- **Inject malware:** Attackers can deliver malicious payloads or prompt users to download infected files.
- **Redirect traffic:** Traffic can be redirected to malicious websites, enabling phishing or further attacks.
- **Capture sensitive data:** Intercept data transmitted by users on the compromised network.

There are several hacking tools commonly used for captive portal attacks:

- **WiFi-Pumpkin:** A versatile tool for creating rogue access points and spoofing captive portals to harvest credentials

- **Wifiphisher:** Specializes in creating fake access points with deceptive captive portals to execute phishing attacks
- **Bettercap:** An advanced network attack tool capable of setting up rogue access points and monitoring traffic
- **Airbase-ng:** Part of the Aircrack-ng suite, creates rogue APs that can serve fake captive portals
- **Responder:** Captures NTLM hashes and other sensitive information during authentication attempts on a rogue portal

There are several use cases for captive portal attacks. The following are three:

- **Phishing credentials in public Wi-Fi:** Attackers set up rogue access points in high-traffic areas like airports or cafes, luring users to connect and log in through fake captive portals that mimic the legitimate network.
- **Compromising corporate networks:** In enterprise environments, a rogue captive portal can trick employees into divulging credentials for internal systems, leading to breaches.
- **Healthcare exploits:** Attackers target hospitals or clinics where patients or staff use guest Wi-Fi networks, capturing credentials or redirecting them to malicious sites that could lead to further attacks.

An example to simulate this attack is that during setup, an attacker deploys Wifiphisher in a hospital parking lot to create a rogue access point named Hospital_Guest_WiFi, identical to the legitimate network. When patients or staff connect, they are presented with a captive portal asking them to log in using their hospital credentials or provide personal details for verification.

Victims unknowingly enter their credentials into the fake portal. The attacker harvests usernames and passwords, potentially gaining access to sensitive hospital systems or patient data. The attacker then uses the stolen credentials to infiltrate the hospital's network, escalate privileges, and launch further attacks, such as ransomware.

How to Mitigate Captive Portal Attacks

Mitigating captive portal attacks requires user education, secure authentication practices, and advanced security measures to protect sensitive information. Educating users is a first line of defense. Training programs should teach individuals how to recognize and avoid rogue networks, particularly those that prompt sensitive information through suspicious captive portals. By promoting awareness, users can better identify potential threats and reduce the likelihood of falling victim to such attacks.

Implementing secure authentication methods, such as MFA, again adds an extra layer of security, making it more difficult for attackers to exploit stolen credentials. This approach ensures that even if login details are compromised, additional verification steps help prevent unauthorized access to sensitive systems. Users should also be instructed to validate captive portals before entering personal information.

This includes checking for HTTPS connections, inspecting URLs, and verifying SSL certificates to confirm the legitimacy of the network.

Organizations should monitor network activity regularly to detect rogue access points and identify unusual traffic patterns indicative of an attack. Employing enterprise-grade wireless intrusion detection and prevention systems (WIDS/WIPS) further enhances security by actively identifying and blocking unauthorized portals or rogue devices attempting to intercept data.

Encrypting data traffic is another crucial mitigation step. Encouraging VPNs on public Wi-Fi networks ensures that even if users connect through a rogue captive portal, their transmitted data remains encrypted and secure. VPNs provide an additional layer of protection, preventing attackers from viewing or manipulating sensitive information during transmission.

By combining user awareness, secure authentication, traffic encryption, and advanced monitoring tools, organizations can reduce the risk of captive portal attacks and safeguard their networks from unauthorized access.

When it comes to captive portal attacks, the following are key things you should take away:

- Captive portal attacks exploit users' trust in public Wi-Fi networks to harvest credentials, inject malware, or intercept sensitive data.
- Tools like Wifiphisher, WiFi-Pumpkin, and Bettercap are commonly used to create rogue access points with fake portals.
- Public Wi-Fi users, particularly in sensitive environments like healthcare or corporate settings, are prime targets for these attacks.
- Mitigation requires user education, secure authentication methods, and network monitoring tools.

PEAP Exchange Vulnerabilities and Attacks

The Protected Extensible Authentication Protocol (PEAP) is widely used in enterprise Wi-Fi networks to provide secure authentication by encapsulating Extensible Authentication Protocol (EAP) in a Transport Layer Security (TLS) tunnel. While PEAP offers significant security improvements over open authentication protocols, it is not immune to vulnerabilities. Attackers can exploit misconfigurations or weaknesses in PEAP exchanges to compromise network security, intercept sensitive data, or gain unauthorized access.

Understanding PEAP Exchange Vulnerabilities

PEAP is widely used to secure wireless network authentication but has some problems. One significant issue is server certificate validation. During the authentication process, PEAP relies on server certificates to establish a trusted TLS tunnel. However, suppose client devices fail to validate the server certificate properly. In that case, attackers can exploit this weakness by deploying rogue access points or conducting MITM attacks, allowing them to intercept sensitive data.

Another vulnerability stems from weak client-side security configurations. Some devices may lack the proper configuration to enforce secure server validation, leaving them susceptible to credential theft. Attackers can impersonate legitimate servers and trick devices into connecting, enabling unauthorized access to network traffic and sensitive information.

The PEAP exchange is also vulnerable to credential harvesting via MITM attacks. If attackers intercept authentication traffic, they can capture usernames and hashed passwords. These credentials are often vulnerable to offline brute-force or dictionary attacks, where attackers attempt to decrypt the hashes to gain access to user accounts. This exploit highlights the importance of enforcing robust authentication policies and hashing algorithms.

A particularly concerning issue arises when using EAP-GTC (Generic Token Card) within PEAP exchanges. EAP-GTC can expose credentials in clear text or weakly hashed formats, making them easy targets for attackers. This weakness can lead to rapid credential theft and network compromise, especially when EAP-GTC is not adequately secured or updated.

Organizations prioritize proper server certificate validation, enforce secure client configurations, and use stronger authentication methods to mitigate these risks. Addressing these vulnerabilities is essential to maintaining the integrity and security of wireless networks that rely on PEAP for authentication.

There are several tools commonly used for PEAP exchange attacks:

- **EvilTwin (Attack Frameworks):** Tools like Airbase-ng (part of Aircrack-ng suite) and Wifiphisher can set up rogue access points that mimic legitimate networks, tricking clients into connecting.
- **EAPeak:** This is designed to analyze and exploit EAP authentication exchanges, including PEAP. It can extract and manipulate EAP packets to discover misconfigurations or weak security implementations.
- **Responder:** This tool captures authentication handshakes and can intercept PEAP authentication data to facilitate credential theft.
- **Hashcat and John the Ripper:** These are used for offline password cracking of PEAP-extracted credentials, allowing attackers to compromise accounts.
- **Wireshark:** This packet analyzer captures and analyzes PEAP exchange traffic to detect vulnerabilities or identify authentication issues.

Some of the use cases of PEAP exchange attacks include the following:

- **Credential harvesting:** Attackers target organizations with improperly configured PEAP to harvest usernames and hashed passwords, which can be cracked offline to access sensitive systems.
- **Network impersonation:** Attackers impersonate legitimate networks by setting up rogue access points. Devices connect automatically due to weak server certificate validation, enabling attackers to intercept sensitive data.

- **Lateral movement:** Gained credentials can escalate privileges within an organization, moving laterally to access critical systems or databases.
- **Healthcare threats:** In a healthcare setting, a compromised PEAP exchange could allow unauthorized access to patient records or critical medical devices that rely on Wi-Fi.

To understand this vulnerability better, the following is an example of an attack on a Hospital's PEAP-Protected Wi-Fi done in five steps:

Step 1: Setup
An attacker deploys a rogue access point in the hospital parking lot using tools like Wifiphisher, mimicking the legitimate network SSID used for internal staff devices.

Step 2: Execution
When staff devices connect to the rogue network, the attacker uses tools like EAPeak to capture authentication traffic. Because staff devices improperly validate their certificates, the connection is established without warnings.

Step 3: Credential Harvesting
Using Responder, the attacker collects usernames and hashed passwords during the PEAP exchange.

Step 4: Password Cracking
The attacker leverages Hashcat to crack weak or poorly hashed credentials offline.

Step 5: Result
With valid credentials, the attacker accesses sensitive systems such as the hospital's EHR platform or medical device networks, compromising patient data and operations.

How to Mitigate PEAP Vulnerabilities

Enforcing strict certificate validation on all client devices is essential to protecting against vulnerabilities in PEAP exchanges. Configurations should require validation of server certificates issued by trusted certificate authorities (CAs) to prevent man-in-the-middle attacks. Strengthening authentication policies is also critical. Organizations should avoid weaker protocols like EAP-GTC and adopt more secure options, such as EAP-TLS, which uses client-side certificates for added protection.

Strong password policies are another critical step to reduce the risk of offline brute-force attacks if credentials are intercepted. Regular security audits and penetration testing should also be conducted to detect vulnerabilities and misconfigurations in Wi-Fi networks before attackers can exploit them. Additionally, enabling MFA adds an extra layer of defense, ensuring that compromised credentials alone are not enough to gain unauthorized access. Together, these strategies help create a more secure wireless network environment.

When it comes to PEAP vulnerabilities, these are the key things you should take away:

- PEAP is a critical protocol for securing Wi-Fi networks, but its effectiveness depends heavily on proper implementation.
- Attackers can exploit misconfigurations or weak encryption within PEAP exchanges to harvest credentials and compromise networks.
- Tools like EAPeak, Wifiphisher, and Hashcat are often used in these attacks, highlighting the importance of robust configurations and regular audits.
- Strengthening certificate validation, upgrading to secure EAP methods, and enforcing strong password policies are essential for mitigating these risks.

Wi-Fi Hacking Tools

Wi-Fi hacking tools have become increasingly sophisticated and powerful, especially recently. While these tools can be used maliciously, they also serve important purposes for cybersecurity professionals conducting penetration testing and security audits. This section will explore my favorite Wi-Fi hacking tools, their capabilities, and some ethical use cases.

Aircrack-ng

The Aircrack-ng suite (www.aircrack-ng.org) is one of the most widely used Wi-Fi hacking toolkits. Designed for penetration testing and security assessments, it provides comprehensive tools to test the security of wireless networks. While the suite is a legitimate tool for ethical hacking and improving network defenses, its capabilities make it attractive to malicious actors. The following are the tools within the suite:

Airmon-ng is designed to enable and manage monitor mode on wireless interfaces. This mode allows an adapter to listen to all network packets, not just those addressed. This capability is handy for scanning and identifying available Wi-Fi networks, setting up wireless cards for data capture, and preparing for further analysis.

Airodump-ng complements Airmon-ng by capturing and displaying wireless packets in real time. It identifies active networks and their properties, such as SSIDs, channels, signal strength, and encryption types, while displaying connected clients and their MAC addresses. It is commonly used for reconnaissance to map networks, identify weak security configurations, and locate hidden SSIDs.

Aireplay-ng is a packet injection tool that manipulates wireless traffic. It performs deauthentication attacks to disconnect clients from access points, forcing them to reconnect and allowing attackers to capture handshake data for password cracking. Additionally, it sends forged packets to stimulate responses, making it ideal for testing network resilience against injection attacks and gathering data for authentication analysis.

Aircrack-ng focuses on cracking WEP and WPA/WPA2-PSK passwords using captured handshake data. It recovers passwords using dictionary attacks, brute-force methods, and statistical techniques, and it offers GPU-based cracking for faster results. This tool is widely used to demonstrate the vulnerability of weak Wi-Fi passwords and validate the effectiveness of encryption settings.

After obtaining the encryption key, airdecap-ng decrypts WEP, WPA, and WPA2-encrypted packets. Once decrypted, it extracts sensitive data such as usernames and passwords from captured traffic, enabling security professionals to analyze risks associated with network encryption protocols and evaluate data exposure vulnerabilities.

Airgraph-ng visualizes wireless network traffic in graph format. It maps connections between access points and clients, highlighting devices with high communication levels that may indicate potential threats. This tool is handy for investigating network topologies, identifying suspicious activity, and educating teams on wireless vulnerabilities.

Airolib-ng offers database-driven support for faster password cracking by storing and organizing password and ESSID information. It precomputes hashes to speed up dictionary-based attacks against WPA/WPA2 networks, making it a valuable tool for streamlining brute force attempts and improving testing efficiency.

Together, these tools form a comprehensive suite for wireless penetration testing, enabling security researchers to assess vulnerabilities, validate encryption settings, and enhance overall network defenses.

An example use case regarding penetration testing on a WPA2-encrypted network is as follows:

1. **Reconnaissance (Airmon-ng and Airodump-ng):**
   - Airmon-ng enables monitor mode on the wireless adapter.
   - Airodump-ng scans and displays networks, identifying a WPA2-protected network with multiple clients.

2. **Packet Injection (Aireplay-ng):**
   - Aireplay-ng performs a deauthentication attack, disconnecting a client from the access point.
   - The attacker captures the four-way handshake data during reconnection.

3. **Password Cracking (Aircrack-ng):**
   - Aircrack-ng uses a precomputed dictionary to brute-force the WPA2-PSK password.
   - If successful, the password provides access to the network.

4. **Traffic Decryption (Airdecap-ng):**
   - Airdecap-ng decrypts captured packets using the cracked key.
   - The attacker analyzes sensitive information, such as user credentials or network activity.
5. **Visualization (Airgraph-ng):**
   - Airgraph-ng maps the network, identifying heavily trafficked devices for further investigation.

Let's look at a demonstration of Wi-Fi vulnerabilities in a hospital. A penetration tester could use the Aircrack-ng suite to highlight risks in a hospital's Wi-Fi network, as follows:

- Airmon-ng and Airodump-ng identify networks and connected IoT devices like infusion pumps or patient monitors.
- Aireplay-ng forces a connection reset on a medical device, capturing the handshake.
- Aircrack-ng demonstrates the risk of weak WPA2 passwords by successfully cracking the network key.
- Airdecap-ng shows how sensitive patient data, such as transmitted EHR details, could be intercepted and decrypted.

The Aircrack-ng suite highlights the need for strong Wi-Fi security measures. Regularly updating firmware, implementing WPA3, using strong passwords, and monitoring rogue devices are crucial to safeguarding networks from such tools. By understanding the suite's capabilities, healthcare organizations can better prepare against real-world threats and ensure patient data remains secure.

Bettercap

Bettercap (www.bettercap.org) is a versatile tool for network monitoring, penetration testing, and security analysis. Unlike single-purpose tools, Bettercap consolidates numerous functionalities into a single framework, making it ideal for advanced network attacks and monitoring scenarios. Its capabilities span wireless networks, wired Ethernet, and Bluetooth, making it a must-have tool for cybersecurity professionals and attackers alike.

Bettercap excels in Wi-Fi network monitoring and attacks, enabling the capture and analysis of wireless traffic through Wi-Fi sniffing. It can also create fake access points using SSID spoofing to lure unsuspecting users into attacks such as Evil Twin attacks. Additionally, Bettercap supports deauthentication attacks, which often force devices off legitimate networks, as a setup for further exploitation.

Bettercap's MITM attack capabilities allow it to intercept and manipulate communication between devices on the same network. By redirecting traffic for malicious purposes, Bettercap enables packet manipulation, phishing, and credential harvesting. It further enhances this by supporting DNS and HTTP spoofing, redirecting users to malicious websites through altered DNS queries or HTTP requests. Thus, Bettercap is a potent tool for phishing campaigns and malware distribution.

Bettercap also includes Bluetooth reconnaissance features, enabling it to detect and analyze nearby Bluetooth devices. This functionality supports attacks like device impersonation or data sniffing, targeting Bluetooth vulnerabilities. Its protocol injection tools allow attackers to inject custom payloads into HTTP or HTTPS streams, which can be used for phishing attacks or delivering malware payloads.

One of Bettercap's standout features is its custom scripting and extensibility, which supports scripts written in Go and Lua. This allows users to adapt the tool for specific scenarios, tailoring its functionality to meet unique security testing requirements. Additionally, Bettercap offers an integrated user interface and reporting system, providing a web-based dashboard for live monitoring and generating reports. This makes it accessible to technical experts and less experienced users, streamlining its use in penetration testing and network security audits.

With its comprehensive toolkit, Bettercap is widely regarded as one of the most effective platforms for assessing wireless, network, and Bluetooth security vulnerabilities. Thus, it is an essential tool for penetration testers and cybersecurity professionals.

These are five everyday use cases for Bettercap:

- **Penetration testing:** Simulates real-world attacks on wireless networks to identify encryption, authentication, or device configuration vulnerabilities.
- **Network reconnaissance:** Maps connected devices, identifying their IP addresses, MAC addresses, and open ports for further analysis.
- **Testing user awareness:** This method simulates phishing attacks by spoofing login pages or injecting malicious scripts to test employee vigilance against social engineering.
- **IoT device security audits:** Evaluates the security posture of IoT devices by analyzing communication patterns and attempting common exploits.
- **Incident response training:** Used in cybersecurity training programs to teach responders how to detect, mitigate, and respond to real-world threats.

Let's examine a five-step example of Bettercap in action. A hospital IT team may hire a penetration tester to assess the security of its wireless network, which supports critical systems like electronic health records and medical devices.

Step 1: Reconnaissance

The tester uses Bettercap to scan the Wi-Fi network, identifying access points and connected devices. This includes detecting unencrypted traffic and open ports on devices.

Step 2: Evil Twin Attack

Using Bettercap's SSID spoofing feature, the tester creates a fake access point mimicking the hospital's Wi-Fi. Staff unknowingly connect to this rogue network.

Step 3: Data Interception

Once connected to the fake access point, the tester uses MITM capabilities to capture sensitive data, such as login credentials for EHR systems.

Step 4: DNS Spoofing

The modified DNS redirects users accessing legitimate hospital portals to a cloned phishing page, harvesting credentials.

Step 5: Findings

The penetration tester identifies weak points, such as the lack of WPA3 encryption and the absence of network segmentation. These findings inform the hospital's remediation efforts.

Strengths of Bettercap

The following are the strengths of Bettercap:

- **All-in-one framework:** It consolidates multiple tools and attack types into a single platform, streamlining the penetration testing process.
- **Cross-protocol capabilities:** It supports Wi-Fi, Ethernet, and Bluetooth, making it versatile across various attack surfaces.
- **Customizable and extensible:** Users can adapt Bettercap to unique scenarios using custom scripts and modules.
- **Ease of use:** Its interactive UI and intuitive commands make it accessible for seasoned professionals and newcomers.

Limitations of Bettercap

The following are the limitations of Bettercap:

- **Steep learning curve:** While powerful, Bettercap's advanced features require a solid understanding of network protocols and attack strategies.
- **Detection risk:** Modern intrusion detection systems (IDS) can detect many Bettercap attacks, such as deauthentication and spoofing.
- **Legal and ethical concerns:** Like any hacking tool, misuse of Bettercap can lead to serious legal consequences.

Key Takeaways Regarding Bettercap

Key takeaways regarding Bettercap include the following:

- **Comprehensive network tool:** Bettercap provides an integrated platform for monitoring, attacking, and analyzing network traffic.

- **Real-world applications:** From penetration testing to training and reconnaissance, Bettercap is invaluable for cybersecurity professionals.
- **Critical for modern security:** As Wi-Fi networks grow more complex and vital in healthcare, education, and enterprise environments, tools like Bettercap are essential for identifying vulnerabilities and improving defenses.

Bettercap's extensive capabilities make it a valuable tool for cybersecurity professionals who want to understand and secure their wireless and wired networks. Whether you're assessing a hospital's Wi-Fi for vulnerabilities or training teams to respond to sophisticated attacks, Bettercap provides the insights and tools you need to stay ahead of modern threats. However, its power comes with a responsibility to ensure its use aligns with ethical guidelines and legal requirements to maximize its capabilities.

coWPAtty

coWPAtty (www.willhackforsushi.com/?page_id=50) is a popular tool in the cybersecurity community for performing brute-force attacks on older WPA and WPA2 pre-shared keys with general options, as shown in Listing 5.1. While it is primarily used in penetration testing to highlight vulnerabilities in Wi-Fi networks, it has also been used maliciously to exploit weak passwords in WPA-protected networks. Its straightforward operation and effectiveness against poorly configured networks make it an essential tool for ethical hackers and penetration testers.

Listing 5.1: coWPAtty Options

```
root@kali :~# cowpatty -h
cowpatty 4.8 - WPA-PSK dictionary attack. <jwright@hasborg.com>

Usage: cowpatty [options]

    -f    Dictionary file
    -d    Hash file (genpmk)
    -r    Packet capture file
    -s    Network SSID (enclose in quotes if SSID includes spaces)
    -c    Check for valid 4-way frames, does not crack
    -h    Print this help information and exit
    -v    Print verbose information (more -v for more verbosity)
    -V    Print program version and exit
```

coWPAtty is designed to crack WPA/WPA2-PSK network passwords through dictionary-based attacks. It works by utilizing a wordlist of potential passwords and systematically comparing hashed values against the captured WPA handshake to identify the correct key. One of its standout features is the ability to use precomputed hash files for specific service set identifiers (SSIDs). This approach accelerates the cracking process by bypassing the need to compute hashes in real time, making it highly effective against networks with predictable SSIDs.

The tool's reliance on SSID-specific precomputed hashes introduces both a limitation and an advantage. While these precomputed hashes can only be applied to networks with identical SSIDs, they enable faster attacks when the SSID is known, highlighting the importance of unique network identifiers for improved security.

coWPAtty also focuses on four-way handshake cracking, which targets the authentication exchange captured when a client connects to a WPA/WPA2 network. By analyzing this handshake, the tool can attempt to decrypt the network key, exploiting weaknesses in password strength or poor configuration. Its capabilities make it a valuable asset for penetration testers assessing legacy Wi-Fi security. However, its efficiency depends heavily on the quality of the dictionary file and whether precomputed hashes are available for the target SSID.

Everyday use cases for coWPAtty include the following:

- **Penetration testing in enterprises:**
  - **Objective:** Evaluate WPA/WPA2 networks' robustness in corporate environments.
  - **Execution:** Ethical hackers use coWPAtty to test whether employees use weak passwords that can be cracked from a dictionary file.
- **Educating organizations on Wi-Fi security:**
  - **Objective:** Demonstrate how easy it is to compromise networks with weak or default passwords.
  - **Execution:** Security teams show how coWPAtty exploits weak keys, motivating organizations to enforce stronger password policies.
- **Pre-audit network security evaluations:**
  - **Objective:** Identify risks in a wireless infrastructure before formal audits.
  - **Execution:** coWPAtty is used to verify if WPA/WPA2 PSK configurations meet organizational security standards.

Example Penetration Test on a WPA2 Wi-Fi Network

A healthcare facility uses WPA2-PSK to secure its guest Wi-Fi network. The penetration testing team is tasked with evaluating its vulnerability to weak passwords.

1. **Capturing the handshake:**
   - The team uses a tool like Airodump-ng to monitor the Wi-Fi network and capture the four-way handshake during a client's connection process.
2. **Using coWPAtty for brute-force attack:**
   - The tester runs coWPAtty, providing the handshake file and a dictionary file of common passwords (e.g., "password123," "guest2023").
   - If the facility uses a weak password that matches an entry in the wordlist, coWPAtty successfully identifies the pre-shared key.

3. **Reporting the results:**
   - The tester documents how a weak password allowed unauthorized access to the network.
   - The report includes recommendations for using unique, complex passwords or upgrading to WPA3 for enhanced security.

Strengths of coWPAtty

The following are strengths of coWPAtty:

- **Simplicity:** coWPAtty is easy to set up and use, making it accessible for penetration testers.
- **Precomputed hash speed:** Cracking speeds increase significantly when precomputed hash files are available for specific SSIDs.
- **Real-world effectiveness:** The tool is highly effective against networks using predictable or weak passwords.

Limitations of coWPAtty

The following are the limitations of coWPAtty:

- **SSID dependency:** Hashes are tied to specific SSIDs, so precomputed files must match the target network's SSID.
- **Resource-intensive:** Without precomputed hashes, the tool's dictionary attacks can be time-consuming and computationally expensive.
- **Ineffectiveness against WPA3:** coWPAtty is designed for WPA/WPA2 networks and cannot target networks using WPA3's enhanced encryption mechanisms.

Key Takeaways Regarding coWPAtty

The effectiveness of coWPAtty underscores the importance of robust password policies and advanced Wi-Fi security protocols. Healthcare facilities, in particular, must prioritize the following:

- **Strong passwords:** Use complex, unique passwords that cannot be found in standard dictionaries.
- **Periodic updates:** Change passwords regularly to prevent unauthorized access.
- **Transition to WPA3:** Adopt WPA3 to mitigate vulnerabilities in WPA/WPA2 and ensure stronger defenses against tools like coWPAtty.

Fern Wi-Fi Cracker

Fern Wi-Fi Cracker (https://github.com/savio-code/fern-wifi-cracker) is a wireless security auditing tool designed with accessibility and usability in mind. Unlike many command-line-driven tools, it provides a user-friendly graphical user interface, as shown in Figure 5-1. This interface enables even those with limited technical knowledge to perform advanced wireless network assessments. This tool is popular among penetration testers and security professionals for its ability to test and exploit vulnerabilities in Wi-Fi networks.

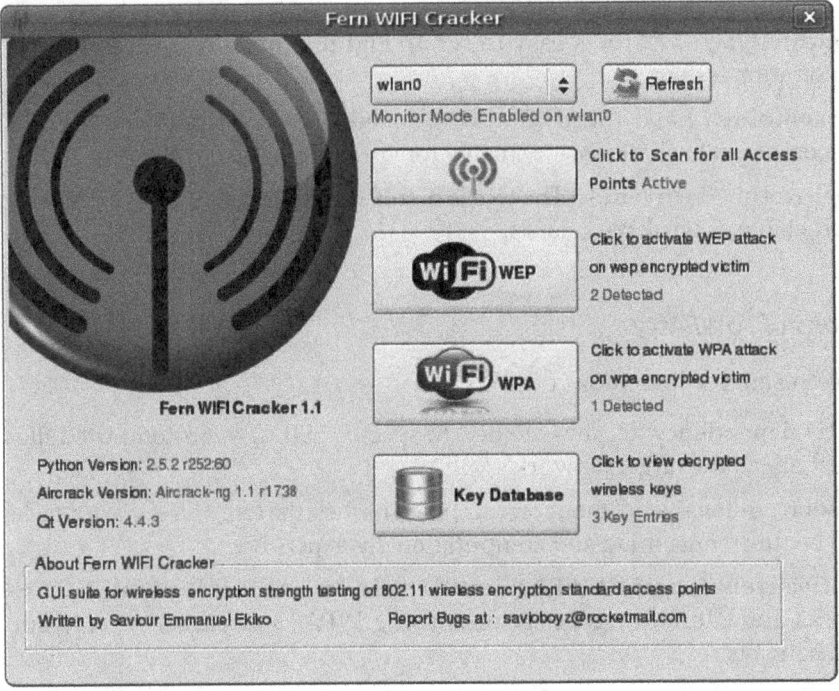

Figure 5-1: Fern WIFI Cracker GUI

The capabilities of Fern Wi-Fi Cracker include the most utilized among good and bad actors:

- **Network scanning and discovery:** Fern Wi-Fi Cracker identifies nearby wireless networks and provides detailed information, such as SSID, signal strength, encryption type, and access points in range.
- **WEP and WPA/WPA2 cracking:** The tool supports automated cracking of WEP, WPA, and WPA2 encryption protocols by capturing and analyzing packets to retrieve the network passphrase.
- **WPS exploitation:** Fern leverages Wi-Fi Protected Setup (WPS) vulnerabilities to brute-force the WPS PIN to gain access to a network, similar to tools like

Reaver. WPS lets devices connect to a network quickly without entering a complex password.

- **Session hijacking:** Fern can intercept and hijack user sessions on unsecured or weakly secured networks, gaining access to sensitive information.
- **MITM attacks:** This allows attackers to perform them by capturing data packets or injecting malicious payloads into the communication stream.
- **Network monitoring:** Fern provides real-time visualization of the network, showing devices connected to the target network and their activity.
- **Modular design:** The tool integrates seamlessly with other hacking tools, such as Aircrack-ng, for advanced functionalities like packet injection and deauthentication.
- **Hash cracking integration:** It supports dictionary-based attacks and integration with hash-cracking tools like Hashcat to decipher WPA2 passphrases.

Some of the typical use cases for Fern Wi-Fi Cracker include the following:

- **Penetration testing:** Security professionals use Fern to identify and exploit weaknesses in corporate or healthcare wireless networks, demonstrating risks and recommending mitigation strategies.
- **Educational demonstrations:** Cybersecurity training programs use the tool to teach students about wireless security, encryption vulnerabilities, and best practices for securing Wi-Fi networks.
- **Network audits:** IT teams use Fern to audit the security of organizational Wi-Fi networks and ensure compliance with regulatory standards, such as HIPAA in healthcare or PCI DSS in retail.

Example of Fern Wi-Fi Cracker in Action

A hospital IT team is concerned about the security of its wireless network, which supports various critical functions, including communication of medical devices, access to patient records, and guest Internet services. They used Fern Wi-Fi Cracker during a penetration testing exercise to address this concern.

The following are the simple steps:

Step 1: Launch Fern Wi-Fi Cracker

The tool is launched on a Linux system with a Wi-Fi adapter capable of monitor mode.

Step 2: Scan for Networks

Fern scans the environment and identifies the hospital's wireless networks. It lists details such as encryption type (e.g., WPA2), signal strength, and active devices.

Step 3: Target Selection

The team selects a guest network secured with WPA2 encryption for testing.

Step 4: Packet Capture and Attack

Fern begins capturing data packets, collecting enough information to attempt a dictionary attack using an integrated wordlist.

Step 5: Result

After a successful attack, the tool retrieves the network passphrase, demonstrating the risk of weak passwords on guest networks.

Step 6: Remediation

The hospital's IT team disables the vulnerable guest network and implements stronger passphrases, WPA3 encryption, and network segmentation to enhance security.

Strengths of Fern Wi-Fi Cracker

The following are the strengths of Fern Wi-Fi Cracker:

- **User-friendly interface:** Simplifies complex wireless attacks, making the tool accessible to beginners and efficient for professionals
- **Comprehensive functionality:** Combines network discovery, encryption cracking, session hijacking, and monitoring in one tool
- **Integration:** Works well with other tools like Aircrack-ng for enhanced capabilities

Limitations of Fern Wi-Fi Cracker

The following are the limitations of Fern Wi-Fi Cracker:

- **Hardware dependency:** It is a compatible Wi-Fi adapter capable of monitor mode and requires packet injection.
- **Limited flexibility:** While the GUI is user-friendly, advanced users may find it less flexible than command-line tools.
- **Not effective on modern security:** WPA3 encryption and robust password policies significantly reduce the tool's effectiveness.

Key Takeaways Regarding Fern Wi-Fi Cracker

These are key takeaways regarding Fern Wi-Fi Cracker:

- **Understanding risks:** Fern Wi-Fi Cracker highlights vulnerabilities in weak encryption protocols, poor password policies, and misconfigured networks.

- **Proactive security:** Organizations should use tools like Fern in controlled environments to identify and fix wireless vulnerabilities before attackers exploit them.
- **Layered security:** Besides strong passwords and encryption, implementing WPA3, disabling WPS, and using network segmentation are critical for robust Wi-Fi security.

Tools like Fern Wi-Fi Cracker emphasize the importance of proactive wireless security. Organizations must regularly test their networks, adopt the latest encryption standards, and educate staff about wireless security best practices. By leveraging tools like Fern responsibly, IT teams can safeguard sensitive data, protect critical systems, and maintain trust in their network infrastructure.

Hashcat

Hashcat (https://hashcat.net/hashcat) is a widely used password-cracking tool in cybersecurity. Known for its versatility and speed, Hashcat supports multiple hashing algorithms and leverages the power of graphical processing units (GPUs) to crack passwords more efficiently. Hashcat is primarily used in Wi-Fi hacking to crack hashed passwords captured during penetration tests of those older, but still in use, WPA/WPA2 networks. Its ability to perform brute-force attacks, dictionary attacks, and rule-based cracking makes it a critical tool in offensive security and defensive assessments.

The capabilities of Hashcat are as follows:

- **Multi-algorithm support:** Hashcat supports more than 200 hashing algorithms, including those used in WPA/WPA2 handshakes (e.g., PBKDF2 with HMAC-SHA1). This makes it highly adaptable for cracking various encrypted data.
- **GPU acceleration:** Hashcat can harness the power of GPUs to crack passwords faster. This capability significantly speeds up the process, especially for WPA2 passwords, which are computationally expensive to crack.
- **Attack modes:**
  - **Dictionary attack:** Hashcat tests passwords from a predefined wordlist, checking them against the captured hash.
  - **Brute-force attack:** Hashcat systematically tries all possible combinations within a specified character set.
  - **Hybrid attacks:** Hashcat combines dictionary and brute-force methods for greater efficiency.
  - **Rule-based attacks:** Hashcat applies transformation rules to a dictionary to generate variations of passwords, such as adding numbers or changing cases.

- **Customizability:** Users can create and modify rules, enabling tailored attacks based on expected password patterns (e.g., common healthcare-related passwords in a medical facility).
- **Compatibility with WPA handshakes:** Hashcat processes WPA/WPA2 handshake files captured using tools like Airodump-ng or Aircrack-ng, extracting the hash for cracking.

Everyday use cases, similar to other tools, for Hashcat, are as follows:

- **Wi-Fi penetration testing:** Hashcat is used to assess the strength of WPA/WPA2 passwords by attempting to crack captured handshakes. This demonstrates the vulnerability of networks with weak passwords.
- **Password policy evaluation:** Organizations can use Hashcat to identify weak passwords within their infrastructure, providing a baseline for enforcing stronger password policies.
- **Research and training:** Security professionals and researchers use Hashcat to understand password patterns and improve password security guidelines.
- **Incident response and forensics:** In security breaches, Hashcat can be used by forensic teams to recover encrypted data or test compromised credentials.

Cracking a WPA2 Wi-Fi Password Example

A cybersecurity consultant is hired to evaluate the security of a hospital's Wi-Fi network. The task is to identify whether the WPA2-PSK password used for the hospital's guest Wi-Fi is vulnerable to cracking.

The simple steps are as follows:

Step 1: Capture the WPA2 Handshake

Using Airodump-ng, the consultant monitors the Wi-Fi traffic and captures the four-way handshake as a device connects to the network.

Step 2: Prepare the Hash

The captured handshake file is converted into a format that Hashcat can process using a tool like hcxpcapngtool.

Step 3: Select a Wordlist

The consultant selects a comprehensive wordlist containing millions of commonly used passwords, such as the RockYou wordlist.

Step 4: Run Hashcat

The consultant uses this command:

```
hashcat -m 2500 captured_hash.hccapx wordlist.txt
```

Here, `-m 2500` specifies WPA/WPA2 cracking mode.

Step 5: Analyze Results

If the password is weak and exists in the wordlist, Hashcat will successfully crack it and display the plaintext password.

The resulting outcome:

- The consultant reports the vulnerability if the password is cracked and recommends a stronger, more complex password.

Strengths of Hashcat

The following are the strengths of Hashcat:

- **Speed and efficiency:** GPU acceleration makes it one of the fastest tools for cracking passwords.
- **Flexibility:** Hashcat supports many hashing algorithms and attack methods, making it highly adaptable.
- **Community and support:** A large community ensures constant updates, resources, and support for new use cases.

Limitations of Hashcat

The following are the limitations of Hashcat:

- **Hardware dependence:** Optimal performance requires high-end GPUs, which might not be accessible to all users.
- **Time-consuming for strong passwords:** Cracking highly complex passwords, such as those using long strings or special characters, can take considerable time.
- **Not effective against WPA3:** WPA3 introduces more robust protections, such as Simultaneous Authentication of Equals (SAE), making cracking attempts with tools like Hashcat ineffective.

Hashcat Key Takeaways

These are the key takeaways regarding Hashcat:

- **Proactive defense:** Hashcat's effectiveness underscores the need for robust password policies. Organizations must enforce unique, long, complex passwords to secure Wi-Fi networks.
- **Upgrading security:** Transitioning to WPA3 is crucial as it addresses vulnerabilities that tools like Hashcat exploit in WPA/WPA2 networks.
- **Training and awareness:** IT teams should use Hashcat to train staff on password security, demonstrating the risks of weak passwords through practical examples.

Wifite

Wifite (https://github.com/kimocoder/wifite2) is another user-friendly tool designed to automate the process of auditing and attacking Wi-Fi networks. It is a favorite among some of my security colleagues and penetration testers due to its ease of use and integration with other tools when auditing legacy wireless networks. By streamlining the execution of Wi-Fi attacks, Wifite, as shown in Listing 5.2, reduces the complexity associated with wireless network assessments. Wifite leverages industry-standard tools like Aircrack-ng, Reaver, and others, enabling a wide range of attack types, from cracking WEP/WPA/WPA2 passwords to exploiting WPS vulnerabilities.

Listing 5.2: Wifite Help Syntax

```
root@kali :~# wifite -h

   .´  .    .   .  ` .   wifite2 2.7.0
 :   :  :  (¯)  :  :  :  a wireless auditor by derv82
  `.  .  ` /¯\ ´  .  .´  maintained by kimocoder
       `  /¯¯¯\   ´      https://github.com/kimocoder/wifite2


options:
  -h, --help                        show this help message and
exit

SETTINGS:
  -v, --verbose                     Shows more options (-h -v).
Prints commands and outputs. (default:
                                    quiet)
  -i [interface]                    Wireless interface to use,
e.g. wlan0mon (default: ask)
  -c [channel]                      Wireless channel to scan
e.g. 1,3-6 (default: all 2Ghz channels)
  -inf, --infinite                  Enable infinite attack mode.
Modify scanning time with -p (default:
                                    off)
  -mac, --random-mac                Randomize wireless card MAC
address (default: off)
  -p [scan_time]                    Pillage: Attack all targets
after scan_time (seconds)
  --kill                            Kill processes that conflict
with Airmon/Airodump (default: off)
  -pow [min_power], --power [min_power]   Attacks any targets with at
least min_power signal strength
  --skip-crack                      Skip cracking captured
handshakes/pmkid (default: off)
  -first [attack_max], --first [attack_max]   Attacks the first attack_
max targets
```

```
  -ic, --ignore-cracked              Hides previously-cracked
targets. (default: off)
  --clients-only                     Only show targets that have
associated clients (default: off)
  --nodeauths                        Passive mode: Never
deauthenticates clients (default: deauth targets)
  --daemon                           Puts device back in managed
mode after quitting (default: off)

WEP:
  --wep                              Show only WEP-encrypted
networks
  --require-fakeauth                 Fails attacks if fake-auth
fails (default: off)
  --keep-ivs                         Retain .IVS files and reuse
when cracking (default: off)

WPA:
  --wpa                              Show only WPA-encrypted
networks (includes WPS)
  --new-hs                           Captures new handshakes,
ignores existing handshakes in hs (default:
                                     off)
  --dict [file]                      File containing passwords for
cracking (default: /usr/share/dict/wordlist-
                                     probable.txt)

WPS:
  --wps                              Show only WPS-enabled networks
  --wps-only                         Only use WPS PIN & Pixie-Dust
attacks (default:
                                     off)
  --bully                            Use bully program for WPS PIN
& Pixie-Dust attacks (default:
                                     reaver)
  --reaver                           Use reaver program for WPS PIN
& Pixie-Dust attacks (default:
                                     reaver)
  --ignore-locks                     Do not stop WPS PIN attack if
AP becomes locked (default:
                                     stop)

PMKID:
  --pmkid                            Only use PMKID capture, avoids
other WPS & WPA attacks (default:
                                     off)
  --no-pmkid                         Don't use PMKID capture
(default: off)
  --pmkid-timeout [sec]              Time to wait for PMKID capture
(default: 300 seconds)
```

```
COMMANDS:
    --cracked                              Print previously-cracked
access points
    --check [file]                         Check a .cap file (or all
hs/*.cap files) for WPA handshakes
    --crack                                Show commands to crack a
captured handshake
```

The capabilities of Wifite include the following:

- **Automated workflow:**
  - Wifite automates scanning, capturing handshakes, and attempting to crack passwords, allowing users to focus on analysis rather than execution.
  - It handles multiple attacks simultaneously, streamlining penetration tests.

- **Tool integration:**
  - Uses Aircrack-ng for handshake cracking
  - Leverages Reaver for brute-forcing WPS PINs
  - Supports Bulldog, PixieWPS, and other tools for exploiting WPS vulnerabilities

- **Flexible target selection:**
  - Users can select specific networks or allow Wifite to attack all vulnerable networks within range.

- **Support for multiple protocols:**
  - It supports WEP, WPA, WPA2, and WPS attacks, making it versatile for various network security assessments.

- **Customizable options:**
  - Users can adjust attack parameters, such as specifying wordlists for WPA/WPA2 cracking or setting attack timeouts.

- **Real-time progress tracking:**
  - It provides real-time feedback on the status of attacks, including handshake captures and cracking progress.

Of course, use cases for Wifite follow a common theme:

- **Wi-Fi penetration testing:** Wifite simplifies testing Wi-Fi network security by automating the entire attack process. Security professionals can identify weaknesses in encryption, authentication, or configuration.

- **Auditing for WPS vulnerabilities:** Wifite can detect and exploit WPS-enabled networks using Reaver and PixieWPS, helping organizations secure against these well-known vulnerabilities.

Chapter 5 ■ Wi-Fi and Other Wireless Protocol Vulnerabilities 137

- **Training and demonstrations:** The tool is ideal for educating IT staff or students about the risks of poorly secured Wi-Fi networks through practical demonstrations.
- **Compliance testing:** Organizations required to adhere to standards like PCI DSS can use Wifite to verify that Wi-Fi networks are securely configured.

As an example of Wifite in action, a penetration tester is hired to evaluate the security of a small business's Wi-Fi network. The goal is to identify potential vulnerabilities and provide recommendations for improvement.

The following simple steps are taken:

Step 1: Launch Wifite

The tester runs Wifite on a Linux-based system with a wireless adapter capable of packet injection.

Step 2: Scan for Networks

Wifite scans the airwaves, listing all available Wi-Fi networks. The tester selects a target network.

Step 3: Capture Handshake

- Wifite deauthenticates connected devices to force a handshake capture for a WPA2-protected network.
- The tool automatically saves the handshake file for further analysis.

Step 4: Crack the Password

Wifite uses Aircrack-ng with a specified wordlist to attempt cracking the captured handshake. If the password is weak, the tool displays it.

Step 5: Test WPS

If the network has WPS enabled, Wifite uses Reaver or PixieWPS to brute-force the WPS PIN, bypassing the need for handshake capture.

The following outcomes result:

- If successful, the tester identifies vulnerabilities such as weak WPA2 passwords or enabled WPS.
- A report is provided to the business, highlighting these issues and recommending strong password policies and WPS deactivation.

Strengths of Wifite

The following are the strengths of Wifite:

- **Ease of use:** Automates complex Wi-Fi attacks, making it accessible to beginners while remaining valuable to professionals
- **Integration with popular tools:** Combines the functionality of multiple tools into one seamless workflow, reducing the need for manual configurations

- **Support for all encryption standards:** Can handle legacy WEP networks, modern WPA/WPA2, and WPS attacks
- **Comprehensive reporting:** Provides detailed logs of actions taken, aiding in reporting and documentation

Limitations of Wifite

The following are the limitations of Wifite:

- **Hardware dependence:** This wireless adapter supports monitor mode and requires packet injection.
- **Time-consuming for strong networks:** Cracking WPA2 networks with strong passwords can be time-intensive, even with automation.
- **No support for WPA3:** Wifite does not address the improved security of WPA3 networks, which resist the attacks it automates.

Wifite Key Takeaways

Key takeaways regarding Wifite include the following:

- **Educational and practical:** Wifite is vital for penetration testers, educators, and security professionals to demonstrate real-world Wi-Fi vulnerabilities.
- **Encourages best practices:** Its effectiveness highlights the importance of strong passwords, disabling WPS, and transitioning to WPA3 for enhanced security.
- **Helps identify risks:** Organizations must regularly audit their Wi-Fi networks using tools like Wifite to identify and remediate vulnerabilities before attackers can exploit them.

Wifite's simplicity and effectiveness make it a cornerstone in Wi-Fi penetration testing. While it demonstrates the dangers of poor security configurations, it also emphasizes the need for proactive measures to safeguard sensitive data and systems.

Kismet

Kismet (www.kismetwireless.net) is an open-source tool for wireless network detection, intrusion detection, and packet sniffing. It operates across multiple wireless standards, including Wi-Fi, Bluetooth, and Software Defined Radio (SDR). Kismet provides a comprehensive solution for auditing and securing wireless networks. Its ability to work passively without transmitting packets makes it particularly effective for stealthy network assessments.

Kismet excels at wireless network detection, identifying Wi-Fi networks across multiple standards (802.11a/b/g/n/ac/ax), Bluetooth devices, and other wireless signals. One of its standout features is its ability to discover hidden SSIDs, or nonbroadcast networks, by capturing association requests and analyzing traffic patterns. This makes it particularly effective for uncovering concealed networks that may otherwise evade detection.

Kismet also supports packet sniffing, capturing raw network traffic, including encrypted and unencrypted packets, for in-depth analysis. It can operate with multiple wireless adapters simultaneously, providing broader coverage and allowing users to monitor several frequency bands simultaneously. Its functionality extends further with an intrusion detection system that monitors suspicious activity, such as deauthentication attacks, disassociation attempts, and rogue access points, flagging anomalies that may indicate intrusion attempts or exploits.

The tool boasts cross-platform compatibility and functions on Linux, macOS, and Windows through the Windows Subsystem for Linux (WSL). Its modular architecture supports plugins and extensions, enabling users to customize features and integrate Kismet with other security tools for enhanced functionality. Beyond Wi-Fi, Kismet provides multiprotocol support, allowing it to monitor Bluetooth, Zigbee, and SDR-based signals, making it particularly useful for IoT device auditing.

Additionally, Kismet incorporates geolocation integration, utilizing GPS data to map discovered networks' locations. This feature is valuable for visualizing wireless infrastructures, identifying coverage gaps, and conducting physical security assessments. With its wide array of capabilities, Kismet remains a critical tool for wireless network analysis, security testing, and intrusion detection, with use cases that include:

- **Wi-Fi security audits:** Organizations can use Kismet to detect rogue access points, unauthorized devices, and misconfigured networks. This is especially critical in healthcare and enterprise environments where sensitive data is transmitted over Wi-Fi.

- **Penetration testing:** Kismet assists penetration testers in identifying vulnerabilities, such as weak encryption protocols or hidden SSIDs, as part of a broader security assessment.

- **Network optimization:** Administrators can optimize Wi-Fi network performance and reduce congestion by analyzing channel usage and interference.

- **IoT device monitoring:** Kismet's ability to detect Bluetooth and Zigbee devices makes it valuable for auditing IoT ecosystems in smart homes, industrial settings, or medical facilities.

- **Educational and research purposes:** Used in academic settings to teach wireless security principles and protocols through hands-on exploration of network traffic.

As an example of Kismet in action, a healthcare facility experiences intermittent Wi-Fi disruptions. The IT team suspects rogue access points or interference but lacks the tools to confirm the issue.

The simple steps taken are as follows:

Step 1: Set Up Kismet

The IT team installs Kismet on a Linux machine equipped with a compatible wireless adapter and configures it to operate in monitor mode for passive traffic analysis.

Step 2: Scan the Network

Kismet detects all nearby wireless networks, including hidden SSIDs and unauthorized access points mimicking the hospital's legitimate network.

Step 3: Identify the Rogue AP

Kismet's IDS flags a rogue access point using the hospital's SSID. After analyzing the traffic, the team determines that an attacker is attempting an Evil Twin attack.

Step 4: Analyze Interference

Kismet maps the facility's Wi-Fi channels and identifies areas with high interference. This allows the team to optimize channel selection for better performance.

Step 5: Remediation

The rogue AP has been disabled, and network configurations have been updated to enhance security. The facility also uses Kismet to monitor for future threats.

The IT team eliminated the rogue AP, optimized network performance, and enhanced Wi-Fi security, ensuring uninterrupted connectivity for critical medical systems.

Strengths of Kismet

The following are the strengths of Kismet:

- **Passive monitoring:** It operates without transmitting packets, making it ideal for stealthy assessments.
- **Wide protocol support:** It works with Wi-Fi, Bluetooth, and IoT devices, offering versatility in wireless security.
- **Customizable:** Modular architecture supports plugins, making Kismet adaptable to specific use cases.
- **Community support:** Regular updates and a strong user community ensure that Kismet remains relevant and practical.

Limitations of Kismet

The following are the limitations of Kismet:

- **Hardware dependence:** It requires wireless adapters that support monitor mode for full functionality.
- **No active attacks:** Kismet focuses on detection and analysis rather than performing active attacks like deauthentication or injection.
- **Steep learning curve:** While powerful, Kismet's interface and configuration options can be complex for beginners.

Kismet Key Takeaways

Key takeaways regarding Kismet include the following:

- **Educational and practical:** Kismet is essential for learning about and securing wireless networks.
- **Versatile applications:** It is effective for both penetration testing and network optimization.
- **Proactive security:** It identifies vulnerabilities and potential threats before attackers can exploit them.

By incorporating Kismet into your cybersecurity strategy, you can help defend against threats, optimize network performance, and ensure the safety of sensitive data in a wireless-first world.

Reaver

Reaver (`https://github.com/t6x/reaver-wps-fork-t6x`) is a powerful and widely used Wi-Fi hacking tool that exploits Wi-Fi Protected Setup (WPS) protocol vulnerabilities. WPS, intended to simplify the process of securely connecting devices to a Wi-Fi network, has inherent design flaws that can be exploited to gain access to those older WPA/WPA2-protected networks. Reaver, whose options are shown in Listing 5.3, targets these weaknesses, making it a valuable tool for penetration testers, network administrators, and, unfortunately, malicious attackers.

Listing 5.3: Reaver Help Command in Kali

```
root@kali :~# reaver -h

Reaver v1.6.6 WiFi Protected Setup Attack Tool
Copyright (c) 2011, Tactical Network Solutions, Craig Heffner <cheffner@tacnetsol.com>
```

```
Required Arguments:
    -i, --interface=<wlan>        Name of the monitor-mode
interface to use
    -b, --bssid=<mac>             BSSID of the target AP

Optional Arguments:
    -m, --mac=<mac>               MAC of the host system
    -e, --essid=<ssid>            ESSID of the target AP
    -c, --channel=<channel>       Set the 802.11 channel for the
interface (implies -f)
    -s, --session=<file>          Restore a previous session file
    -C, --exec=<command>          Execute the supplied command upon
successful pin recovery
    -f, --fixed                   Disable channel hopping
    -5, --5ghz                    Use 5GHz 802.11 channels
    -v, --verbose                 Display non-critical warnings (-vv or
-vvv for more)
    -q, --quiet                   Only display critical messages
    -h, --help                    Show help

Advanced Options:
    -p, --pin=<wps pin>           Use the specified pin (may be arbitrary
string or 4/8 digit WPS pin)
    -d, --delay=<seconds>         Set the delay between pin attempts [1]
    -l, --lock-delay=<seconds>    Set the time to wait if the AP locks
WPS pin attempts [60]
    -g, --max-attempts=<num>      Quit after num pin attempts
    -x, --fail-wait=<seconds>     Set the time to sleep after 10
unexpected failures [0]
    -r, --recurring-delay=<x:y>   Sleep for y seconds every x pin
attempts
    -t, --timeout=<seconds>       Set the receive timeout period [10]
    -T, --m57-timeout=<seconds>   Set the M5/M7 timeout period [0.40]
    -A, --no-associate            Do not associate with the AP
(association must be done by another application)
    -N, --no-nacks                Do not send NACK messages when out of
order packets are received
    -S, --dh-small                Use small DH keys to improve
crack speed
    -L, --ignore-locks            Ignore locked state reported by the
target AP
    -E, --eap-terminate           Terminate each WPS session with an EAP
FAIL packet
    -J, --timeout-is-nack         Treat timeout as NACK (DIR-300/320)
    -F, --ignore-fcs              Ignore frame checksum errors
    -w, --win7                    Mimic a Windows 7 registrar [False]
    -K, --pixie-dust              Run pixiedust attack
    -Z                            Run pixiedust attack
    -O, --output-file=<filename>  Write packets of interest into pcap
file
```

Example:

```
reaver -i wlan0mon -b 00:90:4C:C1:AC:21 -vv
```

Reaver's primary function is cracking WPS PINs through a systematic brute-force attack. Once the PIN is successfully deciphered, the network's WPA/WPA2 credentials can be recovered. This capability provides full access to the target Wi-Fi network, making it a valuable tool for penetration testers assessing wireless security.

One of Reaver's key strengths is its persistence and reliability. It is built to seamlessly resume attacks from where they left off in case of interruptions, ensuring that time and effort are not wasted during lengthy cracking processes. Additionally, Reaver offers broad compatibility, supporting most modern wireless network cards capable of monitor mode and packet injection, which is essential for successful attacks. It works specifically with networks with WPS functionality enabled, often a default setting in many routers.

Reaver also provides customizable options, allowing users to fine-tune parameters such as timing, retries, and other settings to optimize attack performance for specific scenarios. This flexibility makes it suitable for testing environments, from quick scans to prolonged engagements. Furthermore, it features logging and feedback mechanisms that deliver detailed progress reports, including the number of attempts made and time elapsed, giving users real-time insights into the attack's status and efficiency.

With its ability to target WPS vulnerabilities effectively and its user-friendly design, Reaver remains a widely used tool for evaluating and reinforcing wireless network security in these use cases:

- **Penetration testing:**
  - Security professionals use Reaver to test the resilience of WPS-enabled networks and demonstrate vulnerabilities to network administrators.
  - It helps organizations identify insecure WPS configurations and implement necessary fixes.

- **Security training and research:**
  - Reaver is often used in cybersecurity training programs to educate students about the risks associated with weak WPS protocols.

- **Network audits:**
  - IT teams can utilize Reaver to ensure corporate networks are not using insecure WPS implementations.

As an example of Reaver in action, a healthcare facility is concerned about the security of its Wi-Fi network. Many medical IoT devices rely on it for real-time data transmission, and the IT team suspects that WPS may be enabled on some older routers, posing a security risk.

The simple steps to address this are as follows:

Step 1: Setup

The IT team installs Reaver on a Linux-based laptop equipped with a compatible Wi-Fi adapter capable of monitor mode.

Step 2: Network Discovery

Using tools like Airodump-ng, they identify networks with WPS enabled and select a target router for testing.

Step 3: Initiate Reaver

Reaver is launched against the target network with the command:

```
reaver -i wlan0mon -b [BSSID] -vv
```

The tool begins brute-forcing the router's WPS PIN.

Step 4: Result

After a few hours, Reaver successfully cracks the WPS PIN and retrieves the WPA2 passphrase. The IT team uses this information to demonstrate the vulnerability to management.

Step 5: Remediation

To enhance security, WPS is disabled on all routers, and WPA3 is implemented. The IT team educates staff on the risks of outdated protocols.

The organization mitigates a critical vulnerability, ensuring the security of sensitive patient data and the uninterrupted operation of medical devices.

Strengths of Reaver

The following are the strengths of Reaver:

- **Focused attack vector:** Specifically targets WPS vulnerabilities, ensuring high success rates on susceptible networks
- **Ease of use:** Simple command-line interface with detailed progress feedback
- **Persistence:** Automatically resumes interrupted attacks, saving time and resources

Limitations of Reaver

The following are the limitations of Reaver:

- **WPS lockout:** Many modern routers implement a lockout mechanism after repeated incorrect PIN attempts, significantly slowing down attacks.
- **Time-intensive:** Cracking a WPS PIN can take several hours or even days depending on the network and hardware.

- **Reduced effectiveness on modern networks:** With the rise of WPA3 and secure configurations, the use of WPS has declined, limiting Reaver's applicability.

Reaver Key Takeaways

The following are key takeaways from Reaver:

- **Understanding the risk:** Reaver highlights the dangers of WPS-enabled networks. Organizations must disable WPS to protect against brute-force attacks.
- **Proactive defense:** IT teams should routinely audit network configurations and ensure that outdated protocols like WPS are not in use.
- **Security education:** Demonstrating tools like Reaver can help organizations understand their vulnerabilities and implement robust defenses.

Tools like Reaver provide valuable insights into these risks, helping organizations proactively secure their Wi-Fi networks. By disabling WPS and adopting modern protocols like WPA3, organizations can protect sensitive data and ensure the integrity of their wireless infrastructure.

STORM

EC-Council's STORM Mobile Security Toolkit (https://iclass.eccouncil.org/mobile-security-tool-kit) is a comprehensive, portable penetration testing platform for cybersecurity professionals and enthusiasts. It is built on a Raspberry Pi–based touchscreen device and is pre-installed with STORM Linux. This customized Raspbian distribution is loaded with popular hacking tools (including many mentioned in this chapter), making it a versatile solution for on-the-go security assessments. I use this tool occasionally in similar use cases, such as with Kali on my laptop in wireless assessments.

The following are the hardware specifications for STORM:

- Broadcom BCM2711, Quad-core Cortex-A72 (ARM v8) 64-bit SoC at 1.5GHz
- 2GB or 4GB LPDDR4-3200 SDRAM
- Dual-band 2.4 GHz and 5.0 GHz IEEE 802.11ac wireless, Bluetooth 5.0, BLE
- Gigabit Ethernet
- Two USB 3.0 ports and two USB 2.0 ports
- Dual micro-HDMI ports supporting up to 4Kp60
- Micro-SD card slot for OS and data storage
- 5V DC power via USB-C connector
- Operating temperature range: 0–50 degrees Celsius

The software environment for STORM is as follows:

- STORM Linux, a Raspbian-based customized Linux distribution
- Pre-installed with industry-standard penetration testing tools
- Access to the STORM Resource Center, offering video demonstrations, support, and ISO image downloads

Additional accessories include the following:

- Mini water-resistant keyboard
- Field case organizer for gear
- Optional Gale Force 10 Expansion Pack for enhanced capabilities, including independent power sources and Wi-Fi/radio tools for packet sniffing and drone detection

WiFi Pineapple

The WiFi Pineapple (https://shop.hak5.org/products/wifi-pineapple) is a versatile wireless auditing tool designed for penetration testers, security researchers, and ethical hackers. Developed by Hak5, the device (example shown in Figure 5-2) is renowned for its ability to mimic legitimate Wi-Fi networks, conduct advanced wireless attacks, and analyze network vulnerabilities. Despite its professional use cases, the WiFi Pineapple has also garnered attention for its potential misuse by malicious actors, making it a critical tool for understanding Wi-Fi security.

Figure 5-2: Hak5 WiFi Pineapple

Source: From Hak5 LLC / https://shop.hak5.org/products/wifi-pineapple / last accessed March 03, 2025.

The capabilities of WiFi Pineapple are extensive:

- **Rogue access point creation:** The device can mimic legitimate Wi-Fi networks, tricking users into connecting to it instead of the intended network. This forms the basis for phishing, credential theft, and data interception attacks.
- **Man-in-the-middle attacks:** It acts as an intermediary between users and their intended networks, allowing the attacker to capture, modify, or inject data into the communication stream.
- **Wi-Fi scanning and reconnaissance:** This process performs extensive scans to identify nearby Wi-Fi networks, connected devices, and their associated attributes, such as SSID, MAC addresses, and signal strength.
- **Credential harvesting:** It intercepts user login credentials and session cookies by redirecting traffic to malicious login pages or hijacking sessions.
- **Packet sniffing and data analysis:** WiFi Pineapple captures and analyzes real-time network traffic, identifying vulnerabilities or sensitive information transmitted over insecure channels.
- **Customizable modules:** It includes a library of modules for specific attacks, such as DNS spoofing, phishing campaigns, and SSL stripping.
- **Deauthentication attacks:** It forces devices to disconnect from legitimate networks, driving them to connect to the rogue access point instead.
- **Automation and ease of use:** It has a user-friendly web interface, allowing even less experienced users to execute complex wireless attacks with minimal effort.

The WiFi Pineapple's use cases include penetration testing, training and education, network auditing, and use in awareness campaigns.

As an example of WiFi Pineapple in action, an enterprise hospital wants to test its wireless network security and employee awareness about public Wi-Fi threats. They hire a penetration tester to simulate an attack using the WiFi Pineapple.

The simple steps to address this are:

Step 1: Setup

The tester configures the WiFi Pineapple to mimic the hospital's guest network SSID, making it appear as a legitimate access point.

Step 2: Deauthentication Attack

Employees connected to the legitimate guest network are forcibly disconnected, prompting their devices to automatically reconnect to the rogue access point created by the Pineapple.

Step 3: Credential Harvesting

The Pineapple redirects users attempting to log into internal portals or check email to a spoofed login page, capturing their credentials.

Step 4: Data Interception

The tester intercepts unencrypted traffic, analyzing sensitive data such as patient information accessed on unsecured devices.

Step 5: Outcome

The penetration test revealed vulnerabilities in the hospital's Wi-Fi network, such as the lack of WPA3 encryption and improper employee training on identifying rogue access points. To mitigate these issues, it is recommended that WPA3 be enabled, VPNs be used, and regular employee training be conducted.

Strengths of WiFi Pineapple

The following are the strengths of WiFi Pineapple:

- **Comprehensive attack suite:** This suite supports a wide range of attacks, from MITM to phishing, providing a versatile toolkit for security assessments.
- **Ease of use:** The intuitive interface lowers the technical barrier, allowing for quick deployment of advanced attacks.
- **Real-world simulation:** It accurately mimics the tactics used by cybercriminals, helping organizations understand real-world risks.

Limitations of WiFi Pineapple

The following are the limitations of WiFi Pineapple:

- **Ethical concerns:** Malicious actors often exploit the device for illegal activities, highlighting the importance of using it responsibly.
- **Detection:** Modern Wi-Fi networks with strong security measures, like WPA3 and PMF, are less susceptible to Pineapple-based attacks.
- **Hardware dependence:** It requires proximity to the target network and devices for practical use.

WiFi Pineapple Key Takeaways

The following are key takeaways from WiFi Pineapple:

- **Understand the threats:** The WiFi Pineapple demonstrates how attackers exploit unsecured networks, rogue access points, and human behavior to compromise security.
- **Implement mitigations:** To reduce their exposure to such attacks, organizations should adopt WPA3, enable PMF, and segment networks.
- **Educate users:** Employees and users must be trained to identify fake networks and adopt secure browsing practices, such as using VPNs on public Wi-Fi.

The WiFi Pineapple serves as both a warning and a tool for improvement. By responsibly using this device, security teams can uncover vulnerabilities, educate their workforce, and strengthen their defenses against sophisticated wireless attacks.

WiFi-Pumpkin

WiFi-Pumpkin (https://github.com/P0cL4bs/wifipumpkin3) is an auditing tool often used to assess the vulnerabilities of Wi-Fi networks. Its user-friendly interface and wide range of features make it a go-to choice for ethical hackers and penetration testers. However, malicious attackers can exploit the same capabilities to conduct various Wi-Fi attacks, such as phishing, credential harvesting, and session hijacking.

Similar to the WiFi Pineapple (including strengths and weaknesses), here are some of the capabilities of WiFi-Pumpkin:

- **Rogue access point creation:** WiFi-Pumpkin allows users to create rogue access points that mimic legitimate Wi-Fi networks. These rogue APs can lure unsuspecting users into connecting, enabling attackers to intercept their traffic.
- **Custom captive portals:** The tool can host deceptive captive portals, often used to harvest credentials by impersonating legitimate login pages of target networks.
- **Man-in-the-middle attacks:** WiFi-Pumpkin facilitates MITM attacks, allowing attackers to intercept, monitor, and manipulate the traffic of connected users.
- **DNS spoofing:** Users can redirect victims to malicious websites by spoofing DNS responses, a common technique in phishing attacks.
- **Packet sniffing:** The tool supports packet sniffing, enabling attackers to capture and analyze unencrypted data transmitted over the network.
- **SSL stripping:** It can downgrade HTTPS traffic to HTTP, exposing sensitive data such as login credentials or credit card information that would otherwise be encrypted.
- **Network scanning:** WiFi-Pumpkin can identify connected devices and gather details about them, including their MAC addresses and operating systems.
- **Plugin support:** The modular design allows users to add custom plugins, extending its capabilities for specific tasks like social engineering or malware distribution.

Steps During a Clinic Coffee Shop Wi-Fi Network Attack

Let's look at steps from an attack on a clinic's coffee shop's Wi-Fi network. The setup for this scenario is as follows:

- An attacker sets up WiFi-Pumpkin in a nearby location, such as a parked car, to target a popular coffee shop's Wi-Fi network named "Clinic_Coffee_Spot_WiFi."

- The attacker configures a rogue access point using WiFi-Pumpkin and names it "Clinic_Coffee_Spot_WiFi_Free" to entice users.

The execution is as follows:

1. **Luring Users:**
   Unsuspecting patrons connect to the rogue network, believing it to be an extension of the legitimate one.
2. **Captive Portal Attack:**
   Upon connection, users are redirected to a captive portal that mimics the coffee shop's login page and asks for their credentials.
3. **Phishing and Interception:**
   Users input their email addresses and passwords into the fake portal. Simultaneously, the attacker captures their browsing activity and credentials for other online accounts.
4. **Data Harvesting:**
   The attacker uses the captured data to access the victims' accounts or sells the data on the dark web.

In the aftermath of this example, victims may experience account takeovers, data breaches, or even financial theft. Meanwhile, the coffee shop suffers reputational damage for being associated with a breach.

The following are mitigation strategies:

- **Enable HTTPS:**
  Ensure all websites and captive portals use HTTPS to protect users from SSL stripping.
- **Educate Users:**
  Train employees and customers to recognize rogue networks and avoid connecting to unsecured or unfamiliar Wi-Fi networks.
- **Use WPA3 Security:**
  Deploy WPA3 on networks to protect against rogue access points and improve encryption.
- **Implement Wireless Intrusion Detection Systems (WIDS):**
  Use WIDS to monitor and detect rogue access points in the vicinity.
- **Multifactor Authentication:**
  Require MFA for access to sensitive accounts, mitigating the impact of credential theft.

WiFi-Pumpkin Key Takeaways

The following are key takeaways from WiFi-Pumpkin:

- WiFi-Pumpkin is a versatile tool with ethical and malicious applications, offering capabilities such as rogue AP creation, captive portals, and traffic interception.

- It is widely used in penetration testing but poses significant risks when attackers exploit it.
- An example use case is setting up a rogue Wi-Fi network to harvest credentials in public spaces such as coffee shops or airports.
- Mitigation includes education, robust security protocols, and advanced monitoring tools, essential to protect against WiFi-Pumpkin attacks.

Wifiphisher

Wifiphisher (https://wifiphisher.org) is a user-friendly Wi-Fi hacking tool designed to automate phishing attacks on Wi-Fi networks. Unlike tools that rely on brute-forcing passwords or cracking encryption, Wifiphisher focuses on social engineering tactics to deceive users into providing sensitive information or access credentials. Its versatility and effectiveness make it a favorite among penetration testers and, unfortunately, malicious actors, with these capabilities:

- **Rogue access point creation:** This service creates fake Wi-Fi networks that mimic legitimate ones, tricking users into connecting.
- **Captive portal phishing:** It redirects users to fake login pages or captive portals to harvest credentials or sensitive data.
- **Man-in-the-middle attacks:** Once connected to the rogue AP, all user traffic can be intercepted, analyzed, or manipulated.
- **Deauthentication attacks:** It forces users to disconnect from legitimate networks, increasing the likelihood of them connecting to the rogue AP.
- **Custom templates:** This service provides customizable phishing page templates for creating realistic fake login pages or prompts tailored to specific targets.
- **Credential harvesting:** It captures Wi-Fi credentials, email passwords, or other sensitive information users submit on fake portals.

Steps During a Corporate Wi-Fi Network Attack

Let's look at an example. As the setup, an attacker targets a corporate Wi-Fi network named CorpNet. Using Wifiphisher, the attacker configures a rogue access point called CorpNet_Secure with a stronger signal to lure employees.

The execution is as follows:

1. **Deauthentication:**
   The attacker launches a deauthentication attack to disconnect all users from the legitimate CorpNet network.

2. **Rogue Access Point:**
   Now disconnected employees see CorpNet_Secure as an available network and assume it is an official extension or updated version of the corporate Wi-Fi.

3. **Captive Portal:**
   Upon connecting to CorpNet_Secure, employees are redirected to a captive portal that resembles the official corporate login page. The portal requests their network credentials for "security verification."

4. **Credential Harvesting:**
   Employees enter their usernames and passwords, which Wifiphisher immediately captures.

5. **Network Breach:**
   The attacker uses the harvested credentials to access the corporate network, potentially exfiltrating sensitive data or deploying malware.

Mitigation strategies for this scenario would be:

- **Educate Users:**
  Conduct regular training on the risks of connecting to unverified networks and recognizing phishing attempts.

- **Use WPA3:**
  Upgrade to WPA3, which provides enhanced protection against rogue access points and improves encryption.

- **Enable Wireless Intrusion Detection Systems (WIDS):**
  Deploy WIDS to detect and alert rogue access points or deauthentication attacks.

- **Two-Factor Authentication (2FA):**
  Require 2FA to access corporate networks, reducing the impact of credential theft.

- **Verify Network SSIDs:**
  Encourage employees to verify network names and report any suspicious Wi-Fi networks.

Strengths of Wifiphisher

The following are the strengths of Wifiphisher:

- **Automated attack process:** Wifiphisher streamlines the setup of phishing attacks against Wi-Fi networks by automating deauthentication and rogue access point (AP) creation. It simplifies what would otherwise be a multi-step manual process.

- **Customizable phishing scenarios:** It comes with various built-in templates (e.g., firmware upgrade, OAuth login, plugin update) and supports community-built scenarios, making it flexible for different testing contexts.

- **Extensible and open-source:** This community-driven, open-source tool allows users to inspect, modify, and extend its functionality through Python modules. This is an advantage for penetration testers who want to tailor the tool to specific targets or environments.

- **User-friendly interface:** The interactive textual UI guides beginners through the attack setup, lowering the barrier to conducting wireless security assessments.

Limitations of Wifiphisher

The following are the limitations of Wifiphisher:

- **Dependence on user behavior:** Wifiphisher primarily uses social engineering. Its success depends on users ignoring security warnings (for example, when an unencrypted network is presented in place of a secured one). Modern operating systems often alert users if network settings suddenly change.
- **Potential for detection:** The attack might be quickly detected and mitigated in environments with wireless intrusion detection systems (WIDS) or security measures.
- **Operational complexity:** Users sometimes encounter issues with network manager interference or configuration challenges (e.g., needing to disable or reconfigure NetworkManager), which can complicate the attack setup.

Wifiphisher Key Takeaways

Wifiphisher is a powerful social engineering tool that exploits user trust rather than brute-forcing encryption. The following are key takeaways from Wifiphisher:

- **Capabilities:** Rogue AP creation, captive portal phishing, and deauthentication attacks.
- **Use case:** Luring corporate employees into connecting to a rogue network and harvesting credentials.
- **Mitigation:** Educate users, deploy advanced security measures like WPA3 and WIDS, and enforce 2FA.

Wifiphisher highlights the importance of combining technical security measures with user education to combat the growing threat of social engineering-based Wi-Fi attacks.

Wireshark

Wireshark (www.wireshark.org) is one of the most powerful and widely used tools in network security. It is known for capturing and analyzing network traffic in real time. Initially developed for legitimate network troubleshooting and analysis, Wireshark has also become an invaluable tool for penetration testers and hackers, making it a dual-edged sword in cybersecurity. Its capabilities span protocols, providing deep insights into data packets transmitted over wired and wireless networks.

These are the primary capabilities of Wireshark:

- **Packet capture:** Wireshark captures and logs network packets in real time, allowing users to analyze the content of each packet in detail.
- **Protocol analysis:** It supports thousands of network protocols, including HTTP, FTP, DNS, TCP/IP, and Wi-Fi-specific protocols like WPA2 and EAP.
- **Decryption:** It can decrypt specific encrypted traffic if the proper keys or certificates are provided (e.g., WPA2 traffic with the network's Pre-Shared Key).
- **Traffic filtering:** This feature offers advanced filtering options to isolate specific types of traffic or data streams, making it easier to pinpoint issues or vulnerabilities.
- **Real-time and post-capture analysis:** Wireshark enables live network activity monitoring and in-depth analysis of saved capture files.
- **Visualization:** This feature provides packet flow diagrams, stream reconstruction, and traffic statistics to help users understand network behavior holistically.

Wireshark has some additional use cases as well:

- **Network troubleshooting:** Administrators use Wireshark to diagnose network issues, such as identifying dropped packets, connection delays, or misconfigured devices.
- **Security auditing:** Penetration testers employ Wireshark to identify insecure protocols, exposed credentials, and other network vulnerabilities.
- **Forensic analysis:** Cybersecurity teams analyze Wireshark logs during or after a security breach to trace the attacker's activity.
- **Education and training:** It is widely used in cybersecurity training programs to teach students about network protocols and packet-level data analysis.
- **Wireless network auditing:** When used with a compatible Wi-Fi adapter, Wireshark captures wireless traffic, helping auditors evaluate network security and detect suspicious activity.

As an example of Wireshark in action, a hospital IT team discovered that its wireless network has been experiencing slowdowns. Staff reported issues accessing electronic health records, so the team suspected malicious activity, potentially an unauthorized device or rogue access point.

The simple steps are as follows:

Step 1: Capture Setup

The IT team sets up Wireshark on a system connected to the hospital's Wi-Fi network. Using a compatible wireless adapter, they configure it to capture packets on the 2.4 GHz and 5 GHz bands.

Step 2: Packet Analysis

Using Wireshark's filtering capabilities, they isolate traffic from unauthorized devices. The team observes unusually high traffic to a specific unknown MAC address.

Step 3: Protocol Inspection

Further analysis reveals that unencrypted traffic containing sensitive information like usernames and passwords is being sent to an external IP address.

Step 4: Action Taken

The IT team uses the captured data to identify and block the rogue device. They implement encryption protocols to mitigate future attacks and force a network-wide password reset.

Step 5: Outcome

The incident highlights the need for stronger authentication and encryption practices, leading the hospital to adopt WPA3 and enforce regular security audits.

Strengths of Wireshark

The strengths of Wireshark include the following:

- **Granularity:** Provides detailed, packet-level data that can expose even the most subtle network issues or vulnerabilities
- **Protocol coverage:** Supports nearly every protocol used in modern networks, making it an all-in-one solution for analysis
- **Free and open-source:** Easily accessible for professionals and learners, fostering widespread adoption and use in the cybersecurity community
- **Cross-platform:** Available for Windows, macOS, and Linux, ensuring compatibility across various environments
- **Integration with other tools:** Works seamlessly with complementary tools like Aircrack-ng and Kismet for advanced wireless network analysis

Limitations of Wireshark

The following are the limitations of Wireshark:

- **Learning curve:** The tool's advanced features and technical complexity can overwhelm beginners.
- **Data overload:** Capturing traffic on large networks generates an immense amount of data, requiring expertise in filtering and analysis.
- **Encryption challenges:** Encrypted traffic cannot be analyzed without decryption keys.
- **Hardware dependency:** It requires specific hardware, such as wireless adapters, to capture Wi-Fi traffic effectively.

Wireshark Key Takeaways

Key takeaways of Wireshark include the following:

- **Versatility:** Wireshark is indispensable for diagnosing network issues, evaluating security vulnerabilities, and performing forensic analysis.
- **Critical for training:** Its ability to break down complex protocols makes it a cornerstone tool for teaching network security.
- **Proactive defense:** Organizations can use Wireshark to monitor network activity continuously, identifying suspicious behavior before it escalates.

Wireshark is not just a tool but a gateway to understanding the intricacies of network communication. By mastering its capabilities, security professionals can uncover hidden vulnerabilities, respond effectively to threats, and build resilient networks. Whether protecting sensitive patient data in a hospital or ensuring compliance in an enterprise environment, Wireshark empowers you to stay one step ahead of evolving cyber threats.

The Evolution of Tools

While all the tools mentioned are powerful and can be used maliciously, they can also be crucial in identifying and addressing Wi-Fi security vulnerabilities when used ethically. However, it's important to note that using these tools on networks without explicit permission is illegal in many jurisdictions. Therefore, security professionals should always obtain proper authorization before conducting wireless security assessments.

As Wi-Fi technologies evolve, so will the tools used to test and secure them. Staying informed about these developments is crucial for cybersecurity professionals and organizations looking to protect their wireless infrastructure.

Modern Wireless Operational Guide for Healthcare Compliance

In 2025, the healthcare landscape will continue to rely heavily on wireless technology to enable seamless connectivity, from patient monitoring to administrative tasks. However, this dependence introduces significant security and compliance challenges. This section is a guide that outlines best practices, compliance mandates, and practical deployment methods to ensure secure and compliant wireless networks in healthcare environments. It focuses on securing 802.11 Wireless LANs or WLANs within healthcare settings, meeting compliance standards such as HIPAA and HITECH, and limiting the compliance scope of wireless networks while safeguarding sensitive data environments (SDEs).

It also provides actionable recommendations for deploying secure wireless networks while addressing the challenges posed by IoT medical devices, rogue access points, and evolving cyber threats.

Defining the Sensitive Data Environment

The SDE encompasses all systems where protected health information (PHI) is processed, stored, or transmitted. Wireless networks must be secured to prevent unauthorized access or lateral movement into the SDE, even if they do not directly handle PHI. Healthcare organizations must regularly validate their networks to ensure compliance and mitigate risks from rogue devices or misconfigurations.

Key Challenges in Securing Healthcare Wireless Networks

The following are the key challenge areas when securing healthcare wireless networks:

- **Rogue access points:** These unauthorized devices bypass organizational security, potentially exposing PHI. For example, a staff member plugging in a personal Wi-Fi router creates a significant compliance risk.
- **Unsecured IoT devices:** Medical devices such as infusion pumps and telemetry monitors often lack robust security features, leaving them vulnerable to exploitation.
- **Weak authentication protocols:** Using outdated protocols like WPA2-PSK increases susceptibility to brute-force attacks and credential theft.
- **Evolving threat landscape:** Cybercriminals continuously develop sophisticated attacks, such as evil twin networks and advanced phishing campaigns targeting healthcare systems.

Modern Solutions for Wireless Security and Compliance

There are several modern solutions for wireless security and compliance. The following list contains several of these:

- Regular network scanning
    - Identify rogue access points and unauthorized devices.
    - Deploy enterprise-grade wireless intrusion detection/prevention systems (IDS/IPS) for real-time monitoring and automated mitigation.
    - For example, tools like Cisco DNA Center can identify rogue APs and isolate them from the network.
- Network segmentation
    - Isolate medical devices, guest networks, and administrative systems using Virtual LANs and stateful firewalls.
    - For example, telemetry monitors can be placed on a dedicated VLAN with strict access control policies segmented from administrative Wi-Fi.

- Strong authentication and encryption
    - Mandate WPA3-Enterprise with 802.1X authentication for all wireless connections.
    - Enforce multi-factor authentication for administrative access.
    - For example, end-to-end encryption protocols like TLS 1.3 can be used for additional data protection.
- Secure IoT devices
    - Require regular firmware updates and enforce device-specific security policies.
    - For example, partner with vendors to implement secure boot mechanisms and encrypted communication for all IoT devices.
- Advanced threat detection
    - Use AI-driven threat detection tools to analyze wireless traffic for anomalies, such as unusual data patterns or unauthorized connections.
    - For example, Palo Alto Networks' Prisma Access can be implemented to monitor wireless security across multiple healthcare facilities.

Operational Best Practices

The following are operational best practices to consider integrating into your security landscape:

- Physical security
    - Secure access points in tamper-proof enclosures.
    - Deploy tracking systems for portable medical devices like tablets and infusion pumps.
- Policy enforcement
    - Develop wireless usage policies that require management approval, restrict guest access, and mandate device labeling.
    - For example, vendors may be required to use temporary wireless credentials that expire after use.
- Continuous monitoring
    - Enable automated logging and reporting of all wireless activity.
    - Use centralized management platforms for real-time visibility across all healthcare sites.
- Education and training
    - Train healthcare staff on secure Wi-Fi practices, including recognizing phishing attempts and avoiding unauthorized devices.

Additional Compliance Recommendations

The following are additional compliance recommendations you should consider in your organization:

- Encryption standards
  - Use WPA3 with AES-256 encryption for all networks transmitting PHI.
  - Implement end-to-end encryption for critical applications like EHR systems.
- Periodic audits
  - Conduct quarterly wireless audits, including penetration testing, to identify vulnerabilities.
  - Review and update firewall rules bi-annually to ensure alignment with current threats.
- Incident response
  - Establish an incident response plan for wireless threats, detailing steps to isolate rogue devices and secure compromised systems.

Key Takeaways for Healthcare Compliance

The previous information will help serve as a wireless operational guide for healthcare compliance. These are the key takeaways you should glean from this information:

- Wireless networks are integral to healthcare but require rigorous security measures to protect sensitive data and meet compliance mandates.
- Technologies like WPA3, network segmentation, and IoT-specific security policies are essential for modern healthcare environments.
- Continuous monitoring, robust policies, and regular training empower organizations to mitigate risks and anticipate evolving cyber threats.

By adhering to these guidelines, healthcare organizations can build resilient wireless networks that support operational efficiency while safeguarding patient trust and regulatory compliance.

Key Takeaways of Wi-Fi Vulnerabilities and Exploits

This chapter explored the risks associated with healthcare's reliance on Wi-Fi networks. Wireless connectivity is essential for healthcare operations, yet vulnerabilities can compromise sensitive patient data, disrupt critical medical systems, and lead to regulatory penalties.

Key threats were identified, including unencrypted data transmission, weak authentication protocols, rogue access points, outdated firmware, and phishing attacks via Wi-Fi. Real-world case studies highlighted the severe consequences of these vulnerabilities, from operational disruptions to patient safety risks. Organizations must implement encryption, segment networks, enforce strong authentication, and regularly update the firmware to mitigate these threats.

Awareness of Wi-Fi hacking tools like Aircrack-ng and Wifiphisher can help security teams understand potential threats and strengthen defenses. Given the high stakes, securing wireless networks is crucial for protecting patient data, ensuring operational continuity, and maintaining regulatory compliance. Healthcare environments must safeguard all systems handling PHI against unauthorized access. Challenges such as rogue access points, unsecured IoT devices, and outdated security protocols underscore the need for proactive defenses. Modern solutions include network scanning tools like Cisco DNA Center, segmentation strategies using VLANs and firewalls, and authentication measures such as WPA3-Enterprise and MFA.

Threat detection powered by AI can further enhance security. Operational best practices emphasize the physical security of access points, strict policy enforcement, continuous monitoring, and staff training to recognize phishing threats. Compliance measures should include WPA3 with AES-256 encryption, regular wireless audits, and a well-defined incident response plan. By adopting these strategies, healthcare organizations can secure their wireless networks against evolving cyber threats.

CHAPTER 6

Man-in-the-Middle Attacks on Medical Devices

We live in a time when healthcare relies heavily on interconnected medical devices. Therefore, the risks posed by cyberattacks are more severe than ever. Man-in-the-middle (MITM) attacks represent one of the most insidious and dangerous threats to healthcare systems. These attacks involve an adversary secretly intercepting and potentially altering communications between devices and systems without either party realizing the breach. For healthcare organizations, where devices deliver life-critical functions, the implications of MITM attacks extend far beyond data theft. They can compromise patient health, disrupt hospital operations, and jeopardize regulatory compliance.

This chapter covers the mechanics of MITM attacks, exploring how attackers exploit vulnerabilities in communication protocols like Wi-Fi, Bluetooth, and medical IoT-specific connections. I'll uncover the real-world consequences of these attacks, including data theft, device manipulation, and system downtime, with high-level case studies illustrating their impact on patient care. Furthermore, the chapter identifies the root vulnerabilities that make medical devices susceptible to MITM attacks, including outdated encryption protocols, insecure device authentication, and insufficient network design. These weaknesses highlight the urgent need for a multi-layered defense strategy tailored to the unique challenges of healthcare environments.

This chapter also presents another iteration of mitigation strategies to help healthcare organizations strengthen defenses. It outlines actionable steps to safeguard connected medical devices, from leveraging strong encryption and authentication to deploying advanced network monitoring tools and collaborating with vendors. A dedicated section also highlights the critical role of AI-driven anomaly detection, showcasing how proactive tools can help identify and stop attacks in real-time.

Finally, the chapter explores the collaborative role of vendors, regulators, and healthcare providers in addressing MITM vulnerabilities. By prioritizing security in device design, enforcing strict compliance, and fostering open communication, the healthcare industry can build resilient systems that protect patients, data, and operations. MITM attacks are a growing threat that healthcare organizations can no longer afford to ignore. By understanding these risks and implementing comprehensive security measures, healthcare providers can ensure the safety and trust that modern patient care demands.

Understanding Medical Device Man-in-the-Middle Attacks

Medical devices rely on wireless protocols like Bluetooth, Wi-Fi, or Zigbee to communicate with central hospital systems or mobile applications. These communications often include sensitive patient data or real-time commands for device functionality. A MITM attack exploits vulnerabilities in the communication pathway, allowing attackers to accomplish outcomes such as intercepting data. This is where an attacker can capture unencrypted or poorly encrypted data, exposing sensitive information such as patient vitals, medication dosages, or diagnostic results.

If the intercepted communication is encrypted, the attacker may attempt to decrypt it using various techniques, such as exploiting weak encryption keys or using keylogging and other malware tools. In more sophisticated attacks, adversaries can modify commands sent between a medical device and the system it's communicating with, potentially altering medication dosages, changing device settings, or even shutting the device down.

There's also a data replay element where attackers can echo intercepted data packets to simulate a legitimate device response, bypassing authentication protocols or causing system malfunctions. Similar to data interception, in some attacks, the attacker may relay messages between the parties, allowing them to eavesdrop on sensitive communications without altering them, like spying.

Types of MITM Attacks

There are several types of MITM attacks, each exploiting different methods of interception or manipulation, and include the following:

- **Passive MITM attacks:** These attacks involve only eavesdropping or sniffing the communication between devices without altering it. Although these attacks do not immediately disrupt communication, they can still result in data breaches by exposing sensitive health information.

- **Active MITM attacks:** In an active attack, the attacker intercepts and alters the communication. This can include changing commands or data sent to medical devices, injecting malicious data, or disrupting the transmission entirely.
- **Session hijacking:** This involves the attacker taking over an active session between two communicating devices. For instance, an attacker could hijack a remote monitoring session of a critical care device and take control of the system.
- **SSL stripping:** Secure Sockets Layer (SSL) stripping attacks involve downgrading encrypted HTTPS connections to an unsecured protocol such as HTTP, allowing the attacker to eavesdrop on or manipulate the data. This attack is particularly dangerous when medical devices use web interfaces for communication.

Real-World Implications of MITM Attacks on Medical Devices

Attacks on medical devices threaten patient safety, data privacy, and healthcare operations. The potential impact becomes more severe as the healthcare industry increasingly relies on connected devices and IoMT. In this section, I'll explore four real-world implications of MITM attacks in healthcare environments: risks to patient safety, data integrity, and privacy violations. Then, I'll discuss operational disruption.

Patient Safety Risks The most critical concern with MITM attacks on medical devices is the direct threat to patient safety. Attackers who gain control over medical devices can potentially alter their functionality, leading to severe consequences such as the following:

- **Medication delivery systems:** Infusion pumps could be manipulated to deliver incorrect dosages, potentially causing overdoses or underdoses. Insulin pumps might be reprogrammed, leading to dangerous blood sugar levels for diabetic patients.
- **Life support equipment:** Ventilators could have their settings tampered with, impacting the quality of breathing support and potentially endangering patients' lives. Cardiac devices like pacemakers might be vulnerable to remote manipulation, posing life-threatening risks.
- **Diagnostic equipment:** Imaging devices could be compromised, leading to altered results and misdiagnosis. Laboratory equipment might produce inaccurate test results, affecting treatment decisions.

Data Integrity and Privacy Violations MITM attacks can compromise the integrity and confidentiality of sensitive healthcare data, such as the following:

- **Protected health information breaches:** Intercepted patient data could violate HIPAA and similar regulations, resulting in significant legal and financial consequences. Stolen health records might be used for identity theft or sold on the dark web.

- **Diagnostic data tampering:** Altered medical records or test results could lead to misdiagnosis or delayed treatment, potentially harming patients. Manipulated data might impact clinical research, compromising the validity of studies and trials.
- **Prescription fraud:** Attackers could potentially intercept and modify electronic prescriptions, leading to drug diversion or abuse.

Operational Disruption These types of attacks can have productivity-inhibiting effects on healthcare operations, including the following:

- **System downtime:** Critical medical systems might be rendered inoperative, forcing staff to revert to manual methods and slowing care delivery. Extended downtime could lead to patient backlogs and delayed treatments.
- **Ransomware attacks:** MITM tactics could be used as a gateway for launching ransomware attacks, potentially crippling entire healthcare networks. The 2017 WannaCry ransomware attack, which affected the UK's National Health Service, demonstrated the widespread impact of such incidents.
- **Financial losses:** Healthcare organizations might face significant costs related to incident response, system recovery, and potential legal liabilities. As patient trust erodes, reputational damage could lead to long-term financial implications.
- **Regulatory consequences:** Failure to protect against MITM attacks could result in regulatory fines and sanctions, particularly if patient data is compromised.

To mitigate these risks, healthcare organizations should implement robust security measures, which include the following that I've talked about in previous chapters:

- Implementing strong encryption protocols for all connected medical devices
- Regularly updating and patching medical device software and firmware
- Using network segmentation to isolate critical medical systems
- Employing multifactor authentication for device access and management
- Conducting regular security audits and penetration testing
- Developing and maintaining incident response plans specifically addressing MITM scenarios

Key Vulnerabilities Enabling MITM Attacks

MITM attacks exploit vulnerabilities in communication channels, allowing attackers to intercept, alter, or inject malicious data between devices and systems. Understanding the key vulnerabilities that enable these attacks is essential for healthcare organizations to protect patient safety and sensitive medical information. One primary vulnerability allowing this attack vector in healthcare is weak or outdated encryption protocols. Many legacy medical devices, designed before the current emphasis on cybersecurity, rely on encryption methods that are no longer considered secure.

These outdated protocols can be easily compromised, allowing attackers to decode intercepted communications. For example, some older medical devices may still use Wired Equivalent Privacy (WEP) for Wi-Fi security that has been deprecated for a long time due to its vulnerabilities. There has not been a WEP implementation used in production for years, and I have been unable to compromise. Similarly, devices using older versions of SSL or early versions of TLS are at risk, as these protocols have known weaknesses that can be exploited.

The consequences of weak encryption in healthcare can be severe. Attackers who successfully decrypt communications may gain access to sensitive patient data, potentially violating HIPAA regulations and compromising patient privacy. Moreover, compromised communications with devices like infusion pumps or pacemakers could lead to life-threatening situations if an attacker can alter dosages or device settings.

Healthcare facilities often provide Wi-Fi networks for patients, visitors, and staff. While convenient, these networks can become a risk if not adequately secured. Open or poorly configured wireless networks provide an easy entry point for attackers to position themselves between devices and legitimate network access points. In a typical scenario, as discussed in Chapter 5, an attacker might set up a rogue access point posing as the hospital's legitimate network. Unsuspecting users, including medical devices, may connect to this malicious network, allowing the attacker to intercept most, if not all, communications. This type of attack is also known as an evil twin attack.

Password-protected networks may be vulnerable if they use weak encryption methods like WPA2. WPA2 has known vulnerabilities, such as being a target for the KRACK exploit I discussed. To mitigate these risks, healthcare organizations must implement strong network security measures, including the latest WPA3 standard.

Many medical devices, especially those using wireless communication, rely on pairing or authentication to establish secure connections. Weak or improperly configured pairing processes can leave devices vulnerable to MITM attacks, such as the following:

- **Bluetooth pairing:** Insecure Bluetooth pairing mechanisms, such as those that use weak PIN codes or do not adequately authenticate devices, can allow an attacker to intercept or spoof device connections.
- **Lack of Multifactor authentication:** Some medical systems do not use multifactor authentication, which adds a layer of security to prevent unauthorized access to sensitive systems or devices.

I've seen many medical devices, especially older models, that lack strong authentication mechanisms firsthand. This deficiency makes them susceptible to impersonation attacks, where malicious actors can pose as legitimate endpoints in a communication chain. Without proper mutual authentication, a device might connect to an attacker's system, believing it to be a legitimate server or another authorized device. This vulnerability can lead to unauthorized access to sensitive medical data or even allow attackers to send false commands to medical devices. For instance, a study conducted on implantable cardioverter defibrillators found that some devices lacked any form of authentication, allowing researchers to reprogram the devices using off-the-shelf equipment. This lack of authentication could potentially allow attackers to deliver inappropriate shocks or withhold necessary therapy, putting patients' lives at risk.

The lack of network segmentation, which is mentioned several times in this book, is a genuine concern. Colleagues frequently mention lacking or improper segmentation in assessed networks in various chapter or community meetings. In many healthcare organizations, medical devices are often connected to the same network as administrative devices and/or patient data systems. This lack of segmentation increases the risk of a MITM attack spreading across the entire network, allowing an attacker to compromise multiple devices simultaneously.

A flat network design that lacks isolation between critical systems and peripheral devices makes it easier for attackers to move laterally across the network, gaining access to sensitive information and controlling connected devices. Also, without real-time monitoring tools that track device activity, unusual behavior caused by an attack may go undetected until it's too late.

Vendor-specific vulnerabilities and backdoors are another problem. Many medical devices are designed and manufactured by third-party vendors. Vulnerabilities in a device's firmware, software, or hardware could provide attackers with opportunities to exploit or gain unauthorized access, as sourced from these as root causes:

- **Outdated firmware:** Medical devices often run on obsolete firmware that is not regularly patched for security vulnerabilities.
- **Hardcoded credentials:** Some devices come with hardcoded default passwords or other credentials that can be easily guessed or cracked.
- **Backdoors:** Some medical devices may have manufacturer-installed backdoors that attackers can exploit to gain control of the device.

Medical devices are also often designed with ease of use and functionality rather than security. As a result, many devices are shipped with unnecessary features or open ports (such as the following), which attackers typically exploit:

- **Open ports and unused services:** Devices may have open ports or services that are not actively used and are vulnerable to attack.
- **Weak user access control:** Weak or absent user authentication mechanisms can allow unauthorized users to access and control devices.

Many medical IoT devices, designed for specific functions with minimal power consumption, lack the processing power necessary to implement strong encryption or authentication measures. These limitations often result in devices that prioritize functionality over security, leaving them exposed to attacks. For example, a simple health monitoring device might transmit data in plaintext or use weak encryption to conserve battery life, making it an easy target for interception.

Moreover, the sheer number of IoMT devices in a typical healthcare setting—estimated at more than a dozen per hospital bed—creates a deep and wide attack surface. Each device represents a potential entry point for attackers, and their heterogeneous nature makes implementing uniform security measures challenging.

To address these vulnerabilities, healthcare organizations must regularly update and patch all devices and systems to ensure they use the latest security protocols. They must implement strong, segmented network architectures to isolate critical medical devices from potentially compromised networks. In addition, they should utilize current authentication methods, including multifactor authentication, where possible. Regular security audits and penetration testing to identify and address vulnerabilities are also essential. Finally, it's beneficial to work with device manufacturers to develop and implement security features that balance functionality with protection against MITM attacks.

Exploits and Other Potential Impacts of MITM Attacks on Medical Devices

Some of the most common exploits and consequences of MITM attacks on medical devices include data theft, privacy violations, device manipulation, patient safety risks, system downtime, and impacting productivity.

Data Theft and Privacy Violations

One of the primary objectives of MITM attacks against healthcare environments is to intercept and steal sensitive patient data. Attackers can exploit vulnerabilities in the communication protocols used by medical devices to gain unauthorized access to assets, such as the following:

- **Personal health information (PHI):** This includes patient names, medical histories, diagnostic data, and treatment plans. Unauthorized access to PHI can lead to identity theft, blackmail, or fraud.
- **Medical device settings:** Attackers could alter device configurations, potentially leading to incorrect treatments or misdiagnosis.

The consequences of such data breaches extend beyond individual privacy concerns. Healthcare organizations usually face severe penalties, lawsuits, and other reputational damage for violating HIPAA.

Device Manipulation and Patient Safety Risks

These attacks can allow malicious actors to manipulate medical devices, posing direct threats to patient safety. Infusion pump attacks are among them. Studies have demonstrated that attackers can intercept and alter data packets sent to infusion pumps, modifying medication dosages without detection by control systems. Devices like pacemakers, implantable cardioverter defibrillators, and insulin pumps may be susceptible to unauthorized access and manipulation. Attackers could deliver inappropriate shocks or withhold necessary therapy.

MITM attacks on imaging devices or laboratory equipment could lead to altered results, causing misdiagnosis or delayed treatment. These risks are not merely theoretical. For example, former U.S. Vice President Dick Cheney had his doctors disable the wireless capabilities of his pacemaker during implantation in 2007 to prevent a potential assassination attempt.

System Downtime and Operational Disruption

MITM attacks can cause widespread disruption to healthcare operations through denial-of-service. By intercepting and blocking communications, attackers can render critical medical systems inoperable, forcing staff to revert to manual methods and slowing care delivery.

The attacks can also overwhelm network resources, affecting the performance of connected medical devices and potentially disrupting critical services. Data integrity issues also exist. Altered or manipulated data can lead to incorrect clinical decisions, compromising patient care and potentially causing long-term health consequences. Consider the repercussions of system disruption during patient surgery.

Challenges in Securing Medical Devices

I discussed key vulnerabilities earlier, and four primary factors that contribute to the vulnerability of medical devices to MITM attacks are as follows:

- **Legacy systems:** Many healthcare organizations use outdated software and systems, often running on unsupported operating systems without security patches.
- **IoT proliferation:** The average hospital uses thousands of network-connected devices, with estimates suggesting a dozen devices per hospital bed. These IoT devices often lack robust security measures.
- **Limited resources:** Many medical IoT devices have processing power and battery life constraints, making implementing strong encryption or authentication measures challenging.
- **Complexity of mobile devices:** The movement of medical equipment between rooms makes it difficult to maintain a complete inventory and ensure consistent security measures.

Healthcare providers can better prepare for potentially devastating attacks by implementing comprehensive security strategies and staying vigilant against emerging threats. Technology exists that can locate IoMT medical devices and provide data on how often they are used and by whom.

Mitigation Strategies for Healthcare Organizations

Mitigating the risks of MITM attacks should be evident, as these attacks can compromise sensitive patient data, disrupt critical medical systems, and endanger lives. A comprehensive and multi-layered approach to security is essential to protect healthcare environments from such threats. Some of the best strategies I've been using include strong encryption, better authentication, segmentation, regular updating, continuous monitoring, intrusion detection, security awareness training, and collaboration. I'll get into more detail on them in this section, and I'll wrap them into a more significant operational guide of best practices later in this book.

Leverage Strong Encryption for Healthcare Communications

In healthcare environments, where data confidentiality, integrity, and availability (CIA) are critical, leveraging strong encryption is essential to safeguarding patient information and protecting communications between medical devices, networks, and central systems. Encryption ensures that attackers cannot decipher or manipulate sensitive data without the proper decryption keys, even if attackers intercept sensitive data. By adopting modern, strong encryption protocols, healthcare organizations can secure their infrastructure and mitigate risks such as data breaches, unauthorized access, and MITM attacks.

Strengthen Wireless Network Encryption

Wireless networks in healthcare settings are a common target for cyberattacks due to the sensitive data they transmit. Older encryption protocols such as WPA2 have known vulnerabilities, including susceptibility to brute-force attacks and exploits like the KRACK. To address these risks, adopt WPA3 encryption. WPA3, or Wi-Fi Protected Access 3, is the latest wireless security standard and provides significant enhancements over WPA2. It uses SAE for stronger password protection, making it far more resistant to brute-force attacks. Benefits of WPA3 include the following:

- **Improved data privacy:** WPA3 ensures individualized encryption for each device connected to the network, preventing attackers from eavesdropping on other devices' traffic.
- **Forward secrecy:** Even if a device's encryption key is compromised, WPA3 prevents the decryption of past sessions.
- **Ideal for IoT devices:** WPA3 simplifies the secure connection of medical IoT devices, which are common in hospitals and clinics.

An example is a hospital deploying WPA3 across its wireless infrastructure that can protect patient data transmitted between heart monitors and central nursing systems from interception by malicious actors, even in busy public areas like waiting rooms.

Secure Communication for Medical Devices

Medical devices such as infusion pumps, patient monitors, and imaging systems often use wireless communication to exchange critical data with central servers or EHR systems. However, legacy devices may use outdated encryption protocols, leaving them vulnerable to attacks. To ensure secure communication, you should implement modern encryption standards, such as TLS 1.3, for all medical device communication. TLS 1.3 encrypts data in transit using stronger cryptographic algorithms, reducing vulnerabilities associated with earlier TLS versions. Some legacy medical devices may not support newer protocols, requiring careful planning for upgrades or replacements. Compliance with the PATCH Act and updated FDA guidelines is necessary when implementing security measures.

Eliminate legacy protocols by disabling outdated encryption protocols like SSL, TLS 1.0, and 1.1, as they are no longer secure and can be exploited for MITM attacks or data interception. In addition, pair encryption with mutual authentication mechanisms (e.g., certificate-based verification) to confirm that medical devices communicate with legitimate central systems. For example, a healthcare facility may use TLS 1.3 to secure data from imaging devices like MRIs to EHR systems, ensuring that diagnostic results remain private and tamper-proof during transmission. Note that there could be an impact on performance as stronger encryption utilizes more local resources and can add latency.

Encrypt Data in Transit Across All Systems

Data in transit, whether moving between devices, servers, or cloud environments, represents one of the most vulnerable points in the communication chain. Encrypting all data in transit ensures that attackers cannot intercept or alter sensitive patient information, even if they gain access to network traffic. To achieve this, use end-to-end encryption (E2EE). E2EE ensures that data remains encrypted from the moment it is sent to the point it is received. This is critical for sensitive information, such as real-time vital signs, diagnostic test results, and electronic prescriptions.

Implement encryption for video and audio communication channels in telemedicine platforms and remote patient monitoring systems. This safeguards patient interactions and transmitted data from unauthorized interception. Virtual private networks provide an encrypted tunnel for healthcare staff accessing systems remotely, ensuring patient data remains protected from interception, even on unsecured networks. A telemedicine consultation, for example, can use end-to-end encryption to protect video streams and diagnostic information shared between a physician and a remote patient, preventing attackers from accessing the session.

The following are the benefits of strong encryption in healthcare:

- **Data confidentiality:** Strong encryption prevents unauthorized access to sensitive patient data, including PHI, diagnostic reports, and treatment plans.
- **Data integrity:** Strong encryption ensures that patient data is not tampered with or altered during transmission, preserving accuracy and trust in medical information.

- **Compliance:** It helps healthcare organizations comply with regulations such as HIPAA, HITECH, and GDPR, which mandate the encryption of sensitive data in transit.
- **Mitigates cyber threats:** By rendering intercepted data unreadable, it reduces the risks associated with MITM attacks, eavesdropping, and data breaches.
- **Improved patient trust:** Encrypting patient data reassures patients that their private medical information is secure.

Healthcare organizations must modernize their infrastructure by adopting WPA3 for Wi-Fi networks, implementing TLS 1.3 for medical device communication, and encrypting all sensitive data in transit. By combining robust encryption with authentication mechanisms and regular updates, healthcare providers can secure patient information, ensure compliance, and maintain the integrity of life-saving medical systems. Encryption is considered a cornerstone of a resilient and secure healthcare ecosystem.

Implement Robust Device Authentication

Robust device authentication is a critical layer of protection that prevents unauthorized devices from gaining access, minimizes the risk of impersonation attacks, and secures communication pathways between medical devices and control systems. This multi-layered authentication strategy is essential to counter advanced cyber threats targeting healthcare systems.

Secure Pairing with Strong Authentication Mechanisms

I'll start with device pairing since it's the process by which medical devices establish secure connections with central systems or other devices. Weak pairing methods, such as default PINs, weak passwords, or insecure pairing protocols, can be exploited by attackers to impersonate devices or intercept communications. To address this, healthcare organizations must adopt secure authentication methods, such as Public Key Infrastructure (PKI). This uses cryptographic key pairs (public and private keys) to validate device identities. Devices are issued digital certificates from a trusted CA, ensuring only verified devices can communicate on the network. For example, an infusion pump could receive a digital certificate during provisioning, which it uses to authenticate itself to a hospital's control system, ensuring that rogue or counterfeit devices cannot connect.

Digital certificates serve as unique, tamper-proof identifiers for devices. Certificate-based authentication ensures that devices can securely pair and communicate without relying on weak, shared secrets like default PINs. The benefit is that certificates eliminate the risks associated with hardcoded credentials, weak passwords, or shared authentication keys often found in legacy medical devices. Be sure to combine secure authentication with secure boot mechanisms, ensuring that devices are authenticated and validated before running approved software or connecting to the network.

Mutual Authentication for Devices and Central Systems

Mutual authentication requires that both communicating parties verify each other's identities before establishing a secure connection. This two-way validation is critical in healthcare settings to prevent impersonation attacks, where an attacker poses as a legitimate device or central system. It works with the medical device and the central system, exchanging cryptographic keys or digital certificates during authentication.

Only devices with the correct credentials are granted access. A patient monitoring device, for example, authenticates with the hospital's central monitoring station before sharing real-time vitals, and the station verifies the device's legitimacy to ensure it isn't a rogue endpoint. The benefits of mutual authentication include the following:

- **Prevents impersonation attacks:** Attackers cannot spoof devices or systems to gain access.
- **Maintains data integrity:** It ensures that data being exchanged originates from trusted sources, preventing malicious injections or tampering.
- **Mitigates MITM attacks:** Mutual authentication stops attackers from positioning themselves between devices to intercept or alter communications.

A use case would be in a hospital with multiple connected ventilators. Mutual authentication ensures that only authorized ventilators send and receive updates from the central control platform, preventing attackers from issuing malicious commands.

Enforce Multifactor Authentication for Administrative Access

Administrative access to medical devices, network systems, and management platforms poses risks if not adequately secured. Multifactor authentication (MFA) adds an extra layer of security by requiring users to verify their identity using two or more factors before gaining access. Key components of MFA include the following:

- **Something you know:** A password or PIN
- **Something you have:** A physical token, mobile app code, or smart card
- **Something you are:** Biometrics, such as fingerprint or facial recognition

This matters in healthcare due to benefits such as the following:

- **Protection against credential theft:** Even if a user's password is compromised, MFA prevents unauthorized access by requiring a second verification factor.
- **Mitigates insider threats:** MFA ensures only verified personnel can make administrative changes or access sensitive systems.
- **Secures remote access:** MFA allows healthcare staff to authenticate securely when accessing systems remotely, such as telemedicine platforms or cloud-based EHR systems.

A use case is a hospital administrator logging into the central management system for medical devices. The administrator must enter their password and a code generated on their secure mobile authenticator app, reducing the risk of unauthorized access due to stolen credentials.

Integrate Role-Based Access Control

In addition to strong authentication, healthcare organizations should integrate role-based access control (RBAC) to ensure that devices and users only have access to resources relevant to their role. This works where devices, systems, and users are assigned specific roles (e.g., clinician, technician, administrator), each with permissions tailored to their responsibilities. RBAC limits access to critical systems, reducing the risk of insider threats. It also prevents unauthorized devices from performing actions beyond their intended function. For example, a clinician may have read-only access to infusion pump settings, while an administrator can modify configurations after authenticating with MFA.

Continuous Monitoring and Authentication Validation

Authentication is not a one-time event. Continuous validation ensures that devices maintain their authorized status throughout their connection to the network, alongside the following:

- **Session management:** Monitor device sessions to detect anomalies such as unexpected reconnections or failed authentication attempts.
- **Automatic reauthentication:** Devices periodically reauthenticate to confirm their legitimacy and prevent session hijacking.
- **AI-driven monitoring:** Use AI and machine learning tools to identify unusual authentication behaviors or access patterns, such as an unexpected login attempt or a sudden influx of new devices.

An AI-driven system, for example, may detect repeated failed authentication attempts from an infusion pump, flag it as a potential compromise, and then temporarily isolate it until it can be verified.

From my research, the top five benefits of robust device authentication are as follows:

- **Improved security posture:** Prevents unauthorized devices and users from accessing sensitive systems
- **Protection against cyber threats:** Mitigates risks such as device impersonation, credential theft, and MITM attacks
- **Data integrity and privacy:** Ensures that only trusted devices communicate, preserving the integrity of sensitive patient data

- **Compliance with regulations:** Helps healthcare organizations meet the requirements for strong authentication under HIPAA, HITECH, and other regulations
- **Enhanced patient safety:** Protects medical devices from unauthorized tampering, ensuring safe and reliable operation

Robust device authentication is a cornerstone of cybersecurity in healthcare environments. By leveraging secure pairing, mutual authentication, and multifactor authentication, healthcare organizations can ensure that only trusted devices and users interact with critical systems. Pairing these strategies with continuous monitoring and role-based access control creates a layered security approach that protects sensitive patient data and enhances the resilience of life-saving medical devices.

Deploy Network Segmentation and Isolation

In healthcare environments where networked medical devices, administrative systems, and guest access points coexist, network segmentation, enclaving, and/or isolation play crucial roles in mitigating risks and minimizing the impact of breaches. By separating different types of traffic, healthcare organizations can prevent attackers from moving laterally across the network, secure critical systems, protect patient data, and ensure the uninterrupted operation of life-saving devices. A well-implemented segmentation strategy enhances visibility, control, and overall network resilience.

A rule of thumb is to create VLANs or WLANs for traffic segmentation. Virtual networks allow healthcare organizations to segment their networks logically, separating traffic into isolated groups to reduce the attack surface. Each VLAN operates as an independent broadcast domain, ensuring that systems within one segment cannot communicate directly with systems in another segment unless explicitly permitted.

Some examples of how VLANs work in healthcare include the following:

- Medical devices (e.g., infusion pumps and patient monitors) are placed on a dedicated VLAN with strict access controls to isolate traffic from administrative systems, guest networks, and other non-critical devices.
- Administrative systems, such as EHR servers and staff workstations, are placed on a separate VLAN with strict access controls to protect sensitive data.
- Guest Wi-Fi networks are isolated from all internal systems to prevent visitors from accessing the hospital's operational network.

Segmentation ensures that a breach in one virtual network does not immediately compromise the others, containing threats and reducing the risk of lateral movement. Once traffic is segmented, enforcing communication restrictions between VLANs using firewalls and strong access control lists is essential. These help define which devices or systems can interact across segments, ensuring that only authorized traffic flows between isolated areas of the network. Consider these:

- **Firewalls for inter-VLAN communication:** Deploy internal firewalls to monitor and control traffic between VLANs. Granular rules can be set to allow specific communication while blocking unnecessary or potentially malicious traffic. For example, a firewall rule may permit telemetry monitors (e.g., VLAN 40) to communicate only with central monitoring servers (e.g., VLAN 20) but block any attempt to connect to guest Wi-Fi or administrative systems.

- **Access control lists** (ACLs): These rules define what traffic is allowed or denied between segments. They add an enforcement layer to allow only approved devices, IP addresses, and protocols. For example, ACL rules ensure that infusion pumps on VLAN 10 can communicate with control servers on VLAN 30 but cannot interact with guest devices on VLAN 50.

By combining firewalls and ACLs, healthcare organizations can tightly control inter-VLAN traffic, reducing the risk of unauthorized access or malicious activities.

To safeguard life-saving medical devices and mission-critical systems, they must be isolated on highly secure, dedicated network segments with minimal exposure to the broader network. This approach ensures attackers cannot access or disrupt these systems, even if other network parts are compromised. Key isolation techniques include the following:

- **Dedicated VLANs for critical systems:** Devices such as infusion pumps, ventilators, and cardiac monitors are placed on isolated VLANs with strict communication policies.
- **Network address translation (NAT)**: NAT obscures device IP addresses, making it more challenging for attackers to identify or target specific devices.
- **Out-of-band management:** Isolate administrative access for critical systems onto an out-of-band (OOB) network to prevent unauthorized access via the main operational network.

A use case would be a hospital that isolates ventilators and infusion pumps onto a dedicated VLAN that only communicates with a control server. Devices on this VLAN cannot communicate with administrative systems, IoMT devices, or guest networks, limiting their exposure to potential attacks.

Due to their limited security features, IoT medical devices, such as patient monitors, wearable devices, and imaging equipment, introduce security challenges. Segmenting these devices into isolated networks minimizes their threat exposure while maintaining functionality.

For example, telemetry monitors used in ICU rooms can be segmented onto their own VLAN, ensuring they can communicate only with the hospital's central monitoring platform. The segmentation prevents attackers from accessing administrative systems or patient databases if an IoT vulnerability is exploited.

Finally, segmentation should be paired with real-time traffic monitoring to identify and respond to unauthorized communication attempts or suspicious activities. The benefits of network segmentation and isolation are vast, but here are several typical results:

- **Reduced attack surface:** Segmenting the network limits attackers' ability to move laterally, containing breaches to a single segment.

- **Improved data security:** Sensitive systems and devices are isolated, reducing exposure to unauthorized access or data theft.
- **Enhanced compliance:** Network segmentation protects sensitive data and critical systems, helping healthcare organizations comply with HIPAA and HITECH requirements.
- **Operational continuity:** Isolating life-saving medical devices protects their functionality, even if other network parts are compromised.
- **Simplified incident response:** Segmentation helps quickly identify, contain, and remediate breaches within specific segments without disrupting the entire network.

Deploying network segmentation and isolation is a cornerstone of healthcare cybersecurity. By creating VLANs, restricting communication with firewalls and ACLs, and isolating critical systems, healthcare organizations can dramatically reduce the risk of lateral movement and protect sensitive medical systems and data. As medical IoT devices grow in number and sophistication, targeted segmentation strategies are essential to mitigate their vulnerabilities. Combined with real-time monitoring, segmentation creates a layered defense that enhances resilience, ensures operational continuity, and keeps patient safety at the forefront.

Ensure Regular Updates and Patching

Keeping medical devices and systems updated is one of the most fundamental security practices in healthcare environments. Medical devices, such as infusion pumps, heart monitors, imaging systems, and connected IoT devices, are essential for patient care. However, their vulnerabilities, especially in outdated firmware or software, can be exploited by cybercriminals and even automated malware to launch attacks, compromise patient safety, or steal sensitive data. By implementing a proactive update and patch management strategy, healthcare organizations can close security gaps, address known vulnerabilities, and maintain the integrity of their medical systems. This section will review high-level recommendations as I get more granular later in Chapter 16.

Establish a Comprehensive Patch Management Program

A structured patch management process ensures that all devices, systems, and software receive regular updates to mitigate vulnerabilities and protect against emerging cyber threats. You should consider these:

- **Develop a patch schedule:** To ensure consistency, create a rigorous, recurring schedule for firmware and software updates. Consider applying patches during designated maintenance windows to minimize disruptions for critical devices. For example, a hospital's IT team schedules firmware updates for

ventilators and infusion pumps monthly, aligning with vendor release cycles to keep all devices secure.
- **Prioritize patching based on risk:** Not all devices carry the same level of risk. Use a risk-based approach to prioritize updates for devices with critical functions or those connected to sensitive systems.
  - **High-risk devices:** Medical devices that interact directly with patients or handle sensitive PHI, such as infusion pumps or EHR-integrated imaging systems, must be updated immediately.
  - **Lower-risk devices:** Devices with limited connectivity or lower operational impact can follow a secondary schedule.
- **Automate update deployment:** Where possible, use automated patch management tools to streamline the process. Automation reduces manual errors, ensures timely deployment, and simplifies monitoring across extensive device inventories.

Collaborate Closely with Medical Device Vendors

Medical device manufacturers play a key role in providing security updates and patches, but collaboration with healthcare organizations is vital to ensure seamless deployment. Consider these collaborative options:

- **Vendor communication:** Establish open lines of communication with device manufacturers to stay informed about scheduled firmware and software updates, security patches addressing newly discovered vulnerabilities, and end-of-life notifications for unsupported devices.
- **Patch testing and validation:** Collaborate with vendors to test patches in a controlled environment before deploying updates. This ensures compatibility with the hospital's infrastructure and minimizes the risk of operational disruptions. For example, before applying firmware updates to MRI machines, the hospital IT team validates the patch in a sandbox environment to confirm functionality and performance.
- **Proactive vendor partnerships:** Partner with vendors to address vulnerabilities beyond patching, such as enhancing device security features or eliminating hardcoded passwords. Manufacturers should also provide ongoing support for devices throughout their lifecycle, ensuring critical security updates are released promptly. In addition, consider creating a third-party certification process before purchasing devices from a vendor to ensure the devices meet operational and security standards.

Implement Proactive Vulnerability Management

Staying ahead of emerging threats requires continuous vulnerability monitoring and proactive remediation. A good vulnerability management program ensures that newly identified risks are addressed before exploitation. Be sure to consider these in your program:

- **Monitor threat intelligence:** Subscribe to industry threat advisories, vendor security bulletins, and regulatory updates (e.g., FDA medical device alerts) to stay informed about the latest vulnerabilities. Use feeds such as the following:
  - National Vulnerability Database (NVD)
  - Information Sharing and Analysis Centers (ISACs)
  - Vendor-provided threat intelligence reports
- **Conduct regular vulnerability scans:** Automated vulnerability scans on connected medical devices and systems identify outdated firmware, unpatched software, or misconfigurations. For example, weekly scans detect infusion pumps that are still running obsolete firmware. The IT team prioritizes patching these devices before scheduling broader updates.
- **Address zero-day threats:** Develop a plan to respond quickly to zero-day vulnerabilities, where attackers exploit security flaws before patches are available. This includes isolating affected devices or implementing compensating controls until an official patch is deployed.

Overcome Challenges with Legacy Systems

Many healthcare organizations rely on legacy devices not designed with modern cybersecurity standards in mind. These devices often run outdated operating systems or lack vendor support for regular patches. That said, you should do the following:

- **Implement network isolation:** To limit exposure and prevent lateral movement in case of compromise, unsupported legacy devices should be placed on isolated VLANs or restricted networks.
- **Deploy compensating controls:** To safeguard legacy devices that cannot be patched, use additional security measures, such as firewalls, intrusion detection systems, and endpoint protection.
- **Plan for device replacement:** Develop a phased strategy to replace legacy devices with modern, secure alternatives that support ongoing updates and robust security features.

Audit and Monitor Patch Compliance

Regular auditing ensures that updates are applied consistently across the organization and that no device is left vulnerable due to missed patches. Consider using centralized patch management dashboards to track patch deployment progress, identify devices requiring updates, and ensure compliance with organizational security policies.

You should conduct quarterly or bi-annual audits to validate that all devices, including those in remote or off-site facilities, are updated and patched. Include a documented patch history. In other words, maintain detailed records of all applied updates, patch failures, and remediation actions to meet compliance requirements for regulations like HIPAA and HITECH.

A proactive approach to updates and patch management delivers significant benefits for healthcare organizations, including the following:

- **Improved patient safety:** Ensures medical devices operate as intended, minimizing risks of malfunctions caused by security vulnerabilities.

- **Protection against cyber threats:** Reduces the risk of ransomware attacks, malware infections, and unauthorized access resulting from unpatched systems.

- **Regulatory compliance:** Demonstrates adherence to regulatory mandates, such as HIPAA and FDA guidelines, which I'll discuss in Chapter 20. These mandates require timely updates and the safeguarding of PHI.

- **Operational continuity:** Prevents disruptions in critical systems by addressing vulnerabilities before they can be exploited.

A patch management strategy is essential for securing healthcare networks and medical devices in an evolving threat landscape. By establishing a comprehensive update schedule, collaborating with vendors, proactively managing vulnerabilities, and addressing legacy system challenges, healthcare organizations can close security gaps and protect patient data.

Deploy Advanced Monitoring and Intrusion Detection

Advanced monitoring and intrusion detection are great for detecting and mitigating cybersecurity threats like MITM attacks. Healthcare organizations should leverage real-time monitoring capabilities, AI-driven tools, and IDS to identify anomalies, detect unauthorized activities, and respond quickly to potential threats.

Real-time monitoring is essential for maintaining visibility across the network, particularly when securing the communication between medical devices, IoT devices, and hospital systems. By continuously observing network traffic, healthcare IT teams can detect anomalies that may indicate a cyberattack, such as unexpected data delays, packet alterations, or unauthorized connections.

Deploying tools that monitor network behavior for deviations from normal baselines is vital. For example, unusual data spikes, irregular traffic between devices, or unexpected packet loss may indicate a MITM attack or network infiltration. If a telemetry monitor suddenly sends large volumes of data to an unfamiliar IP address, the monitoring tool can flag this anomaly for immediate investigation. Configure systems to trigger automated alerts when suspicious activity is detected. This reduces response time and enables IT teams to act swiftly to contain potential threats.

These days, intrusion detection systems (IDS) and intrusion prevention systems (IPS) are critical. IDS are tools for identifying unauthorized activity on the network.

By analyzing network traffic and comparing it against known attack signatures, IDS tools can detect malicious activity, including MITM attacks, packet injection, and eavesdropping. IPS, a more advanced IDS version, actively blocks or isolates identified threats.

Network-based IDS (NIDS) and host-based IDS (HIDS) are types of IDS recommended for healthcare networks. NIDS monitors traffic across the entire network and flags anomalies. They are ideal for identifying rogue access points, unauthorized devices, or unexpected communication patterns in medical networks. HIDS monitors individual devices, such as infusion pumps, ventilators, and EHR servers, for suspicious behavior or unauthorized changes to system configurations.

For example, a hospital may deploy Snort, an open-source NIDS tool, to monitor real-time network traffic. When an attacker attempts to intercept communications between a heart monitor and the central server, Snort detects anomalous traffic patterns and generates an alert for the IT team. On the other hand, IPS can take proactive measures, such as disconnecting compromised devices or blocking malicious IP addresses, to stop attacks in progress and minimize risk to patient systems.

Reviewing system logs from medical devices, network infrastructure, and access points is essential for identifying signs of an attack. IDS/IPS and other systems can help. For example, healthcare organizations can use centralized monitoring systems to consolidate and analyze logs from multiple sources, ensuring no critical security events go unnoticed. Tools like security information and event management (SIEM) solutions collect, analyze, and correlate logs across the healthcare network, identifying suspicious patterns or anomalies indicative of a MITM attack. Example platforms I've worked with include Splunk, Rapid 7 InsightIDR, IBM QRadar, and Microsoft Sentinel, and each provides centralized log aggregation, real-time alerting, and automated reporting for compliance audits.

Be sure to set automated alerts for unusual activities, such as failed authentication attempts, unauthorized changes to device configurations, or sudden spikes in traffic. Logs should also be regularly audited to identify persistent threats or repeated attempts to compromise medical systems.

Using Artificial Intelligence to Analyze MITM Attacks

Note that artificial intelligence (AI) and machine learning (ML) have become powerful tools in detecting sophisticated cyber threats, such as MITM attacks that may go undetected using traditional monitoring methods. These advanced solutions analyze vast amounts of data, identify patterns, and detect anomalies in real time, providing predictive and adaptive security capabilities. These can often be added features to IDS/IPS and SIEM platforms. Key capabilities of AI-driven threat detection include the following:

- **Behavioral analysis:** AI tools establish baseline behavior for medical devices and network traffic. Any deviation—such as unexpected delays in telemetry data or unusual packet sizes—can be flagged for investigation.

- **Threat prediction:** Machine learning algorithms can identify attack patterns based on historical data, enabling proactive threat mitigation.
- **False positive reduction:** AI tools minimize false alerts by learning from legitimate behaviors over time, ensuring that IT teams focus on real threats.

A hospital that deploys an AI-based threat detection tool, such as Darktrace or Palo Alto Cortex XDR, can monitor real-time communications between connected medical devices. When an attacker intercepts a communication from a patient monitor and attempts to alter vital sign data, the AI system detects the anomaly. It triggers an automated alert, isolating the compromised device from the network.

Integrated Monitoring for IoT and Connected Medical Devices

I'll now talk about integrated monitoring for IoT and connected medical devices. Given the proliferation of medical IoT devices in healthcare settings, advanced monitoring solutions must also focus on the unique vulnerabilities of these systems. IoT-specific tools enable organizations to do the following:

- **Identify and classify devices:** Use tools that automatically detect all connected devices, including infusion pumps, wearable monitors, and imaging systems, to build an accurate inventory.
- **Monitor device-specific behavior:** Track data patterns and operational behaviors for each device type to quickly identify deviations caused by potential attacks.
- **Enforce security policies:** Implement monitoring systems that ensure devices comply with security protocols, such as encryption standards and firmware updates.

An example use case could be a monitoring solution like Armis, Asimily, or Claroty, which detects that a connected MRI machine begins communicating with an external IP address, behavior inconsistent with its baseline traffic patterns. The system flags the anomaly, allowing IT to investigate and isolate the compromised machine before further damage occurs. By deploying advanced monitoring tools and intrusion detection systems, healthcare organizations can do the following:

- **Detect attacks in real time:** Rapid identification of anomalies and suspicious behavior allows IT teams to mitigate threats before they escalate.
- **Protect patient safety:** Prevent the unauthorized manipulation of medical devices, which could impact care delivery or put lives at risk.
- **Ensure regulatory compliance:** Demonstrate proactive security measures to comply with HIPAA, HITECH, and other healthcare regulations.
- **Minimize downtime:** Real-time monitoring reduces the likelihood of prolonged system disruptions caused by cyberattacks.
- **Enhance network visibility:** Centralized monitoring provides comprehensive visibility into network activity, helping IT teams identify vulnerabilities and optimize security strategies.

Deploying advanced monitoring and intrusion detection systems is critical for safeguarding healthcare environments from evolving cyber threats like MITM attacks. By leveraging real-time monitoring tools, intrusion detection systems, centralized log audits, and AI-driven anomaly detection, healthcare organizations can quickly identify and mitigate suspicious activity, ensuring the security of patient data, medical devices, and operational systems.

Conduct Training and Awareness Programs

The human element remains one of the most significant factors in defending healthcare organizations against cyberattacks. While sound technical defenses are essential, they can be undermined if healthcare staff lack the knowledge or awareness to recognize and respond to security threats. A well-rounded and frequently conducted cybersecurity training and awareness program empowers employees to act as the first line of defense, ensuring that medical devices, patient data, and network integrity remain protected. The following are five key strategies for strengthening cybersecurity in healthcare, including fostering a security-first culture, implementing tailored training programs, conducting regular testing and simulations, and reinforcing continuous learning:

1. **Establish a culture of security awareness.**

   Building a culture of security begins with fostering an environment where cybersecurity is everyone's responsibility, not just the IT department's concern. Leadership must emphasize the importance of protecting patient data and systems to ensure secure care delivery. Senior leadership should advocate for cybersecurity awareness, ensuring all staff understand its critical role in patient safety and compliance.

   Reinforcement through communication is key. You should conduct regular town halls or executive briefings to share insights on cyber risks, emerging threats, and the organization's security posture. Also, implement ongoing communication strategies such as newsletters, posters, and updates on recent security incidents, phishing trends, and best practices. Consider using real-world examples to demonstrate the impact of cyberattacks on healthcare, reinforcing the need for vigilance.

2. **Create tailored cybersecurity training programs.**

   Training programs should be customized to the roles and responsibilities of healthcare staff, ensuring that all employees, from nurses and doctors to IT administrators and executives, receive relevant education.

   a. General awareness training for all staff

   All healthcare personnel, regardless of role, must receive foundational cybersecurity training that covers these elements:

- Recognizing signs of compromised devices or networks:
  - Unexpected device behavior includes alarms, configuration changes, or poor performance.
  - Network outages, strange pop-ups, or unresponsive systems may indicate a cyberattack.
- Secure communication practices:
  - Avoid using unsecured networks or public Wi-Fi to access sensitive systems.
  - Use approved communication platforms for sharing patient data and avoid emailing PHI unless encryption is in place.
  - Regularly update passwords and avoid sharing credentials or leaving devices unattended.
- Responding to phishing and social engineering attacks:
  - Recognize common phishing tactics, such as deceptive emails impersonating IT support or external vendors.
  - Avoid clicking suspicious links, downloading unauthorized attachments, or responding to requests for sensitive information.
  - Use real-world phishing simulation tools to train staff on identifying malicious emails.
- Prompt reporting to the IT and security teams:
  - Clearly define procedures for reporting suspicious activity, such as unexpected device behavior, lost or stolen devices, or potential phishing attempts.
  - Create a dedicated incident reporting channel to ensure rapid response from IT teams.

b. Role-based training for technical staff

Technical teams, including IT administrators and biomedical engineers, require advanced training to secure devices, systems, and networks, including the following:

- Identifying and responding to device compromises:
  - Train technical staff to recognize MITM attacks, rogue access points, or unauthorized device communication.
  - Use tools like SIEM solutions to monitor network traffic for anomalies and unauthorized connections.
- Firmware and patch management:
  - Educate teams on the importance of regular device updates and secure patch deployment processes.

- Establish protocols for validating and testing firmware before implementation.
- Incident response readiness:
  - Train IT and security staff to follow detailed incident response playbooks in case of breaches, such as isolating compromised devices, notifying stakeholders, and restoring systems.

c. Targeted training for clinical staff

Medical staff interact directly with devices and systems, making their awareness of security risks critical, and they should understand these:

- Secure use of medical devices:
  - Teach clinicians how to securely log in, use, and recognize abnormalities, such as unexpected configuration changes or unusual alerts. They should also be taught how to secure devices physically.
  - Highlight the risks of unauthorized device usage, such as connecting personal devices or using unsecured USB drives.
- Patient privacy protections:
  - Train staff on safeguarding patient health information using mobile devices, tablets, and EHR systems.
  - Reinforce the importance of logging out after use and locking screens when leaving devices unattended.
- Recognizing social engineering:
  - Educate clinical staff on threats like impersonation (e.g., attackers posing as IT technicians) and how to verify personnel credentials.

3. **Regular Testing and Simulations**

Training programs must include practical exercises to ensure staff are prepared for real-world threats, including the following:

- **Phishing simulations:** Conduct regular, controlled phishing simulations to assess employees' ability to recognize deceptive emails and avoid falling for traps. Provide immediate feedback and targeted retraining for staff who click on simulated phishing links.
- **Incident response drills:** Organize tabletop exercises that simulate cybersecurity incidents, such as a MITM attack, ransomware outbreak, or device compromise. This will allow staff to practice their responses in a controlled environment.
- **Device compromise scenarios:** Work with biomedical teams to simulate device anomalies, such as altered settings or connectivity disruptions, to teach staff how to escalate issues to IT for further investigation.

4. **Continuous learning and reinforcement**

   Cybersecurity threats constantly evolve, and training cannot be a one-time exercise. Continuous education ensures healthcare staff remain aware of emerging risks and best practices, which include the following:

   - **Quarterly refresher training:** Provide regular updates on new threats, such as ransomware techniques, device vulnerabilities, or phishing scams.
   - **Micro-learning modules:** These bite-sized, on-demand training sessions cover password security, secure device use, and phishing awareness. Staff can complete them during breaks.
   - **Recognition programs:** Implement incentives for staff demonstrating strong cybersecurity practices, such as certificates or recognition awards. This will help reinforce positive behaviors.

5. **Emphasizing the patient safety connection**

   Healthcare staff are motivated by patient outcomes, and framing cybersecurity within the context of patient safety increases its relevance. Consider highlighting how cyberattacks can disrupt critical devices, delay care, and jeopardize lives. Try using real-world case studies, such as ransomware attacks on hospitals, to demonstrate the consequences of poor security practices. For example, explain how an unsecured infusion pump could be compromised to deliver incorrect dosages or how a MITM attack could alter patient monitor data, leading to misinformed treatment decisions.

Implementing comprehensive training and awareness programs provides significant benefits to healthcare organizations, such as the following:

- **Improved threat detection:** Staff become capable of identifying compromised devices, unusual network activity, and phishing attempts.
- **Enhanced incident response:** Prompt reporting of suspicious activities enables IT teams to contain threats quickly.
- **Regulatory compliance:** Security training is often required to ensure compliance with HIPAA, HITECH, and other healthcare laws and regulations.
- **Reduced cyber risk exposure:** Educated employees act as an additional layer of defense, reducing the likelihood of successful cyberattacks.
- **Increased patient safety:** Awareness of secure device practices ensures uninterrupted operation of critical medical systems and protection of patient health information.

Cybersecurity in healthcare begins with people. By implementing comprehensive and role-specific training programs, healthcare organizations can empower their staff to recognize threats, follow secure practices, and respond effectively to incidents. Regular simulations, continuous education, and a focus on patient safety ensure that the human element becomes a robust defense against cyberattacks.

Collaborate with Vendors to Enhance Device Security

Collaboration with medical device manufacturers and vendors is essential to ensuring that the devices integrated into healthcare environments meet the rigorous security standards required to protect patient data, maintain operational integrity, and ensure regulatory compliance. This partnership enables healthcare providers to address vulnerabilities proactively and ensure devices are resilient against evolving cyber threats. This section outlines key best practices for securing medical devices, including avoiding hardcoded passwords, providing secure communication protocols, conducting regular security assessments, promoting transparency in product development, supporting lifecycle management, and fostering ongoing collaboration. Healthcare providers can strengthen device security, protect patient safety, and maintain compliance with evolving regulatory standards by implementing these measures within a third-party vendor device vulnerability process.

1. **Avoid hard-coded passwords**

   Hardcoded passwords and preset credentials embedded into device firmware are significant security vulnerabilities. If left unchanged, attackers can exploit these credentials, granting them unauthorized access to medical devices and networks. To mitigate this risk, healthcare providers should:

   - **Demand configurable credentials.** Ensure devices support unique, user-configured administrative and user accounts and passwords. Vendors should eliminate the use of default or hardcoded passwords in device design.
   - **Implement strong password policies:** Collaborate with vendors to enforce password policies that mandate complexity, uniqueness, and periodic updates. Devices should require passwords that include a mix of upper- and lowercase letters, numbers, and special characters.
   - **Promote passwordless solutions:** Explore emerging technologies like biometric authentication or hardware tokens to minimize reliance on passwords altogether.

   For example, in 2017, the FDA issued warnings about pacemakers with hardcoded passwords that made them vulnerable to remote hacking. Collaboration between hospitals and manufacturers led to software updates allowing password customization.

2. **Ensure secure communication protocols**

   Healthcare providers must require vendors to incorporate strong encryption and authentication protocols into their devices to safeguard data transmitted between devices and central systems from interception, tampering, or unauthorized access. To achieve this, devices should adopt industry-standard encryption protocols, such as TLS 1.3 or WPA3, ensuring that data in transit remains secure. Additionally, implementing mutual authentication between devices and central systems is crucial, enabling two-way authentication to verify the legitimacy of communication endpoints before exchanging data. Furthermore, providers should collaborate with vendors to integrate secure boot mechanisms, which validate device firmware and software integrity at startup, preventing unauthorized modifications and enhancing overall security. By enforcing these measures, healthcare organizations can strengthen their cybersecurity posture and protect sensitive patient information from emerging threats.

A telemetry monitoring device, for example, that uses WPA3 encryption and certificate-based authentication ensures that patient vitals are transmitted securely to a central server, minimizing the risk of MITM attacks.

3. **Conduct regular security assessments and updates**

   Medical devices often have extended lifecycles, making regular security assessments and updates essential for maintaining security posture. Healthcare providers should establish collaborative processes with vendors to ensure continuous device improvement, such as the following:

   - **Conduct vulnerability assessments:** Require vendors to perform regular vulnerability assessments and penetration testing on their devices. These tests should be conducted by independent third-party organizations for unbiased evaluations.
   - **Issue security patches promptly:** Develop agreements with vendors to ensure timely delivery of patches and updates for discovered vulnerabilities. This includes rapid response to zero-day threats.
   - **Perform compatibility testing:** Partner with vendors to test updates in sandboxed environments before deployment to avoid disrupting critical operations.
   - **Ensure compliance with standards:** Collaborate to ensure devices align with regulatory standards such as HIPAA, FDA cybersecurity guidance, and international frameworks like ISO 13485 for medical device quality management.

   A good example is a major hospital system that worked with a manufacturer to test and deploy a firmware update for infusion pumps after discovering a vulnerability that allowed attackers to alter medication dosages remotely.

4. **Establish transparency in product development**

   Trust and transparency with vendors ensure that security considerations are prioritized throughout the product lifecycle.

   - **Request security documentation:** This requires detailed documentation of device security features, including encryption methods, authentication mechanisms, and patch management processes.
   - **Secure development practices:** Ensure vendors follow secure software development lifecycle or SDLC practices, incorporating security reviews at every stage of development.

- **Supply chain security:** Collaborate with vendors to vet their supply chains, ensuring that components are sourced from trusted manufacturers and free from embedded vulnerabilities or malware.

  For example, after a vulnerability was discovered in an IoMT device component sourced from a third-party supplier, proactive communication between the healthcare provider and vendor enabled a recall and replacement of the affected components.

5. **Support for lifecycle management**

   Healthcare providers should collaborate with vendors to manage the security of devices throughout their lifecycle, from deployment to decommissioning.

   - **End-of-life planning:** Work with vendors to establish timelines for device support, including when updates and patches are unavailable. Ensure a secure decommissioning process for retiring devices.
   - **Service-level agreements (SLAs):** SLAs with vendors should include cybersecurity expectations and specify responsibilities for patch management, vulnerability disclosure, and incident response support.
   - **Remote monitoring capabilities:** Partner with vendors to deploy remote monitoring systems that provide real-time device health and security updates.

   For example, a healthcare provider worked with a vendor to develop a phased approach to replacing legacy devices nearing end-of-life with updated models, minimizing downtime, and maintaining patient safety.

6. **Foster communication and collaboration**

   Open lines of communication between healthcare providers and vendors are essential for effective security management.

   - **Threat intelligence sharing:** Establish channels for sharing threat intelligence, ensuring both parties are aware of emerging vulnerabilities or attack vectors.
   - **Joint incident response plans:** Develop collaborative incident response plans that define roles and responsibilities in the event of a cybersecurity breach involving medical devices.
   - **User feedback integration:** Create feedback loops to allow healthcare providers to report security concerns or usability issues to vendors, facilitating continuous improvement.

   In this case, an example could be a hospital that reported frequent connectivity issues with a wireless heart monitor to the vendor. This led to a firmware update that resolved the problem and improved device reliability.

As discussed, collaboration between healthcare providers and medical device vendors is a cornerstone of a sound cybersecurity strategy. By addressing vulnerabilities such as hardcoded passwords, ensuring secure communication protocols, conducting regular security assessments, and fostering transparent communication, organizations can build a resilient defense against cyber threats. These partnerships safeguard patient data and medical devices and strengthen trust in the increasingly connected healthcare ecosystem.

Use Case for AI-Driven Detection

I'll examine a use case for AI-driven detections. For background, a hospital might implement an AI-based threat detection system to enhance the security of its medical device network. The detection system would monitor real-time communications between medical devices and the hospital's central network.

Scenario On a busy Tuesday afternoon, the AI-driven detection system identified unusual data patterns in the communication between a patient monitoring system in the Intensive Care Unit and the central nursing station.

Detection The AI system flagged the following anomalies:

- Unexpected latency in data transmission
- Slight alterations in data packet structures
- Unusual routing patterns for device traffic

Immediate Response Upon detecting these anomalies, the AI system:

1. Triggered a high-priority alert to the hospital's IT security team
2. Automatically isolated the compromised patient monitoring device from the network
3. Rerouted critical patient data to a backup monitoring system

Investigation The IT security team quickly investigated and discovered:

- An unauthorized device had inserted itself between the patient monitor and the network.
- The attacker was attempting to intercept and potentially modify patient vital signs data.

Mitigation Thanks to the AI system's rapid detection and response:

- The MITM attack was stopped before any patient data could be compromised.
- The isolated device was physically inspected and reset by the biomedical engineering staff.
- Network logs were analyzed to trace the origin of the attack.

Outcome

The resulting outcomes are as follows:

- Patient safety was maintained throughout the incident.
- The hospital avoided a potential data breach and associated regulatory penalties.
- The security team gained valuable insights to enhance their defenses further.

This case demonstrates the critical role of AI-driven detection in identifying and mitigating sophisticated MITM attacks in healthcare environments, where rapid response is essential for patient safety and data protection.

Key Benefits of a Comprehensive Mitigation Strategy

A comprehensive mitigation strategy offers several key critical benefits for safeguarding healthcare environments. First and foremost, it enhances patient safety by preventing unauthorized alterations to medical device operations, ensuring that care delivery remains accurate, reliable, and uninterrupted. This is particularly vital in environments where patient health depends on the proper functioning of connected devices. It also supports data privacy compliance by protecting sensitive patient information, helping organizations adhere to HIPAA and other laws and regulatory requirements while fostering trust among patients and stakeholders.

Beyond compliance, a strong mitigation strategy ensures operational continuity by reducing risks that could disrupt critical medical services. This minimizes downtime, enabling healthcare providers to maintain seamless operations and uphold confidence in their ability to deliver care. Lastly, it significantly reduces cyber risk exposure by proactively addressing vulnerabilities and implementing defenses against evolving threats. This forward-thinking approach not only strengthens the security posture of healthcare systems but also positions organizations to respond swiftly and effectively to future challenges in an increasingly connected landscape.

MITM attacks, which target the communication pathways of critical medical devices, are a growing threat to healthcare environments. By adopting robust encryption, authentication, network segmentation, and monitoring practices, healthcare organizations can significantly reduce their exposure to these risks. Collaboration between healthcare providers, device manufacturers, and cybersecurity professionals is essential to building resilient defenses that protect patients, data, and operations in an increasingly connected healthcare ecosystem.

Case Study of a MITM Attack on Infusion Pumps

In a simulated attack conducted by ethical hackers, a MITM attack was successfully demonstrated on infusion pumps used to deliver medication in a major hospital. This alarming demonstration highlighted significant vulnerabilities in the security of medical devices and the hospital's network infrastructure, underscoring the urgent need for improved cybersecurity measures in healthcare settings.

The Attack Scenario With the hospital's permission, the ethical hacking team targeted a network of infusion pumps commonly used in critical care settings. These devices, which deliver precise doses of medication to patients, were found to be susceptible to a sophisticated MITM attack.

The attackers exploited weaknesses in the hospital's Wi-Fi network to position themselves between the infusion pumps and the central control system. Once in place, they intercepted and altered data packets transmitted between the devices and the control server.

In a demonstration of the potential consequences, the testers successfully modified the medication dosage instructions sent to an infusion pump, increasing the dose without triggering any alerts in the control system. This scenario highlighted how a malicious actor could harm patients by manipulating critical medical devices.

Vulnerabilities Exposed The successful MITM attack revealed several critical vulnerabilities:

- **Weak encryption:** The infusion pumps used outdated encryption protocols, making it relatively easy for attackers to decrypt and modify the intercepted data.
- **Lack of authentication:** The devices failed to properly authenticate the source of instructions, allowing the attackers to impersonate the control system.
- **Insecure network configuration:** The hospital's Wi-Fi network was not adequately segmented, allowing the attackers to access the medical device network from other system parts.
- **Absence of anomaly detection:** The control system lacked mechanisms to detect unusual changes in medication dosages, failing to alert staff to the modified instructions.

Implications and Risks The implications of this simulated attack are far-reaching. In a real-world scenario, such vulnerabilities could lead to:

- Patient harm due to incorrect medication dosages
- Breach of sensitive patient data
- Disruption of critical care services
- Potential legal and regulatory consequences for the hospital

Mitigation Measures Following the demonstration, the hospital took some immediate steps to address the identified vulnerabilities, including the following:

1. **Encryption upgrade:** All infusion pumps were updated to use strong, modern data-transmission protocols.
2. **Network segmentation:** The hospital implemented strict network segmentation, isolating medical devices on dedicated, secured VLANs.

3. **Device authentication:** Mutual authentication mechanisms were implemented to ensure the legitimacy of both devices and control systems.
4. **Firmware updates:** Regular firmware updates were scheduled for all medical devices to address known vulnerabilities.
5. **Anomaly detection:** AI-driven monitoring tools were deployed to identify unusual communication patterns or device behaviors.
6. **Staff training:** Healthcare staff received comprehensive training on recognizing signs of compromised devices and network irregularities.

This case study serves as a reminder of the critical importance of cybersecurity in healthcare settings. As medical devices become increasingly connected, the potential attack surface expands, necessitating a proactive and comprehensive approach to security.

Healthcare organizations must prioritize implementing robust security measures, including strong encryption, network segmentation, and continuous monitoring. Collaboration between device manufacturers, healthcare providers, and cybersecurity experts is essential to address vulnerabilities and develop more secure medical technologies.

By learning from simulated attacks like this and implementing stringent security protocols, healthcare institutions can better protect their patients, data, and critical infrastructure from the ever-evolving landscape of cyber threats.

The Role of Vendors and Regulators

The responsibility for ensuring medical device security falls on healthcare providers, manufacturers, and regulatory bodies. This section explores the crucial roles that vendors and regulators play in addressing MITM vulnerabilities and safeguarding the healthcare ecosystem. Medical device manufacturers are at the forefront of the battle against attacks. Their role in mitigating these risks begins at the earliest stages of product development and continues throughout the device's lifecycle. Things to consider are:

- **Prioritizing security in design**

    Manufacturers must adopt a security-by-design approach, integrating robust security measures from the initial conceptualization of a device. This includes the following:

    - Implementing strong encryption protocols to protect data transmission
    - Designing devices with secure authentication mechanisms
    - Incorporating tamper-resistant hardware to prevent physical manipulation

- **Regular updates and patch management**

    The cybersecurity landscape is constantly changing, and manufacturers must keep pace. This involves the following:

    - Establishing processes for timely software and firmware updates

- Creating systems for rapid deployment of security patches
- Providing clear guidance to healthcare providers on the update procedures
- **Compatibility with modern security standards**

    As security standards evolve, medical devices must too. Manufacturers should do the following:

    - Ensure compatibility with the latest security protocols (e.g., WPA3 for Wi-Fi devices)
    - Design devices with the flexibility to adapt to future security standards
    - Collaborate with cybersecurity experts to stay ahead of emerging threats

The Regulator's Role

Regulatory bodies, such as the FDA in the United States and HIPAA, which is regulated and enforced by the U.S. Department of Health and Human Services (HHS), specifically through its Office for Civil Rights (OCR), also play a pivotal role in setting and enforcing standards for medical device security. Regulators must establish and maintain rigorous cybersecurity standards for medical devices. This includes the following:

- Mandating comprehensive security risk assessments for all new devices
- Requiring manufacturers to provide detailed cybersecurity plans in premarket submissions
- Enforcing penalties for noncompliance with security standards

As technology advances, regulatory guidelines must keep pace. The FDA's guidance on "Cybersecurity in Medical Devices" exemplifies this approach by:

- Providing detailed recommendations on conducting cybersecurity risk assessments
- Addressing interoperability considerations in an increasingly connected healthcare environment
- Specifying required documentation for premarket submissions related to cybersecurity

Regulators can serve as a central hub for cybersecurity information, fostering collaboration between manufacturers, healthcare providers, and security experts. This can involve the following:

- Creating platforms for sharing threat intelligence and best practices
- Organizing industry-wide cybersecurity exercises and simulations
- Providing resources and training on emerging security threats and mitigation strategies

Collaborative Efforts

As mentioned earlier, addressing MITM vulnerabilities effectively requires a collaborative approach between vendors, regulators, and healthcare providers. Encouraging partnerships between device manufacturers and cybersecurity firms can lead to more robust security solutions. Regulators can facilitate this by doing this:

- Offering incentives for collaborative security research
- Funding joint projects between industry and academia
- Recognizing and rewarding innovative security solutions in medical devices

Industry-wide standards can significantly enhance the overall security posture of medical devices. Regulators and manufacturers should work together to do the following:

- Develop and adopt standard security protocols for medical devices
- Create standardized testing methodologies for assessing device security
- Establish certification programs for cyber-secure medical devices

The threat of MITM attacks on medical devices is not a problem that any single entity can solve. It requires a concerted effort from device manufacturers, regulatory bodies, and healthcare providers. By prioritizing security in device design, enforcing strict compliance requirements, and fostering collaboration across the industry, we can create a more resilient healthcare ecosystem that protects patient safety and data integrity.

As the healthcare sector embraces digital transformation, the importance of addressing MITM vulnerabilities will only grow. Vendors and regulators must remain vigilant, adaptive, and proactive in their cybersecurity approaches. Only through their combined efforts can we ensure that cyber threats do not overshadow the benefits of connected healthcare.

Key Takeaways of Man-in-the-Middle Attacks on Medical Devices

Man-in-the-middle attacks on medical devices significantly threaten patient safety, data integrity, and healthcare operations. These attacks occur when malicious actors intercept and potentially alter communications between medical devices and central systems without detection. Attackers can eavesdrop, manipulate data, or inject harmful commands, compromising patient care and sensitive information.

Common MITM attack types include passive eavesdropping, active data manipulation, session hijacking, and SSL stripping. Key vulnerabilities enabling these attacks are weak encryption protocols, insecure wireless networks, improper authentication, lack of network segmentation, outdated firmware, and limitations of IoT medical devices.

The real-world implications of MITM attacks in healthcare are severe. When attackers alter medical device settings, patient safety is at risk, potentially impacting critical systems like infusion pumps, insulin pumps, ventilators, and pacemakers. Data integrity and privacy violations can lead to HIPAA breaches and identity theft. Operational disruptions caused by manipulated devices or network interference can delay care delivery and serve as entry points for ransomware attacks.

To mitigate MITM threats, healthcare organizations should implement strong encryption (e.g., WPA3 for Wi-Fi, TLS 1.3 for device communication), robust authentication methods, network segmentation, regular updates and patching, and advanced monitoring tools. Collaboration between device manufacturers, regulators, and healthcare providers is crucial for adopting security-by-design approaches, enforcing stricter security requirements, and implementing best practices for encryption, segmentation, and staff education.

By understanding MITM vulnerabilities and implementing comprehensive security strategies, healthcare organizations can enhance patient safety, maintain regulatory compliance, ensure operational continuity, and reduce cyber risks in an increasingly connected healthcare ecosystem.

CHAPTER 7

Replay and Spoofing Attacks in IoMT

Patient care has been modernized with real-time monitoring, automated treatments, and seamless data exchange. Devices like infusion pumps, heart monitors, and insulin delivery systems are now integral to clinical workflows, improving efficiency and patient outcomes. However, this growing reliance on connected medical devices introduces cybersecurity challenges, particularly in the form of replay and spoofing attacks. These attacks exploit vulnerabilities in device communication and authentication.

Replay attacks occur when an adversary intercepts and records legitimate data transmissions, such as medication commands, patient vitals, or authentication tokens, and later replays the data to deceive the receiving system. The system, unable to distinguish between genuine and replayed transmissions, may act on outdated or falsified instructions, potentially causing life-threatening consequences for patients. For instance, replaying an old configuration command to an infusion pump could administer an incorrect medication dosage, while replaying vital sign data from a heart monitor could mask a patient's deteriorating condition.

On the other hand, spoofing attacks involve attackers impersonating legitimate devices, systems, or users to gain unauthorized access or manipulate medical operations. By mimicking trusted devices or communication endpoints, attackers can inject false data, mislead healthcare providers, or even enter critical systems. A spoofed glucose monitor, for example, could send falsified readings to an insulin pump, leading to improper insulin administration. Likewise, a rogue device could impersonate a legitimate system on the network, exfiltrating sensitive patient information or disrupting care delivery.

Replay and spoofing attacks exploit critical vulnerabilities within IoMT ecosystems, such as weak encryption, outdated authentication mechanisms, and insecure device pairing. Legacy systems, insufficient device security, and the complex operational demands of healthcare environments often exacerbate these vulnerabilities.

The implications of these attacks are far-reaching. Beyond immediate risks to patient safety, replay and spoofing attacks can compromise the integrity of diagnostic data, erode clinician trust in connected systems, and result in operational disruptions or regulatory violations. In a sector where every second counts, the consequences of inaccurate data, delayed responses, or compromised devices can be catastrophic.

To safeguard healthcare systems and protect patient lives, it is imperative to understand how replay and spoofing attacks occur, identify the vulnerabilities they exploit, and implement mitigation strategies. This chapter will explore these attacks and provide insights into their real-world implications and potential exploits in healthcare environments. Additionally, it outlines practical defense strategies to build more resilient IoMT ecosystems.

Understanding Replay Attacks in IoMT

As mentioned, a replay attack is a deceptive cyberattack in which an adversary intercepts legitimate data transmissions between two devices or systems, stores that data, and replays it later. The goal is to trick the receiving system into believing the message or data is genuine, leading to unauthorized actions, disruption, or manipulation of the system. These attacks exploit the fact that many systems trust the incoming data without verifying its timeliness or the integrity of the source.

Replay attacks present a significant threat to healthcare within the IoMT ecosystem. Medical devices such as infusion pumps, heart rate monitors, and insulin delivery systems rely on real-time communication with centralized systems or mobile applications. If this communication is intercepted and replayed, it can compromise patient health, the integrity of the data transmitted, and the efficiency of a healthcare system's operations.

How Replay Attacks Work in IoMT Systems

Replay attacks in IoMT systems start with capturing device communications. Attackers begin by positioning themselves within the communication pathway of devices. This is typically achieved through packet sniffing, which uses specialized software to intercept and log network traffic, and MITM attacks (discussed in Chapter 6), which insert themselves between the medical device and its intended recipient. The attacker then captures legitimate data exchanges, such as the following:

- Vital sign transmissions (e.g., heart rate, blood oxygen levels) from patient monitors to nursing stations
- Configuration commands sent to devices for medication dosage control
- Authentication tokens or session identifiers to establish secure connections

Once the attacker has captured valid communications, they can replay this data later. The replayed data often appears legitimate because it matches a previously valid transmission. Many IoMT systems may lack timestamp verification or nonce (number used once) mechanisms, making them vulnerable to accepting outdated commands.

There are many examples of replay attack consequences, but here are two of the most common:

- Replaying an outdated command could lead to incorrect dosage administration.
- Resending old diagnostic data might cause healthcare systems to display inaccurate patient readings, potentially leading to misdiagnosis.

An additional consideration is timing. Attackers may wait for specific moments to replay data, such as during shift changes when vigilance might be lower. They might also choose to replay only certain parts of captured communications to achieve specific malicious goals. Additionally, replay attacks can be used with other techniques, like spoofing or injection attacks, to create more complex and harder-to-detect threats.

Implications of Replay Attacks in Healthcare

As described, replay attacks in healthcare involve intercepting and replaying previously transmitted data, often maliciously, to manipulate medical devices or systems. I'll explore the implications in more detail. Patient safety risks are among the most concerning outcomes of replay attacks, especially when critical medical devices are targeted.

Medication delivery devices like infusion pumps are vulnerable to attackers who can replay instructions to administer repeated or incorrect dosages. This could lead to life-threatening overdoses or ineffective treatments, particularly for patients relying on medications like insulin or chemotherapy drugs. Similarly, implantable devices, such as pacemakers and cardioverter-defibrillators or ICDs, can be manipulated to alter heart rhythms, deliver unnecessary shocks, or disable critical alarms. Such interference could result in immediate harm or even death. Patient monitors in high-acuity environments, such as ICUs, are also at risk. Replay attacks could mask deteriorating conditions by displaying outdated, stable readings or generate false alarms that trigger unnecessary interventions, delaying responses to actual emergencies.

Data integrity and diagnostic errors present another layer of risk. Replay attacks can compromise diagnostic tools by injecting outdated imaging results, such as X-rays or MRIs, leading to missed diagnoses or delayed treatments for progressing conditions. Laboratory systems with replayed test data might produce inaccurate reports, impacting clinical decisions. Additionally, electronic health records can be corrupted when old data packets overwrite recent updates, resulting in errors like incorrect medication orders, overlooked allergies, or outdated treatment plans.

Even clinical decision support systems, which rely on real-time inputs, can be manipulated to suppress critical alerts or trigger inappropriate warnings, undermining the reliability of automated assistance.

The operational disruption caused by replay attacks can also strain healthcare facilities. Device malfunctions are common, with compromised devices freezing, crashing, or behaving erratically, leading to downtime and costly repairs. Attackers can also replay emergency signals, creating false alarms that overwhelm staff with unnecessary alerts, potentially leading to alarm fatigue, where legitimate emergencies are ignored. Additionally, network congestion caused by large-scale replay attacks can flood hospital networks, slowing down systems like EHRs or Picture Archiving and Communication Systems (PACS), essential for accessing real-time diagnostic images and patient data. Scheduling and resource management systems are not immune, either. Replay attacks can introduce old appointment or resource allocation data, resulting in double-booked operating rooms, overcommitted diagnostic equipment, and inefficient staffing schedules that delay patient care.

Use Case of a Replay Attack on an Infusion Pump

An advanced wireless infusion pump system that delivers precise doses of pain medication to patients could be a good use case in a hospital setting. The pumps communicate with a central control system, allowing authorized medical staff to adjust medication dosages remotely.

Attack Execution Steps

1. **Interception:** An attacker posing as a visitor uses a concealed radio frequency (RF) scanner to capture wireless communications between the central system and infusion pumps.

2. **Data Capture:** The attacker intercepts a legitimate command to increase morphine dosage for a post-operative patient from 2mg/hour to 5mg/hour.

3. **Analysis:** The attacker uses specialized software to decode the captured data packet, identifying the command structure and authentication tokens.

4. **Replay:** The attacker replays the intercepted command multiple times over the next hour using a small, disguised transmitter.

Impact

- The infusion pump receives and executes each replayed command, incrementing the dosage by 3mg/hour each time.
- Within an hour, the patient's morphine dosage has increased to dangerous levels (e.g., 20mg/hour).
- The patient experiences severe respiratory depression, requiring emergency intervention.

Detection and Response

- A nurse notices the patient's deteriorating condition during routine checks.
- The discrepancy between the prescribed dosage and the pump's output is discovered upon investigation.
- The hospital's IT security team is alerted and begins analyzing network logs, identifying the repeated, identical commands.

Consequences

- **Patient safety:** The patient suffers potentially life-threatening complications due to opioid overdose.
- **Operational disruption:** The ICU implements manual medication administration procedures while investigating the wireless system.
- **Reputational damage:** News of the security breach erodes patient trust in the hospital's technology.
- **Regulatory penalties:** The hospital faces fines for violating HIPAA security rules and FDA guidelines on medical device cybersecurity.
- **Financial impact:** Costs include potential litigation, cybersecurity upgrades, and extended patient care due to the incident.

This case study demonstrates the critical importance of implementing security measures for wireless medical devices, including strong encryption, authentication, and anomaly detection systems to prevent and rapidly identify replay attacks.

Other Examples of Replay Attacks in IoMT

Some additional examples of replay attacks on IoMT devices include:

- **Heart rate monitor manipulation:** Attackers could intercept data transmitted from a wearable heart rate monitor and replay old, stable readings to healthcare providers, preventing the system from detecting critical changes in a patient's cardiac health.
- **Remote pacemaker attack:** A malicious actor could intercept and replay old commands to a pacemaker, causing the device to deliver incorrect pacing commands to a patient's heart.

Strategies for Mitigation of Replay Attacks

Given the life-and-death nature of healthcare operations, defending against replay attacks requires a comprehensive, multilayered security strategy that addresses technical vulnerabilities and operational safeguards. I'll discuss these more in

Chapter 16 on best practices, but this section provides an overview focusing on reducing the risk of replay attacks.

Implementing strong encryption serves as the foundation for secure communication across medical devices and networks. Healthcare organizations should adopt modern encryption standards, such as TLS 1.3, to protect data in transit, ensuring that information exchanged between devices remains confidential and tamper-proof. End-to-end encryption should be prioritized to safeguard data from the point of origin to its destination, minimizing the risk of interception. Regular audits and updates to encryption algorithms must be part of routine security practices, as they address newly discovered vulnerabilities. Secure key management, including frequent key rotation and proper storage, further strengthen encryption defenses.

Utilizing nonces and timestamps in communication protocols adds another layer of protection against replay attacks. Nonces, which are random numbers used only once, prevent attackers from successfully replaying old messages because each session generates a new identifier. Similarly, timestamps help verify the freshness of transmitted data by enforcing time limits for validity. Nonces and timestamps provide a robust mechanism for validating communication sessions, reducing the risk of unauthorized message reuse. Implementing strict validation processes for these features ensures attackers cannot bypass them.

Mutual authentication is another critical defense, ensuring that the communicating devices and systems verify each other's identities before exchanging data. Healthcare organizations should deploy certificate-based authentication using PKI to establish trust between devices. Multifactor authentication (MFA) further enhances security, particularly for accessing critical systems. Regularly rotating and revoking authentication credentials adds another layer of protection, while device attestation helps verify that devices remain uncompromised and trustworthy during operation.

IDS plays a vital role in identifying replay attacks in real time. Network-based IDS can monitor traffic patterns across medical device networks to detect anomalies, while host-based IDS focuses on individual devices to flag suspicious activity. Advanced tools that leverage machine learning algorithms can enhance detection capabilities by recognizing subtle attack patterns that traditional methods might miss. Integrating these systems into an SIEM platform streamlines monitoring and provides actionable insights for security teams to respond quickly to threats.

Regular device updates and patch management are essential to addressing vulnerabilities in medical devices and associated software. Healthcare organizations should establish strict patch management policies and work closely with vendors to ensure the timely delivery of security updates. Before deployment, updates must be rigorously tested in a controlled environment to avoid unintended disruptions. Automated update mechanisms for devices that support it can further simplify this process while ensuring systems remain up to date against evolving threats.

Securing IoT medical devices, particularly those used in healthcare, such as remote monitors and implantable devices, requires vendor collaboration to implement security-by-design principles. Devices must include built-in encryption, secure communication protocols, and secure provisioning processes during onboarding. Network segmentation can further reduce risk by isolating IoT devices from critical systems, limiting the impact of a potential breach.

What Is a Spoofing Attack in IoMT?

Spoofing attacks in the IoMT exploit the trust relationships between devices, systems, and users in healthcare environments. I'll examine three types of spoofing attacks, explaining how they work and their potential impacts:

- **Device spoofing:** Attackers may create a rogue device that mimics the identity of a legitimate medical device, such as an infusion pump or patient monitor. This fake device could broadcast the same Bluetooth Device Address (BD_ADDR) as the legitimate device, tricking other systems into connecting. Once connected, the attacker could intercept sensitive patient data or inject false information into the healthcare network.
- **Data spoofing:** In this attack, the attacker intercepts and modifies data packets transmitted between IoMT devices. For example, an attacker could alter the readings from a glucose monitor before they reach the insulin pump, potentially causing incorrect insulin dosages. This attack exploits vulnerabilities in the communication protocols IoMT devices use, particularly if they lack strong encryption or authentication mechanisms.
- **User spoofing:** Attackers may impersonate healthcare providers by stealing or guessing login credentials. They could then access EHR systems or medical devices, potentially altering patient data or device settings. This type of spoofing often relies on social engineering tactics or weak authentication protocols in healthcare systems.

Malicious actors might execute these attacks by exploiting weaknesses in the Bluetooth pairing process or vulnerabilities in older encryption protocols. Although Bluetooth's Frequency-Hopping Spread Spectrum (FHSS) can make these attacks more challenging, determined attackers may still find ways to synchronize with the target device's hopping sequence.

How Spoofing Attacks Exploit IoMT Vulnerabilities

Spoofing attacks in the IoMT usually exploit critical security vulnerabilities, targeting gaps in authentication, communication, and device configuration. These attacks enable adversaries to impersonate legitimate devices, users, or systems within healthcare networks, leading to compromised patient safety, data breaches, and operational disruptions. In this section, I'll explain how these vulnerabilities are commonly exploited.

Weak Authentication

One of the most significant vulnerabilities that spoofing attacks exploit is the reliance on weak or outdated authentication mechanisms by IoMT devices and healthcare systems. This happens for several reasons. For example, many IoMT devices are shipped with default credentials (e.g., username: "admin," password: "1234") that are rarely changed, providing attackers with easy access. In addition, some systems do not support or are not in line with MFA. These systems rely solely on passwords, which can be brute-forced, guessed, or stolen in phishing attacks. Some legacy devices lack any form of authentication, enabling attackers to connect directly and impersonate the device without credentials.

An example of exploitation is when an attacker spoofs a glucose monitor by connecting to the network using stolen credentials. Once connected, they could send falsified data to the healthcare system, causing clinicians to make incorrect decisions, such as administering unnecessary or harmful insulin doses.

Lack of Secure Communication Protocols

IoMT devices often use insecure or outdated communication protocols, leaving them vulnerable to data interception and manipulation. These weaknesses enable attackers to inject fake data or impersonate devices on the network. This occurs when there exists unencrypted communication. For example, some IoMT devices transmit data in plaintext or use deprecated encryption protocols like SSL or older versions of TLS, which can be easily intercepted and modified. Insufficient validation is another issue where devices may fail to validate the authenticity of incoming data packets, making them susceptible to data injection attacks. Also, consider what I explained in Chapter 6 about MITM attacks. Attackers intercept communications and insert themselves between a medical device and its control system, relaying and modifying data to impersonate the device.

As an example of exploitation, a spoofing attack on a cardiac monitor could involve an attacker injecting fake heart rate readings into the communication stream. Clinicians relying on this data might miss signs of cardiac distress, delaying critical interventions.

Insecure Device Pairing

IoMT devices often rely on pairing processes to establish secure communication. However, these processes are frequently implemented with weak security practices, leaving them vulnerable to spoofing attacks. These are three common causes of how this happens:

- **Default pairing credentials:** Devices often use factory-default PINs or passwords during pairing, which are easily guessable or available online.
- **Weak pairing protocols:** Some IoMT devices use outdated pairing protocols that lack proper encryption or authentication, making it easy for attackers to impersonate devices during the pairing process.
- **Broadcast discovery:** Devices in discoverable mode may respond to pairing requests indiscriminately, allowing attackers to initiate unauthorized connections.

As an example of exploitation, an attacker could spoof a telemetry device during the pairing process, gaining unauthorized access to sensitive patient data or sending false readings to the control system. For example, an infusion pump configured via insecure pairing could be manipulated to alter medication dosages.

Insufficient Device Hardening

IoMT devices are often designed with functionality as a priority, leading to insufficient security measures that attackers can exploit to carry out spoofing attacks. This can happen because some devices have hardcoded user credentials that cannot be changed, making them easy targets for spoofing.

There's also an issue with unused open ports. Some devices may have open communication ports that attackers can exploit to gain unauthorized access. Furthermore, I've seen legacy devices with firmware vulnerabilities in the field that allow attackers to modify device behavior and impersonate legitimate systems. For example, an attacker might exploit an open port on a ventilator to inject malicious commands, forcing the device to behave erratically or send false telemetry data to the central monitoring system.

Lack of Network Segmentation

Among this book's common themes is the lack of proper network segmentation in healthcare environments. Without segmentation, attackers can move laterally within the network, increasing the scope and impact of spoofing attacks. Without segmentation, all devices share the same network, allowing attackers who spoof one device to access others. Devices may also be configured to communicate with any system on the network, making it easier for spoofed devices to interact with critical systems.

A spoofed device, such as a mobile health monitoring app, could send falsified commands to other connected devices on the same network segment, disrupting multiple systems simultaneously.

Real-World Implications of Spoofing Attacks

Spoofing attacks targeting IoMT devices pose significant threats in healthcare environments, leading to potentially devastating outcomes. Falsified data or malicious commands can result in misdiagnoses, inappropriate treatments, or device malfunctions, jeopardizing patient health and lives. Data breaches are another serious consequence, with attackers impersonating legitimate devices to steal sensitive patient information.

Such incidents violate privacy laws and regulations, such as HIPAA, and can result in financial penalties and long-lasting reputational damage for healthcare organizations. Additionally, operational disruptions caused by spoofed devices can compromise the functionality of essential medical equipment, leading to unexpected system outages, treatment delays, and interruptions in critical patient care.

Mitigation Strategies for Spoofing Attacks in IoMT

Defending against spoofing attacks requires more than standard cybersecurity measures. It requires a multilayered approach that addresses vulnerabilities head-on. To bring this topic to life, I'll break down the key strategies for keeping these systems secure and provide some real-world examples.

I'll start with encryption, the first and most critical defense. Imagine a heart monitor transmitting a patient's vitals to a nurse's station. If that data isn't encrypted, an attacker could intercept it, alter the readings, or even inject false data, potentially leading to a misdiagnosis or harmful treatment. This is where AES-256 encryption and TLS 1.3 protocols come in. These technologies ensure that even if someone manages to capture the data, they won't be able to read or modify it. Hospitals should also implement Mutual TLS (mTLS), which requires both the device and the server to verify each other's identities before sharing information, like a secret handshake to confirm they're talking to the right partner. Implementing mutual authentication between devices and servers is crucial for preventing man-in-the-middle attacks and ensuring the integrity of communications.

Next up is authentication and access control. Think about an infusion pump administering medication to a patient. What if an attacker impersonated the pump to change the dosage? That's where MFA and certificate-based authentication step in. By requiring multiple verification forms, like a password and a digital certificate, devices can prove their identity before connecting to the network. For example, a hospital using PKI certificates ensures that only authorized devices can access the network, making it virtually impossible for attackers to spoof a device without the correct credentials.

Another essential layer of protection is timestamps and sequence numbering. Picture this: a telemetry monitor transmitting a patient's vitals every minute. An attacker captures and replays old data to trick the system into believing the patient is stable when their condition deteriorates. By embedding timestamps and sequence numbers into each data packet, the system can detect and reject any message that's out of order or too old, protecting patients from harmful delays or false alarms.

Next is secure device pairing. Pairing is how devices like glucose monitors or infusion pumps connect to mobile apps or servers. If this process isn't secure, attackers can intercept the pairing attempt and take control of the device. Using Elliptic Curve Diffie-Hellman (ECDH), as mentioned in Chapter 4, key exchanges and disabling factory-default PINs ensure that the pairing process is encrypted and resistant to tampering. For example, when a glucose monitor pairs securely with its app using encrypted credentials, it prevents attackers from hijacking the setup process and manipulating data.

Regular updates and patch management are other key defenses mentioned throughout this book. Outdated firmware is like unlocking the front door, inviting attackers to exploit known vulnerabilities. Hospitals should set up automated patch management systems to update devices without delays. Take this example after discovering a Bluetooth vulnerability. A hospital deployed a firmware update for its patient monitors, closing the security gap and preventing attackers from spoofing devices.

Network segmentation and isolation also play critical roles. Consider separating medical devices into locked rooms rather than leaving them all in one big open space. Virtual LANs prevent attackers from moving laterally across the network, limiting their ability to reach sensitive systems like electronic health records. Imagine infusion pumps isolated on a dedicated VLAN; an attacker who compromises one pump wouldn't be able to access patient databases or disrupt other devices.

Real-time monitoring is the next layer of defense. Hospitals can deploy IDS and AI-driven anomaly detection tools to catch unusual patterns before they escalate. For instance, an IDS might detect multiple failed connection attempts to a vital signs monitor, flagging them as potential spoofing attempts. These systems can then automatically quarantine the suspicious device, stopping the attack.

Finally, let's not forget the human element with training and awareness. Technology alone isn't enough. Healthcare staff need to know how to spot the signs of spoofing, like duplicate readings or devices behaving erratically. For example, a nurse noticing inconsistent vitals from a patient monitor can immediately report it to IT, allowing them to investigate and neutralize the threat. Regular training sessions and clear incident reporting protocols empower staff to act quickly and decisively in emergencies.

Key Takeaways of Replay and Spoofing Attacks in IoMT

This chapter explored the growing cybersecurity threats in the IoMT, focusing on replay and spoofing attacks. While IoMT has revolutionized healthcare through real-time monitoring and automated care, it also introduces significant security risks that can jeopardize patient safety and disrupt medical operations.

Replay attacks occur when malicious actors intercept and retransmit legitimate communications to deceive IoMT systems. This can have serious consequences, such as outdated insulin pump commands being replayed to administer incorrect doses or delayed identification of critical conditions due to manipulated patient vitals. Similarly, spoofing attacks involve an attacker impersonating trusted devices, systems, or users to gain unauthorized access or manipulate operations. Weak authentication and insecure communication channels enable these attacks, leading to falsified glucose readings, exfiltration of sensitive PHI, or disruptions in life-saving medical procedures.

Several vulnerabilities contribute to the success of these attacks, including weak authentication mechanisms, insecure communication protocols, flaws in device pairing, unsegmented networks, and outdated firmware. These weaknesses expose healthcare systems to risks such as compromised patient safety, manipulated medical data, operational downtime, and potential regulatory violations, which can result in severe financial and reputational consequences.

To mitigate these threats, healthcare organizations must implement robust security measures, including encrypting communications with AES-256 and TLS 1.3, enforcing multifactor authentication, deploying timestamps and nonces to prevent replay attacks, and securing device pairing with encrypted protocols. Regular software updates, network segmentation, and advanced monitoring systems can enhance security by detecting and responding to real-time anomalies. Additionally, staff training is crucial in recognizing irregular device behavior and reinforcing best practices for secure device management.

Real-world incidents underscore the urgency of these security concerns. Replay attacks on infusion pumps have led to dangerous overdoses, while spoofing attacks on cardiac monitors have injected false readings, misleading clinicians and delaying critical care. However, AI-driven monitoring and multilayered defense strategies have shown promise in detecting and mitigating such threats before they escalate.

Ultimately, securing IoMT devices requires a proactive, multifaceted approach integrating strong encryption, authentication, network protections, and continuous monitoring. Collaboration with vendors to ensure secure-by-design devices and timely updates is essential, as is fostering cybersecurity awareness among healthcare professionals. By prioritizing these measures, healthcare organizations can safeguard patient data, uphold regulatory compliance, and reinforce trust in the integrity of medical technology.

CHAPTER 8

Denial of Service in Wireless Medical Networks

Integrating wireless into critical healthcare systems introduces security challenges, one of the most disruptive being denial-of-service (DoS) attacks. These attacks target the availability of medical devices, communication networks, or services, rendering them inaccessible and potentially endangering patient health and safety.

A DoS attack involves overwhelming a system with traffic or resource requests, causing it to become slow, unresponsive, or completely unavailable. In wireless medical networks, these attacks can disrupt the normal functioning of medical devices, communication systems, and healthcare operations. They can sometimes prevent critical medical data from reaching healthcare providers, delay medical treatments, or compromise patient outcomes.

This chapter examines the details of DoS attacks in wireless medical networks, including their various forms, the vulnerabilities that enable them, the potential impacts on healthcare services, and strategies for mitigating the risks associated with this attack vector.

Understanding DoS Attacks

As mentioned, a DoS attack is a malicious attempt to disrupt the regular operation of a network, device, or service by overwhelming it with excessive traffic or exploiting vulnerabilities to render it inoperable. In wireless medical networks, which connect critical devices like pumps, patient monitors, and medical imaging systems, a DoS attack can have consequences that include system downtime, delayed patient care, and patient health compromises.

Wireless medical networks are vulnerable due to their reliance on real-time data transmission, constant connectivity, and the spread of IoMT devices. A DoS attack can disrupt these networks and prevent devices from communicating effectively, leading to delayed treatments, loss of critical monitoring data, and operational paralysis within healthcare facilities.

There are many types of DoS attacks, so I'll cover some of the most common types, and I'll try to correlate them in the context of healthcare, such as how they relate to the following:

- **Medical devices:** By overwhelming medical devices with traffic or requests, attackers can disrupt their regular operation and prevent them from transmitting data or receiving commands.
- **Wireless networks:** DoS attacks can also disrupt the wireless communication infrastructure, such as Wi-Fi or Bluetooth networks, preventing medical devices from communicating with healthcare systems or other devices.
- **Healthcare applications:** A DoS attack targeting cloud-based or on-premises healthcare applications can prevent providers from accessing patient records or other critical services.

Common Types of DoS Attacks, Targets, and Device Impact

The most common DoS attacks include flooding, jamming, battery draining, deauthentication, and amplification attacks. The following sections will discuss these topics in more detail:

Flooding Attacks

Flooding attacks are a significant cybersecurity threat that can overwhelm networks or devices by bombarding them with massive traffic volumes, rendering systems unresponsive. In wireless networks, attackers often exploit bandwidth and processing power limitations to disrupt communication and operations. Several techniques are commonly used in these attacks.

Before I describe these techniques, I'll define the protocols. Internet Control Message Protocol (ICMP) is a network layer protocol for error reporting and diagnostics in IP networks. It allows network devices like routers to communicate issues with data transmission, such as unreachable destinations or routing problems. It is used by tools like ping and traceroute for network troubleshooting. UDP is a core transport layer protocol in the Internet Protocol suite. It's a connectionless protocol that doesn't require a handshake before sending data, making it faster but less reliable than TCP. UDP is commonly used in applications where speed is critical and occasional data loss, such as live streaming, is acceptable. TCP is a standard transport layer protocol that ensures reliable, ordered, and error-checked data delivery between applications running on hosts communicating over an IP network. Unlike UDP, TCP is connection-oriented and uses a three-way handshake to establish a connection before data transfer. It's widely used for applications requiring guaranteed delivery, such as web browsing, email, and file transfers. SYN is a control bit in the TCP header that initiates a connection between two devices. It's part of the TCP three-way handshake process:

1. The client sends a SYN packet to the server.
2. The server responds with a SYN-ACK (Synchronize-Acknowledge) packet.
3. The client sends an ACK packet to complete the connection establishment.

SYN packets are crucial for synchronizing sequence numbers between devices and establishing TCP connections.

ICMP floods, or ping floods, involve sending excessive ICMP echo requests to exhaust network resources. UDP floods overwhelm devices by sending large volumes of UDP traffic. In contrast, SYN floods exploit the TCP handshake process by sending repeated SYN requests without completing the connection, tying up resources and leaving systems unable to respond to legitimate requests.

In healthcare environments, flooding attacks often target Wi-Fi access points that connect wireless medical devices, electronic health record servers that manage patient data, and medical telemetry systems for real-time monitoring. The impact of these attacks can be devastating. Devices may lose connection to the wireless network, delaying the transmission of critical data such as patient vitals. Network congestion caused by flooding can render essential equipment, including infusion pumps and heart monitors, unusable, posing life-threatening risks. Additionally, overwhelmed EHR systems may fail to retrieve or display patient records, resulting in diagnosis and care delivery delays. These vulnerabilities highlight the need for healthcare organizations to implement robust defenses, such as traffic filtering, rate-limiting controls, and network segmentation, to safeguard patient safety and operational continuity.

Jamming Attacks

Jamming attacks threaten healthcare environments by using radio frequency interference to disrupt wireless communication between devices and access points. Beyond disrupting communication, sophisticated jamming attacks could lead to data manipulation, causing incorrect clinical decisions. These attacks often target frequency ranges used by Wi-Fi, Bluetooth, or Zigbee-enabled medical devices, compromising their ability to transmit critical data. Attackers may employ various techniques to execute jamming. Constant jamming floods a frequency with continuous noise, effectively blocking legitimate signals. Reactive jamming activates only when legitimate signals are detected, making identifying the source of interference harder. Spot jamming focuses disruption on specific channels or devices, leaving other frequencies unaffected while isolating critical systems.

In healthcare settings, common targets include wireless medical devices like infusion pumps, insulin pumps, patient monitors, Bluetooth-connected wearables that transmit vitals to central monitoring systems, and Wi-Fi-enabled diagnostic tools such as portable ultrasound machines and imaging systems. The impact of jamming attacks can be severe. Critical devices may lose connectivity, interrupting the flow of patient data and halting treatments.

Delayed alarms from telemetry monitors could prevent timely medical interventions, risking patient safety. Furthermore, emergency response systems dependent on wireless communication may fail to activate during life-threatening situations. Given these risks, healthcare organizations must implement defenses such as frequency-hopping technologies, RF shielding, and continuous monitoring systems to detect and mitigate jamming attempts before they disrupt critical operations.

Battery Drain Attacks

Battery drain attacks threaten battery-powered IoMT devices by forcing them to execute unnecessary or repetitive tasks, rapidly depleting their energy reserves. Attackers may use techniques such as sending repeated connection requests, compelling devices to process constant authentication or data transmissions, or exploiting poorly configured systems to trigger frequent status updates and redundant operations. Typical targets include wearable health monitors like continuous glucose monitors, implantable devices such as pacemakers and insulin pumps, and portable diagnostic tools that rely on wireless communication. Battery drain attacks can target not just individual devices but entire networks of IoT nodes, potentially leading to synchronized depletion of multiple devices.

The impact of these attacks can be severe, as battery depletion may cause devices to shut down unexpectedly, compromising patient safety and delaying critical care. Usually these devices have mechanisms to alert a user, but in implantable devices, premature battery drain could necessitate invasive medical procedures for device replacements, adding further risk. Additionally, the failure of monitoring devices could prevent timely detection of life-threatening conditions, underscoring the need for robust security measures to protect against such attacks. Healthcare organizations must prioritize energy-efficient device configurations, implement security protocols to limit unauthorized access, and establish proactive monitoring systems to detect unusual activity before it jeopardizes patient care.

Deauthentication Attacks

Deauthentication attacks threaten Wi-Fi-connected medical devices by exploiting vulnerabilities in wireless networks. These attacks send forged deauthentication frames, tricking devices into disconnecting from their access points. Recall tools like Aircrack-ng, from Chapter 5, that are often used to send these malicious packets, effectively forcing devices offline repeatedly. The attack works by sending forged deauthentication frames, which do not require encryption, even when the session is established with WEP, WPA, or WPA2. This allows attackers to disconnect devices from their access points without needing to be authenticated on the network. It's worth noting that deauthentication attacks can also be used as a precursor to more severe attacks, such as the following:

- Capturing WPA/WPA2 4-way handshakes for password cracking
- Forcing users to connect to rogue access points (evil twin attacks)
- Setting up captive portals for phishing attempts

In healthcare settings, prime targets include patient monitors in ICUs that transmit real-time vitals, medical tablets used by clinicians to access electronic health records during rounds, and smart infusion pumps that depend on continuous connectivity to manage medication dosages. The impact of such attacks can be devastating. Disconnected devices may fail to report critical data, preventing timely interventions, and clinicians could lose access to patient records, delaying diagnoses and treatment.

Even more alarming, network disruptions may prevent life-saving alarms from triggering, leaving deteriorating patient conditions undetected. To safeguard against these risks, healthcare organizations must implement robust encryption protocols, enable network monitoring tools, and adopt strong authentication measures to prevent unauthorized access and ensure the reliability of Wi-Fi-connected medical systems.

Amplification Attacks

Amplification attacks are a significant threat to healthcare networks. They leverage spoofed requests to generate massive server responses and direct the flood of traffic toward targeted devices or systems. This overwhelming volume of data can quickly exhaust resources, causing systems to slow down or crash. Techniques like Domain Name System (DNS) amplification involve sending small DNS queries with a spoofed IP address to a server, which then responds with large packets to the victim. NTP amplification exploits the Network Time Protocol to produce similarly amplified responses.

Key targets in healthcare settings include electronic health record servers, cloud-based data platforms, and network infrastructure components such as routers and firewalls that manage wireless traffic. The impact of these attacks can be severe, such as critical systems that may experience downtime, halting workflows, and delaying access to vital patient data. Additionally, saturated wireless bandwidth can disrupt communication between life-saving devices, while staff may lose access to diagnostic tools and monitoring systems, putting patient safety at risk. To defend against these threats, healthcare organizations must deploy traffic filtering systems, implement rate-limiting measures, and regularly monitor network activity to detect and mitigate potential amplification attacks before they disrupt operations. Additionally, healthcare organizations should consider implementing distributed DoS (DDoS) mitigation solutions, blocking unnecessary ports, using web application firewalls, content delivery networks, and preparing contingency plans for critical assets. That said, let's talk more about DDoS in the next section.

Distributed Denial-of-Service Attacks

In a DDoS attack, multiple compromised devices (often part of a botnet) are used to launch a coordinated attack on the target system. These attacks are more potent than traditional DoS attacks because they leverage many devices, making mitigation harder. Note that between traditional DoS and DDoS attacks, the latter is more common and more complex to mitigate.

Impact of DoS Attacks on Healthcare Operations

The impact of DoS attacks on healthcare operations can be severe and far-reaching, potentially compromising the safety of patients, the integrity of data, operational efficiency, and regulatory compliance. These attacks can have immediate and life-threatening consequences in critical care settings where continuous connectivity is essential for patient monitoring and treatment.

DoS attacks disrupt the connectivity of vital medical devices such as ventilators, preventing the timely delivery of life-critical care. Medication errors could occur if an infusion pump cannot receive updated dosage instructions. Moreover, if emergency alarms and alerts fail to reach clinicians due to network disruptions, critical interventions may be delayed, potentially resulting in adverse patient outcomes.

Data loss and disruption present another challenge. Wireless devices that cannot transmit or receive data may corrupt patient records, compromising the continuity and quality of care. Diagnostic tools that rely on real-time wireless communication may produce inaccurate results due to data transmission failures, potentially leading to misdiagnosis or inappropriate treatment decisions.

Operational delays are also an inevitable consequence of DoS attacks in healthcare environments. When electronic systems are compromised, staff must revert to manual workflows, such as handwritten notes and physical charting. This slows down processes and increases the risk of human errors in documentation and communication. Downtime in critical systems like EHRs, medical imaging platforms, or remote patient monitoring tools can significantly delay treatment decisions, affecting patient care quality and outcomes.

The financial and regulatory consequences of DoS attacks can also be substantial. Extended disruptions can lead to significant economic losses due to canceled procedures, increased labor costs for manual processes, and expenses associated with system recovery and security enhancements. Furthermore, healthcare organizations may face regulatory penalties if the attack results in compromised patient data or noncompliance with regulations such as HIPAA or HITECH. The integrity of patient data and the ability to maintain continuous, secure operations are crucial for meeting these regulatory requirements.

Common Vulnerabilities That Enable DoS Attacks in Wireless Medical Networks

I'll explore key vulnerabilities that make wireless medical networks prone to DoS attacks and how these weaknesses can impact healthcare systems. As discussed from different perspectives in previous chapters, I'm reiterating much of this, but I'll focus on the DoS attack vector.

Insecure Wireless Communication Protocols

As discussed in Part I, many medical devices in healthcare environments rely on wireless communication protocols such as Wi-Fi, Bluetooth, Zigbee, and Near Field Communication to transmit patient data and facilitate seamless operations. While these protocols offer convenience and efficiency, they are often poorly configured or lack strong security measures, leaving them vulnerable to exploitation. Wi-Fi vulnerabilities, for instance, can stem from outdated encryption standards like older WEP or weaker implementations of WPA2, making them susceptible to tools like Aircrack-ng or Bettercap. In a DoS attack, attackers can inject massive traffic volumes to overwhelm access points, disrupting telemetry systems that transmit vital signs to nurse stations. Imagine a scenario where a jamming attack targets Wi-Fi-enabled telemetry monitors in an ICU, severing their connection to central monitoring systems and delaying alerts about a patient's deteriorating condition.

Similarly, Bluetooth and Zigbee weaknesses expose devices to risks like signal jamming and forced disconnections through repeated pairing requests. These low-power communication methods are commonly used in wearable medical devices and smart home health systems, making them attractive targets for attackers. For example, an attacker could exploit an insecure Bluetooth connection in a glucose monitor to disrupt its data transmissions, preventing real-time updates on a patient's blood sugar levels. Likewise, Zigbee-enabled insulin pumps may fall victim to RF jamming, halting dosage delivery and jeopardizing patient safety. These vulnerabilities highlight the need for strong encryption, secure pairing protocols, regular firmware updates, and real-time monitoring to safeguard wireless communications in medical environments.

Lack of Device Authentication and Authorization

Wireless medical devices often suffer from weak authentication and authorization mechanisms, leaving them vulnerable to exploitation. Weak credentials, such as default passwords or simple PINs, create opportunities for unauthorized access. Attackers can exploit these defaults to flood devices with repetitive or malicious connection requests, and with successful authentication, they can disconnect and repeat, overloading their systems and rendering them unresponsive. For example, an innovative infusion pump configured with factory default credentials could be overwhelmed with repeated pairing attempts, causing delays in medication delivery or interruptions in dosage adjustments, potentially endangering patient safety.

Additionally, the lack of mutual authentication, where devices fail to verify the identity of both communicating parties, opens the door for impersonation attacks. In such scenarios, attackers can mimic legitimate devices or access points to hijack connections, disrupt data flow, or reroute traffic. For instance, a spoofed Wi-Fi access point could deceive medical devices into connecting to a malicious network, allowing attackers to intercept data, block critical alerts, or even manipulate treatment commands. These vulnerabilities emphasize the need for stronger authentication protocols, unique device credentials, and encrypted communication to prevent unauthorized access and maintain the reliability of healthcare systems.

Limited Resource Capacity

Many medical devices, especially legacy systems and resource-constrained IoMT devices, operate with minimal processing power, bandwidth, and memory, making them highly vulnerable to resource exhaustion attacks. Resource overload can easily overwhelm these devices, where attackers flood them with high traffic volumes or repetitive connection requests, consuming their limited capacity and rendering them unresponsive. For instance, a portable patient monitor with restricted bandwidth could be targeted with a high-frequency packet flood, causing the device to crash and interrupt clinicians' real-time vital sign data transmission. Such delays could prevent timely interventions, posing serious risks to patient safety.

When inundated with malicious traffic, these devices often experience processing delays, slowing operations or forcing critical systems offline. Their constrained resources make them particularly susceptible to low-cost attacks, where even minimal efforts by attackers can result in significant disruptions. This highlights the urgent need for stronger security measures to protect resource-limited medical systems from malicious exploitation, including traffic filtering, network segmentation, and device hardening.

Legacy Systems and Outdated Software

The continued reliance on legacy medical systems and devices with outdated software or unpatched vulnerabilities poses serious security risks in healthcare environments. Older devices often lack modern security protocols or remain unpatched due to operational constraints, exposing them to known exploits that attackers can leverage to trigger system crashes or service interruptions. For example, an MRI machine running on an outdated operating system could be compromised through a buffer overflow attack, forcing it offline and delaying critical diagnostic imaging for patients needing urgent care. These systems are expensive to replace, so, understandably, they are in operation. However, extra vigilance should be employed in monitoring their security state, as they are susceptible to attack.

Devices no longer supported by vendors face even more significant vulnerabilities, as they cannot receive security updates to address emerging threats. In many cases, legacy systems are deeply integrated with modern infrastructure, serving as entry points for attackers to access broader network environments. This interconnectedness means that compromising a single outdated device, such as a patient monitoring system, could lead to network-wide disruptions, affecting electronic health records or diagnostic tools. These risks emphasize the need for security assessments, network segmentation, and upgrade plans to safeguard critical systems and patient data.

Overloaded Wireless Networks

Wireless networks in hospitals and healthcare facilities often operate under immense strain due to the high number of connected devices required for patient care. These networks must simultaneously support telemetry monitors that transmit real-time vital signs, infusion pumps that deliver precise medication doses, mobile EHR systems clinicians use during rounds, and wearable health devices that monitor patients remotely. When bandwidth is already stretched thin, DoS attacks can amplify network congestion, pushing systems to the brink of failure.

For instance, an attacker could flood the network with excessive traffic, overwhelm Wi-Fi access points in an ICU, and cause disruptions in telemetry monitoring systems. Such an attack could delay critical alarm notifications, leaving clinicians unaware of sudden patient condition changes. The impact can quickly cascade, as multiple devices lose connectivity simultaneously, resulting in system-wide failures that disrupt medication delivery, data access, and monitoring functions. These vulnerabilities highlight the need for network segmentation, traffic monitoring, and prioritized bandwidth allocation to ensure critical medical devices remain operational during high-traffic conditions.

More on the Impact of These Vulnerabilities

When a DoS attack targets wireless medical networks, the consequences can affect patient safety, clinical operations, and regulatory compliance. Patient safety is often the first casualty, as disconnected patient monitors may fail to report critical changes in heart rate, blood pressure, or oxygen levels, delaying life-saving interventions. Similarly, disruptions to infusion pumps or ventilators can halt medication delivery or respiratory support, putting lives at immediate risk.

Beyond safety, operational disruptions can cripple workflows. Clinicians may lose access to EHRs, delaying diagnoses and forcing staff to rely on manual processes, prone to errors, and slower response times. This strain impacts care delivery and increases workloads, leading to staff fatigue and reduced efficiency.

The damage doesn't stop there. Data loss and corruption caused by disconnected devices can compromise the integrity of patient records, leaving gaps in diagnostic histories or fragmented test results. Such failures jeopardize clinical decision-making and continuity of care, further escalating patient risks.

Finally, the regulatory and financial impact can be severe. If a hospital's systems fail to protect sensitive patient data or remain unavailable for extended periods, it may violate HIPAA regulations, resulting in legal penalties and reputational damage. Additionally, hospitals may face significant financial losses due to system recovery costs, downtime, and potential litigation.

Mitigation Strategies for Denial of Service Attacks

Within this book, I repeat many mitigation strategies that correlate with mitigating different types of risks. In this section, I'll explain how healthcare professionals and IT teams can implement measures to prevent DoS attacks in wireless networks.

Implement Strong Network Segmentation and Isolation

Network segmentation limits the blast radius of a DoS attack, preventing it from affecting the entire hospital network. By isolating medical devices, administrative systems and guest networks, healthcare organizations can ensure critical systems remain unaffected during an attack.

- **Virtual LANs (VLANs):** Create dedicated VLANs for medical devices, patient monitoring systems, administrative computers, and guest Wi-Fi networks. Medical devices (e.g., infusion pumps, ventilators, and telemetry monitors) should be isolated on a secure VLAN. For example, a DoS attack targeting guest Wi-Fi would not impact life-critical systems like ICU monitors on a separate VLAN.

- **Access control lists:** Use ACLs to limit communication between segments, allowing only necessary and authorized data flows. ACLs ensure medical devices communicate solely with designated servers and systems.

- **Zero Trust network architecture:** Implement a least privilege approach where every device, user, and system must authenticate before accessing the network. Continuously verify permissions to ensure no unauthorized traffic is introduced. This goes beyond just authentication, including continuous monitoring and verification of all network activities. No user, system, or process is trusted to connect to any device, system, or application, regardless of whose system it is, or where it is on the network. I'll get into Zero Trust later in Chapters 14 and 16.

Deploy Intrusion Detection and Prevention Systems

Intrusion detection and prevention systems (IDSs/IPSs) are critical in identifying and mitigating suspicious activity before they cause network disruption. These systems are network security measures designed to monitor, detect, and respond to potential threats and unauthorized activities in a network. An IDS is a passive system that monitors network traffic and alerts administrators when it detects suspicious activity or security policy violations. It does not take direct action to prevent attacks but provides valuable information for further investigation. An IPS, on the other hand, is an active system that detects potential threats and automatically takes action to prevent them. It can block malicious traffic, terminate dangerous connections, or trigger other security devices to protect the network. The main difference between IDSs and IPSs is their response to detected threats. An IDS focuses on detection and alerting while IPS combines detection with active prevention measures. Both systems use various detection methods, including signature-based, anomaly-based, and stateful protocol analysis, to identify potential security incidents. They are crucial in maintaining network security and can be deployed as stand-alone solutions or integrated into next-generation firewalls and other security tools.

Consider these:

- **Real-time monitoring:** Deploy an IDS/IPS to monitor network traffic for anomalies, such as unexpected spikes in requests or unusual packet flows. These systems can detect signature-based attacks (known threats) and behavior anomalies, flagging potential DoS activity in real time.
- **Automated mitigation:** IPS solutions automatically block malicious IP addresses, rate-limit traffic, or isolate compromised devices during an active attack.
- **AI-driven threat detection:** Integrate AI-powered tools to identify patterns indicative of slow-drip or volumetric DoS attacks. These systems use machine learning to adapt to emerging threats.

For example, tools like Cisco Firepower, Palo Alto Threat Prevention, and Check Point IPS can monitor medical network traffic and block malicious activities.

Prioritize Strong Device Authentication and Authorization

Devices and systems that rely on weak or no authentication are vulnerable to DoS attacks. Strengthening authentication mechanisms ensures that only legitimate devices can access the network. Consider implementing these:

- **Mutual authentication:** Use certificate-based authentication or Public Key Infrastructure (PKI) to verify devices and servers before allowing communication. Devices must validate their identity to the central system, reducing the risks of rogue device attacks.
- **Secure device pairing:** To prevent unauthorized devices from connecting, implement secure pairing protocols, such as Elliptic Curve Diffie-Hellman, for Bluetooth or Wi-Fi devices.
- **Multifactor authentication:** Enforce MFA for access to networked systems and administrative consoles to prevent unauthorized logins that could facilitate DoS attempts.
- **Device whitelisting:** Maintain a whitelist of authorized devices permitted to connect to the network, blocking unapproved endpoints.

Upgrade to Resilient Wireless Infrastructure

Modern wireless infrastructure solutions can help healthcare organizations build a network capable of withstanding DoS attacks, such as the following:

- **WPA3 Security for Wi-Fi:** Upgrade to WPA3 encryption, which includes protections against brute-force attacks and improves resilience to network-based DoS attempts.
- **Bandwidth management:** Use quality of service (QoS) policies to prioritize critical traffic, such as telemetry data, over less essential services like guest Wi-Fi. Quality of service ensures that life-critical data, like patient vitals, flow uninterrupted even during a DoS attempt.
- **Redundant access points and failover systems:** Deploy multiple Wi-Fi access points and implement failover mechanisms to minimize disruptions during an attack. Load-balancing capabilities can help evenly distribute traffic, reducing the impact on any single access point.

Monitor for Anomalies and Implement Rate Limiting

Continuous monitoring and traffic control mechanisms can help reduce the risk of resource exhaustion or flooding attacks. These features are essential to consider:

- **Anomaly detection:** Use network monitoring tools to identify abnormal spikes in traffic, unusual data patterns, or repeated connection requests. Automated alerts allow IT teams to respond to potential attacks in real time.
- **Rate limiting:** Network devices can be configured to restrict the requests a system or endpoint can handle within a specific time frame. This prevents attackers from overwhelming devices or servers with excessive requests.
- **Firewall protections:** Use next-generation firewalls (NGFWs) to detect and block traffic that exhibits DoS-like behavior (e.g., SYN floods or UDP amplification).

Consider DDoS Protection Services

Distributed DoS attacks threaten healthcare environments, where cloud-based platforms, telehealth services, and large-scale medical applications are essential for seamless patient care. Unlike traditional DoS attacks that originate from a single source, DDoS attacks use multiple compromised devices (as mentioned often part of a botnet) to launch a coordinated flood of traffic, overwhelming systems, networks, or applications. Due to their scale and distributed nature, these attacks are more complex, harder to detect, and significantly more challenging to mitigate.

Adopting DDoS protection services is a critical defense strategy for healthcare organizations that depend on uninterrupted access to essential systems and real-time patient data. These services, offered by providers like Cloudflare, AWS

Shield, Microsoft Azure DDoS Protection, and Akamai Prolexic, are designed to absorb, mitigate, and neutralize large-scale attacks before they disrupt operations.

DDoS protection services are a crucial shield between external traffic sources and an organization's critical infrastructure. This is particularly true in healthcare settings, where uninterrupted operations are vital. These services operate at multiple levels, employing advanced techniques to detect and mitigate malicious traffic before it can disrupt essential functions.

One key aspect of DDoS protection is traffic analysis and threat detection. These services continuously monitor incoming traffic patterns to identify anomalies that may indicate a DDoS attack. By utilizing machine learning algorithms and signature-based detection, they can differentiate between legitimate and malicious traffic in real time. For instance, a sudden surge of traffic from multiple IP addresses across different geographic regions could signal a potential attack.

When an attack is detected, traffic scrubbing and filtering mechanisms come into play. Malicious traffic is rerouted to scrubbing centers operated by the DDoS protection provider, where it undergoes thorough analysis and filtering. Techniques such as rate limiting, IP blacklisting, and anomaly-based filtering help ensure that only legitimate requests reach the healthcare network or application.

To counteract large-scale attacks, DDoS protection services rely on their global infrastructure and vast bandwidth capacity to absorb attack traffic. By distributing traffic across geographically dispersed networks, these services prevent any single point of failure. Industry-leading solutions like AWS Shield and Cloudflare can handle terabit-scale DDoS attacks without impacting the targeted system.

Automation plays a significant role in ensuring seamless mitigation. DDoS protection tools can automatically neutralize attacks as they occur, minimizing latency and service disruptions. Simultaneously, they generate real-time alerts for IT and security teams, offering visibility into the scope and impact of the attack. Automation eliminates manual intervention, which is critical in time-sensitive healthcare environments.

Moreover, organizations can enhance their security posture by implementing custom rules and application protection tailored to their needs. Many DDoS protection services offer web application firewalls (WAFs) to secure cloud-based healthcare applications, DNS protection, and API rate limiting. For example, Azure DDoS Protection integrates seamlessly with Microsoft Azure-hosted healthcare systems, ensuring robust application-layer security.

By leveraging these comprehensive protection mechanisms, healthcare organizations can safeguard their critical infrastructure against DDoS attacks and ensure their services' continued availability and reliability.

Healthcare systems are particularly vulnerable to DDoS attacks due to their dependence on uninterrupted network availability and real-time communication. Ensuring continuous access to critical systems is essential, as platforms such as Electronic Health Records (EHR), telehealth applications, and remote patient monitoring must remain accessible at all times. A successful DDoS attack can block access to these crucial systems, delaying diagnoses, interrupting treatments, and endangering patient safety. Additionally, many healthcare organizations rely on cloud-based services to store patient data, run applications, and facilitate telehealth services. Implementing DDoS protection solutions, such as AWS Shield or Azure DDoS Protection, safeguards these cloud environments against volumetric attacks that could disrupt access to vital patient data.

Another significant risk posed by DDoS attacks is operational downtime, as they can paralyze hospital networks, disrupt communications, and force healthcare staff to revert to manual workflows. Automated DDoS mitigation ensures hospital operations remain uninterrupted, even during an attack. Furthermore, healthcare organizations must comply with stringent regulations such as HIPAA and HITECH, which require the protection of patient data. Downtime caused by DDoS attacks can lead to data loss or corruption, resulting in noncompliance and potential legal consequences. Implementing DDoS protection helps maintain data integrity and ensures adherence to regulatory standards.

Beyond compliance, healthcare organizations must also consider the financial and reputational damage associated with DDoS attacks. These attacks can lead to substantial economic losses due to operational delays, incident response costs, and potential legal penalties. Additionally, repeated or successful attacks can erode trust among patients and stakeholders, negatively impacting a healthcare provider's reputation. The evolving nature of cyber threats further underscores the need for strong DDoS defenses, as modern attacks use sophisticated techniques like low-and-slow and multivector attacks that target multiple network layers simultaneously. Scalable DDoS protection services provide adaptive defenses capable of mitigating these evolving threats, ensuring the resilience of healthcare systems against cyber disruptions.

Several industry-leading DDoS protection providers offer solutions tailored to the needs of healthcare organizations. Examples include the following:

- **Cloudflare:** Offers DDoS protection, global traffic scrubbing, and a Web Application Firewall (WAF) to secure web-based healthcare platforms.
- **AWS Shield:** Provides scalable protection for healthcare applications hosted in Amazon Web Services. AWS Shield Advanced offers real-time threat detection, mitigation, and support.
- **Microsoft Azure DDoS Protection:** Integrates seamlessly with Azure-hosted healthcare applications and IoMT platforms, offering comprehensive infrastructure protection.
- **Akamai Prolexic:** Delivers enterprise-grade DDoS protection with global scrubbing centers and advanced mitigation tools.

By leveraging DDoS protection services, healthcare organizations can accomplish the following:

- **Ensure uptime:** Maintain continuous access to critical medical systems, EHRs, and patient monitoring tools.
- **Safeguard patient care:** Prevent disruptions that delay diagnoses, treatments, or emergency interventions.

- **Enhance scalability:** Absorb large-scale attacks without compromising system performance.
- **Achieve regulatory compliance:** Protect data integrity and availability in line with HIPAA and other healthcare regulations.
- **Mitigate financial losses:** Reduce recovery costs and avoid revenue loss caused by operational downtime.
- **Protect reputation:** Demonstrate a strong commitment to cybersecurity, fostering trust among patients and stakeholders.

The consequences of a DDoS attack can be devastating for healthcare organizations, affecting patient care, operational efficiency, and regulatory compliance. Implementing DDoS protection services ensures critical systems remain resilient against large-scale attacks, allowing uninterrupted access to life-saving devices, cloud-based applications, and patient data. Healthcare organizations can proactively defend against evolving threats, safeguard network availability, and protect patient safety by partnering with providers like Cloudflare, AWS Shield, or Microsoft Azure.

Comparison Between DoS and DDoS Attacks in Healthcare

Cyberattacks involving DoS and DDoS targeting healthcare institutions can have severe consequences, including system downtime, delayed patient care, and compromised sensitive data. Table 8-1 compares these two attack types in the healthcare sector.

Table 8-1: DoS vs. DDoS

ASPECT	DOS ATTACK	DDOS ATTACK
Definition	A cyberattack that aims to overwhelm a healthcare system, server, or network with excessive traffic from a single source, making it unavailable to users	A large-scale attack where multiple compromised devices (botnets) flood a healthcare system, server, or network with traffic, making it inaccessible
Attack Source	Single system or attacker	Multiple systems (botnet) controlled by an attacker
Scale & Impact	Localized impact, usually affecting a single system or service	Larger-scale impact, capable of taking down entire hospital networks or telemedicine services
Speed of Attack	Slower, easier to detect and mitigate	Rapid, overwhelming, and harder to counter
Techniques Used	SYN floods, Ping of Death, UDP floods	Botnets, amplification attacks, DNS reflection

ASPECT	DOS ATTACK	DDOS ATTACK
Detection & Prevention	Easier to detect as it originates from a single source; firewalls and rate limiting can help mitigate the attack	More difficult to detect due to multiple attacking sources, requires advanced security solutions like intrusion prevention systems (IPS) and traffic filtering
Impact on Healthcare	Disrupts access to medical records and patient portals, affects appointment scheduling, can be a precursor to data theft	Can cripple entire hospital IT infrastructure, disrupts real-time monitoring devices, prevents access to electronic health records (EHRs) and emergency communication systems
Mitigation Strategies	Firewalls and network monitoring tools, limiting request rates, blocking suspicious IPs	Implementing DDoS protection services (e.g., cloud-based filtering), traffic analysis and anomaly detection, load balancing and redundancy measures

Both DoS and DDoS attacks pose serious threats to healthcare organizations, but DDoS attacks are generally more destructive due to their scale and difficulty in mitigation. Proactive security measures, including robust firewall configurations, network monitoring, and specialized DDoS protection services, are essential to safeguard healthcare networks against these threats.

Ensure Regular Updates and Patch Management

As mentioned, unpatched vulnerabilities are often exploited in DoS attacks, especially legacy medical devices. A patch management strategy ensures systems remain secure and resilient. Consider these:

- **Firmware updates:** Regularly update the firmware of wireless medical devices to address known security vulnerabilities. Partner with vendors to ensure timely updates and patches are applied to all IoMT systems.
- **Software hardening:** Ensure all network equipment (e.g., routers, firewalls, servers) runs the latest security patches.
- **Legacy device mitigation:** Where updates are unavailable for legacy devices, isolate them on dedicated network segments with restricted communication.

Conduct Security Training and Awareness Programs

Healthcare staff can play a crucial role in preventing and mitigating DoS attacks. Proper training equips teams to recognize and respond to unusual activity. Training should help staff to:

- **Recognize symptoms of DoS attacks:** Train staff to identify signs of network disruption, such as devices disconnecting, unresponsive systems, or slow network performance.
- **Report protocols:** Establish clear protocols for staff to report suspicious device behavior or connectivity issues to IT teams.
- **Secure device usage:** Educate staff on securing medical devices, updating passwords, and avoiding unauthorized connections.

Perform Regular Network Audits and Penetration Testing

Proactive testing ensures that vulnerabilities are identified and addressed before attackers can exploit them, including the following:

- **Regular network audits:** Assess the performance and security of wireless networks to identify potential weaknesses. They also monitor bandwidth usage to ensure sufficient capacity to handle peak loads.
- **Penetration testing:** Conduct simulated DoS attacks to evaluate the network's resilience and identify weak points in medical systems or infrastructure.
- **Incident response drills:** Practice incident response plans for DoS scenarios to ensure IT teams and healthcare professionals can respond quickly and effectively. These should include tabletop exercises that address how operations can continue with paper-recorded and documented processes when critical systems are disabled.

Preventing DoS attacks in healthcare wireless networks requires an approach that combines robust infrastructure, proactive monitoring, and continuous education. Most importantly, healthcare professionals must understand that protecting wireless networks is more than just IT security, it's about safeguarding patient lives, ensuring uninterrupted access to critical systems, and maintaining trust in modern healthcare technologies. By staying vigilant, investing in secure systems, and fostering collaboration across clinical and IT teams, healthcare providers can ensure their networks remain reliable, secure, and resilient against DoS threats.

Key Takeaways from DoS in Wireless Medical Networks

In this chapter, I explored DoS attacks, particularly the DDoS variant, and the strategies for mitigating these threats in healthcare environments. A DoS attack is a malicious attempt to disrupt a system, network, or device by overwhelming it with excessive traffic or exploiting vulnerabilities, which can severely impact wireless medical networks by preventing critical medical devices from functioning properly. Attackers often target medical devices like infusion pumps and patient monitors, wireless communication networks, and essential healthcare applications such as electronic health records and telehealth platforms. The consequences of these attacks include delayed medical treatments, data loss, and potential patient safety risks.

Common types of DoS attacks include flooding attacks that overload networks, jamming attacks that interfere with wireless communication, battery drain attacks that force IoMT devices to consume excessive power, deauthentication attacks that disconnect wireless medical devices, and amplification attacks that exploit network vulnerabilities to generate overwhelming traffic. A particularly severe form, DDoS attacks, involves coordinated disruptions from multiple compromised devices, making mitigation more challenging. These attacks are enabled by vulnerabilities such as insecure wireless communication protocols, weak device authentication, limited resource capacity in IoMT devices, outdated software, and overloaded networks.

The impact of DoS attacks on healthcare operations is significant, posing direct risks to patient safety by disrupting life-critical devices such as ventilators and infusion pumps. They also cause operational disruptions by forcing staff to rely on manual workflows, increasing the likelihood of data corruption, leading to financial and regulatory consequences, and creating cascading failures affecting multiple systems simultaneously.

To prevent DoS attacks, healthcare providers should implement network segmentation and isolation through VLANs and Zero Trust Architecture, deploy intrusion detection and prevention systems, and enforce strong authentication mechanisms like mutual certificate-based and multifactor authentication. Upgrading wireless infrastructure with WPA3 encryption, ensuring redundant access points, monitoring for anomalies, and enforcing rate limiting are also crucial steps. Regular updates and patch management help address known vulnerabilities, while security training programs enable staff to recognize attack symptoms. Performing network audits and penetration testing ensures proactive defense against evolving threats.

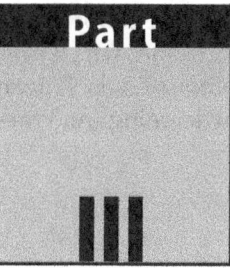

Part III

Case Studies and Real-World Scenarios

In various lunch-and-learns, events, and certification training I've led, my students have always said that the theoretical knowledge I presented is essential and helpful. Still, the real-world examples drive the point home. In Part III, I bridge the gap between concepts and reality by exploring case studies and security incidents that made the news that targeted the healthcare industry. Each chapter highlights specific vulnerabilities in medical devices and healthcare networks, demonstrating the tangible impact of cybersecurity breaches on patient safety, institutional operations, and trust.

These examples underscore the high stakes of protecting modern healthcare systems, from life-saving devices like pacemakers and insulin pumps to hospital-wide IoMT networks and wearable health technologies. By examining real-world attacks, exploits, and their consequences, we gain a clearer understanding of the risks and lessons learned, reinforcing why cybersecurity is not just an IT concern but a critical element of patient care. I'll follow up with mitigation solutions and prevention strategies in later chapters.

Chapter 9 uncovers how vulnerabilities in life-sustaining devices can be exploited and the consequences for patient safety. Chapter 10 explores insulin pump vulnerabilities and exploits weaknesses in these widely used devices, highlighting their potential misuse. Chapter 11 showcases how interconnected medical systems can be gateways for more widespread cyberattacks. Finally, Chapter 12 addresses consumer-driven wearable healthcare technology's growing risks and implications.

These chapters illustrate the critical need for greater security in healthcare environments, where every connected device represents innovation and risk. Healthcare professionals, IT teams, and policymakers can better prepare for emerging threats by learning from these real-world scenarios.

CHAPTER 9

Pacemaker Hacking

Pacemakers, one of the most critical and widely used medical implants, have become a target for cybercriminals due to their wireless connectivity and the increasing amount of data they exchange. The risks associated with pacemaker hacking are not just hypothetical but have been demonstrated through research, simulations, and security breaches.

Pacemakers are life-sustaining devices implanted in patients to regulate their heart rhythm, typically for those with arrhythmias or other cardiac conditions. They work by delivering electrical impulses to the heart when necessary. However, pacemakers have become increasingly connected to wireless networks for monitoring, adjustments, and troubleshooting, making them vulnerable to hacking. Malicious attackers can exploit vulnerabilities to cause harm by tampering with the device's settings or breaching patient data.

This chapter examines pacemakers' key vulnerabilities, presents some case studies, and explores the potential consequences of pacemaker hacking. I'll also discuss the efforts made to secure these devices, the challenges healthcare providers face, and possible solutions to ensure the safety and integrity of patients' lives.

Understanding Pacemaker Technology and Its Risks and Limitations

A pacemaker is a small, implantable medical device that regulates the heart's rhythm when it beats irregularly or too slowly (a condition called *bradycardia*). It acts as an electrical conductor for the heart, ensuring it beats at the correct pace to deliver sufficient blood and oxygen to the body. For many patients, especially those with heart rhythm disorders like arrhythmias, heart block, or sinus node dysfunction, a pacemaker is a life-saving device that restores normal heart function and allows them to live a healthier, more active life.

How Does the Heart Normally Function?

To understand the role of a pacemaker, it's essential first to grasp the basics of how the heart functions. A sophisticated system of electrical signals orchestrates the heart's pumping action. These signals originate in the sinoatrial (SA) node, often referred to as the heart's natural pacemaker, which is situated in the right atrium. From there, electrical impulses spread throughout the heart, dictating when the heart muscle should contract. However, if the SA node becomes damaged, blocked, or malfunctions, it can lead to irregular heart rhythms—either too slow, fast, or erratic. In such cases, an artificial pacemaker becomes crucial, stepping in to restore the proper timing and rhythm of the heart's contractions, effectively taking over the role of the compromised natural pacemaker.

What Is a Pacemaker?

A pacemaker is a compact, battery-powered device designed to monitor the heart's electrical activity and provide electrical stimulation if and when needed. It ensures the heart beats at a healthy rate. Pacemakers are primarily used to treat the following:

- Bradycardia, which is a slow heart rate
- Heart block when electrical signals are delayed or altogether blocked
- Arrhythmias, which are irregular heart rhythms

Modern pacemakers are highly advanced, programmable devices, with built-in sensors and communication systems. While pacemakers can help with some irregular heart rhythms, it's important to note that they are primarily designed for bradyarrhythmia (slow heart rhythms). For tachyarrhythmias (fast heart rhythms), other devices like implantable cardioverter-defibrillators (ICDs) may be more appropriate.

Components of a Pacemaker

Pacemakers are made up of two primary components: the pulse generator and leads (the wires, as shown in Figure 9-1). The pulse generator, often referred to by experts as the brain of the pacemaker, houses the battery and electronic circuitry responsible for producing electrical impulses that regulate the heart's rhythm. The battery typically lasts between 5 to 10 years before requiring replacement. The leads are thin, insulated wires that connect the pulse generator to the heart. These wires transmit electrical impulses to stimulate the heart and relay feedback data about the heart's activity to the generator.

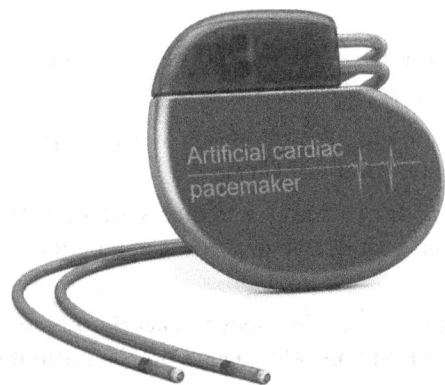

Figure 9-1: Example pacemaker
Source: Alexlmx/Adobe Stock Photos

Depending on the patient's condition, pacemakers may use different configurations of leads. A single-chamber pacemaker stimulates the right atrium or right ventricle, while a dual-chamber pacemaker coordinates stimulation between both chambers to maintain proper timing. For patients with heart failure, a biventricular pacemaker stimulates both ventricles, improving the heart's pumping efficiency. Advancements in technology have also introduced leadless pacemakers, which are entirely self-contained and implanted directly into the heart. These designs eliminate wires, reducing potential complications associated with traditional leads and offering a more minimally invasive solution.

How a Pacemaker Works

A pacemaker continuously monitors the heart's electrical activity in real time. When it detects that the heart rate is too slow or irregular, it delivers a small electrical impulse to stimulate the heart muscle, triggering a heartbeat and maintaining a steady, more appropriate rhythm. Modern pacemakers have different pacing modes to suit individual patients' needs. In Demand Mode, the pacemaker activates only when the heart rate drops below a predefined threshold, providing support only when necessary. In contrast, Rate-Responsive Mode adjusts the pacing rate based on physical activity, breathing patterns, or body temperature, ensuring the heart keeps up with the body's demands during exercise or rest.

These electrical impulses are low-energy, so most patients do not feel them. Still, they are precisely calibrated to be strong enough to sustain a normal heart rhythm without causing discomfort. Pacemakers can help extend people's lives. For example, my best childhood friend has had one (well, a few) since he was very young and still enjoys the benefits of an active lifestyle today.

Pacemakers have evolved dramatically over the years, with advancements in technology improving their efficiency, functionality, and safety. Key features of modern pacemakers include the following:

- **Dual-chamber pacing:** The pacemaker can coordinate timing between all four heart chambers, enhancing overall cardiac function.
- **Miniaturization:** Devices are now smaller, lighter, and easier to implant. Leadless pacemakers are an example of this innovation.
- **Programmability:** Doctors can program the pacemaker to meet each patient's needs. Adjustments to pacing thresholds, sensing levels, and pacing intervals can be done wirelessly.
- **Rate responsiveness:** Pacemakers now use motion sensors, accelerometers, and even respiratory sensors to adjust pacing rates based on the patient's activity level.
- **Remote monitoring:** Modern pacemakers can communicate wirelessly with external monitors or smartphones, allowing healthcare providers to remotely track heart function, battery life, and device performance.
- **Longer battery life:** Lithium-ion batteries are used for reliability and extended life, minimizing the need for frequent replacements.

How Is a Pacemaker Implanted?

A pacemaker implantation is typically a minimally invasive procedure performed under local anesthesia. The steps include the following:

- A small incision is made near the collarbone (usually on the left side).
- Leads are threaded through a vein into the heart under X-ray guidance.
- The pulse generator is placed under the skin in a small "pocket" created during the incision.
- The device is tested and programmed before closing the incision.

The entire late procedure generally takes one to two hours, and patients are often discharged the same day or within 24 hours.

Risks and Limitations

While pacemakers are life-saving devices, they come with risks and considerations that require careful attention. Although rare, device malfunctions can occur due to battery depletion, lead fractures, or software issues, potentially impacting performance. Electromagnetic interference (EMI) from equipment such as MRI machines or industrial devices may temporarily disrupt pacemaker function, necessitating precautions in specific environments.

Additionally, cybersecurity concerns have emerged with modern, connected pacemakers, raising the risk of unauthorized access or hacking. The surgical implantation process also carries risks, including infection, bleeding, or lead displacement, which may require further intervention. Recognizing these limitations is essential for patients, caregivers, and healthcare providers to ensure proper monitoring, maintenance, and device safety over time.

Pacemakers and Patient Quality of Life

Pacemakers play a vital role in improving the quality of life for patients with heart rhythm disorders by restoring normal heart function and alleviating debilitating symptoms. They help patients regain energy and reduce fatigue by maintaining a stable heart rate, allowing the body to receive adequate blood flow and oxygen. By preventing slow or irregular heartbeats, pacemakers significantly reduce symptoms such as dizziness, fainting, and shortness of breath, enhancing overall heart performance. This has greatly benefited my friend.

Modern rate-responsive pacemakers further support an active lifestyle, enabling patients to participate in daily activities, exercise safely, and travel without significant restrictions. As remarkable advancements in medical engineering, pacemakers have revolutionized cardiac care, allowing patients longer, healthier lives. For healthcare professionals, a comprehensive understanding of pacemaker technology, functionality, and risks is essential to delivering effective care, educating patients, and ensuring proper device management.

As technology advances, pacemaker innovations, such as leadless designs, AI-powered monitoring, and enhanced cybersecurity, will further improve patient outcomes and safety. Staying informed about these developments ensures that healthcare professionals are equipped to meet the evolving needs of patients relying on this life-saving technology.

In the following sections, I'll walk through the cybersecurity challenges associated with pacemakers, including cases of pacemaker hacking and the steps needed to protect this vital technology.

Understanding Vulnerabilities in Pacemakers in Today's Connected World

This section will explore pacemakers' critical vulnerabilities and the urgent need for healthcare professionals to understand and address these challenges.

Before diving into vulnerabilities, it's crucial to understand how wireless technology has changed pacemakers and enhanced patient care. Remote monitoring allows doctors to track a patient's pacemaker performance, battery status, and heart rhythm without requiring frequent in-person visits, improving convenience and early detection of issues. Wireless programming enables healthcare providers to adjust pacemaker settings non-invasively using external devices, reducing the need for surgical interventions. Modern pacemakers also leverage Bluetooth, radio frequencies, and near-field communication to seamlessly connect with smartphones, wearables, and monitoring stations, offering patients greater accessibility and control over their cardiac health.

However, while these advancements have streamlined care, they have also introduced new attack surfaces that make pacemakers vulnerable to wireless security threats and cyberattacks, raising critical concerns about patient safety and data integrity. I'll dive into the specific vulnerabilities that impact pacemakers and associated systems, including the following:

Insecure Wireless Communication Many older pacemakers transmit data wirelessly using outdated or unencrypted communication protocols. These protocols may include basic RF transmissions, Bluetooth, or proprietary formats. If the communication is unencrypted, attackers can eavesdrop on the signals exchanged between the pacemaker and its external programmer or monitor. Attackers can intercept sensitive data, such as the device ID, heart rate settings, or patient health information. More critically, they may alter communication signals, causing the pacemaker to misbehave (e.g., change the pacing rate or turn off alarms).

Cybersecurity researchers have recently demonstrated how basic radio equipment could intercept and manipulate unencrypted RF communications in older pacemakers. An attacker intercepting communication could slow the heart rate, deliver unnecessary shocks, or drain the pacemaker's battery.

Weak Authentication Mechanisms Weak authentication refers to insufficient measures to verify the identity of external devices communicating with the pacemaker. Some pacemakers lack two-factor authentication or use hard-coded, unchangeable credentials. Without proper authentication, attackers can impersonate legitimate devices (e.g., a programmer or monitoring tool) to send malicious commands. The lack of encrypted keys allows unauthorized access to device settings.

A study, for example, revealed that some pacemaker programming devices used default PINs or passwords that cannot be changed, allowing unauthorized users to gain control over the device. If an attacker gains control, they can modify pacing thresholds, deliver incorrect shocks, or turn off the pacemaker entirely.

Lack of Security Patches and Updates Many pacemakers, especially older models, do not receive regular software or firmware updates to fix vulnerabilities. Unlike consumer electronics, medical devices are often difficult to update due to regulatory processes or fear of disrupting functionality. Vulnerabilities identified publicly can remain unpatched for years, leaving devices exposed to known exploits. Attackers can exploit these flaws to gain unauthorized access or disrupt device functionality.

In 2017, the FDA recalled nearly 500,000 pacemakers due to a vulnerability that allowed attackers to tamper with the device remotely. The fix required a firmware update, but many patients faced challenges patching their devices. Unpatched vulnerabilities leave pacemakers open to hacking, potentially leading to life-threatening consequences.

Physical Access to Devices While most pacemaker vulnerabilities involve remote access, physical access to the devices or their external programmers introduces another attack vector. If attackers gain physical access to a healthcare setting (e.g., a hospital or clinic), they could manipulate or reprogram pacemakers using legitimate tools. Even patients who access their devices for personal monitoring may unknowingly expose them to tampering.

If hospital programming equipment is compromised, an attacker could reconfigure multiple devices. For instance, malicious actors accessing programming consoles could turn off alarms or modify pacing rates. Hospitals with poor physical security protocols, for example, may allow unauthorized individuals to access sensitive medical equipment or tools.

Lack of Intrusion Detection or Prevention Systems (IDS/IPS) Pacemakers and their monitoring systems often lack advanced tools to detect unauthorized access or abnormal behavior. Without intrusion detection, healthcare providers cannot identify hacking attempts early. Abnormal device behavior, such as a sudden battery drain or erratic pacing rates, may go unnoticed until it impacts the patient's health.

Many current pacemakers provide basic logs but lack real-time alerts or monitoring systems for cyber intrusions. A delayed response to a compromised pacemaker could result in severe health consequences for the patient.

Real-World Case Studies and Impact

Pacemakers represent the convergence of life-saving medical technology and the digital age. Once a theoretical discussion, research and real vulnerabilities have demonstrated the potential for pacemaker hacking, underscoring the critical need for robust security measures.

This section distills the essential insights from the analysis of pacemaker hacking, shedding light on the vulnerabilities, real-world implications, and actionable lessons for securing these vital medical devices. From understanding the technical risks to exploring the strategies that protect patients and healthcare systems, the takeaways highlight the urgency of addressing cybersecurity in the evolving landscape of connected healthcare.

Ethical Hacking Demonstration

Researchers have demonstrated how an attacker could intercept unencrypted communication signals from a pacemaker and manipulate the device using inexpensive radio equipment. They showed that pacing commands could be disrupted, proving the need for encrypted, authenticated communication protocols.

A five-step ethical hacking set of guidelines for a pacemaker hacking demonstration are as follows:

1. **Preparation and legal compliance**

    - Obtain authorization:
        - Secure written consent from all stakeholders, including the device manufacturer, healthcare facility, and patient (if applicable).
        - Ensure compliance with regulations such as HIPAA, FDA guidelines, and local cybersecurity laws.
    - Define scope:
        - Clearly outline the test's objectives, including specific vulnerabilities to assess, such as wireless communication protocols, encryption strength, or remote control features.
        - Identify boundaries to avoid affecting real-world patient data or connected systems.
    - Assemble tools and environment:
        - **Hardware:** Software-defined radios (SDRs) like HackRF One or BladeRF.
        - **Software:** GNU Radio, GQRX, Wireshark, Bettercap, and RFCrack.
        - **Additional tools:** Flipper Zero, SDRSharp, and Kali Linux for protocol sniffing and exploitation.
        - **Isolation:** Conduct tests in a Faraday cage or RF-shielded room to prevent unintentional interference.

2. **Reconnaissance and target identification**

    - Signal scanning:
        - Use SDR tools like HackRF and SDRSharp to identify the radio frequencies used by the pacemaker.
        - Map communication protocols (Bluetooth, RF, or NFC) and record device signals.
    - Protocol analysis:
        - Capture packets using Wireshark or Bettercap to analyze traffic.
        - Identify communication patterns and commands exchanged between the pacemaker and external devices.

- Fingerprinting:
    - Using tools like RFCrack or GATTacker, determine the device model, firmware version, and encryption methods for Bluetooth-enabled devices.
    - Search vulnerability databases (e.g., CVE, Exploit Database) for known exploits related to the identified model.
3. **Exploitation testing**
    - MITM attack simulation:
        - Deploy Bettercap to intercept and manipulate data exchanged between the pacemaker and programmer.
        - Test for unauthorized command injection, such as modifying heartbeat settings.
    - Replay attacks:
        - Capture valid commands using RFCrack or GATTacker and replay them to see if the device executes repeated or unauthorized actions.
        - Test scenarios like activating or disabling therapy modes.
    - Jamming and DoS testing:
        - Use HackRF to simulate RF jamming, assessing the pacemaker's response to signal interference.
        - Measure device resilience to prolonged connectivity loss.
    - Firmware analysis and manipulation:
        - Extract firmware from the pacemaker programmer (if accessible) and reverse-engineer it using tools like IDA Pro or Ghidra.
        - Identify hard-coded keys, vulnerabilities, or backdoors that attackers could exploit.
    - Weak encryption testing:
        - Analyze encryption protocols (e.g., AES) used for data transmission.
        - Attempt brute-force attacks or cryptographic analysis to break encryption keys.
4. **Risk assessment and reporting**
    - Document findings:
        - Details of vulnerabilities were identified, including proof-of-concept demonstrations and their potential impact.
        - Provide logs, screenshots, and code snippets to validate findings.
    - Evaluate impact:
        - Assess the severity of each vulnerability (e.g., device manipulation, patient safety risks, or data exposure).
        - Prioritize risks based on likelihood and impact.

- Propose mitigations:
  - Recommend encryption upgrades, firmware patches, stronger authentication mechanisms, and device isolation strategies.
  - Highlight the need for regular software updates and intrusion detection systems.
- Deliver final report:
  - Present findings to stakeholders, ensuring non-technical summaries are provided for broader audiences.
  - Emphasize proactive security measures and compliance requirements.

5. **Post-test validation and remediation**
   - Verify fixes:
     - Re-test vulnerabilities after patches or updates are applied.
     - Validate that mitigations effectively prevent exploit attempts.
   - Train staff:
     - Conduct training sessions for IT teams and clinicians on recognizing and responding to threats.
   - Implement continuous monitoring:
     - Deploy anomaly detection tools and periodic vulnerability scans to maintain security.

Performing ethical penetration tests on pacemakers highlights potential weaknesses in wireless communication, authentication, and encryption protocols. While these devices improve patient care, they require rigorous security measures to protect against evolving threats. Ethical hacking demonstrations provide insights into vulnerabilities and guide manufacturers and healthcare providers in implementing stronger defenses, ensuring patient safety and data security.

Several real-world cases have highlighted the cybersecurity risks and vulnerabilities associated with pacemakers, underscoring the need for stronger security measures in medical devices. In this section, I will examine a few notable examples from the past decade to paint a picture of decades of risks that are still evolving today.

ICD Study

In 2008, Researchers at the University of Washington and the University of Massachusetts conducted a study to demonstrate vulnerabilities in implantable cardioverter defibrillators or ICDs, which are devices similar to pacemakers. They successfully intercepted wireless communications and manipulated the device. The key risks identified were:

- **Eavesdropping:** Researchers were able to extract sensitive patient data, such as device serial numbers and medical settings.

- **Device control:** Using signal replay techniques, the team sent unauthorized commands to deliver shocks or disable therapy.
- **No encryption or authentication:** The device's communication protocols lacked any form of encryption or access control.

The study proved that pacemakers and ICDs, if unsecured, could become targets for cyberattacks, endangering patient safety and privacy. Medical device manufacturers must adopt encryption and mutual authentication to ensure that only authorized users can interact with these devices.

Barnaby Jack's Ethical Hacking Demonstration

In 2012, well-known cybersecurity researcher Barnaby Jack presented a live demonstration showing how he could remotely hack into a pacemaker and send malicious commands. Jack could manipulate pacemakers within a 30-foot range using a laptop and inexpensive radio equipment. The key risks identified were:

- **Lack of authentication:** The pacemaker accepted signals without verifying their legitimacy.
- **Unsecured communication:** Wireless transmissions between the device and programmer were unencrypted.
- **Device manipulation:** Jack demonstrated that an attacker could send radio signals to deliver inappropriate electrical shocks or disable the pacemaker.

Although this demonstration was ethical and controlled, it highlighted how attackers could potentially cause lethal outcomes by exploiting poorly secured pacemakers. This case emphasized the need for strong authentication protocols and encrypted wireless communication to prevent unauthorized access.

MedSec and St. Jude Medical Controversy

In 2016, cybersecurity firm MedSec claimed that St. Jude Medical's pacemakers and implantable devices had severe vulnerabilities that could allow remote hacking. Their findings were controversial because the claims were released publicly before the vulnerabilities were addressed. The key risks identified were:

- **Unsecured wireless communication:** Signals transmitted to pacemakers were not adequately protected, allowing potential interception.
- **Device manipulation:** MedSec alleged that attackers could exploit these vulnerabilities to modify settings, disrupt functionality, or drain the battery.
- **Patient safety concerns:** Unauthorized control could lead to harmful pacing or therapy delivery changes.

Following an investigation, St. Jude Medical (now part of Abbott) issued a firmware update to enhance security and address the vulnerabilities. This case underscores the ethical concerns around disclosing vulnerabilities while reinforcing the need for collaborative security testing and rapid manufacturer response.

FDA Pacemaker Recall

In 2017, the U.S. FDA issued a recall for 465,000 pacemakers produced by a major medical device manufacturer due to security vulnerabilities. The devices were found to be susceptible to remote hacking, which could allow unauthorized parties to alter device settings, such as pacing rates, or deplete the battery. The following were the key risks identified:

- **Unencrypted communication:** Hackers could intercept wireless signals sent to the pacemaker.
- **Remote reprogramming:** Attackers could send unauthorized commands, causing the pacemaker to behave dangerously.
- **Battery drain:** The vulnerability allowed malicious commands to drain the battery, rendering the device inoperable rapidly.

The manufacturer provided a firmware update to address the security flaws. However, the update required patients to visit their healthcare providers for installation. Although the fix was critical, it posed logistical challenges for patients and hospitals. This case demonstrates the importance of regular security patches and the need for a secure design that prioritizes encryption and authentication mechanisms.

Academic Demonstrations: 2018 Onward

Ongoing research continues to expose vulnerabilities in modern pacemakers. For instance, studies have shown that Bluetooth-enabled pacemakers are susceptible to the following:

- **Signal replay attacks:** Hackers intercept and replay legitimate signals to manipulate device behavior.
- **Denial-of-service:** Repeated connection requests can force the pacemaker to drain its battery or become unresponsive.

Key findings included the following:

- Many devices lack modern encryption standards like TLS 1.3.
- Devices with default PINs or pairing codes are easy targets for unauthorized access.
- Payloads included results with patient information, diagnosis, medical ID number, and the make and model of the device.

Modern pacemakers must implement secure Bluetooth pairing, mutual authentication, and intrusion detection systems to prevent real-world attacks.

Medtronic's Paceart Optima System Risks: 2023

A more recent example of a known reported vulnerability involving pacemakers is the critical flaw detected in Medtronic's Paceart Optima System, which was disclosed in July 2023. According to the Common Vulnerability Scoring System, this vulnerability, identified as CVE-2023-31222, has a severity score of 9.8 out of 10.

The vulnerability affects the Paceart Messaging Service, an optional feature in the Paceart Optima system. If exploited, an unauthorized user could potentially do the following:

- Perform remote code execution
- Launch DoS attacks
- Steal, delete, or modify cardiac device data

The Cybersecurity and Infrastructure Security Agency (CISA) warned about this vulnerability, advising healthcare organizations to work with Medtronic's technical support to install an update that addresses the issue. To mitigate risks, CISA recommended the following actions:

- Minimizing network exposure for control system devices
- Taking affected systems offline when possible
- Using secure virtual private networks for remote access

This vulnerability highlights the ongoing cybersecurity challenges implantable medical devices face and the critical importance of addressing these issues to ensure patient safety and data security.

The Impact of Pacemaker Vulnerabilities

The consequences of pacemaker vulnerabilities are severe and include the following:

- **Patient safety risks:** Unintended shocks, pacing rate changes, or device failures could lead to cardiac events, hospitalization, or even death.
- **Loss of trust:** Patients may lose confidence in healthcare technology, delaying adoption of life-saving devices.
- **Operational risks:** Healthcare institutions may face disruptions if devices or programming tools are compromised.
- **Regulatory consequences:** Hospitals and manufacturers may face lawsuits, recalls, and penalties for failing to secure medical devices.
- **Financial burden:** Recalls and updates can cost healthcare providers and patients millions of dollars.
- **Cybersecurity challenges:** The healthcare industry must continually adapt to address evolving threats.
- **Research and development:** Manufacturers must invest more in security features and testing.

Pacemaker vulnerabilities emphasize the critical need for robust cybersecurity measures to safeguard patient safety. Common issues include a lack of encryption, where devices transmit data in plaintext, making it susceptible to interception and manipulation. Weak authentication protocols, often missing multi-factor authentication, allow attackers to gain unauthorized access to device controls. Unpatched firmware is another risk, as slow responses to known vulnerabilities expose devices to exploitation. Wireless transmissions are particularly vulnerable to signal replay and jamming attacks, enabling attackers to intercept, disrupt, or alter device communications. Additionally, attackers can target battery drain vulnerabilities, overloading devices and depleting their energy reserves, potentially causing malfunctions or failures.

These real-world examples emphasize that securing pacemakers is not optional but essential. Cybersecurity must be a shared priority among manufacturers, healthcare providers, and policymakers to ensure resilient, secure devices that protect patient lives and sensitive data.

In the next section, I'll explore these strategies and technologies that can help mitigate and/or reduce these risks and ensure that pacemakers remain reliable, secure, and life-saving in modern healthcare.

Strategies and Technologies to Mitigate Pacemaker Cybersecurity Risks

To safeguard pacemakers in today's digital healthcare environment, we need a multilayered security strategy that addresses vulnerabilities at every level. This section explores practical mitigation techniques, supported by real-world examples, to protect pacemakers from evolving threats.

Securing Wireless Communication with Strong Encryption

Wireless communication is at the heart of modern pacemaker functionality, enabling remote monitoring and non-invasive adjustments. However, unencrypted data streams are vulnerable to interception and manipulation. Attackers using packet-sniffing tools could eavesdrop on sensitive information or inject malicious commands. To counter this, robust encryption protocols are critical. Adopting AES-256 encryption ensures that data remains secure in transit, while TLS 1.3 provides end-to-end encryption for internet-enabled pacemakers.

For example, a pacemaker transmitting heart rhythm data to a monitoring station can leverage TLS 1.3, making intercepted data unreadable without the proper decryption keys. Dynamic encryption key rotation reduces the risk of reusing compromised keys, ensuring ongoing data protection.

Implementing Strong Authentication and Access Controls

Authentication mechanisms verify that only authorized devices and personnel can access pacemaker settings or data. Weak authentication, such as default passwords, leaves devices vulnerable to impersonation attacks. Modern pacemakers must implement mutual authentication using PKI, where the device and external systems verify each other's identity before sharing data. MFA provides an additional layer of security, combining secure PINs with biometric identifiers like fingerprints.

For instance, a clinician accessing pacemaker settings through a programmer device must use a secure digital certificate and fingerprint scan to validate their identity. Secure pairing protocols, such as Elliptic Curve Diffie-Hellman, protect Bluetooth-enabled pacemakers by encrypting connections during setup to prevent spoofing or eavesdropping.

Regular Firmware Updates and Patch Management

Pacemakers must stay up-to-date with the latest firmware to address vulnerabilities. Many past exploits have targeted devices with outdated software, highlighting the importance of regular updates. Over-the-air updates (OTA) allow vendors to deliver patches without requiring surgical interventions, streamlining maintenance. These updates should be digitally signed to ensure their authenticity and integrity before installation.

For example, if a manufacturer identifies a Bluetooth vulnerability, they can release a digitally signed patch that automatically updates pacemakers, closing the security gap. Hospitals and healthcare providers must also establish a structured process for deploying patches quickly and verifying their effectiveness.

Monitoring for Intrusions and Anomalies

Real-time monitoring and anomaly detection can identify suspicious activity before it escalates. Modern systems can integrate AI-powered IDS to flag irregular patterns, such as repeated unauthorized access attempts or unusual device commands. Event logging enables healthcare IT teams to track all communication with pacemakers, providing valuable forensic data in the event of an attack.

For example, an IDS could detect repeated programming attempts to alter a pacemaker's settings and immediately block the activity while alerting staff. Incorporating tamper-resistant designs that trigger alerts or lockdown modes when interference is detected adds another layer of defense.

Physical Security and Access Controls

Cybersecurity isn't just about digital threats; physical security also matters. Programming devices to adjust pacemaker settings should be kept in secure, access-controlled environments. Hospitals can implement biometric access controls and secure boot technology to ensure that only authorized personnel can operate these tools. Programmed devices stored in locked rooms with fingerprint scanners prevent unauthorized tampering, while time-based locks automatically log out inactive sessions to reduce exposure.

Vendor Accountability and Regulatory Compliance

Manufacturers play a critical role in pacemaker security. Regulatory agencies like the FDA require vendors to follow strict cybersecurity guidelines, including security by design principles during development. Vendors must also provide long-term support, conduct regular vulnerability assessments, and share security updates transparently. Manufacturers must submit post-market cybersecurity plans outlining how to address emerging threats throughout a device's lifecycle. Penetration testing and third-party audits ensure vulnerabilities are identified and fixed before devices reach patients.

Raising Awareness and Training Healthcare Staff

Human error often contributes to security breaches, making education essential. Clinicians need training on secure devices, firmware updates, and incident response procedures. Patients should also be educated about cybersecurity best practices, such as avoiding untrusted networks and reporting unusual device behavior.

For example, a nurse noticing inconsistent data from a pacemaker might identify a potential attack and escalate it quickly, preventing harm. Hospitals should create clear protocols for responding to security incidents to minimize disruption during an attack.

Building a Resilient Future for Pacemakers

Pacemakers are life-critical devices; securing them requires a holistic approach combining encryption, authentication, real-time monitoring, and proactive updates. To future-proof, vendors must prioritize cybersecurity at every stage of development; healthcare providers need training programs, and regulators must enforce compliance standards. Real-world examples, such as OTA updates closing Bluetooth vulnerabilities or AI systems blocking unauthorized commands, demonstrate how these strategies can work in practice. By treating pacemaker security as a shared responsibility, we can protect patients from emerging threats, ensuring these devices remain reliable, resilient, and safe in an increasingly connected world.

More on Consequences of Pacemaker Hacking

The most immediate and dangerous consequence of pacemaker hacking is the compromise of patient health and safety. Since pacemakers regulate the heart's rhythm, any manipulation of the device can lead to the following:

- Inappropriate shocks or pacing, which can cause severe physical harm, including cardiac arrest, arrhythmias, and even death
- Loss of critical data, such as heart rate patterns or medication information, could lead to misdiagnosis or delay in treatment

- Device failure, where attackers drain the pacemaker's battery or prevent it from performing its intended function

The potential for life-threatening consequences makes pacemaker hacking one of healthcare's most dangerous cybersecurity threats.

Breaches of Patient Privacy

Pacemakers are often connected to healthcare systems that transmit sensitive data, including patient heart rhythms, personal health information, and medication histories. Attackers who gain access to these systems could do the following:

- Access private medical information and sell or use it for malicious purposes.
- Compromise patient privacy by exposing personal data or modifying health records.
- Engage in identity theft, using patient data to commit fraud or further attacks. The discovery of Social Security numbers and other patient-sensitive data has been reported.

Ensuring the privacy and confidentiality of patient data is a core requirement for healthcare systems, and a breach involving pacemakers can have far-reaching legal, regulatory, and ethical implications.

Reputation Damage to Healthcare Providers

In addition to the immediate harm to patients, pacemaker hacking can lead to significant reputation damage for healthcare providers. If an organization is found to have failed to secure its medical devices adequately, it will likely face the following:

- **Loss of patient trust:** Patients may feel that their care is compromised, leading to a decline in business and patient retention.
- **Regulatory penalties:** Healthcare providers that fail to secure patient data properly may face sanctions or fines from regulatory bodies, such as the FDA or HIPAA.
- **Increased liability:** Medical facilities could face lawsuits if they are found responsible for allowing an attack to occur or failing

Key Takeaways from Pacemaker Hacking

Pacemaker cybersecurity is a growing concern due to the increasing reliance on wireless connectivity for remote monitoring, diagnostics, and programming. While these advancements improve patient care, they also introduce significant security risks. Real-world cases have demonstrated that pacemakers can be hacked, potentially leading to life-threatening consequences. Several key vulnerabilities make these devices susceptible to attacks, including insecure wireless communication, weak authentication mechanisms, lack of regular security patches, physical access risks, and the absence of intrusion detection systems.

High-profile incidents, such as the 2017 FDA pacemaker recall and cybersecurity demonstrations by ethical researchers, have underscored the dangers of pacemaker hacking. Attackers could intercept and manipulate device settings, drain batteries, or even deliver harmful shocks. Beyond patient safety risks, compromised pacemakers can also result in data breaches, operational disruptions, financial losses, and reputational damage for manufacturers and healthcare providers.

To mitigate these threats, a multilayered cybersecurity approach is essential. Encrypting wireless communication, strengthening authentication mechanisms, ensuring regular firmware updates, and integrating intrusion detection systems can enhance device security. Physical security controls, regulatory compliance, vendor accountability, and patient education contribute to a more resilient ecosystem.

Addressing pacemaker cybersecurity challenges requires close collaboration between manufacturers, healthcare providers, and regulatory agencies. By prioritizing security from the design phase through the device lifecycle, the industry can safeguard pacemakers from cyber threats, ensuring their continued reliability as life-saving medical devices.

CHAPTER 10

Insulin Pump Vulnerabilities and Exploits

Insulin pumps have improved the management of diabetes, particularly for those with Type 1 diabetes, by delivering precise doses of insulin to maintain blood glucose levels. Unlike traditional methods of insulin delivery, such as multiple daily injections, insulin pumps provide continuous subcutaneous insulin infusion (CSII), offering patients greater flexibility and control over their diabetes management. These devices have become an essential part of the daily life of millions of patients worldwide, allowing for improved glycemic control, fewer insulin injections, and a more tailored approach to managing their condition.

As with many medical devices, insulin pumps' increasing connectivity has introduced risks. Insulin pumps are often equipped with wireless communication technologies such as Bluetooth, Wi-Fi, and/or radio frequency signals to allow healthcare providers to monitor the device remotely, adjust settings, or download data. While these capabilities have undeniable benefits regarding patient care and convenience, they also create vulnerabilities that malicious actors can exploit.

The consequences of exploiting vulnerabilities in insulin pumps can be severe, potentially endangering patients' health and safety. Cyberattacks targeting insulin pumps, including changing settings and interrupting communications, could lead to lethal outcomes, such as insulin overdose or underdose, resulting in hypoglycemia (low blood sugar) or hyperglycemia (high blood sugar), both of which can cause acute complications or even death. Given that insulin pumps are integral to managing a life-threatening condition, addressing the cybersecurity risks associated with these devices is critical.

This chapter explores real-world scenarios and case studies of insulin pump vulnerabilities and exploits, examining the risks, consequences of attacks, and efforts to improve device security. It also examines how the healthcare industry, manufacturers, and cybersecurity experts are working to secure insulin pumps and protect patients from harm.

Furthermore, pacemaker and insulin pump vulnerabilities differ in ways based on their function, communication methods, and potential consequences of exploitation. Here's how their vulnerabilities differ:

- **Device function and criticality:**
    - **Pacemaker vulnerabilities:** Pacemakers regulate heart rhythms, making them life-critical devices. A successful exploit could lead to bradycardia (slow heart rate), tachycardia (fast heart rate), or complete heart failure.
    - **Insulin pump vulnerabilities:** Insulin pumps regulate blood sugar by delivering insulin doses, making them metabolically critical but typically not as immediately life-threatening as pacemakers. An exploit could lead to hyperglycemia (high blood sugar) or hypoglycemia (low blood sugar), which can be dangerous over time.

- **Communication and attack surface:**
    - **Pacemakers:** Modern pacemakers often communicate wirelessly with external devices such as programming consoles or patient monitoring systems via Bluetooth or proprietary radio frequencies. This wireless communication opens potential attack vectors where attackers could send malicious commands or interfere with signals.
    - **Insulin pumps:** Insulin pumps also use wireless communication to connect with glucose monitors and smartphone apps, but their communication interfaces are often more exposed to public networks. Vulnerabilities in these networked connections could allow attackers to alter insulin doses remotely.

- **Attack consequences:**
    - **Pacemaker exploits:** Successful attacks could lead to the following:
        - Immediate cardiac arrest
        - Malicious shutdown of the pacemaker
        - Forced irregular heart rhythms, leading to severe health risks or death
    - **Insulin pump exploits:** Potential attack outcomes include the following:
        - Overdosing insulin, causing hypoglycemia, which can rapidly become fatal

- Preventing insulin delivery, causing hyperglycemia and eventual ketoacidosis
- Manipulating glucose data, leading to incorrect dosage adjustments

- **Power and firmware limitations:**
  - **Pacemakers:** Due to their long-term implantation (often 5–15 years), pacemakers have strict power constraints and limited firmware updates. This makes it harder to apply security patches or upgrade encryption methods, making them vulnerable to long-term, unpatched exploits.
  - **Insulin pumps:** Since they are externally worn and rechargeable, they can be updated more frequently. However, they may still lack encryption or authentication mechanisms, leaving them open to cyberattacks.

While both devices share risks in wireless communication vulnerabilities, pacemaker exploits tend to pose an immediate life-threatening risk due to their role in heart function. Insulin pump attacks can result in metabolic crises over time. Insulin pumps often have more frequent software updates and user control, while pacemakers, being long-term implants, are more complex to patch or replace.

Understanding Insulin Pumps and Their Vulnerabilities

An insulin pump is a small, computerized device continuously delivering insulin to people with diabetes. It is typically worn on the body, often attached to a waistband or pocket, and a small catheter is inserted under the skin to deliver the insulin. These pumps can be programmed to provide a basal rate (continuous small doses) and bolus doses (larger doses given at mealtimes), which helps the patient regulate their blood glucose levels throughout the day.

Most modern insulin pumps are connected to other devices, such as continuous glucose monitors (CGMs) mentioned throughout this book, to provide real-time feedback on blood sugar levels and enable automatic adjustments. Some pumps are even integrated into closed-loop systems, which allow for automatic insulin adjustments based on the data received from the CGM, effectively creating an artificial pancreas. Key features of insulin pumps include the following:

- **Basal rate delivery:** Provides a steady flow of insulin to manage blood sugar levels during fasting periods
- **Bolus doses:** Administers additional insulin doses to manage blood sugar spikes after meals

Many pumps now include Bluetooth or RF communication to connect with smartphones, CGMs, or healthcare provider systems. While this connectivity improves usability and remote monitoring, it also introduces vulnerabilities that cyber threats can exploit.

Current Vulnerabilities in Insulin Pumps

While insulin pumps offer benefits in diabetes management, their integration with wireless technologies introduces a range of cybersecurity vulnerabilities. Some of the primary concerns, most of which I touched on earlier, include the following:

- **Insecure wireless communication:** Insulin pumps use wireless protocols like Bluetooth or RF for data transmission and programming. Many devices lack strong encryption or use outdated communication standards. Attackers can intercept unencrypted data transmissions between the pump, CGM, or connected smartphone apps. Attackers could alter insulin dosing instructions or retrieve sensitive health data. A vulnerability was identified in older insulin pump models where attackers could eavesdrop on RF signals and send unauthorized commands to the device.

- **Weak authentication mechanisms:** Many insulin pumps use minimal authentication to access device settings or pair external devices. The lack of MFA allows attackers to impersonate authorized users. Some pumps use default or hardcoded passwords, which are easily exploitable. Research has demonstrated that attackers can access insulin pump settings using publicly available tools due to weak or absent authentication protocols.

- **Vulnerabilities in mobile and cloud integration:** Modern insulin pumps often integrate with mobile apps or cloud platforms for data visualization and remote monitoring. If the app or cloud platform has security flaws, attackers can access sensitive patient data or manipulate device settings. Many apps do not adequately encrypt data during storage or transmission. A study found that some insulin pump apps transmitted user credentials and health data in plaintext, exposing them to interception.

- **Lack of security patches and updates:** Insulin pumps, like other medical devices, often operate on proprietary software. Regular updates to fix vulnerabilities are not always available or implemented. Known vulnerabilities can remain unpatched for years, leaving devices exposed to exploitation. Regulatory hurdles and patient safety concerns may also delay firmware updates. A 2019 recall involved insulin pumps with outdated software, which made them susceptible to unauthorized remote control.

- **Physical access exploits:** If attackers gain physical access to an insulin pump or its programming device, they can manipulate its settings or install malware. Physical tampering can result in altered insulin doses or device malfunctions. Patients who lose or misplace their devices may unknowingly expose them to manipulation. An attacker with physical access could reprogram the pump to deliver incorrect dosages, risking hypoglycemia or hyperglycemia.

- **Denial-of-service attacks:** Insulin pumps with wireless connectivity can be targeted with excessive communication requests, causing the device to crash or stop functioning. A DoS attack could disrupt insulin delivery, putting the patient at immediate risk. Such attacks can drain battery life, requiring premature replacement or servicing. Research has shown how a DoS attack could render an insulin pump inoperable by sending repeated pairing requests.

- **Dependency on legacy systems:** Many healthcare facilities and patients still use older insulin pump models with outdated software and minimal cybersecurity features. These models are more susceptible to known exploits, and legacy systems often cannot support modern security updates or protocols.

- **Software and firmware vulnerabilities:** Some insulin pumps run on outdated or vulnerable software and firmware that may not have been patched to fix known security flaws. Attackers can exploit these weaknesses to gain unauthorized access to the device, potentially causing malfunctions or altering settings that could harm the patient.

- **Limited device security features:** Insulin pumps were not initially designed with robust cybersecurity measures in mind. Many older models lack essential security features such as encryption, multifactor authentication, or the ability to update software remotely to address emerging threats.

- **Limited processing power:** Many IoMT devices, including some insulin pumps, have limited processing power, making it challenging to implement strong security measures. This limitation can affect the ability to use strong encryption or complex authentication mechanisms.

Vulnerability Testing

The first step in testing for insulin pump vulnerabilities is defining the scope and objectives of the test. Identify the specific insulin pump models and versions to be analyzed. Focus on wireless communication, firmware, and data storage vulnerabilities while setting boundaries to avoid accidental harm to patients or devices. Next, obtain formal authorization from manufacturers, healthcare providers, and stakeholders. Ensure compliance with HIPAA, FDA guidelines, and legal requirements before proceeding. Assemble a controlled lab environment that mirrors real-world setups but avoids actual patient connections. Use identical test devices and have an emergency shutdown plan in place.

Once the environment is ready, identify potential attack surfaces. Focus on wireless protocols like Bluetooth, Wi-Fi, RF channels, firmware vulnerabilities, physical access points, and cloud or mobile app connections. Develop threat scenarios, such as unauthorized remote access to pump controls, data interception, DoS attacks, or malicious firmware injection.

Vulnerability testing is where detailed assessments begin. For wireless communication, use tools that I discussed, like Wireshark and Aircrack-ng to analyze traffic and encryption strength. Simulate pairing or replay attacks to uncover weaknesses. Firmware analysis, which is not covered in this book, involves extracting firmware via JTAG or UART interfaces and reverse engineering using tools like Ghidra or IDA Pro to identify insecure code, hardcoded keys, and passwords. The Joint Test

Action Group (JTAG) is a standardized debugging interface that provides low-level access to a device's hardware, allowing for direct manipulation of registers and memory locations, which can be crucial for identifying malfunctions in complex medical implants or monitoring systems. The Universal Asynchronous Receiver Transmitter (UART) is a more straightforward serial communication protocol often used for essential data transfer between a medical device and a computer for data logging or configuration purposes.

Mobile apps should be decompiled with tools like JADX or MobSF to test APIs, encryption flaws, and man-in-the-middle vulnerabilities. Physical security evaluations include inspecting casing protections, identifying debugging ports, and testing tamper resistance.

Controlled exploitation tests help validate vulnerabilities. Frameworks like Metasploit or Burp Suite simulate attacks, including code injections and buffer overflows, while assessing device responses. Evaluate impacts such as unauthorized insulin delivery, data breaches, or device shutdowns and design mitigation strategies to prevent real-world harm.

Metasploit and Burp Suite are two powerful tools used in cybersecurity to simulate attacks and assess device responses, particularly in identifying vulnerabilities such as code injections and buffer overflows. Metasploit, a widely used penetration testing framework, enables security professionals to automate exploit delivery, payload execution, and post-exploitation analysis. It is instrumental in testing for buffer overflow vulnerabilities, where an attacker may attempt to overwrite memory to manipulate program execution. For instance, using Metasploit's built-in modules, a tester can craft malicious payloads to determine if a device is susceptible to memory corruption, allowing them to analyze crash logs and assess exploitability. Additionally, Metasploit can be leveraged for code injection attacks, where adversaries inject malicious code into a running process, often to gain unauthorized access or control over a device.

On the other hand, Burp Suite is a specialized tool for web application security testing, making it particularly effective for identifying SQL injection, cross-site scripting (XSS), and other web-based code injection vulnerabilities. Burp Suite's intruder and repeater modules allow testers to manipulate web requests and inject malicious payloads, simulating real-world attacks against APIs and user input fields. This is particularly valuable when testing medical or IoT devices with web-based management interfaces, as attackers may exploit weak authentication mechanisms or input validation flaws to compromise the system. When used together, Metasploit and Burp Suite provide a comprehensive approach to testing device security by simulating both low-level system exploits (buffer overflows) and application-level attacks (code injections), helping security teams analyze device responses, identify weaknesses, and implement necessary security controls.

Document findings, including reproduction steps, screenshots, and impact analysis. Highlight confidentiality, integrity, and availability risks, and provide actionable recommendations. Suggestions may include stronger encryption, firmware protections, and secure coding practices. Compliance reports should follow FDA and ISO/IEC 27001 standards and shared with manufacturers and regulatory bodies.

The FDA and ISO/IEC 27001 provide essential regulatory and cybersecurity frameworks for ensuring the security and reliability of medical devices in healthcare. The FDA enforces safety and cybersecurity requirements for medical devices to prevent unauthorized access and protect patient data. At the same time, ISO/IEC 27001 establishes an internationally recognized standard for information security management, ensuring confidentiality, integrity, and availability of healthcare systems. Together, these frameworks guide security professionals in identifying vulnerabilities, assessing risks, and implementing necessary controls to safeguard medical devices and healthcare infrastructure.

When assessing medical device security, findings must be documented to ensure repeatability, transparency, and regulatory compliance. Security assessments should include detailed reproduction steps, starting with test case preparation that defines network conditions, device configurations, and attack vectors. Attack execution should involve simulated exploits such as code injection attacks and buffer overflows, using tools like Metasploit for system-level vulnerabilities and Burp Suite for web-based attacks. Observations must be recorded, including network traffic analysis, system logs, and changes in device behavior. Any crash indicators, unauthorized access logs, or unexpected reboots should be documented. Supporting evidence such as screenshots and logs should accompany these findings, including before-and-after images of system behavior, exploit console outputs, and captured network packets from tools like Wireshark.

The impact analysis should assess risks based on the confidentiality, integrity, and availability (CIA) triad. Confidentiality risks include potential data breaches, unauthorized access to patient records, or exposure of sensitive telemetry. Integrity risks may arise from malicious firmware modification, unauthorized software injection, or data tampering that alters device functionality. Availability risks involve threats such as DoS attacks, buffer overflows, or device crashes, potentially disrupting essential medical functions.

Stronger encryption, firmware protections, and secure coding practices should be implemented to mitigate these risks. Devices should use AES-256 encryption for data at rest and TLS 1.3 for data in transit, with mutual authentication between devices and remote platforms. Firmware protections should include secure boot mechanisms, code signing, and integrity checks to prevent unauthorized modifications. Secure coding practices must enforce input validation to avoid buffer overflows and injection attacks, use memory-safe languages like Rust or implement strict memory management in C/C++, and apply least privilege access controls to reduce exploitability.

All findings and remediation steps should be compiled into compliance reports that align with FDA cybersecurity guidance and ISO/IEC 27001 requirements. These reports should include an executive summary, technical details of vulnerabilities, attack vectors, supporting screenshots, risk assessments, and a remediation plan outlining security improvements. Compliance mapping should demonstrate how each identified vulnerability relates to FDA and ISO/IEC 27001 standards. The reports must be securely shared with device manufacturers, healthcare providers, and regulatory authorities to ensure timely mitigation of risks before real-world exploitation occurs.

After identifying vulnerabilities, collaborate with stakeholders to patch issues and implement fixes. Guide developers through secure development practices. Retest vulnerabilities to confirm effectiveness and ensure new problems are not introduced. Regression testing validates that patches function as intended.

Security doesn't end with testing. Establish monitoring protocols to detect anomalies in device activity and deploy intrusion detection systems for wireless and application layers. Train staff on security practices, incident response, and recognizing security risks. Educate end-users to identify potential issues.

Here's a synopsis of findings from a simulated case study example involving a medical campus audit that included IoMT devices, including insulin pumps, in scope. The objective for this project is a black-box penetration test with the following scope:

- **Digital security:** Evaluating network vulnerabilities, application weaknesses, and overall IT infrastructure resilience
- **Physical security:** Assessing the adequacy of physical building security measures
- **Social engineering:** Testing human and procedural vulnerabilities through pretexting, phishing, and on-site manipulation

The goal was to simulate a real-world attack scenario where the team had no prior knowledge of the following environment, mirroring the techniques used by advanced threat actors and included:

- **Facilities:** Six buildings, including the main hospital, research labs, administrative offices, and outpatient care units
- **Systems in scope:** Medical IoT devices, hospital information systems, and connected EHR platforms
- **Physical entry points:** Public and staff entrances, secured labs, server rooms, and parking facilities
- **Human factors:** Testing susceptibility to social engineering attacks, such as phishing emails and in-person impersonation attempts

Given the engagement had particular milestones in scope, with required outcomes, it was executed in many stages, but for brevity, here is a consolidation in three high-level phases:

Phase 1: Reconnaissance

This phase gathers intelligence on the medical campus to identify vulnerabilities and potential attack vectors.

1. Open-source intelligence (OSINT):
   - **Public information:** Identified staff details via LinkedIn and social media
   - **Infrastructure details:** Located IP addresses, DNS records, and publicly accessible subdomains
   - **Employee habits:** Monitored online forums where employees discussed work-related topics
2. On-site observation:
   - **Visitor behaviors:** Observed security practices at entrances and parking areas
   - **Badge systems:** Documented staff movements and badge scanning habits
   - **Physical security:** Identified unlocked access points, lack of surveillance in certain areas, and unattended workstations

Phase 2: Exploitation

In this phase, I simulate attacks to exploit identified weaknesses, covering physical and digital entry points.

Digital Security Testing

1. Network penetration testing:
   - **Wireless access points:** Detected several poorly configured Wi-Fi networks, including guest Wi-Fi with shared passwords
   - **Unencrypted protocols:** Identified unencrypted IoMT communication between devices
   - **Exploited legacy systems:** Accessed an EHR server running outdated software, leading to unauthorized retrieval of patient records
2. Web application testing:
   - **SQL injection:** Found vulnerabilities in the staff portal, allowing unauthorized access to sensitive patient data
   - **Broken authentication:** Exploited weak session management to hijack administrator accounts
3. IoMT Device Exploitation:
   - **Insulin, infusion pumps, and ECG devices:** Manipulated some settings through unsecured APIs, simulating life-threatening scenarios in a controlled environment.

Physical Security Testing

1. Unauthorized entry:
   - **Tailgating:** Successfully entered restricted zones by following legitimate employees during high-traffic periods

- **Impersonation:** Posed as a visiting researcher with forged credentials, gaining access to a research lab
- **Dumpster Diving:** Retrieved sensitive documents, including discarded patient appointment schedules jotted down on paper

2. Device tampering:

- **Unlocked workstations:** Accessed unattended computers in nursing stations and administrative offices.
- **USB drops:** In common areas, USB drives containing harmless payloads labeled "Confidential Payroll" were left. Within a day, two devices were plugged into hospital workstations.

Social Engineering

1. Phishing campaigns:

- **Email phishing:** Emails mimicking IT support requested login credentials to "reset passwords." Just over 4% of recipients responded with their credentials.
- **Voice phishing (vishing):** I called the HR department, which is posing as a vendor, and obtained an employee directory.

2. On-site social engineering:

- **Pretexting:** Convinced security personnel to grant temporary access by claiming to be a new contractor "locked out" of the system
- **Fake maintenance:** Simulated an IT technician inspecting Wi-Fi access points, gaining direct access to network closets

Phase 3: Reporting and Remediation

Deliver a comprehensive report outlining findings, impacts, and remediation strategies in this last phase.

1. **Findings:**

- **Digital security:**
  - Four critical vulnerabilities, including exploitable IoT devices and unpatched servers
  - Multiple instances of weak password policies and shared credentials
- **Physical security:**
  - Unauthorized entry into all six buildings
  - Absence of effective visitor management protocols

- **Social engineering:**
    - Over 10% success rate (attaining some helpful information in perusing various attack vectors) in phishing attempts
    - Security staff lacked proper training to identify imposters
2. **Impact assessment:**
    - Potential for life-threatening scenarios through IoMT tampering
    - Risk of violating HIPAA and incurring regulatory fines due to exposed patient records
    - Reputational damage and legal liabilities from potential breaches
3. **Some of the Key Remediation Recommendations:**
    - **Digital Security:**
        - Implement end-to-end encryption for medical IoT communication
        - Enforce regular software updates and patch management
        - Mandate strong, unique passwords and deploy multifactor authentication
    - **Physical security:**
        - Install access controls with biometric verification in restricted areas
        - Train security personnel to verify identities and deny entry to unauthorized individuals
        - Use shredders for sensitive documents to mitigate dumpster-diving risks
    - **Human training:**
        - Conduct mandatory cybersecurity awareness training for all staff
        - Regularly test staff response to simulated phishing campaigns
    - **Monitoring and audits:**
        - Deploy 24/7 surveillance in high-risk areas
        - Implement centralized logging for IoMT devices and network activity to detect anomalies

The following are the key lessons learned from this case study:

- **Comprehensive testing is crucial:** A holistic approach that combines physical, digital, and human factors uncovers systemic weaknesses often overlooked in isolated testing.
- **User awareness is the first defense:** Social engineering remains one of the most effective attack vectors, emphasizing the need for ongoing education.
- **Regular updates and maintenance:** Unpatched systems and legacy devices are critical vulnerabilities that must be prioritized for upgrades.
- **Collaboration is key:** Security improvements require IT, physical security, and healthcare leadership collaboration.

This engagement served as a wake-up call for the medical campus, leading to a complete overhaul of its security posture. By implementing recommendations, the organization significantly improved its resilience against future cyberattacks, ensuring the safety of its patients, staff, and critical systems.

Implications and Real-World Scenarios of Insulin Pump Exploits

The implications of insulin pump vulnerabilities in modern healthcare settings are far-reaching and potentially life-threatening. Patient safety is the foremost concern, as malicious manipulation of insulin delivery can have severe consequences. Attackers could cause hypoglycemia by administering excessive insulin, leading to dangerous symptoms such as confusion, seizures, or even death in extreme cases. Conversely, insufficient insulin delivery could result in hyperglycemia, potentially triggering diabetic ketoacidosis (DKA) or contributing to long-term complications associated with consistently elevated blood sugar levels.

Beyond immediate health risks, compromised insulin pumps pose threats to data privacy. These devices often store and transmit sensitive patient information, including detailed health records, continuous glucose readings, and personal identifiers. A breach of this data violates patient confidentiality and exposes healthcare providers to potential legal and financial repercussions under privacy laws such as HIPAA and GDPR.

The operational and reputational risks associated with insulin pump vulnerabilities are substantial and multifaceted. A publicized cybersecurity breach involving these critical medical devices can severely erode patient trust in healthcare technology, potentially reducing the adoption of life-saving innovations. Moreover, such incidents often result in increased regulatory scrutiny, potentially leading to costly penalties, mandatory recalls, or stringent new compliance requirements for device manufacturers and healthcare providers. Maintaining the security and integrity of devices like insulin pumps is crucial for advancing patient care.

A cybersecurity breach involving insulin pumps, like with pacemaker hacking, could result in significant financial losses, including the following:

- Costs of resolving the breach include legal fees, regulatory fines, and cybersecurity consultations
- Settlements and damages paid to patients or families affected by the breach or any resulting harm
- Loss of business as patients choose to go elsewhere for care

Several real-world scenarios have highlighted the potential dangers associated with insulin pump vulnerabilities. These cases demonstrate how even the most sophisticated medical devices can be exploited if cybersecurity measures are not implemented adequately.

Security Research

One of the most widely publicized instances of insulin pump vulnerabilities was the 2011 research conducted by Barnaby Jack, a renowned security researcher. At the Black Hat USA cybersecurity conference, Jack demonstrated how insulin pumps could be remotely hacked, showcasing significant vulnerabilities in devices made by manufacturers such as Medtronic.

Jack could intercept and manipulate the communication between an insulin pump and its controller using a wireless transmitter and a custom-designed hacking tool. This allowed him to deliver fatal doses of insulin. Jack showed that an attacker could send commands to the pump to provide an excessive dose of insulin, which could cause a dangerous hypoglycemic reaction (severely low blood sugar). In extreme cases, this could result in coma or death. Jack also demonstrated that the device could be manipulated to alter its programming, such as changing basal or bolus insulin doses. This could result in inappropriate insulin delivery, leading to dangerous blood sugar fluctuations.

Jack's research was a wake-up call to the medical community, highlighting how devices designed to keep people alive could be vulnerable to malicious exploitation. In response, Medtronic and other manufacturers began working to improve the security of their devices, but Jack's demonstration made it clear that many insulin pumps lacked fundamental security protections.

FDA Warning on Insulin Pumps

In 2017, the U.S. FDA issued a safety warning about vulnerabilities in Medtronic's MiniMed 600 Series insulin pumps. The warning came after researchers discovered the devices could be hacked and remotely controlled via their telemetry communication system. According to this Wired article (`https://www.wired.com/story/medtronic-insulin-pump-hack-app`), the researchers built an Android app that could use the flaws in these devices to kill people. They built a universal remote that could be used on these devices worldwide.

Medtronic's insulin pumps were found to be vulnerable, where an attacker, like Jack, intercepts and potentially alters the communication between the pump and its remote controller. The vulnerabilities could allow an attacker to:

- **Modify insulin delivery:** An attacker could manipulate the pump's communication to change insulin delivery rates, resulting in over- or under-delivery of insulin.

- **Disable the device:** In some scenarios, attackers could prevent the insulin pump from receiving commands or updates, effectively disabling the device. Depending on their condition at the time, this could leave patients at risk of dangerously high or low blood sugar levels.

- **Access patient data:** Hackers could potentially access sensitive medical data, such as glucose levels, insulin dosages, and other health information, which they could then sell or exploit.

Due to this vulnerability, Medtronic issued a security patch to fix the issue and updated the firmware of the affected pumps. Additionally, the FDA recommended that patients using these devices avoid using wireless communication features when unnecessary and ensure they use the most current software version.

Ransomware Attack on a Hospital Network Impacting Insulin Pumps

In 2020, cybercriminals launched a ransomware attack on a hospital network, impacting administrative systems, patient data, and several connected medical devices, including insulin pumps. The attack involved installing malicious software that encrypted the hospital's data and demanded a ransom for its release. While this attack primarily targeted hospital operations, it also disrupted the functionality of medical devices, including insulin pumps.

The consequences of this attack were significant because healthcare providers could not access patient data and device settings in real time. This adjustment delay could have led to poor blood glucose control or worsened outcomes for insulin-dependent patients. Although no direct reports of harm were documented, the attack made remote monitoring and adjustments of insulin pumps unavailable, putting patients at risk of complications.

This attack accentuated the increasing cybersecurity risk of connected medical devices in hospitals and healthcare facilities. It also highlighted the potential consequences of cyberattacks that disrupt critical patient care systems, mainly when those systems rely on interconnected devices like insulin pumps.

Mitigation Strategies for Insulin Pump Security

Securing insulin pumps requires a multilayered approach involving manufacturers, healthcare providers, and patients. Strategies are similar in intent with other technologies I discussed and, therefore, include the following:

- **Strong encryption:** Ensure all data transmissions are encrypted with modern standards like AES-256 or TLS 1.3.
- **Robust authentication:** Implement multifactor authentication to access device settings.
- **Regular updates:** Encourage manufacturers to provide timely software and firmware updates.
- **Secure integration:** Ensure mobile apps and cloud platforms follow best practices for data security.
- **Physical security:** Educate patients on safeguarding their devices and programming tools.
- **Anomaly detection:** Integrate real-time monitoring systems to detect unusual activity or unauthorized access attempts.

- **Disabling features:** Disable unnecessary wireless features, such as remote bolus capabilities, when unnecessary.
- **Device isolation and segmentation:** To mitigate the impact of a potential attack, critical devices like insulin pumps should be isolated from less critical systems and protected with firewalls, segmentation, and access controls.

Education and Training for Patients and Healthcare Providers

Because it's often a weakness, I want to emphasize the importance of training. Patients and healthcare providers should receive regular training on the potential risks associated with insulin pumps and how to recognize and respond to suspicious activity or malfunctioning devices.

As insulin pumps become more integrated into connected healthcare ecosystems, the cybersecurity risks they face must be taken seriously. The potential for hacking, data breaches, and malfunctions could have severe consequences for patients, healthcare providers, and the medical device industry. Real-world incidents have already demonstrated the vulnerabilities of these devices, highlighting the need for stronger cybersecurity protections to safeguard patient health and privacy.

By addressing the vulnerabilities associated with insulin pumps, implementing robust security measures, and fostering greater collaboration between cybersecurity experts, manufacturers, and healthcare providers, the medical community can reduce the risks of insulin pump exploits and ensure the continued safety and well-being of diabetes patients worldwide.

Key Takeaways from Insulin Pump Vulnerabilities and Exploits

Insulin pumps have revolutionized diabetes management by providing continuous subcutaneous insulin infusion (CSII), offering precise glycemic control and reducing the need for injections. However, their wireless connectivity—via Bluetooth, Wi-Fi, and RF communication—introduces significant cybersecurity risks. Because these devices are life-critical, any disruption or manipulation can lead to severe health consequences, such as hypoglycemia or hyperglycemia.

Several vulnerabilities exist in insulin pump security. Insecure wireless communication, often lacking encryption, exposes data to interception and manipulation, allowing attackers to alter insulin delivery. Weak authentication mechanisms, such as the absence of multifactor authentication and reliance on hardcoded passwords, make unauthorized access easier. Additionally, integration with mobile apps and cloud platforms increases the risk of patient data breaches. Many pumps operate on outdated software without regular security patches, leaving them vulnerable to known exploits. Physical access threats and denial-of-service attacks further highlight the security risks, with older legacy systems lacking support for modern protective measures.

The real-world impacts of these vulnerabilities are profound. Patient safety is at risk, as insulin manipulation can lead to severe hypoglycemia, seizures, and even death, while inadequate insulin delivery can result in diabetic ketoacidosis. Data privacy is another primary concern, with potential exposure of sensitive health information leading to regulatory violations and identity theft. Hospitals relying on interconnected medical devices also face operational disruptions, care delays, and financial consequences due to regulatory penalties, recalls, and reputational damage.

Several real-world case studies have demonstrated the severity of insulin pump security threats. In 2011, ethical hacker Barnaby Jack showed how insulin pumps could be remotely hacked to deliver fatal doses. In 2017, the FDA issued warnings about vulnerabilities in Medtronic pumps, allowing attackers to alter insulin delivery through man-in-the-middle attacks. More recently, a 2020 ransomware attack on a hospital network disrupted insulin pump monitoring, highlighting the cascading effects of cyberattacks on healthcare systems.

Manufacturers must implement encryption protocols like AES-256 and TLS 1.3 to mitigate these risks, enforce multifactor authentication, provide regular firmware updates, and adopt security-by-design principles. Healthcare providers should isolate insulin pumps on segmented networks, use intrusion detection systems, and train staff on device security. Patients can also take precautions by safeguarding devices, updating software, and turning off unnecessary wireless features.

Education and awareness play crucial roles in enhancing insulin pump security. Both patients and healthcare providers must be vigilant in recognizing suspicious device behavior, securing devices against threats, and responding effectively to cybersecurity incidents. The healthcare industry can strengthen insulin pump security and safeguard patient well-being by implementing these strategies.

CHAPTER 11

Attack Vector Trends and Hospital Network Breaches with IoMT Devices

Hospital network breaches via connected medical devices are a growing threat in healthcare. In recent years, the distribution and implementation growth of IoMT devices has introduced more cybersecurity risks to hospital networks with the increased attack surface. I wrote a novel that depicts some of the latest attack vectors from the perspective of real human impact in a target healthcare environment. It's called *Silent Intrusions*, and you can download it from your favorite marketplaces. As healthcare IT professionals, it's crucial to understand these vulnerabilities and their impact and implement robust security measures.

Connected devices such as insulin pumps, infusion systems, patient monitors, imaging devices, and implantable cardiac devices enhance patient care and clinical efficiency. These devices streamline operations, enable real-time monitoring, and improve outcomes, establishing themselves as critical tools in modern healthcare. However, this technology landscape also introduces a complex array of cybersecurity challenges.

Recent statistics highlight the alarming vulnerabilities inherent in IoMT devices. These vulnerabilities have far-reaching implications, endangering individual patient safety and the integrity of entire healthcare networks. Cybercriminals exploit weaknesses such as outdated software, weak authentication protocols, unencrypted communication, and insufficient patch management. The inherent complexity of healthcare environments exacerbates these issues, where flat network structures, inadequate segmentation, and the rapid adoption of internet-connected devices expand the attack surface.

This chapter examines the risks of IoMT devices, exploring their role in healthcare network breaches and how vulnerabilities arise from technological, procedural, and human factors. As cyber threats grow increasingly sophisticated, healthcare organizations face the urgent challenge of safeguarding patient data, maintaining operational continuity, and building trust in an era of connected care.

Understanding the IoMT Risk Landscape

IoMT devices encompass a wide range of connected medical equipment, including the following:

- Insulin pumps
- Infusion systems
- Patient monitors
- Imaging devices
- Implantable cardiac devices

These devices offer tremendous benefits in patient care but also present unique security challenges. My research from studies has revealed alarming statistics about IoMT device vulnerabilities, such as the following:

- **Infusion pumps:** In general, 75% of infusion pumps were found to have known security gaps that put them at increased risk of being compromised by hackers. Fifty-two percent of analyzed infusion pumps were susceptible to two critical vulnerabilities disclosed in 2019. Twenty-seven percent of infusion pumps have unpatched critical severity CVEs.
- **Medication dispensing systems:** More than 80% contained unpatched vulnerabilities, and more than 30% operated on unsupported Microsoft Windows versions.
- **General medical devices:** On average, each medical device harbors around six vulnerabilities, with more than 40% nearing end-of-life and lacking adequate manufacturer support.

These findings underscore the pressing need for enhanced cybersecurity measures to safeguard patient safety and data integrity in healthcare settings.

Key Vulnerabilities of IoMT and Healthcare Network Breaches

IoMT has introduced vulnerabilities in healthcare networks, leading to breaches compromising patient data and critical systems. These risks arise from outdated infrastructure, weak security protocols, and the complexity of interconnected medical devices.

Many healthcare organizations still use legacy systems that lack modern security features, making them susceptible to cyberattacks. Devices like infusion pumps and imaging systems often run on outdated operating systems without essential security updates, providing attackers with easy entry points. Weak authentication protocols, including default or hard-coded passwords, expose IoMT devices to unauthorized access.

Unencrypted or poorly encrypted communication channels also pose a significant risk, allowing attackers to intercept sensitive patient data or manipulate device functions. Additionally, healthcare institutions often fail to implement timely software patches due to regulatory concerns, leaving vulnerabilities unaddressed for extended periods.

Poor network segmentation enables attackers to move laterally across systems once a single device is compromised. The growing number of internet-connected medical devices increases the attack surface, as many lack built-in security protections. Human error and insider threats further exacerbate cybersecurity risks, with inadequate training leading to unsafe practices such as password reuse and susceptibility to phishing attacks.

Ransomware attacks have become particularly damaging. They exploit IoMT weaknesses to disrupt hospital operations and delay patient care. Third-party vendors' role adds another layer of vulnerability, as security gaps in vendor-supplied devices and services can be exploited to breach healthcare networks.

Mitigating these threats requires a comprehensive approach, including regular software updates, strong authentication measures, robust encryption, network segmentation, and enhanced cybersecurity training for healthcare professionals. Addressing these vulnerabilities is crucial to safeguarding patient data and ensuring the security of interconnected medical systems.

Anatomy of a Healthcare Cyber Attack

I'll get into another case study that's more than just bits and bytes. It's about human ingenuity, both in attack and defense. It's also about the silent guardians who protect our digital lives and the shadowy figures who seek to disrupt them. Imagine for a moment you're sitting at your desk, sipping your morning coffee, when suddenly your computer starts acting strangely. Pop-ups appear out of nowhere, and your browser is redirected to unfamiliar sites. You feel a creeping sense of unease. Something is not right, but you can't put your finger on it. This is how our study begins, not with blaring alarms but with a whisper of doubt.

This isn't science fiction. It's the reality that healthcare professionals can face when a subtle digital intruder infiltrates their systems, slipping past their defenses. As I peel back the layers of this incident, I want you to put yourself in the shoes of these people. A nurse could have unwittingly opened the door to this threat through a seemingly innocent email—the IT professional who first noticed the anomalies and raised the alarm. The cybersecurity team worked tirelessly, piecing together digital breadcrumbs to uncover the full extent of the intrusion.

I'll also explore the human side of threat detection: the late nights, frustration, and breakthrough moments. I'll briefly examine the mindset of both the defenders and the attackers, understanding their motivations, techniques, triumphs, and failures. But this isn't just about looking back. It's about learning, adapting, and growing stronger. Every cyber incident is a teacher if we're willing to listen. I'll discuss the lessons learned, not just in terms of technology but human behavior, organizational culture, and the critical importance of awareness and education.

I encourage you to reflect on your experiences. Have you ever felt that nagging suspicion that something is wrong with your computer? Have you ever been the one to spot an anomaly and raise the alarm? Or perhaps you've been on the other side, part of a team working to unravel a complex cyber incident?

I'll begin our journey into the anatomy of this cyber-attack, which showcases the stages that threat actors typically follow (such as the one shown in Figure 11-1). But as I do, remember that people are behind every line of code, security alert, and incident response. People are working to protect, learning to defend, and striving to create a safer digital world. This is more than just a technical analysis. It's an example of an incident that can have a real impact on people's lives.

Understanding this process is crucial to better defend against and respond to such attacks. Why? Because signs of the early stages of an attack are called *indicators of attack* (IOAs). In the industry, I hear more about indicators of compromise (IOCs). IOCs include malware signatures, suspicious IP addresses, and unusual outbound network traffic. IOAs include unusual enumeration and account behavior, suspicious process execution, and attempts to escalate privileges. The key distinction is that IOCs tell you what happened after (or during) an attack, while IOAs help you detect and potentially stop an attack in progress. IOCs are more reactive, while IOAs are proactive in cybersecurity defense strategies. IOCs and IOAs provide a more comprehensive approach to threat detection and response.

> **Reconnaissance** Let's start with the first stage of most cyber-attacks: reconnaissance. This is where attackers gather information about their target, much like a burglar casing a house before a break-in. The goal is to build a comprehensive picture of the target's digital landscape, identifying potential vulnerabilities and weak points that can be exploited later.
>
> **Enumeration** Once the initial reconnaissance is complete, attackers typically move on to enumeration. This stage involves a more detailed probe of the identified systems and networks. This stage is all about gathering specific technical information that can be used to plan the actual attack. It's like creating a detailed map of the target's digital territory, focusing on identifying weaknesses to attack.
>
> **Penetration** With a clear picture of the target environment, attackers now attempt to gain initial access. This is where they validate and exploit vulnerabilities identified in the previous stages. The goal here is to establish a foothold in the target system, no matter how small.

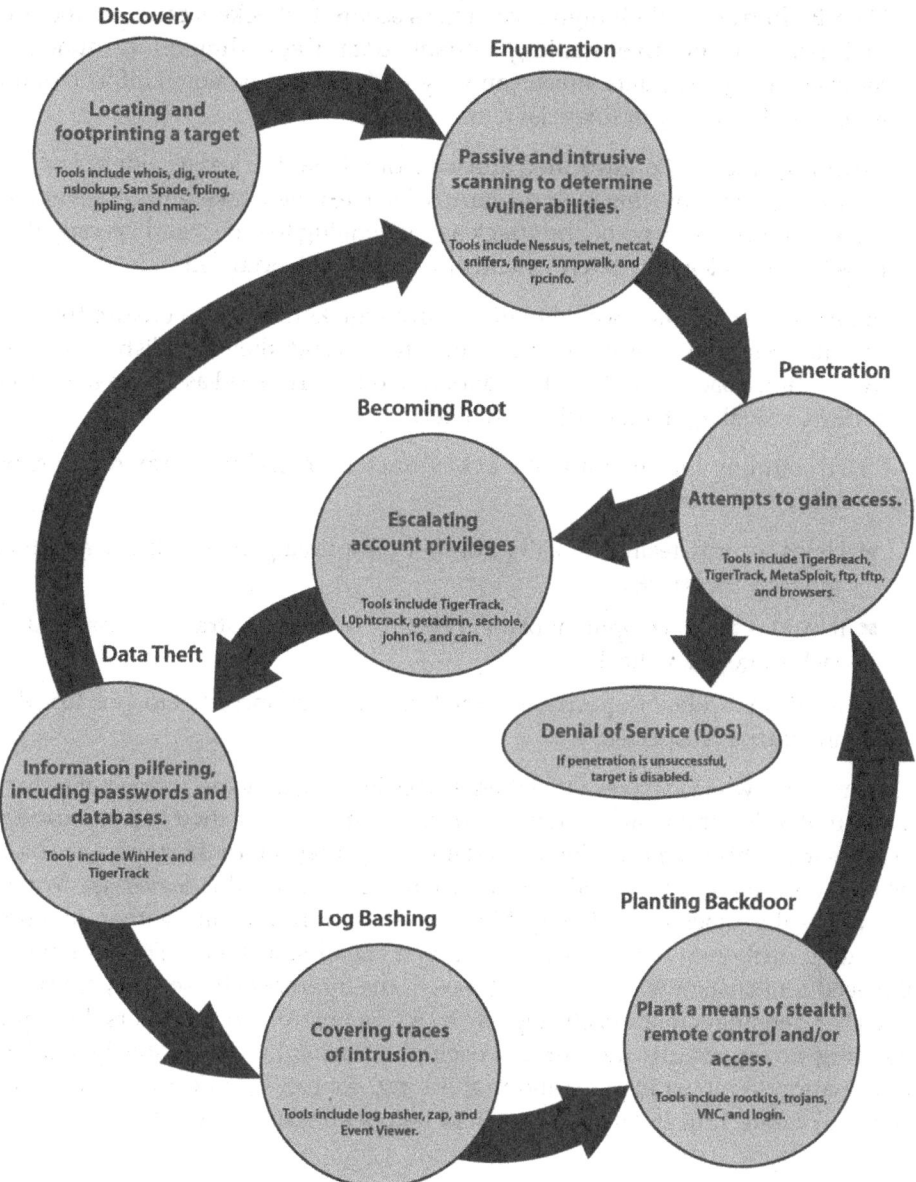

Figure 11-1: Common stages of an anatomy attack

Escalation of Privileges Once inside the system, attackers typically don't have complete access. The next step is to escalate privileges, often aiming to gain root or administrator-level access. Root access is crucial as it gives the attacker full control over the compromised system.

Data Exfiltration With high-level access secured, attackers can now focus on their primary objective: stealing valuable data. Depending on the attacker's motives, the type of data stolen can vary widely, from personal information to intellectual property or financial data.

Covering Tracks Sophisticated attackers don't want to leave evidence of their presence. After achieving their primary objective, they'll take steps to cover their tracks. The goal is to make the attack as challenging to detect and investigate as possible, often leaving defenders unsure if an attack occurred.

Establishing Persistence Finally, many attackers want to ensure they can regain access to the system in the future. To this end, they establish persistence by planting a backdoor. These backdoors are often disguised as legitimate system processes, making them difficult to detect.

Understanding the anatomy of a cyberattack is crucial for many reasons, but here are the top three:

- Helps security teams think like attackers, improving their ability to anticipate and prevent attacks.
- It guides the development of comprehensive defense strategies that address each stage of an attack.
- It aids in incident response, helping teams understand what to look for when an attack is suspected.

Remember, while I've presented these stages linearly, they can overlap or occur in a different order, and many variations and tangents could be their full manuscripts of content. Sophisticated attackers are adaptive and may adjust their approach based on their encounters. Once inside the environment, attackers do not necessarily need to execute the attack immediately. Many prefer to infiltrate and gather data until executing further on the attack chain when most advantageous. This emphasizes the need for constant vigilance on the part of the internal cybersecurity team.

Cyber defenders make each stage as tricky as possible for attackers. By implementing strong security measures at each point, from limiting publicly available information to robust logging and monitoring, we can significantly increase our chances of detecting and stopping attacks before attackers succeed.

Attack Vector Trends and Landscape

I'll dive into the cyberattack landscape because it's been wild. Let's start with the big picture. According to Check Point Research, there's a staggering 75% surge in cyberattacks worldwide toward the third quarter of 2024 compared to the same period the previous year. As shown in Figure 11-2, organizations face an average of more than 1,800 weekly attacks. That's not just a number, folks; it's a wake-up call.

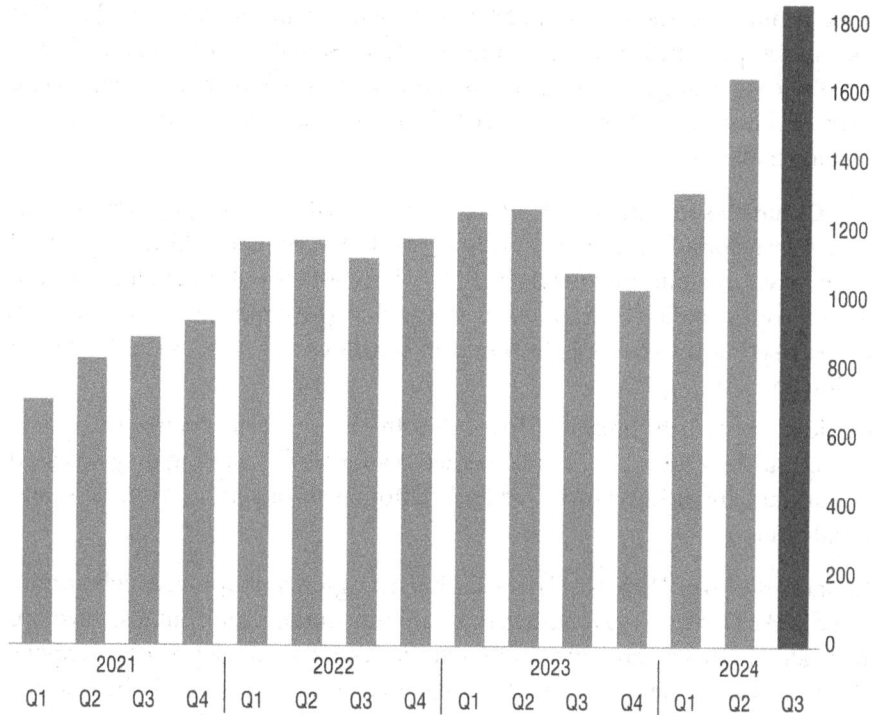

Figure 11-2: Average weekly cyberattacks

This cyberattack activity is undoubtedly staggering, and it correlates with six significant trends:

- Increased sophistication of ransomware attacks
- Rise in cloud-based attacks
- AI-enhanced cyber threats
- Increased targeting of critical infrastructure
- Supply chain and vendor attacks
- Identity-based attacks

I'll briefly talk about identity-based attacks and provide examples from my research.

Increased Sophistication of Ransomware Attacks   Ransomware attacks continue to plague organizations globally. In the first half of 2024, there was a 50% year-on-year increase in ransomware activity. But it's not just about quantity; it's about sophistication. The big story is the rise of double extortion and even triple extortion tactics. Attackers aren't just encrypting data anymore; they're stealing it and threatening to leak it publicly. Some are even contacting the victim's customers or partners to increase pressure.

A prime example is the attack on McLaren Health Care in August 2024. The attackers encrypted critical systems and exfiltrated sensitive patient data, threatening to release it unless a ransom was paid. This attack disrupted healthcare services and put patient privacy at risk. You can read more about this at the HIPAA Journal at www.hipaajournal.com.

Rise in Cloud-Based Attacks   With more organizations moving to the cloud, there is a corresponding rise in cloud-targeted attacks. CrowdStrike reported a 75% increase in cloud intrusions in 2024. These attacks often exploit misconfigurations or use stolen credentials to access cloud environments. Once inside, attackers use legitimate tools to blend in with everyday activities, making detection challenging.

A notable example is the breach of Toyota North America's cloud infrastructure in August 2024. The ZeroSevenGroup claimed responsibility, stating they accessed 240GB of data, including employee and customer information, contracts, and financial data.

AI-Enhanced Cyber Threats   There has been a significant uptick in cybercriminals' use of AI. Generative AI creates more convincing phishing emails, develops sophisticated malware, and even automates parts of the attack process. Artificial intelligence creates new content, such as text, images, music, and code, by learning patterns from large datasets. It uses advanced machine learning models, deep learning, and neural networks to generate human-like outputs.

In early 2024, a sophisticated phishing campaign targeted U.S. government officials. The attackers used AI to generate highly personalized and convincing emails, which increased their success rate in compromising accounts.

Increased Targeting of Critical Infrastructure   Attacks on critical infrastructure have intensified, focusing on energy, healthcare, and government sectors. Many of these attacks have geopolitical motivations. A stark example is the 2023 attack on the Danish power grid, attributed to Russian hackers. This attack caused temporary power outages and highlighted the vulnerability of national infrastructure to cyber threats.

Supply Chain and Vendor Attacks   Cybercriminals are increasingly targeting supply chains and vendors to maximize their impact. By compromising one service provider, attackers can access multiple organizations.

In January 2024, a SolarWinds-style attack on a major IT service provider affected multiple sectors. This attack involved inserting malicious code into software updates, which were then distributed to thousands of clients.

Identity-Based Attacks   Identity threats have exploded, and attackers use sophisticated methods to steal or bypass authentication, including SIM-swapping, MFA bypass, and API keys. The Scattered Spider group has been particularly active in this area. They've been using a combination of social engineering, phishing, and purchased credentials to gain rapid initial access to target systems.

SIM swapping, also known as SIM hijacking, is a form of identity theft where attackers convince a mobile carrier to transfer a victim's phone number to a new SIM card controlled by the attacker. This allows them to intercept calls, text messages, and one-time passwords sent to the victim's phone number, potentially bypassing two-factor authentication on various accounts.

Multifactor authentication (MFA) bypass refers to techniques attackers use to circumvent multi-factor authentication systems. Standard methods include the following:

- Phishing attacks to trick users into revealing MFA credentials
- MFA fatigue attacks, where users are bombarded with authentication requests
- Session hijacking to take more than an active authenticated session
- Exploiting vulnerabilities in MFA implementation or integration

API keys are secret tokens to authenticate and authorize access to APIs or Application Programming Interfaces. When these keys are stolen or leaked, attackers can do the following:

- Access sensitive data or functionality exposed by the API
- Perform unauthorized actions on behalf of the legitimate user or application
- In some cases, such as with cryptocurrency exchanges, they manipulate trades or withdraw funds

Stolen API keys are particularly dangerous because they often grant high access levels and can be challenging to detect if misused. They're frequently targeted in attacks on developers and organizations, often by scanning public code repositories or intercepting network traffic.

Attack Vector Trends Takeaways

So, what do the attack vector trends mean for organizations and individuals? Well, consider these as they correlate with some of the best practices I'll review later in Chapter 16:

- The importance of a robust, multilayered security approach has never been greater. This includes strong endpoint protection, network security, and cloud security measures.
- Employee training is crucial. With the rise of AI-enhanced phishing and social engineering attacks, your staff must be more vigilant than ever.
- Identity and access management should be a top priority. Implement strong authentication methods and regularly audit access privileges.
- Cloud security needs special attention. Ensure your cloud configurations are secure and regularly audited.

- Have a solid incident response plan in place. In the event of an attack, you need to be able to respond quickly and effectively. Exercise this plan regularly to ensure success when the attack occurs.
- Stay informed about the latest threats and trends. The cybersecurity landscape is constantly evolving, and staying up to date is crucial for maintaining effective defenses.

Malware Analysis for Digital Forensics Investigations

Next, before I discuss an actual incident in our case study, I'll walk through the key steps in malware analysis. This process is crucial for understanding how malicious software operates, as it is the root cause in the case study. It helps us develop better defenses and incident response strategies.

Preparation Our first step is preparation, where I set up a secure, isolated environment for our analysis. I typically use virtual machines or sandboxes to contain the malware and prevent it from infecting our main systems. At this stage, I also gather our analysis tools, such as disassemblers, debuggers, and network monitoring software. Remember, safety first! Never run malware on production systems.

Static Analysis Next, I move to static analysis, examining the malware without executing it. I look at things like file metadata, strings within the code, and the overall structure of the executable. Tools like PEiD can help us identify whether the malware is packed or obfuscated. Static analysis gives us our first clues about what the malware might do, but it's limited because many malware samples use sophisticated techniques to hide their true nature.

Dynamic Analysis Dynamic analysis is where things get interesting. In dynamic analysis, I run the malware in our controlled environment. I watch how it behaves: what files it creates or modifies, what registry changes it makes, and what network connections it attempts. Tools like Process Monitor and Wireshark are invaluable here. This step often reveals behaviors that weren't apparent in static analysis.

Memory Analysis After running the malware, I analyzed the system's memory. This can reveal hidden processes, injected code, and other artifacts that the malware leaves behind. Tools like Volatility are great for this. Memory analysis can be particularly useful for detecting sophisticated malware that tries to hide its presence on the system.

Network Analysis With network analysis, I focus on the malware's network activity. I look at DNS queries, IP addresses they connect to, and the data types they send and receive. This can help us identify command-and-control servers, data exfiltration attempts, and other network-based behaviors. Wireshark is a key tool in this step.

Reporting Finally, I compile all my findings into a comprehensive report. This isn't just about documenting what I found; it's about providing actionable intelligence. I include IOCs, details about the malware's capabilities, and recommendations for detection and mitigation. This report becomes a valuable resource for our security teams and potentially for the broader security community.

Remember, malware analysis is often an iterative process. As I uncover new information, I might repeat these steps multiple times. It's like solving a puzzle, where each piece leads to new questions and new investigative areas.

Key Tools and Challenges

Now, let's talk about essential tools, challenges in malware analysis, and some best practices to keep in mind. First, regarding tools in malware analysis, I broadly categorize them into four main types:

- Static analysis tools, like IDA Pro, Ghidra, pestudio, and Joe Sandbox allow us to examine malware without executing it. They're crucial for understanding the structure and potential behavior of malicious code.

- Dynamic analysis tools, such as Cuckoo Sandbox and Any.Run. These tools let us observe malware in action within a controlled environment. They're invaluable for understanding how malware behaves when it's running.

- Memory analysis tools, such as Volatility, help us examine the memory of infected systems. This can reveal hidden processes or data that might not be visible through other means.

- Network analysis tools like Wireshark. These are essential for monitoring and analyzing the network traffic generated by malware, helping us understand its communication patterns and potential command and control infrastructure.

However, malware analysis isn't without its challenges. I'm constantly up against challenges, such as the following:

- **Evolving malware techniques:** Cybercriminals constantly develop new ways to obfuscate their code and evade analysis. Techniques like anti-analysis measures can make our job significantly more difficult.

- **Time constraints:** In cybersecurity, time is often of the essence. I frequently need to analyze malware quickly to prevent further damage or infection.

- **The sheer volume of new malware variants and families:** The volume makes keeping up with the latest threats a constant challenge that requires ongoing learning and adaptation.

To address these challenges and make the most of our tools, I follow some best practices:

- **Always maintain a secure and isolated analysis environment:** This is crucial to prevent accidental infections and to ensure our analysis doesn't impact production systems.
- **Regularly update our analysis tools and knowledge:** The threat landscape is constantly evolving, and so should our tools and skills.
- **Collaborate with other analysts and share threat intelligence:** While no one can keep up with every new threat alone, we can stay ahead of the curve by working together and sharing information.

Remember, malware analysis is as much an art as a science. It requires the right tools, up-to-date knowledge, and a methodical approach. By understanding these key tools, recognizing our challenges, and adhering to best practices, we can effectively analyze and combat the ever-evolving malware threat.

Findings of a Healthcare Security Event

We're all aware of many notable breaches and data compromises. Still, I'll focus on a simulated event with some peppered in forensics and remediation and then think about how many of those trends apply. I'll start with the basics. A security team was brought in to conduct an extensive analysis of a web browser build called Wave Browser. This software was involved in a breach that affected dozens of healthcare clinics.

The Wave Browser has mixed reviews because there are many versions or builds, and it is customizable for good or not-so-good. Some say it's safe, some say it's a potentially unwanted program (PUP) such as adware, and others say it's malware. It's not out there; it's primarily breaching networks or holding data for ransom. But that doesn't mean it's harmless. Overall, Wave Browser has been reported to facilitate unwanted pop-up ads, create new tabs, redirect links, and modify browser settings. I would classify this behavior under two risk categories: Adware and Evader.

So, there were two versions of the Wave Browser in a production environment—the original and one after it was updated. Reverse engineering revealed some other concerns:

- The browser is connected to a domain that injects ads into search results. Malvertising has been reported in banner and other ads.
- Wave Browser used a software updater domain and was hosted on one of the world's leading cloud platforms.
- Wave Browser was able to be installed without elevated user rights or consent.

Now, let's talk about patient zero in the affected clinic network. How did Wave Browser get in?

The culprit was determined to be a malicious ad embedded in a phishing email. It's important to note that at the time of installation, a Windows 10 desktop had several n-day vulnerabilities that made it an easy target since their patching cycle was 60 days. These included the following:

- A security feature bypass vulnerability allowing attackers to bypass Microsoft Office macro policies
- A remote code execution vulnerability in Microsoft Word
- A remote code execution vulnerability in the Windows Graphics Component
- A vulnerability in Windows Common Log File System that could allow attackers to achieve SYSTEM privileges

So, these vulnerabilities appear to have rolled out the red carpet for Wave Browser.

In a malware analysis, 55 sources were utilized, and only 4 flagged anything but safe. Two identified four files associated with Wave Browser as low-to-medium risk, categorizing them as potentially unwanted programs and two as malware.

Now, let's discuss what Wave Browser was doing on the network. Through sandboxing, reverse engineering, and disassembly, the browser was programmed to access a long list of domains and subdomains, including variations of `wavebrowser.com`, `wavebrowserbase.com`, and `mywavehome.net`.

If I rewind the clock and reiterate, the analysis revealed that Wave Browser first appeared in the environment two months before the investigation. It was installed on a desktop in a clinic and used by a nurse. The installation originated from personal web browsing and email use through an affected advertisement correlated with a low-rated phishing attack that is assumed, based on some indicators, to have been crafted using AI.

The Wave Browser was also set as the default browser on this machine, and logs show that the user was accessing online applications via `office.com` and `office.net` using the browser. However, after the software was updated, logs indicated callouts and payloads pointed to China-hosted known malware repositories. One final note is that at a point, bad actors also attempted to leverage known RMM software, in this case called Landesk, used by a partner to support eScreen readers on the nurses' desktops. The eScreen readers were used to assist in reading and processing electronic medical records, health documents, and test results.

Technical Analysis

Let's dig into more of the technical analysis of the clinics and affected assets. At the time, and somewhat even today, the industry did not categorize the Wave Browser as a computer infection, Trojan horse, or a file encrypting malware that can impair computers. While the Wave Browser isn't reported as doing anything malicious, it has been reported as facilitating unwanted pop-up ads, new tabs, page redirect links, and browser modifications.

I'll walk through a technical analysis of the incident, starting with the software and working my way into the injection point and malicious intent. I'll also discuss the real impact. As mentioned, the Wave Browser software behavior correlates with two cybersecurity risk classification categories: *Adware* and *Evader* and *PUP with Adware and Browser Hijacker Characteristics*.

Reverse engineering of the software depicts the behavior of a connection to `api.wavebrowserbase.com`, which injects ads into web search results. It is important to note that the Wave Browser can be installed without elevated user privileges or user consent. This is an extract from the Joe Security platform analysis. You can search their website for detailed reports on the Wave Browser.

Behavioral Analysis:

- **Process manipulation:**
  - Creates threads in other processes (thread injection).
  - Creates processes in suspended mode, likely for code injection.
  - These behaviors are often associated with malware attempting to hide its activities.
- **Anti-analysis techniques:**
  - Attempts to detect debuggers and virtual machines.
  - Contains functionality for execution timing checks.
  - These are common evasion tactics used by malware to avoid detection and analysis.
- **Data harvesting:**
  - Tries to harvest browser information (history, passwords).
  - Contains capabilities for clipboard reading.
  - This suggests potential privacy and security risks for users.
- **System control:**
  - Can launch processes as different users.
  - Has system shutdown/reboot functionality.
  - These capabilities could be used for legitimate purposes but also malicious activities.

These characteristics, especially the invalid checksum and nonstandard sections, often indicate potentially malicious software.

Network activity also suggests potential command-and-control communication or data exfiltration with ingress and egress to locations in China. While this does not directly address "ChinaNet," it illustrates a pattern of cyber activities associated with some bad actors in China. These activities involve malware, vulnerability exploitation, and attempts to compromise critical infrastructure and communication networks. The activities range from pre-installed malware on hardware to sophisticated state-sponsored cyber operations targeting various sectors.

I mentioned that clinics have eScreen reader devices that communicate with the escreen.com domain, which a third party manages. However, this traffic correlates with the Wave Browser events from a timeframe perspective, which could indicate attackers may have tried to leverage the platform. These included unencrypted pages that allow for the download and installation of the LANDesk agents (for remote control) without any form of authentication. There's also a link to a console that pulls in an authentication form.

A note about next generation security information and event management (SIEM) platforms. I mentioned them in previous chapters, but know that they significantly enhance digital forensics investigations in the following ways:

- **Comprehensive data collection:** Next-gen SIEMs collect and centralize data from various sources across an organization's IT infrastructure, providing investigators with a holistic view of the environment.
- **Advanced analytics:** These platforms use machine learning and AI to detect anomalies and patterns that might indicate a security incident, helping investigators focus on relevant data.
- **Automated attack timelines:** Next-gen SIEMs can automatically piece together elements of an attack and present them on a visual timeline, speeding up the investigation process.
- **User and entity behavioral analytics (UEBA):** By establishing baselines of regular activity, these systems can highlight suspicious behaviors that may be part of an attack.
- **Rapid search and correlation:** Investigators can quickly search through large volumes of data and correlate events across different systems, aiding in root cause analysis.
- **Forensic data preservation:** Next-generation SIEMs often include features to ensure the immutability of collected data, which is crucial for maintaining the integrity of evidence.
- **Incident reconstruction:** These platforms can help reconstruct the sequence of events leading up to and following a security incident.
- **Integration with threat intelligence:** Next-gen SIEMs can provide context to potentially malicious activities by incorporating up-to-date threat intelligence.
- **Automated reporting:** They can generate detailed reports that can be used as evidence in investigations or for compliance purposes.

By leveraging these capabilities, digital forensics investigators can conduct more thorough and efficient investigations, uncovering evidence that might be missed with traditional methods. In this case, I'm focusing on Rapid7 InsightIDR, a platform I'm very familiar with, which can create forensics reporting in many ways, including the following:

- **Comprehensive data collection:** InsightIDR collects data from various sources across an organization's IT infrastructure, including endpoint devices, authentication logs, and network security tools.

- **Unified data view:** The platform aggregates and normalizes data, attributing events to specific users and assets, providing a holistic view of the environment.
- **Automated investigation timelines:** InsightIDR automatically creates detailed, visual investigation timelines for each alert, correlating events across different data sources.
- **Endpoint forensics:** The Insight Agent allows real-time endpoint scanning and collecting forensic data such as running processes, DNS cache, installed services, and registry keys.
- **Log analysis:** InsightIDR enables searching and analyzing raw logs, which can be added to investigations for context.
- **UEBA:** The platform uses behavioral analytics to detect anomalies and suspicious activities.
- **Customizable reporting:** Users can generate detailed reports on threat trends and the overall effectiveness of the security team.
- **Integration with DFIR tools:** For advanced forensic capabilities, InsightIDR Ultimate integrates with Velociraptor, a Digital Forensics and Incident Response (DFIR) tool.
- **Automated response actions:** The platform supports automation workflows for actions like quarantining assets or creating tickets, which can be included in forensic reports.
- **Data export:** InsightIDR allows for exporting of investigation data, enabling the creation of customized forensic reports.

By leveraging these features, InsightIDR enables security teams to create comprehensive forensic reports that include detailed timelines, endpoint data, log analysis, and behavioral insights. These reports provide a thorough overview of security incidents for investigation and compliance purposes.

The framework approach monitors all devices spanning to the edge and sends logs, vitals, running processes, and traffic to a local collector. The collector will securely send data for analysis that federates alarms to folks. This is a synopsis of key steps to take when running a digital forensics investigation using a log analysis tool:

1. **Identification and preservation:**
    a. Identify all relevant log sources (servers, applications, network devices, etc.)
    b. Ensure logs are preserved and secured to maintain chain of custody
    c. Create forensic copies/images of log data to work from
2. **Collection:**
    a. Ingest logs into the log analysis tool
    b. Verify data integrity during ingestion
    c. Apply any necessary parsing or normalization to standardize log formats

3. **Analysis:**
   a. Use the tool's search and filtering capabilities to identify relevant events
   b. Look for indicators of compromise or suspicious activity patterns
   c. Correlate events across different log sources to build a timeline
   d. Apply any built-in threat detection or anomaly detection capabilities
   e. Use visualization features to identify trends or anomalies
4. **Documentation:**
   a. Document all steps taken during the investigation
   b. Record search queries used and results obtained
   c. Capture screenshots of relevant findings
   d. Maintain an audit trail of all investigative actions
5. **Reporting:**
   a. Use the tool's reporting capabilities to generate investigation summaries
   b. Include key findings, timelines, and supporting evidence
   c. Ensure reports are clear and understandable for non-technical stakeholders
6. **Presentation:**
   a. Prepare visualizations or dashboards to present findings
   b. Be ready to explain the methodology and tools used
   c. Ensure all presented evidence maintains integrity and chain of custody

Strict access controls must be maintained throughout the process on the log data and investigation results to preserve confidentiality and integrity. The log analysis tool should provide features to support each of these steps in a forensically sound manner.

Another benefit of InsightIDR is its centralized deception technology. This allows us to create an illusion for attackers that they have found something of interest within our customer's environment. When intruder traps are deployed on a network, they act as a virtual trip wire. Once an attacker is tricked into touching the trap, InsightIDR fires an alert to our team.

So why is this useful? Some stealthy attacks can be difficult to discern from regular activity, allowing attackers to sneak past security controls. Distracting intruders by placing traps often helps us find them earlier and take action to block them.

In conclusion, Wave Browser and the folks from China didn't cause catastrophic damage in the scenario, as it was detected and mitigated just after updating. Those connections serve as a wake-up call. They remind us that threats can come in many forms, and even seemingly benign software can pose significant risks to our networks and data.

Among a long list of recommendations, for brevity, the organization would implement stricter controls on personal web use, enhance email filtering, conduct more frequent vulnerability assessments, and ensure assets are patched within 30 days of release after an upgrade to Windows 11. The customer would also implement GEO blocking and start doubling down on user education because, as this incident shows, the users were the first line of defense and the weak link.

Post-Event Lessons Learned

This simulated case highlights many of the severe consequences of cybersecurity breaches in healthcare, affecting not only the financial stability of organizations but also the quality and continuity of patient care and the overall trust in the healthcare system. Here is an overview of the average (some say on the low side) financial and human impacts on healthcare organizations from the example:

- Financial Impacts:
  - Direct cost is approximately $300,000.
  - Lost revenue due to service disruptions and operational downtime for weeks.
  - Increased cybersecurity insurance premiums can rise by approximately 26%.
- Human Impacts:
  - Disruption to patient care includes delayed treatments, surgeries, and inability to access and transfer some patient records.
  - Stress and increased workload for healthcare and IT staff dealing with the aftermath of attacks and implementing workarounds.
  - Some reported job losses are likely due to organizational financial and operational strain.
  - The erosion of trust between some affected patients and the healthcare provider could lead to patients avoiding or delaying necessary care.
  - Delayed advancements in patient treatments and therapies.

Key Takeaways from Hospital Network Breaches with IoMT Devices

This chapter highlights the urgent need for a multilayered, proactive approach to securing IoMT devices and healthcare networks. Lessons from past breaches serve as a roadmap for preventing future incidents and safeguarding healthcare systems. While IoMT has significantly improved patient care through technologies like infusion pumps, patient monitors, and imaging systems, these advancements also introduce substantial cybersecurity risks. The interconnected nature of these devices creates a broad attack surface, making them prime targets for cybercriminals. Many IoMT devices operate with outdated software, unpatched vulnerabilities, and weak security features, such as default credentials and insufficient encryption, exposing them to exploitation.

One critical risk is poor network segmentation, which allows attackers to move laterally across hospital systems after compromising a single IoMT device. Flat network structures connect critical systems, such as electronic health records and imaging devices, making them accessible from a single breach point. Additionally, human error, including weak password practices and falling victim to phishing attacks, remains a major factor in cybersecurity incidents. Insider threats, whether intentional or accidental, further increase the risk of system compromises.

The rise of publicly accessible IoMT devices has expanded the attack surface, exposing them to external scanning and exploitation. Cybercriminals increasingly employ sophisticated tactics such as ransomware and man-in-the-middle attacks to target these vulnerable systems. Attacks typically progress through multiple stages, including reconnaissance, penetration, privilege escalation, data exfiltration, and persistence, emphasizing the need for early threat detection. Case studies, such as ransomware attacks on healthcare institutions and third-party vendor breaches, illustrate the devastating impact of IoMT vulnerabilities, leading to operational disruptions, data breaches, and financial losses. Beyond monetary damages, cyberattacks delay surgeries, disrupt patient care, and erode public trust in healthcare providers.

To address these risks, healthcare organizations must implement strategic defense measures. Network segmentation can help isolate IoMT devices from critical systems, reducing the potential attack surface. Timely patching, updates, and strong collaboration with manufacturers are essential for mitigating vulnerabilities. Advanced detection and response mechanisms, including intrusion detection systems and anomaly detection, can identify and neutralize threats proactively. Continuous cybersecurity education for healthcare staff is crucial in minimizing human error, while vendor accountability ensures that third-party providers uphold stringent security standards.

A proactive approach to threat management, integrating IOAs with IOCs, enables healthcare organizations to detect, respond to, and prevent cyber threats more effectively. Emerging technologies, such as deception techniques, behavioral analytics, and centralized monitoring, further enhance security. Ultimately, securing IoMT devices requires collaboration between healthcare providers, device manufacturers, cybersecurity experts, and regulatory agencies. By adopting industry best practices, including secure-by-design principles and zero-trust architectures, the healthcare sector can significantly reduce cybersecurity risks and ensure the safety and integrity of connected medical devices.

CHAPTER 12

Wearable Medical Device Security Challenges

Devices such as smartwatches, continuous glucose monitors, wearable ECG monitors, smart inhalers, and fitness trackers are now commonplace, allowing individuals to track everything from heart rate and blood oxygen levels to sleep patterns and blood glucose levels. These devices are often connected to the Internet or paired with smartphones and other systems to provide real-time feedback, remote monitoring, and analysis. The data collected can help healthcare providers make more informed decisions about diagnosis, treatment, and prevention. However, the growing reliance on wearable medical devices has raised concerns about security and privacy. As these devices increasingly store, transmit, and interact with sensitive health data, they have become prime cyberattack targets.

This chapter provides an overview of the security challenges surrounding wearable medical devices. It examines vulnerabilities and their implications for patient safety, data privacy, and healthcare systems. The chapter also offers practical recommendations for mitigating these risks, including further advancements in leveraging AI.

The Rise of Wearable Medical Devices

Wearable medical devices are electronic devices that individuals wear on their bodies to monitor or assist with healthcare-related tasks. These devices collect real-time data about the user's health and provide users and healthcare providers with insights into their health status. Wearable medical devices include the following types:

- **Smartwatches:** Devices like the Apple Watch or Fitbit monitor heart rate, steps, and calories burned, and some even offer ECG readings
- **Continuous glucose monitors:** Devices such as Dexcom or Freestyle Libre that monitor blood glucose levels continuously throughout the day for people with diabetes
- **Wearable ECG monitors:** Devices like the KardiaMobile that track heart activity and can detect irregular heart rhythms, including atrial fibrillation
- **Wearable sleep trackers:** Devices that monitor sleep patterns, including the quality and duration of sleep
- **Smart Inhalers:** Devices that help individuals with asthma or COPD track their medication usage and inhaler techniques

These devices are often equipped with sensors, and they communicate with other devices (such as smartphones) via Bluetooth, Wi-Fi, or cellular networks to send health data to healthcare providers or cloud storage for analysis, tracking, and reporting.

Key Benefits of Wearable Devices

The continuous flow of real-time data offers numerous benefits but introduces cybersecurity vulnerabilities, which will be discussed next. Some of the key benefits of wearable devices include the following:

- **Remote patient monitoring:** Healthcare providers can remotely monitor a patient's vital signs, such as heart rate, blood pressure, and glucose levels, without requiring in-person visits. This can improve patient outcomes, especially for chronic conditions.
- **Personalized treatment:** Continuous monitoring allows healthcare professionals to adjust treatment plans in real time based on accurate, up-to-date data.
- **Early detection of health issues:** Wearables can detect irregularities in a patient's health, such as abnormal heart rhythms or elevated blood glucose levels, and alert the patient and healthcare provider before the situation becomes critical. This also facilitates cost savings.
- **Convenience and patient engagement:** Wearables offer patients convenience by allowing them to actively participate in their health management, monitor progress, and track their lifestyle choices without regularly visiting a doctor.
- **Modernization:** Wearables generate large amounts of health data for research and innovation in healthcare.

Security Challenges of Wearable Medical Devices

Continuous glucose monitors and wearable ECGs are widely integrated into healthcare ecosystems. As these devices connect to networks, smartphones, and cloud-based platforms, they face escalating cybersecurity threats. This section analyzes some of the most common security challenges.

Key Vulnerabilities in Wearable Medical Devices

I'll explore five significant vulnerabilities in connected wearables and discuss why they matter, how attackers exploit them, and what can be done to protect them.

Weak or No Encryption   Let's start with encryption, or its lack thereof. Wearable medical devices transmit sensitive health data wirelessly using technologies like Bluetooth, Wi-Fi, or, in some cases, proprietary protocols. Attackers can intercept this data if it isn't encrypted with strong algorithms such as AES-256 or TLS 1.3. Imagine someone listening in on your private conversations, which would be the digital equivalent.

Emerging threats in 2024 have revealed that attackers are exploiting unencrypted connections in real time. For instance, they've modified insulin pump settings or interfered with cardiac monitors, putting patients at risk. This highlights the urgent need for strong encryption to keep data secure.

Insecure Communication Protocols   As mentioned in the previous chapters, communication protocols like Bluetooth Low Energy and Zigbee, while power-efficient, are widely used and have well-known weaknesses:

- BLE pairing can sometimes be bypassed with tools called sniffer devices.
- Replay attacks allow attackers to resend captured signals, potentially disrupting device functionality or gaining unauthorized access.
- Proprietary protocols can also pose risks because they may not undergo rigorous security testing, leaving unknown vulnerabilities.

To reduce these risks, manufacturers must secure these protocols, and users must keep their devices updated.

Lack of Robust Authentication   Another significant issue is weak authentication. Many wearable devices ship with default passwords that users are never required to change. Others don't support multifactor authentication, which leaves them vulnerable to unauthorized access. For example, attackers may use social engineering to steal credentials or exploit QR codes for device pairing. As these attacks become more sophisticated, it's critical for manufacturers to enforce stronger authentication mechanisms and for users to adopt safer practices.

Unpatched Firmware and Software   Wearables often run on proprietary firmware that may not receive regular updates. Why? This lack of updating could be due to strict regulatory processes for healthcare devices, manufacturer negligence, or simply because users don't know updates are available. A 2024 study found that 30% or more of wearable devices had vulnerabilities left unpatched for over a year. This means attackers could exploit old flaws that haven't been fixed. Regular updates are crucial to patch security holes and protect users.

Weak Access Controls   Many devices lack proper access controls. Some don't use biometric authentication, like fingerprints, or fail to log users out after a certain period. This leaves devices open to physical or remote attacks. Without safeguards, attackers can tamper with settings or extract sensitive information. Imagine an attacker gaining access to a heart monitor and altering its readings—this could have life-threatening consequences.

In summary, wearable medical devices offer incredible benefits, but their vulnerabilities cannot be ignored. The lack of standardization and regulation in the IoMT ecosystem contributes to these vulnerabilities. Weak encryption, insecure protocols, poor authentication, unpatched software, and weak access controls make them attractive targets for attackers.

Data Privacy Risks

I'll focus on four significant data privacy risks related to wearable medical devices: unauthorized data access, data sharing practices, cloud vulnerabilities, and third-party app misuse.

Unauthorized Data Access   Wearable medical devices store and transmit personal health data, including glucose levels, heart rate, and sleep patterns. They may also track your location and store identifiable details like your name, age, and medical history. If a device gets hacked, this information can fall into the wrong hands.

Even more concerning is how attackers are using advanced AI tools in 2024. These tools analyze stolen data to create highly personalized phishing attacks or even blackmail campaigns targeting sensitive health conditions. Imagine someone threatening to reveal a private health issue unless you pay them. This is a real risk, so protecting devices with strong encryption and authentication is essential.

Data Sharing and Selling Practices   Next, consider how data is shared and sold. Many wearable manufacturers and their partners collect and share user data with third parties, such as marketers and insurance companies. What's the problem with this? Often, users aren't fully aware of how their data is used. For example, some companies may sell anonymized data, but studies show that anonymized data can often be re-identified. In 2023, one major manufacturer was investigated for sharing anonymized health data that advertisers could trace back to individuals. This sparked regulatory actions and public outcry.

Regulations like HIPAA in the United States and GDPR in the EU require companies to protect user data and obtain explicit consent before sharing it. Failure to comply can result in hefty fines and damage to a company's reputation. Users should always review privacy policies carefully before using these devices.

Cloud and API Vulnerabilities The cloud and APIs also present vulnerabilities. Most wearable devices store data on cloud servers or allow access through APIs, which are connections between applications. While this setup is convenient, it's also risky. Misconfigured cloud storage can expose data, allowing unauthorized users to access sensitive information.

Weak API security, such as missing rate limits or improper authentication, can also make it easy for attackers to breach systems. For example, early last year, a global fitness app suffered an API breach, exposing the heart rate and fitness data of more than 1 million users. To reduce these risks, companies need to implement stronger encryption, regularly audit their systems, and use secure tokens for authentication.

Data Misuse by Third-Party Apps Let's remind ourselves about the risks of third-party apps. Most wearables rely on companion apps to function, but these apps can introduce security gaps. Some apps request excessive permissions, like access to your contacts, messages, or location, even if they don't need it for core functions. Many apps fail to encrypt locally stored data, making it easier for attackers to extract information if they gain access to your device. In some cases, apps share data with advertisers without adequately disclosing this to users. It's important only to download apps from trusted sources and to check what permissions they request. Manufacturers must also test their apps thoroughly and follow best encryption and data handling practices.

Regulatory and Compliance Challenges

Regulatory and compliance challenges surrounding wearable medical devices are increasingly complex, particularly as these devices become more integrated into healthcare ecosystems. One central area of concern is adherence to healthcare data regulations. HIPAA mandates the privacy and security of protected health information or PHI, while GDPR imposes strict rules for safeguarding personal health data and ensuring explicit user consent. However, many wearable devices operate in a regulatory gray area, primarily when the data they collect extends beyond their primary medical purpose, raising questions about how these rules apply and how compliance should be enforced.

Global variability in cybersecurity standards adds to this complexity. Manufacturers face the challenge of navigating a patchwork of regulations across jurisdictions. A wearable device designed to meet stringent cybersecurity benchmarks in one region may fail to satisfy the requirements of another, creating significant hurdles for globally distributed products and increasing the risk of compliance lapses.

Another pressing issue is managing devices nearing the end of their lifecycle. Many wearable devices continue to be used even after manufacturers cease providing software updates or security patches. These unsupported devices become systemic vulnerabilities, exposing users and healthcare networks to emerging cyber threats. The lack of a clear strategy for addressing end-of-life devices underscores the need for coordinated efforts between regulators, manufacturers, and healthcare providers to ensure that security remains a priority throughout the device lifecycle.

Global compliance gaps in wearable medical devices highlight inconsistencies, limitations, and challenges in ensuring uniform security, privacy, and regulatory standards across different jurisdictions. These gaps expose patients, healthcare providers, and manufacturers to cybersecurity risks, data privacy violations, and legal liabilities. I'll cover 10 of the key global compliance gaps.

Variability in regulations across regions presents significant challenges for wearable medical device manufacturers. Different countries impose distinct regulatory requirements, creating inconsistencies in compliance frameworks. For instance, while the HIPAA in the United States emphasizes the privacy and security of protected health information, the GDPR in the European Union prioritizes user consent and data minimization. Compliance with one regulation does not necessarily ensure adherence to the other. International cybersecurity and data protection standards in wearable medical devices remain largely unharmonized. Unlike regulations governing medical device safety and efficacy, cybersecurity guidelines vary widely across regions. As a result, manufacturers must customize their devices for different markets, increasing costs and complexity.

The limited scope of existing regulations further exacerbates regulatory gaps. Many wearable devices collect non-medical data, such as fitness tracking information, that is not directly linked to diagnosis or treatment. These devices often fall outside the purview of strict medical regulations, creating a vacuum in privacy and security protections. Furthermore, rapid technological advancements, including artificial intelligence-driven insights and Internet of Things (IoT) integration outpace current regulatory frameworks. These innovations are not always covered under existing laws, leaving significant gaps in oversight and accountability.

Enforcement mechanisms for healthcare cybersecurity regulations are often inadequate. Many countries have no strict penalties for noncompliance, which undermines regulatory effectiveness. Additionally, resource constraints hinder the ability of regulatory bodies, particularly in low—and middle-income countries, to implement necessary oversight. Without sufficient resources and expertise, ensuring the cybersecurity of wearable devices becomes increasingly complex, leaving consumers vulnerable to potential threats.

Another significant concern is the insufficient coverage of data transfers, especially in cross-border transactions. Wearable devices frequently transmit user data to cloud platforms hosted in different countries. While frameworks like GDPR regulate such transfers, many regions lack equivalent protections, making data susceptible to interception or misuse during international transit. Moreover, data sovereignty conflicts arise in countries with strict data localization laws, such as China and India. These regulations pose significant challenges for global manufacturers, who must navigate multiple, often conflicting, legal requirements.

The absence of standards for end-of-life management also contributes to cybersecurity risks. Many wearable devices remain used long after manufacturers discontinue software updates and security support, creating systemic vulnerabilities. Current regulatory frameworks do not adequately address the risks associated with legacy devices. Additionally, there are no globally enforced requirements mandating manufacturers to notify users about end-of-life device use or to provide secure disposal and deactivation protocols. This lack of regulation increases the potential for cybersecurity threats from outdated devices.

The integration of third-party systems into wearable medical devices introduces further security risks. Many wearables interact with external platforms, including mobile applications and cloud systems. However, no comprehensive regulations ensure these third parties adhere to equivalent security and compliance standards. Furthermore, data collected by wearable devices is often shared with third-party companies for analytics, marketing, or research purposes without stringent oversight. This unregulated data sharing raises concerns about how securely such information is handled and whether user privacy is adequately protected.

Emerging markets face additional regulatory gaps, often lacking effective cybersecurity regulations for medical devices. The absence of stringent oversight makes it easier for poorly secured wearables to enter these markets, increasing cybersecurity vulnerabilities. Moreover, while international frameworks such as those from the International Medical Device Regulators Forum (IMDRF) provide regulatory guidance, their adoption and implementation vary widely across different regions. This inconsistency further contributes to a fragmented global regulatory landscape.

Incident response and reporting standards for wearable medical devices remain inadequate. While regulations such as HIPAA and GDPR mandate breach reporting, there is no globally unified protocol dictating when, how, or to whom breaches should be reported. As a result, some regions experience delays in responding to security incidents, allowing breaches involving wearable devices to go unreported for extended periods. This lack of standardized breach protocols increases user risks, as security incidents may not be promptly addressed.

Security benchmarking for wearable medical devices also lacks uniformity. There is no global baseline for cybersecurity requirements, leading to variations in encryption, authentication, and patch management protocols across regions and manufacturers. Additionally, startups and smaller manufacturers in under-regulated markets prioritize rapid deployment over security compliance. This rush to market without adequate security measures introduces vulnerabilities, exposing users to potential cybersecurity threats.

Finally, accountability frameworks for wearable medical devices are fragmented, leading to ambiguity in responsibility. The division of accountability between device manufacturers, healthcare providers, and end-users is often unclear, particularly in multi-jurisdictional deployments. Additionally, gaps in liability for data misuse remain a pressing concern. Many regions lack clear regulations defining who is responsible for mishandling wearable device data, whether manufacturers, service providers, or data handlers. This lack of accountability creates uncertainty and limits users' ability to seek redress in data breaches or misuse cases.

By addressing these gaps, the healthcare industry can better manage the risks associated with wearable medical devices while maintaining patient trust and compliance with evolving global standards. Here is a short list regarding those standards:

- **International harmonization efforts:** Bodies like the World Health Organization (WHO) and International Electrotechnical Commission (IEC) drive standardized guidelines for cybersecurity in wearables.

- **Explicit data use regulations:** Governments should ensure that wearables are covered by health data regulations, even when their primary purpose is non-medical.
- **Lifecycle management requirements:** Global standards enforce secure end-of-life policies, including notifications, safe disposal, and patching obligations.
- **Cross-border collaboration:** Unified data transfer protocols and incident response protocols can help address wearables' global cybersecurity risks.

New Trends and Threats in Wearable Device Security

Wearable medical devices have transformed healthcare by providing continuous monitoring and personalized insights into patient health. The latest trends highlight how cybercriminals adapt their strategies to exploit wearable ecosystems. Some correlate with the previous chapter's attack trends and landscape, underscoring the urgent need for advanced security measures. I'll discuss the top four further by emerging threats and real-world implications.

AI-Powered Attacks

Cybercriminals are increasingly leveraging artificial intelligence to enhance the sophistication of their attacks, making them more effective and challenging to detect. AI is used to identify vulnerabilities in wearable ecosystems, such as insecure communication protocols or unpatched software, enabling attackers to exploit these weaknesses. Additionally, AI is automating phishing campaigns targeting wearable users, creating highly personalized and convincing schemes that trick individuals into revealing credentials or installing malicious applications. Another significant threat is the development of adaptive malware capable of bypassing traditional security measures, such as static antivirus systems or predefined intrusion detection rules. The real-world implications of AI-powered attacks are substantial, as they can dramatically increase the efficiency and success rate of breaches, threatening user privacy and device functionality. For instance, attackers could exploit wearables that interface with hospital networks, introducing broader system-wide vulnerabilities that jeopardize critical healthcare operations.

IoMT Botnets

Attackers are hijacking wearable medical devices to form IoMT botnets, taking advantage of their always-on connectivity and relatively weak security measures. These botnets are deployed for various malicious purposes, including distributed denial-of-service (DDoS) attacks. Cybercriminals can overwhelm servers with excessive traffic by commandeering wearables connected to healthcare networks, causing system outages that disrupt patient care and hospital operations. Another major threat is covert data harvesting, where botnets systematically exfiltrate sensitive patient data from compromised networks, leading to potential privacy violations and data breaches. The real-world implications of such attacks are severe, as seen in the Mirai botnet incident, which demonstrated how IoT devices could be weaponized at scale. Similar exploits in the context of wearables could compromise critical medical operations, disrupt emergency services, and expose millions of patient records to unauthorized access.

Data Poisoning

Attackers are employing data poisoning techniques to inject false data into wearable devices or the cloud systems they connect to, posing serious risks to healthcare and medical analytics. This type of attack can corrupt medical records and skew health monitoring data, leading to incorrect diagnoses, inappropriate treatments, or even life-threatening medical decisions. Furthermore, data poisoning undermines AI-powered healthcare analytics by feeding maliciously altered data into machine learning models, negatively impacting predictive accuracy and care recommendations. The consequences of such manipulation can be dire; for example, an attacker could alter glucose readings from a connected wearable, leading healthcare providers to administer inappropriate insulin dosages to diabetic patients. This could result in severe health complications, illustrating the dangerous potential of data poisoning in the medical and wearable technology sectors.

Supply Chain Exploits

Cybercriminals are increasingly targeting the supply chains of wearable devices, embedding malware or backdoors into products before they even reach consumers. These attacks often involve tampering, where malicious actors compromise the firmware during manufacturing or distribution, granting them control over devices post-deployment. Another common tactic is exploiting vulnerabilities in third-party software or hardware components integrated into wearables, creating security gaps that attackers can later exploit. The real-world implications of such supply chain exploits are significant, as evidenced by a 2023 breach involving compromised firmware in wearable fitness trackers. This incident highlighted how attackers could gain unauthorized access to user data globally. Supply chain exploits pose systemic risks, as compromised devices may be distributed widely before vulnerabilities are detected, challenging mitigation efforts.

Proactive Measures for Mitigating Wearable Device Threats

Addressing these emerging security challenges is essential as wearable medical devices become integral to healthcare. The following measures are critical to building a resilient and secure wearable ecosystem:

- **End-to-end encryption:** Encrypt data in transit and at rest to prevent unauthorized access during communication between wearables, cloud systems, and mobile apps.
- **Strong authentication:** To prevent unauthorized access, implement advanced protocols such as multifactor authentication, biometric verification, and device attestation.
- **Segmentation:** Enclave medical device networks from general IT networks to reduce the attack surface and prevent lateral movement within the network.
- **Least Privilege segmentation:** Enclave medical device networks from general IT networks to reduce the attack surface and prevent lateral movement within the network.
- **Timely software updates:** Ensure regular software and firmware updates to patch vulnerabilities promptly and communicate these updates clearly to users to ensure adoption.
- **Supply chain security:** Monitor supply chain partners closely and enforce stringent security requirements to prevent tampering or malware insertion during manufacturing. Ensure proper testing of proprietary protocols.
- **Threat detection and monitoring:** Deploy advanced AI-powered threat detection systems to monitor wearable ecosystems for unusual activity and mitigate risks in real time.
- **Regulatory compliance:** Adhere to evolving global standards, including HIPAA, GDPR, and regional cybersecurity guidelines, to ensure patient data privacy and device security.
- **User education:** Train users on best practices, such as recognizing phishing attempts, securing devices with strong passwords, and avoiding unverified apps or connections.

In 2025, wearable medical devices continue to unlock transformative possibilities in patient care, but their growing adoption and connectivity bring unprecedented cybersecurity risks. Cybercriminals are becoming more sophisticated, leveraging AI, botnets, and supply chain exploits to compromise these devices. Addressing these threats requires a collaborative effort between manufacturers, healthcare providers, cybersecurity experts, and regulators. By implementing comprehensive security measures and fostering awareness, we can harness the full potential of wearable medical devices while safeguarding patient safety and data integrity. Proactive vigilance is no longer optional; it is the foundation of trust in the healthcare technology landscape. In the next section, I will review how AI can help.

How AI Can Help

AI provides advanced tools for threat detection, prevention, and system optimization, helping to keep wearable medical devices safe. Here, I'll briefly examine how AI can improve wearable security.

Anomaly Detection and Real-Time Threat Identification AI systems are excellent at analyzing massive amounts of data in real time. They can quickly spot unusual behavior that might indicate a security threat. For example, AI can flag this immediately if a wearable device suddenly sends unexpected signals or connects to an unauthorized network. It can then alert users or administrators to take quick action and prevent further damage.

Predictive Analytics for Threat Prevention AI doesn't just respond to threats; it can also predict them. AI algorithms can identify vulnerabilities before they are exploited by studying device behavior, usage patterns, and historical attack data. For instance, AI can warn manufacturers about firmware weaknesses, allowing them to fix problems through updates or patches before attackers can take advantage.

Adaptive Authentication Mechanisms AI can make authentication more innovative and more flexible. Instead of relying on fixed passwords, AI analyzes user behavior, like login patterns and device usage to detect unusual activity. If a wearable is accessed from an unknown location, AI can trigger multifactor authentication or temporarily block access until the user verifies their identity.

Enhancing Encryption Standards AI can optimize encryption processes, ensuring that sensitive data stays secure while balancing the limited processing power of wearable devices. For example, AI can dynamically adjust encryption protocols based on the data's sensitivity. This approach ensures that even real-time data, like ECG readings, remains protected without slowing down performance.

AI-Powered Firmware Integrity Checks Wearable devices rely on firmware, which can be vulnerable to tampering. AI can continuously monitor firmware integrity, checking for unauthorized changes or malware. If an issue is detected, AI can trigger immediate responses, such as rolling back the firmware to a secure version or isolating the device from the network.

Advanced Threat Intelligence Integration AI can analyze global threat intelligence to update wearable devices against the latest attack methods. For example, AI can identify new vulnerabilities in Bluetooth protocols and automatically adjust security settings to counter those threats, providing continuous protection.

Secure Data Management and Privacy AI can play a crucial role in protecting data privacy. It can anonymize user data while making it useful for analytics and decision-making. For example, AI can filter sensitive health information and ensure that only anonymized data is shared with cloud systems or third parties, maintaining privacy without sacrificing functionality.

Proactive Botnet Mitigation AI can detect and respond to botnet attacks, where devices are hijacked and used in large-scale attacks. If a wearable starts behaving suspiciously, like sending large amounts of traffic to unknown servers, AI can block its network access or isolate it until the issue is resolved.

Personalized Security Configurations AI can customize security settings based on user habits, preferences, and environments. For instance, if a wearable connects to a public Wi-Fi network, AI can automatically tighten security by disabling unsecured connections or enforcing stronger encryption.

Autonomous Incident Response When a threat is detected, AI can respond immediately without human intervention. For example, suppose malware is detected on a wearable device. In that case, AI can disconnect it from the network, alert the user, and restore its firmware to a safe version, all executed automatically.

Enhanced Supply Chain Security AI can also analyze the supply chain for vulnerabilities, identifying counterfeit components or tampered firmware before they are installed in devices. For example, AI can scan device components and flag mismatched serial numbers or suspicious suppliers, ensuring that only trusted parts are used.

Continuous Learning and Adaptation AI systems continuously learn and adapt as new threats emerge. They analyze incidents globally and update defenses in real time. AI systems constantly improve and keep up with new attack strategies, including AI-driven hacking attempts.

The following are some notable products exemplifying these advancements:

- **Eko Health's CORE500 Digital Stethoscope:** This integrates AI to provide high-fidelity audio, a full-color display, and a three-lead electrocardiogram (ECG). It is compatible with Eko's Sensora platform, which utilizes AI for cardiac disease detection, ensuring accurate and secure monitoring of heart conditions.

- **AliveCor's KardiaMobile 6L:** As the first FDA-cleared six-lead personal ECG device, KardiaMobile 6L employs AI algorithms to detect atrial fibrillation and normal sinus rhythm. Its design allows for secure data transmission and analysis, enhancing the reliability of cardiac monitoring.

- **Empatica's Embrace2 Smartwatch:** Designed to detect generalized tonic-clonic seizures, the Embrace2 uses AI to monitor physiological signals such as electrodermal activity and movement. It provides caregivers with real-time alerts, enhancing patient safety and response times.

- **Ceribell's Rapid Response EEG System:** This system features a headband device with an AI seizure-detection algorithm. It enables quick identification of seizures in hospital settings, which is crucial for preventing serious brain injuries and improving patient outcomes.

- **Nanox.AI's Imaging Solutions:** Nanox.AI utilizes AI to analyze routine medical CT scans, aiding in the early detection of asymptomatic chronic conditions such as heart, bone, and liver issues. This proactive approach facilitates timely interventions and enhances patient care.

In summary, AI offers a game-changing approach to securing wearable medical devices. With its ability to detect threats in real time, predict vulnerabilities, and respond autonomously, AI helps protect sensitive data, ensures system integrity, and safeguards patient safety. By integrating AI into the design and management of wearable devices, manufacturers and healthcare providers can build a safer and more secure future for connected healthcare technologies.

Key Takeaways from Security Challenges of Wearable Medical Devices

Wearable medical devices have transformed healthcare by enabling real-time health monitoring and personalized treatment. Smartwatches, continuous glucose monitors, and wearable ECG monitors integrate seamlessly into healthcare ecosystems, enhancing patient engagement and remote management of chronic conditions. However, their connectivity also introduces significant cybersecurity vulnerabilities. These risks range from weak encryption and insecure communication protocols to authentication weaknesses, unpatched firmware, and insufficient access controls. End-of-life devices that no longer receive updates compound security concerns, as they remain in use without proper decommissioning guidelines.

Data privacy is another major challenge, with unauthorized access to sensitive health data, opaque data-sharing practices, and cloud security vulnerabilities posing significant threats. Many manufacturers share user data with third parties without precise consent mechanisms, and gaps in regulatory compliance, such as HIPAA and GDPR, create inconsistencies in data protection. Emerging threats, including AI-powered cyberattacks, IoMT botnets, data poisoning, and supply chain exploits, further increase the risks associated with wearable devices. The regulatory landscape remains fragmented, with global security requirements inconsistencies and limited end-of-life management guidance.

Healthcare organizations and manufacturers must adopt proactive security strategies to mitigate these risks. Strengthening security practices through end-to-end encryption, multifactor authentication, regular software updates, and AI-driven threat detection can significantly reduce vulnerabilities. Enhancing supply chain security, advocating for more explicit global regulations, and educating users on device security are crucial steps toward a safer healthcare ecosystem. AI is increasingly important in wearable security, offering anomaly detection, predictive analytics, adaptive authentication, and firmware integrity monitoring capabilities.

As wearable medical devices evolve, collaboration between manufacturers, healthcare providers, regulators, and cybersecurity experts is essential to addressing security challenges. Implementing robust security and compliance measures will safeguard patient data and foster trust and innovation in the rapidly advancing field of healthcare technology.

Part IV

Detection and Prevention

Part IV examines strategies, technologies, and practices to safeguard IoMT networks. Chapter 13 introduces the pivotal role of intrusion detection and prevention systems (IDPSs) in securing IoMT environments. By understanding IoMT ecosystems and deploying tailored IDPS solutions alongside integrating threat hunting that encapsulates indicators of attack (IOAs) and tactics, techniques, and procedures (TPPs) with indicators of compromise (IOCs), healthcare organizations can better detect and mitigate cyber threats in real time. Case studies and best practices provide actionable insights into risk assessment, layered security, AI-powered detection, and incident response. Emerging trends, such as behavioral analytics and edge-based IDSs, demonstrate how innovation shapes the future of intrusion prevention.

The evolution of wireless communications demands more sophisticated approaches to detecting and mitigating attacks. Therefore, Chapter 14 covers how machine learning (ML) enhances wireless attack detection through anomaly detection, feature extraction, and real-time analysis. It discusses various ML techniques, including supervised, unsupervised, and deep learning, and their applications in securing wearable devices, rogue access point detection, and denial-of-service prevention. Challenges such as adversarial ML attacks and resource constraints are addressed alongside future directions like federated learning and explainable AI or XAI.

Chapter 15 focuses on ensuring data confidentiality, integrity, and authentication through protocols like TLS, DTLS, and IPsec. Key topics include encryption algorithms, key management, and authentication mechanisms such as multifactor authentication and digital certificates. The chapter also revisits secure device pairing, regulatory compliance, and emerging trends, offering practical guidance to protect patient data and device functionality in an interconnected medical landscape.

Chapter 16 culminates in a synopsis of key best practices for IoMT device security, providing a framework to safeguard medical technologies. Topics include network enclaving, regular updates, AI-powered analytics, Zero Trust architecture, and improved employee training. Additionally, the chapter addresses the physical and digital scopes of security, such as secure onboarding, encryption, and compliance with regulatory standards. These practices ensure resilience against cyber threats while maintaining patient safety and continuity in operations.

By combining technical expertise with practical case studies, Part IV equips healthcare professionals, IT teams, and decision-makers with the tools and knowledge to help secure IoMT networks. This part can be used as a guide to navigating the complexities of detection and prevention in medical device security.

CHAPTER 13

Intrusion Detection and Prevention for IoMT Networks

As the reliance on IoMT grows, so does the need for better security solutions beyond traditional IT measures. Intrusion detection and prevention systems (IDPSs) have become necessary tools for securing environments. These systems monitor network traffic, detect suspicious activities, and even take proactive measures to prevent harm.

This chapter examines the role IDPS plays in safeguarding medical network ecosystems. It explores how these solutions address unique challenges in healthcare environments, their methodologies for protecting critical systems, and the innovation shaping their future. From understanding the vulnerabilities inherent in IoMT to examining real-world case studies and best practices, this chapter provides a foundation for selecting and implementing effective intrusion detection and prevention for interconnected medical devices.

Introduction to Intrusion Detection and Prevention Systems for IoMT

As healthcare technology evolves, wearable insulin pumps, ECG monitors, and smart infusion pumps are staples in modern healthcare. These innovations provide improved outcomes and convenience; however, they also come with heightened cybersecurity risks. In the first half of this book, I reviewed many of those. We learned that the sensitive nature of IoMT systems makes them prime targets for cyberattacks.

IDPSs have become critical components in securing environments as these systems monitor network traffic, identify suspicious activities, and respond to mitigate threats. I'll describe the role of IDPSs, challenges they address, methodologies they employ, and some integration options into healthcare ecosystems. But first, in the landscape of healthcare cybersecurity, I talked about the strategy of integrating indicators of compromise (IOCs) with indicators of attack (IOAs), but I'll add tactics, techniques, and procedures (TTPs), as well as proactive threat hunting with IDPSs. The reason is that this creates a better framework for detecting and mitigating threats. This integrated approach ensures healthcare organizations can stay ahead of attackers while maintaining the integrity and availability of data. I'll break these down.

IOCs are the digital breadcrumbs attackers leave behind, such as unusual file hashes, IP addresses, or domain names associated with malicious activities. These reactive measures help detect known threats by correlating them against IDPS databases. In healthcare, where sensitive data such as PHI is a prime target, implementing IOC-driven detection helps ensure that any known malware or suspicious network activity is flagged, allowing teams to act before breaches escalate.

While IOCs focus on after-the-fact evidence, IOAs examine ongoing activities that signal potential threats, such as unusual lateral movement or privilege escalation. This proactive layer is critical for healthcare systems connected to the IoMT, which often operate in real time. IDPS solutions incorporating IOAs can identify behaviors that may indicate an attack in progress, such as unauthorized access to medical device networks, enabling healthcare organizations to mitigate risks before damage occurs.

Now, understanding TTPs provides deeper insights into an attacker's methodology. In healthcare, TTPs might include ransomware delivered via phishing emails targeting hospital staff or supply chain attacks aimed at IoMT devices. Integrating TTP analysis into an IDPS allows for advanced detection of novel attacks by identifying patterns aligned with known adversarial techniques, even if specific IOCs or IOAs have not been previously recorded.

While an IDPS offers automated detection, threat hunting adds a proactive, human-led dimension to cybersecurity. Skilled analysts use tools like threat intelligence feeds, anomaly detection systems, and network data to uncover hidden threats. For healthcare organizations, threat hunting focuses on identifying low-and-slow attacks, such as advanced persistent threats (APTs), that may evade traditional IDPS detection. For example, hunters might uncover a compromised third-party vendor's credentials being used to access sensitive databases.

An IDPS is the backbone of healthcare threat detection. By integrating IOCs, IOAs, TTPs, and threat hunting methodologies, it evolves from a stand-alone tool into a dynamic ecosystem. In healthcare environments, this means detecting and blocking known threats and recognizing abnormal traffic indicative of insider threats, lateral movements, or data exfiltration attempts targeting electronic health records.

Here are five good reasons the combined effectiveness of these technologies improves healthcare threat detection:

- **Enhanced real-time detection:** IDPSs powered by IOC and IOA intelligence detect threats faster, reducing the exposure window for critical healthcare systems.

- **Proactive threat response:** TTP-focused IDPSs and threat hunting enable organizations to identify and mitigate novel attacks before they manifest into significant incidents.
- **Comprehensive visibility:** The combination of automated and manual threat detection ensures all vectors, from phishing campaigns to IoMT vulnerabilities, are monitored and addressed.
- **Regulatory compliance:** Robust detection capabilities help healthcare organizations comply with strict regulatory requirements and laws, such as HIPAA, which mandates safeguarding patient data.
- **Incident investigation:** Integrating TTPs and threat hunting streamlines incident analysis, offering granular insights into how an attack occurred and how to prevent recurrence.

A synergistic approach that combines IOCs, IOAs, TTPs, threat hunting, and IDPS enables organizations to stay ahead of increasingly sophisticated cyber threats.

Understanding IoMT Ecosystems

If you skipped the first part or two, IoMT refers to interconnected medical devices and systems that facilitate real-time monitoring, diagnostics, and treatment. We know some of the unique characteristics of IoMT environments create specific security challenges:

- **Device diversity:** IoMT encompasses various devices, from wearable health trackers to implantable pacemakers with different capabilities and vulnerabilities.
- **Data sensitivity:** IoMT handles protected health information (PHI), which is governed by strict regulations like HIPAA in the United States and GDPR in the EU.
- **Critical dependencies:** Many IoMT devices are life-critical, meaning disruptions can directly impact patient health and safety.
- **Always-on connectivity:** IoMT devices rely on constant connectivity to transmit data to healthcare providers or cloud platforms, increasing exposure to cyber threats.

As I have discussed, these challenges require an organized level of due diligence to ensure that device breaches, exfiltration of sensitive data, or disruption to service do not occur.

What Is Intrusion Detection and Prevention in IoMT Environments?

An intrusion detection and prevention system is a cybersecurity tool designed to monitor network and device activities, detect malicious behavior, and proactively take measures to prevent harm. Intrusion detection systems, or the IDS part, focus on monitoring and alerting administrators to suspicious activity without necessarily taking direct action. Generally speaking, an IDS is a cybersecurity tool that monitors network traffic and system activities for malicious activity or policy violations. When a threat is detected, the IDS usually alerts security administrators, enabling them to take appropriate action. The key components of IoMT IDS include the following:

- **Data collection:** Gathering network traffic data from IoMT devices and systems
- **Analysis engine:** Processing collected data to identify patterns and anomalies
- **Knowledge base:** Leveraging a repository of known attack signatures and typical behavior patterns for event correlation
- **Reporting system:** Generating alerts and reports on detected threats
- **Sensors or agents:** Monitoring and analyzing activity; sensors for networks, agents for hosts
- **Management servers:** Handling and managing information from sensors/agents
- **Database servers:** Repositories for event information
- **Consoles:** Interfaces for IDPS users and administrators

Historically, IDS is categorized into two main types. The first is host-based IDSs (HIDS), which can be installed on individual devices to monitor internal operations and system calls. Network-based IDSs (NIDSs) are the second leading type deployed at strategic network points to monitor traffic between devices. In IoMT, a NIDS is typically more prevalent, as it enables monitoring of interconnected devices on a network. Advanced techniques in an IoMT IDS incorporate deep learning by utilizing neural networks for more accurate threat detection, ensemble learning combining multiple machine learning models to improve overall performance, and federated learning by enabling collaborative learning across distributed IoMT devices.

Intrusion prevention systems, or the IPS part, detect and actively block or mitigate identified threats. When an IPS is integrated with an IDS, we end up with an IDPS, which creates a comprehensive approach to securing IoMT environments and balancing real-time monitoring with automated threat response. These are often incorporated into SIEM platforms, which I also discussed previously. The role of IDPS in IoMT is to secure a complex ecosystem where traditional IT security measures may fall short. These are some key functions:

- **Real-time monitoring:** Continuous analysis of network traffic and device activities to identify deviations from normal behavior
- **Threat detection:** Using advanced techniques like signature-based detection for known threats and anomaly-based detection for unknown or emerging risks
- **Automated prevention:** Blocking unauthorized access, isolating infected devices, and preventing malicious activity before it can propagate
- **Regulatory compliance:** Ensuring adherence to healthcare data security standards by providing detailed audit trails and incident response capabilities

Intrusion detection and prevention systems are essential in securing connected medical networks by addressing critical risks. Unauthorized access is a prevalent threat, as attackers exploit weak or absent authentication protocols to gain control over devices, potentially altering their functions or compromising sensitive data.

MITM attacks further exacerbate vulnerabilities by intercepting and manipulating data transmissions between IoMT devices and healthcare systems, undermining the integrity and confidentiality of patient information. Ransomware poses another significant risk, where cybercriminals encrypt data or disrupt the functionality of IoMT devices, leveraging these actions to demand ransoms, which can halt critical medical services and endanger patient lives. I recently covered DoS attacks that target the operational stability of IoMT networks by overwhelming them with traffic, leading to service interruptions that compromise timely patient care. Lastly, data exfiltration remains a concern as unauthorized access to PHI violates patient privacy and exposes healthcare organizations to severe regulatory penalties and reputational damage. By detecting and mitigating these risks in real time, IDPSs help ensure the resilience and security of IoMT networks.

Here's a breakdown of key IDPS features for IoMT:

- **Signature-Based Detection:**
    - Compares activity against a database of known attack signatures.
    - Effective for detecting well-documented threats.
    - Limitation: Cannot detect new (e.g., zero-day and some n-day) or unknown threats.

- **Anomaly-Based Detection:**
    - Machine learning is used to establish a baseline of normal behavior for IoMT devices.
    - Detects deviations indicative of zero-day attacks or insider threats.
    - Example: Identifying abnormal data flows from an insulin pump at odd hours.

- **Hybrid Detection Models:**
    - Combines signature and anomaly-based detection for comprehensive threat coverage.
    - Balances accuracy and adaptability.

- **Behavioral Analytics:**
    - Monitors user and device behaviors to identify patterns associated with malicious activities.
    - Example: Alerting administrators if a wearable ECG device starts communicating with an unauthorized external IP address.

- **Deception Technology:**
    - Deploys decoy devices or data to lure attackers and analyze their behavior without compromising real systems.

Implementing intrusion detection and prevention systems in IoMT networks can be challenging due to the unique demands and constraints of healthcare environments. One hurdle is resource constraints, as many IoMT devices possess limited computational power. Deploying traditional IDPS directly onto these devices can also be challenging. Organizations can leverage edge computing or cloud-based IDPS solutions to address this, which offload processing tasks to more capable infrastructure while maintaining low-latency protection.

Another common issue is false positives, where overly sensitive detection systems generate excessive alerts, overwhelming security teams and reducing operational efficiency. Using AI and machine learning, IDPS can help refine detection accuracy, minimize noise, and prioritize actionable threats. Additionally, encrypted traffic presents a challenge, as encrypted data streams can obscure threats, allowing them to bypass some security measures unnoticed. Integrating SSL/TLS decryption proxies within the IDPS framework enables secure traffic inspection while preserving data integrity.

The diversity of IoMT devices further complicates IDPS implementation. These devices vary widely in capabilities, operating systems, and configurations, making creating universal security policies difficult. To counter this, security teams can develop device-specific baselines and detection rules, tailoring IDPS functionality to each device type's unique behaviors and vulnerabilities.

Lastly, there is the challenge of compliance pressure. IDPS must align with regulations such as HIPAA and GDPR, among others, that I mentioned in earlier chapters, to ensure patient data privacy and security. Integrating these regulatory frameworks directly into the IDPS design helps organizations remain compliant while addressing evolving threats. Overcoming these challenges requires a combination of innovative technologies, adaptive strategies, and adherence to industry standards, ensuring strong protection for IoMT ecosystems.

Case Study: Implementing IDPS in a Healthcare Environment

Let's review details from a simulated IDPS implementation in a healthcare environment. The scenario is a large hospital heavily reliant on IoMT devices such as smart infusion pumps and wearable glucose monitors that have reported unusual spikes in network activity. The irregularities coincided with delayed device responses and intermittent disruptions in patient monitoring systems. These anomalies raised alarms about potential cyberattacks targeting critical IoMT infrastructure, prompting immediate action to safeguard patient safety and ensure regulatory compliance. There was an identification of a ransomware attempt and a target of outdated firmware on some connected medical technologies.

Actions Taken:

- **Deployment of a network-based IDPS:**
  The hospital implemented an IDPS to monitor all network traffic between IoMT devices and central servers. The network-based approach allowed

continuous surveillance without imposing additional computational strain on the resource-constrained IoMT devices.

- **Adoption of hybrid detection techniques:**
  The IDPS was configured to utilize signature-based detection to identify known threats and behavioral anomaly detection to uncover unknown or evolving attack vectors. By integrating these methods, the system could handle routine cyber risks and sophisticated zero-day exploits targeting IoMT devices.

- **Integration of AI-powered anomaly detection:**
  The hospital enhanced its IDPS with AI and machine learning algorithms to address the challenge of high false positive rates. These systems analyzed historical and real-time data to establish device-specific baselines, allowing the detection of deviations genuinely indicative of malicious activity. This refinement reduced the burden on the hospital's security operations center (SOC) and improved the accuracy of alerts.

- **Real-time automated responses:**
  The IDPS was further enhanced with automated response capabilities. When threats were identified, the system could execute real-time actions, such as blocking malicious IP addresses, quarantining compromised IoMT devices, and isolating suspicious network segments. These measures ensured that threats were neutralized before they could propagate or disrupt patient care.

Outcomes:

- **Successful threat mitigation:**
  The IDPS detected and thwarted another sophisticated ransomware attack aimed at their IoMT devices. The attack exploited vulnerabilities in older firmware versions of smart infusion pumps to gain initial access, intending to encrypt patient data and disrupt device functionality. The IDPS flagged the anomalous behavior early, blocking malicious traffic and isolating affected devices before the ransomware could spread.

- **Enhanced incident response times:**
  AI-powered anomaly detection reduced the time required to identify and address potential threats. With real-time automated responses, the hospital's SOC could focus on higher-priority tasks without being overwhelmed by false alarms or routine monitoring.

- **Operational continuity maintained:**
  Rapidly detecting and mitigating threats ensured minimal disruption to critical healthcare operations. Aside from a temporary quarantine caused by the incident mentioned, patient monitoring systems remained functional. Care delivery proceeded without any impactful delays, preserving patient trust and safety.

- **Regulatory compliance achieved:**
  The IDPS generated detailed logs and audit trails that allowed the hospital to demonstrate adherence to healthcare regulations, including HIPAA and GDPR. The system's ability to document threat detection and mitigation activities bolstered compliance efforts and prepared the organization for audits.

- **Proactive risk management:**
  The IDPS provided actionable insights into the hospital's cybersecurity posture, enabling proactive measures such as firmware updates for IoMT devices and network segmentation. These actions strengthened the hospital's defenses against future threats.

Key Lessons Learned:

- **Hybrid detection is essential.**
  Combining signature-based and behavioral anomaly detection ensures comprehensive threat identification, particularly in dynamic IoMT environments where threats evolve rapidly.
- **AI can be a game-changer.**
  AI-powered anomaly detection proved critical in reducing false positives and enhancing detection accuracy, enabling faster and more effective responses to real threats.
- **Automation minimizes risk.**
  Real-time automated responses are crucial for mitigating threats in high-stakes environments like healthcare, where every second counts.
- **Regular firmware updates are vital.**
  The original ransomware attempt exploited outdated IoMT device firmware, underscoring the importance of timely software and firmware updates across all connected devices.
- **Regulatory compliance benefits security.**
  Aligning IDPS systems with regulatory frameworks ensures compliance and strengthens the overall security posture through detailed documentation and accountability measures.

This case study highlights how a proactive intrusion detection and prevention approach can safeguard IoMT ecosystems. By integrating cutting-edge solutions like AI and automation, the hospital protected its infrastructure, ensured patient safety, and maintained operational resilience in the face of escalating threats.

IDPS Solutions

We know that securing IoMT networks requires specialized systems that can address some of the unique challenges of interconnected medical devices. There are many products and solutions available today to consider:

- BluVector
- Check Point
- Cisco NGIPS
- Fail2Ban

- Fidelis Network
- Fortinet
- Hillstone Networks
- NSFOCUS
- OpenWIPS-NG
- OSSEC
- Palo Alto Networks
- Sagan
- Samhain
- Security Onion
- Semperis
- Snort
- SolarWinds
- Splunk
- Suricata
- Trellix
- Trend Micro
- Vectra Cognito
- Zeek
- ZScalar

Table 13-1 presents a brief product comparison of four tools based on details from each tool's website and/or personal experience.

Table 13-1: Comparison of IDPS Solutions

FEATURE	TREND MICRO TIPPINGPOINT	CISCO SECURE IPS	FORTINET FORTIGATE IPS	PALO ALTO THREAT PREVENTION
Threat Intelligence	Digital Vaccine (DVL)	Cisco Talos	FortiGuard Labs	WildFire
Virtual Patching	Yes	Yes	Yes	Yes
Behavioral Analytics	Limited	Advanced (AI/ML)	Moderate	Moderate
Edge Capabilities	Minimal	Moderate	Advanced	Moderate
Scalability	High	High	High	Moderate
Ease of Deployment	Easy	Moderate	Easy	Moderate

In the following sections, I'll provide more granular details about more IDPS solutions that align with IoMT environments from my research, but in no particular order. For most of these solutions, I'll pepper in features, strengths and weaknesses, challenges and considerations, and even example use cases focusing on in-scope IoMT networks. The goal is to help you make informed decisions regarding technologies and integrated solutions.

Cisco Secure IPS

Cisco Secure Intrusion Prevention System (NGIPS), as shown in Figure 13-1, is a next-generation security solution that combines advanced threat detection, real-time prevention capabilities, and comprehensive network visibility. In the context of IoMT networks, it addresses the specific challenges of safeguarding sensitive healthcare data, ensuring device integrity, and maintaining operational continuity. The following is an in-depth evaluation of Cisco Secure IPS tailored for IoMT environments.

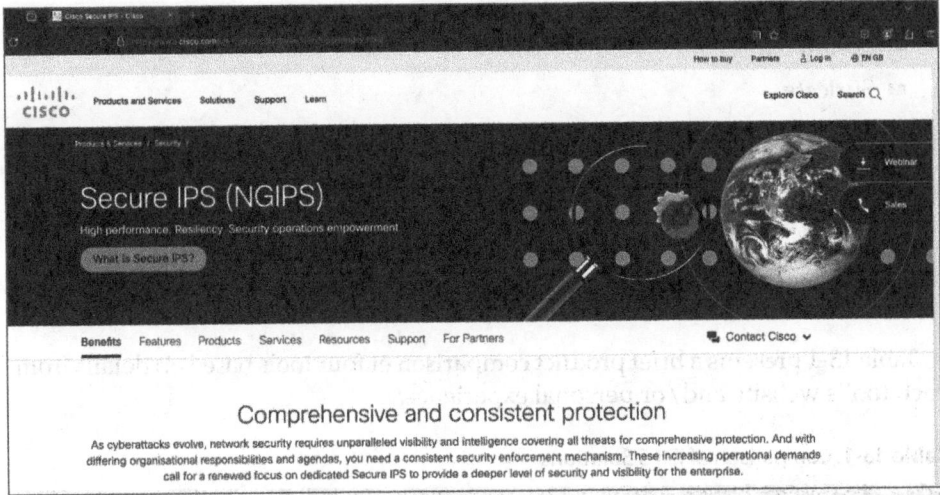

Figure 13-1: Cisco NGIPS website

Core Features and Benefits Deep Visibility into Network Traffic

- **Capabilities:** Cisco Secure IPS provides granular visibility into all network activities, including east-west and north-south traffic flows. It uses deep packet inspection (DPI) to analyze both encrypted and unencrypted traffic for anomalies.
- **IoMT relevance:** IoMT networks are characterized by constantly transmitting sensitive data between devices, cloud platforms, and healthcare servers. This visibility is critical for identifying unusual patterns, such as unexpected data spikes or unauthorized communication attempts from medical devices.

- **Example use case:** Monitoring traffic from a wearable ECG monitor to its healthcare provider's system could reveal potential MITM attacks or data exfiltration attempts.

Advanced Threat Detection

- **Capabilities:** Cisco Secure IPS integrates with Cisco Talos Threat Intelligence to leverage real-time updates on emerging threats. Its machine learning algorithms analyze behavioral patterns and detect zero-day vulnerabilities.
- **IoMT relevance:** IoMT networks face evolving threats such as ransomware, targeted attacks, and device exploitation. Cisco's ML-enhanced detection identifies anomalies specific to medical devices, like sudden changes in firmware behavior or unauthorized access attempts.
- **Example Use Case:** Detecting malware embedded in an IoMT device's firmware update file could disrupt an infusion pump's operations.

Automated Network Security and Response

- **Capabilities:** Cisco Secure IPS automates threat response with real-time actions such as isolating compromised devices, blocking malicious IPs, and applying virtual patches to vulnerable devices.
- **IoMT relevance:** Automated responses are critical in healthcare, where a delayed reaction to an intrusion could jeopardize patient safety. The system ensures that threats are neutralized without human intervention, minimizing potential disruptions.
- **Example use case:** When a ransomware attack targets IoMT devices, Cisco Secure IPS can isolate infected systems, block the attacker's communication channels, and protect other devices in the network.

Integration with Cisco's Security Suite

- **Capabilities:** Cisco Secure IPS integrates seamlessly with other Cisco security tools, such as SecureX, Cisco Umbrella, and Secure Firewall. This interoperability enables a cohesive, layered defense strategy.
- **IoMT relevance:** IoMT networks often span multiple sites (e.g., hospitals, remote clinics) and rely on cloud services. Unified integration ensures that threats are detected and mitigated across the entire network.
- **Example use case:** Coordinating responses to threats detected in a multisite hospital system, ensuring consistent security policies for all IoMT devices.

Customizable Policies for Diverse Devices

- **Capabilities:** Cisco Secure IPS allows administrators to create and apply custom detection and prevention policies tailored to specific device types and network zones.

- **IoMT relevance:** The diversity of IoMT devices, from wearable monitors to imaging systems, requires adaptable security policies. Cisco's flexibility supports device-specific configurations without compromising network performance.
- **Example use case:** Setting stricter security rules for implantable cardiac devices than general-purpose hospital IoT systems.

Strengths in IoMT Context

- Scalability
  Cisco Secure IPS is well-suited for small healthcare facilities and large hospital networks. Its scalability ensures comprehensive protection as IoMT deployments grow.
- Real-Time Threat Intelligence
  The integration with Cisco Talos delivers up-to-date threat intelligence, providing proactive defense against global cybersecurity trends.
- AI and ML Capabilities
  Advanced analytics enhances detection accuracy, reducing false positives and ensuring timely responses.
- Regulatory Compliance Support
  Cisco Secure IPS offers logging and reporting capabilities to help users comply with healthcare regulations such as HIPAA, GDPR, and FDA cybersecurity guidelines.

Challenges in IoMT

- Complex Configuration:
  - IoMT networks require device-specific policies, which can be challenging to configure without specialized expertise.
  - **Recommendation:** Engage security teams with IoMT experience to optimize deployment.
- Resource Demands:
  - While Cisco Secure IPS is highly effective, its advanced features may require significant computational resources.
  - **Recommendation:** Use cloud or hybrid configurations to offload processing from resource-constrained IoMT devices.
- Cost:
  - The comprehensive features of Cisco Secure IPS are expensive, which may be a barrier for smaller healthcare providers.
  - **Recommendation:** Evaluate potential ROI by comparing the system's cost to the financial and reputational risks of a cyberattack.

Use Case in IoMT Networks In a hospital, Cisco Secure IPS was deployed to protect a network of interconnected IoMT devices, including insulin pumps, patient monitors, and imaging systems. After implementation:

- The system detected and blocked a ransomware attack targeting older IoMT devices.
- Behavioral analytics identified and flagged unauthorized firmware updates attempted on several infusion pumps.
- Automated responses isolated compromised devices, preventing lateral movement within the network.
- Regulatory reporting features demonstrated compliance with HIPAA and GDPR standards during an audit.

Cisco Secure IPS is a powerful and versatile solution for securing IoMT networks. Its deep traffic visibility, advanced threat detection, and automated responses align well with healthcare environments' unique needs. While configuration complexity and cost may present challenges, its benefits in safeguarding patient data, ensuring device integrity, and maintaining regulatory compliance make it a strong contender for healthcare organizations seeking stronger IoMT security.

A note on Talos, as described in Wikipedia: Cisco Talos, or Cisco Talos Intelligence Group, is a cybersecurity technology and information security company based in Fulton, Maryland. It is part of Cisco Systems Inc. Talos' threat intelligence powers Cisco Secure products and services, including malware detection and prevention systems. Through several open-source products, including the Snort intrusion prevention system and ClamAV antivirus engine, Talos provides Cisco customers and internet users with customizable defensive technologies and techniques. The company is known for its involvement in several high-profile cybersecurity investigations.

Trend Micro TippingPoint

Trend Micro TippingPoint (also known as Trend IPS, as shown in Figure 13-2) is an Intrusion Prevention System designed to provide comprehensive protection against a wide range of cyber threats. Its real-time threat intelligence, streamlined automation, and high performance make it a compelling choice for securing IoMT networks. The following is an in-depth analysis of its features, capabilities, and relevance to IoMT environments.

Core **Features and Capabilities**   Real-Time Threat Intelligence
Trend Micro TippingPoint leverages the Threat Digital Vaccine (DVL) service, which delivers up-to-the-minute threat intelligence from the Trend Micro Smart Protection Network. This feature ensures that IoMT environments are protected against the latest vulnerabilities and attack vectors, including zero-day threats.

- IoMT relevance:
    - Medical devices such as infusion pumps and wearable monitors require continuous protection against evolving threats. DVL's real-time updates help safeguard these devices from new exploits.
    - **Example:** If a widely used vulnerability in a glucose monitor is discovered, TippingPoint can quickly release a virtual patch to block the exploit.

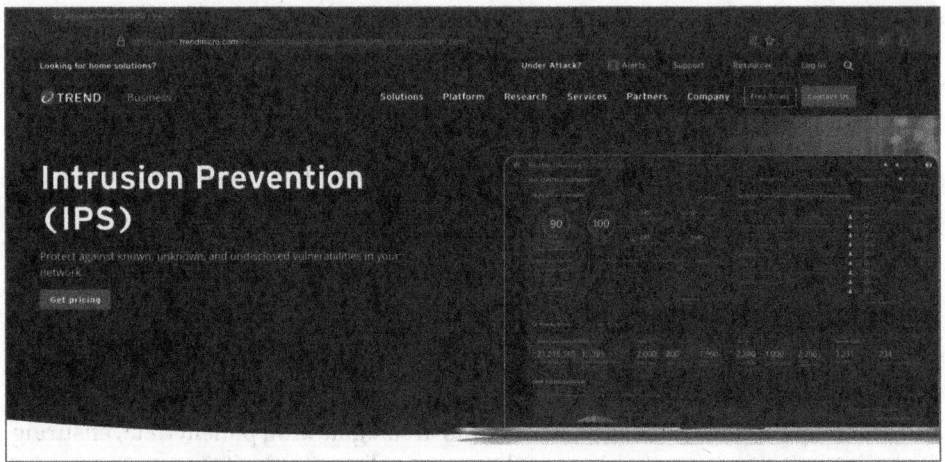

Figure 13-2: Trend IPS Website

Automated Responses
TippingPoint excels in delivering proactive security by automating responses to identified threats. The system can block malicious traffic, isolate compromised devices, and prevent unauthorized access without manual intervention.

- **IoMT relevance:**
  - In healthcare, immediate response to threats is critical to ensure patient safety. Automated responses can prevent ransomware from encrypting device data or disrupting essential operations.
  - **Example:** If TippingPoint detects unusual traffic from a networked ECG monitor, it can isolate the device to prevent lateral movement within the network.

High-Performance Traffic Analysis
With DPI and low-latency processing, TippingPoint is built to handle high volumes of network traffic without impacting performance.

- **IoMT relevance:**
  - IoMT networks generate substantial traffic from interconnected devices transmitting sensitive patient data. TippingPoint's real-time inspection of traffic ensures seamless healthcare operations while maintaining security.
  - **Example:** Monitoring traffic from hundreds of wearable devices in a hospital ward without slowing network communication.

Virtual Patching
Trend Micro's virtual patching capability is a standout feature. It offers immediate protection against vulnerabilities without requiring downtime for physical patch deployment.

- **IoMT relevance:**
  - Many IoMT devices have limited support for traditional software updates. Virtual patching provides an effective way to secure these devices against known vulnerabilities without disrupting their functionality.
  - **Example:** A virtual patch can protect a smart infusion pump with outdated firmware from exploitation.

Scalability and Customization
TippingPoint supports scalability and tailored security policies to address the diverse needs of IoMT networks, which range from small clinics to large hospital systems.

- **IoMT relevance:**
  - Healthcare organizations with diverse device ecosystems benefit from customizable security rules that cater to specific IoMT device behaviors and vulnerabilities.
  - Example: Custom rules can be set to monitor and secure communication protocols unique to pacemakers or insulin pumps.

Strengths in **IoMT** *Context*

Essential for time-sensitive IoMT operations, such as real-time monitoring and device communication.

Protects against ransomware, denial-of-service attacks, data exfiltration, and more.

Compatible with existing healthcare IT infrastructure, simplifying deployment in IoMT networks.

Assists healthcare organizations in meeting requirements such as HIPAA, GDPR, and FDA guidelines through detailed logging and automated security measures.

Challenges in IoMT Implementations

- Focus on Signature-Based Detection:
  - While TippingPoint provides behavioral analysis, its reliance on signature-based detection may limit its effectiveness against sophisticated zero-day threats compared to AI-driven solutions.
  - **Recommendation:** Supplement TippingPoint with machine learning-based anomaly detection tools for comprehensive security.
- Limited Edge Capabilities:
  - Unlike some competitors, TippingPoint does not natively support edge-based processing for IoMT devices located in remote or distributed settings.
  - **Recommendation:** Pair with edge computing solutions to ensure coverage for decentralized IoMT networks.

- Cost Considerations:
  - The licensing and operational costs may be challenging for smaller healthcare providers.
  - **Recommendation:** Evaluate total cost of ownership and prioritize critical IoMT assets to optimize implementation.

Use Case *in IoMT Networks* A metropolitan hospital experiences unusual traffic from several connected glucose monitors, raising concerns about data exfiltration.

- **Detection:**
TippingPoint identifies and flags the unusual traffic pattern as a potential breach using its DPI capabilities.
- **Response:**
The system automatically isolates the compromised devices and blocks the associated IP addresses.
- **Outcome:**
Patient data remains secure, and healthcare operations continue without disruption.

Trend Micro TippingPoint is an IDPS solution that provides real-time protection, automated threat response, and high-performance traffic analysis. Its virtual patching feature is particularly valuable for IoMT networks, where traditional updates can be impractical. While it may not match the advanced AI-driven capabilities of systems like Cisco Secure IPS, it remains a strong contender for healthcare organizations seeking a reliable, scalable, easy-to-deploy security solution. With proper integration and complementary technologies, TippingPoint can effectively secure complex IoMT ecosystems against a broad spectrum of cyber threats.

Check Point IPS

The Check Point Intrusion Prevention System/Quantum, shown in Figure 13-3, is a powerful tool for detecting and mitigating cybersecurity threats. It is particularly well-suited for Internet of Medical Things networks. With its advanced threat detection capabilities, real-time blocking, and comprehensive reporting features, Check Point IPS addresses the unique challenges of securing interconnected medical devices in healthcare environments.

Core Features and Capabilities Integrated Intrusion Prevention

- **Real-time detection and blocking:** Check Point IPS continuously monitors network traffic to identify and block malicious activities. It combines signature-based and behavioral analysis to detect known and emerging threats.

- **Zero-day protection:** By leveraging Check Point ThreatCloud, the system identifies and mitigates vulnerabilities before they are widely exploited. This is critical for IoMT devices that may have unpatched firmware.
- **Granular controls:** Customizable policies allow for precise threat management tailored to the specific needs of IoMT environments, such as prioritizing high-risk devices like infusion pumps and wearable monitors.

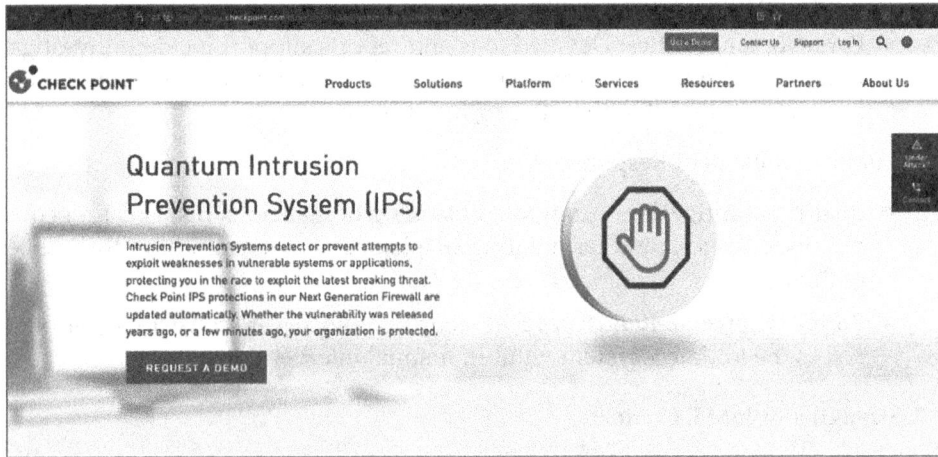

Figure 13-3: Check Point Intrusion Prevention System/Quantum website

Tailored for Healthcare and IoMT

- **Healthcare-specific threat intelligence:** Check Point IPS integrates threat intelligence focused on medical environments, identifying attacks targeting IoMT devices or exploiting healthcare-specific vulnerabilities.
- **Support for regulatory compliance:** Detailed logging and reporting features facilitate compliance with healthcare regulations like HIPAA and GDPR, providing audit trails and security insights to satisfy regulatory requirements.
- **Segmented IoMT security:** The IPS integrates seamlessly with Check Point's broader security framework, enabling network segmentation to isolate IoMT devices and reduce the attack surface.

Advanced Threat Intelligence

- **Check Point ThreatCloud integration:** The system relies on one of the world's largest collaborative threat intelligence networks, providing real-time updates on emerging threats.
- **Behavioral analytics:** Machine learning algorithms detect anomalies in device and network behavior, such as unusual data flows or unauthorized access attempts, which are essential for IoMT systems where traditional detection methods may fall short.

Comprehensive Visibility and Reporting

- **Detailed network insights:** Provides granular visibility into traffic patterns and device activity, enabling proactive threat management and early risk identification.
- **Customizable dashboards:** The platform allows healthcare IT security or operations teams to tailor dashboards to monitor critical IoMT devices and track potential vulnerabilities.
- **Forensic capabilities:** Detailed logs and reports support incident investigation and remediation efforts, particularly important in healthcare where breaches can have life-threatening implications.

Automated Incident Response

- **Real-time mitigation:** Automated blocking of malicious IPs, isolating compromised devices, and terminating suspicious sessions minimize the impact of threats.
- **Policy enforcement:** Ensures that security protocols are consistently applied across the IoMT ecosystem without manual intervention.

Strengths in IoMT Context

- **Enhanced Security for Critical IoMT Devices**
  Check Point IPS is particularly effective in securing life-critical IoMT devices such as insulin pumps, pacemakers, and wearable ECG monitors. Its ability to identify and block threats in real-time ensures that patient care is not disrupted by cyberattacks.

- **Simplified Compliance**
  With built-in reporting tailored for healthcare regulations, Check Point IPS reduces the burden of maintaining compliance. Automated audit logs and security summaries streamline the process for regulatory inspections.

- **Scalability**
  The solution is highly scalable, making it suitable for both small clinics and large hospital campuses. This adaptability ensures consistent security across diverse IoMT deployments.

- **Integration with Healthcare Ecosystems**
  Check Point IPS integrates seamlessly with other Check Point solutions, such as firewalls and endpoint protection, enabling a unified security strategy for healthcare organizations.

Challenges in IoMT Implementation

- **Resource Constraints**
  IoMT devices often have limited computational power, which can impact the implementation of security measures. While Check Point IPS operates at the network level, its effectiveness can be reduced if endpoint devices lack proper baseline configurations.

- **Encrypted Traffic Inspection**
  Encrypted data streams can obscure potential threats. While Check Point IPS offers SSL/TLS decryption capabilities, deploying these features requires careful planning to balance performance and security.
- **Complexity of Management**
  For organizations with limited IT resources, managing an advanced IPS like Check Point may require additional training and expertise to fully utilize its capabilities.

Deployment in Healthcare Example   A large hospital network with interconnected IoMT devices, including wearable monitors, infusion pumps, and imaging systems, implemented Check Point IPS to address increasing cyber threats targeting healthcare infrastructure.

- Outcomes:
  - **Reduced risk:** The system blocked multiple ransomware attempts targeting IoMT devices.
  - **Improved visibility:** Security administrators gained detailed insights into network traffic, allowing for proactive security adjustments.
  - **Regulatory compliance:** Automated reporting ensured compliance with HIPAA and GDPR, avoiding potential penalties and reputational damage.
- **Key Benefits for IoMT Networks**

  - **Real-time protection:** Proactively detects and blocks threats targeting IoMT ecosystems.
  - **Regulatory Support:** Simplifies adherence to healthcare regulations through reporting and auditing tools.
  - **Threat intelligence:** Leverages global intelligence to stay ahead of emerging threats.
  - **Customizability:** Tailored security policies address the unique needs of IoMT devices.
  - **Resilient design:** Ensures uninterrupted device functionality and patient safety during cyber incidents.

Check Point IPS is a solution for securing IoMT networks, offering advanced threat detection, real-time protection, and healthcare-specific features. While implementation may require careful planning and expertise, its comprehensive capabilities and seamless integration with other security tools make it an excellent choice for healthcare organizations aiming to safeguard sensitive medical devices and patient data.

Palo Alto Networks Threat Prevention

Palo Alto Networks Threat Prevention, as shown in Figure 13-4, is a leading intrusion detection and prevention system that provides advanced threat detection, real-time prevention, and a suite of cybersecurity features. Designed to cater to the complex needs of large enterprises, its capabilities align seamlessly with the demands of IoMT networks. Its scalability, advanced analytics, and deep integration with healthcare security requirements make it an excellent option for securing interconnected medical devices in healthcare settings.

Figure 13-4: Palo Alto Networks Threat Prevention website

Core Features and Capabilities Advanced Threat Detection

- **Signature-based detection:** Utilizes an extensive database of known attack signatures to identify and block well-documented threats targeting IoMT devices.
- **Anomaly-based detection:** Employs machine learning to detect deviations in device or network behavior, identifying zero-day threats or sophisticated attacks such as ransomware and APTs.
- **Real-time intelligence integration:** Constantly updated with threat intelligence from the Palo Alto Networks Threat Intelligence Cloud, ensuring that it stays ahead of evolving attack vectors.

Real-Time Threat Prevention

- **Automated blocking:** Proactively prevents unauthorized access, data exfiltration, and malware deployment by halting threats before they reach critical IoMT devices.
- **Inline threat prevention:** Functions seamlessly in real time to stop threats without causing noticeable latency, a critical factor in healthcare environments where downtime can impact patient care.
- **Decryption and inspection:** Supports SSL/TLS decryption to inspect encrypted traffic without compromising device or data integrity, ensuring threats cannot hide within secure communications.

Scalability for Large IoMT Deployments

- **Centralized management:** Offers centralized control for monitoring and managing security policies across multiple healthcare facilities and IoMT networks.
- **Cloud and on-premises integration:** Can be deployed on-premises or in hybrid cloud environments, making it suitable for healthcare organizations with diverse network architectures.
- **Support for diverse IoMT devices:** Accommodates a wide range of IoMT devices, from wearable monitors to large imaging systems, through flexible configurations and granular policies.

Healthcare-Specific Features

- **Regulatory compliance support:** Facilitates adherence to HIPAA, GDPR, and FDA guidelines by offering detailed logging, reporting, and audit capabilities.
- **Medical device security policies:** Enables tailored security policies for IoMT devices, ensuring that life-critical equipment is prioritized and continuously monitored.
- **Network segmentation:** Supports micro-segmentation to isolate IoMT devices, limiting the lateral spread of threats and enhancing overall security posture.

Enhanced Visibility and Reporting

- **Comprehensive analytics:** Provides in-depth visibility into network traffic, device communications, and potential vulnerabilities, enabling proactive security measures.
- **Customizable dashboards:** Allows healthcare IT or security teams to create dashboards specific to IoMT device monitoring, helping them quickly identify and address issues.
- **Incident reporting:** Generates detailed reports for compliance and forensic investigations, streamlining response efforts during and after a cyber incident.

Strengths in IoMT Context

- **Proactive Threat Mitigation**
  Palo Alto Networks Threat Prevention stands out for its ability to neutralize threats in real time, significantly reducing the risk of cyberattacks affecting critical IoMT devices such as infusion pumps, pacemakers, and wearable glucose monitors. Its inline threat prevention capabilities ensure that malicious traffic is blocked before reaching sensitive devices.

- **Seamless Integration with Healthcare Systems**
  This solution integrates seamlessly with other Palo Alto Networks products, such as firewalls and endpoint protection, creating a unified security

architecture. It supports the unique requirements of healthcare environments, where patient safety and data privacy are paramount.

- **Scalable for Large Enterprises**
  With centralized management and support for hybrid deployments, Palo Alto Networks Threat Prevention is ideal for large healthcare organizations managing extensive IoMT networks across multiple locations.

Challenges in IoMT Implementation

- **High Resource Requirements**
  IoMT devices often have limited processing power, and while the system itself operates at the network level, organizations may face challenges deploying advanced features like SSL/TLS decryption, which require additional computational resources.

- **Cost Considerations**
  As a premium solution, Palo Alto Networks Threat Prevention may represent a significant investment. Smaller healthcare organizations with limited budgets may find it challenging to adopt, despite its robust capabilities.

- **Configuration Complexity**
  While its feature set is comprehensive, configuring and managing the system requires a high level of expertise. Healthcare organizations may need to invest in additional training or hire specialized staff to optimize its use.

Use Case: IoMT Deployment in a Large Healthcare Enterprise A multi-campus healthcare organization relied on hundreds of interconnected IoMT devices, including imaging systems, wearable devices, and infusion pumps. The organization faced increased cyber threats, including ransomware attempts and data exfiltration risks, prompting them to deploy Palo Alto Networks Threat Prevention.

- **Outcomes:**
  - **Enhanced security:** The system identified and blocked multiple ransomware attempts targeting IoMT devices. Its real-time prevention capabilities ensured uninterrupted patient care.
  - **Regulatory compliance:** Detailed reporting and audit logs facilitated compliance with HIPAA and GDPR, reducing the organization's regulatory risk.
  - **Improved visibility:** Comprehensive network insights enabled the IT team to proactively address vulnerabilities and enhance overall security posture.
  - **Operational continuity:** The solution's low-latency performance ensured no disruptions to critical IoMT functions, maintaining trust and reliability in patient care.

- **Key Benefits for IoMT Networks:**
  - **Real-time threat detection and prevention:** Protects IoMT devices from both known and emerging threats.
  - **Compliance support:** Simplifies adherence to healthcare regulations through reporting and audit capabilities.
  - **Scalability:** Accommodates large and complex IoMT networks with centralized management and hybrid deployment options.
  - **Integrated security architecture:** Works seamlessly with other Palo Alto Networks solutions for a unified and comprehensive security approach.
  - **Advanced analytics:** Provides actionable insights for proactive risk management and threat prevention.

Palo Alto Networks Threat Prevention is a reliable IDPS solution for IoMT networks, offering advanced threat detection, real-time prevention, and tailored healthcare features. While its high resource requirements and cost may pose challenges for smaller organizations, its scalability and effectiveness make it a top choice for large healthcare enterprises managing complex and sensitive IoMT deployments. By ensuring real-time protection and compliance with regulatory standards, it enables healthcare providers to maintain secure, resilient operations and safeguard patient trust.

OSSEC HIDS

OSSEC (Open Source Security) HIDS, at the web address in Figure 13-5, is a widely used, open-source security tool designed to monitor individual systems by analyzing logs, checking file integrity, and sending real-time alerts for suspicious activities. Its lightweight, flexible, and open-source nature makes it an attractive option for healthcare organizations seeking an effective solution for securing Internet of Medical Things devices. While OSSEC HIDS is traditionally used for general host-based monitoring, its capabilities align well with specific requirements for protecting IoMT devices in distributed healthcare environments.

Core Features and Capabilities   Host-Based Monitoring

- **Log analysis:** OSSEC analyzes logs from IoMT devices, servers, and applications to detect unusual activities. For instance, it can identify unauthorized access attempts, configuration changes, or suspicious data transmissions from IoMT devices like wearable monitors or infusion pumps.
- **File integrity checking:** Ensures critical files on IoMT devices remain unaltered, which is essential for identifying unauthorized changes or malware infections.
- **System monitoring:** Tracks processes and system calls on IoMT devices to identify potential threats like malicious scripts or unapproved applications.

Figure 13-5: OSSEC (Open Source Security) HIDS Website

Real-Time Alerting

- **Automated alerts:** Provides immediate notifications to administrators when a suspicious activity is detected, enabling rapid response to potential threats targeting IoMT systems.
- **Customizable rules:** Users can create tailored detection rules specific to the behavior of IoMT devices, improving accuracy and reducing false positives.

Scalability and Flexibility

- **Agent-based architecture:** OSSEC uses lightweight agents deployed on IoMT devices or connected systems, which communicate with a centralized server for analysis.
- **Cross-platform support:** Compatible with a variety of operating systems, including Windows, Linux, and macOS, which is beneficial for managing diverse IoMT environments.

Open-Source Benefits

- **Cost-effective:** As an open-source solution, OSSEC eliminates licensing fees, making it accessible for organizations with budget constraints, including smaller healthcare providers.
- **Customizability:** Allows extensive customization to address the unique requirements of IoMT networks, including integration with other security tools and healthcare applications.

Strengths in IoMT Context

- **Tailored Security for Individual Devices**
  OSSEC's host-based approach is particularly effective for securing individual IoMT devices, such as wearable monitors, insulin pumps, or imaging systems.

By monitoring the device's internal logs and file system, OSSEC can detect localized threats that may bypass network-based intrusion detection systems.

- **Cost-Effectiveness for Resource-Constrained Environments**
  Many healthcare organizations face budget limitations when implementing IoMT security. OSSEC's open-source nature and lightweight agents make it a viable choice for such settings, offering proactive monitoring without significant financial or computational overhead.

- **Real-Time Protection**
  Real-time alerting ensures that threats to critical IoMT devices are detected and mitigated promptly, minimizing disruptions to patient care or the risk of compromised PHI.

Challenges in IoMT Implementation

- **Limited Network Visibility**
  OSSEC HIDS is designed for host-based monitoring and lacks built-in capabilities for analyzing network traffic or detecting threats that exploit vulnerabilities in the broader IoMT ecosystem. Pairing it with a NIDS is often necessary for comprehensive coverage.

- **Resource Constraints**
  IoMT devices often have limited computational resources, and installing OSSEC agents may impact device performance, particularly for resource-intensive monitoring tasks such as real-time file integrity checks.

- **High Configuration Overhead**
  While OSSEC is highly customizable, setting up tailored rules and policies for diverse IoMT devices can be time-consuming and requires significant expertise, especially in environments with a wide range of device types and operating systems.

- **No Built-In Threat Intelligence Integration**
  Unlike some commercial IDPS solutions, OSSEC lacks direct integration with real-time threat intelligence feeds, limiting its ability to proactively identify emerging threats or adapt to evolving attack patterns without manual updates.

Use Case: OSSEC in a Healthcare Environment A smaller hospital deployed OSSEC to monitor critical IoMT devices such as wearable glucose monitors and networked infusion pumps, after noticing an increase in unauthorized access attempts on its systems.

- **Actions Taken:**
  - **Agent deployment:** Lightweight OSSEC agents were installed on IoMT devices capable of running the software, as well as on connected servers managing device communications.

- **Customized rules:** Device-specific monitoring rules were created to detect abnormal behaviors, such as changes to configuration files or unexpected data transmissions.
- **File integrity monitoring:** OSSEC was configured to ensure that firmware and critical application files on IoMT devices remained unchanged, alerting administrators to any unauthorized modifications.

- **Outcomes:**
  - **Improved device security:** OSSEC detected and alerted administrators to multiple unauthorized access attempts and prevented potential compromise of sensitive devices.
  - **Operational continuity:** By addressing threats promptly, the hospital maintained uninterrupted IoMT operations, safeguarding patient care and data integrity.
  - **Cost savings:** The open-source nature of OSSEC allowed the hospital to enhance its IoMT security without incurring substantial costs, making it an ideal solution for resource-constrained environments.

- **Key Benefits for IoMT Networks**
  - **Localized threat detection:** Provides granular insights into individual IoMT device activities, making it ideal for detecting device-specific anomalies.
  - **Customizability:** Allows for the development of tailored security rules to address the unique vulnerabilities and behaviors of various IoMT devices.
  - **Real-time alerts:** Facilitates rapid response to threats, ensuring minimal impact on healthcare operations.
  - **Cost-effective deployment:** Open-source and lightweight, OSSEC is suitable for organizations with limited budgets or resources.

- **Limitations in IoMT Context**
  - **Lack of network-level analysis:** Requires pairing with a NIDS to address broader network-based threats.
  - **Performance impact on devices:** May strain the limited computational resources of some IoMT devices.
  - **Manual updates and maintenance:** Customization and maintenance require significant expertise, particularly in diverse IoMT environments.

OSSEC HIDS is a flexible tool for securing IoMT networks, especially for organizations prioritizing host-level monitoring and real-time alerts on individual medical devices. Its open-source nature and cost-effectiveness make it a viable option for small to mid-sized healthcare providers. However, its limitations in network visibility and lack of integrated threat intelligence highlight the need for complementary solutions to ensure comprehensive IoMT security. By carefully deploying OSSEC alongside other tools and investing in customization and expertise, healthcare organizations can leverage its strengths to protect their IoMT ecosystems effectively.

Snort

Snort, at the address shown in Figure 13-6) is one of the most widely adopted open-source network intrusion detection and prevention systems, renowned for its real-time traffic analysis, packet logging, and customizable rulesets. Developed and maintained by Cisco, Snort offers flexibility and scalability, making it a valuable tool for securing IoMT networks. Its ability to detect a variety of threats, from protocol anomalies to complex cyberattacks, makes it a compelling choice for healthcare organizations seeking security solutions for IoMT environments.

Figure 13-6: Snort Website

Core Features and Capabilities   Real-Time Traffic Analysis

- **Network traffic monitoring:** Snort captures and analyzes packets in real time, identifying potential threats such as unauthorized access, anomalous data flows, and malicious payloads.
- **Protocol analysis:** Ensures compliance with expected communication protocols, which is critical for IoMT devices like infusion pumps and wearable monitors that rely on specific standards for data transmission.
- **Pattern matching:** Uses signature-based detection to identify known attack patterns and anomalies in IoMT network traffic.

Customizable Rules Engine

- **Rule-based detection:** Snort allows administrators to create and modify detection rules tailored to the unique requirements of IoMT networks, such as monitoring device-specific behavior or identifying unauthorized connections.

- **Community and proprietary rulesets:** Access to both open-source and Cisco-maintained rulesets enables healthcare organizations to stay updated on emerging threats.

Versatility in Deployment

- **IDS and IPS modes:** Operates as either an intrusion detection system (monitoring and alerting) or an intrusion prevention system (actively blocking threats), depending on the healthcare network's security needs.
- **Scalability:** Can be deployed across small clinic networks to large hospital systems with extensive IoMT infrastructures.

Packet Logging and Forensics

- **Detailed packet logging:** Captures and stores packet-level data for post-incident analysis, supporting forensic investigations into IoMT-related security breaches.
- **Integration with SIEM:** Logs can be integrated with Security Information and Event Management tools for centralized monitoring and analysis.

Strengths in IoMT Context

- **Adaptability to IoMT Traffic**
  Snort's customizable rules allow it to adapt to the unique communication patterns and security requirements of IoMT devices. For example, it can monitor and flag irregularities in data flows between medical devices and cloud platforms, ensuring that abnormal traffic is detected early.

- **Real-Time Threat Detection**
  IoMT networks, which handle sensitive patient data and critical device operations, require real-time detection to mitigate threats before they disrupt care. Snort's packet-level analysis ensures immediate identification of potential threats like malware or unauthorized access attempts.

- **Cost-Effectiveness**
  As an open-source tool, Snort eliminates licensing costs, making it accessible for smaller healthcare providers. Its compatibility with commodity hardware further reduces implementation expenses, allowing even resource-constrained organizations to secure their IoMT networks effectively.

- **Community and Industry Support**
  Snort benefits from an extensive user community and active support. Regular updates and a vast library of rules help organizations stay ahead of evolving cyber threats.

Challenges in IoMT Implementation

- **Resource Demands**
  - **High-performance requirements:** Real-time packet analysis and logging can be resource-intensive, potentially overwhelming healthcare networks with high volumes of IoMT traffic.
  - **Dedicated hardware or optimization needed:** Deploying Snort in environments with extensive IoMT devices may require specialized hardware or optimized configurations.

- **False Positives**
  - **Noise from anomalies:** Snort's reliance on predefined rules can lead to false positives, especially in dynamic IoMT environments where device behavior may vary.
  - **Mitigation:** Advanced rule tuning and integration with machine learning tools can reduce unnecessary alerts.

- **Limited Native Threat Intelligence**
  - **Static detection capabilities:** While effective at detecting known threats, Snort lacks built-in capabilities for integrating real-time threat intelligence or predictive analytics, which are increasingly essential for proactive IoMT security.
  - **Supplementary tools required:** Organizations may need to pair Snort with external threat intelligence feeds or advanced analytics platforms.

- **Complexity in Rule Management**
  - **High customization overhead:** Writing and managing rules for diverse IoMT devices requires significant expertise, particularly in healthcare networks with a variety of devices and protocols.
  - **Specialized knowledge needed:** Administrators must have in-depth knowledge of IoMT traffic patterns and Snort rule syntax to optimize performance and accuracy.

Use Case in a Healthcare Environment A regional hospital deployed Snort to secure its IoMT network, which included wearable ECG monitors, infusion pumps, and patient tracking systems. After experiencing abnormal data transmissions from several devices, the hospital sought a real-time solution to detect and prevent potential security breaches.

- **Actions Taken:**
  - **Custom rule development:** Snort rules were customized to monitor device-specific behaviors, such as data transmission schedules for infusion pumps and authentication requests for wearable devices.

- **Real-time packet analysis:** Snort was deployed in IPS mode, actively blocking traffic from unauthorized IP addresses and alerting administrators to protocol anomalies.
- **Integration with SIEM:** Snort's logs were integrated with the hospital's SIEM platform, enabling centralized analysis and cross-referencing with other security tools.

■ Outcomes:
- **Successful threat detection:** Snort identified and blocked several unauthorized access attempts targeting IoMT devices, preventing potential data breaches and operational disruptions.
- **Enhanced visibility:** Detailed packet logs provided insights into network behavior, helping the hospital refine its security policies and improve device configurations.
- **Cost-effective security:** The open-source nature of Snort allowed the hospital to secure its IoMT infrastructure without incurring significant expenses.

■ Key Benefits for IoMT Networks
- **Customizable rules:** Tailored detection rules ensure precise monitoring of device-specific traffic patterns and vulnerabilities.
- **Scalable deployment:** Suitable for both small clinics and large hospitals with extensive IoMT ecosystems.
- **Real-time protection:** Detects and prevents threats before they compromise sensitive medical data or device functionality.
- **Community-driven updates:** Regular updates and ruleset contributions keep Snort aligned with evolving threats.

■ Limitations in IoMT Context
- **Resource intensiveness:** Requires significant processing power for real-time packet analysis in high-traffic networks.
- **False positives:** Predefined rules may generate excessive alerts in dynamic healthcare environments.
- **Lack of native AI/ML integration:** Relies on static rules, limiting its ability to adapt to novel or evolving threats without external tools.
- **Complex rule management:** Customizing and maintaining rules for diverse IoMT devices is time-consuming and requires expertise.

Snort is a versatile IDPS solution for IoMT networks, providing real-time packet analysis, customizable rules, and cost-effective deployment. Its adaptability and extensive community support make it a strong contender for securing healthcare environments, particularly when combined with complementary tools for threat intelligence and machine learning. While challenges such as resource demands and false positives exist, these can be mitigated with careful configuration and supplementary technologies. For healthcare organizations seeking an open-source solution to enhance IoMT security, Snort offers a proven and effective framework.

Suricata

Suricata, as shown in Figure 13-7, is a high-performance, open-source IDPS known for its multithreaded architecture and advanced features. It offers real-time network traffic analysis, packet logging, and threat detection capabilities. With its ability to handle high-throughput environments efficiently, Suricata is particularly well-suited for securing IoMT networks, which are characterized by diverse medical devices, sensitive data, and constant connectivity. Its adaptability and scalability make it a compelling choice for healthcare organizations aiming to protect critical IoMT infrastructure.

Figure 13-7: Suricata IDPS Website

Core Features and Capabilities Multithreaded Architecture

- **Parallel processing:** Suricata's multithreaded design allows it to process large volumes of network traffic efficiently, ensuring minimal latency in high-throughput IoMT environments.
- **Optimized for scalability:** Ideal for hospitals and healthcare networks, where IoMT devices generate continuous streams of data, such as wearable monitors, infusion pumps, and imaging systems.

Protocol Awareness

- **Deep packet inspection:** Suricata goes beyond traditional packet inspection by understanding protocols like HTTP, HTTPS, SMB, FTP, and DNS. This is critical in IoMT networks where diverse devices communicate using various protocols.
- **Custom protocol detection:** Supports customization for IoMT-specific communication protocols, ensuring accurate monitoring of medical devices.

Versatile Threat Detection

- **Signature-based detection:** Leverages rule sets to identify known threats, providing a strong defense against well-documented attack patterns.
- **Anomaly-based detection:** Identifies deviations from normal network behavior, flagging potential zero-day exploits or unauthorized access attempts.
- **File extraction and malware analysis:** Extracts files from network traffic for in-depth analysis, helping detect malicious payloads targeting IoMT devices.

Integration with Threat Intelligence

- **Real-time updates:** Incorporates external threat intelligence feeds to enhance detection capabilities and stay updated on emerging threats.
- **Community rule sets:** Utilizes community-contributed and third-party rule sets to detect the latest attack vectors targeting IoMT environments.

Event Logging and Reporting

- **Detailed logs:** Generates comprehensive logs for forensic analysis and compliance reporting, including details of threats detected, device behavior, and network anomalies.
- **Flexible output formats:** Supports various output formats, including JSON, enabling easy integration with SIEM systems and healthcare analytics tools.

Strengths in IoMT Context

- **High Performance in Healthcare Networks**
  Suricata's multithreaded architecture ensures efficient processing of the continuous data streams generated by IoMT devices. Its ability to handle large-scale traffic with minimal latency is crucial for maintaining the performance of medical systems that rely on real-time data transmission.
- **Advanced Protocol Awareness**
  IoMT networks involve diverse devices communicating through multiple protocols. Suricata's protocol awareness allows it to accurately analyze and protect these communications, reducing false positives and enhancing detection accuracy.

- **Threat Detection Flexibility**
  The combination of signature-based and anomaly-based detection makes Suricata highly effective against both known and emerging threats. This dual approach ensures comprehensive protection for IoMT devices, which are often targeted by ransomware, denial-of-service attacks, and data exfiltration attempts.

- **Open-Source Advantage**
  As an open-source solution, Suricata provides cost-effective security without sacrificing functionality. This is particularly advantageous for smaller healthcare facilities with limited cybersecurity budgets.

- **Extensibility**
  Suricata's ability to integrate with threat intelligence feeds, SIEM platforms, and other security tools enhances its functionality, making it a central component of a layered defense strategy in IoMT networks.

Challenges in IoMT Implementation

- **Resource Demands**
  - **High CPU and memory requirements:** Despite its efficiency, Suricata's multithreaded architecture can be resource-intensive, especially in environments with extensive IoMT deployments.
  - **Mitigation:** Requires deployment on optimized hardware or integration with cloud-based infrastructure to manage processing loads effectively.

- **Rule Management Complexity**
  - **Extensive ruleset maintenance:** Suricata's effectiveness depends on well-maintained and updated rulesets. Managing these rules for diverse IoMT devices can be time-consuming and requires expertise.
  - **Solution:** Automating rule updates through trusted sources can help reduce the management burden.

- **Encrypted Traffic Challenges**
  - **Inspection limitations:** Suricata cannot inspect encrypted traffic directly, which may allow certain threats to bypass detection.
  - **Solution:** Integration with SSL/TLS decryption proxies ensures comprehensive traffic analysis while preserving data integrity.

- **Limited IoMT-Specific Features**
  - **Generalized threat detection:** While highly capable, Suricata is not specifically tailored for IoMT networks and may require customization to address device-specific vulnerabilities and communication patterns.
  - **Solution:** Custom rules and protocol configurations can bridge this gap, ensuring compatibility with IoMT environments.

Use Case: Suricata in a Healthcare Environment A midsize hospital with a growing IoMT network, including wearable glucose monitors, ECG devices, and infusion pumps, sought a scalable IDPS solution to secure its infrastructure against ransomware attacks and unauthorized access.

- **Actions Taken:**
  - **Deployment in a Hybrid Mode:**
    Suricata was deployed in both IDS and IPS modes to monitor traffic across the network and actively block malicious activity targeting IoMT devices.
  - **Custom Protocol Configuration:**
    Tailored Suricata's protocol detection capabilities to include healthcare-specific communication protocols used by IoMT devices.
  - **Integration with Threat Intelligence:**
    Linked Suricata to real-time threat feeds to enhance detection of emerging threats, including ransomware strains targeting medical devices.
  - **Enhanced Logging and Analytics:**
    Configured detailed logging to integrate with the hospital's SIEM for centralized monitoring and compliance reporting.
- **Outcome:**
  - **Successful threat mitigation:** Suricata identified and blocked multiple unauthorized access attempts and detected anomalous traffic indicative of malware activity, preventing breaches.
  - **Improved network visibility:** The hospital gained a clearer understanding of IoMT device behavior and communication patterns, enabling proactive risk management.
  - **Operational continuity maintained:** Secured IoMT devices remained functional throughout the implementation, ensuring uninterrupted patient care.
- **Key Benefits for IoMT Networks**
  - **Scalable performance:** Handles high-throughput traffic efficiently, even in large IoMT networks.
  - **Protocol adaptability:** Monitors a wide range of protocols, ensuring comprehensive protection for diverse IoMT devices.
  - **Cost-effective security:** Open-source nature makes it accessible for organizations of all sizes.
  - **Threat intelligence integration:** Real-time updates enhance detection capabilities against sophisticated cyber threats.
  - **Extensive logging:** Detailed logs provide valuable insights for compliance, forensic investigations, and proactive security measures.

- **Limitations in IoMT Context**
    - **Resource requirements:** Demands significant processing power, particularly in large-scale deployments.
    - **Encrypted traffic challenges:** Limited native capabilities for inspecting encrypted communications.
    - **Customization needs:** Requires tailored configurations and rules to fully align with IoMT-specific security needs.
    - **Expertise dependency:** Effective deployment and maintenance require skilled personnel familiar with Suricata and IoMT environments.

Suricata is a powerful and versatile IDPS solution well-suited for securing IoMT networks. Its high performance, protocol awareness, and threat detection flexibility make it a valuable tool for healthcare organizations aiming to protect sensitive medical devices and patient data. While challenges such as resource demands and customization requirements exist, these can be addressed with proper planning and deployment strategies. For healthcare facilities seeking an open-source, high-performance security solution, Suricata offers good protection and scalability, ensuring the resilience of IoMT networks against evolving cyber threats.

Best Practices for IoMT IDPS Deployment

Implementing IDPS into IoMT networks requires a strategic, layered approach to ensure the security of interconnected medical devices. The following best practices provide a head start to creating a runbook for deploying and managing IDPS in a healthcare environment.

Conduct a Risk Assessment

- **Identify critical IoMT assets:** Begin by cataloging all IoMT devices and their roles within the healthcare network. This includes devices such as infusion pumps, wearable monitors, and imaging systems.
- **Evaluate vulnerabilities:** Assess each device's potential weaknesses, such as outdated firmware, weak encryption, or insecure communication protocols.
- **Data flow:** Analyze the data flow between IoMT devices and other systems to identify potential security gaps.
- **Analyze attack vectors:** Consider possible threats, including ransomware, denial-of-service attacks, and data exfiltration, and evaluate the potential impact of these threats on patient safety and operational continuity.
- **Prioritize risks:** Rank vulnerabilities based on their potential impact and likelihood to ensure critical assets are protected first.

Adopt Layered Security

- **Defense in depth:** Deploy IDPS as part of a broader security architecture that includes firewalls, endpoint protection, and network segmentation.
- **Authentication protocols:** Implement multi-factor authentication and role-based access controls to minimize the risk of unauthorized access to IoMT devices and systems.
- **Encryption standards:** Use strong encryption (e.g., AES-256 or TLS 1.3) to secure data in transit and at rest, ensuring confidentiality and integrity. Consider implementing a cluster-based user authentication protocol like 3ECAP, which includes phases for setup, medical staff registration, sensor registration, login and authentication, and password/biometric updates.
- **Network segmentation:** Isolate IoMT devices into dedicated network zones to limit the impact of breaches and reduce lateral movement by attackers.

Utilize AI and Machine Learning

- **Enhanced threat detection:** Leverage AI-powered IDPS solutions to analyze large volumes of data in real time, detecting anomalies and patterns indicative of malicious activity.
- **Behavioral baselines:** Use machine learning to establish normal behavior profiles for IoMT devices and flag deviations that may signal threats.
- **False positive reduction:** AI algorithms can minimize noise by refining detection rules and prioritizing alerts, allowing security teams to focus on genuine risks.

Regularly Update Policies

- **Threat intelligence feeds:** Integrate up-to-date threat intelligence feeds to stay informed about emerging vulnerabilities and attack vectors.
- **Custom detection rules:** Continuously refine detection rules to address new threats and adapt to changes in the IoMT ecosystem.
- **Patch management:** Regularly update IoMT device firmware and IDPS software to address known vulnerabilities and enhance functionality.

Integrate with Incident Response Plans

- **Seamless integration:** Ensure the IDPS is fully integrated with the organization's incident response (IR) framework to enable rapid detection, containment, and recovery.
- **Automated responses:** Configure automated actions, such as isolating compromised devices or blocking malicious IP addresses, to minimize the impact of attacks.
- **Log analysis and forensics:** Use IDPS-generated logs to support forensic investigations and improve future incident response capabilities.

Educate Staff

- **Training programs:** Provide comprehensive training to healthcare professionals and IT staff on how to interpret IDPS alerts and take appropriate actions.
- **Awareness campaigns:** Raise awareness about cybersecurity risks specific to IoMT devices and the role of IDPS in mitigating these risks.
- **Simulated exercises:** Conduct regular drills to test staff readiness in responding to IDPS alerts and coordinating with incident response teams.
- **Collaboration:** Foster a culture of collaboration between IT and healthcare teams to ensure that all stakeholders understand the importance of security measures.

Deploying an effective IDPS for IoMT networks is a critical step. By conducting thorough risk assessments, adopting layered security measures, leveraging AI capabilities, and keeping policies updated, organizations can build resilient defenses. Integrating IDPS with incident response plans and training staff helps ensure that healthcare providers can respond swiftly and effectively to potential threats.

Modern Innovations in IoMT IDS

Now that we understand IDPS for IoMT and walked through some great options plus some of the best practices, I'll explore a bit more on some of the cutting-edge innovations transforming IDS technologies. These are making them more effective, proactive, and adaptable for securing IoMT environments. I'll talk about AI-powered detection, behavioral analytics, edge-based IDS, integrating with threat intelligence, adding deception technology, emerging trends, regulatory compliance, and future directions.

AI-Powered Detection

The incorporation of artificial intelligence into IDSs has been a game-changer. Machine learning algorithms can analyze enormous volumes of network traffic and device data in real time, uncovering patterns and anomalies that would be impossible for humans to detect. Regarding threat prediction, by studying historical data, AI can predict emerging vulnerabilities, allowing preemptive defenses. There's also adaptive learning, where AI systems continuously improve their detection capabilities by learning from new data and evolving threats. Imagine an IDS that instantly recognizes when an infusion pump is behaving abnormally, such as delivering an unauthorized dosage, and triggers an alert before harm can occur.

Behavioral Analytics

Modern IDSs use behavioral analytics to establish normal activity profiles for IoMT devices by monitoring communication patterns, data volumes, and operational hours. Deviations from these baselines, such as unexpected IP communications, trigger alerts, enhancing threat detection. This approach minimizes false positives and identifies subtle threats like insider attacks and stealthy malware.

Edge-Based IDSs

Traditional centralized IDS systems often struggle with latency and bandwidth issues in IoMT networks, where real-time monitoring is most critical. An edge-based IDS addresses this challenge by deploying detection capabilities closer to the devices themselves. Benefits include low latency as threats are identified and addressed locally, minimizing delays.

There's also decentralized monitoring, where each node monitors its surrounding environment, ensuring that even the most remote IoMT devices are protected. For example, in a hospital, an edge-based IDS can monitor wearable devices or infusion pumps directly on the ward, ensuring that anomalies are detected and addressed without delays caused by sending data to a central server.

Threat Intelligence Integration

Today's IDS systems don't work well in isolation. Real-time threat intelligence feeds provide them with up-to-date information on the latest global cyber threats. Dynamic updates facilitate IDS to receive live data on emerging attack methods, malicious IP addresses, and new vulnerabilities. This intelligence also allows IDS to preemptively block known threats before they impact the network with a proactive defense. An example would be a ransomware strain targeting IoMT devices globally, which is flagged in a threat feed, enabling the IDS to block its command-and-control servers within seconds.

Deception Technology

Deception technology represents a sophisticated and proactive layer of cybersecurity, enhancing IDS in networks. By integrating honeypots and decoys, deception technology serves as both a shield and a learning tool, offering unique advantages in threat detection, mitigation, and intelligence gathering.

These decoy devices are designed to resemble legitimate IoMT devices, such as smart infusion pumps, glucose monitors, or patient wearables. Some can replicate typical device behaviors, including data transmission patterns, network activity, and operational characteristics, making them indistinguishable from real devices in the eyes of an attacker that is not familiar with the target infrastructure. The result is a diversion of malicious activity away from actual IoMT assets, reducing the risk of compromise. By incorporating these decoys, healthcare networks transform from passive defenders to active participants in cybersecurity, effectively luring attackers into controlled environments and away from critical systems.

One of the most significant advantages of deception technology lies in its ability to facilitate in-depth attack analysis. When an attacker compromises a decoy device, the system captures valuable intelligence about the intruder's methods, tools, and objectives. This includes the techniques used to exploit the device, malware payloads, and command sequences employed during the attack, and details about the attacker's network traffic and communication endpoints. This wealth of information enables security teams to identify vulnerabilities within the IoMT network, develop targeted mitigation strategies, and reinforce defenses against similar threats in the future.

Unlike traditional intrusion detection systems, which focus primarily on detecting and reporting anomalies, deception technology can actively engage attackers. This proactive approach allows security teams to observe and understand cybercriminal behaviors in real-time, offering deeper insights into evolving tactics and techniques. By leveraging the intelligence gathered from decoy devices, organizations can stay ahead of threats, fortify their IoMT networks, and ensure the security and functionality of critical healthcare operations.

An illustration of deception in action is, for example, a hospital that deploys a decoy wearable glucose monitor within its IoMT network. This device is programmed to simulate all typical functionalities of a real monitor, including communication with the hospital's servers and data transmissions to the cloud. A cybercriminal scans the hospital's network and identifies a decoy glucose monitor, mistakenly believing it to be a real device. Attempting to exploit the monitor, the attacker injects malware or tries to intercept its data streams. However, the decoy device logs the attacker's actions, capturing crucial details such as IP addresses, malicious payloads, and commands. The intrusion detection system quickly flags the activity as a threat, isolating the attacker's IP to prevent lateral movement within the network. Security teams then analyze the collected intelligence to develop targeted countermeasures. As a result, the attacker's methods are exposed without compromising actual patient devices or data, allowing the hospital to strengthen its defenses and eliminate vulnerabilities.

Key benefits of deception technology include the following:

- **Risk mitigation:** Diverts attackers away from critical systems, reducing the risk of real asset compromise. Also provides an additional layer of defense beyond traditional IDS mechanisms.

- **Enhanced threat intelligence:** Collects detailed information on attacker behavior and methodologies, enabling continuous improvement of security measures. Also supports predictive analysis by identifying trends and recurring threat patterns.

- **Minimized operational impact:** By engaging attackers in a controlled environment, prevents disruptions to patient care and hospital operations.

- **Proactive defense strategy:** Transforms IoMT networks from reactive to proactive security environments, where threats are actively studied and neutralized.

Deception technology is a powerful addition to IoMT IDS frameworks, leveraging decoys and honeypots to lure attackers, gather intelligence, and protect critical healthcare systems. By turning cyberattacks into opportunities for learning and defense enhancement, deception technology not only safeguards patient data and device functionality but also equips organizations with the tools needed to stay ahead.

Emerging Trends in IoMT IDS

The evolution of IDS for IoMT networks is being driven by technologies and methodologies aimed at enhancing security with efficiency. As described, one notable trend is the development of AI-driven adaptive IDS, which leverages artificial intelligence and machine learning to autonomously adjust to emerging threats and network changes. These systems continuously learn from data patterns, enabling real-time detection and response to evolving cyber threats.

Another innovation is the implementation of blockchain-based IDS, which utilizes distributed ledger technology to ensure secure and tamper-proof logging of security events. This approach enhances the integrity and traceability of security data, providing protection against malicious modifications. Additionally, the edge computing in IDSs I discussed is gaining traction, where data is processed closer to IoMT devices, significantly reducing latency and enabling faster threat detection and response. By bringing computing power closer to the source, edge computing ensures more timely protection for critical medical systems.

Future Directions in IoMT IDS

The future of IoMT IDS is set to be shaped by advancements in technology and an expanding range of applications. The integration of beyond 5G technology, such as 6G, provides faster and more efficient communication between IoMT devices, enabling enhanced IDS capabilities with reduced latency and improved scalability. As IoMT devices continue to evolve, there is a growing need for IDS solutions specifically tailored to emerging technologies like ingestible sensors and smart implants, which require specialized detection mechanisms to address their unique vulnerabilities. Moreover, there is an increasing focus on predictive analytics within IDS systems. By analyzing historical and real-time data, these systems aim to anticipate and prevent potential security breaches before they occur, shifting the paradigm from reactive to proactive defense. Together, these developments represent a transformative approach to securing IoMT ecosystems in the face of dynamic threats.

Key Takeaways from IDPS for IoMT Networks

The increasing adoption of Internet of Medical Things devices, such as wearable glucose monitors and smart infusion pumps, is revolutionizing patient care by enabling real-time monitoring and data exchange. However, this connectivity also makes IoMT networks highly vulnerable to cyber threats, necessitating tailored security measures beyond traditional IT protections. Intrusion detection and prevention systems play a crucial role in securing IoMT environments by monitoring network traffic, detecting unauthorized access, mitigating ransomware attacks, and safeguarding PHI. Key IDPS techniques include signature-based detection for known threats, anomaly-based detection leveraging machine learning to identify zero-day attacks, hybrid models for comprehensive threat coverage, behavioral analytics to track suspicious activity, and deception technology, such as honeypots, to lure and study attackers.

Despite their effectiveness, implementing IDPSs for IoMT presents challenges, including resource constraints due to limited device computational power, false positives that can overwhelm security teams, encrypted traffic obscuring threats, the diversity of IoMT devices requiring customized detection rules, and the complexity of regulatory compliance with frameworks like HIPAA and GDPR. To enhance IDPS capabilities, modern innovations such as AI-powered detection, edge-based IDS for low-latency responses, behavioral analytics to improve accuracy, and real-time threat intelligence integration are being adopted. Case studies demonstrate how hospitals leveraging hybrid IDPS solutions have successfully thwarted ransomware attacks, reduced false positives through AI-driven anomaly detection, and implemented proactive security measures such as firmware updates and network segmentation.

To effectively deploy IDPS in IoMT environments, healthcare providers must conduct risk assessments, adopt layered security approaches, integrate AI and machine learning for better detection accuracy, maintain updated security policies, align IDPS with incident response plans, and educate staff on responding to alerts. Additionally, adherence to regulatory standards, including FDA cybersecurity guidelines, is essential to ensure data privacy and device integrity. Looking ahead, advancements such as 5G integration will enhance IDS scalability, predictive analytics will enable proactive threat detection, and tailored solutions will be developed for emerging IoMT technologies like ingestible sensors and smart implants. Ultimately, robust IDPS deployment is vital for protecting patient safety, securing sensitive data, and maintaining trust in healthcare operations, making continuous updates, proactive risk management, and staff training indispensable for long-term security resilience.

CHAPTER 14

Machine Learning Approaches to Wireless Attack Detection

Machine learning (ML) enables advanced data analysis, predictive modeling, and automation across various applications. In medical imaging and diagnostics, ML algorithms analyze X-rays, MRIs, and CT scans to detect anomalies like tumors or fractures. At the same time, image recognition tools support early disease detection, such as cancer or diabetic retinopathy. Predictive analytics uses ML to assess patient risk, optimize population health management, and predict equipment maintenance needs, ensuring efficiency and safety.

Personalized medicine also benefits from ML by tailoring treatments to individual genetic and lifestyle profiles, expediting drug discovery, and advancing pharmacogenomics for more precise medication matching. Clinical decision support systems (CDSSs) enhance real-time recommendations and symptom analysis, while remote patient monitoring uses wearables to detect irregular health patterns and manage chronic conditions. Natural language processing (NLP) automates clinical documentation, enables speech recognition, and analyzes patient sentiment, reducing administrative burden while enhancing care delivery. Virtual assistants and chatbots streamline patient engagement, from scheduling to symptom triage in telemedicine.

Operational efficiencies are also achieved by predicting patient volume, optimizing workflows, and managing supply chains. ML also bolsters fraud detection in insurance claims and strengthens cybersecurity by identifying irregular network patterns. In behavioral health, ML monitors mental health markers and delivers personalized therapeutic interventions. Surgery and rehabilitation robots use ML to enhance precision and tailor recovery programs. Finally, clinical trials and research leverage ML to match patients to studies, predict outcomes, and identify disease biomarkers. With its integration into these technologies, ML is reshaping healthcare by improving outcomes, reducing costs, and personalizing care.

Regarding security, ML has also been reforming wireless attack detection, especially in healthcare networks and the IoMT. Wireless communication enables real-time data exchange between medical devices, healthcare systems, and cloud platforms, making it critical for delivering modern, efficient care. However, the dependence of medical devices on wireless protocols exposes healthcare networks to myriad security threats. In my review of eavesdropping, spoofing, and denial-of-service attacks, malicious actors exploit vulnerabilities in wireless communication to compromise sensitive patient data, disrupt operations, and jeopardize patient safety. ML addresses these challenges by leveraging advanced algorithms to process vast volumes of wireless data, detect anomalies, and identify malicious activities in real time.

An entire book could be dedicated to machine learning, but in this chapter, I'll explore its role in securing wireless communications within IoMT environments. I'll cover some key advancements in ML, its integration with existing security infrastructure, ethical considerations, and case studies that help highlight its impact on healthcare cybersecurity.

Introduction to Machine Learning for Wireless Attack Detection

ML for wireless attack detection is a cutting-edge approach to securing healthcare networks. In these environments, wireless connectivity enables real-time data exchange between medical devices, healthcare systems, and cloud platforms. However, relying on wireless communication introduces vulnerabilities, making these systems attractive targets for attackers. Machine learning leverages advanced algorithms to analyze large amounts of wireless communication data, detect anomalies, and identify malicious activities in real time, thus bolstering the security of IoMT networks.

Why ML Is Critical for Wireless Attack Detection

Machine learning addresses traditional security methods' limitations by providing real-time, adaptive, and scalable defense. IoMT networks heavily rely on wireless communication protocols such as Wi-Fi, Bluetooth, Zigbee, and others to connect medical devices, patient wearables, and centralized healthcare systems. For any technology, the dependence on wireless protocols creates vulnerabilities that attackers can exploit. For example, recall that eavesdropping attacks can intercept sensitive health information, while spoofing and man-in-the-middle attacks can manipulate or disrupt device communications. Additionally, denial-of-service attacks can overwhelm IoMT networks, leading to system downtime and jeopardizing patient safety.

Machine learning addresses vulnerabilities by analyzing real-time wireless communication patterns and identifying deviations that could signal potential threats. Unlike static rule-based systems, ML models can detect subtle anomalies such as unusual signal behaviors, unauthorized access points, or irregular data flows. ML models in wireless attack detection are algorithms trained to identify patterns and anomalies in network data to detect cyber threats. These models can be categorized into supervised, unsupervised, semi-supervised, and reinforcement learning approaches. Supervised models, such as decision trees, random forests, support vector machines (SVMs), and neural networks, require labeled datasets to classify normal and malicious activities. Unsupervised models, including clustering algorithms and autoencoders, detect anomalies without predefined attack labels. Semi-supervised models leverage small, labeled datasets with more extensive unlabeled data for improved detection, while reinforcement learning models dynamically adapt to evolving threats. ML models are used in IDS, behavioral analysis, and anomaly detection to identify attacks. However, their effectiveness is affected by challenges such as data imbalance, adversarial attacks, feature selection, and computational overhead. Addressing these challenges is crucial for enhancing ML-based wireless security solutions.

By continuously monitoring and analyzing the wireless environment, ML ensures that IoMT networks remain more resilient against evolving threats. In this context, static, rule-based intrusion detection systems are often inadequate. They rely on predefined rules that may fail to recognize new or advanced threats. For instance, an emerging attack technique that mimics legitimate device behavior may go undetected by conventional systems.

Machine learning is a solution that adapts to the changing threat landscape. By learning from historical attack data and real-time network activity, ML algorithms develop a comprehensive understanding of normal and malicious behaviors, like a baseline. Supervised learning techniques can identify known attack patterns, while unsupervised methods detect previously unseen anomalies. This adaptability enables ML-driven systems to stay ahead of attackers, recognizing and mitigating threats before they cause significant harm. In an IoMT context, this might involve detecting a novel Bluetooth spoofing attack targeting wearable glucose monitors or identifying an unusual pattern of connection attempts to a medical server.

Networks generate enormous amounts of data these days due to the continuous operation of interconnected devices. My research showed that the average enterprise could generate up to a daily terabyte in log data. Each device produces data streams that should be monitored for anomalies, from wearable heart monitors and infusion pumps to imaging systems and diagnostic tools. This data's sheer volume and complexity make manual monitoring impractical and overwhelm some traditional detection systems. As mentioned, ML shines in processing large volumes of high-dimensional data. ML can analyze traffic patterns, signal integrity, and device behaviors to identify threats with exceptional speed and accuracy. For example, ML can pinpoint irregularities in data transfer rates that indicate a potential DoS attack or detect anomalous device communication that suggests an unauthorized access attempt. By automating the analysis of complex data streams, ML not only improves the efficiency of attack detection but also reduces the burden on human analysts, allowing them to focus on other tasks.

How Machine Learning Enhances Wireless Attack Detection

ML provides innovative tools for detecting, mitigating, and predicting wireless attacks in complex networks. In this section, I'll explore how ML enhances wireless attack detection, focusing on anomaly detection, feature extraction, real-time analysis, and attack prediction features. The goal is to help you make more informed decisions about choosing technologies and solutions incorporating machine learning features.

Anomaly Detection

Anomaly detection is one of the foundational applications of ML in wireless security. ML models are trained to establish baselines for normal network behavior by analyzing parameters such as signal strength, data transfer rates, and device activity patterns over time. These baselines create a reference framework for distinguishing legitimate operations from potential threats.

ML algorithms, particularly those based on unsupervised learning, monitor network traffic continuously to detect deviations from established baselines. For instance, a sudden drop in signal strength, unexplained packet loss, or the appearance of unauthorized access points may signal a potential attack.

An example would be in an IoMT network, where an anomaly detection model might flag unusual data flows originating from a wearable insulin pump that suddenly starts communicating with an unknown IP address. This could indicate a man-in-the-middle attack or a rogue command injection attempt. By identifying these anomalies in real time, ML systems provide early warnings, enabling healthcare organizations to respond quickly before the anomalies escalate into full-scale attacks.

Feature Extraction and Classification

Feature extraction and classification are also critical components of ML-based wireless attack detection. These techniques involve analyzing specific attributes or features of network traffic to classify activities as benign or malicious. ML algorithms extract and evaluate features such as signal integrity, device identifiers, communication protocols, and connection durations. The system classifies these activities into predefined categories using the supervised learning techniques, helping differentiate normal operations from suspicious behaviors.

Detecting rogue access points is a practical application of feature extraction. By analyzing deviations in signal characteristics, such as unusual signal strength variations, unexpected connection patterns, or mismatched device identifiers, ML can pinpoint unauthorized devices attempting to infiltrate the network. The ability to classify activities with high precision ensures that legitimate actions are not mistakenly flagged as threats, reducing false positives and enhancing overall network reliability.

Real-Time Analysis

The real-time analysis capabilities of machine learning are also a game-changer for wireless attack detection. Advanced ML models, including those based on deep learning, process large amounts of data in real time to instantly identify and respond to threats. Deep learning models, such as convolutional neural networks (CNNs) and recurrent neural networks (RNNs), excel at processing complex datasets like those generated by wireless IoMT networks. These models also analyze real-time traffic patterns, device interactions, and signal characteristics, detecting anomalies or attack signatures as they emerge.

Consider a Bluetooth spoofing attack targeting a wearable glucose monitor. A deep learning model could detect discrepancies in device pairing protocols or unauthorized data transmissions, triggering automated mitigation measures like device isolation or network segmentation. Real-time analysis minimizes the window of opportunity for attackers.

Attack Prediction

Another powerful application of machine learning, especially in wireless security, is attack prediction. Predictive analytics uses ML to anticipate potential threats by analyzing historical data, current conditions, and trends. Predictive models employ algorithms like time-series analysis and regression to identify patterns and correlations that may indicate an impending attack. These models continuously update their predictions based on new data, improving their accuracy.

An ML system could forecast the likelihood of a DoS attack on a hospital's Wi-Fi network by analyzing traffic spikes, unauthorized connection attempts, and historical patterns of denial-of-service attacks. This early warning would allow security administrators to allocate resources preemptively or implement defenses, such as rate-limiting or load balancing.

Machine Learning Feature Engineering for Wireless Attack Detection

Feature engineering is essential in building machine learning models for wireless attack detection. By carefully transforming raw data into meaningful features, we can significantly improve a model's ability to identify and mitigate security threats. In this section, I'll discuss key features in wireless attack detection, how to collect and preprocess data, and the metrics used to evaluate model performance.

I'll start with network traffic features. These features provide insights into how wireless communications behave. For example, packet size anomalies might signal malicious activity, such as unusually large packets used in data theft or small packets in denial-of-service attacks. Another key feature is inter-arrival time, which can highlight irregular traffic patterns, like sudden bursts of small packets that might indicate a SYN flood attack targeting IoMT devices.

Next, there are protocol-specific features. Different wireless protocols, like Wi-Fi, Bluetooth, and Zigbee, have unique behaviors that can reveal anomalies. For instance, identifying the protocol type can help distinguish regular traffic from malicious communication. Header fields, including sequence numbers and source or destination addresses, can also be analyzed to uncover spoofing or replay attacks. For example, a mismatch in sequence numbers in Bluetooth connections may indicate a replay attack, where attackers attempt to resend captured data to gain access.

Another category of features concerns signal strength and quality indicators. Wireless attacks often affect signal characteristics, such as the Received Signal Strength Indicator (RSSI) and/or Signal-to-Noise Ratio (SNR). A sudden drop in RSSI might signal a spoofing or jamming attack, while degraded SNR could suggest interference or malicious activity. For example, fluctuations in RSSI during communication may indicate an MITM attack.

Temporal features, which analyze patterns over time, also play a vital role in attack detection. Irregularities in connection durations or timestamps can reveal malicious activity. For instance, a wearable device attempting connections outside its regular operational hours might be compromised. Similarly, identifying patterns during peak attack hours can help predict and prevent recurring threats.

Spatial features focus on devices' physical and logical locations. They can reveal inconsistencies, such as devices connecting through unexpected or rogue access points. Tracking device mobility can also highlight suspicious behavior. For example, a stationary medical device that suddenly connects to multiple access points may be a victim of spoofing.

Device behavior patterns add another layer of analysis. IoMT devices follow consistent behavior patterns so that deviations can indicate compromise. Monitoring activity frequency, such as unexpected spikes or drops in usage, and analyzing command patterns can detect unauthorized commands or unusual sequences. For example, an infusion pump receiving unauthorized instructions may signal a security breach.

Now, I'll talk about data collection and preprocessing. Tools like Wireshark and tcpdump are essential for capturing network traffic, allowing us to collect raw data for feature extraction and model training. Model training is teaching a machine learning model to recognize patterns in data by adjusting its parameters using a training dataset. During training, the model learns from input data and corresponding outputs (in supervised learning) or identifies structures and anomalies (in unsupervised learning). It optimizes its performance by minimizing errors using gradient descent and backpropagation techniques. The trained model can then predict or classify new, unseen data. Practical training requires high-quality data, appropriate feature selection, and careful tuning of hyperparameters to prevent overfitting or underfitting. Simulators like NS-3 and OMNeT++ can generate synthetic data to mimic attack scenarios, such as a DoS attack on Zigbee networks. Cleaning and normalizing data is just as important. Removing duplicates, fixing incomplete entries, and scaling features to uniform ranges ensure data quality and fairness in model performance.

Feature selection and dimensionality reduction further optimize data for machine learning. Techniques like correlation analysis or mutual information help identify the most relevant features. Dimensionality reduction tools, such as principal component analysis (PCA), simplify complex data while retaining key information, improving computational efficiency and model accuracy.

Evaluating model performance is the final step. Accuracy measures the proportion of correct predictions but can be misleading in imbalanced datasets. Precision minimizes false alarms by calculating the true and predicted positives ratio. Recall emphasizes identifying as many attacks as possible, ensuring minimal missed threats. There's an F1-Score element that balances precision and recall, while metrics like the Area Under the ROC Curve (AUC) evaluate the model's ability to distinguish between attack and regular traffic. It's also essential to monitor the False Positive Rate (FPR) to avoid unnecessary alerts and the False Negative Rate (FNR) to ensure critical threats are not overlooked.

To summarize, feature engineering is the foundation of machine learning models for wireless attack detection. By leveraging diverse features, ranging from network traffic patterns and protocol behaviors to device activity, and combining them with advanced preprocessing techniques, we can build models capable of effectively detecting and mitigating threats. Performance metrics ensure these models remain reliable and practical for real-world deployment, especially in sensitive environments like IoMT networks.

Types of Machine Learning Techniques

ML enables organizations to address increasingly sophisticated threats with more adaptive and proactive solutions. By leveraging different ML techniques, such as supervised, unsupervised, reinforcement, and deep learning, security systems can identify, mitigate, and prevent a wide range of wireless attacks. I'll examine some of these techniques in more detail and discuss their applications in wireless attack detection, particularly in the context of IoMT networks and healthcare.

Supervised Learning Supervised learning is one of the most established ML techniques, relying on labeled datasets to train models to distinguish between normal and malicious activities. It is particularly effective for detecting known attack patterns. It depends on the datasets to train models to classify activities as benign or malicious with several algorithms. These are the ones that excel in this domain, including the following:

- Support vector machines create decision boundaries to classify data points, making them effective for detecting known wireless threats like spoofing or DoS attacks.

- By aggregating multiple decision trees, random forests enhance prediction accuracy and robustness. They are handy for distinguishing between normal and anomalous traffic patterns.

- Decision Trees offer interpretable results, making them ideal for environments requiring clear explanations of detected threats, such as unauthorized access points.
- Neural networks can identify intricate patterns in high-dimensional data and are effective for complex attack scenarios like MITM attacks.
- K-nearest neighbors (KNN) classifies data based on its proximity to labeled examples. This method is beneficial for identifying similarities to known attack signatures in wireless communication.

Supervised learning models are trained using datasets that include examples of both legitimate and malicious activities, with each instance labeled accordingly. Once trained, the model can associate specific features with corresponding labels, such as packet size, signal strength, or transmission frequency. During operation, the model evaluates incoming data against its training to classify activities as usual or indicative of an attack.

- Use Case:
  - Detecting known wireless attack types like MAC address spoofing or Wi-Fi jamming.
  - For example, a supervised learning model can analyze traffic logs and identify a Wi-Fi jamming attempt by recognizing the distinct packet patterns associated with such an attack, compared to regular wireless activity.
- Advantages:
  - High accuracy in identifying previously encountered threats.
  - Reliable in environments with well-documented attack histories.
- Limitations:
  - Inability to detect zero-day attacks or unknown threat patterns.
  - Dependence on the quality and comprehensiveness of the labeled training data.

Unsupervised Learning Unsupervised learning is particularly effective in scenarios where labeled datasets are unavailable. It focuses on identifying patterns and anomalies within data, making it a tool for detecting novel or zero-day wireless attacks. Unlike supervised learning, which relies on predefined labels, unsupervised learning works with unlabeled datasets to uncover hidden structures and irregularities that may indicate malicious activities.

One commonly used algorithm is K-means clustering, which partitions data into groups or clusters based on similarities. This method is beneficial for identifying unusual communication patterns that deviate from established norms, making detecting potential threats in wireless networks more manageable. Another approach is hierarchical clustering, which organizes data into nested clusters, creating a hierarchy that can reveal relationships between devices and highlight irregular network behaviors indicative of attacks.

PCA is another essential technique in unsupervised learning. It reduces the dimensionality of network traffic data, allowing analysts to visualize patterns and pinpoint anomalies that could signal security breaches. By simplifying complex datasets, PCA enhances the ability to detect deviations that may go unnoticed in higher-dimensional data.

Autoencoders, a type of neural network, are also widely used for anomaly detection. These networks compress data more straightforwardly and then attempt to reconstruct it. Instances where the reconstructed output deviates significantly from the original data often signal malicious activity. This approach effectively identifies subtle variations indicating an ongoing or emerging attack.

In summary, the unsupervised learning algorithms provide a framework for detecting anomalies in wireless network traffic without requiring labeled data. Techniques such as K-means clustering, hierarchical clustering, PCA, and autoencoders enable security systems to uncover hidden patterns, visualize irregularities, and flag potential threats. These methods are instrumental in safeguarding wireless networks against evolving threats, including zero-day attacks.

- Use Case:
  - Discovering novel or zero-day attacks that deviate from established communication norms.
  - For example, an unsupervised learning model might detect a sudden surge in unusual packet headers or unauthorized devices attempting to connect to a medical IoT network, signaling a potential attack.
- Advantages:
  - Effective in detecting unknown threats.
  - Does not require pre-labeled datasets, making it more adaptable to dynamic environments.
- Limitations:
  - Higher rates of false positives due to the lack of predefined labels.
  - Requires careful tuning to avoid misclassifying legitimate deviations as threats.

Semi-supervised Learning   Semi-supervised learning bridges supervised and unsupervised methods, combining the strengths of both approaches to improve detection accuracy in scenarios where labeled data is limited. It leverages small, labeled datasets alongside larger, unlabeled datasets, enabling machine learning models to generalize better and identify threats more effectively. This approach is helpful in wireless attack detection, where acquiring labeled data can be costly and time-consuming.

One common technique is self-training, an iterative process that begins with a model trained on labeled data. This initial model is then used to label additional data points, progressively refining its detection capabilities as more labeled data becomes available. Another method, co-training, employs multiple classifiers trained on different feature sets. By combining insights from these classifiers, co-training enhances the robustness of detection systems, making it effective for identifying threats like rogue access points and signal spoofing.

Graph-based methods represent wireless networks as graphs, where nodes represent devices and edges represent communication links. These approaches analyze network topologies and communication flows to identify anomalous device interactions, providing deeper insights into network behavior. These semi-supervised learning techniques offer a scalable and adaptive framework for enhancing wireless security, effectively addressing modern anomaly detection and threat mitigation challenges.

Reinforcement Learning Reinforcement learning (RL) is a powerful and dynamic approach that enables systems to learn optimal defense strategies through trial and error. It is particularly well-suited for developing adaptive intrusion prevention systems that respond to evolving cybersecurity threats. In RL, an agent interacts with the wireless network environment, learning from the outcomes of its actions. The agent receives rewards for security-enhancing actions, such as successfully blocking an attack and penalties for ineffective actions. Over time, this process allows the agent to develop policies that respond effectively to various attack scenarios.

A key application of RL in wireless security is real-time intrusion prevention. For instance, an RL-based system can detect and mitigate a DoS attack on an IoMT network by dynamically adjusting bandwidth allocation and isolating malicious devices. The primary advantage of RL in cybersecurity is its continuous learning capability, which enables it to adapt to evolving threats without requiring constant human intervention. Additionally, RL systems operate autonomously, making them highly effective in real-time security scenarios. However, RL has challenges, including its computational intensity, as training an RL model requires significant resources. Furthermore, its initial learning phase can be slower than supervised learning techniques, making it less effective in environments requiring immediate results. Despite these limitations, RL remains a promising tool for enhancing wireless security in healthcare and other critical infrastructures.

Deep Learning Deep learning analyzes complex and high-dimensional data, effectively detecting advanced and stealthy threats in wireless communication systems. It's especially well-suited for handling wireless data's dynamic and temporal nature, which is common in IoMT networks. Temporal data refers to data indexed or organized based on time, meaning observations depend on the order in which they occur. This type of data captures patterns, trends, and dependencies over time, making it crucial for tasks such as time series forecasting, anomaly detection, and sequential decision-making. Examples include stock prices, weather data, sensor readings, and patient vitals. Temporal data is often processed using specialized models like recurrent neural networks (RNNs), long short-term memory (LSTM) networks, and transformers, which can effectively capture time-based dependencies and long-term patterns. I'll closely examine some key deep learning models and their applications.

Convolutional neural networks (CNNs) are excellent at analyzing spatial patterns, such as signal spectrums. They can detect interference and spoofing attacks in wireless protocols like Wi-Fi and Bluetooth. For example, CNNs can spot anomalies in signal frequencies that might indicate an attacker trying to jam or impersonate a legitimate signal.

RNNs are designed for sequential data analysis, making them ideal for identifying time-series anomalies such as irregular packet timing or unexpected bursts of signal transmissions. They also help detect patterns that unfold over time, like sudden surges in network activity.

A specialized form of RNNs, LSTM networks, is even better at learning long-term dependencies. These are highly effective for identifying sustained attacks, such as persistent denial-of-service attempts or slow-drip data exfiltration, where small amounts of sensitive information are leaked over time.

Another approach, deep belief networks (DBNs), excels at learning hierarchical patterns within data. They help analyze encrypted or compressed wireless traffic and uncover hidden patterns that may indicate security threats.

Deep learning models use layers of interconnected neurons to process intricate datasets, including signal patterns, encrypted traffic, and multi-protocol communication streams. They stand out for their ability to automatically extract features and identify subtle anomalies or correlations that traditional machine learning techniques might miss.

For instance, imagine a MITM attack targeting a wearable glucose monitor. A deep learning model could detect unusual changes in encryption handshakes or unexpected delays in data transmission, alerting administrators to the threat before harm occurs.

While deep learning offers several advantages, including high accuracy and the ability to process large volumes of real-time data with minimal human oversight, it does come with limitations. These models often require large datasets and significant computational resources for training. Additionally, they can act as a black box, making it difficult to interpret how decisions are made.

In summary, deep learning provides a framework for wireless attack detection in IoMT networks. Its ability to handle spatial and temporal data, detect advanced threats, and operate with minimal human intervention makes it a valuable tool for securing modern wireless communications. However, its reliance on large datasets and its lack of interpretability highlights the need for careful deployment and monitoring.

Transfer Learning Transfer learning is an advancement that allows models trained on one task or dataset to be repurposed for another, enhancing efficiency and reducing resource demands. In wireless security, this technique is proper for deployment in IoMT networks, where labeled datasets of attack scenarios are often limited.

Transfer learning leverages knowledge from pre-trained models developed on large datasets, such as general network traffic or attack patterns, and applies it to new environments with minimal retraining. It eliminates the need to collect and label extensive datasets specific to each healthcare network, saving time and resources. Models can quickly adapt to new wireless protocols or IoMT devices without complete retraining. For example, a pre-trained model designed to detect anomalies in enterprise Wi-Fi networks can be fine-tuned to identify rogue access points or MITM attacks in a hospital's IoMT ecosystem. Transfer learning enables faster deployment and greater adaptability.

Graph Neural Networks (GNNs) Graph neural networks are a specialized class of deep learning models designed for processing and learning from graph-structured data. They represent a breakthrough in understanding and analyzing the relationships within complex systems, such as wireless network topologies. GNNs model wireless networks as graphs, representing devices as nodes and connections (e.g., Wi-Fi, Bluetooth links) as edges. This structure allows the model to analyze how devices interact and detect anomalies in these interactions. The effectiveness of GNNs in wireless security can be further improved by integrating them with other machine learning techniques and considering physical layer information.

GNNs excel at identifying attacks that exploit network structures, such as MAC spoofing or routing-based attacks, by recognizing unusual patterns in device connectivity or communication paths. These models can adapt to network topology changes, such as adding new IoMT devices and ensuring continuous monitoring. In a healthcare setting, GNNs can monitor how wearable devices connect to access points, flagging suspicious connections that deviate from the standard network structure.

Quantum Machine Learning Quantum machine learning (QML) is an emerging field (I'll talk about quantum computing in Chapter 18) that combines the computational power of quantum computing with ML techniques, offering the potential to revolutionize wireless attack detection.

QML utilizes quantum computers' ability to process vast amounts of data simultaneously, solving optimization problems that are computationally prohibitive for classical machines. This capability is helpful in wireless security, where complex attack scenarios often require multidimensional analysis.

To detect subtle attack signatures, QML can process high-dimensional data, such as signal variations or encrypted traffic patterns. Quantum algorithms can rapidly identify the best defensive actions, such as rerouting traffic or isolating compromised devices, even in highly dynamic environments. Potentially, QML could solve challenges like optimizing wireless network configurations in real time to minimize exposure to attacks or rapidly identifying coordinated multi-vector attacks targeting IoMT ecosystems. Though still in its infancy, quantum machine learning represents a promising edge that could redefine the limits of wireless security.

> **NOTE** Ensemble methods combine multiple models to enhance overall detection performance, reducing false positives and negatives in wireless attack detection. There's bagging (bootstrap aggregating) that builds multiple models on random subsets of data and averages their predictions, increasing robustness against overfitting and noise. Boosting sequentially trains models, focusing on correcting the errors of previous ones, making it highly effective for identifying subtle or hard-to-detect threats. Then, stacking combines predictions from multiple base models using a meta-model, delivering improved accuracy and generalization for detecting diverse wireless attack scenarios.

Each type of machine learning technique offers unique strengths and applications for wireless attack detection. Supervised learning is ideal for detecting known threats, while unsupervised learning excels at uncovering unknown vulnerabilities. Reinforcement learning adapts dynamically to evolving attack scenarios, and deep learning delivers unparalleled accuracy for advanced threat detection in complex environments. By leveraging these techniques, organizations can enhance their wireless security capabilities.

Machine Learning Applications in Healthcare and IoMT

From securing wearable devices and detecting rogue access points to preventing DoS attacks and enhancing network segmentation, ML provides healthcare organizations with the tools to protect sensitive data, ensure operational integrity, and safeguard patient lives. As wireless protocols and IoMT devices evolve, ML's adaptability and predictive capabilities will remain critical in maintaining better security frameworks.

With IoMT networks connecting a wide range of medical devices, the application of ML has proven vital in addressing unique security and operational integrity challenges. In the following subsections, I discuss key areas where ML is transforming, particularly in healthcare and IoMT security.

Securing Wearable Devices

Wearable medical devices such as ECG, glucose monitors, and insulin pumps are pivotal for real-time patient monitoring. However, as discussed throughout this book, their wireless connectivity makes them vulnerable. ML models monitor wireless communication patterns to detect anomalies that could signify unauthorized access attempts. Also, the challenge of distinguishing between rogue APs and legitimate but misconfigured APs provides a more comprehensive ML-based solution. ML can identify threats such as MITM attacks by analyzing device behavior and data transmission patterns, where an attacker intercepts and manipulates data during transmission.

For example, a wearable ECG monitor transmitting real-time patient data may be targeted by an MITM attack. The ML system identifies irregularities in the encryption handshake or communication latency, flags the activity as suspicious, and triggers an alert or blocks the connection. The impact includes the following:

- Enhanced patient safety by ensuring uninterrupted, secure data transmission
- Early detection of potential breaches that could compromise sensitive health data

Rogue Access Point Detection

Unauthorized wireless access points (APs) threaten healthcare environments by allowing attackers to intercept or inject malicious traffic into IoMT networks. ML algorithms analyze wireless signals, device association behaviors, and network configurations to identify anomalies that indicate unauthorized APs. By continuously learning from network traffic patterns, ML systems can differentiate between legitimate and rogue APs.

A rogue access point, for example, can be set up within a hospital to capture sensitive data from IoMT devices. The ML system identifies anomalies based on signal strength, unusual traffic patterns, or lack of proper authentication protocols and alerts the security team. The impact includes the following:

- Mitigation of risks associated with unauthorized data access or malicious injection attacks
- Preservation of network integrity in dynamic healthcare environments

Preventing Denial-of-Service Attacks

IoMT devices are increasingly targeted by DoS attacks, which overwhelm devices or networks with excessive traffic, causing disruptions in critical healthcare operations. ML models analyze traffic patterns to establish baselines for expected behavior. Sudden spikes in connection requests or unusual packet sizes are flagged as potential DoS attacks. ML can take preventive measures by identifying these anomalies in real time, such as blocking malicious IPs or rate-limiting traffic to affected devices. It's important to note that the potential for ML to generate false positives and the need for human oversight facilitates a balanced program.

A flood attack targeting smart infusion pumps is detected when the ML system notices a rapid increase in connection attempts. The system automatically isolates the malicious traffic, ensuring the pumps remain operational. The impact includes the following:

- Minimization of disruptions to life-critical medical services
- Enhanced resilience of IoMT networks to volumetric and application-layer attacks

Bluetooth and Zigbee Security

Wireless protocols like Bluetooth and Zigbee are widely used in IoMT devices for short-range communication, but their vulnerabilities can expose devices to spoofing, replay, and eavesdropping attacks. ML algorithms analyze communication patterns and protocol integrity to detect anomalies such as duplicate packets (indicative of replay attacks) or altered device identifiers (signaling spoofing attempts). These systems can monitor encryption performance and signal strength to ensure secure communication.

A Zigbee-based smart thermometer, for example, may experience a spoofing attack where an attacker tries to impersonate a legitimate device. The ML model detects the spoofing attempt by identifying inconsistencies in device identifiers and communication patterns, preventing the attack. The impact includes the following:

- Improved security for low-power, high-efficiency wireless protocols integral to IoMT
- Protection of sensitive data transmitted over these protocols

Enhanced Network Segmentation

Proper network segmentation is critical to isolating devices and ensuring secure communication in complex IoMT environments. By automating segmentation, ML systems can work together to analyze device behaviors, communication patterns, and data streams to identify legitimate devices and connections—ML groups devices with similar risk profiles or operational roles, reducing the attack surface.

For example, an ML model identifies that specific devices (e.g., infusion pumps) communicate only with particular servers. It segments these devices into a dedicated network zone, preventing unauthorized lateral movement in the event of a breach. The impact includes the following:

- Reduced exposure to lateral movement attacks within healthcare networks
- Streamlined management of device clusters based on operational needs and risk profiles

Challenges in Applying ML to Wireless Security in IoMT

While ML holds promise for enhancing wireless security in the IoMT, its application comes with challenges. These challenges stem from the unique characteristics of IoMT networks, including resource-constrained devices, highly sensitive data, and the critical need for operational continuity. In addition, the skill set required by the security professionals to leverage ML capabilities may be challenging for healthcare organizations to address. Therefore, I read that many organizations leveraging service providers that can be an extension of IT to fill that skill gap. Addressing these obstacles is essential to maximize the effectiveness of ML in securing IoMT environments.

One of the most pressing challenges is dealing with imbalanced datasets, where attack events are rare compared to the overwhelming volume of regular network traffic. This imbalance can lead to biased models that favor regular traffic, resulting in missed detection of critical threats. For example, a DoS attack or MAC address spoofing attempt may represent less than 1% of total network activity, making it difficult for the ML model to identify these anomalies accurately. Techniques like oversampling the minority class, synthetic data generation, or employing cost-sensitive learning algorithms are necessary to mitigate this issue and enhance the model's sensitivity to rare attack patterns.

Adversarial Machine Learning Attacks Attackers are increasingly leveraging adversarial techniques to exploit vulnerabilities in ML models. These attacks involve manipulating input data to deceive the detection system, such as subtly altering packet features or injecting malicious traffic that mimics benign patterns. In the context of IoMT, an attacker could craft adversarial samples to bypass detection and compromise critical medical devices. To counteract these threats, ML models must incorporate adversarial training and feature extraction methods to detect and withstand such manipulations effectively.

Concept Drift and Model Adaptation Wireless networks, especially in dynamic environments like healthcare, frequently experience concept drift, which is a change in the underlying data distribution over time. For instance, introducing new IoMT devices or updates to wireless protocols can alter traffic patterns, rendering pre-trained ML models less effective. Ensuring that models remain adaptive requires continuous retraining or online learning techniques, where the model updates itself incrementally with new data. Failing to address concept drift can lead to increased false negatives and a reduced ability to identify evolving attack vectors.

Real-Time Detection Requirements Wireless attack detection demands real-time processing to prevent or mitigate threats effectively. However, the computational complexity of ML models can introduce latency, making them unsuitable for immediate response in time-sensitive environments like healthcare. For example, detecting and mitigating a MITM attack targeting a wearable glucose monitor must occur in seconds to avoid compromising patient safety. Optimizing algorithms for low-latency processing, leveraging edge computing, and employing lightweight models such as decision trees or ensemble methods are critical for meeting real-time detection requirements.

Resource Constraints in Wireless Devices Many wireless devices, particularly IoMT devices, are resource-constrained, with limited computational power, memory, and battery life. Deploying sophisticated ML models directly on such devices can strain their resources and degrade performance. For instance, a wearable heart rate monitor may be unable to run deep learning models locally. To address this challenge, offloading computations to edge or cloud-based systems while maintaining data transmission efficiency is essential. Another approach to overcoming this limitation is designing lightweight algorithms operating within these devices' resource constraints.

Privacy Concerns in Data Collection and Sharing Privacy concerns are vital in ML-based wireless attack detection, especially in healthcare environments involving PHI. Collecting and sharing network traffic data for training ML models can expose sensitive patient information to potential breaches or misuse. For example, analyzing data from wearable devices might inadvertently reveal patient identity or medical conditions. Data anonymization, federated learning, and differential privacy must be employed to protect sensitive information while enabling effective ML model training and deployment. Additionally, strict adherence to regulations like HIPAA and GDPR is required to maintain trust and compliance.

Data Quality and Quantity ML models rely on large, high-quality datasets for effective training, as they must learn to differentiate between normal and malicious behaviors. In IoMT networks, collecting such datasets poses several challenges, such as:

- **Limited data availability:** Many IoMT networks lack comprehensive logs or historical data that capture a variety of wireless attack scenarios. The rarity of specific attack types, such as zero-day exploits, makes providing enough examples for training challenging.
- **Heterogeneous data sources:** IoMT networks have diverse devices with varying communication protocols, such as Wi-Fi, Bluetooth, and Zigbee. This heterogeneity complicates data collection and integration.
- **Data privacy concerns:** IoMT networks handle sensitive health information, which must be anonymized or encrypted before being used for ML training, adding complexity to data preparation.

Potential solutions include using synthetic data generation to simulate attack scenarios and supplement real-world datasets. Federated learning, which allows ML models to train across distributed IoMT devices without exposing sensitive data, is also possible.

Device Resource Constraints Many IoMT devices, such as wearable monitors and implantable medical devices, are designed for low power consumption and minimal computational overhead. These constraints make deploying resource-intensive ML algorithms directly on these devices challenging. IoMT devices may lack the resources required for real-time ML-based intrusion detection, and frequent ML computations could drain their batteries, reducing their operational lifespan.

For example, a smart infusion pump with limited resources may not support the local execution of complex ML models for wireless threat detection. Potential solutions include edge computing, such as deploying ML models on edge devices or gateways that sit closer to the IoMT devices, providing faster processing without burdening the devices. Consider cloud-based processing to offload data to cloud platforms for intensive ML computations, ensuring that IoMT devices remain lightweight and efficient. You can also develop specialized, low-complexity ML algorithms tailored for resource-constrained environments.

Encrypted Traffic IoMT networks use encryption protocols like SSL/TLS to secure wireless communications. While encryption enhances privacy, it also poses a challenge for ML-based threat detection systems, including encrypted traffic that conceals packet contents, making it difficult for ML models to analyze data and identify potential threats. Without decryption, ML models must rely solely on metadata, such as packet size, frequency, and timing, which may not provide enough information to detect sophisticated attacks. An attacker might use an encrypted channel to launch a data exfiltration attack, bypassing ML detection because the model cannot analyze the encrypted payload.

Potential solutions include the following:

- **SSL/TLS decryption proxies:** Integrate decryption proxies within the network to enable the inspection of encrypted traffic before feeding it into ML systems.
- **Feature engineering:** Focus on metadata analysis and behavioral patterns, such as traffic anomalies, to detect threats without decrypting content.
- **Homomorphic encryption:** Explore advanced encryption methods that allow data processing while maintaining confidentiality, enabling secure ML analysis.

False Positives and Negatives Achieving a balance between detection sensitivity and accuracy, such as false positives, is one of the most significant challenges in applying ML to wireless security in IoMT networks. Overly sensitive ML models may generate numerous alerts for benign activities, overwhelming security teams and leading to alert fatigue. An example is a wearable ECG monitor connecting to a new Wi-Fi access point, which could be flagged suspicious if the ML model lacks context for legitimate behavior changes. There are also false negatives, where less sensitive ML models may fail to detect subtle or sophisticated threats, leaving the network vulnerable to undetected attacks. An advanced persistent threat may disguise malicious activity as regular traffic, bypassing a poorly tuned ML system.

Potential solutions include the following:

- **Human oversight:** Combine ML with expert analysis to fine-tune detection thresholds and validate alerts.
- **Ensemble learning:** Use multiple ML models with different strengths to improve detection accuracy.
- **Feedback loops:** Implement systems that learn from missed threats and false positives to refine their accuracy continually.

Applying machine learning to wireless security in IoMT networks presents unique challenges that require innovative solutions. The issues of data quality, device resource constraints, encrypted traffic, and false positives/negatives must be addressed to unlock the full potential of ML in securing these critical environments. By leveraging technologies like edge computing, federated learning, and SSL/TLS proxies, and by balancing automation with human expertise, healthcare organizations can build more robust ML-driven defenses.

Future Directions of Machine Learning for Attack Detection in Healthcare

Integrating machine learning into wireless security offers transformative potential, but the field is still evolving. Addressing adversarial attacks, real-time processing, and privacy concerns requires innovative research and adaptable solutions. By focusing on these future directions, the cybersecurity community can enhance the efficacy of ML models, ensuring more secure and resilient wireless networks. In the following subsections, I explore emerging directions that promise to redefine how healthcare organizations defend against evolving cyber threats.

Federated Learning

As mentioned earlier in this chapter, federated learning is revolutionizing ML by enabling collaborative training across distributed IoMT devices and healthcare organizations without requiring centralized data storage. This approach addresses privacy concerns and regulatory requirements while fostering collective security advancements. Federated learning trains ML models locally on IoMT devices or within individual healthcare institutions. Only anonymized model updates, not raw data, are shared with a central aggregator, ensuring patient confidentiality.

Hospitals in different regions, for example, share attack pattern insights from their IoMT networks to collectively enhance detection capabilities without exposing sensitive patient data. This benefits data privacy, such as complying with regulations like HIPAA and GDPR by keeping patient data localized. Scalability enables global collaboration to tackle complex threats while maintaining decentralized data management. Finally, improved accuracy combines diverse datasets to create models capable of detecting sophisticated and regional-specific attacks.

Explainable AI

As machine learning becomes integral to healthcare cybersecurity, explainable AI (XAI) will improve trust and transparency. XAI focuses on making ML models interpretable and providing clear explanations for their decisions.

XAI systems break down ML predictions into human-readable explanations, showing why a particular activity was flagged as suspicious. This enables security teams to understand the decision-making process and assess whether alerts are accurate. For example, a wearable insulin pump triggers an alert due to unusual data transmission patterns. XAI explains that the decision was based on a combination of factors, including atypical packet size and an unrecognized IP address.

The benefits include trust-building, as healthcare providers are more likely to adopt ML systems when they can understand and validate decisions. XAI also supports audit requirements by providing traceable reasoning for security actions. Operational efficiency is another benefit, as it reduces false positives by helping teams fine-tune ML models based on explicit feedback.

Edge AI

Edge AI represents a shift by bringing machine learning capabilities closer to the IoMT devices, enabling real-time attack detection and response. This approach addresses latency issues and minimizes dependence on centralized systems. Lightweight ML models are deployed on edge devices or gateways, analyzing data locally and responding to threats instantly. It reduces the need to send large volumes of data to cloud servers for processing. An example application would be an IoMT device, such as a wearable ECG monitor, that detects an anomaly in its wireless communication patterns and blocks unauthorized access within milliseconds.

The benefits include real-time detection with immediate responses to threats, which is critical in healthcare settings where delays could endanger lives. We can also expect reduced latency, as it minimizes the time to detect and mitigate attacks by processing data locally. There's also energy efficiency, as optimized ML models ensure low power consumption, preserving the battery life of IoMT devices.

Machine Learning Integration with Existing Security Infrastructure

Integrating machine learning into traditional security frameworks helps organizations detect, mitigate, and respond to cyber threats. By augmenting established security systems with ML capabilities, enterprises can enhance their ability to process large volumes of data, detect subtle patterns, and adapt to evolving threats. I'll explore how ML enhances core components of security infrastructure.

    Combining ML with Traditional Intrusion Detection Systems (IDS) Traditional IDS rely heavily on signature-based or rule-based detection methods to identify threats. While effective for known attack vectors, these systems struggle with detecting new, sophisticated, or zero-day threats. Integrating ML into IDS offers several advancements, such as:

- **Enhanced anomaly detection:** ML algorithms, such as unsupervised learning, establish baselines for normal network behavior and flag deviations that could indicate malicious activity. This allows the system to detect threats that don't match predefined signatures.

- **Reduced false positives:** Traditional IDS can overwhelm security teams with false positives, especially in dynamic environments. ML models refine detection accuracy by analyzing contextual data, minimizing noise, and prioritizing real threats.
- **Adaptive learning:** ML-augmented IDS can evolve, adapting to new attack patterns without manual intervention. This is useful in fast-changing environments like IoMT networks.

In a healthcare setting, for example, an ML-integrated IDS can detect unusual communication patterns from IoMT devices, such as an infusion pump connecting to an unrecognized server, and raise alerts before a breach occurs.

Incorporating ML-Based Detection into SIEM Systems Security information and event management (SIEM) systems collect and analyze logs from multiple sources to provide a centralized view of an organization's security posture. Integrating ML with SIEM systems transforms its capabilities, such as with:

- **Real-time threat correlation:** ML enhances SIEM by analyzing large volumes of log data in real time and identifying correlations between seemingly unrelated events. For example, an unusual login attempt combined with data exfiltration activity can trigger a high-priority alert.
- **Behavioral analytics:** ML-powered SIEM systems use historical data to build user, device, and application profiles. Anomalous behavior, such as a user accessing sensitive data outside of business hours, is flagged automatically.
- **Automated incident response:** ML allows SIEM systems to predict potential threats based on current activities and historical patterns. This enables automated mitigation actions such as isolating affected devices or blocking malicious IP addresses.

For example, a SIEM system integrated with ML can detect low-level alerts, such as unusual IoT device behavior and a firewall rule violation, and escalate it to a coordinated attack, such as a lateral movement within the network.

Enhancing Firewalls and Access Control Systems with ML Capabilities Firewalls and access control systems form the frontline of network defense, but their static nature can limit their effectiveness against dynamic and evolving threats. ML integration enhances these systems by introducing intelligence and adaptability, including:

- **Dynamic rule generation:** ML models can analyze traffic patterns and automatically update firewall rules to block emerging threats, such as DoS attacks or malicious payloads.
- **Behavior-based access control:** ML enables adaptive access control systems that evaluate contextual factors like user behavior, location, and device type

before granting or denying access. For instance, a login attempt from a known device in a familiar location is permitted, while an attempt from an unknown location triggers multi-factor authentication.

- **Deep packet inspection (DPI):** Traditional firewalls often rely on packet headers for decision-making. ML-powered DPI inspects payloads for suspicious content, such as encoded malware or phishing links, providing a deeper level of scrutiny.

In a corporate environment, an ML-enhanced firewall could detect and block an attacker attempting to exfiltrate data using encrypted traffic by recognizing packet size and timing anomalies.

Integrating machine learning into security infrastructure is critical in modernizing cyber defenses. By augmenting IDS, SIEM systems, and firewalls with ML capabilities, organizations can achieve greater visibility, faster response times, and improved adaptability against emerging threats.

Integration with Zero Trust Architectures

As discussed previously, Zero Trust Architecture (ZTA) is becoming a cornerstone of healthcare cybersecurity, emphasizing the principle of *never trust, always verify*. ML can enhance ZTA by continuously validating the legitimacy of wireless communications and device behavior. In other words, ML models monitor IoMT networks for anomalies and verify every access request, even from trusted devices or users. Behavioral analytics ensure that device activities align with established norms. An example is a smart infusion pump communicating with a hospital server. ML verifies the device's credentials, behavior patterns, and network activity before granting access, blocking discrepancies.

Its benefits include continuous validation, which ensures that no device or user is implicitly trusted, reducing the risk of insider threats and advanced persistent threats. ML also adapts to changing network conditions and evolving attack methods, reinforcing ZTA principles. Enhancing compliance is also worth considering because it aligns with regulatory frameworks by ensuring strong access controls and monitoring.

Future Research Directions for Machine Learning in Wireless Security

As attackers employ sophisticated tactics, research must focus on enhancing ML models to anticipate, detect, and mitigate vulnerabilities effectively. The following introduces key future directions for ML research in wireless attack detection:

Developing Robust ML Models Against Adversarial Attacks Adversarial machine learning, where attackers craft inputs designed to deceive ML models, presents a significant challenge. Future research must focus on developing resilient ML algorithms that can withstand such attacks without compromising accuracy. Techniques like adversarial training, which involves exposing models to adversarial examples during the learning phase, can enhance robustness. Additionally, integrating XAI methods can help security teams understand how models make decisions, making it easier to identify and counter adversarial manipulations.

Improving Real-Time Detection Capabilities for High-Speed Wireless Networks The proliferation of high-speed wireless networks, such as 5G and Wi-Fi 6, has increased the demand for real-time security solutions. ML models must evolve to process and analyze vast amounts of data with minimal latency. Future research should explore lightweight ML architectures and edge computing solutions to enable real-time detection at the network edge. Techniques like online learning, where models adapt incrementally as new data becomes available, can enhance responsiveness in dynamic wireless environments.

Enhancing Privacy-Preserving ML Techniques for Sensitive Wireless Environments Data privacy is paramount in wireless security, particularly within IoMT and healthcare settings. Traditional ML models often require access to raw data, which can conflict with privacy regulations like HIPAA and GDPR. Future research should prioritize privacy-preserving ML techniques, such as federated learning and homomorphic encryption. These approaches enable collaborative learning across distributed systems while keeping sensitive data secure, ensuring that patient and user information is not exposed during training or inference.

Exploring Hybrid Approaches That Combine Multiple ML Techniques for Improved Accuracy No single ML technique is universally effective for all wireless attack scenarios. Future research should explore hybrid approaches that combine the strengths of various ML methodologies. For example, supervised learning can detect known attacks, while unsupervised learning identifies novel threats. Ensemble methods, such as stacking and boosting, can further improve detection accuracy by leveraging multiple models simultaneously. Integrating ML with traditional rule-based systems can also provide a layered defense mechanism.

Investigating the Use of ML in Proactive Threat Hunting and Predictive Analytics Rather than merely reacting to detected threats, ML can play a pivotal role in proactive threat hunting and predictive analytics. Future research should focus on developing ML models to identify potential vulnerabilities and forecast attack trends. By analyzing historical data, network behavior, and emerging threat patterns, these models can provide actionable insights to preempt attacks. Techniques like reinforcement learning and deep learning can be instrumental in building proactive security systems that adapt to evolving threat landscapes.

Ethical and Legal Considerations for Machine Learning in Wireless Security

As with any emerging technology that correlates with sensitive information, organizations must consider ethical and legal considerations when harnessing the power of machine learning in wireless security while maintaining fairness, compliance, and trust. These principles are essential for fostering innovation and ensuring the responsible deployment of ML-based solutions in increasingly connected and sensitive environments:

Bias in ML Models and Their Impact on Fairness in Attack Detection Bias in machine learning models pose significant ethical concerns, particularly in wireless attack detection, where models must distinguish between benign and malicious activities. If training data is skewed, perhaps overrepresenting certain types of devices, network protocols, or user behaviors, the resulting model may unfairly favor or penalize specific scenarios. For example, a biased model might disproportionately flag legitimate traffic from particular regions or devices as suspicious, leading to false positives and unnecessary disruptions. Addressing bias involves careful data collection, representative sampling, and ongoing evaluation to ensure equitable treatment across all user groups and network types.

Compliance with Data Protection Regulations Machine learning-based wireless security systems often collect extensive data to identify patterns and detect anomalies. This practice must comply with data protection regulations like the GDPR and HIPAA. These laws mandate the secure handling, anonymization, and restricted use of sensitive data, including user activity and device metadata. Organizations must implement privacy-preserving techniques, such as data anonymization and federated learning, to protect individual rights while enabling effective model training and operation.

Responsible Disclosure of Vulnerabilities Discovered Through ML Techniques Machine learning systems often uncover new vulnerabilities while analyzing network traffic and device behavior. Ethical considerations dictate that these vulnerabilities must be responsibly disclosed to affected parties, such as device manufacturers, software developers, or network operators. Responsible disclosure involves providing detailed reports of the issue, potential impacts, and recommendations for mitigation without exposing the vulnerability to malicious actors. This practice fosters a culture of collaboration and trust within the cybersecurity community while minimizing the risk of exploitation.

Ethical Use of ML in Offensive Security Research and Penetration Testing Using machine learning in offensive security research and penetration testing presents unique ethical challenges. While these activities are intended to identify and remediate security weaknesses, the misuse of ML techniques, such as automated attack generation or exploitation of discovered vulnerabilities, can cause significant harm. Researchers and practitioners must adhere to strict ethical guidelines, ensuring that ML tools are used solely for defensive purposes. This includes obtaining proper authorization for penetration testing, maintaining confidentiality, and prioritizing the safety of users and systems during experiments.

Machine Learning Case Studies in Healthcare

I'll end this chapter with some case studies of ML in healthcare applications that I researched in the industry. These case studies demonstrate the potential of machine learning to address diverse wireless security challenges in healthcare. Organizations can help safeguard IoMT devices, wireless networks, and patient data against emerging threats by employing advanced ML techniques.

IoT Botnet Detection Using Deep Learning A large healthcare provider experienced unusual spikes in network traffic originating from IoT devices, including smart thermometers and connected patient monitors. These devices were suspected to be part of an IoT botnet.

Implementation:

- A deep learning model, specifically a LSTM network, was trained to analyze traffic patterns and detect botnet activity. The model focused on features such as traffic volume, packet size, and frequency of connections.
- Data was collected from a simulated environment using IoMT devices, and previously identified botnet traffic patterns were used to create labeled datasets for supervised learning.

Outcome:

- The LSTM model achieved a high detection accuracy of over 95%, identifying malicious traffic within seconds.
- The healthcare provider deployed the model in its network security operations center (SOC), which enabled the early detection and isolation of compromised devices.
- This approach reduced the risk of large-scale disruptions caused by DDoS attacks and ensured uninterrupted patient care.

Wireless Intrusion Detection in 5G Networks An innovative hospital leveraging 5G networks for real-time patient monitoring and remote surgeries faced concerns about unauthorized access to its wireless network.

Implementation:

- A supervised machine learning model using SVM was implemented to monitor 5G network traffic for abnormal behavior. Features such as session duration, signal strength fluctuations, and connection handovers were analyzed.
- The training data included a mix of legitimate and malicious 5G traffic collected from network simulators.

Outcome:

- The SVM model accurately identified unauthorized access attempts at 92%, enabling the IT team to block rogue connections in real time.
- The system's capability to analyze high-speed 5G traffic without significant latency protected critical healthcare operations.

Drone-Based Wireless Attacks and ML-Based Countermeasures A research team investigated the risk of drones conducting wireless eavesdropping and jamming attacks near a hospital campus.

Implementation:

- A CNN was used to detect anomalies in signal strength and communication patterns caused by drone-based attacks.
- Data was collected using wireless signal simulators to mimic drone interference with IoMT devices operating on Bluetooth and Wi-Fi.

Outcome:

- The CNN model achieved 90% accuracy in distinguishing between regular and drone-induced interference.
- The hospital implemented the model in their wireless monitoring system, enabling early detection of drone-based threats.
- This proactive measure ensured secure communication between IoMT devices and reduced the risk of patient data breaches.

Smart Home Device Fingerprinting for Anomaly Detection A healthcare organization partnered with patients using smart home medical devices, such as connected blood pressure monitors and glucose trackers, raising concerns about device tampering and unauthorized access.

Implementation:

- A K-means clustering algorithm was employed to analyze features such as MAC addresses, communication protocols, and typical usage patterns for device fingerprinting.
- Anomaly detection was achieved by identifying deviations from the expected behavior of each device.

Outcome:

- The system identified anomalies, such as unauthorized firmware updates and unusual data transfer rates, with an 88% detection rate.
- Patients were alerted to potential threats, and compromised devices were isolated from the network to prevent further risks.
- This approach enhanced patient trust in using smart home medical devices and ensured compliance with healthcare security regulations.

Key Takeaways from Machine Learning Approaches to Wireless Attack Detection

Machine learning is set to transform wireless security in healthcare by enabling proactive defense mechanisms, adaptive system responses, and privacy-conscious solutions. These advancements enhance patient safety and operational resilience within the IoMT ecosystem. Machine learning is critical in securing IoMT networks by providing sophisticated attack detection methods, including anomaly detection, predictive analytics, and real-time threat response. It is particularly valuable in handling complex wireless communication protocols such as Wi-Fi, Bluetooth, and 5G. Machine learning techniques contribute to these efforts: supervised learning models like SVMs and random forests detect known threats. At the same time, unsupervised methods such as K-means clustering and Autoencoders identify novel attacks. Deep learning architectures, including CNNs and LSTM networks, further improve detection accuracy for complex threats like man-in-the-middle attacks or signal spoofing.

In healthcare applications, machine learning secures IoMT devices like wearable ECG monitors and smart infusion pumps by detecting unauthorized access and anomalous behavior. Proactive security measures enhance hospital network defenses, including rogue access point detection and Bluetooth spoofing mitigation. However, challenges persist, including imbalanced datasets that can bias models, adversarial attacks targeting machine learning systems, and the evolving nature of network behavior that requires adaptable solutions. Resource constraints in IoMT devices and privacy concerns regarding data collection also hinder widespread implementation. Emerging advancements such as transfer learning, GNNs, and quantum machine learning are pushing the boundaries of wireless security by improving attack detection and optimization capabilities.

Ethical and legal considerations remain essential in deploying machine learning for wireless security. Ensuring fairness in ML models, complying with data protection regulations like GDPR, and maintaining ethical standards in security research are necessary for responsible innovation. Future research will likely focus on improving ML defenses against adversarial attacks, enhancing real-time detection in high-speed networks, and refining privacy-preserving techniques. Hybrid machine learning approaches and proactive threat-hunting strategies are expected to advance the field. Real-world case studies demonstrate the practical impact of machine learning in healthcare security, with applications such as IoT botnet detection using deep learning, wireless intrusion prevention in 5G networks, and ML-based countermeasures against drone-based attacks. Smart home device fingerprinting with ML also underscores its potential in patient-monitoring systems. As machine learning continues to evolve, it promises to redefine the security landscape of IoMT environments, ensuring resilience and compliance in an increasingly connected healthcare ecosystem.

CHAPTER 15

Secure Communication Protocols for Medical Devices

Secure communication protocols for medical devices are essential to protecting sensitive patient data, ensuring device integrity, and helping maintain the overall security of healthcare systems. As medical devices become connected and integrated into broader healthcare networks, the importance of secure protocols has never been greater. This chapter explores the various aspects, challenges, and best practices related to secure communication protocols, focusing on medical devices.

Importance of Secure Communication in Medical Devices

The role of secure communication in medical devices is critical, and the types of medical devices I talked about earlier in this book that require secure communication include the following:

- Implantable devices
- Wearable health monitors
- Diagnostic equipment
- Telemedicine devices
- Hospital information systems
- Mobile health applications

There are many reasons why secure communication is essential, but I'll focus on an overview of some of the most critical purposes here, such as patient data privacy, device integrity and functionality, compliance with regulations, preventing unauthorized access, and maintaining trust.

Protection of Patient Data Privacy Medical devices collect and transmit sensitive patient information and if communication channels are not secured, this data becomes vulnerable to interception by malicious actors. Patient privacy breaches undermine trust and expose patients to identity theft and medical fraud risks. Implementing encryption protocols like TLS and AES helps ensure that patient data remains confidential and inaccessible to unauthorized entities.

Ensuring Device Integrity and Functionality Secure communication safeguards the integrity and proper functionality of medical devices. Cyberattacks that compromise device communication can lead to altered data readings or the insertion of malicious commands. For example, a hacked insulin pump could deliver incorrect dosages, while a compromised pacemaker might fail to operate as intended. By authenticating communication channels and ensuring data integrity through cryptographic techniques, healthcare providers can better protect patients from these risks.

Compliance with Healthcare Regulations Regulatory frameworks like HIPAA and GDPR mandate strict security measures to protect patient data and device communications. Secure communication protocols help organizations comply with these regulations, avoiding fines and inevitable reputational damage. Furthermore, adhering to these standards demonstrates a commitment to patient safety and data security.

Preventing Unauthorized Access and Control Medical devices connected to wireless networks can be appealing targets for cybercriminals. Unauthorized access to these devices can cause harmful outcomes, such as tampering with treatment settings or causing service disruptions. Secure communication mechanisms, such as strong authentication and encrypted channels, help ensure that only authorized personnel and systems can access and control medical devices.

Maintaining Trust in Healthcare Technology Healthcare technology adoption hinges on trust, and patients and healthcare providers must feel confident in the security of medical devices. Secure communication protects patients and fosters trust in digital health innovations. When patients are assured their data and devices are safe, they are more likely to embrace advancements in healthcare technology, such as new remote monitoring and telemedicine solutions.

The bottom line is that secure communication in medical devices is not optional. It is a fundamental requirement for protecting patient privacy, ensuring safety, and maintaining the integrity of healthcare devices and systems. By prioritizing this, healthcare organizations can comply with regulatory standards, prevent unauthorized access, and strengthen trust in technology, transforming patient care.

Key Security Requirements for Medical Device Communication

The unique demands of healthcare environments require security measures to address the multiple dimensions of data and device protection. Some of the most common threats to medical device communication, which I discussed in prior chapters, include the following:

- Eavesdropping and data interception
- Man-in-the-middle attacks
- Replay attacks
- Denial of Service attacks
- Malware and ransomware
- Social engineering attacks
- Physical tampering

That said, there are a variety of key security requirements for medical device communication. There are six principles from best practices that I'll also cover later: confidentiality, data integrity, authentication, authorization, availability, and nonrepudiation. Let's walk through a synopsis of each of these:

Confidentiality Confidentiality ensures unauthorized individuals or systems cannot access sensitive data, such as health metrics or medical histories. Medical devices often transmit data over wireless networks, making them susceptible to eavesdropping attacks. Employing encryption protocols like AES-256 and TLS ensures that the data remains unreadable to attackers even if the communication channel is intercepted. TLS 1.2 or higher is recommended for HIPAA compliance. Additionally, encryption should be applied not just during transmission but also for data at rest. This is critical in maintaining patient privacy and complying with strict confidentiality regulations.

Integrity Data integrity is vital so that information exchanged between medical devices and systems is not altered during transmission. Tampered data could lead to incorrect diagnoses, inappropriate treatments, or compromised device functionality. For instance, a corrupted signal from an insulin pump could endanger the patient. Cryptographic hash functions and digital signatures help verify that data remains unaltered from its source to its destination.

Hash functions generate a fixed-size hash value (or digest) from input data. A good hash function ensures that even a small change in the input produces a vastly different output, enabling tamper detection. Recommended hash functions include the following:

- **SHA-256 (Secure Hash Algorithm 256-bit):** Part of the SHA-2 family, SHA-256 is widely adopted and provides a high level of security for healthcare data integrity. It is used with electronic health record systems, secure messaging, and data archiving.

- **SHA-3 (Keccak):** The latest standard from NIST, SHA-3 offers added resistance to specific cryptographic vulnerabilities and is ideal for next-generation applications in healthcare.
- **HMAC (Hash-Based Message Authentication Code):** This combines a cryptographic hash function (e.g., SHA-256) with a secret key to provide integrity and authentication. It helps ensure that data transmitted between healthcare devices is untampered with and sent by an authorized source.

Digital signatures ensure data authenticity and nonrepudiation by cryptographically binding the sender's identity to the transmitted data. This is critical for protecting sensitive healthcare data during transmission. Recommended digital signature algorithms include the following:

- **RSA (Rivest-Shamir-Adleman):** A widely used standard for digital signatures in healthcare applications. It's typically implemented with key sizes of 2048 bits or higher for long-term security. It's suitable for signing documents like medical prescriptions, clinical reports, or insurance claims.
- **Elliptic Curve Digital Signature Algorithm (ECDSA):** This algorithm offers strong security with smaller key sizes, making it ideal for resource-constrained environments like IoMT devices. It's recommended for secure device-to-device communication in healthcare networks.
- **Edwards-Curve Digital Signature Algorithm (EdDSA):** A newer algorithm offering enhanced speed and security over traditional RSA or ECDSA. It's useful for applications where performance and energy efficiency are priorities.

Example applications in healthcare are as follows:

- **Data integrity verification:** Use cryptographic hashes (e.g., SHA-256) to create digests of EHRs, diagnostic images, or test results, ensuring any changes can be detected.
- **Secure data transmission:** Combine hash functions with digital signatures (e.g., RSA or ECDSA) to sign and verify transmitted healthcare data such as lab reports or referrals.
- **IoMT device security:** Employ HMACs and EdDSA to secure communication between interconnected medical devices and ensure data integrity in real-time monitoring systems.
- **Blockchain in healthcare:** Leverage SHA-256 and digital signatures to store and verify transaction records in healthcare blockchain applications securely.

Authentication Authentication ensures that only authorized devices and users can communicate within the network. Medical devices must confirm the identity of the systems they interact with to prevent, for example, impersonation attacks. Strong authentication methods, such as multifactor authentication (MFA), certificates, and secure device pairing protocols, provide confidence that data is exchanged between legitimate parties.

Multifactor authentication is a foundational approach that requires users to verify their identity through at least two factors: something they know (password), something they have (security token or smartphone app), or something they are (biometric verification like fingerprint or facial recognition).

Digital certificates also play a role by leveraging Public Key Infrastructure to authenticate devices, users, and systems. In the context of IoMT, digital certificates are cryptographic credentials used to authenticate devices, secure communications, and ensure data integrity. They function as electronic passports, verifying the identity of IoMT devices, encrypting sensitive medical data, and preventing unauthorized access to networks and systems. Certificates are issued by trusted certificate authorities and are used to establish secure communication channels via encryption. For example, when a healthcare provider accesses an electronic health record system, the server's certificate ensures the data exchanged is encrypted and trusted.

Secure device pairing protocols, especially for IoMT devices, add another layer of confidence. These protocols, such as Bluetooth Secure Simple Pairing or NFC-based pairing, ensure that only authorized devices connect to the healthcare network. Methods like out-of-band authentication, where the pairing process requires physical proximity or manual confirmation, mitigate the risk of man-in-the-middle attacks.

By combining MFA for user authentication, digital certificates for system trust, and secure pairing for device validation, healthcare organizations create a suitable framework ensuring data exchange integrity and confidentiality.

Authorization Authorization governs what actions an authenticated user or device can perform. This ensures that even if a system is authenticated, it can only access the data or functions permitted. For instance, a monitoring system might read patient data but not alter device settings. Implementing role-based access control (RBAC) and least privilege principles ensures that sensitive functions are tightly controlled.

RBAC assigns access permissions based on a user's role within the organization, ensuring that individuals can only access the information and systems necessary to perform their job functions. For example, a nurse may access patient medical records relevant to their care but not the hospital's financial systems or other unrelated areas. This segmentation reduces the risk of unauthorized access and ensures accountability by aligning access with responsibilities.

The principle of least privilege complements RBAC by further limiting permissions to the minimum level required for a specific task or role. For instance, a medical intern may need temporary access to review patient records but not the ability to modify them. Similarly, administrative staff might be permitted to process billing data without access to clinical records. By restricting permissions to the bare minimum, healthcare organizations reduce the attack surface and mitigate the impact of potential insider threats or compromised credentials.

To implement these measures effectively, you should conduct regular audits to ensure role assignments and access permissions align with job responsibilities. Automation tools can help streamline the process, revoking unnecessary access when roles change and flagging deviations from established policies. This is critical for ensuring that employees' onboarding and offboarding (removal) are managed appropriately. Additionally, monitoring and logging mechanisms ensure access is continuously tracked and anomalous behavior can be identified quickly.

Availability to Ensure Continuous Access to Critical Information and Services Availability is critical in healthcare, where delays in accessing medical data or device malfunctions can have life-threatening consequences. Medical devices must be resilient against DoS/DDoS attacks, network outages, or hardware failures. Redundant systems, failover mechanisms, and distributed architectures help ensure that medical devices and their data remain accessible during disruptions.

Nonrepudiation for Preventing Denial of Sent or Received Communications Nonrepudiation ensures that the origin and receipt of data cannot be denied. This is crucial for maintaining accountability and trust within healthcare systems. For example, if an alert about a patient's deteriorating condition is sent, there must be a record proving that it was transmitted, received, and by whom. Digital signatures and blockchain-based logging are practical tools for achieving nonrepudiation.

These requirements, confidentiality, integrity, authentication, authorization, availability, and nonrepudiation, work together to create a more secure ecosystem. By addressing these aspects, healthcare providers and manufacturers can protect patient data, ensure compliance with regulatory standards, and maintain the trust essential for advancing medical technology.

Secure Communication Protocols for Medical Devices

Several key communication protocols are tailored to the unique needs of medical device networks. These include TLS, DTLS, IPsec, IEEE 802.11i, BLE security, ZigBee security, HL7 FHIR, and DICOM. Later, I will walk through best practices where you'll see these integrated into various solutions. Here is an overview of each of these:

- **Transport Layer Security (TLS)/Secure Sockets Layer (SSL)**

    TLS is a widely used protocol for securing Internet communications. However, it's important to note that SSL is an older, deprecated protocol that TLS has replaced. Modern systems should use TLS exclusively. It provides encryption to protect data during transit, ensuring data integrity and authentication between communicating parties. These protocols are well-suited for web-based medical applications and telemedicine platforms where sensitive health information is transmitted over the Internet. For instance, TLS can secure interactions between a patient portal and a hospital's electronic health record system, preventing unauthorized data interception.

- **Datagram Transport Layer Security (DTLS)**

  DTLS secures UDP-based communications, offering the same level of security as TLS but optimized for real-time and latency-sensitive applications. It's useful for resource-constrained medical devices such as wearable monitors that rely on efficient and low-latency communications. For example, DTLS can secure data streams from a wearable ECG monitor to a clinician's real-time dashboard.

- **Internet Protocol Security (IPsec)**

  Operating at the IP layer, IPsec ensures secure communications across potentially untrusted networks by creating encrypted tunnels. These tunnels are often used for VPNs in healthcare networks. IPsec is ideal for securing large-scale data transfers, such as remote clinics and centralized hospital servers. It safeguards data integrity, confidentiality, and authentication, making it a cornerstone for establishing secure remote connections in telemedicine.

- **IEEE 802.11i (WPA2/WPA3)**

  Securing Wi-Fi communications is essential for medical devices operating in wireless environments. WPA2 and WPA3 protocols help ensure encrypted wireless communications, preventing unauthorized access and eavesdropping on network traffic. For instance, these protocols protect data transmitted between infusion pumps or imaging systems and hospital networks. WPA3, however, is the recommended option and offers additional resilience against password-guessing attacks, making it the preferred choice for modern healthcare facilities.

- **Bluetooth Low Energy (BLE) Security**

  BLE is a cornerstone for short-range communication in wearable medical devices like glucose monitors or fitness trackers. Secure pairing methods, including passkey authentication, Just Works pairing, and BLE's encryption capabilities protect data exchanged between devices. For example, BLE security can ensure the confidentiality of real-time glucose readings sent to a patient's smartphone app.

- **ZigBee Security**

  ZigBee is a lightweight communication protocol optimized for low-power devices, making it suitable for medical sensor networks. It incorporates encryption and secure key exchange to protect communication in medical environments like remote patient monitoring systems. For instance, ZigBee can securely transmit data from a network of sensors monitoring a patient's vital signs in a hospital room.

- **HL7 FHIR (Fast Healthcare Interoperability Resources)**

    HL7 FHIR is designed to standardize the exchange of healthcare information across systems. It incorporates built-in security measures, such as OAuth2 for authentication and data encryption, to protect sensitive healthcare information. For example, FHIR enables secure sharing of patient lab results between labs, hospitals, and physicians' EHR systems, facilitating seamless and secure interoperability.

- **DICOM (Digital Imaging and Communications in Medicine)**

    DICOM is the standard protocol for medical imaging devices. It ensures the secure exchange of sensitive medical images, such as X-rays, CT scans, and MRIs. To protect against unauthorized access and tampering, DICOM includes features for encryption, authentication, and data integrity. For example, it can secure the transfer of patient imaging data from an MRI machine to a radiologist's workstation.

These protocols address the diverse requirements of medical device communications, from securing short-range connections to safeguarding large-scale data exchanges. By adopting these protocols, healthcare organizations can help ensure protection against cyber threats, maintain regulatory compliance, and foster trust in their ecosystems.

Encryption Algorithms and Key Management

Encryption algorithms and effective key management practices form the backbone of these protocols, ensuring confidentiality, integrity, and trust in the data being transmitted and stored. The following are overviews of standard encryption algorithms and management practices, including symmetric and asymmetric encryption, hash functions, key exchange protocols, PKI, and secure key storage with rotation practices.

Symmetric Encryption Symmetric encryption involves a single key shared between communicating parties for encryption and decryption. Its efficiency and speed make it ideal for resource-constrained medical devices. AES is the gold standard for symmetric encryption, offering strong security with key lengths of 128, 192, and 256 bits. It is widely used for encrypting patient data stored on devices and during wireless transmission. ChaCha20 is a lightweight alternative to AES and is particularly suitable for low-power medical devices, such as wearable monitors, due to its high performance and resistance to side-channel attacks. In the context of IoMT and symmetric encryption, side-channel attacks are cyberattacks that exploit indirect information leaked by a cryptographic system rather than break the encryption algorithm itself. To infer secret keys, these attacks analyze physical or behavioral characteristics such as power consumption, electromagnetic emissions, or timing variations during encryption operations. Since medical devices are often resource-constrained and operate in real-time environments, they can be particularly vulnerable to such attacks. ChaCha20, as mentioned, is designed to resist side-channel attacks, making it a strong choice for securing low-power medical devices.

Asymmetric Encryption Asymmetric encryption uses a pair of keys—public and private—for secure communication. While computationally intensive, it's essential for establishing secure connections. RSA (Rivest-Shamir-Adleman) secures initial handshakes and key exchanges between devices and central servers in medical networks. Its long-standing reliability makes it a trusted choice.

Elliptic Curve Cryptography (ECC), on the other hand, provides equivalent security to RSA with much smaller key sizes, reducing computational overhead. This makes it ideal for implantable devices and IoMT networks with limited processing capabilities.

Hash Functions Hash functions ensure data integrity by generating a fixed-length hash value from input data. They are crucial for verifying that transmitted data has not been tampered with. SHA-256 is the widely used cryptographic hash function, providing strong collision resistance. It is suitable for securing electronic health records and digital signatures in medical devices. SHA-3 is the next generation of secure hashing, designed to offer enhanced protection against emerging cryptographic vulnerabilities.

Key Exchange Protocols Securely exchanging encryption keys is critical for initiating secure communication channels between devices. Diffie-Hellman (DH) is a foundational protocol for secure key exchange over public networks, often used with symmetric encryption for session keys.

ECDH, discussed before, is an optimized version of DH leveraging ECC, and ECDH is highly efficient for resource-constrained medical devices, ensuring secure key establishment without excessive computational demands.

Public Key Infrastructure (PKI) PKI provides the framework for managing digital certificates and public-private key pairs, enabling trust in secure communication. A CA is a trusted third party that issues digital certificates to medical devices, verifies their authenticity, and secures communications. PKI ensures that only authorized devices can join a network, reducing the risk of unauthorized access or rogue devices.

Secure Key Storage and Rotation Practices Proper management of encryption keys is critical for maintaining long-term security. Secure key storage is also essential. Medical devices should use dedicated hardware security modules (HSMs) or Trusted Platform Modules (TPMs) to securely store encryption keys and prevent unauthorized extraction. Key rotation is also essential, as regularly rotating encryption keys mitigates the risk of key compromise. Automated systems for key rotation ensure that devices remain secure without manual intervention.

The following are a few practical applications for using encryption algorithms and key management in medical devices:

- **Secure Data Transmission:** AES encrypts data transmitted between wearable devices and healthcare providers, ensuring patient privacy during wireless communication.
- **Authentication and Access Control:** RSA or ECC provides secure authentication, ensuring only authorized personnel can access critical device functions.
- **Data Integrity Verification:** SHA-256 generates hash values for transmitted medical data, confirming that it remains unaltered during transmission.

Effective encryption and key management are the foundations of secure communication protocols in medical devices. Symmetric and asymmetric encryption, hash functions, and secure key management practices protect patient data against unauthorized access and tampering. As healthcare systems evolve, adopting advanced cryptographic techniques like ECC and integrating PKI frameworks will further enhance the security and reliability of medical devices.

Authentication Mechanisms

In secure communication, authentication helps ensure that only authorized parties can access sensitive medical data or interact with devices. For medical devices, strong authentication mechanisms are critical for protecting patient privacy, maintaining device integrity, and ensuring compliance with regulations. I'll review some key authentication mechanisms to secure communication in this space.

Multifactor Authentication

MFA has been discussed already, and we know it strengthens security by requiring users to present two or more verification factors. As of 2025, MFA has become a standard requirement for healthcare organizations to comply with HIPAA and other regulatory standards. Healthcare providers should implement MFA for all user types, including care providers, administrative staff, and patients accessing EHRs. It can be implemented for healthcare professionals accessing device management systems or patients interacting with wearable health monitors. For example, a physician logging into a patient monitoring system may need to use both a password and a mobile app-generated code. Benefits include mitigating the risk of unauthorized access and enhancing protection against phishing and credential theft.

Biometric Authentication

Biometric authentication relies on unique physical or behavioral traits such as fingerprints, facial recognition, or voice patterns to verify identity. Biometric sensors can be embedded into insulin pumps or smart infusion systems. For instance, fingerprint scanners could ensure that only authorized medical staff can adjust dosage settings.

The benefits of biometric authentication include the following:

- Convenient for users as they don't require remembering passwords or carrying physical tokens
- Provides high levels of security since biometric traits are difficult to replicate

Digital Certificates

Digital certificates use PKI to authenticate devices and encrypt communications. A device presents its certificate to verify its identity to another device or server. Digital certificates are widely used for securing communication between medical devices and cloud servers. For example, an ECG monitor transmitting patient data to a hospital system can use a certificate to authenticate and encrypt the data transfer.

The benefits of digital certificates include the following:

- Provides a strong mechanism for device-to-device and device-to-server authentication
- Ensures data confidentiality and integrity during transmission

Consider using short-lived certificates to reduce the risk of compromise. Also, automated certificate management systems should be employed to handle renewals and revocations.

OAuth 2.0 and OpenID Connect for Authorization

OAuth 2.0 is an open standard for access delegation, allowing secure API access without sharing credentials. OpenID Connect extends OAuth 2.0 for authentication, enabling single sign-on (SSO) capabilities. These protocols are beneficial in multi-application ecosystems. For example, a patient may use a wearable glucose monitor connected to an app that integrates with a hospital's electronic health record system. OAuth 2.0 can ensure secure authorization for such cross-platform interactions.

The benefits of these include the following:

- Simplifies user authentication across multiple systems
- Reduces the need to store and manage passwords in individual applications

RADIUS and TACACS+ for Network Device Authentication

Remote Authentication Dial-In User Service (RADIUS) and Terminal Access Controller Access-Control System Plus (TACACS+) are protocols that authenticate users accessing network resources. In a hospital environment, RADIUS or TACACS+ can authenticate devices like ventilators, infusion pumps, or diagnostic tools connecting to the hospital's secure wireless network.

The benefits include the following:

- Centralized authentication management simplifies device and user administration.
- Provides logging and tracking access attempts, aiding in compliance and audits.

RADIUS is ideal for environments requiring authentication, authorization, and accounting (AAA) processes. Meanwhile, TACACS+ offers granular control over command authorization, making it suitable for managing administrative access to network devices.

Authentication mechanisms are vital for ensuring the secure operation of medical devices, protecting sensitive patient data, and maintaining trust in technology. While each method has unique strengths, combining them into layered security frameworks can address many threats. For instance, integrating biometric authentication with OAuth 2.0 and PKI certificates can ensure user and device authentication in complex IoMT ecosystems.

Secure Device Pairing and Onboarding

Secure communication begins with strong pairing and onboarding protocols. These protocols ensure that devices are authenticated, trusted, and protected from unauthorized access, establishing a secure foundation for their operation. This is especially critical in healthcare environments, where compromised device communication could jeopardize patient safety, data privacy, and regulatory compliance. I'll explore modern methods that make secure device pairing and onboarding practical and effective.

Out-of-Band Authentication Methods

Out-of-band (OOB) authentication enhances security using a secondary, independent channel to verify the pairing process. This might involve sending a code to a smartphone or using a physical token in medical devices. For example, a patient onboarding a wearable glucose monitor may receive a verification code via email or SMS, which must be entered during device pairing. This method reduces the risk of attacks such as man-in-the-middle, as the secondary channel is typically independent of the primary communication pathway.

QR Code-Based Pairing

QR codes have become a popular method for initiating secure communication between devices. They allow quick and easy sharing of cryptographic keys or device-specific credentials. The medical device generates a QR code containing secure pairing data, which the user scans with a companion app on a trusted device.

The benefits of QR code-based pairing include the following:

- Simplifies the setup process for nontechnical users
- Reduces the likelihood of pairing errors due to manual input
- Helps mitigate risks of eavesdropping by ensuring encrypted information is exchanged visually rather than wirelessly

A use case would be home healthcare devices like blood pressure monitors or smart inhalers for seamless patient setup.

Near Field Communication for Secure Setup

In the early chapters, I discussed near field communication (NFC) as a short-range communication technology that uses secure, proximity-based pairings for medical devices. NFC-enabled devices initiate communication when brought within a few centimeters of each other, automatically exchanging encryption keys or device credentials. Some advantages include the following:

- Extremely low risk of interception due to the short range.
- Fast and user-friendly pairing process, especially for elderly or nontechnical users.
- Ideal for environments where secure pairing needs to be quick and foolproof.
- NFC is more intuitive and user-friendly, especially for elderly users.
- It's beneficial for quick, secure interactions in clinical settings.

A use case would be onboarding implantable devices like insulin pumps or temporary medical patches in clinical settings.

Bluetooth Low Energy Secure Connections

Given that I discussed Bluetooth Low Energy (BLE) in detail, I'll reiterate the secure pairing features, which include the following:

- **Elliptic Curve Diffie-Hellman (ECDH):** Ensures cryptographic key exchange without exposing sensitive information
- **Passkey Entry or Just Works Modes:** Adds user-based verification or streamlines the pairing process depending on the security requirements
- **Bonding and Key Storage:** Ensures paired devices recognize each other in future sessions, preventing unauthorized reconnection

These are well-suited for wearable devices like ECG monitors or fitness trackers that rely on long-term connectivity. They provide layered security, protecting against replay attacks and eavesdropping.

The Importance of Secure Pairing and Onboarding

Secure pairing and onboarding processes establish the foundation for protecting sensitive medical data and ensuring the reliability of device communications. One key reason secure pairing matters is confidentiality. By implementing strong encryption protocols during setup, secure pairing prevents the unauthorized interception of sensitive patient information, such as vital signs or medication delivery schedules. This protection is essential to maintaining patient privacy and preventing data breaches.

Secure onboarding promotes data integrity and confidentiality. It safeguards devices against tampering during the initial communication setup, ensuring that the information exchanged between the device and the network remains authentic and unaltered. This is especially important in healthcare, where compromised data could lead to incorrect diagnoses or treatments.

Building trust is another vital aspect of secure pairing and onboarding. Patients and healthcare providers depend on medical devices to function correctly and safely. A seamless and secure setup process reassures users that their devices are trustworthy and capable of performing as intended without risk of interference or compromise.

Finally, secure pairing supports compliance with regulatory frameworks like HIPAA and GDPR. These regulations require strict security measures to protect sensitive health data. By demonstrating secure onboarding practices, organizations can meet compliance standards, avoid penalties, and reinforce their commitment to safeguarding patient information.

Regulatory Compliance and Standards

In today's healthcare landscape, ensuring the secure communication of medical devices is a technical and regulatory requirement. Medical devices operate in sensitive environments, handling critical patient data and performing life-saving tasks. Therefore, adhering to established compliance frameworks and standards is essential for protecting patient safety, ensuring data security, and maintaining trust in healthcare technology. I'll walk through some of the most popular standards. I'll get more into the weeds later in Chapter 20.

FDA Guidance on Cybersecurity for Medical Devices

The U.S. Food and Drug Administration (FDA) has outlined comprehensive guidance on cybersecurity for medical devices, emphasizing the importance of secure communication protocols. This includes pre-market expectations, where manufacturers must demonstrate that their devices incorporate security features such as encryption, secure authentication, and firmware update mechanisms. There are also post-market responsibilities, and the mandate includes ongoing monitoring, vulnerability assessments, and timely device patching. Secure communication is necessary to mitigate remote monitoring and data exchange risks.

HIPAA Security Rule Requirements

The Health Insurance Portability and Accountability Act (HIPAA) 1996 governs aspects such as handling Protected Health Information or PHI. The HIPAA Security Rule sets specific standards for securing electronic PHI or ePHI, which directly applies to medical device communication:

- **Confidentiality:** Encryption of transmitted data to protect PHI from unauthorized access
- **Integrity:** Mechanisms to ensure that data has not been altered in transit
- **Availability:** Measures to ensure critical medical information is accessible when needed

EU Medical Device Regulation (MDR)

The European Union's Medical Device Regulation (MDR) enforces these strict cybersecurity requirements for medical devices sold within the EU:

- **Safety and performance:** Devices must demonstrate that they are secure against known cyber threats and vulnerabilities.
- **Risk management:** Manufacturers must integrate cybersecurity into their risk management processes throughout the device lifecycle.
- **Transparency:** Clear labeling and documentation of cybersecurity features are required.

For example, a cloud-connected blood glucose monitor must ensure compliance with MDR by encrypting communication with cloud services and providing documentation on its security protocols.

ISO/IEC 27001 Information Security Management

ISO/IEC 27001 is an internationally recognized standard for information security management. It provides a structured approach to securing communication in medical devices by:

- **Implementing security controls:** Ensuring encryption, secure authentication, and access controls are in place for device communication.
- **Risk assessment:** Identifying and mitigating device connectivity and data transmission risks.
- **Auditable framework:** Regular audits to ensure compliance and improve security practices.

An example is a hospital's IoMT network, which includes infusion pumps and patient monitoring devices. The network can adhere to ISO/IEC 27001 with secure communication channels.

IEC 62304 Medical Device Software Life Cycle Processes

IEC 62304 focuses on the development and maintenance of medical device software, including its communication protocols, which are:

- **Software Security by Design:** Incorporating secure communication features during the development phase
- **Risk analysis:** Evaluating and mitigating risks specific to software vulnerabilities and communication pathways
- **Maintenance:** Ensuring that software updates address emerging cybersecurity threats

For example, a remote diagnostic imaging device must adhere to IEC 62304 by implementing secure software updates that address vulnerabilities in its data transmission protocols.

Key Points Regarding Regulatory Compliance

There are several key points to remember regarding regulatory compliance. Simply put, compliance drives security. Adhering to regulations like FDA guidance, HIPAA, and EU MDR ensures communication security in medical devices. International standards enhance overall trust. Implementing frameworks like ISO/IEC 27001 and IEC 62304 builds confidence in device reliability and security.

Secure communication is not a one-time effort; it requires continuous risk management, monitoring, and updates. In addition, manufacturers targeting multiple markets must integrate diverse regulatory requirements into their development and operational processes. By aligning with these standards and regulations, manufacturers and healthcare providers can ensure secure, reliable communication for medical devices, ultimately protecting patient safety and maintaining compliance.

Challenges in Implementing Secure Communication Protocols

Implementing secure communication protocols for medical devices is essential; however, this task is difficult, given the unique constraints and complexities of healthcare environments. Here are the six top challenges, in order of constraint level, based on my interviews and research in healthcare:

1. **Resource constraints of medical devices:** Medical devices often operate under strict resource limitations, including limited power, processing capability, and memory. Secure communication protocols, such as encryption and

authentication, require computational resources, which can drain battery life or slow down device performance. For instance, an implantable cardiac monitor may struggle to implement advanced encryption algorithms without compromising its primary real-time monitoring function. This necessitates lightweight cryptographic solutions specifically designed for resource-constrained environments.

2. **Balancing security with usability and functionality:** While security measures are critical, they should not impede the usability or functionality of medical devices. Overly complex protocols can create barriers for healthcare providers, delaying critical treatments or interventions. For example, requiring frequent re-authentication for a ventilator during an emergency can introduce unacceptable delays. Designing protocols that ensure security without disrupting clinical workflows is a delicate balancing act.

3. **Interoperability between devices and systems:** Healthcare ecosystems are becoming increasingly interconnected, comprising devices from various manufacturers that must communicate seamlessly. Interoperability challenges arise when proprietary protocols conflict with open standards, creating vulnerabilities in data exchange. Ensuring secure communication across diverse devices, such as infusion pumps, patient monitors, and electronic health record systems, requires adopting universally compatible yet robust security standards.

4. **Legacy device integration and security upgrades:** Many healthcare organizations still rely on legacy medical devices not designed with modern security requirements. Retrofitting these devices with secure communication protocols is often infeasible due to hardware limitations or a lack of manufacturer support. These legacy systems create security gaps, exposing the entire network to potential breaches. In many cases, they are prohibitively expensive to replace, requiring them to remain in service. Organizations must prioritize segmenting these devices and incorporating compensatory controls to minimize risk.

5. **Rapid evolution of threats and attack vectors:** Cyber threats targeting medical devices are evolving, from ransomware attacks on hospital networks to exploitation of communication vulnerabilities in IoT-enabled devices. Secure protocols must be adaptable to counter emerging threats while ensuring continuous protection. However, this requires frequent updates and patch management, which can be logistically challenging for medical devices deployed in critical care settings.

6. **Complexity of healthcare IT environments:** Integrating medical devices into complex IT ecosystems adds another layer of difficulty. Medical devices often share networks with other critical systems, such as EHR platforms and imaging devices, which can introduce additional attack surfaces. Ensuring secure communication within this multifaceted environment requires network segmentation, traffic monitoring, and threat detection capabilities, all adding to implementation complexity.

Implementing secure communication protocols for medical devices involves navigating intricate challenges. Resource constraints, usability demands, interoperability issues, legacy devices, evolving threats, and the complexity of healthcare IT environments require careful consideration. The challenge of securing communication in medical devices is not just technical but also involves human factors, such as user training and awareness. Overcoming these hurdles requires a multidisciplinary approach combining innovative technologies, adherence to regulatory standards, and collaboration between manufacturers, healthcare providers, and cybersecurity experts.

Best Practices for Secure Medical Device Communication

From safeguarding patient data to maintaining device functionality, a comprehensive approach to security is essential. Here are some of the key best practices for securing medical device communication, but are also based on healthcare leadership feedback:

- **Implement defense-in-depth strategies:** A multilayered security approach protects against various threats. Defense-in-depth strategies include employing multiple layers of security measures, such as firewalls, intrusion detection systems, and endpoint protection, working together to ensure redundancy and mitigate single points of failure. Consider the principles of Zero Trust, which I discuss more in Chapter 16.

- **Use strong, standardized encryption protocols:** Encrypting data during transmission is critical to maintaining confidentiality and integrity. Protocols like TLS 1.3 and AES-256 ensure that sensitive data, including patient information and device commands, is protected against eavesdropping and unauthorized modifications. Always prioritize using standardized and widely tested encryption protocols over proprietary solutions.

- **Update and patch communication software regularly:** Like any other connected technology, medical devices are susceptible to vulnerabilities that attackers can exploit. Regularly updating and patching device firmware and software ensures that known vulnerabilities are addressed promptly, reducing the risk of exploitation. This requires close collaboration between device manufacturers, healthcare organizations, and regulatory bodies.

- **Conduct thorough security and vulnerability assessments:** Comprehensive security testing, including penetration testing and vulnerability scanning, should be performed throughout a device's lifecycle. These assessments help identify communication protocol and system configuration weaknesses, allowing organizations to address them before attackers exploit them.

- **Implement secure boot and code signing for device integrity:** Secure boot mechanisms ensure that only trusted software is loaded during a device's startup, protecting against malware and unauthorized code execution. Code signing further enhances security by verifying the authenticity of software updates and ensuring they have not been tampered with.

- **Use network segmentation to isolate medical devices:** Segmenting networks helps contain potential breaches and limits attackers' lateral movement. Medical devices should be placed on isolated network segments with restricted access to critical healthcare systems. This reduces their exposure to external threats while enabling secure communication within the isolated environment.
- **Implement robust logging and monitoring systems:** Comprehensive logging and real-time monitoring are essential for detecting and responding to potential security incidents. Logs should include details of device communication, access attempts, and system changes, enabling forensic investigations and proactive threat detection.
- **Develop and maintain incident response plans:** Preparedness is key to mitigating the impact of security breaches. An incident response plan should outline clear steps for identifying, containing, and recovering from security incidents involving medical devices. Regular drills and updates ensure the plan remains effective against evolving threats.
- **Provide cybersecurity training for healthcare staff:** Human error remains a significant security risk. Training healthcare staff on best practices for securing medical devices, recognizing phishing attempts, and understanding the implications of poor cybersecurity hygiene is crucial. Empowered and informed staff are the first line of defense in protecting device communication and the overall healthcare infrastructure.

Following these best practices can enhance the security of medical device communication. This ensures compliance with laws and regulations like HIPAA and GDPR, protects patient safety, and maintains trust.

Emerging Technologies and Future Trends

Several emerging technologies and trends are shaping the future of secure medical device communication. These advancements address current and future challenges in protecting sensitive health data, ensuring device functionality, and enabling seamless communication within healthcare systems. Key technologies and trends include 5G networks, quantum-resistant cryptography, blockchain, AI, edge computing, and post-quantum cryptography. I'll look at each:

5G Networks and Their Impact on Medical Device Communication The rollout of 5G networks has already improved medical device communication. With ultra-low latency, higher bandwidth, and improved reliability, 5G enables real-time data transmission between medical devices, healthcare providers, and cloud systems. This enhanced connectivity will benefit from applications such as remote surgeries, continuous patient monitoring, and telemedicine.

However, with increased connectivity comes an expanded attack surface, making it essential to implement security protocols to protect health data and ensure device functionality. Beyond 5G (with 6G) aims to improve bandwidth and reliability and add additional security controls.

Quantum-Resistant Cryptography for Long-Term Data Protection As quantum computing advances, traditional encryption methods risk becoming obsolete. Quantum-resistant cryptography is being developed to future-proof medical device communication by creating encryption algorithms resistant to quantum attacks. These algorithms will play a critical role in ensuring the confidentiality and integrity of health data, safeguarding it from computational breakthroughs that could compromise current encryption techniques.

Blockchain for Secure Data Exchange and Device Management Blockchain technology offers a decentralized and tamper-proof framework for managing medical device communication and data exchange. Blockchain can automate device authentication, secure data sharing, and compliance verification processes by utilizing smart contracts. For example, blockchain can enforce strict access controls, allowing only authorized healthcare providers to access patient data while maintaining an immutable record of interactions. This approach enhances both security and accountability within medical systems.

AI and Machine Learning for Anomaly Detection AI and ML are becoming essential tools for detecting and mitigating threats in medical device communication. AI systems can process vast amounts of data to identify anomalies, such as unauthorized access attempts or irregular data flows. These technologies continuously learn and adapt to new threats, enabling a proactive approach to securing medical device ecosystems. With AI-powered anomaly detection, healthcare organizations can respond to threats more quickly and effectively.

Edge Computing for Localized and Secure Data Processing Edge computing brings data processing closer to the end device, reducing latency and minimizing the need to transmit sensitive data to centralized servers. By processing data locally, devices such as wearables can provide real-time insights without exposing patient information to potential threats during transmission. This localized approach enhances security and privacy and ensures compliance with regulations like HIPAA and GDPR, which mandate strict control over sensitive information.

Post-Quantum Cryptography for Future-Proof Security Post-quantum cryptography focuses on developing encryption methods that remain secure even against future quantum computing threats. Medical devices, which often have long lifecycles, must be equipped with cryptographic techniques capable of withstanding advancements in quantum computing. By adopting post-quantum encryption, healthcare organizations can ensure long-term security for device communication.

In summary, the future of secure medical device communication lies at the intersection of these emerging technologies. Adopting 5G and beyond networks, quantum-resistant cryptography, blockchain, AI, edge computing, and post-quantum cryptography will enable healthcare organizations to build resilient systems capable of protecting sensitive data, maintaining device functionality, and preserving trust in medical technologies.

Secure Communication Strategies

In healthcare, the security of medical device communication can be a matter of life and death. The increasing reliance on connected devices and systems makes confidentiality, integrity, and availability of data and device functions critical. Here are notes from four unique case studies that specifically highlight the application of secure communication strategies in healthcare environments.

- **Securing Implantable Cardiac Devices Against Wireless Attacks**

    Wireless-enabled implantable cardiac devices, such as pacemakers and defibrillators, have evolved patient care by allowing remote monitoring and programming. However, these devices are vulnerable to wireless attacks, including unauthorized control or data interception. A notable case involved the discovery of vulnerabilities in pacemakers that allowed attackers to deliver harmful commands or deplete device batteries.

    To address this, researchers implemented a secure communication protocol using strong encryption (in this case, AES-256) and mutual authentication techniques. The protocol ensured that only authorized devices could communicate with the cardiac implants, preventing unauthorized access. Additionally, device firmware was updated to include intrusion detection mechanisms that alert healthcare providers to suspicious activity.

- **Implementing End-to-End Encryption in Telemedicine Platforms**

    Telemedicine has seen exponential growth but comes with unique security challenges. A primary telemedicine provider faced concerns over the privacy of patient consultations and data transmission. Without robust security, sessions were vulnerable to eavesdropping, and patient health records were at risk of being intercepted.

    The provider implemented end-to-end encryption (E2EE) across its platform, ensuring only authorized participants could access the communication. Secure key exchange protocols, such as Diffie-Hellman, were utilized to protect against man-in-the-middle attacks. Furthermore, multifactor authentication was introduced to verify users' identities before they could access sessions or records.

- **Securing Large-Scale Hospital Networks with Diverse Medical Devices**

    Integrating various connected medical devices, including infusion pumps, imaging systems, and patient monitors, in a large hospital created a sprawling network vulnerable to cyberattacks. A penetration test revealed weaknesses in communication protocols, such as unencrypted transmissions and weak authentication mechanisms.

To secure the network, the hospital deployed a unified communication security framework. This included TLS for encrypted data transmission, role-based access controls to limit device access, and digital certificates for device authentication. Network segmentation was also implemented to isolate critical medical devices from less secure systems, minimizing the risk of lateral movement during a breach. This comprehensive approach mitigated risks and ensured compliance with security standards.

- **Addressing Vulnerabilities in Insulin Pump Communications**

    Insulin pumps have been targeted by attackers who exploit wireless communication channels to alter dosages. In one high-profile case, a vulnerability allowed attackers to hijack the communication between the pump and its controller. A solution involved re-engineering the communication protocol to include strong encryption and frequent key rotation. Authentication mechanisms were enhanced using cryptographic tokens that ensured only the authorized user and healthcare provider could control the pump. Additionally, real-time monitoring tools were implemented to detect and alert users of any anomalies in communication. This multilayered approach effectively secured the devices while maintaining ease of use for their patients.

These case studies illustrate the need for secure communication in medical devices. By employing advanced security measures, such as encryption, authentication, and network segmentation, healthcare organizations protect patient data, ensure device functionality, and maintain regulatory compliance. Each example underscores the importance of a proactive and layered approach to securing the interconnected systems that underpin modern healthcare.

Ethical Considerations

The healthcare industry should adopt many ethical considerations to ensure that secure medical device communication protects patient data and device functionality and upholds the values of fairness, privacy, and accessibility. In this section, I'll end the chapter with the four most popular and debated ethical concerns. These were highlighted in my research and touched on protecting sensitive patient data, ensuring devices remain accessible, addressing the privacy implications of data collection, being responsible for the disclosure of vulnerabilities, and ensuring that security solutions are scalable and affordable.

- **Balancing Security Measures with Patient Care and Device Accessibility**

    Healthcare systems have a dual responsibility: protecting sensitive patient data while ensuring devices and systems remain accessible in critical situations. Security features, such as multifactor authentication and strict access controls, are essential to prevent unauthorized access. However, these measures can sometimes create barriers, delaying access to life-saving data or devices during emergencies.

For example, imagine an ER physician needing immediate access to a ventilator's controls, but a lengthy authentication process causes delays. Such scenarios highlight the need to design security protocols that integrate seamlessly into medical workflows. Security should never compromise patient outcomes. Instead, healthcare organizations must adopt flexible, role-based access systems that balance security with operational efficiency. In this way, we safeguard patient data while empowering providers to deliver timely care.

- **Privacy Implications of Secure Data Collection and Transmission**

Modern medical devices collect and transmit health metrics, diagnoses, and treatment plans. Encryption and secure communication protocols protect this data, but ethical concerns arise regarding its collection, use, and storage. Patients have a fundamental right to know how their data is being used.

Transparent policies that require informed consent before data collection are critical to maintaining trust. Patients must be assured that their data will not be misused or shared without permission. Additionally, even anonymized data carries risks, as advanced re-identification techniques can sometimes reveal personal information. Healthcare organizations must adopt stringent policies for handling de-identified data and periodically review privacy safeguards to stay ahead of evolving threats.

Another ethical aspect is the long-term storage of patient data. Data retention policies should balance the need for historical records with minimizing exposure risks. Organizations must also consider the ethical challenges associated with secondary data use, such as research applications, and ensure that data-sharing agreements protect individual privacy.

- **Ethical Hacking and Responsible Disclosure of Vulnerabilities**

Identifying and fixing security vulnerabilities in medical devices is critical to protecting patient safety. Ethical hacking, also known as penetration testing, plays a vital role in this process. Ethical hackers simulate attacks to uncover weaknesses, helping manufacturers address vulnerabilities before malicious actors exploit them. However, ethical hacking must follow responsible disclosure practices. Ethical hackers should report vulnerabilities to device manufacturers and regulatory bodies before publicizing findings.

This approach allows time for patches and updates, protecting devices and patients from unnecessary risks. Furthermore, healthcare organizations must foster collaboration with cybersecurity researchers, create safe channels for vulnerability reporting, and incentivize proactive security testing.

An essential ethical question arises when vulnerabilities are identified in legacy systems still in use. In such cases, healthcare providers must weigh the risks of disclosure against the costs of system replacements or upgrades, ensuring patient safety remains the priority.

- **Equitable Access to Secure Medical Technologies**

    Security measures should not widen the gap between different patient populations. Due to cost constraints, underserved or economically disadvantaged patients often rely on older, less secure medical technologies. As we push for better security standards, we must ensure that protections are scalable and affordable.

    Manufacturers and policymakers must collaborate to standardize security practices across all devices, from high-end hospital equipment to affordable consumer health devices. Equitable access requires creative solutions, such as subsidized upgrades for vulnerable populations and open-source security tools that lower costs. Security must be treated as a fundamental component of healthcare, not a privilege limited to well-funded institutions.

In summary, ethical considerations in healthcare security encompass more than just protecting data; they also involve ensuring accessibility, privacy, and fairness. Security protocols must align with medical workflows to avoid hindering patient care. Transparent data practices and informed consent protect privacy, while ethical hacking and responsible disclosure strengthen device security. Finally, equitable access to secure technologies ensures that all patients, regardless of economic background, benefit from advancements in healthcare security.

Key Takeaways from Secure Communication Protocols for Medical Devices

Secure communication protocols are essential for ensuring medical devices' safety, reliability, and trustworthiness in modern healthcare. By addressing security challenges and implementing best practices, healthcare organizations can protect patient data, maintain compliance with regulatory requirements, and enhance overall system resilience. Secure communication is the foundation for safeguarding sensitive information, preventing unauthorized access, and ensuring the proper functionality of critical devices such as insulin pumps, pacemakers, and telemedicine platforms.

A comprehensive security framework must incorporate confidentiality, integrity, authentication, authorization, availability, and nonrepudiation to mitigate risks like data breaches, service disruptions, and denial-of-service attacks. Strong encryption protocols such as TLS, DTLS, WPA3, and ZigBee are crucial in securing data transmission between devices and healthcare systems. However, implementation challenges, including resource constraints, interoperability issues, and legacy device integration, require adaptive solutions that balance security with usability to avoid disruptions in patient care.

Best practices for secure communication include a defense-in-depth approach, strong encryption, vulnerability assessments, and continuous monitoring. Techniques such as secure device pairing, network segmentation, and multifactor authentication further strengthen the resilience of medical device ecosystems. Emerging technologies like 5G, blockchain, quantum-resistant cryptography, and AI-driven anomaly detection are shaping the future of secure medical communications, offering proactive defenses against evolving cyber threats.

Regulatory compliance with frameworks such as HIPAA, GDPR, FDA guidelines, and ISO standards ensures a standardized approach to medical device security. Real-world case studies highlight the successful implementation of secure protocols to protect patient health and hospital networks. Ethical considerations also play a role, because balancing security with usability, safeguarding patient privacy, and responsibly addressing vulnerabilities are critical for maintaining trust in healthcare technology.

Looking ahead, ongoing research into advanced security models, post-quantum cryptography, and hybrid security approaches will drive continued innovation. Collaboration among manufacturers, healthcare providers, and policymakers is essential to fostering a secure, scalable, and equitable healthcare ecosystem that can meet the growing demands of modern patient care.

CHAPTER 16

Best Practices for IoMT Device Security

Throughout this book, mitigation strategies were highlighted from the perspective of a particular technology. This chapter consolidates all those best practices but in more detail. Adhering to best practices like those mentioned in this chapter will help you and your organization comply with industry regulations such as HIPAA, GDPR, and FDA guidelines and, in many cases, ensure that devices remain secure throughout their lifecycle.

Proactively implementing security measures builds trust among patients, providers, and stakeholders while enabling healthcare organizations to fully leverage the benefits of IoMT technology without compromising security or privacy. Entire books could be written on best practices, and in some cases, they have been. This chapter will focus on more prominent ones that correlate with healthcare environments.

I'll start with the ripple security logic for healthcare infrastructure. This logic envisions a pond where a single drop of water creates ripples that expand outward, symbolizing the interconnected layers of healthcare infrastructure. Security controls must be strategically implemented to counter specific threats at each layer, starting from the endpoint, rippling out to the perimeter, and extending into the cloud.

The core, or endpoint security, focuses on securing medical devices, workstations, and mobile devices. Key practices include endpoint detection and response (EDR) for real-time monitoring, antivirus and anti-malware solutions, secure boot processes, device encryption, application whitelisting, and regular patch management. Equally important are role-based access controls and user awareness training to minimize exposure and mitigate social engineering risks.

The first ripple, network security, connects these endpoints and demands robust defenses. Network segmentation isolates IoMT devices and critical systems to limit lateral movement. IDPS, firewalls, and Zero Trust network architecture ensure that only authenticated users and devices gain access. Data loss prevention (DLP) and network access control (NAC) further protect sensitive data and enforce strict device authentication policies. DLP is critically important because it helps protect sensitive patient data, such as electronic health records (EHRs) and protected health information (PHI), from unauthorized access, leakage, or theft. IoMT devices—like connected monitors, insulin pumps, and imaging systems—constantly collect and transmit data, often over wireless networks, increasing the risk of data breaches.

DLP solutions monitor, detect, and block the movement of sensitive data across devices and networks, ensuring compliance with regulations like HIPAA. They help healthcare organizations prevent accidental or malicious data leaks, safeguard patient privacy, and maintain trust in digital healthcare systems.

The second ripple, perimeter security, forms the boundary between the healthcare network and external environments. Web application firewalls (WAFs) defend against web-based attacks, while distributed denial-of-service protection prevents service disruptions. Email security gateways block phishing and malware attempts, and physical security measures such as biometric controls safeguard the facility. Deception technologies, like honeypots, detect and redirect attackers.

The outer ripple encompasses cloud security, addressing the shared responsibility model for data stored and processed in the cloud. Controls include cloud access security brokers (CASBs) for visibility and policy enforcement, encryption for data at rest and in transit, and identity and access management (IAM) systems. MFA ensures secure access, while configuration and cloud security posture management (CSPM) automate risk detection. Backup and disaster recovery strategies maintain data availability, and logging and monitoring tools enhance event detection.

Integration across all layers forms a cohesive defense. Cross-layer incident response planning, compliance monitoring for regulations like HIPAA and GDPR, and centralized log analysis via SIEM systems ensure unified protection. Threat hunting and data flow mapping proactively identify vulnerabilities and secure data movement between layers.

This holistic approach emphasizes that each security layer must function harmoniously and be tailored to healthcare's unique requirements. Organizations can strengthen their defenses against evolving threats by adopting ripple security logic and safeguarding sensitive healthcare data and critical systems.

Endpoint Security Best Practices

Endpoint security best practices for healthcare IoMT devices are the foundation of a secure healthcare infrastructure, as they directly protect the core elements—medical devices, servers, workstations, and mobile endpoints—where patient data is accessed, processed, and transmitted. To secure these critical endpoints, healthcare organizations should implement EDR solutions that provide real-time monitoring, threat detection, and automated response to potential security incidents. Antivirus and anti-malware software must be deployed and regularly updated to guard against known threats and emerging malware targeting IoMT devices. Secure boot processes are essential to ensure that devices start with verified and trusted software, preventing tampering at the firmware level. Device encryption, both at rest and in transit, protects sensitive data stored on endpoints from unauthorized access in the event of theft or loss. In addition, application whitelisting allows only approved software to run on devices, reducing the risk of malware or unauthorized applications compromising system integrity.

Regular patch management is another critical best practice, ensuring all endpoint devices receive timely updates to address known vulnerabilities that cyber attackers often exploit. Role-based access controls (RBACs) should be enforced to limit user access based on job responsibilities, minimizing the attack surface and reducing the potential impact of compromised accounts. User awareness training is crucial in educating healthcare staff and device users about security best practices, phishing threats, and social engineering tactics that could compromise endpoints complementing these technical measures. By fostering a culture of cybersecurity awareness and applying these layered security controls, healthcare organizations can significantly strengthen their endpoint defenses and protect sensitive data at its source in an increasingly interconnected IoMT ecosystem.

Network Security Best Practices

Network security best practices are essential in healthcare environments to protect the communication pathways connecting IoMT devices, clinical systems, and sensitive patient data. The first line of defense is network segmentation, which isolates IoMT devices, critical systems, and sensitive data repositories into separate zones or VLANs. This limits lateral movement in the event of a breach, containing potential threats and reducing their impact. Complementing segmentation, firewalls, and intrusion detection and prevention systems (IDPSs) continuously monitor network traffic for suspicious activity and block unauthorized access. A zero-trust network architecture (ZTNA) further enhances security by requiring strict identity verification for every device and user attempting to access the network, operating under the principle of "never trust, always verify."

In addition to access controls, DLP tools such as EHRs and PHI are key in monitoring and controlling the flow of sensitive patient data. DLP policies ensure that sensitive information is not transmitted insecurely or leaked outside of the organization, supporting compliance with healthcare regulations like HIPAA. NAC solutions enforce strict authentication and posture assessment policies, allowing only authorized and compliant devices to connect to the healthcare network. This minimizes the risk of unauthorized devices introducing vulnerabilities or malware.

Continuous network monitoring and traffic analysis help detect anomalies and potential breaches in real time. Secure communication protocols, such as HTTPS and VPNs with strong encryption, should protect data in transit across wired and wireless networks. Wireless security should be bolstered with WPA3 encryption and segmented guest networks to separate public access from internal healthcare systems. Regular vulnerability assessments and penetration testing are critical to identifying and addressing weaknesses in the network before they can be exploited.

By implementing these comprehensive network security practices, healthcare organizations can create defenses that protect interconnected IoMT environments from external threats, prevent unauthorized access, and safeguard sensitive patient data while ensuring the availability and integrity of critical healthcare services.

Perimeter Security Best Practices

Perimeter security best practices are a critical component of a layered defense strategy in healthcare environments, acting as the boundary that protects internal networks and systems from external threats. A robust perimeter security framework begins with deploying next-generation firewalls (NGFWs) and Web Application Firewalls WAFs to filter incoming and outgoing traffic, inspect application-level data, and block malicious requests targeting healthcare web portals and applications. WAFs are especially important in defending against common web-based attacks such as SQL injection and cross-site scripting (XSS), which could expose sensitive healthcare data or disrupt critical services.

DDoS protection mechanisms should be implemented to defend against volumetric and application-layer attacks that overwhelm healthcare systems and disrupt access to critical services. Email security gateways are essential for filtering out phishing emails, malicious attachments, and links that could be vectors for ransomware or credential theft. Since email is a common entry point for attackers, advanced threat detection capabilities like sandboxing and machine learning-based anomaly detection help identify and quarantine suspicious messages before they reach end users.

Physical security controls at the perimeter are equally important. Healthcare organizations should enforce strict access controls to data centers and network hardware through biometric authentication, smart card systems, and video surveillance, ensuring that only authorized personnel can physically access critical infrastructure. Deception technologies, such as honeypots and decoy systems, add another layer of security by luring attackers into controlled environments where their tactics can be monitored and analyzed without putting actual systems at risk.

Furthermore, network IDPSs should be deployed at the perimeter to monitor and block suspicious traffic in real time. VPNs with strong encryption protocols must be enforced for remote access, ensuring that external connections to the healthcare network are secure and authenticated. Security information and event management (SIEM) tools should aggregate and analyze logs from perimeter defenses to provide centralized visibility and support rapid incident detection and response.

Implementing these comprehensive perimeter security best practices can strengthen healthcare organizations' defenses against external threats, protect sensitive healthcare data, and ensure the continuity and resilience of their critical systems and services.

Cloud Security Best Practices

Cloud security best practices are essential in healthcare environments where sensitive data such as EHRs and PHI are stored, processed, and transmitted via cloud services. The cornerstone of adequate cloud security is understanding the Shared Responsibility Model, which clarifies the security obligations of the healthcare organization and the cloud service provider. Healthcare organizations must implement strong IAM controls, enforcing multifactor authentication (MFA) to prevent unauthorized access to cloud resources and sensitive data. IAM policies should follow the principle of least privilege, granting users and applications only the access they need to perform their roles.

Data encryption is critical, both at rest and in transit. Strong encryption standards, such as AES-256 for storage and TLS 1.3 or higher for data transmission, ensure that sensitive healthcare data remains protected even if intercepted or accessed without authorization. Cloud access security brokers (CASBs) provide visibility into cloud usage, enforce security policies, and detect risky activities, helping organizations maintain control over their cloud environments. CASBs can also aid in compliance monitoring for healthcare regulations like HIPAA and GDPR.

To further reduce risk, organizations should implement cloud security posture management (CSPM) tools that continuously monitor cloud configurations and ensure they adhere to security best practices and compliance requirements. CSPM solutions help identify and remediate misconfigurations, such as open storage buckets or improperly configured access controls, which are common causes of data breaches. Regular vulnerability assessments and penetration testing of cloud environments are essential to uncover weaknesses and ensure cloud infrastructure remains secure against evolving threats.

Logging and continuous monitoring are vital for detecting and responding to security incidents in the cloud. Healthcare organizations should integrate cloud audit logs into a SIEM system for centralized analysis and real-time alerting. Backup and disaster recovery plans must be in place to ensure data availability and resilience, with frequent testing to verify recovery processes. Configuration management practices should include automated tools and templates to deploy secure, standardized cloud resources, minimizing human error and ensuring consistent security across environments.

By following these comprehensive cloud security best practices, healthcare organizations can protect sensitive data, maintain regulatory compliance, and ensure their cloud-based services and systems' integrity, confidentiality, and availability.

Network Segmentation

Now, let's return to a critical aspect of securing IoMT devices: network segmentation or enclaving. The IoMT ecosystem connects medical devices to healthcare networks. If proper safeguards, like network segmentation, are not implemented, a compromised device could jeopardize an entire healthcare system. Let's explore this practice in more detail, breaking it down into three key principles: isolation, risk reduction, and strategic controls.

Isolate IoMT Devices into Separate Network Segments Network segmentation divides a more extensive network into smaller, isolated sub-networks or segments. Each segment usually operates independently, and data and traffic are strictly controlled between them if allowed.

Believe it or not, folks have asked me, "Why should I isolate IoMT devices in particular?" The answer is that IoMT devices often have unique vulnerabilities such as limited processing power, which restricts advanced security measures, outdated or unpatched software due to FDA clearance complexities, and lack of built-in features compared to other standard IT devices. By isolating these devices into dedicated network segments, we:

- Prevent general-purpose devices like laptops or smartphones from interacting directly with IoMT devices.
- Reduce the exposure of sensitive IoMT devices to broader network vulnerabilities.
- Create controlled environments for monitoring and securing IoMT device traffic.

Throughout this book, I have referenced a simple example: an IoMT segment that might include infusion pumps, patient monitors, and imaging devices. These devices are restricted to communicating only with authorized hospital systems, not the hospital's public Wi-Fi or external Internet.

Reduce the Risk of Breaches Spreading Across Systems I'll talk a bit more about threat containment. In cybersecurity, breaches are sometimes unavoidable. However, network segmentation limits their impact. If an attacker compromises one segment, the attack could be contained within that segment, protecting other network parts. IoMT-specific scenarios, obviously depending on their specific access controls, include:

- **Ransomware attacks:** A breach targeting an administrative asset will not immediately affect life-critical IoMT devices.
- **Data exfiltration:** Patient data on medical imaging systems remains protected even if another segment is compromised.
- **IoT botnets:** Devices in one segment are shielded from being commandeered to participate in distributed denial-of-service attacks.

A real-world example is a hospital network with IoMT devices in one segment, administrative systems in another, and public-facing services (e.g., patient portals) in a third. If a phishing attack compromises the public-facing segment, the segmented IoMT network could remain insulated, safeguarding patient data and ensuring uninterrupted operation of those critical devices.

Implement Firewalls and Access Controls Between Segments Firewalls can serve as gatekeepers between network segments. They monitor and control traffic based on predefined security rules. For IoMT devices, firewalls enforce that only necessary protocols (e.g., HL7, DICOM) are allowed. Unauthorized traffic, like file-sharing or web browsing protocols, is blocked. In other words, access controls ensure that only authorized personnel or systems can interact with IoMT devices. This includes:

- RBAC to restrict user access
- NAC to allow only authorized devices onto the network

Let's also not forget Zero Trust architecture, which offers benefits such as adopting a never-trust, always-verify approach. Each communication between segments would be authenticated and authorized before being permitted.

Generally speaking, practical implementation tips include using VLANs/WLANs to create virtual segments, employing intrusion detection/prevention systems to identify and respond to suspicious activity, and regularly auditing firewall rules and access controls to ensure their currentness.

Let's face it, network segmentation is not just a technical best practice, it's a cornerstone of a proactive security strategy for IoMT devices. By isolating IoMT devices, reducing the risk of spreading breaches, and implementing firewalls and access controls, healthcare organizations can protect patient safety, maintain regulatory compliance, and safeguard sensitive data.

Strong Authentication and Access Controls

It is important to defend against cyber threats via strong authentication and access controls. Organizations can significantly reduce the risk of unauthorized access and data breaches by implementing more authentication methods and fine-tuned access controls. I'll examine the key practices for achieving this level of security.

Use MFA for Device Access What is MFA? Well, in short, MFA requires users to verify their identity using at least two out of three factors, which could be:

- Something they know (e.g., a password)
- Something they have (e.g., a smart card, token, or even mobile app)
- Something they are (e.g., a fingerprint or facial recognition)

Why should you use MFA for IoMT devices? Well, IoMT devices often control critical functions or hold sensitive patient data. Without MFA, a single compromised password could give attackers unrestricted access. It's a best practice to require MFA to access all administrative interfaces of IoMT devices. An example would be to use mobile-based authenticators or physical tokens for added security. A technician accessing a medical imaging system should enter a password and verify their identity through a fingerprint scanner or other factor. Even if the password is compromised, the attacker cannot gain access without the biometric factor.

Implement Role-Based Access Controls RBAC is necessary for IoMT security because it reduces insider threats by preventing unauthorized access to sensitive systems and limiting the potential impact of compromised accounts.

Simplified steps when implementing RBAC are to:

1. Define clear roles and responsibilities for all staff interacting with IoMT devices.
2. Assign permissions only to those roles that require them.
3. Continuously audit and adjust roles as responsibilities evolve.

An example would be a nurse who may have access to patient monitoring systems to view real-time data but cannot alter device configurations. With RBAC, only biomedical engineers can perform updates or maintenance on these devices.

Regularly Review and Update User Permissions Regular reviews are necessary because user roles and responsibilities usually change. Without them, former employees or contractors might retain access, even inadvertently. Permissions may also exceed current needs, increasing security risks.

Some of the best practices for this would be to:

- Conduct quarterly or biannual audits of user permissions.
- Immediately revoke access for employees who leave or change roles.
- Use automated tools to generate and review access reports.

For example, during an audit, you might discover that a former technician still has remote access to IoMT devices. To eliminate the risk of misuse, you might promptly revoke their credentials.

Avoid Default Usernames and Passwords To simplify the problem with defaults, IoMT devices often come with well-documented default usernames and passwords, which attackers can exploit. These defaults exist to make out-of-the-box access and configurations easier for people. However, people often overlook those defaults when disabling or changing credentials.

That said, some best practices are to:

- Immediately change default credentials during device setup.
- Use unique usernames for all accounts.

An attacker, for example, that scans for IoMT devices using known default credentials like "admin/admin" could be thwarted. Changing these defaults impedes such attempts before they can succeed.

Enforce Strong, Unique Passwords for All Devices and Systems There are many characteristics of strong passwords, depending on the methodology or regulatory intent, but based on research, the average is to enforce that passwords are:

- At least 12 characters long.
- A mix of upper- and lowercase letters, numbers, and special characters.
- Avoid dictionary words, names, and common patterns.

Unique passwords are essential because reusing them across devices or systems increases the risk of credential stuffing attacks, where attackers use stolen credentials from one breach to access other systems.

Implementation tips are to:

- Establish organization-wide password policies.
- Require periodic password changes (but avoid overly frequent resets, which can lead to weak habits).

An example might be an IoMT system that requires a strong and unique password, such as Il0v3Str0ngPwds2025. This password should not be reused on any other device or system.

Entropy refers to a password's randomness and unpredictability, which directly correlates to its difficulty in cracking. The higher the entropy, the more possible combinations an attacker would need to guess or brute-force it. Entropy is typically measured in bits, and each bit doubles the number of possible guesses required to crack a password.

Now, password length has a massive impact on entropy. Simply put, longer passwords exponentially increase the number of possible combinations, making brute-force attacks far less feasible. For example, if you have a password composed of lowercase letters, there are 26 possible characters for each position. A 6-character password has 26^6 (about 308 million) possible combinations. However, the potential combinations skyrocket when you increase the length to 13 or 14 characters.

Let's look at an example using a 94-character set (which includes uppercase, lowercase, numbers, and symbols):

- A 10-character password has 94^{10}, or about 5.4 quadrillion possible combinations.

- A 13-character password jumps to 94^{13}, or about 2.3 septillion combinations.
- A 14-character password goes to 94^{14}, which is over 218 septillion combinations.

That's an exponential increase in difficulty. Even with powerful modern hardware, the time and computational effort to crack a password of 13 or 14 characters (assuming decent randomness and complexity) are astronomically higher than shorter ones. In practical terms, a password of this length and complexity can move an attacker's effort from hours or days to thousands or millions of years, depending on the method used.

This is why security best practices recommend longer, more complex passwords. Even better, passphrases—a series of random words strung together—can be highly secure and easier to remember while providing high entropy.

Use Password Management Tools to Facilitate Secure Credential Management Password management tools securely store and generate unique passwords for all accounts, reducing the likelihood of human error and password reuse. IoMT security benefits include simplifying the management of complex passwords, automatically generating strong passwords during account creation, and reducing the burden on IT staff and end users.

Implementation tips are to:

- Use enterprise-grade password managers.
- Educate staff on the use of these tools.
- Enable password auditing features to identify weak or potentially reused passwords.

Many hospital IT departments use a password manager to store unique credentials for the vast number of IoMT devices. This ensures secure access while avoiding the risk of lost or forgotten passwords.

In enterprise-grade password management, Microsoft Entra is an example solution that plays a pivotal role by providing a comprehensive Identity and Access Management (IAM) solution that enhances security, simplifies user authentication, and reduces reliance on traditional passwords. Microsoft Entra encompasses services like Entra ID (formerly Azure Active Directory), which enables organizations to implement passwordless authentication methods such as Windows Hello for Business, FIDO2 security keys, and the Microsoft Authenticator app, significantly lowering the risk of credential theft and phishing attacks. Additionally, Entra supports adaptive access policies and Conditional Access, allowing enterprises to enforce granular controls based on user risk, location, device compliance, and behavior patterns. Entra provides password protection features for organizations still using passwords, including banned password lists and smart password lockout policies to defend against brute-force and password spray attacks. Integration with Privileged Identity Management (PIM) further secures administrative accounts by enforcing just-in-time access and multifactor authentication for high-risk operations. Through Entra's centralized identity platform, enterprises can streamline access management, enhance security posture, and move towards a Zero Trust architecture, all while maintaining compliance with industry regulations like HIPAA, GDPR, and ISO standards.

Regular Updates and Patching

Regular updates and patching are among the most effective ways to protect IoMT devices. I'll explore why updates and patching are vital and discuss how to implement this best practice effectively. I'll focus on four key elements: establishing a patch management process, keeping software and firmware up-to-date, routinely scanning for missing patches, applying patches promptly, and monitoring security advisories.

> **Establish a Robust Patch Management Process** Patch management involves identifying, testing, and applying software updates or patches, addressing vulnerabilities and improving functionality. A process is necessary because IoMT devices operate in complex environments where unplanned updates could disrupt critical functions. A structured process ensures updates are managed systematically and with minimal risk. Simplified steps to establish a process are as follows:
>
> 1. **Inventory devices:** Maintain an up-to-date inventory of all IoMT devices, software versions, and patch histories.
>
> 2. **Prioritize devices:** Categorize devices based on their criticality and threat exposure. For example, life-support systems should be prioritized over non-critical devices.
>
> 3. **Patch risk assessment:** Regular vulnerability scans and monitoring of vendor patch releases are crucial to identifying necessary patches and assessing their risk level.
>
> 4. **Test patches:** Test updates in a controlled environment to ensure compatibility with existing systems.
>
> 5. **Schedule updates:** Plan updates during maintenance windows to minimize disruptions.
>
> Furthermore, a concise policy is essential. It should outline the procedures, responsibilities, and timelines for patch management and include patch prioritization, testing, deployment, and documentation guidelines.

To that end, a simple example would be a hospital implementing a monthly review process where the IT team assesses available patches, tests them in a sandbox environment, and then schedules updates during off-peak hours.

Keep Software and Firmware of IoMT Devices Up-to-Date This is important for many reasons, but the most popular is that outdated software and firmware are common entry points for attackers. Many cyberattacks exploit vulnerabilities that have already been patched but were not applied by the organization. Some of the best practices in this category are to:

- Work with device manufacturers to understand the update schedule.
- Enable automatic updates if the feature is available and tested for reliability.
- Ensure legacy devices, which may no longer receive updates, are isolated from critical systems.

It's important to highlight that medical device updates require regulatory approval, which can delay patches. Work with manufacturers to understand the approval timelines and implement compensating controls, like network segmentation, for devices awaiting updates.

Apply Security Patches Promptly to Address Known Vulnerabilities Security patches address vulnerabilities that attackers could exploit to gain unauthorized access or disrupt device functionality. Prompt application matters because delays in applying patches leave devices exposed to attacks, especially for publicly disclosed vulnerabilities. You should monitor the Common Vulnerabilities and Exposures (CVE) database for vulnerabilities affecting your devices and develop a timeline for patch application based on the severity of the vulnerability (e.g., apply the most critical patches within 24–48 hours).

When a manufacturer, for example, releases a patch for a known ransomware vulnerability targeting infusion pumps, the IT team rapidly deploys the patch across all affected devices in the network to reduce the risk.

Monitor Security Advisories Related to IoMT Devices As implied in the previous section, security advisories are alerts issued by manufacturers, regulators, or cybersecurity organizations about vulnerabilities, threats, and recommended actions. Staying informed allows healthcare organizations to anticipate and respond proactively to emerging threats. Sources of security advisories include:

- Manufacturers' official websites or email alerts.
- The U.S. Cybersecurity and Infrastructure Security Agency (CISA) advisories.
- Industry forums and professional organizations.

Consider assigning a team or individual to monitor advisories regularly, integrate advisory updates into the patch management process, and maintain communication with device manufacturers for those real-time updates I reviewed.

Often, a manufacturer issues a security advisory for a critical asset, like an ultrasound machine, detailing a vulnerability and providing a patch. The IT team immediately downloads, tests, and deploys the patch while following the advisory's guidelines.

Regular updates and patching are indispensable for IoMT device security. By establishing a good, working, and practiced patch management process, keeping software and firmware up-to-date, promptly applying security patches, and monitoring security advisories, healthcare organizations can safeguard their devices and systems against evolving threats.

AI-Powered Monitoring and Analytics

Traditional cybersecurity measures alone are no longer sufficient to protect IoMT devices, given their complexity and the sophistication of modern cyber threats. This section will focus on an emerging AI-powered monitoring and analytics best practice. This innovative approach leverages artificial intelligence and machine learning to enhance IoMT device security by enabling real-time analysis, anomaly detection, and predictive threat identification.

Implement AI-Driven Tools for Real-Time Behavior Analysis At events, some people ask me what real-time behavior analysis is. I tell them that, in short, AI-driven tools monitor the activities of IoMT devices continuously, learning their normal behavior and identifying deviations that might indicate a threat. This is important because IoMT devices generate massive volumes of data, making manual monitoring impractical. AI processes this data at scale, providing immediate insights and faster response times. This works for IoMT because many of those devices operate in life-critical environments, where every second matters.

Practical implementation recommendations are to:

- Deploy AI-enabled monitoring solutions that integrate with your IoMT ecosystem.
- Configure tools to establish a baseline of normal device behavior, such as network traffic patterns and usage metrics.
- Use AI to automatically flag activities outside the baseline, such as unexpected data transfers or abnormal device commands.
- Integrate AI-powered tools with existing security systems, such as IDSs, IPSs, and SIEM systems. This ensures that AI insights are actionable and can trigger appropriate responses across the security infrastructure.

I recently read about an AI-driven tool that detected an infusion pump sending data to an unfamiliar IP address. It immediately alerted IT staff, who investigated and blocked the suspicious connection.

Detect Unusual Patterns That Could Indicate a Breach AI identifies patterns in many ways but excels at identifying subtle patterns in vast datasets that might go unnoticed by human analysts. It correlates multiple signals, such as failed login attempts, unusual traffic spikes, or changes in device performance, to identify potential breaches. This matters for IoMT security because IoMT devices often have predictable usage patterns. Sudden deviations, such as a diagnostic device operating outside working hours, might indicate unauthorized access.

Some key steps to consider are:

- Use AI tools to monitor traffic between IoMT devices and the broader network.
- Enable AI to analyze both real-time data and historical logs for irregularities.
- Combine AI insights with human expertise to validate and respond to alerts.

For example, an AI system notices unusually high data requests from a single imaging device during a holiday weekend, triggering an investigation. The IT team discovers and neutralizes malware attempting to exfiltrate patient data.

Use Advanced Analytics for Anomaly Detection in Device Behavior Anomaly detection focuses on identifying unusual events or behaviors within a dataset. AI and advanced analytics enhance this process by applying statistical models, neural networks, and clustering techniques. Important applications in IoMT devices involve detecting hardware malfunctions before they impact patient care, identifying unauthorized configuration changes, and even flagging devices communicating with unknown or blacklisted domains.

Some of the best practices are to:

- Train AI models using device-specific datasets to improve accuracy.
- Prioritize alerts based on risk level, automate responses to low-risk events, and refine AI models to reduce false positives.
- Incorporate feedback loops where flagged anomalies are reviewed and categorized to refine future detection.
- Use anomaly detection as an early warning system for security and operational issues.

An anomaly detection tool, for example, flagged a ventilator drawing more power than usual. Upon inspection, technicians discovered tampered hardware, preventing a potential sabotage incident.

Leverage Machine Learning Algorithms for Threat Detection Machine learning was covered in more depth in a prior chapter, but, in short, it enables systems to learn from data and improve their accuracy over time without explicit programming. ML algorithms can predict and identify cyber threats by analyzing patterns and trends.

Types of ML algorithms for IoMT security include:

- **Supervised learning:** Trains on labeled data to classify known threats.
- **Unsupervised learning:** Identifies unknown or emerging threats by clustering similar behaviors.
- **Reinforcement learning:** Adapts to evolving threats by continuously improving through feedback.

There are numerous advantages of ML in IoMT security. One is that it identifies zero-day threats by detecting patterns that resemble known attacks. Another is that it adapts to the unique behaviors of IoMT devices, reducing false positives. Finally, it provides actionable insights, such as prioritizing the most critical threats.

An example is a model that detects a ransomware attack targeting hospital servers by identifying encryption processes similar to previous attacks. The system isolates affected devices, minimizing damage.

AI-powered monitoring and analytics represent a powerful, proactive approach to securing IoMT devices. By implementing real-time behavior analysis, detecting unusual patterns, leveraging advanced anomaly detection, and using machine learning algorithms, healthcare organizations can stay ahead of new threats.

Zero Trust Security Model

Zero Trust has a lot of fantastic content, but I'll summarize the model here. This approach can enhance the security of IoMT ecosystems. Specifically, I'll discuss the principles of *never trust, always verify*, continuous verification, and restricting device access to the broader network.

Adopt a Never Trust, Always Verify Approach Zero Trust operates on the principle that no user, device, or application should be trusted by default, even if it resides within the network perimeter. Every access request must be verified before being granted, regardless of whether the system connects from within or outside the network or who the user is. This is important for IoMT security because IoMT devices often connect to hospital networks alongside administrative and public-facing systems. A breach in one area could easily compromise these critical devices unless strict trust boundaries are enforced.

Core principles include the following:

- Treat every device, user, and connection as a potential threat.
- Require authentication and authorization for every access request and actively monitor this activity.
- Enforce the least privilege principle, ensuring access is limited to what is strictly necessary.

A healthcare provider, for example, implementing Zero Trust, ensures that a diagnostic imaging device does not communicate with unrelated systems, such as the hospital's email server, even if both are on the same network.

Implement Continuous Verification Before Granting Access You may ask yourself, what is continuous verification? My answer is that traditional security relies on one-time authentication. In contrast, Zero Trust continuously evaluates the security posture of users, devices, and applications throughout a session, ensuring that access is only granted and maintained under secure and trusted conditions. Continuous verification enhances security by regularly checking the device's compliance with security policies (e.g., firmware updates and endpoint security tools). It also detects compromised devices or accounts in real-time, preventing them from escalating privileges or accessing sensitive systems. It can identify and respond to unusual activity during ongoing sessions.

Simplified steps to implement continuous verification could be to:

1. Deploy tools like multifactor authentication for all access requests.
2. Use identity and access management or IAM systems to monitor and enforce security policies.
3. Integrate endpoint detection and response solutions to ensure IoMT devices maintain secure configurations.

For example, an IoMT infusion pump requires authentication from a technician to access its settings. Continuous verification monitors the technician's activity and detects anomalies, such as an unusual attempt to alter network configurations, prompting an immediate lockout.

Restrict Device Access to the Broader Network In Zero Trust, IoMT devices are segmented (recall that recommendation throughout this book) and given access only to the systems and data they require. This limits the attack surface and minimizes the impact of potential breaches. We want to restrict network access because IoMT devices often have limited security features. By isolating these devices from the broader network, the likelihood of lateral movement, where attackers use one compromised device to infiltrate others, is significantly reduced.

Ways to restrict access would be to:

- Use network segmentation to isolate IoMT devices into dedicated VLANs or subnets.
- Employ micro segmentation, where even devices within the same network segment are individually restricted.
- Implement firewalls and access control lists or ACLs to regulate device communication strictly.

For example, an IoMT blood pressure monitor could be restricted from communicating only with its management server and cannot connect to other devices or internet-facing services. This restriction ensures that, even if compromised, it cannot spread malware across the network.

The Zero Trust security model is a shift in how we approach IoMT device security. By adopting a never trust, always verify approach, implementing continuous verification, and restricting device access to the broader network, healthcare organizations can significantly mitigate risks and enhance security. As cyber threats continue to evolve, embracing Zero Trust is no longer optional; it is essential for protecting patient data, maintaining operational integrity, and ensuring the safe and reliable operation of medical devices.

Encryption and Data Protection

Another cornerstone of IoMT security is encryption and data protection. This practice ensures that even if data is intercepted or accessed by unauthorized individuals, its content remains secure and unreadable. In this section, I'll examine strong encryption, end-to-end encryption for sensitive data, and pseudonymization techniques to protect patient identities.

Use Strong Encryption for Data in Transit and at Rest Encryption is the process of converting readable data (aka plaintext) into an unreadable format (called ciphertext) using cryptographic algorithms. Only authorized parties with the decryption key can revert the data to its original form. The idea is to encrypt data in transit because IoMT devices often transmit sensitive data over networks. Without encryption, this data is vulnerable to exposure during transmission. Additionally, you should encrypt data at rest because stored data, such as patient records or device logs, can be a target for attackers if left unprotected.

Some best practices for strong encryption are to:

- Use industry-standard encryption protocols like AES-256 for data at rest and TLS 1.3 for data in transit.
- Avoid deprecated protocols, such as SSL or older versions of TLS, which are vulnerable to attacks.
- Regularly update and manage encryption keys securely to prevent unauthorized access.

For example, a hospital's IoMT system encrypts all patient monitoring data transmitted between devices and central servers using TLS. Stored data, such as historical readings, is encrypted with AES-256, ensuring security even if storage systems are compromised.

Implement End-to-End Encryption for Sensitive Data Transmission End-to-end encryption (E2EE) ensures that data is encrypted at the source and remains encrypted until it reaches its intended destination. Only the sender and recipient have the keys to decrypt the data. One of the benefits of E2EE for IoMT devices is that it prevents interception or tampering by unauthorized parties, even if the communication network is compromised. E2EE also helps ensure compliance with healthcare data privacy regulations, such as HIPAA or GDPR, because it protects highly sensitive data, such as real-time telemetry or medical imaging results.

Recommendations regarding E2EE implementation are to:

- Choose IoMT devices and platforms that support E2EE natively.
- Use cryptographic libraries and APIs to implement E2EE in custom applications.
- Regularly audit encryption implementations to ensure proper configuration.

For example, a wearable heart monitor would transmit data directly to a physician's secure dashboard. The data is encrypted on the device, remains encrypted during transmission, and is only decrypted when accessed by the physician.

Consider Pseudonymization Techniques to Protect Patient Identities Pseudonymization replaces identifiable information in a dataset with artificial identifiers, such as codes or tokens, reducing the risk of exposing patient identities. It matters because pseudonymization ensures that patient identities remain protected if data is intercepted or accessed without authorization. It also enables secure data sharing for research and analytics without compromising privacy and aligns with data protection regulations emphasizing patient anonymity, such as GDPR.

Some pseudonymization practices are to:

- Before data is transmitted or stored, patient identifiers (e.g., names and social security numbers) should be replaced with unique tokens.
- Maintain a secure mapping system that links tokens to actual identities, accessible only by authorized personnel.

For example, consider an IoMT device that collects patient data for a clinical study. Before transmitting the data to researchers, the system replaces patient identifiers with randomly generated codes, ensuring anonymity while preserving the data's usability.

Three key considerations for pseudonymization implementation are as follows:

1. **Compliance with regulations:** Encryption and pseudonymization must comply with the requirements of healthcare data protection laws, such as HIPAA, GDPR, or HITECH.

2. **Performance impact:** Evaluate the performance of IoMT devices when implementing encryption to avoid latency or reduced functionality, especially in real-time applications.

3. **Key management:** Secure encryption keys should use hardware security modules (HSMs) or secure key management software. Rotate keys periodically and immediately replace compromised keys.

Encryption and data protection are non-negotiable in securing IoMT devices and safeguarding sensitive patient data. By using strong encryption for data in transit and at rest, implementing end-to-end encryption for sensitive transmissions, and applying pseudonymization techniques to protect identities, healthcare organizations can significantly enhance their cybersecurity posture.

Asset Inventory and Management

Asset inventory and management involves maintaining an up-to-date inventory, tracking connected devices, and leveraging automated tools to identify new or unauthorized devices. Here, I'll focus on a foundational best practice for IoMT security that incorporates asset inventory and management.

Maintain a Comprehensive Inventory of All IoMT Devices Comprehensive inventory is essential because IoMT ecosystems are diverse, including devices like infusion pumps, patient monitors, diagnostic imaging systems, and wearable health trackers. Each device represents a potential entry point for attackers, so having a complete inventory is the first step in securing them. Key components of an IoMT device inventory might include:

- **Device details:** Make, model, serial number, firmware, and software versions.
- **Location:** Physical or virtual location within the network.
- **Purpose:** Description of the device's function and role in patient care.
- **Owner/administrator:** Identify who is responsible for maintaining and securing the device.

A comprehensive inventory facilitates quick identification of vulnerable or unpatched devices. It also ensures compliance with healthcare security standards and regulations and simplifies incident response by providing immediate visibility into affected devices.

A hospital, for example, would maintain a database listing all IoMT devices, including infusion pumps in ICU rooms, with details on their firmware version and last update date. This allows the IT team to identify devices needing updates when a vulnerability is disclosed.

Regularly Update the Inventory to Track All Connected Devices Regular updates are essential because IoMT environments are dynamic. Devices are frequently added, moved, or decommissioned, and failure to keep the inventory updated can lead to security blind spots. Establish a routine update schedule, such as monthly or quarterly reviews. You should also integrate device inventory updates into the onboarding process for new devices. Finally, a best practice is to conduct periodic audits to ensure all devices are accounted for and properly categorized.

Consider busy healthcare environments that often add devices without notifying IT teams. Implementing workflows requiring all new devices to be registered in the inventory before deployment would be a benefit. For example, during a quarterly audit, an IT team discovers several portable diagnostic devices were added to the network without proper registration. This should trigger a process such that the team updates the inventory and applies the necessary security measures.

Use Automated Discovery Tools to Identify New or Unauthorized Devices Automation is critical for manual tracking of IoMT devices that are time-consuming and error-prone, especially in large or multisite healthcare organizations. Automated tools streamline this process by continuously monitoring the network for connected devices. Some of the features of automated discovery tools are:

- **Real-time monitoring:** Identifies devices as soon as they connect to the network
- **Device fingerprinting:** Classifies devices based on attributes like MAC addresses, protocols, and traffic patterns
- **Alerts for unauthorized devices:** Flags devices that are not registered in the inventory or deviate from normal behavior

Automation reduces the risk of rogue or unauthorized devices going unnoticed. It enhances security by enabling faster responses to potential threats. It also frees up IT resources for higher-level tasks. An automated discovery tool, for example, could detect a new device on the network, such as a diagnostic tool brought in by a visiting specialist. The system flags the device as unauthorized, prompting the IT team to investigate and secure or block its connection.

There are many popular automated discovery tools available that healthcare organizations can implement to enhance visibility and security over their IoMT and network-connected devices. Medigate by Claroty is a popular choice in healthcare, specifically designed for identifying, monitoring, and securing IoMT devices. It provides real-time device discovery, classification, and risk assessment tailored to clinical environments. Another strong option is Armis, an agentless security platform that delivers comprehensive visibility and continuous monitoring of medical, operational technology (OT), and traditional IT devices. Armis excels in device fingerprinting and offers detailed insights into device behavior and potential vulnerabilities. Forescout is also widely used in healthcare for its automated network access control and device discovery capabilities. It continuously monitors the network, identifying authorized and unauthorized devices, and enforces access policies without requiring agents on devices.

Additionally, Cisco Cyber Vision provides detailed visibility into IoT and IoMT environments, integrating with Cisco's broader security and network infrastructure for streamlined management. Lastly, Ordr delivers real-time discovery and classification of every connected device, combined with automated policy enforcement, to segment and protect devices based on their risk profile. Each of these tools helps healthcare organizations maintain a secure, up-to-date device inventory while enabling the rapid detection and response to unauthorized or potentially malicious devices.

Implementation tips for asset inventory and management are to:

- **Centralize the inventory:** Use a centralized platform or database to store and manage device information. Ensure accessibility to both IT and clinical engineering teams.

- **Integrate with other security tools:** Link the inventory to vulnerability management systems to prioritize security updates for critical devices.

- **Train staff on inventory processes:** Educate clinical and administrative staff on registering devices. Create clear procedures for reporting new devices or decommissioning old ones.

Asset inventory and management are fundamental practices for IoMT device security. By maintaining a comprehensive inventory, regularly updating it, and using automated discovery tools, healthcare organizations can gain complete visibility into their IoMT ecosystems. This visibility is essential for identifying vulnerabilities, responding to incidents, and ensuring compliance with security regulations.

Vendor Management and Third-Party Risk Assessment

Most IoMT ecosystems depend on vendors and third-party integrations in today's healthcare landscape. While these partnerships enable innovation and efficiency, they also introduce security risks. In this section, I'll focus on the best practices for vendor management and third-party risk assessment in IoMT device security. I'll cover how to evaluate vendor security practices, assess third-party risks, and ensure that vendors adhere to security best practices and compliance requirements.

Evaluate the Security Practices of IoMT Device Manufacturers Vendor security practices and policies are important because IoMT devices are often proprietary and tightly integrated with manufacturer-provided software. If the vendor's security practices are inadequate, the devices become weak links in the network. Key areas to evaluate include the following:

- **Product security features:**
  - Encryption for data in transit and at rest
  - Secure boot mechanisms and firmware updates
  - Support for modern authentication methods (e.g., MFA)

- **Vulnerability management:**
  - Frequency and transparency of patch releases
  - Speed in addressing newly discovered vulnerabilities
  - Availability of detailed security documentation
- **Vendor security policies:**
  - How does the vendor secure their own systems and supply chains?
  - Do they follow recognized standards, such as ISO 27001 or NIST CSF?
  - Are they transparent about past security breaches and remediation steps?

Simplified practical implementations include using detailed questionnaires or audits to gather information on vendor practices. One option is to require vendors to provide software bills of materials (SBOMs) to identify potential vulnerabilities in third-party software components.

An example would be a hospital evaluating the manufacturer's security track record before purchasing infusion pumps, discovering their firmware updates are delayed compared to industry standards. The hospital chooses an alternative vendor with a more vigorous update process.

Assess the Risks Associated with Third-Party Integrations IoMT devices rarely operate in isolation. Instead, they integrate with third-party systems, such as electronic health records, cloud platforms, or analytics tools. Each integration increases the attack surface, making third-party risk assessments crucial.

Here are four steps to consider when assessing risks:

1. **Identify integration points:**
   - Map out all third-party connections for each IoMT device.
   - Include APIs, cloud services, and software dependencies.
2. **Evaluate data handling practices:**
   - What type of data is exchanged with third parties?
   - Is sensitive data encrypted during transmission and storage?
3. **Assess security controls:**
   - Does the third-party solution have strong access controls and logging mechanisms?
   - How do they handle incidents, breaches, or downtime?
4. **Review contracts and service level agreements (SLAs):**
   - Include clear clauses on data protection, breach notification, and compliance requirements.

A diagnostic imaging device, for example, may connect to a third-party cloud service for data storage and processing. During the assessment, the healthcare organization discovered that the cloud service lacked encryption for stored data. They worked with the vendor to address the issue before deployment.

Ensure Vendors Follow Security Best Practices and Compliance Requirements Vendors must adhere to industry best practices and regulatory requirements, such as HIPAA or GDPR. Noncompliance can result in legal penalties and reputational damage. Some best practices to consider for enforcing vendor compliance are to:

- **Incorporate security in contracts:** Require vendors to comply with specific standards, such as OWASP IoT Security Guidelines. Mandate regular security audits and penetration tests.
- **Monitor ongoing compliance:** Conduct periodic reviews to ensure vendors maintain security commitments. Automate compliance monitoring using third-party risk management platforms.
- **Establish incident response expectations:** Define roles and responsibilities for handling security incidents. Include breach notification timeframes and remediation requirements in contracts.

An example would be a hospital that contracts with a vendor for wearable health monitors. The contract specifies compliance with HIPAA and requires the vendor to conduct annual security assessments, ensuring that both parties are aligned on protecting patient data.

Three simplified implementation tips for effective vendor management are to:

1. **Develop a vendor risk assessment framework:**
   - Create a checklist or scoring system to evaluate and compare vendors.
   - Include criteria for security, compliance, and performance.
   - Consider continuous monitoring for real-time risk management.
2. **Foster collaborative relationships:**
   - Work with vendors to address identified security gaps rather than immediately terminating contracts.
   - Encourage joint incident response planning to improve overall security posture.
3. **Educate stakeholders:**
   - Train procurement, IT, and clinical teams to understand vendor-related security risks.
   - Involve all stakeholders in vendor selection and risk assessment processes.

Vendor management and third-party risk assessment are vital components of IoMT security strategies. By evaluating manufacturers' security practices, assessing the risks of third-party integrations, and ensuring compliance with security standards, healthcare organizations can mitigate vulnerabilities and build more secure IoMT ecosystems.

Compliance with Regulatory Standards

This section focuses on compliance with regulatory standards for IoMT security. Specifically, I'll discuss adherence to key regulations like HIPAA, GDPR, and FDA guidelines, the application of standards such as the NIST Cybersecurity Framework for IoT devices, and the need to stay informed about evolving regulatory landscapes.

Adhere to Relevant Regulations and Guidelines Adhering to healthcare regulations is essential for organizations entrusted with safeguarding sensitive patient data and securing critical medical devices. Noncompliance can lead to significant consequences, including financial penalties, legal liabilities, reputational damage, and, most importantly, compromised patient safety. Healthcare organizations, operating within the IoMT ecosystem, must align with multiple regulatory frameworks to ensure compliance and security. Key regulations include:

- **Health Insurance Portability and Accountability Act (HIPAA):**
  - Governs U.S.-based healthcare organizations and their business associates.
  - Protects electronic protected health information or ePHI by enforcing technical safeguards such as encryption, multifactor authentication, audit controls, and incident response protocols.
  - Emphasizes the importance of securing patient data during storage and transmission, particularly for IoMT devices.
  - The proposed 2025 updates to the HIPAA Security Rule emphasize risk analysis, contingency planning, and regular compliance audits.
- **General Data Protection Regulation (GDPR):**
  - It applies to organizations handling the personal data of EU citizens, regardless of where the organization is located.
  - It focuses on principles like data minimization, collecting only necessary data, obtaining explicit consent for data processing, and granting individuals the right to access, correct, and erase their data.
  - It requires IoMT devices to adopt privacy-by-design and privacy-by-default approaches, ensuring patient data protection is integral to their architecture.
- **U.S. Food and Drug Administration (FDA) guidelines:**
  - Sets standards for the cybersecurity of medical devices during their lifecycle.

- Mandates manufacturers to conduct pre-market risk assessments, implement design controls, and release post-market security updates to address emerging threats.
- Encourages transparent communication between manufacturers and healthcare providers regarding device vulnerabilities and mitigation measures.

■ **Health Information Technology for Economic and Clinical Health Act (HITECH):**
- Expands HIPAA's requirements to include stricter penalties for data breaches and encourages the adoption of secure electronic health record systems.
- Holds organizations accountable for safeguarding health information, especially in systems integrated with IoMT devices.
- Incentivizes healthcare organizations to improve IT security infrastructure through financial incentives.

■ **California Consumer Privacy Act (CCPA):**
- Provides privacy rights to California residents, including access to, deleting, and controlling personal information.
- California requires healthcare organizations operating in California to ensure transparency in data collection and implement safeguards for personal or medical data processed through IoMT devices.

■ **ISO 14971 and IEC 62304:**
- ISO 14971 focuses on risk management for medical devices, including IoMT, ensuring identified risks are mitigated and documented.
- IEC 62304 outlines requirements for developing medical device software, emphasizing lifecycle security and reliability.
- These standards ensure that identified risks are mitigated and documented throughout the device lifecycle.

■ **NIST Frameworks:**
- Provide guidelines for managing and reducing cybersecurity risks in critical sectors, including healthcare.
- Recommends using tools like continuous monitoring, encryption, secure device pairing, and role-based access controls tailored for environments such as IoMT.

By adhering to these and other relevant regulations, healthcare organizations ensure compliance and build a security posture that protects patient data, fosters trust, and enhances the overall integrity of the healthcare ecosystem. Regular audits, employee training, and the integration of secure technologies further reinforce adherence to these frameworks, minimizing risks and supporting patient safety.

A hospital, for example, should ensure its IoMT devices meet HIPAA requirements by encrypting all transmitted ePHI and implementing access controls. For GDPR compliance, they pseudonymize patient data transmitted by devices used in cross-border research studies.

Follow Standards like the NIST Cybersecurity Framework for IoT Devices The NIST Cybersecurity Framework provides a structured approach to managing cybersecurity risks, including those specific to IoT devices. It is widely regarded as a best practice framework, even when not mandated by regulations. The five core functions of the NIST framework are as follows:

1. **Identify:** Understand and document IoMT device assets, risks, and dependencies.
2. **Protect:** Implement safeguards such as strong encryption, firewalls, and access controls.
3. **Detect:** Deploy monitoring systems to identify potential threats or vulnerabilities.
4. **Respond:** Establish an incident response plan to address security breaches effectively.
5. **Recover:** Develop processes to restore normal operations following an incident.

The NIST guidelines for IoT specifically emphasize secure device configurations, regular software updates and patching, and secure communication protocols. For example, a healthcare organization uses the NIST framework to assess risks associated with IoMT devices, implement strong security controls, and develop a response plan to mitigate ransomware attacks targeting diagnostic equipment.

Stay Informed About Evolving Regulatory Requirements Staying informed about cybersecurity is critical. IoMT security and data privacy regulations constantly evolve to address new threats, technologies, and public concerns. Organizations must be proactive in adapting to these changes to maintain compliance.

Here are three common ways to stay updated:

1. **Subscribe to official channels:**
   Follow updates from regulatory bodies like the FDA, EU regulators, and NIST.
   Stay connected with industry organizations and professional associations.
2. **Engage in continuous training:**
   Train IT, clinical, and administrative teams on updated compliance requirements.
   Use webinars, workshops, and certification programs to ensure staff remain knowledgeable.
3. **Perform regular audits:**
   Conduct periodic reviews of IoMT security policies and practices.
   Compare current processes against the latest regulatory requirements and best practices.

For example, when the European Data Protection Board issues updated guidelines on using health data under GDPR, a hospital should revise its data-sharing policies for IoMT devices to ensure compliance.

Compliance with regulatory standards is not just a legal obligation, it's a cornerstone of IoMT device security. By adhering to regulations like HIPAA, GDPR, and FDA guidelines, following frameworks like NIST, and staying informed about evolving requirements, healthcare organizations can protect patient data, ensure device integrity, and maintain trust.

Continuous Monitoring and Incident Response

Continuous monitoring and incident response are effective ways to safeguard devices. I'll discuss three essential components of this best practice: implementing 24/7 monitoring, developing and maintaining incident response plans, and conducting regular security assessments and penetration testing.

Implement 24/7 Monitoring of IoMT Devices and Network Traffic IoMT devices operate around the clock and handle critical patient data and operations. Any lapse in security monitoring could allow a breach to go undetected, compromising patient safety and data integrity. Some of the core objectives of continuous monitoring are to:

- Detect anomalies in device behavior or network traffic that may indicate a security incident.
- Identify unauthorized devices or connections attempting to access the network.
- Track performance and compliance with security policies.

When implementing continuous monitoring, be sure to consider the following:

- **Deploying monitoring tools:**
  - Use network monitoring systems (NMS) to oversee traffic flows.
  - Implement IoMT-specific security solutions that analyze device behaviors and flag anomalies.
- **Leveraging AI and machine learning:**
  - Use AI-powered tools to identify patterns and detect subtle signs of compromise.
  - Apply machine learning to adapt monitoring rules based on evolving threats.
- **Integrating with a security operations center (SOC):**
  - Centralize monitoring efforts within a SOC that operates 24/7.
  - Provide real-time alerts and actionable intelligence for immediate response.

Develop and Maintain Incident Response Plans An incident response plan or IRP is a documented process outlining how an organization will detect, respond to, and recover from cybersecurity incidents. Key components of an IRP for IoMT security include the following four steps:

1. **Preparation:**
   Identify critical IoMT assets and potential threats.
   Define roles and responsibilities for incident response teams.

2. **Detection and analysis:**
   Establish procedures for identifying security incidents.
   Use monitoring data to assess the scope and severity of incidents.

3. **Containment, eradication, and recovery:**
   Contain the impact by isolating affected devices or network segments.
   Remove the root cause (e.g., malware) and restore normal operations.

4. **Post-incident review:**
   Analyze the incident to identify lessons learned.
   Update the IRP to address gaps or improve processes.

Some best practices for maintaining the IRP are to:

- Regularly review and update the IRP to align with emerging threats and organizational changes.
- Conduct tabletop exercises and simulations to test the plan's effectiveness.
- Integrate vendor and third-party contacts into the IRP for devices under external management.

An example would be a ransomware attack targeting a network segment housing IoMT devices. The incident response team follows the IRP, isolates the affected segment, restores backups, and communicates with the manufacturer to apply security patches.

Conduct Regular Security Assessments and Penetration Testing Security assessments are essential, given that IoMT devices often face many threats due to their connectivity and critical functions. Regular security assessments help identify vulnerabilities and ensure devices remain resilient. Some of the most common types of security assessments include these:

- **Vulnerability scanning:**
    - Automated tools scan devices and networks for known vulnerabilities.
    - Provides a baseline understanding of security risks.

- **Penetration testing:**
  - Ethical hackers simulate real-world attacks to uncover exploitable weaknesses.
  - Tests both device security and broader network defenses.
- **Configuration audits:**
  - Assess device settings to ensure compliance with security policies and best practices.
  - Verify that features like encryption and access controls are correctly implemented.

When incorporating these assessments into IoMT security, be sure to:

- Schedule regular assessments, such as quarterly vulnerability scans and annual penetration tests.
- Prioritize testing for devices handling sensitive data or performing life-critical functions.
- Collaborate with third-party security experts for unbiased evaluations.

Some key tips known from successful implementations involve:

- **Investing in technology and expertise:**
  - Deploy advanced monitoring tools that integrate seamlessly with IoMT devices.
  - Train IT and clinical staff to recognize security threats and follow incident response protocols.
- **Fostering collaboration:**
  - Involve all stakeholders in monitoring and response efforts, including clinical teams, IT staff, and device manufacturers.
  - Establish clear communication channels for reporting and managing incidents.
- **Measuring and improving continuously:**
  - To evaluate performance, use metrics such as mean time to detect (MTTD) and mean time to respond (MTTR).
  - Incorporate feedback from incidents and assessments into ongoing security improvements.

Continuous monitoring and incident response are indispensable practices for securing IoMT devices. By implementing 24/7 monitoring, developing and maintaining comprehensive incident response plans, and conducting regular security assessments and penetration testing, healthcare organizations can protect their devices, networks, and, most importantly, patient safety.

Employee Training and Awareness

While advanced technologies and protocols are essential, they can only succeed if knowledgeable and vigilant employees support them. In this section, I examine some of the best practices for employee training and awareness of IoMT device security. These include educating staff on risks, conducting regular cybersecurity training, and fostering a culture of security awareness throughout the organization.

Educate Staff on IoMT Security Risks and Best Practices Education in this context is crucial because IoMT devices are often managed or interacted with by diverse teams, including clinicians, IT professionals, and administrative staff. Many breaches occur due to unintentional mistakes, such as clicking on phishing emails or failing to follow security protocols. Educating staff is the first step in mitigating these risks, and key topics to cover include:

- **IoMT device security basics:**
  - What IoMT devices are and their role in patient care.
  - Common threats, such as malware, ransomware, and unauthorized access.
  - Potential consequences of a security breach, including compromised patient safety and data loss.
- **Best practices for device security:**
  - Proper handling of IoMT devices to prevent physical tampering.
  - Adherence to network segmentation protocols.
  - Avoiding the use of default credentials and ensuring strong password management.
- **Recognizing threats:**
  - Identifying phishing emails or suspicious communications.
  - Reporting unusual device behavior or network activity.

For implementation, consider developing role-specific training programs tailored to the unique responsibilities of clinical, IT, and administrative staff. Also, be sure to use real-world examples to highlight the potential risks and consequences of lapses in security. A training session that demonstrates how a phishing attack could lead to unauthorized access to patient monitoring systems. Staff should learn how to recognize and report phishing attempts promptly.

Conduct Regular Cybersecurity Training Sessions Cyber threats constantly evolve, and employees must stay updated with the latest security practices. Regular training reinforces key concepts and introduces new strategies to counter emerging threats. Some components of more effective training include:

- **Interactive sessions:**
  - Include hands-on activities, such as mock phishing exercises and role-playing scenarios.
  - Provide opportunities for employees to ask questions and clarify doubts.
- **Simulation-based learning:**
  - Use simulated cyberattacks to test and improve employees' responses to real-world scenarios.
  - Analyze results to identify areas for improvement.
- **Policy reviews:**
  - Regularly review and update staff on changes to security policies and procedures.
  - Ensure employees understand their role in protecting IoMT devices and data.

It's recommended that training sessions be conducted at least quarterly. Consider using a mix of in-person workshops, webinars, and self-paced online courses to accommodate different schedules and learning preferences. During a quarterly training session, for example, staff participate in a simulated ransomware attack, practicing isolating affected devices and notifying the IT team. Post-simulation, employees discuss lessons learned to enhance future readiness.

Foster a Culture of Security Awareness in the Organization A security-aware culture ensures that every employee views cybersecurity as a shared responsibility and integrates secure practices into daily routines. Four steps to consider that help foster security awareness are:

1. **Leadership involvement:**
   - Leaders should actively champion cybersecurity initiatives, setting an example for the rest of the organization.
   - Regularly communicate the importance of IoMT security through town halls, newsletters, or memos.
2. **Incentivize secure behavior:**
   - Recognize and reward employees who demonstrate proactive security practices.
   - Use gamification techniques, such as leaderboards or quizzes, to encourage engagement.
3. **Integrate security into daily operations:**
   - Make security discussions a regular part of team meetings.
   - Provide easy access to resources for addressing security concerns, such as quick reference guides or helplines.

4. **Open reporting channels:**
   - Create a nonpunitive environment where employees feel comfortable reporting security incidents or potential threats.
   - Ensure timely feedback and resolution for reported issues.

   An example would be a hospital implementing a "Security Hero of the Month" program, recognizing employees who take proactive steps to report security risks or suggest improvements to IoMT device protocols.

Some of the key benefits of employee training and awareness are:

- **Reduced human error:**
  Training equips staff with the knowledge and skills to avoid common mistakes, such as weak passwords or falling victim to phishing.
- **Enhanced incident response:**
  Educated employees can recognize and respond to threats faster, minimizing potential damage.
- **Stronger organizational resilience:**
  A security-aware workforce becomes a proactive defense layer against cyber threats, complementing technical measures.

Healthcare organizations can significantly enhance their cybersecurity posture by educating staff on risks and best practices, conducting regular training sessions, and fostering a culture of security awareness.

Secure Device Onboarding and Decommissioning

As healthcare organizations continue to expand their IoMT ecosystems, the processes for onboarding new devices and decommissioning outdated ones play a critical role in maintaining security. Without proper protocols, these devices can become entry points for attackers or sources of data breaches. This section contains some of the best practices for onboarding and decommissioning, covering secure processes for adding new devices to the network and ensuring proper data wiping and disposal when devices are retired.

Implement Secure Processes for Adding New Devices to the Network Secure onboarding matters because IoMT devices often contain sensitive patient data and connect to networks critical for healthcare operations. Insecure onboarding processes can expose these devices to vulnerabilities right from the start. Four key steps for secure onboarding consideration are to:

1. **Authenticate devices:**
   - Verify the authenticity of each device before adding it to the network.
   - Use unique credentials for each device to prevent unauthorized access.

2. **Assign to segmented networks:**
   - Place IoMT devices on dedicated, segmented networks to isolate them from administrative or public-facing systems.
   - Use VLANs or microsegmentation to restrict device communication to only necessary endpoints.
3. **Apply security policies:**
   - Configure devices with secure settings, such as enabling encryption, disabling unnecessary ports and services, and enforcing strong passwords.
   - Ensure the device's firmware and software are up-to-date before activation.
4. **Log device details:**
   - Record essential information such as the device's make, model, serial number, assigned IP address, and location in a centralized inventory system.
   - Track its configuration and update history for future reference.

Consider using network access control solutions to automate onboarding, ensuring devices meet security requirements before connecting. Creating an isolated network segment, often called a quarantine or remediation zone, is a critical best practice for managing IoMT and other connected devices that fall out of compliance with security policies. This isolated environment allows healthcare organizations to safely remove noncompliant, unpatched, or potentially compromised devices from the production network without disrupting clinical operations. Once identified—typically by automated discovery tools or NAC solutions—these devices are automatically redirected to the isolated segment, where their activity can be closely monitored and assessed. Within this controlled zone, IT and security teams can perform necessary actions such as installing firmware updates, applying security patches, adjusting configuration settings, or conducting malware scans, all without risking exposure to the primary healthcare network. After remediation, the device undergoes validation checks to ensure it meets security policies before rejoining the production environment. This approach minimizes the risk of spreading vulnerabilities, maintains the network's integrity, and ensures regulatory compliance, while enabling efficient lifecycle management of connected medical devices and other critical assets.

Many healthcare organizations use fingerprinting tools to identify and classify IoMT devices automatically. A hospital, for example, would implement a secure onboarding process for new infusion pumps. Before being added to the inventory, each pump is authenticated using a unique device certificate, assigned to a secure VLAN, and configured to use encrypted communication protocols.

Ensure Proper Data Wiping and Secure Disposal of Decommissioned Devices IoMT devices store sensitive data, such as patient records and usage logs, which could be exploited if improperly handled during disposal. Secure decommissioning prevents data leaks and ensures compliance with regulations like HIPAA and GDPR. Four key steps for secure decommissioning are:

1. **Data backup and wiping:**
   - Back up essential data, ensuring it is stored securely.
   - Use certified data-wiping tools to permanently erase sensitive information from the device's memory and storage.
2. **Reset to factory defaults:**
   - After wiping, reset the device to factory settings to remove any configurations tied to the healthcare organization's network.
3. **Physical destruction (if necessary):**
   - For devices with nonremovable storage or highly sensitive data, physically destroy the storage medium to prevent data recovery.
4. **Document the process:**
   - Maintain a record of all decommissioned devices, including the steps to secure and dispose of them.
   - Ensure documentation complies with legal and regulatory requirements.

Consider working with certified vendors. In other words, partner with accredited vendors to securely dispose and recycle medical devices. That said, proof of destruction, such as certificates, is required for accountability. An example is a wearable health monitor that is retired after its lifecycle. The IT team backs up its logs, securely wipes its memory using certified software, and ensures its physical components are responsibly recycled through an authorized vendor.

Some additional considerations for both onboarding and decommissioning include:

- **Training and awareness:**
  - Educate IT and clinical staff on the importance of secure onboarding and decommissioning processes.
  - Provide clear guidelines and checklists for handling devices.
- **Regular audits:**
  - Periodically audit the onboarding and decommissioning processes to identify and address any gaps.
  - Verify that decommissioned devices are no longer active or connected to the network.
- **Policy integration:**
  - Incorporate onboarding and decommissioning protocols into the organization's broader IoMT security policies.
  - Ensure these processes align with regulatory requirements and industry standards.

Benefits of secure onboarding and decommissioning are vast, but here are a few key ones:

- **Improved security posture:** Mitigates the risk of unauthorized access or data breaches during the device's lifecycle.
- **Regulatory compliance:** Ensures adherence to legal requirements for data protection and device handling.
- **Operational efficiency:** Streamlined processes reduce errors and downtime during device onboarding and decommissioning.
- **Environmental responsibility:** Secure disposal practices contribute to environmentally friendly recycling and waste management.

Secure device onboarding and decommissioning are vital components of a good IoMT security strategy. By implementing authentication and segmentation during onboarding, wiping data securely, and ensuring responsible disposal, healthcare organizations can protect patient data, maintain regulatory compliance, and mitigate potential risks.

Physical Security Measures

One critical but sometimes overlooked area in IoMT device security is physical security. Protecting IoMT devices from unauthorized physical access or tampering is vital to maintaining their integrity, availability, and security. I'll focus on some of the best practices for physical security measures, covering how to implement physical access controls and secure devices against tampering or unauthorized access.

Implement Physical Access Controls for IoMT Devices Physical access controls are important because IoMT devices are often in public or semi-public areas, such as hospital rooms, clinics, or patients' homes. These devices are vulnerable to theft, tampering, or misuse without proper physical access controls. Some of the key strategies are to:

- **Restrict access to authorized personnel:**
  - Control access to rooms or areas where IoMT devices are stored or operated using physical locks, card readers, or biometric scanners.
  - Maintain a list of authorized personnel who can access these devices.
- **Secure storage for portable devices:**
  - When not in use, store portable IoMT devices, such as diagnostic tools or wearable monitors, in locked cabinets or secured areas.
  - Use tethering solutions to prevent unauthorized removal of devices.
- **Monitor access:**
  - Install surveillance cameras in areas housing IoMT devices.
  - Use logging systems to record when and by whom devices are accessed.

- **Use identification badges:**
  - Require staff to wear badges for easy identification, ensuring only authorized individuals have physical access to IoMT equipment.

During implementation, consider combining physical access controls with cybersecurity measures for layered protection. Also, regularly review and update access permissions to reflect changes in staff roles and responsibilities. In a hospital, all IoMT devices in critical care units should be stored in rooms with restricted access. Only authorized clinicians and biomedical engineers can enter using ID cards and PIN-based locks.

Secure Devices Against Tampering or Unauthorized Physical Access Physical tampering can lead to device malfunctions, data breaches, or even unauthorized network access. Securing devices against tampering protects both patient safety and data confidentiality. Tamper resistant measures include these popular options:

- **Tamper-evident seals:**
  - Seals should be applied to IoMT devices to indicate if a device has been opened or altered visually.
  - Inspect seals regularly for signs of tampering.
- **Enclosures and locking mechanisms:**
  - Use tamper-proof enclosures or hardware to prevent unauthorized opening of devices.
  - Install locking mechanisms on ports or interfaces to restrict physical connections.
- **Physical placement:**
  - Position IoMT devices in secure areas where unauthorized individuals cannot easily access them.
  - Avoid placing devices near publicly accessible locations, such as waiting rooms or hallways.
- **Tamper detection:**
  - Integrate sensors into IoMT devices that trigger alerts if physical tampering is detected.
  - Configure devices to lock or disable themselves if unauthorized physical access is attempted.

It's important to secure cables, ports, and other connections to IoMT devices to prevent interception or unauthorized access for devices that must remain stationary, use cable locks, or secure mounting solutions. A diagnostic imaging device, for example, in a radiology department, should be housed in a locked, tamper-proof enclosure. Tamper-evident seals are applied to access panels, and the device triggers an alert if the seal is broken or the enclosure is opened. Some additional and common considerations for physical security are the following:

- **Educate staff:**
  - Train staff on the importance of physical security for IoMT devices and how to recognize signs of tampering or unauthorized access.
  - Provide clear guidelines on reporting physical security incidents.
- **Conduct physical security audits:**
  - Periodically review the physical security of IoMT devices to identify vulnerabilities or lapses in protective measures.
  - Test the effectiveness of physical access controls through simulated incidents.
  - This will align with maintaining a comprehensive inventory of IoMT devices, which is crucial for effective security management, including physical security.
- **Integrate physical and cybersecurity policies:**
  - Ensure that physical security measures complement cybersecurity protocols.
  - For example, require physical presence and authentication for certain IoMT device operations, such as firmware updates.
- **Plan for theft or loss:**
  - Develop protocols for responding to the theft or loss of IoMT devices, including immediate deactivation or tracking if applicable.
  - Use asset tracking tools to locate and recover lost devices.

The benefits of strong physical security measures are numerous, but here are four key ones:

- **Enhanced device integrity:** Protects devices from tampering, theft, or damage, ensuring reliable operation.
- **Reduced risk of data breaches:** Prevents unauthorized access to sensitive patient data stored on or transmitted by devices.
- **Improved patient safety:** Ensures that IoMT devices operate as intended without interference, safeguarding patient care.
- **Compliance with regulations:** Meets physical security requirements outlined in HIPAA, GDPR, and NIST standards.

Physical security is a vital yet often underestimated aspect of IoMT device protection. By implementing access controls, using tamper-resistant measures, and regularly auditing physical security practices, healthcare organizations can safeguard their IoMT ecosystems against physical threats.

Backup and Recovery

Like any technology, IoMT systems are vulnerable to disruptions from cyberattacks, hardware failures, or natural disasters. Therefore, Backup and Recovery are critical best practices for ensuring operational continuity and data integrity. I'll discuss implementing effective backup and recovery strategies, focusing on two essential components: regularly backing up device configurations and critical data and establishing disaster recovery plans for IoMT systems.

Regularly Backup Device Configurations and Critical Data Backups are essential because IoMT devices often contain configurations, logs, and patient data critical to healthcare operations. Losing this data can disrupt patient care, compromise regulatory compliance, and incur significant recovery costs. That said, some of the key backup best practices are to:

- **Identify backup priorities:**
  - Determine which data and configurations are critical for patient care and device functionality.
  - Prioritize backups of patient data, device configurations, and software/firmware versions.
- **Schedule regular backups:**
  - Set up automatic backups to run at consistent intervals (e.g., daily or weekly).
  - Align backup frequency with the criticality of the data or device.
- **Use redundant backup systems:**
  - Store backups in multiple locations, including on-premises servers and secure cloud storage.
  - Ensure geographic redundancy to protect against regional disasters.
- **Encrypt backup data:**
  - Use strong encryption to protect backups from unauthorized access.
  - Ensure encryption keys are securely managed and regularly rotated.
- **Test backups regularly:**
  - Conduct regular restoration tests to verify the integrity and usability of backup data.
  - Identify and address any issues in the backup or recovery process.

During implementation, some tips are to use backup software that integrates with IoMT devices and central management platforms. Also, maintain a log of backup activities for audit and compliance purposes. A hospital, for example, should back up configuration data for its infusion pumps daily and store the backups in a secure local server and an encrypted cloud repository. During a ransomware attack, the hospital quickly restores the pumps' settings to continue patient care without disruption.

Implement Disaster Recovery Plans for IoMT Systems Disasters, whether natural (e.g., floods, earthquakes) or artificial (e.g., cyberattacks), can incapacitate IoMT systems. A well-crafted disaster recovery plan or DRP minimizes downtime and ensures the rapid restoration of critical services. Six key components of a DRP include the following:

1. **Risk assessment:**
   - Identify potential risks to IoMT systems, such as power outages, ransomware attacks, or hardware failures.
   - Evaluate the impact of each risk on healthcare operations.
   - Monitor backup systems and regular maintenance to ensure they remain effective over time.

2. **Define recovery objectives:**
   - Recovery Time Objective (RTO): The maximum acceptable downtime for IoMT systems.
   - Recovery Point Objective (RPO): The maximum acceptable amount of data loss.

3. **Develop recovery procedures:**
   - Outline step-by-step instructions for restoring device configurations, software, and data.
   - Include procedures for restoring network connectivity and secure device communication.

4. **Assign roles and responsibilities:**
   - Clearly define the roles of IT staff, clinical teams, and external vendors in disaster recovery.
   - Establish a chain of command for decision-making during an incident.

5. **Maintain an inventory of resources:**
   - Keep a detailed list of IoMT devices, backup locations, and recovery tools.
   - Ensure spare parts and replacement devices are readily available.

6. **Conduct regular DRP drills:**
   - Simulate disaster scenarios to test the plan's effectiveness and refine processes.
   - Incorporate lessons learned into updated versions of the DRP.

An example of a disaster recovery scenario is a cyberattack that compromises a segment of the hospital network, disabling several IoMT devices. The IT team activates the disaster recovery plan, isolating affected systems, restoring devices from encrypted backups, and re-establishing network connectivity within the RTO of 2 hours.

Benefits of effective backup and recovery strategies include:

- **Minimized downtime:** Enables rapid restoration of critical devices and services, ensuring continuity of patient care.
- **Data integrity and compliance:** Protects patient data from permanent loss and ensures adherence to regulatory requirements like HIPAA and GDPR.
- **Cost savings:** Reduces the financial impact of extended outages, data recovery efforts, and potential legal penalties.
- **Improved resilience:** Demonstrates disaster preparedness, fostering trust among patients, staff, and regulatory bodies.

There are many implementation challenges and solutions. For example, a common challenge is ensuring compatibility with diverse IoMT devices. A solution might be to use backup solutions designed specifically for healthcare environments, capable of integrating with heterogeneous device ecosystems. Another common challenge is balancing backup frequency with resource constraints. Optimizing schedules by prioritizing critical devices and data for more frequent backups could help in that case. A final challenge could be securing backups from cyberattacks. A solution mentioned throughout this book is to encrypt backups, store them in isolated environments, and implement strict access controls.

Backup and Recovery are indispensable for securing IoMT devices and ensuring operational continuity. By regularly backing up device configurations and critical data and implementing disaster recovery plans, healthcare organizations can mitigate the impact of disruptions and maintain patient care despite challenges.

Secure Communication Protocols

As discussed in this book, using secure communication protocols is one of the most effective ways to protect data in transit and ensure the integrity of device communications. In this section, I'll focus on two key aspects of this best practice, using secure protocols for device communication and implementing certificate-based authentication for device-to-device interactions.

Use Secure Protocols for Device Communication (e.g., TLS, DTLS) IoMT devices exchange sensitive information, including patient health data and real-time telemetry. Attackers can exploit unsecured communication channels to intercept, alter, or inject malicious data, compromising patient safety and data privacy.

Key secure protocols include:

- **Transport Layer Security (TLS):**
  - TLS ensures encrypted communication between devices and servers.
  - Protects against eavesdropping, tampering, and impersonation.
  - Widely used for secure HTTP (HTTPS) and other application-level protocols.

- **Datagram Transport Layer Security (DTLS):**
  - Designed for secure communication over datagram protocols like UDP.
  - Suitable for IoMT devices requiring low-latency or real-time data exchange, such as patient monitors and wearable devices.
- **Secure Shell (SSH):**
  - Provides encrypted remote access to IoMT devices for management and troubleshooting.
  - Ensures remote users' authentication before granting access.
- **IPsec (Internet Protocol Security):**
  - Encrypts and authenticates communication at the IP layer, securing device-to-network or device-to-device traffic.

During implementation, ensure that all communication channels use the latest versions of protocols (e.g., TLS 1.3) to avoid vulnerabilities in outdated versions. Also, don't forget to configure devices to disable insecure protocols, such as SSL or TLS 1.0/1.1. Use cryptographic libraries that comply with industry standards to implement these protocols.

Implement Certificate-Based Authentication for Device-to-Device Communication Certificate-based authentication uses digital certificates to verify the identity of devices during communication. Certificates are issued by a trusted Certificate Authority (CA) and contain cryptographic information used for authentication. Certificate-based authentication helps prevent unauthorized devices from connecting to the network or communicating with legitimate devices. It also protects against impersonation attacks (e.g., man-in-the-middle attacks) and enables mutual authentication, where both communicating devices verify each other's identities.

Here is a simplified depiction of its functionality in three steps:

1. **Certificate issuance:**
   - Each IoMT device is issued a unique digital certificate during manufacturing or onboarding.
   - A trusted CA signs certificates to ensure authenticity.
2. **Handshake process:**
   - During device-to-device communication, devices exchange certificates and verify their authenticity using the CA's public key.
   - If authentication is successful, an encrypted communication channel is established.
3. **Certificate management:**
   - Certificates have expiration dates and must be renewed periodically.
   - Organizations should implement automated tools for certificate provisioning, renewal, and revocation.

Some implementation tips to consider are:

- Use secure key storage mechanisms, such as Trusted Platform Modules (TPMs) or Hardware Security Modules (HSMs), to protect private keys associated with certificates.
- Establish a Public Key Infrastructure to manage certificates efficiently.
- Regularly audit and revoke certificates for decommissioned or compromised devices.

Additional considerations for the actual secure communication protocols include the following:

- **Encryption algorithms:**
  - Strong encryption algorithms should be used, such as AES-256 for data encryption and RSA or ECC for key exchange.
  - Avoid weak algorithms like DES or RC4.
- **Secure firmware updates:**
  - Use secure protocols to transmit firmware updates to devices, ensuring updates are not intercepted or tampered with.
- **Monitor and audit communications:**
  - Implement tools to monitor network traffic for signs of insecure communication or malicious activity.
  - Regularly audit communication logs to identify and address vulnerabilities.
- **Integration with network segmentation:**
  - Combine secure communication protocols with network segmentation to limit the potential impact of a compromised device.

There are many benefits of using secure communication protocols, but here are the top four:

- **Data confidentiality:** Protects sensitive patient data from being intercepted or stolen during transmission.
- **Integrity:** Ensures that data transmitted between devices remains unchanged.
- **Authentication:** Verifies the identities of devices and servers, preventing unauthorized access.
- **Compliance:** Meets regulatory requirements for securing electronic protected health information under standards like HIPAA and GDPR.

Secure communication protocols are the backbone of IoMT device security, ensuring data confidentiality, integrity, and authenticity in transit. By using modern protocols like TLS and DTLS and implementing certificate-based authentication, healthcare organizations can significantly reduce the risk of data breaches and unauthorized device interactions.

Data Minimization and Retention Policies

IoMT generates large amounts of data critical to improving healthcare outcomes. However, if not managed properly, this data carries significant security and privacy risks. A best practice to mitigate these risks is implementing data minimization and retention policies. Here, I'll explore how to balance the value of data with the need for security and privacy by focusing on two key principles: collecting and retaining only necessary data and implementing data retention policies that comply with regulatory requirements.

Collect and Retain Only Necessary Data Data minimization limits data collection and storage to only what is essential for the intended purpose. This reduces the risk of data breaches, minimizes regulatory exposure, and simplifies compliance efforts. It is also important because it reduces the attack surface. Let's face it: the less data you collect and store, the fewer attackers can steal. Data minimization also protects patient privacy, as collecting excessive or unnecessary data can lead to privacy violations. Regulations like GDPR and HIPAA require organizations to collect only necessary information and avoid over-retention.

Some of the best practices for data minimization are to:

- **Evaluate data needs:**
  - Assess the specific data required for each IoMT device's function.
  - Avoid collecting extraneous information that does not directly contribute to patient care or operational goals.

- **Anonymize or pseudonymize data:**
  - Whenever possible, remove or replace identifiable information to protect patient privacy.
  - Use pseudonymization techniques to make data useful for analysis while reducing privacy risks.

- **Avoid storing duplicate data:**
  - Eliminate redundant data storage by centralizing data management.
  - Use secure integration methods to share data across systems without creating unnecessary copies.

- **Design devices with data minimization in mind:**
  - Configure IoMT devices to collect and transmit only the data they need to perform their tasks.
  - Work with device manufacturers to ensure compliance with data minimization principles during design.

A wearable heart monitor, for example, is configured to collect real-time ECG data and alert physicians only when readings deviate from normal. This avoids collecting nonrelevant patient information, such as demographic data, which is not essential for its operation.

Implement Data Retention Policies in Compliance with Regulations Data retention policies define how long data is stored, how it is securely archived, and when and how it is permanently deleted. These policies ensure that organizations retain data only for as long as it is legally or operationally required. Retention policies are essential, and here are a few reasons to consider:

- **Regulatory compliance:** Laws like GDPR, HIPAA, and local health regulations often specify data retention periods and requirements for secure deletion.
- **Cost management:** Retaining unnecessary data increases storage costs and management complexity.
- **Data security:** Longer retention periods increase exposure to breaches and unauthorized access.

Four simplified steps to implement effective retention policies are to:

1. **Understand regulatory requirements:**
    - Identify regulations governing your organization, such as HIPAA (U.S.), GDPR (EU), or other local laws.
    - Document the minimum and maximum retention periods for each type of data.
2. **Classify data:**
    - Categorize data based on sensitivity, usage, and regulatory requirements.
    - Define retention periods for each category, such as clinical data, device logs, or operational records.
3. **Automate retention policies:**
    - Use data management tools to enforce retention periods automatically.
    - Set up alerts for data nearing its retention limit to ensure timely action.
4. **Delete securely:**
    - Implement processes to delete data at the end of its retention period permanently.
    - Use certified data-wiping tools or physical destruction methods for decommissioned storage devices.

A hospital, for example, should implement a policy to retain patient monitoring data for seven years, as HIPAA requires. After this period, data can be automatically deleted from the system, ensuring compliance and reducing storage costs.

Some common key challenges and solutions are:

- **Balancing operational needs with data minimization:** A solution could be to engage clinical, IT, and compliance team stakeholders to identify essential data needs while avoiding overcollection.

- **Managing data across diverse IoMT devices:** A good solution might be using centralized data management systems to standardize retention policies and minimize duplication.
- **Keeping up with evolving regulations:** In this case, a solution would be regularly reviewing retention policies to ensure they align with updated legal requirements and industry best practices.

Some benefits of data minimization and retention policies are:

- **Enhanced security:** Reduces the volume of sensitive data, limiting the potential impact of breaches.
- **Improved privacy protection:** Demonstrates respect for patient privacy by handling data responsibly.
- **Regulatory compliance:** Aligns with legal mandates, reducing the risk of fines or legal action.
- **Cost savings:** Lowers storage and data management expenses by eliminating redundant or outdated data.
- **Operational efficiency:** Simplifies data management processes, making locating and using critical information easier.

Data Minimization and Retention Policies are essential for IoMT device security and data management. By collecting and retaining only necessary data and implementing retention policies in compliance with regulations, healthcare organizations can protect patient privacy, enhance security, and streamline operations.

Cybersecurity Insurance

In the context of healthcare organizations, a key best practice is integrating comprehensive cybersecurity insurance as part of the overall risk management strategy. Given the sensitive nature of PHI and the critical reliance on IoMT devices and digital healthcare systems, cybersecurity insurance provides an essential financial safety net in case of a data breach, ransomware attack, or other cyber incidents. Healthcare organizations should carefully assess policies to cover various threats, including data breaches, business interruption, extortion demands, legal fees, regulatory fines, and reputational damage.

Working with insurers who understand the healthcare sector's unique regulatory and operational complexities, such as HIPAA compliance and patient safety concerns, is important. Additionally, organizations should regularly review and update their coverage as their IT environment evolves, and align their cybersecurity controls with policy requirements—many insurers require adherence to best practices like regular security assessments, employee training, and incident response planning. By incorporating cybersecurity insurance as part of a layered security strategy, healthcare organizations can mitigate the financial impact of cyberattacks while demonstrating due diligence in protecting patient data and critical systems.

Regular Security Audits

A cornerstone of maintaining IoMT security is performing regular security audits. This chapter closes with a discussion on the importance of conducting periodic security audits of IoMT devices and infrastructure and how to address vulnerabilities promptly to ensure an effective security posture.

Conduct Periodic Security Audits of IoMT Devices and Infrastructure A security audit systematically evaluates IoMT devices, networks, and associated systems to identify vulnerabilities, assess compliance with security standards, and ensure effective protective measures. The ability to pass a third-party audit is critical to any healthcare operation. Security audits are essential for many reasons because they:

- **Identify risks:** Detect weaknesses in devices or configurations before attackers exploit them.
- **Ensure compliance:** Meet regulatory requirements such as HIPAA, GDPR, or FDA guidelines.
- **Maintain operational integrity:** Prevent disruptions by proactively identifying and mitigating security gaps.

Some of the key components of an IoMT security audit are as follows:

- **Inventory and assessment:**
    - Compile a complete inventory of IoMT devices, including their configurations, firmware versions, and network connectivity.
    - Assess each device's security controls and its role in the network.
- **Vulnerability scanning:**
    - Use automated tools to scan devices and infrastructure for known vulnerabilities.
    - Focus on unpatched firmware, outdated protocols, and misconfigurations.
- **Penetration testing:**
    - Simulate real-world attacks to evaluate the resilience of devices and systems.
    - Identify potential points of entry and paths for lateral movement within the network.
- **Compliance checks:**
    - Compare security measures against regulatory requirements and industry standards, such as the NIST Cybersecurity Framework.
    - Document areas of noncompliance for corrective action.
- **Network traffic analysis:**
    - Monitor network activity to identify unusual patterns or unauthorized communication between devices.

- **Physical security review:**
  - Assess the physical security of IoMT devices to ensure they are protected against tampering or theft.

Regarding audit frequency, consider conducting comprehensive audits at least annually, with additional reviews after significant changes, such as adding new devices or updating software. For example, a hospital should perform an annual security audit of its IoMT ecosystem. The audit may reveal that several diagnostic devices are running outdated firmware. These devices are then promptly flagged for updates, reducing their exposure to potential threats.

Address Identified Vulnerabilities Promptly Prompt remediation is crucial because delays in addressing vulnerabilities expose systems to potential exploitation. A timely response minimizes risks and ensures continued compliance with security standards. Five common steps to address vulnerabilities are to:

1. **Prioritize based on risk:** Use a risk-based approach to prioritize vulnerabilities. Focus first on critical risks impacting patient safety or leading to data breaches.
2. **Patch and update:** Work with device manufacturers to apply patches and updates for identified vulnerabilities. Schedule updates during maintenance windows to minimize disruption.
3. **Reconfigure devices:** Address insecure configurations, such as open ports, default credentials, or unnecessary services. Align configurations with security best practices.
4. **Mitigation measures:** For vulnerabilities without immediate patches, implement compensating controls, such as network segmentation or stricter access controls, to reduce risk.
5. **Validate remediation:** After addressing vulnerabilities, test devices, and systems to ensure the fixes are effective and do not introduce new issues. Update audit logs to document the resolution process.

For continuous improvement, use insights from security audits to refine security policies, enhance training programs, and improve incident response plans. For example, penetration testing might uncover a misconfigured IoMT ventilator during a security audit that allows unauthorized remote access. The IT team should reconfigure the device quickly, apply the latest firmware update, and restrict its access to a secure network segment, effectively mitigating the vulnerability.

Some key benefits of regular security audits include the following:

- **Proactive risk management:** Identifies vulnerabilities before attackers exploit them.
- **Enhanced compliance:** Demonstrates adherence to regulatory requirements, reducing the risk of fines or legal penalties.

- **Improved incident response:** Provides insights into potential weaknesses, helping organizations prepare for and respond to security incidents.
- **Increased trust:** Builds confidence among patients, staff, and stakeholders by demonstrating a commitment to security.

There are many challenges and solutions to incorporating regular security audits. Consider large-scale IoMT environments. One solution could be to use automated tools to streamline vulnerability scanning and inventory management. Another common challenge is limited resources. In this case, focus audits on high-risk devices and network segments first, gradually expanding the scope over time. This book also mentions manufacturer dependencies as a challenge. Establishing strong vendor relationships and requiring timely updates and patches through contracts or service agreements may help.

Key implementation tips for effective audits are to:

- **Develop a standardized audit framework:** Use established frameworks like NIST or ISO 27001 to guide audit processes and ensure consistency.
- **Engage cross-functional teams:** To better understand risks and operational impacts, involve IT, clinical staff, and device manufacturers in the audit process.
- **Document findings and actions:** Maintain detailed records of audit findings, remediation efforts, and compliance checks for future reference and accountability.
- **Stay informed:** Regularly monitor security advisories, industry reports, and emerging threats to update audit protocols and priorities.

Regular security audits are essential for maintaining the integrity, availability, and security of IoMT devices and infrastructure. By systematically evaluating devices and networks and promptly addressing vulnerabilities, healthcare organizations can mitigate risks, enhance compliance, and better protect patient safety.

Key Takeaways of Best Practices for IoMT Device Security

By implementing the best practices outlined in this chapter, healthcare organizations can significantly enhance the security of their IoMT devices, protect sensitive patient data, and maintain the integrity of their healthcare systems. IoMT security is not a one-time effort but an ongoing process that requires continuous monitoring, adaptation, and improvement to counter evolving cyber threats. Key strategies include segmenting networks to isolate IoMT devices and limit lateral movement, enforcing strong authentication and role-based access controls, and maintaining a rigorous patch management process to address vulnerabilities promptly.

Leveraging AI-powered monitoring tools enables real-time behavior analysis and anomaly detection, while adopting a Zero Trust security model ensures continuous verification of users and devices. Encryption of data in transit and at rest, along with secure communication protocols, safeguards sensitive information. A comprehensive asset inventory, vendor risk assessments, and compliance with regulatory standards like HIPAA and GDPR are essential components of a security program. Incorporating security-by-design principles in device development, continuous monitoring, and well-defined incident response plans further strengthen defenses.

Employee training, secure onboarding and decommissioning of devices, physical security measures, reliable backup and recovery processes, data minimization policies, and regular security audits round out an integrated, multilayered approach to IoMT security. By following these practices, healthcare organizations can mitigate risks, ensure regulatory compliance, and build a resilient, secure IoMT ecosystem.

Part V

Future Trends and Emerging Threats

Healthcare technology is evolving rapidly, driven by advancements in connectivity, computing power, and artificial intelligence. While these innovations promise improvements in patient care and operational efficiency, they also introduce various security challenges and other emerging threats. Part V probes into the technologies shaping the future of healthcare, such as 5G and beyond, quantum computing, and AI, while addressing their implications for security and resilience in this sector.

Chapter 17 begins by exploring 5G and beyond technologies and their impact on the IoMT. 5G's capabilities, including enhanced connectivity, ultra-low latency, and support for massive IoT networks, open new possibilities for real-time patient monitoring, telemedicine, and AI-driven diagnostics. However, these advancements also expand the attack surface and introduce vulnerabilities, requiring adherence to regulatory frameworks, industry collaboration, and research to mitigate risks proactively.

Chapter 18 focuses on quantum computing, a groundbreaking technology threatening traditional security systems. Because it can potentially disrupt widely used cryptographic methods, quantum computing necessitates the adoption of quantum-resistant cryptography, quantum-safe network protocols, and innovative approaches such as quantum-enhanced anomaly detection.

This part concludes with Chapter 19 and examines AI-driven attacks and defenses in healthcare, highlighting AI's role in enabling and countering cyber threats. While AI has empowered attackers to execute sophisticated phishing, ransomware, and impersonation attacks, it also offers advanced defenses such as predictive threat detection, automated incident response, and intelligent access control. The chapter addresses the challenges of implementing AI-driven defenses, ethical considerations, and the future AI-powered trends in cybersecurity. By exploring these topics, Part V provides an understanding of the emerging technologies and threats poised to redefine healthcare security.

CHAPTER 17

5G and Beyond and Implications for IoMT Security

The IoMT is at the forefront of healthcare delivery, making it more efficient, personalized, and connected. With the arrival of 5G and beyond technologies, the potential is set to reach new heights. These technologies promise advancements in connectivity, data transmission, and medical applications. This chapter discusses these technologies and some new challenges, especially concerning security.

Introduction to 5G and Beyond Technologies

5G, or the fifth generation of cellular network technology, represents a leap forward in wireless communication. It offers higher data transfer speeds, lower latency, and enhanced connectivity than earlier generations, such as 4G LTE. 5G technology supports a broader range of applications, from mobile broadband to mission critical communications and massive IoMT medical deployments.

The key features of 5G include the following:

- **Enhanced Mobile Broadband (eMBB):** This feature supports exceptionally high data rates, enabling seamless streaming, virtual reality (VR), augmented reality (AR), and other data-intensive applications. eMBB improves user experiences by delivering faster downloads and uninterrupted connectivity.

- **Ultra-Reliable Low-Latency Communications (URLLC):** URLLC is designed for mission-critical applications that demand minimal delay and high reliability. It supports applications like autonomous vehicles, remote surgeries, and industrial automation, where real-time communication is essential.
- **Massive Machine-Type Communications (mMTC):** mMTC facilitates large-scale connectivity for IoT devices. It enables networks to handle billions of connected devices, making it ideal for smart cities, agriculture, and environmental monitoring.

While 5G represents a big step forward, sixth generation (6G) technologies are expected to expand communication capabilities even further. These advancements address emerging needs in speed, capacity, intelligence, and security. Planned 6G technology is expected to integrate enhanced sensing capabilities alongside ultra-fast data transmission. One of the key focuses of 6G will be on providing exact location services and developing advanced sensor networks. Unlike current systems, 6G aims to enable centimeter-level positioning accuracy, which will be crucial for applications such as autonomous vehicles, smart cities, healthcare monitoring, and industrial automation. Enhanced sensing features will allow networks to communicate data and sense their environment, enabling capabilities like object detection, gesture recognition, and even environmental monitoring. These innovations will be made possible through technologies such as terahertz (THz) communication, intelligent reflecting surfaces (IRSs), and AI-driven network management.

As for the estimated timeline, 6G development is in its early research and standardization phases. Many industry experts and organizations predict that the first commercial 6G networks will begin rolling out around 2030, following extensive testing and standard development throughout the late 2020s. In the meantime, the focus remains on advancing beyond 5G (B5G) technologies, which aim to enhance the performance of current 5G networks by improving speed, reducing latency, and enabling more reliable connectivity. B5G deployment and innovations are anticipated to be widespread between 2025 and 2028, bridging the gap toward the eventual launch of 6G.

The key features of 6G include:

- **Terahertz (THz) communications:** 6G is expected to utilize terahertz frequency bands, enabling data rates up to 100 times faster than 5G. THz communication will support ultra-high-definition holographic displays, extended reality (XR), and advanced imaging applications.
- **Artificial intelligence or AI integration:** AI will be deeply embedded into 6G networks, enabling intelligent resource allocation, predictive maintenance, and automated decision-making. AI-driven networks will improve efficiency, adaptability, and responsiveness.
- **Quantum communications:** Leveraging the principles of quantum mechanics, 6G aims to introduce quantum encryption and ultra-secure communication channels. This feature will enhance data security and ensure resistance to hacking attempts, even with advances in quantum computing.

- **Holographic communications:** 6G is estimated to include introducing holographic communication systems, which allow realistic 3D projections for remote meetings, telemedicine, and virtual collaboration and provide immersive experiences.

The evolution from 5G to 6G represents a shift toward faster, more intelligent, and more secure communication systems. While 5G has already started transforming industries with enhanced broadband and low-latency capabilities, 6G promises to push boundaries further with terahertz communication, AI integration, and quantum security. These technologies will reshape how we connect, communicate, and drive innovations in healthcare, smart cities, and beyond.

Impact of 5G on IoMT

I'll look at the impact of 5G and beyond technologies on IoMT. In the following sections, I'll focus on how these technologies enhance connectivity, enable real-time data transmission, and improve healthcare outcomes through advanced applications like telemedicine, medical imaging, and AI-driven diagnostics:

Increased Connectivity for Comprehensive Patient Monitoring   IoMT systems often consist of massive networks of connected devices. Traditional networks struggle to handle the volume and density of these connections. At a minimum, the impact of 5G incorporates the following:

- **Support for more IoT networks:** 5G networks can support up to 1 million devices per square kilometer, ensuring seamless connectivity for many medical devices. This capability allows comprehensive patient monitoring in hospitals, homes, and remote areas.

- **Seamless interoperability:** 5G enables better integration between IoMT devices, electronic health records, and other systems, creating a holistic view of patient health.

For example, a rural clinic with limited resources can connect multiple wearable health monitors and diagnostic tools to a central system via 5G, providing doctors real-time insights into patients' health.

Real-Time Data Transmission for Critical Medical Operations   In healthcare, milliseconds can matter. IoMT devices often require real-time data transfer to support critical applications such as remote surgeries and emergency monitoring. The impact that 5G brings to the table includes:

- **Ultra-low latency:** 5G networks offer latency as low as 1 millisecond, enabling near-instantaneous communication between IoMT devices. This is crucial for applications like robotic-assisted surgeries and rapid response systems.

- **Continuous data flow:** This feature enables uninterrupted monitoring of vital signs, ensuring that anomalies are detected and addressed in real time.

An example would be a cardiac patient's wearable monitor, which can instantly alert healthcare providers of irregularities, allowing immediate intervention and potentially saving lives.

Enhanced Telemedicine Through High-Quality Connectivity Telemedicine has become a post-pandemic cornerstone of modern healthcare. Its success hinges on higher-quality communication. 5G facilitates telemedicine with:

- **High-definition videoconferencing:** 5G's high bandwidth supports HD and 4K video streams with minimal buffering, improving the quality of remote consultations.
- **AR/VR applications:** This technology enables augmented and virtual reality tools for remote medical training and patient engagement, enhancing the effectiveness of telemedicine.

For example, a specialist in an urban center can use VR tools to guide a rural healthcare worker through a complex procedure, ensuring better outcomes in remote areas.

Improved Medical Imaging with Faster Data Transfer Medical imaging technologies like MRIs and CT scans produce considerable data, which can be challenging to transfer and analyze quickly. With 5G, we get improvements such as:

- **Rapid data transmission:** 5G supports gigabit-level speeds, enabling the swift transfer of large imaging files.
- **Cloud-based processing:** Facilitates real-time analysis of imaging data via cloud-based AI tools, accelerating diagnostics and treatment planning.

For example, a radiologist can instantly access and review an MRI scan from a remote imaging center, providing faster diagnoses and improving outcomes.

AI-Driven Diagnostics for Personalized Healthcare We know that artificial intelligence is central in the evolution of IoMT, offering capabilities like predictive analytics and personalized treatment recommendations. 5G helps that initiative with:

- **Real-time data analysis:** The high speeds and low latency of 5G allow AI models to analyze patient data in real time, detecting conditions like arrhythmias or early signs of sepsis.
- **Personalized treatment plans:** AI-driven insights tailored to individual patients can be delivered instantly, improving the precision of interventions.

An example use case would be a wearable device for diabetic patients that analyzes glucose levels in real time, integrates the data with AI algorithms, and recommends insulin adjustments. This would be facilitated by 5G connectivity.

While there are many benefits of 5G for IoMT, they also bring unique challenges and security considerations such as:

- **Expanded attack surface:** With more connected devices, the potential entry points for cyberattacks increase.
- **Data privacy concerns:** Rapidly transmitting and storing sensitive medical data require better encryption and access controls.
- **Reliability:** Ensuring uninterrupted 5G connectivity is critical for applications like remote surgery.

Part IV's recommendations include implementing network slicing to isolate critical IoMT traffic, using AI-driven intrusion detection systems to identify and mitigate threats in real time, and adopting zero-trust architectures to ensure only authorized devices and users access the network.

Security Implications for IoMT

This section will focus on the security implications of 5G and beyond technologies for IoMT, examining how these advancements introduce vulnerabilities that healthcare providers must address. I'll look at the obvious implications of an expanded attack surface, network slicing, edge computing security, AI, and quantum computing threats. I'll break these out into security implications versus mitigation options to counteract them and end with an example.

Expanded Attack Surface The IoMT ecosystem is growing with 5G, enabling the connection of more devices. While this supports better patient care, it also creates a larger attack surface for potential cyber threats. For up-to-date and reliable projections on the growth of the IoMT ecosystem, particularly about 5G-enabled connectivity, several industry reports and sources provide solid data and forecasts. Here are some reputable references you can look into:

- **MarketsandMarkets' IoMT Market Report:** Their reports often forecast the IoMT market size and growth. For example, they project the IoMT market to grow from $41 billion in 2020 to over $176 billion by 2026. They also cover how 5G will support more connected medical devices, enabling real-time data transmission and remote care.
- **Fortune Business Insights' IoMT Market Research Report:** This report predicts significant growth, estimating the market will reach $187.60 billion by 2028, driven by 5G connectivity, AI, and telemedicine expansion.
- **Ericsson Mobility Report:** While not specific to IoMT alone, Ericsson frequently discusses how 5G will expand IoT applications across industries, including healthcare. They offer projections for the number of cellular IoT connections, which are expected to surpass 5 billion by 2028, with healthcare being a primary use case.
- **Statista's IoMT and Connected Devices Statistics:** Statista provides data on the increasing number of connected medical devices. For example, they report that by 2030, the number of connected IoMT devices could reach 50 billion, reflecting rapid adoption due to 5G's capabilities.

- **Deloitte Insights' 5G in Healthcare:** Deloitte offers detailed reports on how 5G will impact healthcare, including expectations for device connectivity and market growth. They emphasize how 5G will enable remote patient monitoring and real-time diagnostics, driving IoMT expansion.
- **International Data Corporation (IDC):** IDC often releases forecasts on IoT and healthcare devices. They predict healthcare IoT spending will reach $176 billion by 2026, much of it fueled by 5G-enhanced connectivity and data handling.

Security implications include:

- **More entry points for attackers:** Each connected device represents a potentially exploitable vulnerability.
- **Device heterogeneity:** IoMT devices range from wearable monitors to complex imaging systems, each with varying security capabilities.
- **Insecure devices:** Many IoMT devices lack security features due to resource constraints, making them easy targets for attackers.

Mitigation strategies include:

- Conduct regular device audits to ensure all devices meet minimum security standards.
- Network segmentation isolates IoMT devices from broader networks, limits lateral movement during attacks, and/or breaks the larger ecosystem into smaller targets.
- Implement zero trust architecture, ensuring each device must authenticate before accessing network resources.

For example, a cyberattack targeting a hospital exploits vulnerabilities in older IoMT devices, allowing attackers to infiltrate critical systems. Proper network segmentation could have contained the attack.

Network Slicing Vulnerabilities Network slicing in 5G allows operators to create virtualized network segments tailored for specific applications, such as IoMT. Each slice can have dedicated resources and performance requirements. Network slicing is a key feature in 5G, allowing multiple virtual networks to exist within the same physical network.

Security implications include:

- **Inter-slice attacks:** Misconfigurations or vulnerabilities in one slice could allow attackers to breach it and move laterally to other slices.
- **Isolation challenges:** Ensuring complete isolation between slices is complex and requires specific security policies.
- **Slice-specific threats:** IoMT slices, carrying sensitive healthcare data, may become high-value targets for attackers.

Mitigation strategies include:

- Use stricter access controls and real-time monitoring to detect and prevent unauthorized access to slices.
- Regularly audit slice configurations to identify and address vulnerabilities.
- Implement AI-powered monitoring tools to identify anomalies specific to IoMT slices.

A misconfigured network slice, for example, that is used for IoMT monitoring, allows unauthorized access to another slice hosting patient data, resulting in a data breach.

Edge Computing Security Edge computing in 5G brings data processing closer to the source, such as IoMT devices, reducing latency and improving performance. 5G adds high bandwidth and low latency capabilities for edge computing.

Security implications include:

- **Decentralized security risks:** Maintaining consistent security policies becomes challenging with data processed at multiple edge locations.
- **Physical security:** Edge nodes in less secure environments may be vulnerable to tampering or theft.
- **Data breaches:** Compromised edge nodes can expose sensitive patient data or disrupt critical services.

Mitigation strategies include:

- Deploy tamper-proof hardware and secure enclosures for edge devices.
- Use stronger encryption for data in transit and at rest to protect information processed at the edge.
- Implement zero trust principles at the edge, ensuring continuous authentication and monitoring.

An example would be a physically tampered-with edge node at a remote clinic, which exposed sensitive data. Tamper-proof hardware and encryption could have prevented this breach.

AI-Related Threats AI is integral to IoMT, enabling advanced analytics, predictive diagnostics, and personalized treatment. However, it introduces vulnerabilities, which I will explain in Chapter 19.

Security implications include:

- **Adversarial attacks:** Attackers can manipulate input data to deceive AI models, leading to incorrect diagnoses or alerts.
- **Biased decision-making:** Poorly trained models may inadvertently prioritize certain patient groups, undermining trust in AI-driven systems.
- **Data poisoning:** Attackers can introduce malicious data during training, compromising the model's accuracy and reliability.

Mitigation strategies include:

- Train AI models using diverse and high-quality datasets to minimize bias.
- Deploy adversarial machine learning defenses to detect and mitigate manipulated inputs.
- Use explainable AI or XAI to ensure transparency in AI decision-making processes.

For example, an adversarial attack manipulates an AI system analyzing ECG data, causing false alarms. Regular testing and the use of adversarial defenses can safeguard such systems.

Quantum Computing Threats While still in their infancy, quantum computers have the potential to break classical encryption methods, posing a significant risk to IoMT data security.

Security implications include:

- **Vulnerability of current encryption:** Many IoMT systems rely on RSA and ECC encryption, which quantum computers could eventually decrypt.
- **Future-proofing IoMT:** Transitioning to quantum-resistant cryptographic algorithms is necessary to ensure long-term security.

Mitigation strategies include:

- Begin adopting post-quantum cryptography (PQC) algorithms designed to resist quantum attacks.
- Use hybrid encryption systems, combining classical and quantum-resistant methods for gradual transitions.
- Stay informed about advancements in quantum computing and update security policies proactively.

For example, a healthcare provider may implement quantum-resistant encryption for IoMT data, ensuring its security even in the face of future quantum computing threats.

Regulatory Considerations

Now that I have reviewed some of the leading security implications of 5G and beyond, I'll discuss the regulatory considerations, focusing on updated security standards, privacy regulations, interoperability requirements, and certification programs. Understanding these aspects is essential for ensuring compliance, safeguarding patient data, and fostering trust in this advancing landscape.

Updated Standards for 5G and IoMT Security Updated security standards have become a top priority with the rapid adoption of 5G networks and IoMT devices. 5G introduces new capabilities such as low latency, massive connectivity, and network slicing, enabling healthcare applications like remote patient monitoring and telemedicine. However, these advancements also create new vulnerabilities that demand tailored security measures. To address these challenges, regulatory bodies are focusing on three primary areas.

First, it is critical to develop 5G-specific security standards. These standards define protocols to secure network slicing, edge computing, and IoMT data transmission. They also anticipate emerging threats, including vulnerabilities posed by quantum computing and AI-driven attacks, ensuring resilience against evolving risks.

Second, global coordination of security standards is essential to supporting international healthcare operations and collaborations. Aligning standards across regions allows seamless data exchange and interoperability vital in emergencies and multinational research efforts.

Finally, standards must remain dynamic. Continuous updates are necessary to keep pace with evolving technologies and threats and maintain the integrity of healthcare ecosystems. Several frameworks provide a foundation for securing 5G and IoMT devices. The National Institute of Standards and Technology (NIST) Cybersecurity Framework offers comprehensive guidelines for protecting IoMT networks and devices, focusing on risk assessment, mitigation, and incident response. Similarly, the 3rd Generation Partnership Project (3GPP) standards address 5G-specific security needs, including enhanced authentication mechanisms and robust encryption protocols to safeguard sensitive communications.

Despite these advancements, implementing security standards comes with challenges. One hurdle is balancing security with performance, especially for IoMT devices with limited processing power and battery life. Ensuring compliance across a diverse range of devices and manufacturers also complicates the process, requiring flexible yet rigorous approaches to enforcement.

As we progress, regulatory bodies must work closely with industry stakeholders, including device manufacturers, healthcare providers, and security researchers. Collaboration is key to developing practical, enforceable standards that address real-world 5G and IoMT security challenges.

Privacy Regulations for Data Protection Privacy is a fundamental concern in healthcare as systems collect and transmit sensitive health data. The enhanced data collection and connectivity enabled by 5G networks make protecting patient privacy critical. Ensuring compliance with privacy regulations is essential to safeguard patient trust and data security. Several privacy regulations set the foundation for protecting sensitive medical data. GDPR applies to organizations handling data of EU citizens, regardless of location. It emphasizes data minimization, consent management, and patient rights, giving individuals greater control over their data. Organizations must ensure transparency and accountability in collecting, processing, and storing data.

HIPAA mandates electronically protected health information safeguards, including encryption, access controls, and audit trails to prevent unauthorized access. These safeguards are especially crucial for IoMT devices that store or transmit patient data.

Recognizing the unique challenges IoMT poses, several countries are also developing laws tailored to these technologies. Emerging IoMT-specific regulations address device tracking, remote monitoring, and real-time data transmission risks. These regulations aim to protect patient privacy while enabling the benefits of connected medical technologies.

Compliance can be challenging despite clear regulations, especially for global deployments of IoMT systems. Cross-border compliance is a significant hurdle, as privacy laws vary across regions. Companies must navigate these differences to ensure seamless operation while adhering to legal requirements.

Real-time data processing further complicates compliance, especially with 5G networks enabling rapid transmission of health information. Organizations must implement measures to secure data as it moves across networks while meeting the demands of privacy regulations.

To address these challenges, organizations should adopt privacy-by-design principles during device development. This approach integrates privacy safeguards into the design and architecture of devices from the outset, ensuring compliance is built-in rather than added later. Encryption and access controls should be implemented to protect data at rest and in transit. In addition, regular audits and assessments of IoMT systems are essential. Continuous monitoring helps identify vulnerabilities and ensures compliance with evolving regulations. For example, a hospital using encrypted 5G networks to transmit patient data securely can comply with HIPAA and GDPR, demonstrating a proactive approach to privacy protection.

Interoperability Requirements for Secure IoMT Systems Interoperability is another requirement for secure IoMT systems. 5G's high-speed, low-latency capabilities enable the connection of diverse devices, forming an interconnected ecosystem where different devices must securely communicate and share data. However, these connections can introduce vulnerabilities without clear interoperability standards, risking data breaches and operational failures. Ensuring seamless communication among devices while maintaining security is essential for advancing patient care and protecting sensitive health information.

To address these challenges, regulatory frameworks emphasize several goals to establish secure interoperability. First, standardized protocols like HL7 Fast Healthcare Interoperability Resources (FHIR) and Digital Imaging and Communications in Medicine (DICOM) are critical for defining secure methods of data exchange. These protocols ensure that devices can share information consistently and securely, regardless of the manufacturer or application.

Another key goal is device certification. Before entering the market, regulatory bodies require devices to meet established interoperability and security standards. Certification processes validate compliance, ensuring devices can handle secure communication and data protection.

Cross-vendor compatibility is also a priority. Regulations mandate that devices from different manufacturers must securely interact within the same network. This requirement prevents vendor lock-in and supports scalable, flexible healthcare ecosystems where technologies can evolve without sacrificing security or performance.

The adoption of interoperability standards brings several benefits to IoMT systems. First, it reduces the risk of miscommunication or data loss between devices, improving reliability and accuracy in healthcare delivery. Standardized protocols ensure that data is transferred in a consistent format, minimizing errors caused by incompatible systems.

Interoperability enables seamless system integration. For example, wearable devices, diagnostic tools, and electronic health record systems can share encrypted data over 5G networks in real time. This integration streamlines workflows, enhances clinical decision-making, and improves patient outcomes while maintaining data security.

Next, managing security risks during data exchanges between devices is a challenge with varying security capabilities. While modern devices may support advanced encryption and authentication methods, legacy systems often lack these features, creating vulnerabilities.

Another challenge is ensuring that legacy devices can securely integrate with modern systems. Many older devices were not designed with interoperability or cybersecurity, requiring updates or additional security layers to meet current standards. Organizations must carefully plan and invest in secure transition strategies to bridge the gap between old and new technologies.

Imagine an IoMT ecosystem where wearable devices, diagnostic imaging tools, and EHR systems seamlessly exchange encrypted data over a 5G network. In this scenario, interoperability standards enable secure and accurate data sharing, reducing errors and improving clinical efficiency. For example, a wearable glucose monitor can transmit real-time data to an EHR system, alerting healthcare providers about abnormal readings and triggering timely interventions.

Standardized protocols, device certification, and cross-vendor compatibility provide the foundation for safe and scalable healthcare networks. While challenges like legacy system integration remain, the benefits of improved patient care and operational efficiency underscore the importance of adopting and enforcing interoperability standards.

Certification Programs for IoMT Security Certification programs ensure that devices meet established security standards. These certifications help reduce vulnerabilities, protect sensitive health data, and build trust among healthcare providers, regulators, and patients. Given the critical nature of IoMT systems, certification provides assurance that devices are designed and tested to withstand potential threats.

Effective certification programs incorporate several key features to evaluate and maintain the security of these devices. The foundation is comprehensive testing, which assesses devices for encryption strength, authentication mechanisms, and resistance to known vulnerabilities. This testing identifies weaknesses before devices reach the market, minimizing the risk of exploitation.

Another essential feature is ongoing monitoring. Security threats evolve, making periodic certification renewal necessary. This approach ensures that devices are updated and compliant with the latest standards. Additionally, certifications should be globally recognized to streamline compliance for manufacturers operating across multiple regions. Standardized global acceptance reduces duplication of efforts and simplifies regulatory approval processes.

Several certification programs and frameworks currently guide IoMT security practices. The FDA Premarket Guidance mandates that manufacturers address cybersecurity risks during device design and submission phases in the United States. This proactive approach ensures that security is integrated into products from the outset.

The ISO/IEC 27001 standard focuses on information security management and applies to IoMT systems. It provides a systematic framework for managing sensitive data, identifying risks, and implementing controls to mitigate potential threats.

The UL Cybersecurity Assurance Program (CAP) is another example, specifically evaluating IoT and IoMT devices for cybersecurity resilience. It assesses products against industry best practices, certifying them based on their ability to withstand real-world attacks.

Despite their benefits, implementing certification programs present challenges. The rapid pace of innovation in technologies like 5G and IoMT often inhibits the ability of certification processes to keep up. New features and functionalities may introduce vulnerabilities that existing frameworks do not address. Small-scale manufacturers may face difficulties meeting stringent certification requirements due to limited resources. This can lead to delays in product releases or a lack of compliance in resource-constrained markets.

To address these challenges, tiered certification programs can be introduced. These programs would establish security standards based on device complexity, ensuring that simpler devices meet appropriate levels of security without imposing unnecessary burdens. Public-private partnerships can also help streamline certification development and enforcement. Collaboration between governments, industry leaders, and academic institutions can accelerate the creation of adaptable frameworks that keep pace with technological advancements.

Consider an IoMT manufacturer developing a 5G-enabled wearable device for continuous patient monitoring. By undergoing UL certification, the manufacturer ensures that its product complies with global security standards, enhancing marketability and patient trust. The certification process also prepares the device for regulatory approval in multiple regions, simplifying global rollout.

Future Research Directions

The future of 5G and IoMT security relies on research areas that address emerging threats and vulnerabilities as these systems become more integrated and data-intensive, advancements in post-quantum cryptography. AI-based anomaly detection, secure edge computing, blockchain integration, and biometric authentication should be considered. These technologies aim to enhance data protection, improve threat detection, and create resilient systems to safeguard patient safety.

Quantum computing, which I'll discuss in more detail in Chapter 18, poses a challenge to traditional encryption methods. Quantum computers could break these encryption standards, necessitating the development of quantum-resistant cryptographic techniques. Research efforts focus on creating algorithms like lattice-based, hash-based, and code-based cryptography that can withstand quantum attacks. Hybrid cryptographic systems are also being explored to combine traditional methods with quantum-resistant algorithms, enabling a gradual transition without compromising backward compatibility. Additionally, researchers are designing efficient implementations of these algorithms that can operate on resource-constrained IoMT devices without impacting performance.

Despite these advancements, challenges remain, such as balancing computational complexity with device limitations and ensuring interoperability between legacy systems and quantum-secure technologies. Organizations like NIST are already working on standardizing post-quantum cryptographic algorithms to prepare IoMT systems for the future.

AI, which I'll visit in Chapter 19, offers advanced capabilities to monitor and secure IoMT systems by detecting unusual patterns that may indicate threats. Research focuses on developing machine learning models, including unsupervised and reinforcement learning algorithms, to detect unknown and evolving threats. Explainable AI (XAI) is also prioritized to ensure that anomaly detection systems produce interpretable results for healthcare professionals. Behavioral analytics and AI can establish baselines for device activity and flag deviations, improving threat detection. Additionally, AI models are optimized for real-time processing in low latency 5G environments.

However, reducing false positives and negatives remains challenging, as does preserving data privacy while using patient information to train AI models. AI-powered anomaly detection systems, such as those that monitor wearable devices for unusual activity, demonstrate how these technologies can prevent breaches and protect sensitive data.

With 5G enabling edge computing, data processing is moving closer to IoMT devices. While this reduces latency and enhances performance, it also introduces new risks. Research is focused on designing edge-specific security architectures, such as lightweight, decentralized protocols tailored for edge environments. Zero Trust frameworks, which require continuous authentication and monitoring of devices, are also being developed to secure edge nodes. Data privacy remains a key priority, with efforts to process sensitive data locally without compromising confidentiality. Additionally, AI integration within edge nodes enhances real-time threat detection and response capabilities.

Some other challenges include protecting edge nodes from physical and cyber tampering and maintaining consistent security policies across decentralized networks. Standards like those from ETSI on multi-access edge computing (MEC) are helping address these issues. Blockchain technology offers a decentralized, tamper-proof ledger to enhance the security and transparency of systems. It provides solutions for secure data sharing, authentication, and compliance tracking. Research is exploring the use of blockchain to verify the authenticity and integrity of medical data and decentralized identity management for secure device authentication. Smart contracts automate compliance and data-sharing agreements, improving efficiency and security. Efforts are underway to develop lightweight blockchain solutions capable of handling the high transaction volume in IoMT networks.

Additional challenges include addressing blockchain's computational and energy demands for resource-constrained devices and ensuring compatibility with existing infrastructure. Applications such as blockchain-based systems for securely recording patient data interactions illustrate its potential for improving trust and security.

Biometric authentication provides a secure and user-friendly alternative to passwords, ensuring that only authorized users can access devices and data. Research is focused on multi-modal biometrics, which combines multiple identifiers, such as fingerprints, iris scans, and voice recognition, for enhanced security. Biometric encryption is also being explored, using biometric data as cryptographic keys to secure devices and information. Wearable integration is another area of interest, as well as embedding biometric sensors into IoMT devices for continuous authentication. AI is being leveraged to improve the accuracy and reliability of biometric systems.

Other challenges include securely storing biometric data to prevent theft or misuse and addressing biases or accessibility issues in biometric technologies. Integrating biometric authentication in smartwatches to grant access to health data highlights how this approach can improve security without sacrificing usability.

Industry Collaboration and Knowledge Sharing

Securing the IoMT in the 5G era and beyond requires more than isolated efforts. It demands collaboration across industries, public and private sectors, and academic disciplines. Stakeholders can build more secure and resilient ecosystems by pooling resources, expertise, and knowledge. In this section, I'll discuss the importance of collaboration, focusing on public-private partnerships, information-sharing platforms, and cross-disciplinary research as essential strategies for addressing security challenges and driving innovation.

Public-private partnerships are vital in securing IoMT systems. They unite government agencies, healthcare providers, and technology companies, each bringing unique expertise. Government agencies contribute regulatory oversight, funding, and national security insights. Healthcare providers offer practical perspectives on IoMT implementation, while technology companies provide the infrastructure, devices, and security solutions.

Key collaborative actions include policy development, where governments work with industry leaders to establish security standards for 5G-enabled IoMT systems. For instance, the U.S. FDA collaborates with device manufacturers to define cybersecurity guidelines for medical devices. Joint funding initiatives like the EU's Horizon Europe program also drive innovation. These initiatives support research into secure IoMT technologies like post-quantum cryptography and AI-based monitoring tools. In addition, coordinated incident response frameworks help address large-scale cyberattacks, ensuring swift action to protect healthcare systems.

The benefits of these partnerships are clear. They streamline regulatory compliance, accelerate the deployment of innovative security solutions, and improve resilience against national and global cyber threats. For example, during the COVID-19 pandemic, public-private partnerships enabled the rapid deployment of secure telemedicine platforms, demonstrating the value of collaboration in crisis response.

Consider information-sharing platforms essential for exchanging threat intelligence, best practices, and lessons learned. Threat intelligence sharing allows organizations to share real-time data on vulnerabilities and exploits. For example, healthcare providers can notify others about ransomware attacks, enabling them to reinforce their defenses. Centralized repositories of best practices and case studies also help organizations implement proven security strategies. Collaborative incident databases document security events, providing insights into trends and recurring vulnerabilities.

Existing initiatives, such as the Health Information Sharing and Analysis Center (H-ISAC), enable organizations to exchange information specific to healthcare cybersecurity. Government-led platforms, like the U.S. Cybersecurity and Infrastructure Security Agency (CISA), support information sharing across critical infrastructure sectors, including healthcare.

Challenges in information sharing include concerns over privacy and competition. Organizations may hesitate to share sensitive data, fearing misuse. Solutions such as anonymized data sharing and legal protections can address these concerns. Another challenge is the lack of standardization in data formats, which can be resolved by adopting frameworks like STIX (Structured Threat Information Expression). Effective information sharing reduces response times to vulnerabilities, increases awareness of emerging threats, and strengthens collective defenses against cyberattacks. Organizations can avoid evolving threats by promoting collaboration and enhancing overall security. Medical professionals and cybersecurity experts can also work together to design secure IoMT devices. For example, creating an infusion pump that prioritizes both functionality and security requires input from clinicians and security engineers. Similarly, network engineers and device manufacturers can optimize 5G infrastructure while integrating strong security features into IoMT devices.

Academic institutions also play a key role, partnering with industry to prototype and test innovative technologies like AI-powered anomaly detection systems.

Encouraging more collaboration through joint research programs and hackathons is a practical approach. Government and industry stakeholders can fund collaborative projects focused on IoMT security challenges. Initiatives like the U.K.'s Digital Catapult promote innovation by supporting 5G and IoMT research. Hackathons and competitions also bring together experts to tackle specific security problems, accelerating innovation and knowledge transfer.

By fostering collaboration, the healthcare industry can build resilient, secure, and scalable IoMT ecosystems capable of addressing evolving threats. Students preparing to work in this field must recognize the importance of teamwork, communication, and shared knowledge in driving advancements in security.

Key Takeaways of 5G and Beyond and Implications for IoMT Security

This chapter highlights the dual-edged nature of 5G and beyond technologies in the IoMT, emphasizing the vast opportunities for advancing healthcare and the pressing need for more robust security measures. The transformational impact of these technologies includes enhanced connectivity that supports seamless integration of IoMT devices, enabling real-time patient monitoring and interconnected healthcare systems. Ultra-low latency facilitates instant communication vital for remote surgeries and emergency alerts, while high bandwidth enhances telemedicine and rapid transmission of large medical imaging files. AI-driven diagnostics leverage real-time data to enable personalized treatments and early disease detection.

However, the proliferation of connected devices also expands the attack surface, exposing vulnerabilities in network slicing, edge computing, and AI systems, with future quantum computing posing additional encryption threats. Regulatory bodies must develop updated security standards to address these risks and ensure privacy compliance while fostering interoperability across diverse IoMT ecosystems. Future research must focus on post-quantum cryptography, AI-based anomaly detection, secure edge computing, blockchain integration, and biometric authentication to fortify IoMT environments. Moreover, public-private partnerships and cross-disciplinary collaboration are essential for knowledge sharing, policy development, and effective cybersecurity responses. Ultimately, balancing innovation and security through proactive collaboration, continuous research, and comprehensive regulations is key to unlocking the full potential of 5G-enabled IoMT while safeguarding patient safety, data privacy, and healthcare operations.

CHAPTER 18

Quantum Computing in Medical Device Security

Quantum computing represents a paradigm shift in computational power and capabilities, with implications for various medical device security fields. As quantum computers become more advanced and accessible, they present opportunities and challenges for securing medical devices and associated data. This chapter explores the intersection of quantum computing with medical device security, covering key concepts, potential applications, challenges, and future directions. The goal is to arm you with knowledge to help you prepare for the quantum era.

Fundamentals of Quantum Computing

This chapter on quantum computing gets a bit in the weeds, technically, and therefore, I'll start with a simplified synopsis in this section on the fundamentals. If you choose to read my overview and then move on to the next chapter, know that there are great books and other resources you can find online offering various perspectives, with some boiling the concepts down to the basics.

That said, imagine you're using a super-advanced computer that doesn't just follow the usual on-or-off logic of regular computers. Well, quantum computers use qubits that can be both on and off simultaneously, thanks to a property called *superposition*. This makes them incredibly fast and powerful for solving complex problems, like analyzing vast amounts of data or cracking encryption.

Now, here's the kicker for healthcare and other industries. This same power could threaten the way we protect sensitive data. For instance, quantum computers could break standard encryption to secure medical records and device communications. This means attackers could access private patient information or take control of medical devices.

The healthcare industry is investigating quantum-resistant encryption to protect against this, a new type of security that even quantum computers can't crack. One example is Quantum Key Distribution, which uses quantum physics rules to send encryption keys securely. Because the quantum state changes, the system immediately knows if anyone tries to intercept these keys. It's like having an alarm system built into the data.

Quantum technology also helps with security in other ways. Quantum random number generators create truly random numbers for stronger encryption, and quantum machine learning can detect unusual patterns in data, like someone tampering with a device.

But quantum isn't just about risks; it also opens doors to amazing possibilities. For example, quantum sensors could make MRIs so sensitive that they detect diseases earlier than ever. Another example would be quantum clocks, which could make surgeries even more precise by perfectly syncing medical devices.

Of course, there are challenges. Quantum computers are still experimental, and building systems to work with them takes time. Healthcare organizations must start preparing now, exploring quantum-safe technologies, and staying ahead of the curve to protect patients and keep systems secure. This exciting future requires thoughtful planning and collaboration across the industry.

Consider this for the more technical reader: unlike classical computers that rely on binary bits representing 0s and 1s, quantum computers use quantum bits (the previously mentioned qubits). Qubits harness the principles of quantum mechanics, enabling them to exist simultaneously in multiple states, known as superposition. This property allows quantum computers to process a massive number of possibilities at once, providing an exponential increase in computational power compared to classical systems. For example, while a classical computer processes data sequentially, a quantum computer can evaluate many solutions simultaneously, making it exceptionally powerful for tasks like cryptographic analysis or complex simulations.

Another fundamental concept in quantum computing is quantum entanglement, where pairs or groups of qubits become interconnected, such that the state of one qubit is directly related to the state of the others, regardless of distance. This entanglement enables enhanced computational capabilities and is a cornerstone of quantum algorithms and secure quantum communication protocols. For medical device security, entanglement could pave the way for more secure communication methods by allowing encrypted messages to be transmitted and decoded using quantum keys that are inherently tamper aware. If an attacker attempts to intercept the communication, the quantum state of the entangled particles changes, alerting the system to the intrusion.

Despite its potential, quantum computing faces challenges, the chief one of which is quantum decoherence. Decoherence occurs when qubits lose their quantum properties due to interactions with the surrounding environment, such as temperature fluctuations or electromagnetic interference. This instability results in errors and limits the practical usability of quantum computers. Overcoming decoherence requires highly controlled environments and advanced correction techniques, which are major hurdles in building large-scale quantum systems. For the healthcare industry, addressing decoherence will be critical to ensure the reliability and accuracy of quantum-powered security solutions for medical devices.

Understanding the fundamentals of quantum computing, such as qubits, entanglement, and decoherence, is essential for leveraging its potential in medical device security. By employing these principles, quantum technology promises to enhance encryption, optimize device functionality, and bolster the overall resilience of healthcare systems against evolving cyber threats.

Potential Applications in Medical Device Security

Quantum computing holds potential for medical device security by addressing some of the most pressing challenges in safeguarding systems. One of the most promising applications is quantum cryptography, mainly through quantum key distribution (QKD). QKD leverages the principles of quantum mechanics to securely distribute encryption keys between devices, ensuring that any interception attempt alters the quantum state and immediately alerts the parties involved. This method provides (theoretically) unbreakable encryption, making it an ideal solution for protecting sensitive medical data transmitted between devices, such as electronic health records or real-time telemetry from wearable health monitors.

Another application is quantum random number generation (QRNG), which generates true random numbers by utilizing the inherently unpredictable behavior of quantum particles. Unlike traditional random number generators that rely on deterministic algorithms, QRNG produces fundamentally unpredictable numbers, significantly enhancing the strength of encryption keys and other security protocols. For medical devices, QRNG can ensure that cryptographic systems remain resilient against even the most sophisticated attacks, providing an added layer of security for patient data and device communication.

With Quantum Machine Learning (QML), quantum computers promise to enhance anomaly detection and data analysis. By processing large datasets with quantum algorithms, QML can identify complex patterns and subtle irregularities in device behavior, enabling proactive identification of cybersecurity threats. For instance, QML could detect unusual network traffic patterns or anomalies in device functionality that may indicate a potential breach. Moreover, its real-time medical data analysis supports advancements in personalized medicine, optimizing both security and patient outcomes.

Quantum simulation offers new capabilities for modeling complex biological systems and predicting cybersecurity threats. Quantum computers can simulate molecular interactions and biological processes, accelerating drug discovery and the development of personalized treatments. In medical device security, quantum simulation could model attack scenarios, anticipate vulnerabilities, and design more robust countermeasures before threats materialize. Healthcare organizations can stay ahead of emerging cybersecurity challenges by understanding and predicting potential attack vectors. My colleagues and I are incredibly excited about the proactiveness we can expect from this technology.

Challenges Posed by Quantum Computing

Quantum computing poses some challenges to the security of medical devices in the context of cryptography, data integrity, authentication protocols, and long-term data security. These challenges necessitate action to safeguard sensitive healthcare systems from future quantum-enabled threats.

One of the concerns is cryptographic vulnerabilities due to Shor's algorithm, which can efficiently factor large numbers and solve discrete logarithms. This capability directly threatens widely used public-key cryptography systems such as RSA (Rivest-Shamir-Adleman) and ECC (Elliptic Curve Cryptography), which underpin the security of many medical devices. These cryptosystems are crucial for securing device communication, encrypting patient data, and authenticating users. A quantum computer equipped with Shor's algorithm could decrypt these systems, exposing sensitive medical data and enabling unauthorized control of critical devices. Transitioning to quantum-resistant cryptographic algorithms, such as lattice-based cryptography, is essential to mitigate this risk. If you are unfamiliar with Shor's algorithm, it was developed by mathematician Peter Shor in 1994. Since it is designed to factorize large integers, it solves a computationally difficult problem, and in some cases, impossible, for classical computers.

Another challenge is maintaining data integrity. Quantum algorithms could weaken the effectiveness of traditional hash functions used for integrity checks, creating vulnerabilities in medical device logs and data storage systems. In this context, hash functions are cryptographic algorithms that take an input (or "message") and produce a fixed-size string of characters, typically a sequence of numbers and letters, known as a hash value or digest. They are designed to represent data uniquely and are commonly used to verify data integrity—ensuring that information, such as medical device logs and stored records, has not been tampered with or altered. If even a tiny change occurs in the input data, the hash function will produce a vastly different output, signaling potential data corruption or unauthorized modifications. However, quantum algorithms threaten to undermine the security of traditional hash functions by making it easier to find two different inputs that produce the same hash (a collision), potentially compromising their effectiveness in safeguarding data integrity.

Ensuring the authenticity and accuracy of data is critical in healthcare, as even minor errors could lead to incorrect diagnoses or treatment plans. To address this, quantum-resistant hash functions that can withstand the computational power of quantum systems while maintaining the lightweight nature required for IoMT devices, which lack resources, are needed.

Authentication protocols will also be vulnerable in the upcoming quantum age. Many current systems rely on cryptographic primitives that are not resistant to quantum attacks, such as key exchange mechanisms (again based on RSA or ECC). Quantum computing could enable attackers to bypass these protocols, leading to unauthorized access to medical devices or systems. Developing and deploying quantum-safe authentication mechanisms, such as those based on lattice-based or code-based cryptography, will be crucial.

Hardware limitations are among the most pressing issues in the context of implementation challenges. Many IoMT devices, such as wearable monitors, implantable sensors, and remote diagnostic tools, are built with minimal processing power, limited memory, and strict energy constraints to maximize patient comfort and device longevity. These limitations make it challenging to integrate quantum-resistant algorithms, which often require more computational resources and larger key sizes than traditional encryption methods. Additionally, the lack of universally accepted standards for quantum-resistant cryptography in the IoMT sector complicates the situation further. Healthcare providers and medical device manufacturers face uncertainty about which cryptographic protocols to implement, how to maintain interoperability among diverse systems, and how to comply with evolving regulatory requirements. This absence of clear, standardized guidelines delays widespread adoption and increases the risk of inconsistent security measures across different devices and networks. Moreover, the cost implications of upgrading IoMT infrastructures are significant. Updating firmware or replacing hardware to support new cryptographic methods can be prohibitively expensive, particularly for healthcare systems managing extensive networks of medical devices. These financial challenges are compounded by the need to minimize downtime and avoid disruptions in patient care. As a result, healthcare organizations must carefully weigh the costs and logistical complexities of upgrading their IoMT ecosystems against the imperative to protect sensitive patient data from emerging quantum threats.

Finally, long-term data security poses a unique challenge. Quantum computers could facilitate a harvest now and decrypt later attacks, where attackers collect encrypted data and decrypt it when quantum capabilities become available. This concerns healthcare organizations, as patient data often needs to be stored securely for decades. To counter this, it is essential to adopt encryption schemes that offer forward secrecy, which ensures that past data remains secure even if encryption keys are compromised in the future.

Quantum Attack on IoMT Firmware

I've established the foundational threat landscape and the inherent vulnerabilities. Now, I'll visualize a practical, albeit hypothetical, quantum attack. This walkthrough details how a sophisticated adversary might exploit these weaknesses, leveraging the power of a future, sufficiently advanced quantum computer. The attack focuses on a common IoMT scenario: a firmware update process for a smart home medical device. This scenario is chosen for its relative simplicity, yet it encapsulates the core vulnerabilities of many other IoMT devices.

The attack unfolds in several stages: interception, decryption, modification, and re-signing. Each phase relies on specific weaknesses, often related to inadequate cryptographic protections and the target device's limited resources.

Stage 1: Interception

The hypothetical attacker begins by passively monitoring the network traffic between the smart target device and the manufacturer's update server. This is often achievable through network sniffing tools, especially in poorly secured home networks. Many IoMT devices use insecure communication protocols, making the interception process surprisingly straightforward. The attacker captures the firmware update package, typically a digitally signed file containing the new firmware code. This interception is facilitated by the frequently overlooked absence of end-to-end encryption in firmware updates for many IoMT devices. The lack of stronger TLS or similar secure transport protocols renders the communication vulnerable to eavesdropping. This is a critical vulnerability, even independent of quantum computing.

Stage 2: Decryption

The captured firmware update is digitally signed to verify its authenticity and integrity. However, many IoMT devices employ weak cryptographic algorithms for this digital signature, often relying on Elliptic Curve Cryptography (ECC) with relatively short key lengths or RSA with similarly inadequate key sizes. While sufficient against classical computing power, these algorithms are highly vulnerable to a sufficiently powerful quantum computer using Shor's algorithm.

In a quantum application, Shor's algorithm for factoring large numbers and solving the discrete logarithm problem can break these cryptographic schemes exponentially faster than any known classical algorithm. This means that a quantum computer with enough qubits and sufficient error correction could efficiently break the digital signature within a reasonable timeframe, effectively decrypting the firmware update and revealing its contents.

The specific vulnerability here is the choice of a quantum-vulnerable algorithm coupled with insufficient key length, a common oversight in many legacy IoMT devices. The attacker uses their simulated quantum computer (representing future capabilities) to run Shor's algorithm on the intercepted digital signature, breaking the encryption and revealing the original firmware update's contents. The ability to perform this decryption relies heavily on the future availability of sufficiently powerful quantum computers. While current quantum computers are not yet at this stage, the potential threat is undeniable, necessitating proactive measures. This highlights the need for post-quantum cryptography.

Stage 3: Modification

The attacker modifies the code once the firmware update's contents are revealed. The specific modifications depend on the attacker's goals. For instance, the attacker might introduce a backdoor, enabling remote access to the target device. This could allow the attacker to manipulate the target device's settings remotely, potentially for personal gain or malicious purposes. Another possibility is to install a keylogger to steal sensitive data, like Wi-Fi passwords or personal preferences. Even more damaging would be the introduction of malware to allow the target device to participate in a botnet, carrying out distributed denial-of-service (DDoS) attacks on a much larger scale.

The simplicity of the modification step underscores the need for vigorous integrity checks and rigorous code signing practices. The ability to modify the firmware highlights another critical vulnerability: the lack of thorough code signing and verification processes on many older IoMT devices. The success of this step depends heavily on the attacker's knowledge of the device's firmware architecture and ability to modify the code without obvious errors or malfunctions. This stage demands a level of reverse engineering skill, but the inherently limited resources and often poorly documented firmware of many IoMT devices make it feasible.

Stage 4: Re-signing

After modifying the firmware, the attacker must re-sign it to make it appear legitimate to the target device. The attacker cannot simply use the original signature because they've altered the firmware; the signature would no longer be valid. Therefore, the attacker attempts to forge a new digital signature using the same algorithm. This forging process is made possible by breaking the original signature in stage 2. With the original cryptographic keys compromised via Shor's algorithm, the attacker can effectively generate a new digital signature that appears perfectly valid to the target device.

This step requires extensive technical expertise. It involves mimicking the original digital signature algorithm and generating a convincing forgery. However, the inherent weaknesses in many security mechanisms make this a potentially feasible task. The success of this stage is directly linked to the weaknesses exploited in stage 2. Weak cryptographic algorithms and insufficient key lengths make the signature vulnerable to forgery.

Stage 5: Installation and Damage Assessment

Finally, the attacker transmits the modified, re-signed firmware update to the smart target device. Because the target device's weak verification mechanisms fail to detect the forged signature, it installs the malicious firmware. The attacker now has complete control over the target device and can exploit the backdoor or malicious code previously embedded. The consequences can range from inconvenience to life-threatening.

The damage assessment phase evaluates the attack's impact, considering the potential consequences of compromised functionality and data breaches. In more critical scenarios, these could include financial loss, personal data theft, disruptions in medical support, or even physical harm. The successful culmination of the attack highlights the systemic risks associated with vulnerable IoMT firmware and the urgency of mitigating such threats through post-quantum cryptographic solutions and robust security practices. The attack also highlights the importance of adopting quantum-resistant cryptographic algorithms and implementing strong security measures throughout the firmware update lifecycle.

Quantum-Resistant Cryptography for Medical Devices

As quantum computing advances, it threatens traditional cryptographic systems used in medical devices, requiring the transition to quantum-resistant cryptography. These emerging cryptographic approaches, designed to withstand quantum attacks, hold promise for securing the IoMT. In this section, I'll explore key quantum-resistant cryptographic methods, including lattice-based cryptography, hash-based signatures, code-based cryptography, and multivariate cryptography, and their applications in securing medical devices.

Lattice-Based Cryptography Lattice-based cryptography is one of the most promising candidates for post-quantum cryptography. Its security is based on the hardness of lattice problems, such as Learning With Errors (LWE) issues, which are resistant to attacks by both classical and quantum computers.

Lattice-based schemes offer several advantages for medical devices. They are versatile, supporting encryption, digital signatures, and even advanced functionalities like fully homomorphic encryption, which enables computations on encrypted data without decryption. Furthermore, lattice-based algorithms are computationally efficient and can be implemented on resource-constrained hardware. For example, secure patient data exchange between wearable monitors and hospital systems could benefit from lattice-based encryption, ensuring resilience against quantum-enabled attacks.

Hash-Based Signatures Hash-based signatures provide a quantum-resistant approach to digital signatures, which are critical for authenticating devices, verifying firmware updates, and enabling secure boot processes. These signatures derive their security from the collision resistance of cryptographic hash functions, making them inherently resistant to quantum attacks. One widely studied scheme is the Merkle signature scheme, which uses hash trees for efficient verification. Hash-based signatures are well-suited for medical devices because of their simplicity and minimal computational requirements.

Code-Based Cryptography Code-based cryptography offers another alternative for quantum-resistant encryption. Its security is based on the difficulty of decoding random linear codes, a problem that remains intractable even for quantum computers. Code-based schemes, such as the McEliece cryptosystem, are highly efficient for encryption and decryption operations, making them suitable for resource-constrained medical devices. These schemes benefit applications requiring low latency and secure communication, such as real-time telemetry from implantable devices or secure transmission of diagnostic data.

Multivariate Cryptography Multivariate cryptography leverages the difficulty of solving systems of multivariate polynomial equations over finite fields. This approach is well-suited for lightweight cryptography, which is essential for IoMT devices with limited computational power and energy constraints. Multivariate schemes, such as those based on the Rainbow signature scheme, can provide fast signature generation and verification, making them practical for authenticating devices in a dynamic IoMT ecosystem. For instance, wearable health monitors could use multivariate cryptography to authenticate themselves to a hospital network securely and efficiently.

These quantum-resistant cryptographic methods offer unique advantages for securing medical devices in this space. For example, lattice-based cryptography excels in versatility and efficiency, hash-based signatures provide robust authentication, code-based cryptography supports low-latency encryption, and multivariate cryptography enables lightweight security solutions. By adopting these methods, the healthcare industry can ensure that its IoMT systems remain secure against quantum-enabled threats.

Quantum Sensing and Metrology in Medical Devices

I'll briefly review other quantum technologies in healthcare. Quantum computing is not the only technology that has reshaped the medical field. Quantum sensing and metrology, leveraging the principles of quantum mechanics, are unlocking precision and sensitivity in medical devices. Quantum advancements are poised to revolutionize diagnostics, treatment, and healthcare delivery by enhancing technologies like MRI, biosensors, and timing systems. This section explores the potential of quantum-enhanced sensing and metrology in medical devices.

Enhanced magnetic resonance imaging (EMRI) is one of healthcare's most promising quantum sensing applications. Quantum sensors, such as nitrogen-vacancy (NV) centers in diamonds, enable MRI systems to achieve significantly higher resolution and sensitivity than conventional technologies. These sensors exploit quantum properties like superposition and entanglement to detect minute magnetic fields accurately. This enhanced sensitivity allows for earlier and more accurate disease detection, even at the molecular or cellular level. For example, quantum-enhanced MRI could identify cancerous tissues or neurological disorders at much earlier stages, enabling timely intervention and improving patient outcomes. Additionally, the increased resolution of quantum sensors supports more detailed imaging, aiding in complex surgical planning and precision treatments.

Quantum-enhanced biosensors are another innovation, offering ultra-sensitive detection of biomarkers that indicate disease or physiological changes. These sensors utilize quantum effects to achieve detection thresholds far below traditional biosensors, making them capable of identifying extremely low concentrations of molecules like proteins, DNA, or metabolites. For instance, quantum biosensors could detect the early presence of Alzheimer's-related biomarkers in blood or cerebrospinal fluid years before symptoms appear. Similarly, they can improve the accuracy and reliability of diagnostic devices used for rapid testing, such as those for infectious diseases or metabolic conditions. By providing more precise and early diagnostics, quantum-enhanced biosensors pave the way for personalized medicine and more targeted therapeutic approaches.

Precise timing in medical devices is where quantum metrology offers substantial benefits. Quantum clocks, which utilize the oscillations of atoms or ions to measure time with unparalleled precision, are redefining synchronization capabilities in distributed medical systems. In telemedicine, devices across different locations must work harmoniously, and quantum clocks ensure precise synchronization, enabling seamless patient data integration from various sources. Additionally, time-sensitive medical procedures, such as robotic-assisted surgeries or advanced imaging techniques, rely heavily on precise timing for accuracy and safety. Quantum clocks can enhance the precision of these procedures, reducing errors and improving outcomes. For instance, in proton therapy for cancer treatment, quantum timing systems could ensure the precise delivery of radiation doses to target tissues while sparing healthy surrounding areas.

Quantum-Safe Network Protocols for Medical Devices

Developing quantum-safe network protocols is essential to safeguard IoMT systems against quantum-enabled threats. This section explores advancements in quantum-safe network protocols, including post-quantum TLS, quantum-resistant VPNs, and hybrid cryptographic approaches.

Post-quantum Transport Layer Security is at the forefront of quantum-safe communication protocols for medical devices. I talked about how TLS is widely used to secure data in transit, such as communication between wearable health monitors and healthcare databases. However, current versions of TLS rely on public-key cryptographic methods like RSA or ECC, which we know are vulnerable to quantum attacks. Post-quantum TLS aims to replace these vulnerable algorithms with quantum-resistant alternatives, such as lattice-based or hash-based cryptographic methods. Doing so ensures the long-term security of sensitive medical data, even as quantum computers become more capable. Implementing post-quantum TLS in medical devices is essential for providing secure communication of electronic health records and real-time patient monitoring data.

Quantum-resistant virtual private networks can protect remote access to medical devices and systems. VPNs are essential for securely connecting off-site healthcare professionals to hospital networks or IoMT systems. However, traditional VPN encryption methods are also at risk of being broken by quantum computers. Quantum-resistant VPNs leverage quantum-safe cryptographic algorithms to secure these remote connections against quantum-enabled eavesdropping. This is critical for protecting sensitive data like diagnostic results or surgical plans accessed remotely. Additionally, quantum-resistant VPNs are essential for maintaining the security of telemedicine services, which rely on encryption to ensure the confidentiality of doctor-patient communications.

Hybrid cryptography approaches provide a practical transition strategy toward quantum-safe protocols by combining classical cryptographic algorithms with quantum-resistant counterparts. This hybrid model enables medical devices and systems to maintain compatibility with existing infrastructure while preparing for quantum threats. For instance, a hybrid cryptographic approach could involve using RSA and a lattice-based algorithm to encrypt communication. While RSA provides compatibility with legacy systems, the lattice-based algorithm ensures that data remains secure even if quantum attacks become viable. This approach allows for a phased adoption of quantum-resistant protocols, minimizing disruption to healthcare operations. Moreover, hybrid cryptography can be integrated into IoMT systems to secure firmware updates, device authentication, and real-time data transmission. By ensuring backward compatibility, hybrid methods facilitate a smoother transition to a quantum-safe future while maintaining the highest security standards for medical devices.

Regulatory and Standardization Efforts

As quantum computing advances, regulatory bodies and standardization organizations are shaping the future of medical device security. Ensuring that medical devices remain secure in a quantum-enabled world requires the proactive development of quantum-resistant measures and global standards. This section explores three key aspects of these efforts: the NIST Post-Quantum Cryptography Standardization initiative, anticipated FDA guidance on quantum computing, and the international efforts led by ISO/IEC in standardizing quantum-safe cryptography.

> **NIST Post-Quantum Cryptography Standardization** The National Institute of Standards and Technology (NIST) is spearheading an effort to standardize quantum-resistant cryptographic algorithms, a cornerstone for future-proofing the security of medical devices. This initiative, which began in 2016, aims to identify and formalize cryptographic methods that can withstand attacks from quantum computers. NIST has shortlisted candidate algorithms, focusing on lattice-based, hash-based, code-based, and multivariate polynomial cryptography. I should also mention that NIST and NSA (National Security Agency) collaborate on developing and standardizing post-quantum cryptography.

Once finalized, these standardized algorithms will serve as the backbone for quantum-resistant security protocols in medical devices. For the medical industry, adopting NIST-recommended algorithms will be critical to ensuring compliance with future security regulations. These algorithms will likely influence encryption standards for electronic health records, secure device communication, and patient data protection. As medical devices increasingly connect through the IoMT, integrating NIST-approved quantum-resistant cryptography will be essential for maintaining secure operations.

FDA Guidance on Quantum Computing The U.S. FDA has historically provided guidance on cybersecurity for medical devices, emphasizing the need to address emerging threats. While specific guidance on quantum computing has yet to be formalized, and the FDA anticipates that it will issue recommendations or requirements to address the unique challenges of quantum-enabled threats.

International Standards: ISO/IEC Efforts On the global stage, ISO and the IEC are actively developing standards for quantum-safe cryptography. These efforts are crucial for establishing a consistent framework that ensures the security of medical devices across different regions and regulatory environments.

ISO/IEC standards aim to provide guidelines for implementing quantum-resistant cryptographic algorithms, secure key management, and system interoperability. These standards will likely influence global security requirements for medical devices, ensuring that devices meet consistent security benchmarks regardless of where they are manufactured or deployed. This is important for multinational healthcare organizations that rely on a diverse array of medical devices operating across borders.

The impact of ISO/IEC efforts extends to fostering international collaboration in addressing quantum computing challenges. By aligning standards with initiatives like NIST's post-quantum cryptography program, ISO/IEC ensures that global medical device security strategies remain cohesive and interoperable. This alignment also facilitates faster adoption of quantum-safe measures, enabling manufacturers to streamline compliance processes and accelerate innovation.

Regulatory and standardization efforts are foundational to addressing the challenges posed by quantum computing in medical device security. The NIST Post-Quantum Cryptography Standardization initiative lays the groundwork for secure algorithms that will become integral to future devices. Anticipated FDA guidance will likely set the stage for mandatory quantum-resistant measures, ensuring the security and safety of patients in the U.S. healthcare system. On the global front, ISO/IEC standards aim to standardize quantum-safe protocols, creating a unified approach to medical device security worldwide.

Ethical and Privacy Considerations

Integrating quantum computing into medical device security introduces capabilities that raise ethical and privacy considerations. As these technologies reshape how sensitive medical data is protected and processed, healthcare stakeholders must address challenges around data privacy, equitable access, and the widespread adoption of quantum-secured medical technologies. This section explores two crucial dimensions of these considerations: ensuring data privacy in the quantum era and fostering equitable access to quantum-enhanced medical security.

Data Privacy in the Quantum Era Quantum computing challenges in existing encryption methods can compromise the long-term confidentiality of medical data. Once quantum computers achieve sufficient computational power to break these algorithms, current encryption standards could become obsolete. This raises the urgent need for healthcare systems to adopt quantum-resistant cryptographic measures to protect patient data.

Ensuring the long-term privacy of medical data involves transitioning to quantum-safe encryption and addressing how data is managed and shared across connected healthcare systems. Data utility must be balanced with security, which is how effectively data can be used for diagnostics, treatment planning, and research. Techniques such as differential privacy and homomorphic encryption, combined with post-quantum cryptography, can allow healthcare organizations to utilize patient data while maintaining its confidentiality securely.

The ethical challenge lies in the transition period. Medical data currently encrypted with vulnerable algorithms could be targeted in a harvest now, decrypt later attack, where attackers collect encrypted data now and decrypt it in the future using quantum computers. This creates a pressing need for healthcare organizations to act proactively, re-encrypting sensitive data with quantum-resistant methods to ensure its privacy for years. Organizations that delay this transition risk not only regulatory penalties but also breaches of patient trust.

Equitable Access to Quantum-Enhanced Medical Technologies Quantum computing adoption risks create disparities in access to secure healthcare. Quantum-secured medical devices and systems may initially be expensive and resource-intensive to implement, potentially limiting their availability to well-funded healthcare institutions or regions with advanced technological infrastructures. This could exacerbate existing inequalities in healthcare access.

Governments, industry leaders, and nongovernmental organizations must collaborate to ensure the equitable distribution of quantum-secured medical technologies. Subsidies, public-private partnerships, and open-source initiatives for quantum-resistant software could help bridge the gap between resource-rich and resource-limited healthcare settings. Ensuring widespread access to these advancements is not just an ethical imperative but also a practical one, as unprotected systems in underfunded regions could serve as entry points for global cybersecurity threats.

Additionally, standardizing quantum-safe security measures is crucial for achieving equity. International standards must be designed to accommodate the varying capabilities of healthcare organizations worldwide, allowing smaller institutions to adopt baseline protections while enabling larger ones to implement advanced features. Ethical frameworks should also guide the rollout of quantum-secured technologies, emphasizing inclusivity, fairness, and the prioritization of patient safety.

Future Research Directions

Future investigations must focus on developing quantum-safe solutions tailored for medical devices, leveraging quantum technologies for advanced security, and exploring revolutionary paradigms like the quantum internet. This section examines four pivotal research directions: quantum-resistant lightweight cryptography, quantum-enhanced anomaly detection, quantum-safe secure boot and firmware updates, and the quantum internet for healthcare.

Quantum-Resistant Lightweight Cryptography Medical devices often operate under resource constraints, with limited processing power, memory, and energy. Developing efficient quantum-safe cryptographic algorithms that meet these limitations is essential for securing IoMT devices against quantum-era threats. I discussed that traditional post-quantum cryptography methods, such as lattice-based algorithms, may require significant computational resources, making them impractical for low-power medical devices.

Future research must prioritize lightweight cryptographic algorithms that balance security with performance. These algorithms should offer quantum resistance while optimized for resource-constrained environments like wearable devices and implantable sensors. Techniques such as streamlined key generation, efficient encryption/decryption processes, and reduced computational overhead ensure these devices remain secure and operationally efficient.

Quantum-Enhanced Anomaly Detection Anomaly detection is a cornerstone of device security, identifying unusual patterns in device behavior and network traffic that may indicate threats or malfunctions. Quantum computing, especially quantum machine learning, has the potential to advance this field by enabling advanced threat detection capabilities. QML algorithms can process and analyze large datasets more efficiently than classical methods, uncovering complex correlations and patterns that traditional systems might miss.

Research in this area should focus on developing quantum algorithms for real-time security monitoring in medical device networks. These algorithms can enhance the accuracy and speed of detecting anomalies, such as unauthorized access, abnormal device behavior, or unusual data flows.

Quantum-Safe Secure Boot and Firmware Updates Secure boot mechanisms and authenticated firmware updates are standard practices, but they rely on classical cryptographic methods vulnerable to quantum attacks. These mechanisms must be updated to incorporate quantum-resistant techniques in a post-quantum era. Future research should focus on developing quantum-safe code signing and verification methods to ensure the authenticity and integrity of software updates. This includes creating efficient algorithms for digital signatures that can withstand quantum decryption attempts. Additionally, these methods should be designed to accommodate the unique constraints of medical devices, ensuring that secure boot and firmware update processes remain feasible and efficient without compromising on quantum resistance.

Quantum Internet for Healthcare The concept of a quantum internet, which is leveraging quantum communication technologies to transmit information securely, holds great potential for healthcare. Quantum key distribution, a foundation of quantum internet research, offers theoretically unbreakable encryption, ensuring the confidentiality and integrity of medical data during transmission. Future research should explore how a quantum internet could change medical device security by enabling ultra-secure communication between devices, healthcare providers, and cloud-based systems.

Key areas of investigation include developing quantum repeaters and memory to facilitate long-distance quantum communication and overcome the limitations of photon loss and decoherence. Researchers should also evaluate how quantum internet infrastructure can be integrated into healthcare networks to enable seamless and secure data exchange. The implications for applications such as telemedicine, real-time diagnostics, and global health data sharing are profound, paving the way for a new era of secure healthcare.

Preparing the Healthcare Industry for the Quantum Era

Preparing the healthcare industry for the quantum era is crucial to ensure patient safety, data integrity, and operational continuity. While the full-scale realization of quantum computing threats may still be years away, experts estimate that quantum computers capable of breaking widely used cryptographic algorithms could emerge within the next 10 to 20 years. However, the healthcare industry cannot afford to wait for these advancements to materialize before taking action. Given the long development cycles and extended lifespans of many medical devices—often remaining in use for over a decade—preparations for quantum resilience must begin immediately. Organizations are encouraged to adopt a phased approach, with short-term goals focused on education, awareness, and initial risk assessments over the next 1 to 3 years. Mid-term strategies, spanning 3 to 7 years, should prioritize piloting and integrating hybrid cryptographic solutions that combine classical and post-quantum algorithms. Long-term efforts, extending beyond 7 years, will involve a broader migration to fully quantum-resistant systems, informed by evolving standards from regulatory bodies and advancements in quantum-safe technologies. Proactive planning and adherence to these timelines are essential to safeguarding healthcare data integrity and ensuring uninterrupted patient care in the quantum era. This section focuses on three critical aspects in preparation: education and training, risk assessment and migration strategies, and collaboration and knowledge sharing.

Education and Training A foundational step in preparing the healthcare industry for the quantum era is developing quantum computing literacy among professionals responsible for medical device security. Healthcare IT professionals, medical device engineers, and cybersecurity specialists must be equipped with the knowledge to address quantum-related challenges proactively. Educational programs should emphasize the principles of quantum computing and its implications for cryptography and device security. Training courses for healthcare IT teams can highlight quantum vulnerabilities in encryption and authentication systems and strategies for implementing quantum-resistant solutions.

Incorporating quantum security concepts into medical device engineering curricula is equally important. Future engineers must understand how to design quantum-safe devices that balance security with performance and usability. This integration will ensure that upcoming generations of medical device developers are equipped to address the unique challenges of quantum technology.

Risk Assessment and Migration Strategies Evaluating the quantum threat landscape for existing medical devices is critical for developing a proactive response. Many devices currently rely on cryptographic algorithms, which are vulnerable to quantum attacks. Healthcare organizations must conduct thorough risk assessments to identify which devices and systems are most at risk. These assessments should consider device lifecycles, data sensitivity, and network dependencies.

The next step is to develop migration strategies. Transitioning to quantum-safe technologies requires careful planning to minimize disruptions while ensuring security. Organizations should prioritize high-risk systems and devices for early migration to post-quantum cryptographic algorithms. Hybrid approaches combine classical and quantum-resistant algorithms and can serve as an interim solution, offering backward compatibility while preparing for a quantum-secure future. Comprehensive roadmaps, including timelines and resource allocation, will be essential for successful implementation.

Collaboration and Knowledge Sharing Preparing for the quantum era is complex and necessitates collaboration across industries and disciplines. Partnerships between quantum computing experts and medical device manufacturers can drive innovation and create tailored solutions for the healthcare sector. These collaborations can explore practical applications of quantum-resistant cryptography, secure quantum communications, and advanced quantum-enhanced security measures.

Establishing forums for sharing best practices in quantum-safe medical device security is equally important. Industry conferences, working groups, and online platforms can facilitate the exchange of knowledge and strategies.

Collaborative efforts can also address common challenges, such as the resource constraints of IoMT devices, and ensure that advancements in quantum security are accessible to all stakeholders, including smaller healthcare providers and device manufacturers.

Preparing the healthcare industry for the quantum era requires education, strategic planning, and collaboration. By developing quantum computing literacy, conducting thorough risk assessments, and fostering partnerships across sectors, the healthcare industry can navigate the challenges of quantum technology while leveraging its innovation potential.

Key Takeaways from Quantum Computing in Medical Device Security

This chapter highlights the transformative impact of quantum computing on medical device security, emphasizing its potential benefits and risks. Quantum computing's revolutionary processing power offers advancements in encryption, diagnostics, and system optimization while simultaneously threatening traditional cryptographic methods. Core principles like superposition and entanglement enable new capabilities but introduce challenges such as error mitigation. Applications in medical device security include quantum cryptography, random number generation, machine learning for threat detection, and quantum simulations.

However, quantum threats jeopardize current cryptographic algorithms, data integrity, authentication protocols, and long-term data security, driving the need for immediate adoption of quantum-resistant solutions. Emerging post-quantum cryptographic methods, quantum sensing technologies, and quantum-safe network protocols are critical to safeguarding the Internet of Medical Things. Regulatory bodies like NIST, FDA, and ISO/IEC are developing standards for global security compliance. Ethical considerations focus on data privacy and equitable access to quantum technologies.

Future research aims to create lightweight cryptography, quantum-enhanced cybersecurity, and secure quantum communication networks. Preparing for the quantum era requires education, risk assessment, strategic migration plans, and industry collaboration to protect healthcare systems while leveraging quantum innovations.

CHAPTER 19

AI-Driven Attacks and Defenses in Healthcare

AI-driven attacks are an evolving threat to healthcare organizations. The good news, however, is that AI also offers powerful tools for defense. This chapter introduces the risks and opportunities AI presents in cybersecurity. Healthcare organizations can better protect their systems, data, and patient safety. The key lies in the proactive adoption of AI-driven security measures, continuous learning, and a balanced approach that considers both AI's technological and ethical implications in healthcare. This chapter intends to provide a guide for making AI-based decisions regarding technology features and integrations into your environments.

AI-driven attacks represent a new frontier in cybersecurity. These attacks leverage artificial intelligence and machine learning techniques to create more sophisticated, targeted, and difficult-to-detect threats. The healthcare sector is vulnerable due to its valuable data, critical infrastructure, and often outdated security measures. I'll examine the different types of AI-driven attacks.

Types of AI-Driven Attacks in Healthcare

AI attacks, some mentioned previously in Chapter 11, exploit advanced capabilities like natural language processing (NLP), machine learning, and deep learning to bypass traditional defenses, posing unprecedented risks to the healthcare sector. In this section, I'll explore their methods and implications for phishing, ransomware, impersonation attacks, malware, social engineering, password attacks, and DDoS.

AI-Enhanced Phishing Phishing, one of the most common attack vectors out there, has been enhanced by AI. Using NLP, attackers craft compelling phishing emails that mimic legitimate communications. These emails often leverage personalization, drawn from analysis of the target's online behavior, social media activity, or professional background, to increase their effectiveness. For instance, a phishing email to a healthcare professional may reference recent medical conferences or patient cases, making it appear authentic. Furthermore, AI enables the automated generation of phishing content at scale, allowing attackers to target multiple victims simultaneously with tailored messages. In healthcare, where email communications are frequent and often urgent, this attack can trick employees into revealing sensitive information or downloading malicious attachments.

AI-Powered Ransomware Ransomware attacks have evolved with the help of AI, becoming more targeted and adaptive. AI-powered ransomware uses algorithms to identify and encrypt high-value data, such as patient records, imaging files, or proprietary research data. These attacks also often employ adaptive encryption techniques to evade detection by antivirus programs, ensuring that the ransomware remains undetected until its mission is complete. Some ransomware even integrates automated negotiation capabilities, where AI bots communicate with victims to demand and settle ransom payments. In the healthcare sector, where access to critical data can mean life or death, these intelligent ransomware attacks are devastating, forcing many organizations to pay ransom quickly to restore operations.

AI-Driven Impersonation Attacks Powered by AI, impersonation attacks use deepfake technology to create convincing audio and video impersonations of healthcare professionals, administrators, or patients. Attackers can also use voice cloning to conduct vishing (voice phishing) attacks, impersonating a trusted individual to extract sensitive information or authorize fraudulent transactions. For example, a deepfake video of a hospital director might instruct staff to transfer funds or share confidential data. These AI-driven impersonations exploit the trust inherent in healthcare environments, making them effective and difficult to detect.

AI-Generated Malware AI has modernized malware creation. Attackers can now design polymorphic malware that evolves its code continuously to avoid detection by traditional security systems. These malware programs leverage machine learning to identify specific vulnerabilities in healthcare systems, such as outdated software or unpatched devices, and adapt their attack strategies accordingly. Additionally, some AI-generated malware is self-propagating, learning from its environment to spread efficiently across networks. In a hospital setting, such malware could disable critical medical devices or compromise patient data, causing widespread disruption.

AI-Assisted Social Engineering Social engineering attacks rely on manipulating human behavior and have become more effective with AI assistance. Attackers use AI to analyze social media profiles, public records, and organizational data to craft highly convincing pretexts for their schemes. AI can also automatically identify high-value targets within healthcare organizations, such as executives, IT administrators, or researchers, who have access to sensitive data or systems. With this information, attackers generate tailored scripts to manipulate victims into revealing passwords, transferring funds, or granting unauthorized access.

AI-Powered Password Cracking AI has also enhanced traditional password-cracking methods. Attackers now use machine learning algorithms to optimize their guessing techniques, identifying patterns commonly used by healthcare professionals. For example, AI can analyze datasets of leaked passwords to identify trends like the use of medical terminology, job titles, or standard date formats. This allows attackers to guess passwords more efficiently, compromising accounts and gaining unauthorized access to sensitive systems.

AI-Enhanced DDoS Attacks Distributed denial-of-service attacks, which overwhelm systems with traffic to render them inoperable, are now being augmented by AI. Attackers use AI to intelligently target critical healthcare infrastructure, such as electronic health record systems, telemedicine platforms, or hospital networks. These attacks employ adaptive patterns that evolve during the attack, bypassing traditional defenses and maximizing disruption. In healthcare, such attacks can delay patient care, disrupt operations, and even threaten lives if they target emergency services or critical care systems.

It should be clear that AI-driven healthcare attacks represent a new cybersecurity threat. These attacks combine advanced technology with malicious intent to exploit the sector's vulnerabilities. From AI-enhanced phishing and ransomware to deepfake impersonations and intelligent malware, these attacks are more sophisticated, targeted, and challenging to defend against than their traditional counterparts.

Impact of AI-Driven Attacks on Healthcare

The rise of AI-driven attacks presents challenges for the healthcare sector, impacting data security, operational efficiency, financial stability, reputational standing, and patient safety. These sophisticated attacks exploit advanced AI capabilities, creating unprecedented risks for healthcare organizations. I'll explore the impact of AI-driven attacks on healthcare by focusing on data breaches, operational disruption, financial losses, reputational damage, and patient safety risks.

Data Breaches AI-driven attacks have amplified the scale and sophistication of data breaches, increasing the risk of large-scale theft of sensitive patient data. With the ability to analyze and exploit vulnerabilities in healthcare networks, attackers can infiltrate systems to extract electronic health records, insurance information, and proprietary research data. The exposure of such information compromises patient privacy and places individuals at risk of identity theft, fraud, or discrimination. For instance, stolen medical records can be sold on the dark web for malicious purposes, such as fraudulent insurance claims or blackmail. Furthermore, breaches of research data, such as clinical trial results or drug formulations, can undermine years of scientific work and cause financial harm to healthcare organizations.

Operational Disruption AI-driven attacks can potentially disrupt critical healthcare services, jeopardizing timely care delivery. By targeting medical devices, hospital networks, or administrative systems, attackers can cause interruptions in healthcare operations. For example, AI-powered ransomware can lock down patient records, delaying diagnoses and treatments. Similarly, DDoS attacks, enhanced by AI, can overwhelm hospital networks, rendering telemedicine platforms and EHR systems inoperable. Disruptions to medical devices, such as infusion pumps or diagnostic tools, can exacerbate operational challenges in emergency settings where timely interventions are crucial. Such disruptions compromise the quality of care and can have life-threatening consequences for patients.

Financial Losses The financial implications of AI-driven attacks on healthcare are immense, driven by both the sophistication of these attacks and their frequency. Healthcare organizations face increased costs for detecting, mitigating, and recovering from cyberattacks. AI-powered ransomware attacks pose financial risks due to their targeted nature and high ransom demands. These attacks often lock down critical systems or data, forcing organizations to pay substantial sums to regain access. Additionally, healthcare providers may incur costs related to regulatory fines, legal fees, and compliance audits following a data breach. Beyond immediate financial losses, long-term expenses arise from investments in enhanced cybersecurity measures and cybersecurity insurance premiums to prevent future incidents.

Reputational Damage The reputational fallout from AI-driven attacks can be severe, eroding trust between healthcare organizations and their patients. Data breaches and service disruptions can damage the perception of an organization's ability to safeguard sensitive information and provide reliable care. Patients may be reluctant to share personal information or seek services from an organization with a history of cybersecurity incidents. In addition, regulatory investigations and lawsuits stemming from data breaches or operational failures can amplify reputational harm. For healthcare organizations, reputational damage affects patient retention and undermines partnerships with insurers, research institutions, and technology providers, further complicating recovery efforts.

Patient Safety Risks The most alarming consequence of AI-driven attacks is their direct impact on patient safety. Attackers' Manipulation of medical data or devices can lead to incorrect diagnoses, inappropriate treatments, or adverse health outcomes. For instance, altering patient records could result in administering incorrect medications or dosages, posing serious risks to patient health. Moreover, disruptions to critical care systems, such as ventilators or monitoring equipment, can delay lifesaving interventions. In extreme cases, attackers could exploit vulnerabilities in connected devices, such as pacemakers or insulin pumps, to cause physical harm to patients. The potential for such scenarios underscores the urgency of addressing AI-driven threats to safeguard human lives.

The impact of AI-driven attacks on healthcare is profound, spanning data breaches, operational disruptions, financial losses, reputational damage, and patient safety risks. These attacks exploit the interconnectedness and digitization of modern healthcare systems, targeting vulnerabilities for maximum impact. For healthcare organizations, addressing these challenges requires a proactive and comprehensive approach to cybersecurity, including adopting advanced defenses, regulatory compliance, and a culture of vigilance. Please refer to the chapter on best practices for mitigation strategies. I'll discuss some of these at a high level in the next section.

AI-Driven Defenses in Healthcare

AI-powered cybersecurity tools enable healthcare organizations to anticipate, detect, and respond to emerging threats. This section explores key aspects of AI-driven defenses in healthcare, including AI-powered threat detection, automated incident response, enhanced access control, dynamic security policy management, vulnerability and patch management, phishing defense, and network segmentation.

AI-Powered Threat Detection AI-powered threat detection leverages machine learning algorithms to identify anomalies in network traffic, user behavior, and system activity. Unlike traditional methods, which rely on predefined rules, AI systems continuously learn from vast amounts of data to detect subtle patterns indicative of potential threats. These systems analyze security data in real time, enabling healthcare organizations to identify and respond to attacks before they escalate. Predictive analytics further enhance these capabilities by anticipating potential threats based on historical trends and current indicators. For instance, an AI system might detect unusual access attempts from an employee's account, flagging it as a possible credential compromise. This proactive approach significantly reduces the time attackers can remain undetected within a network.

Automated Incident Response AI-driven tools are pivotal in automating the incident response process, ensuring swift action against cyber threats. These systems can triage security incidents by categorizing alerts based on severity and initiating containment measures. Several AI-driven tools are streamlining and accelerating how organizations detect, prioritize, and respond to cyber threats. Prime examples are Security Orchestration, Automation, and Response (SOAR) platforms such as Cortex XSOAR, IBM Security QRadar SOAR, and Splunk SOAR. These platforms integrate with various security systems to automate the triage of incidents, prioritize alerts, and orchestrate comprehensive response actions. They can automatically isolate infected devices, block malicious IP addresses, and even initiate patch management workflows, ensuring that vulnerabilities are addressed swiftly. By automating routine tasks, SOAR tools significantly reduce the burden on security teams and allow them to focus on more complex threats.

Endpoint detection and response (EDR) and extended detection and response (XDR) solutions are also vital AI-driven tools in automated incident response. Products like CrowdStrike Falcon Insight, Microsoft Defender XDR, and SentinelOne Singularity XDR use advanced machine learning algorithms to detect threats in real time, assess the severity of incidents, and automatically initiate containment measures. These might include quarantining compromised devices or cutting off their network access to prevent the spread of malware. EDR and XDR platforms help reduce alert fatigue by correlating signals across various vectors, allowing analysts to focus on high-priority threats.

Threat intelligence platforms like Recorded Future and ThreatConnect leverage AI to process vast amounts of data, delivering real-time insights and prioritizing threats based on risk relevance to the organization. These platforms often integrate with SOAR solutions to automate actions like blocking indicators of compromise or updating firewall rules, ensuring an immediate and intelligent response to emerging threats.

AI-powered vulnerability management and patch automation tools are essential to an automated incident response strategy. Solutions like Qualys VMDR, Tenable.io with Nessus, and Ivanti Neurons for Patch Management utilize AI to assess and prioritize vulnerabilities. They can also automatically deploy patches or enforce system configurations, addressing weaknesses before attackers exploit them.

Tools such as Abnormal Security, Darktrace Antigena Email, and Microsoft Defender for Office 365 excel at detecting phishing attempts and other malicious communications. These tools can automatically quarantine or delete suspicious emails, block compromised accounts, and trigger investigation workflows, reducing the risk of successful social engineering attacks.

Finally, in Splunk and Microsoft Sentinel, behavioral analytics and insider threat detection tools such as Exabeam and the User and Entity Behavior Analytics (UEBA) capabilities use AI to monitor user activity and detect anomalies that may indicate insider threats or compromised accounts. These systems can automatically trigger alerts, lock accounts, or launch further investigations, adding an essential layer of proactive defense.

These systems can triage security incidents by categorizing alerts based on severity and initiating containment measures. Automated patch management and system updates strengthen defenses by addressing vulnerabilities before they can be exploited. Additionally, AI systems prioritize security alerts intelligently, ensuring that critical issues are addressed promptly while reducing alert fatigue for IT teams. By automating routine tasks, AI frees cybersecurity professionals to focus on other activities.

AI-Enhanced Access Control—Ensuring secure access to healthcare systems and data is vital, and AI can enhance access control mechanisms. Behavioral biometrics, such as keystroke dynamics and mouse movement patterns, enable continuous authentication of users, detecting anomalies that indicate compromised accounts. Contextual and risk-based access management adds another layer of security by adjusting permissions based on location, device type, and behavior patterns. For example, an employee accessing sensitive patient data from an unfamiliar location might trigger additional verification steps. AI also excels at detecting and mitigating the use of compromised credentials by analyzing login patterns and cross-referencing them with threat intelligence feeds.

AI-Driven Security Policy Management AI simplifies the complexity of managing security policies in dynamic environments. AI systems can dynamically adjust security policies by analyzing real-time threat intelligence to counter evolving risks. For example, if a specific type of malware is prevalent, the system can tighten firewall rules or enforce stricter authentication for affected systems. AI-driven tools also streamline compliance monitoring and reporting by continuously auditing systems for adherence to regulatory standards. This ensures that healthcare organizations remain compliant with frameworks such as HIPAA and GDPR, reducing the risk of penalties and data breaches.

AI-Powered Vulnerability Management Vulnerability management is critical for preventing cyberattacks, and AI enhances this process by intelligently scanning and prioritizing vulnerabilities. Traditional vulnerability scanning tools generate extensive reports that can overwhelm IT teams. AI systems, however, analyze potential exploit paths and prioritize vulnerabilities based on factors such as severity, likelihood of exploitation, and impact on critical systems. Predictive analysis enables organizations to address vulnerabilities proactively, reducing the window of opportunity for attackers. For example, an AI-powered system might flag an unpatched server with access to patient data as a high-priority target, ensuring it receives immediate attention.

AI-Enhanced Phishing Defense AI offers advanced defenses against the phishing threat. Using NLP, AI-powered email filters can detect subtle signs of phishing attempts, such as suspicious wording, anomalous sender behavior, or misleading links. These systems also analyze user behavior to identify unusual interactions with emails, such as clicking on unexpected links or downloading unfamiliar attachments. By combining real-time analysis with behavioral insights, AI reduces the likelihood of successful phishing attacks, protecting employees and patients from data breaches.

AI-Driven Network Segmentation Network segmentation is a critical strategy for minimizing the spread of cyber threats, and AI brings new levels of intelligence to this process. AI-driven tools enable intelligent micro-segmentation by analyzing real-time threat data and segmenting networks accordingly. Sensitive systems, such as those managing patient data or connected medical devices, can be isolated from less critical systems. Automated enforcement of least-privilege access ensures that users and devices only have access to the resources they need, reducing the risk of lateral movement by attackers.

AI-driven defenses are redefining how healthcare organizations protect themselves against sophisticated threats. By leveraging machine learning and intelligent automation, these tools enhance threat detection, streamline incident response, strengthen access controls, and optimize security policy management. AI also improves vulnerability management, phishing defense, and network segmentation, creating a stronger and more adaptive security posture.

Integrating AI into your systems, whether for cybersecurity or other business functions, starts with defining your objectives. It's important to clarify what problems you aim to solve with AI. For example, you might want to automate threat detection and response, reduce alert fatigue for your IT team, streamline repetitive tasks, or enhance data analysis. Knowing your goals will help determine which AI tools and approaches best fit your organization.

The next step is assessing your current environment. Look closely at your existing IT infrastructure, security tools, and workflows. Consider what tools you already use—such as firewalls, SIEM systems, endpoint protection, or antivirus—and whether they can integrate with AI-driven solutions. Additionally, evaluate whether you can access the data these AI systems need to function effectively. Many AI tools rely on large amounts of data to analyze patterns and detect anomalies, so understanding your data readiness is key.

Once you have a clear picture of your environment, you can select the right AI tools. If you're focusing on cybersecurity and incident response, some of the leading AI-powered solutions include SOAR platforms like Cortex XSOAR, IBM QRadar SOAR, and Splunk SOAR. These tools help automate and orchestrate responses to security incidents. You might also consider EDR or XDR tools like CrowdStrike Falcon, SentinelOne, or Microsoft Defender XDR. Platforms, like Recorded Future or ThreatConnect, are highly effective for organizations interested in enhancing their threat intelligence. Beyond cybersecurity, if you're exploring AI for other business areas, you can look into AI chatbots (like ChatGPT or Microsoft Copilot), process automation tools (like UiPath with AI), or custom AI solutions through cloud providers such as Azure AI, AWS AI/ML, or Google Vertex AI.

There are generally two approaches to integration: out-of-the-box solutions or custom development. Many modern AI tools are designed for easy integration and offer APIs, plug-and-play connectors, and cloud-based deployment options that simplify the process. If you prefer to develop custom AI models tailored to your unique needs, platforms like Azure Machine Learning, AWS SageMaker, and Google Vertex AI provide frameworks for building and training your AI systems. However, custom development typically requires data science expertise and high-quality data.

Deployment is another important consideration. You can opt for cloud-based AI services, which are scalable, fast to deploy, and managed by the provider. This is often a good choice for organizations that need flexibility and lower upfront costs. Alternatively, you may need more control over your data due to compliance or security concerns. In that case, on-premises AI deployment might be the better option, though it requires more infrastructure and in-house expertise.

Once you have chosen your AI tools, it's time to integrate them into your existing systems. Most AI-powered platforms offer APIs that enable connecting with your SIEM, ticketing systems like ServiceNow or Jira, email platforms, and more. Many solutions also feature low-code or no-code interfaces that make integration accessible, even without deep technical skills.

Successful AI implementation also depends on having the right people and skills. Whether you're working with cybersecurity professionals to manage AI-driven security tools or data analysts and engineers to develop custom models, investing in training and building your team's expertise is essential for long-term success.

It's often a good idea to start small with a pilot project, such as automating phishing response or patch management, and then scale up as you measure success and refine your approach. Working with vendors or managed service providers (MSSPs) can ease the process. These partners can handle much of the deployment, integration, and management of AI systems, particularly if your in-house resources are limited.

For example, if you already use Microsoft Sentinel as your SIEM platform, you could add Microsoft Defender XDR to automatically detect and respond to threats across your endpoints and identities. You might then integrate Cortex XSOAR to automate actions like isolating compromised endpoints or resetting user credentials. Alerts can be automatically sent to your ticketing system, such as ServiceNow, to generate and manage incident tickets. With this setup, you'd have a fully automated, AI-driven incident response process.

Challenges in Implementing AI-Driven Defenses

Implementing the previously mentioned AI-driven defenses in healthcare comes with its challenges. These challenges span data privacy concerns, integration with legacy systems, managing false positives and alert fatigue, addressing skill gaps, and navigating ethical considerations. Understanding and addressing these obstacles is critical for ensuring AI's effective and ethical deployment in healthcare cybersecurity.

Data Privacy Concerns AI systems rely on large datasets to train models and detect anomalies effectively, but the use of patient data must comply with strict privacy regulations. Healthcare organizations must ensure that AI tools do not inadvertently expose or misuse sensitive medical information. Data anonymization, differential privacy, and federated learning can help mitigate these concerns by allowing AI models to learn from data without directly accessing identifiable information. However, implementing these methods requires careful planning and a thorough understanding of regulatory requirements, adding complexity to the deployment process.

Integration with Legacy Systems Healthcare IT environments often include legacy systems and outdated infrastructure not designed with modern AI-driven solutions in mind. Integrating AI tools into these environments can be challenging due to compatibility issues and the lack of standardization across systems. For example, many medical devices and electronic health record systems use proprietary protocols or outdated software, which can hinder the deployment of AI-driven defenses. This fragmentation creates gaps in security coverage, leaving specific systems more vulnerable to attacks. To address this challenge, organizations must invest in updating and standardizing their IT infrastructure while ensuring that new AI tools are compatible with existing systems. This requires significant financial and technical resources and collaboration between AI developers, healthcare IT teams, and medical device manufacturers.

False Positives and Alert Fatigue AI-driven cybersecurity systems are highly effective at detecting threats but can also generate excessive false positives, overwhelming IT teams with unnecessary alerts. In the healthcare context, where timely responses are critical, false alarms can divert attention from genuine threats and lead to alert fatigue among security personnel. This problem is exacerbated when AI models are not fine-tuned to the specific contexts of healthcare environments, such as the unique network behaviors of medical devices. Organizations must invest time and effort in training AI models using healthcare-specific data and scenarios to mitigate this challenge. Continuous monitoring and refinement of these models are essential to improve their accuracy and reduce false positives. Additionally, implementing tiered alert systems that prioritize critical incidents can help manage the volume of alerts and ensure that resources are focused on the most pressing issues.

Skill Gap The successful implementation of AI-driven defenses requires cybersecurity professionals with specialized knowledge of AI technologies and their applications. However, there is a significant shortage of such expertise in the industry. Many healthcare organizations struggle to recruit and retain professionals skilled in AI and cybersecurity, leaving them ill-equipped to deploy and manage advanced security tools. Furthermore, existing IT and security staff may lack the training to effectively use AI-driven solutions, creating a gap between the technology's potential and its practical application. Addressing this challenge requires a multifaceted approach, including investments in training programs, partnerships with academic institutions, good partners with in-house skills, and developing user-friendly AI tools requiring minimal technical expertise.

Ethical Considerations AI-driven security tools raise important ethical considerations that healthcare organizations must navigate carefully. For example, AI algorithms used in threat detection and response must be designed to avoid biases that could lead to unfair or discriminatory outcomes. Biases in training data, for instance, could result in disproportionate scrutiny of specific users or devices, undermining trust in the system. Additionally, critical security decisions, such as isolating devices or shutting down systems, must involve human oversight to ensure that automated actions do not inadvertently compromise patient care or safety. Establishing clear guidelines for the ethical use of AI in cybersecurity and maintaining transparency in AI decision-making processes are essential steps toward addressing these concerns.

To sum up, balancing security needs with patient privacy, integrating AI with legacy systems, managing false positives, addressing skill gaps, and navigating ethical considerations are critical hurdles that healthcare organizations must overcome. By adopting a strategic approach that includes investment in training, infrastructure upgrades, and ethical frameworks, the healthcare sector can harness the power of AI to build resilient and secure systems while maintaining trust, compliance, and operational integrity. Furthermore, collaboration with other healthcare organizations, AI developers, and regulatory bodies can facilitate the development of standardized guidelines and best practices for AI deployment.

Future Trends in AI-Driven Healthcare Cybersecurity

The integration of AI into healthcare is not only transforming how threats are detected and mitigated but also paving the way for innovative solutions that address emerging challenges. This section explores future trends in AI-driven healthcare cybersecurity, focusing on quantum-resistant cryptography (in case you skipped it in the last chapter), federated learning for threat intelligence, AI-driven security automation, explainable AI for security, AI-enhanced threat hunting, and the integration of AI with blockchain for data integrity.

Quantum-Resistant Cryptography With the advent of quantum computing, traditional encryption methods face vulnerabilities. Quantum computers have the potential to break widely used cryptographic algorithms, posing a risk to the confidentiality of sensitive healthcare data. AI-assisted quantum-resistant cryptography is emerging as a key trend to address this threat. By leveraging AI, healthcare organizations can design and implement quantum-safe encryption methods that are both efficient and scalable. AI can assist in optimizing post-quantum cryptographic algorithms, tailoring them to the resource constraints of medical devices and ensuring seamless integration into existing healthcare infrastructures.

Federated Learning for Threat Intelligence Collaboration among healthcare organizations is critical for combating cyber threats, but sharing sensitive data for joint analysis poses privacy risks. Federated learning offers a solution by enabling AI models to learn from distributed datasets without sharing raw data. In the context of threat intelligence, federated learning allows multiple healthcare organizations to collaboratively train AI models on diverse threat patterns while maintaining data privacy and compliance with regulations such as HIPAA. This approach enhances the effectiveness of threat detection and fosters a culture of shared responsibility in addressing cybersecurity challenges.

AI-Driven Security Automation and Orchestration AI-driven security automation and orchestration promise to modernize healthcare organizations' cybersecurity defense management. Fully automated security operations centers powered by AI can handle tasks like threat detection, incident response, and vulnerability management with minimal human intervention. These AI-driven systems can analyze massive amounts of security data in real time, prioritize threats based on severity, and automatically initiate appropriate countermeasures. This level of automation reduces response times and alleviates the burden on human security teams, allowing them to focus on strategic initiatives and complex problem-solving.

Explainable AI for Security While AI is highly effective in detecting and mitigating threats, its decision-making processes often lack transparency, leading to challenges in trust and accountability. Explainable AI is emerging as a trend in healthcare, with the aim of making AI models more interpretable and understandable. XAI systems can provide clear rationales for their security decisions, such as why a specific action was taken, or an alert was generated. This transparency is essential for ensuring security professionals can trust AI-driven systems and validate their outputs. In the healthcare context, XAI can also aid in compliance with regulations that require documentation of decision-making processes, further reinforcing the role of AI as a reliable partner in cybersecurity.

AI-Enhanced Threat Hunting Proactive threat hunting is vital in modern cybersecurity strategies, and AI is transforming this field by enabling the more accurate and efficient identification of hidden threats. AI-enhanced threat hunting uses advanced techniques, such as machine learning and pattern recognition, to uncover subtle indicators of compromise that traditional methods might miss. AI can detect anomalies and provide actionable insights for preemptive action by analyzing historical data, network traffic, and user behavior.

Integration of AI with Blockchain for Data Integrity Finally, integrating AI with blockchain technology represents a collaboration for enhancing data integrity and security. Blockchain's decentralized and tamper-proof nature ensures that medical data remains secure and unaltered. At the same time, AI adds a layer of intelligence by monitoring the blockchain for anomalies or suspicious activities. For example, AI can analyze transaction patterns on a blockchain to detect unauthorized access or fraudulent activities. This combination also supports secure data sharing among healthcare stakeholders, enabling trust and collaboration without compromising privacy. As healthcare organizations increasingly adopt blockchain for medical records, supply chain management, and IoMT device authentication, AI will play a pivotal role in optimizing and safeguarding these systems.

Best Practices for Healthcare Organizations

Implementing best practices tailored to the unique challenges of healthcare cybersecurity can help organizations harness the power of AI while mitigating associated risks. This section focuses on key best practices, including investing in AI-driven security solutions, continuous education, collaboration, regular security assessments, ethical frameworks, zero-trust architectures, and data quality assurance.

Invest in AI-Driven Security Solutions Healthcare organizations must prioritize adopting AI-powered threat detection and response tools to stay ahead of increasingly sophisticated threats. AI systems excel at analyzing large amounts of data in real time, detecting anomalies, and predicting potential attacks. By integrating machine learning-based threat detection tools into their infrastructure, healthcare providers can proactively identify and mitigate risks. For instance, AI-powered solutions can monitor network traffic to detect unusual patterns or flag potential breaches before they escalate. Investing in these tools enhances security and reduces the workload on human security teams, allowing them to focus on strategic initiatives.

Employ Continuous Education and Training The dynamic nature of AI-driven cyber threats necessitates ongoing education and training for healthcare security teams. Professionals must stay informed about the latest developments in AI-based attack techniques, such as deepfake technology, AI-enhanced ransomware, and cutting-edge defense strategies. Regular workshops, certifications, and simulation exercises can equip teams with the skills to deploy and manage AI-driven security tools effectively. Additionally, fostering a culture of cybersecurity awareness among all staff members, including clinicians and administrative personnel, ensures that the organization is vigilant against threats.

Encourage a Collaborative Approach Collaboration is essential for addressing the complex challenges of healthcare cybersecurity. Participating in information-sharing initiatives within the healthcare sector can give organizations valuable insights into emerging threats and best practices. Platforms like the Health Information Sharing and Analysis Center (H-ISAC) enable healthcare providers to share threat intelligence, learn from real-world incidents, and develop collective defense strategies. A collaborative approach extends to partnerships with technology providers, academic institutions, and government agencies, fostering innovation and enhancing the sector's overall resilience.

Perform Regular Security Assessments Regular security assessments are critical for identifying vulnerabilities and ensuring that defenses remain effective. AI-assisted penetration testing and vulnerability assessments can simulate sophisticated attacks, uncover weaknesses, and provide actionable recommendations for improvement. These assessments should be performed frequently and cover all aspects of the organization's digital ecosystem, including medical devices, electronic health records systems, and network infrastructure.

Develop an AI Ethics Framework As healthcare organizations increasingly rely on AI, guidelines for the ethical use of this technology must be established. An AI ethics framework should address transparency, accountability, and fairness in AI decision-making processes. Ethical guidelines also promote trust in AI tools and ensure their deployment aligns with the organization's mission to protect patients and uphold regulatory compliance.

Implement a Zero Trust Architecture Zero-trust architecture is a modern security model that assumes no user, device, or application can be trusted by default. Healthcare organizations can leverage AI to implement continuous verification and authentication. AI systems can analyze contextual factors such as user behavior, device health, and access requests in real time and grant or deny access based on dynamic risk assessments. By adopting this, organizations can minimize the impact of breaches and limit attackers' ability to move laterally within networks. Refer to Chapter 16 for more on Zero Trust.

Focus on Data Quality Finally, AI security models are only as effective as the data on which they are trained. Ensuring high-quality, diverse datasets for training AI-driven cybersecurity systems is crucial for their accuracy and reliability. Poor-quality data can lead to false positives, missed threats, and biased decision-making. Healthcare organizations should invest in good data management practices, including data validation, anonymization, and integration of diverse threat intelligence sources. Organizations can maximize the effectiveness of AI-driven defenses by maintaining a strong focus on data quality.

Organizations can strengthen their defense against threats by investing in AI-driven security solutions, fostering continuous education, adopting a collaborative approach, and conducting regular security assessments. Implementing ethical frameworks, Zero Trust architectures, and ensuring data quality further strengthen the foundation for AI-driven cybersecurity. These best practices protect sensitive healthcare systems and data and enable healthcare organizations to navigate the complexities of AI-enhanced threats confidently.

Key Takeaways from AI-Driven Attacks and Defenses in Healthcare

AI presents both significant challenges and valuable opportunities for healthcare cybersecurity. As cyber threats become more sophisticated through AI, healthcare organizations must adopt advanced AI-driven defenses to safeguard their systems, sensitive data, and patients. Cyberattackers leverage AI to develop more effective phishing schemes, ransomware, malware, deepfake-based impersonation attacks, and AI-assisted social engineering tactics. These threats pose serious risks to patient data privacy, disrupt critical healthcare services, and can compromise patient safety, resulting in financial losses and reputational damage. Healthcare organizations use

AI-powered threat detection, automated incident response, and advanced access control measures like behavioral biometrics to strengthen their defenses.

Despite these advancements, implementing AI solutions comes with challenges, including balancing privacy with security, integrating AI with legacy systems, managing false positives, and addressing the shortage of AI and cybersecurity expertise. Emerging technologies such as quantum-resistant cryptography, federated learning, and explainable AI are expected to shape the future of healthcare cybersecurity. To avoid evolving threats, healthcare organizations should invest in AI-driven security tools, foster continuous staff training, participate in threat intelligence sharing initiatives, and implement best practices such as Zero Trust architectures and ethical AI frameworks.

Part VI

Legal and Ethical Considerations

IoMT brings an array of legal and ethical challenges. These interconnected systems pose data security, privacy, and patient safety risks. To address these complexities, it is essential to establish legal frameworks and ethical guidelines that mitigate risks and promote innovation and trust in healthcare.

Part VI examines some aspects of navigating modern healthcare's regulatory and ethical landscape. Chapter 20 explores some of the regulatory frameworks for IoMT security, reviewing the roles of some key regulatory bodies, the legal requirements for compliance, and the ethical principles that guide decision-making. By understanding these frameworks, stakeholders can align innovation with patient safety and trust.

The discussion then transitions to Chapter 21 with guidelines for ethical hacking in healthcare, recognizing ethical hackers' role in uncovering healthcare systems' vulnerabilities. This chapter highlights the importance of proactive cybersecurity, provides best practices for conducting ethical hacking, and explores the legal, ethical, and practical considerations essential for ensuring effective engagements.

This part integrates regulatory knowledge, ethical insights, and practical strategies to provide a guide for the complex intersection of technology, law, and ethics in healthcare. It aims to empower device manufacturers, healthcare providers, regulators, and ethical hackers to collaboratively foster a secure and ethical healthcare environment based on patient care.

CHAPTER 20

Regulatory Frameworks for IoMT Security

This book recognizes that the IoMT has made a difference in healthcare delivery but also introduces security and privacy risks. Regulatory frameworks for IoMT security aim to protect patient data, ensure device integrity, and maintain public trust in healthcare technology. This chapter introduces some of these frameworks, which aim to balance innovation with safety, privacy with data utility, and security with usability.

Key Regulatory Bodies and Frameworks

Regulatory frameworks play a role in addressing challenges and ensuring that IoMT devices and systems operate securely while protecting patient data and maintaining compliance with legal and ethical standards. The following focuses on some of the more common regulatory bodies and frameworks in the United States, the European Union, and internationally:

United States The regulatory landscape in the United States is defined by a combination of agencies and laws that ensure the security, functionality, and privacy of devices, systems, and data.

- **Food and Drug Administration (FDA)**
  The FDA is the central authority that regulates medical devices. It provides guidance on cybersecurity, emphasizing secure design, risk management,

and incident response. Key FDA initiatives include premarket direction for incorporating cybersecurity during device development and postmarket recommendations for maintaining device security throughout its lifecycle. The FDA also mandates manufacturers to provide a cybersecurity bill of materials detailing software and components used to aid in risk assessment.

- **Health Insurance Portability and Accountability Act (HIPAA)**
  HIPAA governs the privacy and security of protected health information or PHI in the U.S. IoMT systems that handle PHI must comply with HIPAA's Security Rule, which mandates administrative, physical, and technical safeguards to protect data. For instance, IoMT devices transmitting patient data must employ encryption, access controls, and audit capabilities to ensure confidentiality and integrity.

- **Federal Trade Commission (FTC)**
  The FTC enforces consumer protection laws and holds manufacturers accountable for deceptive practices, including inadequate cybersecurity measures. It can penalize organizations that fail to secure consumer data or misrepresent their security practices. The FTC's emphasis on transparency and accountability complements both FDA and HIPAA regulations.

European Union   The European Union employs regulations to secure devices and protect patient data, focusing on privacy and system resilience. We have these to consider:

- **General Data Protection Regulation (GDPR)**
  GDPR is a cornerstone of data privacy in the EU. It requires organizations to safeguard personal data and ensure transparency in data processing. For IoMT devices, GDPR mandates strong encryption, data minimization, and explicit user consent for data collection. Noncompliance can result in fines, making it essential for manufacturers and healthcare providers to prioritize data protection.

- **Medical Device Regulation (MDR)**
  The MDR governs the safety and performance of medical devices, including IoMT systems. It requires manufacturers to address cybersecurity risks during device design and document security features. The regulation emphasizes the traceability of medical devices and their components, aiding in identifying vulnerabilities and facilitating recalls if necessary.

- **Network and Information Systems (NIS) Directive**
  The NIS Directive establishes a framework for improving cybersecurity across critical infrastructure, including healthcare. It requires healthcare organizations to implement security measures for networked systems and report significant cybersecurity incidents. The directive promotes collaboration between EU member states to enhance resilience against cyber threats.

International   At the global level, standardization organizations provide guidelines and frameworks to balance IoMT security practices across borders, such as:

- **International Organization for Standardization (ISO)**
  ISO develops international standards that serve as benchmarks for security and quality. For IoMT, ISO/IEC 27001 (Information Security Management) and ISO/IEC 27701 (Privacy Information Management) are particularly relevant. These standards outline best practices for securing devices and managing sensitive data, providing a foundation for global compliance.

- **International Electrotechnical Commission (IEC)**
  The IEC focuses on standards for electronic and electrical technologies, including IoMT devices. IEC 62304, which addresses the software lifecycle processes of medical devices, and IEC 60601, which pertains to the safety and performance of medical electrical equipment, are critical for ensuring systems' secure and reliable operation. These standards align with ISO guidelines, creating a cohesive framework for international implementation.

Some key regulatory bodies and frameworks in the United States, the European Union, and internationally form the backbone of IoMT security, addressing challenges related to device integrity, data privacy, and system resilience. Healthcare organizations and manufacturers can ensure compliance, protect patient safety, and build trust by adhering to these regulations. However, the dynamic nature of cybersecurity threats necessitates continuous updates to these frameworks, emphasizing the need for proactive collaboration among regulators, manufacturers, and healthcare providers worldwide.

Legal Considerations

The IoMT operates at the intersection of healthcare, technology, and legal systems. These devices handle sensitive patient data and provide critical care functions, so they must navigate a complex web of legal considerations. This section examines some of the key legal aspects of IoMT security, focusing on data protection, device certification, cybersecurity requirements, liability, cross-border data transfers, and intellectual property protection.

Data Protection and Privacy Data protection laws like the GDPR and the California Consumer Privacy Act or CCPA establish stringent requirements for handling personal data, including sensitive health information managed by IoMT devices. Organizations must ensure compliance with these regulations by implementing privacy measures.

Main legal principles include:

- **Patient consent:** Patients must consent to collecting, processing, and sharing their data. The consent forms should be transparent and detail the data's use, who will access it, and the patient's right to revoke consent.

- **Data minimization:** Devices should collect only the data necessary for their intended purpose. For example, a wearable device monitoring heart rate should not collect unrelated personal information.

- **Purpose limitation:** Data collected by in-scope systems must only be used for explicitly stated purposes, preventing misuse or unauthorized secondary processing.

Noncompliance with data protection laws can result in fines and reputational damage, emphasizing the need for privacy governance frameworks.

Device Certification and Approval Before entering the market, IoMT devices must undergo certification and approval to meet safety and performance standards. Regulatory bodies like the FDA and the European Medicines Agency (EMA) oversee these processes.

Key considerations include:

- **Pre-market approval:** Manufacturers must demonstrate that devices comply with relevant standards, including those related to cybersecurity. This involves submitting detailed documentation, risk assessments, and evidence of security measures.
- **Post-market monitoring:** Even after approval, manufacturers must continuously monitor devices for vulnerabilities or adverse events. Regular software updates and patch management are often mandated.
- **Device risk classifications:** IoMT devices are categorized based on the risk they pose to patients. High-risk devices, such as implantable cardiac monitors, face more stringent regulatory requirements than low-risk devices like fitness trackers.

Failure to comply with certification processes can delay market entry and expose manufacturers to legal liabilities.

Cybersecurity Requirements In many jurisdictions, the cybersecurity of IoMT devices is not just a best practice but a legal obligation. Regulatory frameworks require mandatory security controls, incident reporting, and vulnerability management.

Some fundamental aspects include:

- **Mandatory security controls:** Manufacturers must adopt best practices such as encryption, access controls, and secure software development lifecycle (SDLC) practices to protect devices and data.
- **Incident reporting:** Organizations must notify regulatory bodies, affected patients, and stakeholders of a security breach within prescribed timeframes. For example, GDPR requires breach notifications within 72 hours.
- **Vulnerability disclosure policies:** Manufacturers must establish mechanisms for identifying and addressing vulnerabilities, including engaging with ethical hackers and security researchers.

Liability and Responsibility Determining liability for IoMT-related issues, such as device malfunctions or data breaches, complex legal challenges. These systems often involve multiple stakeholders, including manufacturers, healthcare providers, and patients.

Key considerations include:

- **Device malfunctions:** Manufacturers may be held liable for defective devices that cause harm to patients. However, healthcare providers may share the liability if they fail to follow proper usage protocols or maintain the device.
- **Data breaches:** Liability for breaches often depends on the source of the vulnerability. If a breach occurs due to a flaw in the device, the manufacturer may be responsible. Conversely, if the breach results from inadequate security practices by a healthcare provider, then liability may fall on them.
- **Shared responsibility models:** Transparent contracts and agreements are essential to delineate responsibilities among all parties involved, reducing disputes in the event of incidents.

The legal landscape around liability is evolving, emphasizing the need for clarity and proactive risk management.

Cross-Border Data Transfers IoMT systems often operate across international borders, raising legal challenges related to data transfers. Regulations like GDPR impose strict requirements on transferring personal data outside approved jurisdictions.

Some considerations include:

- **Adequacy decisions:** Data can be transferred only to countries deemed to provide adequate protection by regulatory bodies. For example, GDPR recognizes certain countries, such as Canada and Japan, as having adequate data protection frameworks.
- **Appropriate safeguards:** Organizations transferring data to nonapproved jurisdictions must implement safeguards like standard contractual clauses (SCCs) or binding corporate rules (BCRs) to ensure compliance.

Healthcare organizations must carefully assess the legal implications of data flows, notably when partnering with international IoMT service providers.

Intellectual Property Protection Manufacturers must balance protecting their innovations with the need for security transparency. Intellectual property (IP) considerations are crucial in fostering innovation while ensuring device security.

Considerations include:

- **Patent protection:** Patents safeguard proprietary technology but must not impede vulnerability disclosures. Open communication with security researchers is vital to address potential flaws without violating IP laws.

- **Open-source software:** Many IoMT devices rely on open-source components. Organizations must ensure compliance with licensing requirements while securing these components against vulnerabilities.

Balancing IP protection with security disclosure promotes innovation and accountability, ensuring that IoMT solutions remain cutting-edge and secure.

Legal considerations for IoMT security are multifaceted, spanning data protection, device certification, cybersecurity, liability, cross-border data transfers, and intellectual property. Navigating this complex landscape requires a proactive approach integrating legal compliance with security measures.

Ethical Considerations

Integrating the IoMT into healthcare raises ethical questions that healthcare providers, policymakers, and technologists must address. These considerations span patient autonomy, data ownership, algorithmic fairness, equitable access, privacy trade-offs, human oversight, and posthumous data management. Ethical frameworks are essential to ensure that systems align with healthcare's fundamental values of beneficence, nonmaleficence, justice, and respect for autonomy.

Patient Autonomy and Informed Consent Patient autonomy is the basis of ethical healthcare practice. For IoMT devices, this principle mandates that patients understand the risks and benefits of these technologies and can make informed decisions about their use. Healthcare providers and manufacturers must present clear and accessible information about how devices collect, store, and use data. This includes detailing the potential for data breaches, secondary uses of data, and the security measures to protect sensitive information. Informed consent processes should avoid technical jargon and prioritize transparency, ensuring patients fully comprehend their choices. Ethical implementation respects patient autonomy by prioritizing informed, voluntary participation.

Data Ownership and Control The question of who owns the data generated by devices is central to ethical debates in digital health. Patients often assume they own their health data, but device manufacturers, healthcare providers, and cloud service operators may also claim ownership or control. Ethical frameworks must establish that patients have primary rights over their data, including the ability to access, correct inaccuracies, and request deletion.

Transparent data governance policies should ensure that patients retain control while balancing the needs of stakeholders like researchers or public health agencies. Providing patients with intuitive tools to manage their data fosters trust and respects their rights.

In the healthcare context, where AI and LLMs might be used to support clinical decision-making or personalize treatments, knowing the origin of the data that feeds these systems is essential for several reasons:

- **Ethical use and consent:** If third-party data is being used, it's essential to ensure that the individuals whose data is involved have given proper consent for their information to be used in AI training. This aligns with respecting patient autonomy and data rights.
- **Data legitimacy and ownership:** Organizations must confirm that they have the legal rights and licenses to use external data. Misuse or unauthorized use of data can lead to ethical breaches and legal consequences, undermining trust and violating privacy laws like GDPR or HIPAA.
- **Bias and fairness:** Understanding data sources is key to identifying potential biases in AI models. If LLMs are trained on unrepresentative or biased data sets (especially from third parties), this can result in unfair or discriminatory outcomes in healthcare decision-making, raising serious ethical concerns.
- **Transparency and accountability:** Patients, healthcare providers, and regulators increasingly expect transparency about AI-driven decisions. Knowing and disclosing where the data comes from helps build trust and allows for accountability if the system behaves in ways that need scrutiny or correction.
- **Data quality and reliability:** The quality of third-party data directly affects the performance and reliability of AI systems. Decisions in healthcare can have life-altering consequences, so it's ethically imperative to ensure that the data used is accurate, relevant, and validated.

It's ethically and legally important to know the data sources feeding any AI or LLM systems being used in healthcare and to confirm that the organization has the proper rights and controls. Clear governance frameworks should extend to third-party and external data, just like they do for patient-generated data.

Algorithmic Bias and Fairness IoMT systems increasingly rely on AI and machine learning (ML) to analyze data and support clinical decisions. However, biases in these algorithms can lead to unfair or harmful outcomes. For example, training data that underrepresents certain demographic groups can result in inaccurate diagnoses or treatment recommendations for those populations.

Ethical practices demand rigorous testing of AI models for bias and implementing measures to mitigate disparities. Transparency in algorithmic decision-making is also critical, ensuring that patients and providers understand how decisions are made and can challenge or override them when necessary. Fairness in AI strengthens trust and ensures equitable care.

Digital Divide and Equitable Access The digital divide, the gap between those with access to advanced technologies and those without, presents a significant ethical challenge. Patients in low-income, rural, or underserved areas may lack access to devices or the secure networks needed to support them. Additionally, implementing advanced security measures could increase the cost of IoMT solutions, exacerbating healthcare inequities.

Ethical frameworks should address these disparities by promoting equitable access to IoMT technologies. This could involve subsidizing costs, developing low-resource alternatives, or investing in infrastructure for underserved communities. Security measures must be designed to protect all patients, regardless of socioeconomic status.

Privacy vs. Public Health IoMT systems often collect and share data for purposes beyond individual care, such as public health monitoring or disease surveillance. This raises ethical tensions between protecting personal privacy and maximizing societal benefits. For instance, during pandemics, devices may be used for contact tracing or monitoring disease spread, requiring some data sharing. Ethical practices must balance these competing priorities by ensuring that data sharing is proportional, minimally invasive, and anonymized where possible. Transparent communication about how data will be used, as well as safeguards against misuse, can help reconcile privacy with public health goals.

Human Oversight and Autonomy As systems become more automated, the ethical question of human oversight becomes increasingly important. While automation can improve efficiency and reduce errors, it also risks eroding human autonomy and judgment. For example, automated diagnostic systems might recommend treatments clinicians are hesitant to override, or IoMT devices might make autonomous decisions without patient input. Ethical frameworks should delineate clear boundaries for automation, emphasizing the importance of human oversight in critical decisions. Patients and providers must retain the ability to intervene or override automated processes to ensure that care remains personalized and aligned with individual values.

End-of-Life Considerations IoMT devices raise unique ethical issues at the end of a patient's life. After death, questions arise about the appropriate handling of data and devices. Should data be retained for research purposes or deleted to respect the deceased's privacy? Ethical policies should provide clear guidance on these matters, respecting the preferences of patients and their families. The physical devices must be securely decommissioned to prevent misuse or data breaches. Transparent and respectful end-of-life data policies ensure patients' rights are honored even after passing.

I only covered a handful of ethical considerations. However, in IoMT security, they are integral to building trust, ensuring fairness, and protecting patients in an increasingly digital healthcare landscape. By addressing autonomy, data ownership, algorithmic fairness, equitable access, privacy, human oversight, and end-of-life care, healthcare organizations can navigate the complex ethical challenges posed by IoMT technologies. Incorporating these principles into regulatory frameworks, device design, and operational policies ensures that IoMT systems uphold the highest standards of ethics.

Challenges in Regulatory Framework Development

Developing regulatory frameworks for the IoMT is critical to medical devices' security, privacy, and functionality. However, the complexity and rapid evolution of IoMT technologies present challenges for regulators, healthcare organizations, and device manufacturers. Addressing these challenges requires a careful balance between fostering innovation and ensuring strong protections for patients and systems. This section explores key challenges in regulatory framework development, including rapid technological advancement, interoperability, global harmonization, resource constraints, and legacy device integration.

Rapid Technological Advancement One of the most pressing challenges in IoMT regulation is the speed at which technology evolves. Devices are constantly being enhanced with new features, connectivity options, and capabilities, often outpacing regulatory bodies' ability to update their frameworks. For example, advances in AI, machine learning, and 5G connectivity enable more sophisticated devices while introducing new security vulnerabilities and privacy risks.

Regulatory frameworks must remain adaptable to accommodate these innovations while ensuring security and privacy protections keep pace. Achieving this balance requires proactive engagement with industry stakeholders, continuous monitoring of technological trends, and the development of flexible, principles-based regulations that can evolve alongside the technology.

Interoperability and Standardization Interoperability enables seamless communication between devices, platforms, and healthcare providers. However, ensuring interoperability without compromising security poses a regulatory challenge. Different manufacturers often use proprietary communication protocols, creating compatibility issues that can hinder secure data exchange. Regulatory frameworks must promote the development of common standards for secure device communication while encouraging collaboration among stakeholders. For example, frameworks could mandate standardized encryption protocols or authentication mechanisms that ensure compatibility and security. At the same time, standards must be robust enough to protect against threats without stifling innovation or creating barriers to entry for smaller manufacturers.

Global Harmonization IoMT is a global industry, with devices and systems often crossing national borders. However, regulatory requirements vary significantly between jurisdictions, creating challenges for manufacturers and healthcare providers operating internationally. For example, GDPR imposes strict data privacy standards, while regulations like HIPAA focus more on healthcare-specific requirements. These differences can lead to conflicts, duplicative compliance efforts, and increased costs. Global harmonization of regulations is essential to address these issues. This involves aligning standards and requirements across regions, fostering international collaboration, and addressing conflicts between national and international laws. Harmonization not only simplifies compliance for manufacturers but also ensures consistent security and privacy protections for patients worldwide.

Resource Constraints Resource constraints are a challenge for smaller healthcare providers and manufacturers, which may lack the financial or technical capacity to comply with complex regulations. For example, implementing advanced security measures, conducting regular audits, and maintaining compliance with evolving standards can be prohibitively expensive for smaller organizations. Regulatory frameworks must account for these constraints by offering scalable requirements or tiered compliance models based on organizational size and risk level. Additionally, governments and industry associations can provide support through funding, training, and access to shared resources, such as threat intelligence platforms or security toolkits.

Legacy Device Integration Many healthcare organizations rely on older medical devices that are not designed with modern cybersecurity requirements in mind. These legacy devices often lack basic security features, such as encryption or remote update capabilities, making them vulnerable to attacks. Developing regulatory frameworks that address the risks posed by legacy devices is a challenge. On the one hand, requiring immediate compliance with modern standards may be unrealistic, given the cost and logistical challenges of replacing or retrofitting existing devices. On the other hand, ignoring these risks leaves healthcare systems exposed to potential breaches. A balanced approach involves creating phased compliance timelines, incentivizing replacing high-risk devices, and developing security guidelines tailored for legacy systems.

Developing regulatory frameworks for IoMT security is a challenge that requires balancing innovation with protection, fostering interoperability, aligning global standards, and addressing practical constraints. Rapid technological advancement, the need for standardized communication, and the integration of legacy devices add complexity to this task. By adopting flexible, collaborative, and scalable approaches, regulators can create frameworks that support the growth of IoMT while ensuring that patient safety, data privacy, and system integrity remain top priorities.

Best Practices for Regulatory Compliance

Compliance with security and privacy regulations protects patients and their data, builds trust, and ensures the long-term success of technologies. Adopting best practices for regulatory compliance is essential for manufacturers, healthcare providers, and other stakeholders. In addition, most organizations understand the need for a chief security officer (CSO). Still, healthcare also requires a chief privacy officer who works with the CSO and the chief legal counsel on these practices. Some of the most popular practices include privacy by design, a risk-based approach, continuous monitoring, transparency, accountability, and collaboration.

Employ Privacy by Design Privacy by design is a proactive approach that integrates privacy and security considerations into the earliest stages of IoMT device development. Rather than treating security as an afterthought, manufacturers must embed safeguards throughout the design process. For example, devices should initially incorporate data encryption, secure authentication, and access controls.

Privacy by design also involves minimizing data collection to what is strictly necessary for device functionality and ensuring that collected data is anonymized wherever possible. This approach aligns with regulatory requirements like the GDPR, which emphasizes the importance of building privacy into the core of systems. By adopting privacy by design, organizations meet compliance standards and enhance their devices' resilience and trustworthiness.

Use a Risk-Based Approach A risk-based approach tailors security measures to the specific risks associated with each IoMT device or system. Not all devices face the same level of threat. For example, an implantable cardiac device may require stricter protections than a wearable fitness tracker due to its potential impact on patient safety.

Regulators like the FDA encourage a risk-based methodology, where manufacturers assess the potential vulnerabilities and consequences of a device's compromise. This assessment informs the development of appropriate security controls, such as encryption, intrusion detection systems, or physical safeguards. A risk-based approach ensures that resources are allocated efficiently, addressing the most critical risks while avoiding unnecessary overregulation of low-risk devices.

Integrate Continuous Monitoring and Updates Regulatory compliance is not a one-time achievement but an ongoing process that requires continuous monitoring and improvement. This book has repeatedly reiterated that cyber threats evolve rapidly, and IoMT devices must be equipped to respond to emerging vulnerabilities. Organizations should establish processes for regular security assessments, including penetration testing, vulnerability scans, and compliance audits with relevant standards.

Equally important is the ability to deploy updates and patches quickly and securely. Devices should support over-the-air updates to address vulnerabilities without requiring physical intervention. Continuous monitoring also involves tracking changes in regulatory requirements and adapting compliance efforts accordingly.

Embrace Transparency and Accountability Transparency and accountability are foundational to regulatory compliance and patient trust. Organizations must communicate their security practices, data usage policies, and compliance efforts to patients, regulators, and other stakeholders. For example, providing patients with accessible information about collecting, storing, and sharing data can help build confidence in IoMT technologies. Similarly, maintaining detailed records of compliance activities, such as risk assessments and incident response measures, demonstrates accountability to regulators. Organizations should also establish clear lines of responsibility for cybersecurity and regulatory compliance within their teams. This ensures everyone understands their role in maintaining security and compliance, reducing the risk of oversight or negligence.

Leverage a Collaborative Approach   Regulatory compliance is not achieved in isolation. It requires collaboration across the healthcare and IoMT ecosystem. Engaging with regulators, industry peers, and cybersecurity experts can help organizations navigate complex regulatory requirements and stay ahead of emerging threats. Participation in industry working groups, such as those led by the International Organization for Standardization or the Health Information Sharing and Analysis Center, allows organizations to share knowledge and best practices. Collaboration with regulators during the design and approval process can also ensure that devices meet compliance standards without unnecessary delays. A collaborative approach fosters innovation while maintaining the highest standards of security and privacy.

Future Trends in IoMT Security Regulation

The increasing integration of advanced technologies like artificial intelligence, quantum computing, blockchain, and 5G (plus beyond or 6G), coupled with the rise of personalized medicine, is reshaping the healthcare security landscape. Future regulations must balance the need for innovation with patient safety, privacy, and data integrity protections. This section explores popular trends in IoMT security regulation, including AI and machine learning governance, quantum-safe cryptography standards, blockchain-based health data management, next-generation wireless technologies, and securing personalized medical data.

AI and Machine Learning Governance   AI-driven medical devices, such as those enabling predictive diagnostics or real-time anomaly detection, require frameworks to ensure reliability, transparency, and fairness. Future regulations must address algorithmic accountability, bias in AI models, and the interpretability of AI decision-making processes. For instance, regulators may mandate that AI systems used in healthcare provide explainable outputs, enabling clinicians to understand and trust their recommendations. Additionally, continuous validation of AI models in real-world settings will be essential to maintain accuracy and relevance over time.

Quantum-Safe Cryptography Standards   The upcoming quantum computing paradigm threatens traditional cryptographic methods, necessitating the development of quantum-safe cryptography standards. IoMT devices, which often handle highly sensitive patient data, must have encryption protocols resilient to quantum attacks. Future regulations will likely mandate the adoption of quantum-resistant algorithms for securing medical devices and health data. For example, initiatives like NIST's Post-Quantum Cryptography Standardization project are laying the groundwork for such protocols. Regulatory frameworks must establish timelines and guidelines for transitioning to these new cryptographic standards, ensuring that healthcare organizations are prepared for the quantum era without disrupting operations.

Decentralized Identity and Blockchain Blockchain technology offers promising applications in health data management. However, its regulatory implications are still being explored. Future frameworks must address decentralized identity solutions that allow patients to control access to their data without relying on centralized systems. Regulations must define data integrity, interoperability, and privacy standards in blockchain-based systems. For instance, establishing protocols for verifying the authenticity of health records while ensuring compliance with privacy laws like GDPR will be critical. Blockchain's potential for tracking device lifecycles and securing IoMT device identities also calls for targeted regulatory oversight to prevent misuse or data tampering.

5G and Beyond Future regulations must also address the vulnerabilities associated with 5G and beyond, such as network slicing and edge computing security. Guidelines for securing these infrastructures will need to cover aspects like secure device onboarding, stronger encryption for data in transit, and protections against distributed denial-of-service attacks. Additionally, regulators may require IoMT manufacturers to demonstrate how their devices interact securely within 5G or 6G-enabled networks to ensure interoperability without compromising security.

Personalized Medicine and Genomic Data The rise of personalized medicine and the growing use of genomic data and unique, permanent genetic makeup reveal deeply personal health information, making their protection vital. Future regulatory frameworks must establish standards for securely storing, processing, and sharing personalized medical data. For instance, laws may require stringent encryption, controlled access, and consent mechanisms for genomic data usage. Additionally, frameworks must address ethical concerns, such as preventing discrimination based on genetic information and ensuring equitable access to personalized medical treatments. As personalized medicine expands, regulations must evolve to safeguard patient data and public trust.

Governance frameworks for AI-driven devices, quantum-safe cryptography standards, blockchain-based health data management, next-generation wireless technologies, and personalized medicine will play an essential role in ensuring the security and efficacy of IoMT systems. By proactively addressing these trends, regulators can adopt innovation while upholding the healthcare sector's highest safety, privacy, and trust standards.

Examples of Benefits from Regulation Implementation

Examining the benefits can help us better understand the successes and challenges of applying regulatory principles to IoMT security. The following sections present case studies on the U.S. FDA Pre-Certification Program, the European Union's Medical Device Regulation, and the GDPR in healthcare.

FDA Pre-Cert Program: Regulating Software as a Medical Device (SaMD) The FDA's Pre-Certification Program is a pilot initiative designed to streamline the regulatory oversight of Software as a Medical Device (SaMD). SaMD refers to software intended for medical purposes that operate independently of a physical medical device, such as diagnostic apps or machine learning algorithms for patient monitoring. Given the rapid pace of updates and iterations, traditional regulatory pathways for medical devices can be cumbersome for software. The Pre-Cert Program addresses this by focusing on the developer's trustworthiness rather than solely evaluating the software product.

Through this program, the FDA assesses organizations for excellence in five key areas: product quality, patient safety, clinical responsibility, cybersecurity responsibility, and proactive culture. Once pre-certified, organizations can more efficiently bring SaMD products to market while committing to post-market monitoring and ongoing engagement with the FDA. The program illustrates the balance between encouraging innovation and maintaining rigorous safety standards. For IoMT developers, this approach underscores the importance of integrating security measures and a commitment to transparency throughout the software lifecycle.

EU MDR Implementation: Stricter Security Requirements for Manufacturers The EU MDR, which was enacted in May 2021, overhauls the EU's regulatory framework for medical devices. One of its defining features is the emphasis on cybersecurity, which recognizes the growing threat landscape connected medical technologies face. The MDR imposes stricter requirements on manufacturers, mandating comprehensive risk management systems encompassing a device's entire lifecycle, from design and production to maintenance and decommissioning.

Under the MDR, manufacturers must demonstrate that their devices are designed to withstand cyber threats, incorporating secure communication protocols, encryption, and regular software updates. The regulation also requires detailed technical documentation, including a cybersecurity report, as part of the conformity assessment process. The MDR has prompted many manufacturers to reevaluate their development practices, invest in stronger security measures, and collaborate closely with notified bodies responsible for certification. While the stricter requirements have raised compliance costs, they have also driven innovation and improved trust in IoMT devices across the European market.

GDPR in Healthcare: IoMT Data Practices in Europe The GDPR has profoundly impacted European healthcare data practices, particularly for IoMT devices that collect, process, and transmit sensitive patient information. The GDPR emphasizes data protection, privacy, and accountability, holding organizations accountable for handling personal data. For IoMT, this has meant a greater focus on secure data processing practices, explicit patient consent for data use, and robust data access, correction, and deletion mechanisms.

One of GDPR's key principles, data minimization, has led to changes in how IoMT devices collect and store information. Manufacturers and healthcare providers are encouraged to collect only the data necessary for a specific purpose and to anonymize or pseudonymize data where possible. GDPR's breach notification requirements have also motivated organizations to implement stronger incident detection and response protocols. Noncompliance can result in fines, as demonstrated by several high-profile penalties imposed on healthcare entities.

The GDPR has also highlighted the importance of cross-border data transfers, especially for multinational healthcare organizations using IoMT. To comply, these entities must implement safeguards such as standard contractual clauses or obtain adequacy decisions for data transfers outside the EU. While GDPR has added complexity to IoMT data management, it has also enhanced patient trust by ensuring their data is handled responsibly and securely.

These case studies illustrate the evolving landscape of regulatory frameworks for IoMT security. The FDA Pre-Cert Program demonstrates a forward-thinking approach to regulating rapidly changing software technologies, while the EU MDR underscores the importance of lifecycle-wide cybersecurity measures. GDPR exemplifies the critical role of data protection and privacy in fostering trust in IoMT devices. These frameworks highlight the need for dynamic, collaborative, and patient-centered approaches to IoMT regulation, ensuring that security and innovation coexist in the digital healthcare ecosystem.

Recommendations for Stakeholders

Device manufacturers, healthcare providers, patients, and policymakers are critical in safeguarding IoMT ecosystems against cyber threats and ensuring compliance with regulatory frameworks. The following are some actionable recommendations for each stakeholder group that can foster a secure and resilient IoMT environment.

Device Manufacturers and Leading with Security by Design Device manufacturers are at the forefront of IoMT innovation and are responsible for ensuring that security is embedded in their products from the start of their design and development phases. Security-by-design principles should guide every stage of product development, from concept to deployment. This includes implementing secure communication protocols, strong encryption, and authentication mechanisms while designing devices to minimize vulnerabilities. Regular risk assessments and penetration testing should also be integral to the development process.

Manufacturers must also engage proactively with regulatory bodies to ensure their products meet current compliance standards. This involves maintaining transparency about device capabilities and limitations, submitting comprehensive technical documentation, and participating in pre-market approval processes where required. Collaborating with regulators during the development phase can help manufacturers align their innovations with evolving security expectations and avoid costly redesigns or delays in bringing products to market.

Healthcare Providers Building Organizational Resilience Healthcare providers play a critical role in securing devices within clinical settings. To effectively manage these technologies, providers must develop comprehensive security policies that address device management, network segmentation, data protection, and incident response. These policies should be informed by both regulatory requirements and the unique risks posed by the organization's IoMT ecosystem.

Additionally, it is essential to invest in staff training on regulatory compliance and cybersecurity awareness. Clinicians, IT personnel, and administrative staff should know how to identify potential threats, adhere to best practices, and respond effectively to incidents. This includes training on data privacy regulations, safe device usage, and recognizing phishing attempts or other common attack vectors.

Patients Advocating for Security and Transparency As the end-users of IoMT devices, patients have a vested interest in ensuring their security and responsible use. They should stay informed about the security features of their medical devices, such as encryption, data access controls, and update mechanisms. Patients should not hesitate to ask healthcare providers and manufacturers about the measures they are taking to protect their data and ensure the safety of their devices.

Furthermore, patients can advocate for transparency in data usage and security practices by requesting clear, accessible information about how their health data is collected, stored, and shared. Understanding their rights under regulations like GDPR or HIPAA empowers patients to make informed decisions about their care and data. This advocacy also encourages manufacturers and providers to prioritize security and compliance as key components of patient trust.

Policymakers Enabling Collaboration and Innovation As mentioned, policymakers shape the regulatory landscape for IoMT security. To address the dynamic nature of this field, they should foster collaboration between industry, academia, and government in developing regulations. Collaborative initiatives can help policymakers understand the challenges faced by manufacturers and providers while also drawing on cutting-edge research to create forward-thinking security standards.

At the same time, policymakers must ensure that regulations are flexible enough to accommodate technological advancements without stifling innovation. This requires adopting a risk-based approach that modifies requirements to the complexity and criticality of devices while providing clear pathways for compliance. Policymakers should also establish frameworks for regular review and regulation updates, ensuring they remain relevant in emerging technologies like AI, quantum computing, and blockchain.

Key Takeaways from Regulatory Frameworks for IoMT Security

The regulatory landscape for the IoMT is complex and continually evolving to keep pace with advancements in healthcare technology. Effective frameworks aim to balance innovation with robust security and privacy protections, ensuring that connected medical devices enhance patient care without compromising data integrity. Regulatory bodies across regions play critical roles—such as the FDA, HIPAA, and FTC in the United States, the GDPR, MDR, and NIS Directive in the European Union, and international standards from ISO and IEC—each establishing requirements for data protection, device certification, cybersecurity, and cross-border data transfers. Legal considerations address informed consent, liability, and intellectual property, while ethical concerns emphasize patient autonomy, data ownership, fairness in AI systems, and equitable access to secure healthcare technologies.

Developing effective regulations presents challenges, including keeping up with rapid technological changes like AI and 5G, promoting interoperability, and integrating legacy devices. Best practices for compliance involve adopting privacy by design, using risk-based security approaches, ensuring continuous monitoring, and fostering collaboration among stakeholders. Future regulatory trends include governance of AI and machine learning, quantum-safe cryptography, blockchain for secure data management, and frameworks to protect personalized medicine and genomic data. Case studies, such as the FDA's Pre-Cert Program and the EU's MDR, highlight the importance of adaptive regulation and cybersecurity throughout a device's lifecycle. Ultimately, collaboration among manufacturers, healthcare providers, patients, and policymakers is essential to create rules that protect patients and support innovation in connected healthcare.

CHAPTER 21

Guidelines for Ethical Hacking in Healthcare

Ethical hacking involves intentionally probing applications, networks, and devices for vulnerabilities and exploiting them if they are in scope, with the owner's permission. In healthcare, this practice is crucial for identifying and addressing security weaknesses before malicious actors can exploit them. Given the sensitive nature of healthcare data and the potential impact on patient safety, ethical hacking in this sector requires special considerations and strict guidelines. This chapter provides an overview of the most common boundaries.

Importance of Ethical Hacking in Healthcare

Ethical hacking plays a critical role in strengthening cybersecurity in the healthcare sector. As healthcare organizations increasingly adopt interconnected systems and devices, the risk of cyberattacks targeting sensitive patient data and critical operations grows. Ethical hacking often enables organizations to identify and address vulnerabilities proactively before attackers can exploit them. This practice is a technical necessity and a basis for patient safety, regulatory compliance, and organizational trust.

Protecting patient data is one of the most compelling reasons for ethical hacking in healthcare. Electronic health record systems, which store sensitive personal health information (PHI), are prime targets for cybercriminals seeking to steal, ransom, or exploit this valuable data. Ethical hackers simulate real-world attacks to uncover vulnerabilities in these systems, network configurations, and data storage practices. By identifying and addressing weaknesses, healthcare organizations can safeguard patient confidentiality and prevent unauthorized access. That said, proactive measures through ethical hacking reduce the risk of data breaches.

Regarding ensuring medical device safety, malicious tampering with devices, such as insulin pumps, pacemakers, and diagnostic equipment, could lead to incorrect dosages, false readings, or even life-threatening situations. Ethical hacking is essential for testing the security of these devices, both during development, after deployment, and after critical changes in clinical environments. Ethical hackers help identify vulnerabilities in communication protocols, software, and hardware components, enabling manufacturers to implement better security measures. This ensures that devices perform as intended and remain secure against potential cyberattacks.

Adherence to data protection and cybersecurity regulations is a legal requirement for healthcare organizations. Ethical hacking helps organizations meet these regulatory standards by uncovering and mitigating compliance gaps. For example, penetration testing can reveal deficiencies in encryption methods, access controls, or breach notification processes, allowing organizations to address these issues before regulators discover them. Demonstrating due diligence in cybersecurity efforts through ethical hacking also provides evidence of a proactive approach to risk management, which can reduce or mitigate penalties and reputational damage in the event of an incident.

System downtime in healthcare can have dire consequences, delaying treatments, disrupting surgeries, or compromising emergency response capabilities. Ethical hacking helps healthcare organizations identify weaknesses that could lead to operational disruptions, such as vulnerabilities in network configurations, backup systems, or disaster recovery plans. Ethical hackers help organizations strengthen their defenses against incidents that could compromise service availability by simulating ransomware attacks or distributed denial-of-service attacks. Furthermore, ethical hacking informs business continuity planning by identifying potential points of failure and ensuring robust backup systems. Regular testing and updates of systems and protocols are crucial to address evolving threats. Collaboration between IT teams and clinical staff is also essential to ensure that technical and clinical perspectives are considered in maintaining system resilience. This comprehensive approach protects against technical failures and enhances staff awareness and preparedness, ultimately preserving the continuity of critical healthcare services.

In a time where data breaches and cyberattacks frequently make headlines, demonstrating a commitment to security is essential for maintaining trust with patients, partners, and stakeholders. Ethical hacking provides tangible proof that an organization is taking proactive steps to protect sensitive data and ensure the safety of its systems and devices. Healthcare organizations enhance their reputation for prioritizing security and patient care by addressing vulnerabilities before they can be exploited. This trust is vital for fostering long-term relationships with patients and partners and maintaining a competitive edge.

Scope of Ethical Hacking in Healthcare

Ethical hacking in healthcare encompasses various activities designed to identify and mitigate vulnerabilities across the sector's technological, physical, and human elements. The scope of ethical hacking is defined by the diverse components that contribute to the security of healthcare systems, including network infrastructure, application security, medical devices, physical security, and social engineering. Each area is critical in maintaining the confidentiality, integrity, and availability of sensitive healthcare data and services. I'll look at each of these areas:

Network Infrastructure A secure network infrastructure is the backbone of any healthcare organization, enabling the safe transmission and storage of sensitive data. Ethical hackers focus on testing firewalls, routers, and other network devices to identify misconfigurations, outdated software, or exploitable vulnerabilities. They assess whether firewalls adequately protect critical systems or whether intrusion detection systems function effectively.

Additionally, with healthcare facilities increasingly relying on wireless networks, ethical hacking evaluates the security of Wi-Fi systems, ensuring they are protected against unauthorized access and eavesdropping. Techniques like penetration testing and vulnerability scans help organizations fortify their networks against potential breaches.

Application Security Healthcare applications, such as electronic health record systems, patient portals, and telemedicine platforms, are prime targets for cyberattacks due to the sensitive information they handle. Ethical hacking involves evaluating these applications for vulnerabilities, such as SQL injection, cross-site scripting (XSS), and inadequate authentication mechanisms.

Testing mobile health apps is equally important, as these apps often collect and transmit personal health information. Ethical hackers simulate attacks to uncover weaknesses in data storage, encryption, authentication, authorization flaws, and communication protocols. By addressing these vulnerabilities, organizations can protect patient data and ensure the reliability of critical applications.

Medical Devices Ethical hacking in the IoMT domain involves assessing the security of devices such as infusion pumps, pacemakers, and diagnostic tools to ensure they are protected against tampering or unauthorized access. Security engineers test communication protocols, software updates, and hardware configurations to identify potential attack vectors. Ethical hacking also evaluates how these devices interact within broader hospital networks to ensure they do not become entry points for cyberattacks.

Physical Security Physical security is a critical yet often overlooked aspect of healthcare cybersecurity. Ethical hacking involves evaluating access controls to sensitive areas such as data centers, server rooms, and administrative offices. For example, ethical hackers may test whether physical access systems like keycards, biometric scanners, or surveillance systems can be bypassed. They also assess the security of physical servers and workstations, ensuring that devices storing sensitive information are protected against theft or unauthorized tampering.

Social Engineering Human error remains among the weakest links in healthcare cybersecurity, making social engineering a vital component of ethical hacking. Ethical hackers conduct tests that may include phishing, vishing, and smishing simulations to evaluate staff susceptibility to deceptive emails, phone calls, or messages designed to extract sensitive information. They also test staff awareness and adherence to security policies through tactics such as impersonation or baiting. These activities highlight potential employee training and organizational culture weaknesses, providing actionable insights for improving security awareness programs.

Legal and Regulatory Considerations

Ethical hacking must be conducted within strict legal and regulatory frameworks. These frameworks ensure that testing activities align with laws protecting patient privacy, device safety, and organizational accountability. Key considerations include compliance with HIPAA, adherence to FDA regulations, awareness of state and local laws, and alignment with international regulations like GDPR and ISO standards. I'll look at each of these:

HIPAA Compliance The Health Insurance Portability and Accountability Act (HIPAA) sets rigorous standards for protecting patient information in the United States. Ethical hacking activities must fully adhere to HIPAA's Privacy and Security Rules, which govern the handling of PHI. Before accessing PHI systems, ethical hackers must obtain authorization from healthcare organizations and ensure that all testing activities are documented and approved.

Testing methodologies should include effective safeguards to prevent unauthorized access, data breaches, or accidental exposure of patient information. For example, any data accessed during testing must be encrypted and anonymized wherever possible. Ethical hackers must also provide detailed reports demonstrating how their testing aligns with HIPAA requirements, helping organizations maintain compliance and protect patient trust.

FDA Regulations For medical devices, ethical hacking must consider the guidelines established by the U.S. FDA. The FDA requires that testing activities do not interfere with the safety or functionality of medical devices, particularly those that are life-sustaining or critical to patient care. Ethical hackers must follow FDA recommendations for cybersecurity assessments, including pre- and postmarket guidance. For example, testing should validate the effectiveness of a device's security controls without jeopardizing its certification status. Ethical hackers should also work closely with device manufacturers to ensure that any identified vulnerabilities are addressed in a way that complies with FDA documentation and risk management standards.

State and Local Laws   In addition to federal regulations, ethical hacking activities must comply with state data protection and cybersecurity laws. For example, states like California have enacted laws like the California Consumer Privacy Act (CCPA), which mandates strict data handling and breach notification requirements. As of March 2025, 20 U.S. states have enacted comprehensive data privacy laws to protect residents' personal information. These laws generally apply across various industries, with certain exceptions, and grant individuals specific rights regarding how businesses collect, use, and share their data. Notable examples include California's CCPA and laws in Virginia, Colorado, Connecticut, Utah, Iowa, Indiana, Tennessee, Texas, Florida, Montana, Oregon, Delaware, New Hampshire, New Jersey, Kentucky, Nebraska, Rhode Island, Washington, and Nevada. These regulations typically provide residents with rights such as accessing their data, requesting its deletion, and opting out of its sale to third parties.

Additionally, many of these laws require businesses to maintain transparent privacy policies that clearly outline their data collection practices. The specifics of each law vary by state, so organizations conducting ethical hacking or handling data must ensure compliance within each jurisdiction where they operate. Staying informed about state-level privacy requirements is essential for avoiding legal risks and maintaining responsible data security practices. Reliable resources like the International Association of Privacy Professionals' US State Privacy Legislation Tracker offer valuable, up-to-date insights on these evolving laws. Ethical hackers conducting testing in specific jurisdictions must understand and adhere to these local regulations, ensuring that testing activities do not violate state-mandated privacy protections. Furthermore, state and local laws may impose additional requirements for reporting security incidents or coordinating with law enforcement during vulnerability assessments. Awareness of these laws helps organizations avoid legal pitfalls and ensures ethical hacking practices remain compliant across different regions.

International Regulations   For healthcare organizations operating globally, ethical hacking must account for international regulations, such as the GDPR. It imposes stringent requirements on data privacy and security for organizations handling the personal data of EU citizens, regardless of where the organization is based. Ethical hackers working with such organizations must ensure that testing activities comply with GDPR's data minimization principles, explicit consent, and breach notification. For example, when testing a system that handles EU patient data, testers must anonymize sensitive information and obtain explicit authorization for all testing activities.

Global standards like ISO 27001 also influence ethical hacking practices. ISO 27001 provides a framework for information security management, emphasizing risk assessment, continuous monitoring, and secure data handling. Ethical hackers can align their methodologies with ISO standards to ensure consistency and credibility in their testing processes, particularly for multinational healthcare organizations.

Ethical Boundaries and Guidelines

Ethical hacking in healthcare must be conducted within clear ethical boundaries. These guidelines ensure that ethical hackers act with integrity, protect patient safety and data, and uphold the trust placed in them by healthcare organizations. These principles foster a secure and professional partnership where vulnerabilities can be addressed responsibly and effectively. Ethical hackers should keep the following boundaries and guidelines in mind:

Obtain Explicit Permission Ethical hacking should begin with securing explicit written authorization from the healthcare organization's leadership. This authorization ensures that all activities are sanctioned and aligned with organizational priorities. The scope of testing, including its objectives, limitations, and timeline, must be clearly defined and agreed upon in advance. For example, testing may focus solely on a specific network segment or exclude certain critical systems to avoid potential disruptions. Ethical hackers can prevent misunderstandings and ensure compliance with organizational policies and legal requirements by clearly outlining expectations and boundaries.

Protect Patient Data A foundational principle of ethical hacking is protecting patient data. Ethical hackers must avoid accessing patient data unless necessary and only with explicit permission. Whenever possible, anonymized or synthetic data should be used during testing to eliminate the risk of exposure. For example, testing an electronic health record system should utilize simulated patient profiles to replicate real-world scenarios without compromising data. This approach ensures that patient privacy is upheld, aligning with legal and ethical obligations.

Minimize Operational Impact Healthcare operations are often critical and time-sensitive, making it essential to minimize disruptions during testing. To reduce the risk of interfering with patient care, ethical hackers must schedule tests during low-traffic periods, such as after-hours or planned maintenance windows. Additionally, there should be a predefined plan to immediately halt testing if there is any indication that patient safety or system functionality could be compromised. For instance, if testing inadvertently affects the performance of a connected medical device, ethical hackers must cease activities and notify the appropriate personnel immediately.

Maintain Confidentiality Maintaining confidentiality is also essential. Ethical hackers must handle discovered vulnerabilities with discretion, sharing findings only with authorized personnel within the organization. Any data collected during testing, including logs or system configurations, must be securely stored and disposed of once no longer needed. This ensures that sensitive information does not fall into the wrong hands and that trust between the tester and the organization is preserved.

Do not Exploit for Personal Gain Ethical hackers must never exploit discovered vulnerabilities for personal or financial gain. Their role is to identify and report weaknesses, not to misuse them. Critical vulnerabilities that pose immediate risks to patient safety or data integrity must be reported promptly to the organization's designated contact. For example, if a vulnerability allows unauthorized access to an EHR system, ethical hackers must notify the relevant personnel immediately and refrain from further testing until directed. This principle ensures that ethical hackers act in the organization's and its patients' best interests.

Conduct Professionalism Professional conduct is essential throughout the entire ethical hacking engagement. Ethical hackers should adhere to recognized codes of conduct, such as the EC-Council Code of Ethics, emphasizing integrity, responsibility, and respect for privacy. This includes maintaining clear and respectful communication with stakeholders, adhering to agreed-upon protocols, and transparently documenting all activities. Upholding professionalism builds trust and ensures a productive working relationship with the healthcare organization.

Provide Detailed Documentation and Reporting A key deliverable of ethical hacking is a detailed, actionable report on the findings. This report should include a comprehensive analysis of discovered vulnerabilities and their potential impact and prioritized remediation recommendations. Ethical hackers must ensure their advice is practical and within the organization's policies and procedures, avoiding overstepping their bounds or assuming roles outside their expertise. For example, while ethical hackers can suggest specific security measures, they should not attempt to dictate internal policies or strategies.

By adhering to these ethical boundaries and guidelines, ethical hackers can provide invaluable insights into healthcare cybersecurity while respecting patients' rights, the integrity of systems, and the trust of the organizations they serve.

Best Practices for Ethical Hacking in Healthcare

Adhering to best practices ensures that ethical hacking engagements are effective, minimize risks, and provide actionable insights to enhance security. Consider these practices focusing on planning, risk management, communication, documentation, and continuous improvement. They enable healthcare organizations to protect sensitive data and critical systems effectively.

Begin with Comprehensive Planning A successful engagement begins with comprehensive planning. Developing a detailed test plan with clearly defined objectives ensures that all stakeholders understand the scope and purpose of the testing. This plan should outline the systems to be tested, the methodologies used, and the desired outcomes. Identifying key stakeholders, such as IT administrators, compliance officers, and clinical staff, and establishing clear communication channels ensures alignment and readiness. Effective planning minimizes misunderstandings, reduces disruptions, and provides a testing process that aligns with organizational goals and regulatory requirements.

Conduct a Risk Assessment Conducting a thorough risk assessment before testing is essential to understand the potential impact of ethical hacking activities on healthcare operations. This assessment identifies critical systems, high-risk areas, and vulnerabilities that require priority attention. For example, systems handling patient data, such as electronic health records or medical imaging devices, should be treated with heightened caution. By focusing on areas that pose the most significant risk, ethical hackers can maximize the value of their efforts while minimizing unnecessary disruptions.

Implement a Staged Approach A staged approach to ethical hacking allows for controlled testing that reduces risks to operational systems. The process should begin with less intrusive tests, such as vulnerability scans, and gradually increase in intensity with more aggressive penetration testing techniques. This phased methodology identifies potential issues early without compromising critical services. For instance, testing the security of a hospital network may start with basic network scans before progressing to simulated attacks on specific devices or systems. A staged approach provides a systematic way to uncover vulnerabilities while safeguarding patient care and organizational operations.

Utilize Effective Tools and Techniques Aligned with Real-World Threats In any ethical hacking engagement, selecting and applying the right tools and techniques is critical for accurately assessing a customer's security posture. A core principle is to test using the same tools and methods an attacker would use. By leveraging tools commonly found in the arsenals of real-world threat actors—whether open-source, commercial, or custom—you ensure that your testing reflects realistic attack scenarios. This includes utilizing frameworks like Metasploit and Cobalt Strike (in a controlled, authorized context), open-source tools like Nmap, Burp Suite, and OWASP ZAP, and advanced techniques like social engineering or phishing simulations, depending on the scope.

It's also important to stay current with emerging tactics, techniques, and procedures (TTPs) documented in frameworks like MITRE ATT&CK. Incorporating these modern adversary behaviors ensures your testing goes beyond known vulnerabilities and assesses an organization's resilience against advanced threats.

Additionally, a balanced approach that combines automated scanning tools with manual testing techniques often yields the most comprehensive results. Automation can identify common issues at scale, while manual testing can uncover complex logic flaws, chained exploits, and business logic vulnerabilities that automated tools typically miss.

Using attacker-grade tools and methodologies—within the boundaries of a well-defined scope and with proper authorization—gives customers a realistic view of their security risks and actionable insights to improve their defenses.

Maintain Real-Time Communication Maintaining open lines of communication with IT staff and other relevant personnel during testing is crucial for addressing any immediate issues. Ethical hackers must report critical vulnerabilities in real time to prevent potential exploitation. For example, if a significant weakness in a patient portal is discovered that could expose sensitive data, it should be escalated immediately to the appropriate team for mitigation. Regular updates on progress and findings help build trust and ensure stakeholders are informed and engaged throughout the process.

Provide Comprehensive Documentation Detailed documentation is critical. Maintaining logs of all activities, including the methods used, systems tested, and vulnerabilities identified, ensures transparency and accountability. These logs serve as a valuable resource for understanding the testing process and addressing any issues. Final reports should be clear and actionable, and recommendations should be prioritized based on the severity and potential impact of vulnerabilities. For instance, the report might highlight a critical vulnerability in an EHR system that requires immediate patching alongside suggestions for longer-term improvements, such as enhancing access controls or staff training.

Provide Post-Test Support Ethical hacking does not end with identifying vulnerabilities. Guiding remediation efforts ensures that organizations can effectively address the issues. This may include recommending specific security tools, policies, or practices to mitigate risks. Conducting follow-up tests to verify that fixes have been implemented correctly and that no new vulnerabilities have been introduced is also essential. Post-test support demonstrates a commitment to improving security and reinforces the value of engagements.

Enable Continuous Learning Ethical hackers must stay updated on the latest healthcare-specific risks, such as vulnerabilities in telemedicine platforms or IoMT devices. Regularly updating testing methodologies and tools ensures that ethical hacking remains effective and relevant. Engaging in continuous learning through certifications, industry conferences, and collaboration with peers enhances ethical hackers' expertise and the quality of their work.

By adhering to these best practices, ethical hacking in healthcare can effectively identify vulnerabilities, enhance security, and protect patient safety and data integrity. Comprehensive planning, risk assessment, a staged approach, real-time communication, thorough documentation, post-test support, and a commitment to continuous learning create a framework for successful and impactful ethical hacking engagements. These practices strengthen organizational security and build trust and resilience in digital healthcare environments.

Challenges in Healthcare Ethical Hacking

The healthcare sector operates under strict regulatory requirements, deals with highly sensitive patient data, and depends on the continuous availability of systems and devices for patient care. Ethical hackers should carefully consider navigating this section's complexities to ensure effective testing without compromising operational integrity or patient trust.

Balancing Security with Availability One of the most common challenges in healthcare ethical hacking is ensuring that security testing does not disrupt the availability of critical services. Healthcare systems must always remain operational to deliver patient care. Ethical hackers must carefully plan and execute tests to minimize the risk of system downtime or service interruptions. For example, scheduling penetration tests during off-peak hours or using simulated environments can help balance the need for security assessments with maintaining service availability.

Legacy Systems Many healthcare organizations rely on outdated software or hardware that is not designed to handle modern threats. These systems are often fragile, poorly documented, and lack basic security features like encryption or remote update capabilities. Ethical hackers must approach these systems with extreme caution, as overly aggressive testing, even aggressive discovery scanning, could cause crashes or data loss. It is essential to develop tailored testing strategies that account for the limitations and vulnerabilities of legacy systems.

Diverse Ecosystem Healthcare environments typically consist of a diverse ecosystem of systems and devices, such as IoMT, hospital networks, cloud-based applications, and third-party vendor platforms. This complexity poses a challenge for ethical hacking, as vulnerabilities in one system can cascade into others. Ethical hackers must comprehensively understand the interconnected nature of healthcare technologies and carefully assess how vulnerabilities in one area might impact the broader ecosystem. For instance, testing a connected infusion pump requires assessing the device and evaluating its integration with the hospital's network and patient monitoring systems.

Regulatory Compliance As mentioned, ethical hacking activities must adhere to regulations such as HIPAA, GDPR, and other local laws. Ensuring compliance involves obtaining proper authorization for testing, documenting all activities, and avoiding unnecessary access to PHI. Ethical hackers must also consider the regulatory implications of their findings and ensure that their reports are detailed enough to support organizations in meeting compliance obligations.

Sensitivity of Data Accessing or exposing PHI, even during authorized testing, carries legal and reputational risks. Ethical hackers must take every precaution to avoid accessing actual patient data unless necessary and should use anonymized or synthetic data whenever possible. When PHI must be accessed, strict safeguards, such as encryption and secure handling protocols, must be in place to ensure data confidentiality. Additionally, ethical hackers must navigate the ethical implications of discovering vulnerabilities that could expose sensitive patient information and determine how to report and address these issues responsibly.

Resource Constraints Many healthcare organizations operate with limited cybersecurity budgets and resources, and this can hinder the scope and effectiveness of ethical hacking. Smaller organizations may struggle to allocate sufficient funding for comprehensive testing or to address identified vulnerabilities. Ethical hackers must work within these constraints by prioritizing high-risk areas and providing cost-effective recommendations for remediation. Building awareness of the importance of cybersecurity among healthcare leadership can also help secure the necessary resources for ongoing security improvements.

Emerging Trends and Future Considerations

As technology transforms the industry, ethical hacking must evolve to address new challenges and leverage emerging tools and methodologies. The bombardment of AI, the increasing number of IoMT devices, the adoption of cloud-based services, quantum computing, and expanding telemedicine create opportunities and complexities for security testing. This section explores these trends and future considerations in ethical hacking within the healthcare sector.

Artificial Intelligence and Machine Learning AI and ML are becoming integral, enabling more sophisticated and automated penetration testing. AI-driven tools can analyze massive datasets to identify patterns and anomalies indicative of vulnerabilities, reducing the time required for manual assessments. For example, machine learning algorithms can identify potential attack vectors by analyzing network traffic or system logs. Additionally, AI can simulate complex attack scenarios, providing deeper insights into potential weaknesses. However, using AI in ethical hacking also raises ethical considerations, such as ensuring that these tools are used responsibly and do not inadvertently cause harm.

IoMT Security The growth of the IoMT presents challenges and opportunities for ethical hacking. IoMT devices, such as connected infusion pumps, wearable health monitors, and implantable medical devices, often operate with limited computational resources and are deployed in life-critical environments. Ethical hackers must develop specialized techniques to test these devices without disrupting their functionality or endangering patients. For example, testing could focus on evaluating communication protocols, data encryption, and integration with hospital networks.

Cloud Security in Healthcare Cloud environments host critical applications, such as electronic health records systems, telemedicine platforms, and data analytics tools, making them targets for cyberattacks. Ethical hackers must adapt their practices to assess cloud infrastructure security, including configurations, access controls, and data encryption. Special attention should be paid to multitenancy risks, where vulnerabilities in one organization's cloud instance could potentially expose the data or systems of other tenants. As healthcare organizations rely more heavily on cloud services, ethical hacking must also address emerging threats, such as container vulnerabilities and misconfigured APIs, to ensure the integrity and confidentiality of patient data.

Quantum Computing Implications   Quantum computing threatens current cryptographic standards. As quantum computing technology advances, ethical hackers must prepare for a future where these methods may become obsolete. This involves testing healthcare systems for vulnerabilities that could be exploited by quantum-powered attackers and recommending transitions to quantum-resistant cryptographic algorithms. Ethical hackers should also stay informed about developments in quantum-safe encryption standards, such as those emerging from NIST's Post-Quantum Cryptography Standardization project.

Ethical Hacking in Telemedicine   Telemedicine has become a big part of modern healthcare due to the growing demand for remote care delivery. However, this shift introduces security challenges that ethical hackers must address. Telemedicine platforms rely on video conferencing, remote monitoring, and data-sharing tools, all potential attack vectors. Ethical hackers should focus on testing the security of these platforms, including end-to-end encryption, user authentication, and secure data transmission. Additionally, they must consider the privacy implications of telemedicine, ensuring that patient consultations and health data are protected from eavesdropping or unauthorized access.

Training and Certification for Healthcare Ethical Hackers

The critical nature of healthcare cybersecurity requires ethical hackers to possess specialized knowledge and skills tailored to the unique challenges of protecting sensitive medical data, connected devices, and critical systems. Training and certification are essential for developing competent professionals who can identify vulnerabilities while adhering to the ethical and regulatory standards of the healthcare sector. This section focuses on the importance of specialized certifications, continuous education, and ethical training for healthcare ethical hackers.

Specialized Certifications

Obtaining relevant certifications is a foundational step for ethical hackers seeking to specialize in healthcare. Certifications such as the Healthcare Information Security and Privacy Practitioner (HCISPP) and the Certified Ethical Hacker (CEH) with a healthcare focus provide the necessary technical and contextual knowledge to address healthcare-specific security challenges.

The HCISPP certification, offered by the International Information System Security Certification Consortium (ISC)², is tailored for professionals working in healthcare information security. It emphasizes key areas such as healthcare regulations, privacy laws, risk management, and security best practices. This certification is valuable for ethical hackers who need to navigate the regulatory landscape of healthcare, including HIPAA, GDPR, and other compliance frameworks.

The CEH certification, offered by the EC-Council, equips ethical hackers with advanced penetration testing techniques and tools. Focusing on healthcare, this certification ensures that professionals are proficient in testing electronic health record systems, IoMT devices, and telemedicine platforms while prioritizing patient safety and data integrity.

Continuous Education

Continuous education is essential for maintaining expertise. In short, ethical hackers must stay informed about the latest trends in healthcare-specific security threats, such as ransomware attacks targeting hospitals, vulnerabilities in connected medical devices, and emerging IoMT challenges. Participating in industry conferences, such as the Healthcare Information and Management Systems Society (HIMSS) conference or the Health-ISAC Summit, provides opportunities to learn from experts, network with peers, and explore innovative solutions. Workshops and online courses focused on healthcare cybersecurity also offer practical training on new tools, attack techniques, and defensive strategies.

In addition to technical skills, ethical hackers should familiarize themselves with healthcare regulations and standards updates, ensuring their practices align with evolving legal requirements. Ethical hacking carries unique responsibilities due to the potential impact on patient safety and privacy. Ethical training should emphasize these responsibilities, ensuring that testers understand the profound implications of their work. The top three aspects of ethical training, in this context, include:

- **Patient-centered focus:** Ethical hackers must prioritize protecting patients above all else. This involves avoiding unnecessary access to sensitive data, using anonymized datasets for testing whenever possible, and ensuring that testing does not disrupt critical healthcare services.

- **Regulatory adherence:** Ethical training should instill a strong understanding of compliance with healthcare regulations, such as HIPAA and GDPR, emphasizing the importance of protecting personal health information during testing.

- **Professional conduct:** Ethical hackers should adhere to established codes of conduct, such as those provided by the EC-Council or (ISC)², maintaining professionalism and integrity in all aspects of their work.

Training and certification are crucial for ethical hackers in healthcare. They equip them with the specialized knowledge, technical skills, and ethical mindset to navigate the sector's unique challenges. By pursuing certifications like HCISPP and CEH, engaging in continuous education, and prioritizing ethical considerations, professionals can contribute to the security and resilience of healthcare systems.

Case Studies

Examining case studies allows us to appreciate the tangible impact of ethical hacking and the lessons it offers. This section focuses on a synopsis of successful ethical hacking engagements that have improved healthcare security and the takeaways from incidents where ethical hacking revealed critical vulnerabilities.

Successful Ethical Hacking Engagements

Ethical hacking has consistently demonstrated its value in uncovering vulnerabilities before malicious actors can exploit them. One notable example involves a hospital system in the United States that conducted a comprehensive penetration test as part of its cybersecurity overhaul. Ethical hackers identified multiple vulnerabilities, including unencrypted communication between IoMT devices and central servers, weak default passwords on infusion pumps, and outdated software on critical care equipment.

Through detailed reporting and collaboration with the hospital's IT team, these vulnerabilities were addressed by implementing encrypted communication protocols, enforcing strong password policies, and applying necessary software patches. The engagement bolstered the hospital's cybersecurity posture and demonstrated compliance with regulations like HIPAA.

Another case involved an ethical hacking firm working with a telemedicine provider. The testers discovered a flaw in the platform's authentication system, which allowed unauthorized access to patient consultation records. They demonstrated the potential impact by simulating an attack, prompting the provider to implement two-factor authentication and encrypt sensitive data at rest and in transit. This engagement prevented a possible breach that could have compromised the PHI of thousands of patients.

Ethical hacking engagements often reveal critical lessons for improving cybersecurity practices. A significant case involves a major healthcare network that commissioned ethical hackers to test its electronic health record system. The testers uncovered a severe vulnerability in the system's user access controls, which allowed employees to access patient records beyond their job requirements. This discovery led to role-based access controls and regular access audits, ensuring that employees could only access the information necessary for their roles. This case underscores the importance of granular access management to protect sensitive data.

Another key lesson emerged from an incident involving IoMT devices in a hospital. Ethical hackers found that multiple devices shared the same default credentials, a common oversight in large deployments. This weakness could have allowed attackers to gain control of devices like cardiac monitors and infusion pumps. Following the report recommendations, the hospital implemented a policy requiring unique, strong passwords for all devices and conducted staff training on cybersecurity best practices. This case highlights the risks associated with default configurations and the importance of customizing security settings during deployment.

In some engagements, ethical hacking has also revealed weaknesses in physical security. At a healthcare facility, ethical hackers successfully bypassed access controls to a server room by exploiting lax enforcement of badge-checking protocols. This breach highlighted the need for stricter enforcement of physical security measures, such as biometric authentication and surveillance systems, to protect critical infrastructure.

These case studies illustrate that ethical hacking is an invaluable tool for identifying and mitigating cybersecurity risks in healthcare. They demonstrate the importance of regular security assessments, strong access controls, and the need for a holistic approach that addresses both digital and physical vulnerabilities. Moreover, they highlight the critical role of collaboration between ethical hackers and healthcare organizations in fostering a proactive security culture.

Key Takeaways from Ethical Hacking in Healthcare

Ethical hacking is vital in securing healthcare systems and protecting sensitive patient data. However, due to the unique sensitivities of the healthcare environment, it must be conducted with the highest ethical standards and in strict compliance with legal and regulatory requirements. Ethical hacking practices must also adapt to address emerging threats as healthcare technology evolves—through adopting IoMT devices, telemedicine, cloud-based services, and AI. Ethical hackers in healthcare are tasked with safeguarding critical infrastructure, ensuring the safety and functionality of medical devices, and maintaining the privacy of patient information, all while minimizing operational disruption and adhering to frameworks such as HIPAA, GDPR, and FDA guidelines.

A comprehensive ethical hacking approach spans network infrastructure, application security, physical security, and even human factors like social engineering. Successful engagements rely on meticulous planning, risk assessments, real-time communication, and thorough documentation. Ethical hackers must maintain professionalism, secure explicit authorization, and ensure confidentiality. They also face significant challenges, such as balancing security with service availability, dealing with legacy systems, and navigating complex healthcare ecosystems, often under resource constraints.

Continuous learning, certification (such as HCISPP and CEH), and staying current with cybersecurity trends—like quantum computing and advanced threat tactics—are essential for maintaining effective, ethical hacking practices. Real-world case studies highlight the value of ethical hacking in revealing vulnerabilities such as weak access controls and poor credential management, reinforcing the need for ongoing assessments and robust security strategies. Ultimately, ethical hacking helps healthcare organizations build resilient, secure, and trusted environments that protect patient safety, ensure data privacy, and meet regulatory obligations.

Conclusion

In conclusion, the intersection of medical IoT, healthcare, and cybersecurity presents challenges and opportunities. Throughout this book, I traversed the complex landscape of IoMT security, from its foundational aspects to attack vectors and defense strategies. As discussed in Part I, the rapid evolution of wireless technologies in medical devices has modernized healthcare delivery and introduced new vulnerabilities. Next, the attack vectors in Part II revealed the sophistication of threats facing IoMT devices, underscoring the critical need for strong security measures. The scenarios and case studies presented in Part III focused on these threats, demonstrating the potential impact of successful attacks on medical systems. From pacemaker hacking to hospital network breaches, these examples serve as reminders of the high stakes involved in IoMT security.

In response to these challenges, Part IV introduced detection and prevention strategies. Integrating machine learning, advanced intrusion detection systems, and secure communication protocols offers promising enhancements for IoMT security. However, as explained, technology alone is not enough, and best practices and human vigilance remain crucial components of a comprehensive security strategy. Part V examined emerging trends such as 5G networks (and beyond with 6G), quantum computing, and AI-driven attacks and defenses. These developments promise to reshape the IoMT security landscape with their challenges and solutions. Finally, discussing legal and ethical considerations in Part VI highlighted the regulatory environment surrounding IoMT security. The need to balance innovation with patient safety, privacy, and ethical considerations will continue challenging the healthcare industry.

It's crucial to recognize that IoMT security is not static. The threats, technologies, and strategies discussed here will continue to evolve. Therefore, this book should be a foundation for ongoing learning and adaptation. The security of IoMT devices is not just a technical challenge; it's a matter of patient safety, privacy, and public health. As cybersecurity professionals, healthcare leaders, IT specialists, and researchers, we are all responsible for safeguarding these critical systems.

Moving forward, collaboration across disciplines is key. Cybersecurity experts, healthcare providers, device manufacturers, policymakers, IT, healthcare leadership, and ethicists must continue to work together to create a more secure ecosystem. We strive for a future where the benefits of connected healthcare can be realized without compromising security or patient trust. In the face of threats, our vigilance, creativity, and commitment to ethical practices will be our most potent defenses. As we continue to innovate and adapt, let us remember that the goal is to secure systems and protect and improve human lives. This book has equipped you with knowledge, insights, and motivation to contribute to this mission.

Finally, suppose you're interested in a fast-paced fictional depiction of the latest in healthcare attack vectors. In that case, you can find my novel, *Silent Intrusions*, in various marketplaces online or scan the following QR code:

Index

A

Abnormal Security, 481
academic demonstrations, of pacemaker vulnerabilities, 240
access control lists (ACLs), 108, 175, 217
access controls
 AI-enhanced, 482
 best practices, 397–401
 improving with machine learning, 358–359
 for IoMT devices, 19, 112–113
 as a mitigation strategy for pacemaker vulnerabilities, 242–243
 for spoofing attacks, 205
 MITM attacks and, 166
 with RFID technology, 36
 weak, as a vulnerability of wearable medical devices, 285
 Wi-Fi networks and, 108–109
access points (APs), 53, 219
accountability, 499, 503–504
active MITM attacks, 163
active tags, 28
adaptability, as a strength of Snort, 324
address randomization, with Bluetooth, 70–71
addressing zero-day threats, 178
adequacy decisions, 497
administrative access, enforcing multifactor authentication (MFA) for, 172–173
adopting
 hybrid detection techniques, 303
 layered security, 332
advanced analytics, 277
advanced diagnostics, using IoMT devices, 17
advanced monitoring, deploying, 179–182
advanced threat detection, as a capability of Cisco Secure IPS, 307
advanced threat intelligence integration, wearable devices and, 292
adversarial attacks, 449
adversarial machine learning attacks, 353, 359–360
AES-128 encryption, 102
AES-256 encryption, 19, 205, 242, 253

527

agent-based architecture, as a capability of Open Source Security (OSSEC) HIDS, 320
agents, as key components of IoMT IDS, 300
aggregating, 344
AI algorithms, 12–13
AI-assisted social engineering, 477–478
AI-driven attacks
  impact of on healthcare, 478–480
  impersonation, 477
  types, 476–478
AI-driven defenses
  about, 480–484
  best practices, 488–489
  challenges in implementing, 484–486
  future trends in, 486–487
AI-driven monitoring, continuous validation and, 173
AI-driven network segmentation, 482–483
AI-driven security automation and orchestration, 487
AI-driven security policy management, 482
AI-driven threat detection, for DoS attacks, 218
AI-enhanced access control, 482
AI-enhanced phishing, 477, 482
AI-enhanced threat hunting, 487
AI-generated malware, 477
AI-powered anomaly detection, integrating, 303
AI-powered attacks, on wearable devices, 289
AI-powered detection, IDS and, 333
AI-powered firmware integrity checks, wearable devices and, 292
AI-powered monitoring and analytics, best practices, 403–405
AI-powered password cracking, 478
AI-powered ransomware, 477
AI-powered threat detection, 480
AI-powered vulnerability management, 482
Airbase-ng, 116
Aircrack-ng suite, 83, 85, 86, 120–122, 214
AI-related threats, 449–450
Aireplay-ng, 120–121
Airgeddon, 84, 85
Airgraph-ng, 121
Airmon-ng, 120
Airodump-ng, 120
Airolib-ng, 121
Akamai Prolexic, 221
alert fatigue, as a challenge in implementing AI-driven defenses, 485
algorithmic bias, 499
AliveCor's KardiaMobile 6L, 293
always-on connectivity, 299
amplification attacks, 212–213
analysis engine, as key component of IoMT IDS, 300
anomaly detection
  AI-powered, 303
  as a capability of Palo Alto Networks Threat Prevention, 316
  as a capability of Suricata, 328
  as a key IDPS feature, 301
  machine learning and, 341
  as a mitigation strategy
    for DoS attacks, 219
    for insulin pumps, 260
    for pacemaker vulnerabilities, 243
  smart home device fingerprinting for, 363–364
  wearable devices and, 292
anti-analysis techniques, 276
Any.Run, 273
API keys, 271
API vulnerabilities, as a data privacy risk of wearable medical devices, 286
applications
  of Bluetooth in healthcare, 52

ethical hacking, 512
machine learning, 350–352
of quantum computing, 461–462
of Wi-Fi in healthcare, 56–58
appropriate safeguards, 497
architecture, of Bluetooth Low Energy (BLE), 50
Area Under the ROC Curve (AUC), 344
artificial intelligence (AI)
  about, 40
  analyzing MITM attacks using, 180–181
  for anomaly detection, 385
  Bluetooth attacks, 61–63
  for ethical hacking, 520
  governance in, 504
  IDPS deployment and, 332
  integrating with 6G, 444
  IoMT and, 20
  as a strength of Cisco Secure IPS, 308
  wearable devices and, 291–294
  Wi-Fi attacks and, 61–63
asset management, 17, 409–411
asymmetric encryption, 374
attack modes, as a capability of Hashcat, 131
attack prediction, machine learning and, 342
attack surfaces
  about, 447–448
  for insulin pumps, 248
  for pacemakers, 248
  reduced, as a benefit of network segmentation and isolation, 175
attack vectors
  about, 65–66, 263–264
  analyzing, 331
  as a challenge of implementing secure communication protocols, 382
  landscape and, 268–272
audits
  best practices, 436–438

Kismet for, 139
as a mitigation strategy for DoS attacks, 224
monitoring and, 257
patch compliance, 178–179
Wifite for, 136
Wireshark for, 154
augmented reality (AR), IoMT and, 21
authentication
  about, 332
  artificial intelligence and, 62
  best practices, 397–401
  with Bluetooth, 70
  broken, 255
  as a challenge
    for IoMT devices, 111, 112
    of quantum computing, 463
    in securing healthcare wireless networks, 157
  in CIA triad, 68–70
  lack of
    as a vulnerability enabling DoS attacks, 214–215
    as a vulnerability of pacemakers, 239
    as a vulnerability of wearable medical devices, 284
  mechanisms for, 375
  as a mitigation strategy
    for DoS attacks, 218
    for insulin pumps, 260
    for pacemaker vulnerabilities, 242–243
    for spoofing attacks, 205
    for wearable devices, 291
  mutual, 172
  pairing and, 171
  as a security requirement for communication, 369–370
  with smart pill bottles/dispensers, 37
  for telemedicine, 34
  weak
    as a vulnerability of insulin pumps, 250

as a vulnerability of
pacemakers, 234
as a vulnerability of spoofing
attacks, 202–203
wearable devices and, 292
Wi-Fi networks and, 108–109
authentication, authorization, and
accounting (AAA), 377
authentication validation, 173–174
authorization
lack of, as a vulnerability enabling
DoS attacks, 214–215
as a mitigation strategy for DoS
attacks, 218
as a security requirement for
communication, 370–371
autoencoders, 346
automation
automated alerts as a capability of
Open Source Security (OSSEC)
HIDS, 320
automated attack timelines, 277
automated blocking as a capability of
Palo Alto Networks Threat
Prevention, 316
automated incident response,
314, 480–481
automated investigation
timelines, 278
automated mitigation for DoS
attacks, 218
automated network security and
response as a capability of Cisco
Secure IPS, 307
automated prevention as key
function of IDPS in IoMT, 300
automated response actions, 278
automated responses as a capability
of Trend Micro TippingPoint, 309
as a capability of WiFi Pineapple, 147
as a capability of Wifite, 136
continuous validation and automatic
reauthentication, 173
for reporting, 277

autonomous incident response,
wearable devices and, 293
autonomy, 500
AWS SageMaker, 483
AWS Shield, 221
Azure Machine Learning, 483

B

BackBox Linux, 85–86, 87
backdoors, MITM attacks and, 166
backup and recovery, best
practices, 428–430
bandwidth management, for DoS
attacks, 219
Barnaby Jack's Ethical Hacking
Demonstration, 239
basal rate delivery, for insulin
pumps, 249
battery
battery drain attacks, 211, 240
life, as a key feature of
pacemakers, 232
limitations, as a disadvantage of
wireless devices, 24, 39
optimization, as a best practice for
wireless technology
implementation, 44
battery service, 51
behavioral analysis
about, 276
as a capability of AI-driven threat
detection, 180
as a capability of Check Point
IPS, 313
IDS and, 333–334
as a key IDPS feature, 301
best practices
about, 391–392
AI-powered monitoring and
analytics, 403–405
asset inventory and
management, 409–411
authentication and access
controls, 397–401

backup and recovery, 428–430
cloud security, 395
compliance with regulatory
    standards, 414–417
continuous monitoring and incident
    response, 417–419
cybersecurity insurance, 435
data minimization and retention
    policies, 433–435
employee training and
    awareness, 420–422
encryption and data
    protection, 407–409
endpoint security, 392–393
ethical hacking, 516–518
healthcare organizations, 488–489
IoMT IDPS deployment, 331–333
network security, 393–394
network segmentation, 396–397
perimeter security, 394–395
physical security measures,
    425–427
regular security audits, 436–438
regulatory compliance, 502–504
secure communication
    protocols, 430–432
secure device onboarding and
    decommissioning, 422–425
secure medical device
    communication, 383–384
updates and patching, 401–403
vendor management and third-party
    risk assessment, 411–414
Wi-Fi, 158
wireless technology
    implementation, 43–44
Zero Trust security model, 405–407
Bettercap, 83, 86, 116, 122–125, 214
bias, 499
biased decision-making, 449
biometric authentication, 375–376
BlackArch Linux, 84–85, 86
blockchain technology, 21, 41, 385,
    456, 487

blood pressure, IoMT devices for
    monitoring, 6
BlueBorne case study, 102–103
bluejacking, 58, 81
Bluelog, 84, 85, 90–91
BlueMaho, 84, 86, 98
bluesmacking, 80
Bluesnarfer, 83, 85, 86
bluesnarfing, 58, 79–80
Bluetooth
  about, 23, 25, 46–47, 48
  disabling, 101
  hacking tools
    about, 82
    BlueLog, 90–91
    BlueMaho, 98
    BlueZ, 88–89
    btCrawler, 92–93
    BtleJack, 95–96
    BTScanner, 93–94
    Flipper Zero, 87–88
    GATTacker, 96–97
    HCIDump, 98–99
    Linux distributions, 83–87
    PyBluez, 99–101
    Ubertooth One, 94–95
  in healthcare, 47–52
  machine learning and, 352
  mitigating vulnerabilities, 100–103
  mitigation planning, 67–103
  MITM attacks and pairing, 165
  security
    about, 58–63, 68–70
    authentication, 70
    challenges of, 71
    encryption, 70
    pairing, 70
    privacy features, 70–71
  vulnerabilities
    about, 67–103
    bluejacking, 81
    bluesnarfing, 79–80
    Bluetooth forward and future
        secrecy (BLUFFS) attacks, 76–79

Bluetooth impersonation attacks (BAIS), 72–75
Bluetooth Remote Code Execution (RCE), 81–82
data interception, 71–72
denial-of-service (DoS) attacks, 80–81
man-in-the-middle (MITM) attacks, 75–76
Bluetooth Basic Rate/Enhanced Data Rate (BR/EDR), 48–49
Bluetooth Classic, 48–49, 89
Bluetooth Core Specifications, 49
Bluetooth forward and future secrecy (BLUFFS) attack, as a common Bluetooth vulnerability, 76–79
Bluetooth impersonation attacks (BIASs), 58
Bluetooth Low Energy (BLE), 48, 49–51, 89, 95–96, 372, 378
Bluetooth Remote Code Execution (RCE), as a common Bluetooth vulnerability, 81–82
bluetoothd, 89
bluetooth-meshd, 89
BluetoothScanner, 83
BlueZ Utilities, 84, 86, 88–89
bolus doses, for insulin pumps, 249
bonding, 378
broadcast discovery, 203
brute-force attacks, 60, 132
btCrawler, 92–93
BtleJack, 95–96
BTScanner, 93–94
Bully, 86
Burp Suite, 252

C

California Consumer Privacy Act (CCPA), 415, 514
captive portal attacks
about, 115–117
as a capability of Wifiphisher, 151
as a capability of WiFi-Pumpkin, 149

capturing sensitive data, 115
case studies
about, 227–228
attack vector trends and hospital network breaches with IoMT devices, 263–281
Bluetooth vulnerabilities, 102–103
for ethical hackers, 523–524
implementing IDPS in healthcare environments, 302–304
insulin pump vulnerabilities and exploits, 247–262
machine learning, 362–364
MITM attack on infusion pumps, 190–192
pacemaker hacking, 229–246
replay attack on infusion pumps, 199–200
wearable medical device security challenge, 282–294
cellular technologies, 23, 27–28
centralized management, as a capability of Palo Alto Networks Threat Prevention, 317
Ceribell's Rapid Response EEG System, 293
Certificate Authority (CA), 431
certificate-based authentication, 431–432
certification programs, 453–455
Certified Ethical Hacker (CEH), 521–522
ChatGPT, 483
Check Point Intrusion Prevention System/Quantum, 312–315
Chirillo, John (author)
Silent Intrusions, 263
CIA triad, 68–70, 253, 380
Cisco Secure Intrusion Prevention System (NGIPS), 306–309
clinical decision support systems, replay attacks and, 199
cloning attacks, with RFID technology, 36

cloud
  integration
    as a capability of Palo Alto
      Networks Threat
      Prevention, 317
    as a vulnerability of insulin
      pumps, 250
  security
    best practices, 394
    for ethical hacking, 520–521
  vulnerabilities
    as a data privacy risk of wearable
      medical devices, 286
    rise in cloud-based attacks, 270
cloud access security brokers
  (CASB), 392
cloud security posture management
  (CSPM), 392, 395
Cloudflare, 221
code signing, 383–384
code-based cryptography, 466–467
collaboration
  about, 504
  as a best practice, 488
  fostering, 188
  policymakers enabling, 508
  quantum computing and, 474–475
communication
  about, 366
  best practices, 383–384, 430–432
  challenges in implementing,
    381–383
  device pairing, 377–379
  emerging technologies and future
    trends, 384–386
  encryption algorithms and key
    management, 373–377
  ethical considerations, 387–389
  fostering, 188
  importance of, 366–367
  for insulin pumps, 248
  for medical devices, 371–373
  onboarding, 377–379
  for pacemakers, 248

  regulatory compliance and
    standards, 379–381
  security requirements for, 368–371
  strategies for, 386–387
  unsecured
    as a vulnerability of
      pacemakers, 239
    as a vulnerability of spoofing
      attacks, 203
    as a vulnerability of wearable
      medical devices, 284
  with vendors, 186–187
community rulesets
  as a capability of Snort, 324
  as a capability of Suricata, 328
community support, as a strength of
  Snort, 324
compatibility, as a capability of
  Hashcat, 132
compensating controls, deploying, 178
complexity challenges
  of implementing secure
    communication protocols, 382
  of Palo Alto Networks Threat
    Prevention, 318
  of securing medical devices, 168
  of Snort, 325
compliance
  as a benefit of strong encryption, 171
  improved, as a benefit of network
    segmentation and isolation, 175
  with regulatory standards, 57
  Wifite for testing, 137
compliance mapping, 253–254
comprehensive analytics, as a
  capability of Palo Alto Networks
  Threat Prevention, 317
comprehensive data collection, 277
comprehensive mitigation strategy,
  benefits of, 190–194
comprehensive testing, 257
comprehensive visibility, 299, 314
compromising corporate
  networks, 116

Computer Fraud and Abuse Act
    (CFAA), 88
concept drift, 353
confidentiality
  in CIA triad, 68–70
  maintaining during ethical
    hacking, 515–516
  as a security requirement for
    communication, 368
connectivity, from DoS attacks, 213
consoles, as key component of IoMT
    IDS, 300
constant jamming, 210
continuous glucose monitors, 283
continuous learning
  artificial intelligence and, 62
  as a best practice, 488
  for ethical hacking, 518, 522
  wearable devices and, 293
continuous monitoring
  about, 173–174, 503
  as a benefit of wireless devices, 29–30
  best practices, 417–419
  for IoMT devices, 5–7, 19
convenience, as a benefit of wearable
    devices, 283
convolutional neural networks
    (CNNs), 342, 348
corporate networks,
    compromising, 116
Cortex XSOAR, 483, 484
cost
  as a challenge
    of Cisco Secure IPS, 308
    of Palo Alto Networks Threat
      Prevention, 318
    of Trend Micro TippingPoint, 311
  as a strength
    of Bluetooth, 52
    of Open Source Security (OSSEC)
      HIDS, 320–321
    of Snort, 324
  Ubertooth One, 95
covering tracks, IOCs, IOAs and, 268

coWPAtty, 125–127
credential harvesting
  about, 115
  as a capability of WiFi Pineapple, 147
  as a capability of Wifiphisher, 151
  PEAP exchange attacks and, 118
  preventing, as a benefit of MFA, 172
critical dependencies, 299
critical infrastructure, increased
    targeting of, 270
cross-border data transfers, regulatory
    frameworks and, 497
cross-platform support/compatibility
  as a capability of Open Source
    Security (OSSEC) HIDS, 320
  with PyBluez, 100
cross-site scripting (XSS), 252, 394
cross-vendor compatibility, 453
CrowdStrike Falcon Insight, 481, 483
Cuckoo Sandbox, 273
custom templates, as a capability of
    Wifiphisher, 151
customizable alerts, with
    BlueMaho, 98
customizable reporting, 278
cyber attacks, anatomy of, 265–268
cyber threats
  AI-enhanced, 270
  mitigating, as a benefit of strong
    encryption, 171
  protection
    as a benefit of device
      authentication, 173
    improved, as a benefit of update
      and patch management, 179
cybersecurity
  challenges, as a risk of
    pacemakers, 241
  regulatory frameworks and
    requirements for, 496
  training and awareness programs for
    reduced risk exposure, 185
  training in, 384
cybersecurity insurance, 435

D

Darktrace Antigena Email, 481
data analysis, as a capability of WiFi Pineapple, 147
data at rest, 19, 407
data breaches, 478–479, 497
data collection, 300, 343, 354, 388
data confidentiality, as a benefit of strong encryption, 170
data exfiltration, 268, 396
data export, 278
data flow, 331
data harvesting, 276
data in transit, 19, 170–171, 407
data integrity
  as a benefit
    of device authentication, 173
    of mutual authentication, 172
    of strong encryption, 170
  as a challenge of quantum computing, 462
  integration of AI and blockchain for, 487
  man-in-the-middle (MITM) attacks and violations of, 163–164
  replay attacks and, 198
data interception, 32, 71–72
data legitimacy, 499
data loss, from DoS attacks, 213
data loss prevention (DLP), 392
data minimization, 34, 433–435, 495
data misuse, as a data privacy risk of wearable medical devices, 286
data ownership, 498–499
data poisoning, 290, 449
data privacy
  as a benefit
    of device authentication, 173
    of WPA3, 169
  as a challenge
    in implementing AI-driven defenses, 484
    of wearable medical devices, 285–286, 292
    for quantum computing, 471
  regulatory frameworks and, 495–496
data protection
  best practices, 407–409
  privacy regulations for, 451–452
  regulatory frameworks and, 495–496
data quality/quantity, 354, 389, 399
data reliability, 499
data security, improved, as a benefit of network segmentation and isolation, 175
data sensitivity, 299, 519–520
data sharing, 285, 354
data spoofing, 202
data theft, MITM attacks and, 167
data transmission
  as a primary use of Bluetooth Classic, 49
  privacy implications of, 388
  as a security risk in telemedicine, 33
database servers, as key component of IoMT IDS, 300
data-driven decisions, as a benefit of wireless devices, 24
data-driven insights, using IoMT devices for, 12–14
Datagram Transport Layer Security (DTLS), 372, 431
deauthentication attacks
  about, 211–212
  as a capability
    of WiFi Pineapple, 147
    of Wifiphisher, 151
  as a challenge for IoMT devices, 111, 114
decentralized identity and blockchain, 505
deception technology, 301, 334–336
decision trees, 345
decommissioning best practices, 422–425
decryption, 154, 316
deep learning, 347–348, 362
deep packet inspection (DPI), 328, 359

defense in depth, 332, 383
defense strategy, as a key benefit of deception technology, 335
Deloitte Insights' 5G in Healthcare, 448
denial-of-service (DoS) attacks
  about, 58, 208–209
  amplification attacks, 212–213
  battery drain attacks, 211
  as a common Bluetooth vulnerability, 80–81
  common vulnerabilities, 214–217
  deauthentication attacks, 211–212
  distributed denial-of-service (DDoS) attacks, 213, 222–223
  flooding attacks, 209–210
  impact of on healthcare operations, 213
  jamming attacks, 210–211
  mitigation strategies for, 217–224
  preventing with machine learning, 351
  types of, 209–213
  as a vulnerability
    of insulin pumps, 250–251
    of pacemakers, 240
deploying
  advanced monitoring, 179–182
  compensating controls, 178
  intrusion detection, 179–182
  network controls, 102
  network segmentation and isolation, 174–176
  network-based IDPS, 302–303
  security solutions, 102
devices
  authentication
    about, 102
    implementing, 171–174
  behavior patterns, 343
  certification and approval, 496
  challenges in securing, 168
  compromise scenarios, 184
  control, as a risk of pacemakers, 239
  discovery of
    as a challenge of Bluetooth security, 71
    with PyBluez, 100
  diversity of, 299
  ethical hacking, 512
  hijacking, as a risk of wireless remote patient monitoring, 32
  information service, 51
  insufficient hardening, as a vulnerability of spoofing, 204
  isolation and segmentation of, 261
  malfunctions of, 497
  management of, 110–111
  manipulation of
    MITM attacks and, 167–168
    as a risk of pacemakers, 239
  MITM attacks and, 167
  pairing
    about, 377–379
    for DoS attacks, 218
    insecure, as a vulnerability of spoofing, 203–204
    as a mitigation strategy for spoofing attacks, 205
  replacement plans, 178
  risk classification, 496
  scanning with BlueMaho, 98
  security features of, 251
  spoofing, 202
  tampering, 256
  tracking
    with BlueMaho, 98
    as a challenge of Bluetooth security, 71
  whitelisting for DoS attacks, 218
DFIR tools, integration with, 278
diagnostics
  impact of 5G on, 446–447
  man-in-the-middle (MITM) attacks and, 163, 164
  replay attacks and, 198
dictionary attacks, 60, 132

Diffie-Hellman (DH) key
  exchange, 54, 374
digital certificates, 171, 370, 376
Digital Imaging and Communications
  in Medicine (DICOM), 373, 452
digital divide, 499–500
digital security, 254, 256, 257
disabling
disassociation attacks, as a challenge
  for IoMT devices, 111, 114
discoverability, limiting, 102
distributed denial-of-service
  (DDoS) attacks
  about, 213
  AI-enhanced, 478
  denial-of-service (DoS) attacks
    compared with, 222–223
distributions, Linux, 83–87
diverse ecosystems, as a challenge of
  ethical hacking, 519
DNS spoofing, as a capability of
  WiFi-Pumpkin, 149
documentation, for ethical hacking,
  516, 518
Domain Name System (DNS), 212
downgrade attacks, as a key feature of
  BLUFFS attacks, 77
downtime, advanced monitoring tools
  for minimizing, 181
drone-based wireless attacks,
  363
dual-chamber pacing, as a key feature
  of pacemakers, 232
dumpster diving, 256
dynamic analysis, 272, 273
dynamic application Security testing
  (DAST), 19

E
EAP Tunneling (Sycophant), as a
  Wi-Fi security risk, 59
EAPeak, 118
early detection, 14, 283
ease of use

  as an advantage of Bluetooth, 52
  as a capability of WiFi Pineapple, 147
eavesdropping
  with RFID technology, 36
  as a risk of pacemakers, 238
  as a risk of Wi-Fi security, 59
  as a risk of wireless remote patient
    monitoring, 32
ecosystems, IoMT, 299
Edge AI, 357
edge computing
  about, 40
  for data processing, 385
  IoMT and, 21
  security for, 449
edge-based IDSs, 334
Edwards-Curve Digital Signature
  Algorithm (EdDSA), 369
802.11ac standard, 53
802.11ax standard, 53
802.11n standard, 53
Eko Health's CORE500 Digital
  Stethoscope, 293
electromagnetic interference (EMI), 39
electronic health records
  (EHRs), 10–12
Elliptic Curve Cryptography
  (ECC), 374
Elliptic Curve Diffie-Hellman
  (ECDH), 70, 205, 243, 378
Elliptic Curve Digital Signature
  Algorithm (ECDSA), 369
email phishing, 256
emerging trends
  about, 441–442
  for ethical hacking, 520–521
  in IoMT IDS, 336
  for medical device
    communication, 384–386
  for wireless devices, 40–41
Empatica's Embrace2 Smartwatch, 293
enabling strong encryption, 102
enclaving, 108
encrypted traffic, 329, 355

encryption
  algorithms for, 373–377
  artificial intelligence and, 62
  best practices, 407–409
  with Bluetooth, 70
  for data at rest, 407
  for data in transit, 170–171, 407
  enabling strong, 102
  for healthcare
    communication, 169–171
  for IoMT devices, 19
  lack of, as a risk of pacemakers, 239
  as a mitigation strategy
    for insulin pumps, 260
    for replay attacks, 201
    for spoofing attacks, 205
  protocols for, 383
  with RFID technology, 36
  with smart pill bottles/dispensers, 37
  standards for, 292, 332
  for telemedicine, 34
  weak, as a vulnerability of wearable
    medical devices, 284
  for Wi-Fi, 56–57, 169
  for wireless remote patient
    monitoring, 33
end-of-life considerations, 500
end-of-life planning, 188
endpoint detection and response
  (EDR), 391
endpoint forensics, 278
endpoint security, best
  practices, 392–393
end-to-end encryption (E2EE)
  about, 170
  as a mitigation strategy
    for replay attacks, 201
    for wearable devices, 291
  for sensitive data transmission,
    408
  in telemedicine platforms, 386
enforcing multifactor authentication
  (MFA) for administrative
  access, 172–173

Enhanced Mobile Broadband
  (eMBB), 443
ensemble learning, 350, 355
Enterprise-grade 802.1X
  authentication, Wi-Fi and, 109
enumeration, IOCs, IOAs and, 266
environmental monitoring, using
  IoMT devices, 17
equipment location, RFID for, 28
equitable access, 471, 499–500
Ericsson Mobility Report, 447
escalation of privileges, IOCs, IOAs
  and, 267
establishing persistence, IOCs, IOAs
  and, 268
ethical considerations
  about, 491
  as a best practice, 489
  as a challenge in implementing
    AI-driven defenses, 485–486
  for communication, 387–389
  for ethical hacking, 515–516
  for machine learning in wireless
    security, 361–362
  for quantum computing, 470–472
  regulatory frameworks and, 498–500
ethical hacking
  about, 388
  best practices, 516–518
  case studies, 523–524
  challenges in, 519–520
  emerging trends and future
    considerations, 520–521
  ethical boundaries and
    guidelines, 515–516
  importance of, 510–511
  legal and regulatory
    considerations, 513–515
  for pacemakers, 236–241
  scope of, 512–513
  training and certification, 521–522
European Medicines Agency
  (EMA), 42
European Union (EU), 494

European Union (EU) Medical Device Regulation (EU MDR), 17, 39, 41–42, 380, 494, 506
evil twins, 59, 111
EvilTwin (Attack Frameworks), 118
explainable AI (XAI), 356–357, 487
extended detection and response (CDR), 481
extensibility, as a strength of Suricata, 329
Extensible Authentication Protocol (EAP), 59, 117

F

failover systems, for DoS attacks, 219
fairness, 499
false negatives, machine learning and, 355–356
False Positive Rate (FPR), 344
false positives
  as a challenge in implementing AI-driven defenses, 485
  of Snort, 325
  machine learning and, 355–356
  reducing, as a capability of AI-driven threat detection, 181
FDA Pacemaker Recall, 240
feature engineering, 342–344, 355
feature extraction and classification, machine learning and, 341
Federal Trade Commission (FTC), 494
federated learning, 356, 486
Fedora Security Spin, 86, 87
feedback loops, 355
Fern Wi-Fi Cracker, 85, 128–131
files
  extraction as a capability of Suricata, 328
  integrity checking as a capability of Open Source Security (OSSEC) HIDS, 319
  transfer capabilities with BlueMaho, 98

financial losses
  about, 479
  from DoS attacks, 213
  from man-in-the-middle (MITM) attacks, 164
  as a risk of pacemakers, 241
fingerprinting, 61
firewalls
  about, 19
  for DoS attacks, 219
  enhancing with machine learning, 358–359
  for inter-VLAN communication, 174–175
  for telemedicine, 34
  for wireless remote patient monitoring, 33
firmware
  as a challenge for IoMT devices, 111, 113–114
  for DoS attacks, 223
  as a mitigation strategy for pacemaker vulnerabilities, 243
  MITM attacks and, 166
  quantum attack on, 463–466
  unpatched, as a vulnerability of wearable medical devices, 284–285
  as a vulnerability of insulin pumps, 251
5G
  about, 27, 40, 362–363, 384–385, 443–445, 505
  future research directions, 455–456
  impact on IoMT, 445–447
  industry collaboration, 456–458
  IoMT and, 20
  knowledge sharing, 456–458
  regulatory considerations, 450–455
  security implications for IoMT, 447–450
flexibility
  as a capability of Open Source Security (OSSEC) HIDS, 320

as a capability of Suricata, 328, 329
as a capability of Wifite, 136
Flipper Zero, 87–88
flooding attacks, 209–210
Food and Drug Administration (FDA), 17, 41, 42, 240, 252–253, 259–260, 379–380, 414–415, 470, 493–494, 506, 513–514
forensic analysis
  as a capability
    of Check Point IPS, 314
    of Snort, 324
  IDPS deployment and, 332
  Wireshark for, 154
forensic data preservation, 277
Fortune Business Insights' IoMT Market Research Report, 447
forward secrecy
  about, 57
  as a benefit of WPA3, 169
  as a key feature of BLUFFS attacks, 77
freedom of movement, as a benefit of wireless devices, 24, 29
frequency bands/channels, for Wi-Fi, 53
functionality, as a challenge of implementing secure communication protocols, 382
future trends
  about, 441–442
  for ethical hacking, 520–521
  for medical device communication, 384–386
  in regulatory frameworks, 504–505
  secrecy violations as a key feature of BLUFFS attacks, 77
  for wireless devices, 40–41

G

GATTacker, 96–97
General Data Protection Regulation (GDPR), 414, 494, 506–507, 514
general medical devices, 264
Generic Access Profile (GAP) layer, for Bluetooth Low Energy (BLE), 50
Generic Attribute Profile (GATT) protocol, 50, 96–97
Generic Token Card (GTC), 118
genomic data, 505
Ghidra, 273
global harmonization, as a challenge of regulatory frameworks, 501
glucose levels, IoMT devices for monitoring, 6
Google Vertex AI, 483
GPU acceleration, as a capability of Hashcat, 131
granular controls, as a capability of Check Point IPS, 313
graph neural networks (GNNs), 349
Great Scott Gadgets, 94
Grimwepa, 84

H

hardcoded credentials, MITM attacks and, 166
hard-coded passwords, 186
hardware limitations, as a challenge of quantum computing, 463
hardware security modules (HSMs), 374
hash cracking integration, Fern Wi-Fi Cracker for, 129
hash functions, 374
Hash-Based Message Authentication Code (HMAC), 369
hash-based signatures, 466
Hashcat, 118, 131–133
Hciconfig, 83
HCIDump, 98–99
hcxdumptool/hcxtools, 83
Health Information Technology for Economic and Clinical Health (HITECH) Act, 38–39, 156, 221, 415
Health Insurance Portability and Accountability Act (HIPAA), 17, 38–39, 109, 156, 221, 380, 414, 494, 513

health thermometer service, 51
healthcare industry
  Bluetooth in, 47–52
  exploits, 116
  impact of IoMT in, 5–16
  IoMT in, 3–22
  IoT devices case study, 103
  mitigation strategies for, 169–194
  PEAP exchange attacks and, 119
  preparing for quantum
    computing, 473–475
  Wi-Fi in, 52–58
Healthcare Information Security and
  Privacy Practitioner
  (HCISPP), 521–522
hearing aids, NFC for, 29
heart rate monitors, 6, 200
high configuration overhead, as a
  challenge of open Source Security
  (OSSEC) HIDS, 321
high resource requirements, as a
  challenge of Palo Alto Networks
  Threat Prevention, 318
high-performance traffic analysis, as a
  capability of Trend Micro
  TippingPoint, 309–310
HIPAA Journal, 270
HL7 Fast Healthcare Interoperability
  Resources (FHIR), 39, 373, 452
holographic communications, 6G
  and, 445
homomorphic encryption, 355
hospital equipment management,
  targeted RFID in, 35–36
hospital wristbands, NFC for, 28
host-based IDS (HIDS), 180, 300
host-to-controller (HCI) interface, for
  Bluetooth Low Energy (BLE), 50
human oversight, 355, 500
human training, 257
hybrid attacks, Hashcat for, 132
hybrid cryptography, 469
hybrid detection techniques, 301, 303
hydration levels, IoMT devices for
  monitoring, 6

I
IBM QRadar SOAR, 483
ICD Study, 238–239
IDA Pro, 273
identification badges, 426
identity and access management
  (IAM) systems, 392
identity-based attacks, 270
IDPS solutions
  about, 304–306
  Check Point Intrusion Prevention
    System/Quantum, 312–315
  Cisco Secure Intrusion Prevention
    System (NGIPS), 306–309
  Open Source Security (OSSEC)
    HIDS, 319–323
  Palo Alto Networks Threat
    Prevention, 315–319
  Snort, 323–327
  Suricata, 327–331
  Trend Micro TippingPoint, 309–312
IEC 62304 Medical Device Software
  life cycle processes, 381, 415
IEEE 802.11i (WPA2/WPA3), 372
imaging systems, vulnerabilities
  of, 37–38
impact assessment, 257
impersonation attacks
  about, 256
  as a common Bluetooth
    vulnerability, 72–75
  preventing, as a benefit of mutual
    authentication, 172
implantable medical devices (IMDs)
  cardiac devices, 386
  pacemakers, 232
  replay attacks on, 198
  security concerns with, 35
implementing
  defense-in-depth strategies,
    383
  device authentication, 171–174
  errors, as a challenge of Bluetooth
    security, 71
  network isolation, 178

proactive vulnerability
    management, 177–178
role-based access control
    (RBAC), 398
incident response
  about, 188, 384
  as a benefit of network segmentation
    and isolation, 175
  best practices, 417–419
  Bettercap for training in, 122
  drills for, 184
  drills for DoS attacks, 223
  Hashcat for, 133
  IDPS deployment and, 332
  incident investigation, 299
  incident reconstruction, 277
  incident reporting, 317, 496
  for IoMT devices, 20
  for telemedicine, 34
  training and awareness programs for
    enhanced, 185
indicators of attack (IOAs), 266, 298
indicators of compromise (IOCs),
    266, 298
individualized data encryption, 57
Industrial, Scientific, and Medical
    (ISM) band, 48
industry collaboration, 5G
    and, 456–458
industry support, as a strength of
    Snort, 324
informed consent, 498
infusion pumps, 264
Initial Reconnaissance stage, in
    BLUFFS attacks, 77
injecting malware, 115
inline threat prevention, as a
    capability of Palo Alto Networks
    Threat Prevention, 316
innovation, policymakers
    enabling, 508
insider threats, 32, 172
Institute of Electrical and Electronics
    Engineers (IEEE), 42

insulin pump vulnerabilities and
    exploits case studies
  about, 247–249, 387
  education and training, 261
  FDA warning on insulin
    pumps, 259–260
  mitigation strategies, 260–261
  ransomware attacks, 260
  security research, 259
  vulnerabilities in insulin
    pumps, 249–258
integrity
  in CIA triad, 68–70
  as a security requirement for
    communication, 368–369
intellectual property protection,
    regulatory frameworks
    and, 497–498
interception risk
  with RFID technology, 36
  of surgical and imaging systems, 38
interference, as a risk of wireless
    remote patient monitoring, 32
International Data Corporation
    (IDC), 448
International Electrotechnical
    Commission (IEC), 288, 495
International Organization for
    Standardization (ISO), 42, 495
international regulations, 514–515
Internet Control Message Protocol
    (ICMP), 209
Internet of Medical Things (IoMT)
  about, 1–2
  applications of, 16–17
  best practices for security of, 18–20
  challenges and considerations in
    adoption of, 17–18
  future trends in, 20–22
  in healthcare, 3–22
  how it works in healthcare, 16–17
  impact of, in healthcare, 5–16
  impact of 5G on, 445–447
  replay attacks, 197–201

risk landscape, 264–268
secure device management, 110
security implications for, 447–450
spoofing attacks, 197–198, 202–206
vulnerabilities of, 264–265
Internet of Things (IoT)
  Bettercap for device security audits, 122
  botnets, 396
  Kismet for device monitoring, 139
  proliferation, as a challenge in securing medical devices, 168
Internet Protocol Security (IPsec), 372, 431
interoperability
  as a challenge of implementing secure communication protocols, 382
  as a challenge of regulatory frameworks, 501
  as a challenge of wireless devices, 24
  requirements for 5G, 452–453
interslice attacks, 448
intrusion detection and prevention systems (IDSs/IPSs)
  about, 297–299
  best practices for IDPS deployment, 331–333
  case study, 302–304
  deploying, 179–182, 217
  ecosystems, 299
  innovations in, 333–336
  integrating machine learning with, 357–358
  in IoMT environments, 299–302
  lack of, as a vulnerability of pacemakers, 235
  as a mitigation strategy
    for pacemaker vulnerabilities, 243
    for replay attacks, 201
  solutions, 304–331
  for telemedicine, 34
  for wireless remote patient monitoring, 33

inventory and management, best practices, 409–411
IoMT botnets, wearable devices and, 289–290
IoMT device exploitation, 255
ISM band, 68
ISO 14971, 415
ISO/IEC 27001 standards, 252–254, 380–381, 454, 470, 514–515
isolation, deploying, 174–176
Ivanti Neurons for Patch Management, 481

J

Jack, Barnaby (researcher), 259
jamming, 96, 210–211
Jira, 484
Joe Sandbox, 273
John the Ripper, 118
Joint Test Action Group (JTAG), 251–252
Just Works Modes, 378

K

Kali Linux, 83, 86
Kcitool, 83
key compromise, as a key feature of BLUFFS attacks, 76–77
key exchange protocols, 374
Key Extraction and Analysis stage, in BLUFFS attacks, 77
key management, 373–377
Key Negotiation of Bluetooth (KNOB) attack, 58
Key Reinstallation Attack (KRACK) exploit, 54, 57, 62
key storage, 378
Kismet, 85, 86, 138–141
K-nearest neighbors (KNN), 345
knowledge sharing
  5G and, 456–458
  as key component of IoMT IDS, 300
  quantum computing and, 474–475

L

lateral movement, PEAP exchange attacks and, 119
lattice-based cryptography, 466
layered security, adopting, 332
least privilege principle, 370
least privilege segmentation, as a mitigation strategy for wearable devices, 291
legacy systems
  as a challenge
    of Bluetooth security, 71
    of ethical hacking, 519
    of implementing AI-driven defenses, 484–485
    of implementing secure communication protocols, 382
    of regulatory frameworks, 502
    in securing medical devices, 168
  for DoS attacks, 223
  exploited, 255
  as a vulnerability
    enabling DoS attacks, 215–216
    of insulin pumps, 251
legal considerations
  about, 491
  for ethical hacking, 513–515
  for machine learning in wireless security, 361–362
  regulatory frameworks and, 495–498
lessons learned, Bluetooth vulnerabilities, 102–103
liability and responsibility, regulatory frameworks and, 497
life support equipment, man-in-the-middle (MITM) attacks and, 163
lifecycle management, support for, 188
limited resources, as a challenge in securing medical devices, 168
limiting discoverability, 102
Link protocol, of Bluetooth Low Energy (BLE), 50
Linux distributions, 83–87
local laws, 514
locking mechanisms, 426
log analysis
  about, 278
  as a capability of Open Source Security (OSSEC) HIDS, 319
  IDPS deployment and, 332
logging and monitoring systems, 384
Logical Link Control and Adaptation Protocol (L2CAP)
  about, 88–89
  for Bluetooth Low Energy (BLE), 50
  with PyBluez, 100
Long Range Wide Area Network (LoRaWAN), 23, 27
long-term data security, as a challenge of quantum computing, 463
LootyBooty (EAP-GTC Downgrade), as a Wi-Fi security risk, 59
loss of trust, as a risk of pacemakers, 241

M

machine learning (ML)
  about, 12–13, 40, 338–339
  for anomaly detection, 385
  applications in healthcare and IoMT, 350–352
  case studies, 362–364
  challenges in applying to wireless security in IoMT, 352–356
  ethical and legal considerations, 361–362
  for ethical hacking, 520
  feature engineering for wireless attack detection, 342–344
  future directions, 356–360
  governance in, 504
  how it enhances wireless attack detection, 341–342
  IDPS deployment and, 332
  importance of for wireless attack detection, 339–341
  IoMT and, 20
  as a strength of Cisco Secure IPS, 308

techniques, 344–350
malware
  AI-generated, 477
  as a capability of Suricata, 328
  for digital forensics investigations, 272–280
  injecting, 115
  as a risk of wireless remote patient monitoring, 32
  of surgical and imaging systems, 37–38
management complexity, as a challenge of Check Point IPS, 315
management servers, as key component of IoMT IDS, 300
mandatory security controls, 496
man-in-the-middle (MITM) attacks
  about, 161–162
  advanced monitoring for, 179–182
  as a capability
    of WiFi Pineapple, 147
    of Wifiphisher, 151
    of WiFi-Pumpkin, 149
  as a challenge of Bluetooth security, 71
  challenges in securing medical devices, 168
  collaboration with vendors for, 186–190
  as a common Bluetooth vulnerability, 75–76
  data theft, 167
  device authentication for, 171–174
  device manipulation, 167–168
  encryption for healthcare communication, 169–171
  Fern Wi-Fi Cracker for, 129
  impacts on medical devices of, 167–168
  intrusion detection systems (IDSs) for, 179–182
  intrusion protection systems (IPSs) for, 179–182
  key benefits of mitigation strategy, 190–194
  as a key feature of BLUFFS attacks, 77
  key vulnerabilities enabling, 164–167
  mitigation strategies
    as a benefit of mutual authentication, 172
    for healthcare organizations, 169–190
  network segmentation and isolation for, 174–176
  operational disruption, 168
  patient safety risks, 167–168
  privacy violations, 167
  real-world implications of, 163–164
  as a risk of wireless remote patient monitoring, 32
  system downtime, 168
  training and awareness programs for, 182–185
  types of, 162–163
  updates and patching for, 176–179
  as a Wi-Fi security risk, 59
MarketsandMarkets' IoMT Market Report, 447
Massive Machine-Type Communications (mMTC), 444
McLaren Health Care, 270
Medical Device Regulation (EU MDR), 17, 39, 41–42, 380, 494, 506
medical devices. *See* devices
medical imaging, impact of 5G on, 446
medication delivery systems
  about, 264
  man-in-the-middle (MITM) attacks and, 163
  replay attacks on, 198
medication management, using IoMT devices, 17
MedSec and St. Jude Medical Controversy, 239–240
Medtronic's MiniMed 600 Series insulin pumps, 259–260

Medtronic's Paceart Optima System
  Risks, 241
memory analysis, for malware
  analysis, 272, 273
Metasploit, 252
metrology, in medical devices, 467–468
micro-learning modules, 185
Microsoft Azure DDoS Protection, 221
Microsoft Copilot, 63, 483
Microsoft Defender for Office 365, 481
Microsoft Defender XDR, 481, 483, 484
Microsoft Sentinel, 481, 484
miniaturization, as a key feature of
  pacemakers, 232
mitigation strategies
  about, 60–61
  with Bluetooth, 71, 100–103
  captive portal attacks, 116–117
  for DoS attacks, 217–224
  for healthcare organizations, 169–194
  for insulin pumps, 260–261
  for pacemaker
    vulnerabilities, 242–244
  PEAP vulnerabilities, 119–120
  quantum computing and, 474
  for replay attacks, 200–201
  for spoofing attacks, 205–206
  vulnerabilities, 67–103
  for wearable device threats, 290–291
MITRE ATT&CK, 517
mobile integration, as a vulnerability
  of insulin pumps, 250
MobSF, 252
model adaptation, 353
modernization, as a benefit of
  wearable devices, 283
modular design, Fern Wi-Fi
  Cracker of, 129
multi-algorithm support, as a
  capability of Hashcat, 131
multi-dongle support, with
  BlueMaho, 98
multifactor authentication (MFA)
  about, 271, 370, 375

  for DoS attacks, 218
  enforcing for administrative
    access, 172–173
  as a mitigation strategy for replay
    attacks, 201
  MITM attacks and, 165
  using for device access, 397–398
  Wi-Fi and, 109
multiple protocol support, as a
  capability of Wifite, 136
multivariate cryptography, 467
mutual authentication
  about, 172
  for DoS attacks, 218
  as a mitigation strategy for replay
    attacks, 201
Mutual TLS (mTLS), 205

N

nanotechnology, IoMT and, 21
Nanox.AI's Imaging Solutions, 293
National Institute of Standards and
  Technology (NIST), 451, 469–470
National Security Agency (NSA), 469
natural language processing
  (NLP), 476
Near Field Communication (NFC), 24,
  28–29, 378
network access control (NAC), 392
network address translation
  (NAT), 175
Network and Information Systems
  (NIS) Directive, 494
Network of the National Library of
  Medicine (NNLM), 80
network segmentation and isolation
  about, 332, 384
  AI-driven network, 482–483
  best practices, 396–397
  as a capability of Palo Alto Networks
    Threat Prevention, 317
  as a challenge for IoMT devices,
    111, 113
  deploying, 174–176

enhanced with machine learning, 352
implementing
  about, 178
  as a mitigation strategy for DoS attacks, 217
  for IoMT devices, 19
  lack of, as a vulnerability of spoofing, 204
  as a mitigation strategy for spoofing attacks, 206
  Wi-Fi and, 54, 107–108
networks
  analysis, for malware analysis for digital forensics investigations, 272
  analysis tools for malware analysis, 273
  audits
    for DoS attacks, 223
    Fern Wi-Fi Cracker for, 129
    Reaver for, 143
  best practices for security of, 393–394
  Bettercap for reconnaissance, 122
  breaches
    about, 263–264
    vulnerabilities of, 264–265
  deploying controls, 102
  ethical hacking infrastructure, 512
  Fern Wi-Fi Cracker for monitoring, 129
  Kismet for optimizing, 139
  network-based IDPS, 302–303
  network-based IDS (NIDS), 180
  PEAP exchange attacks and impersonation, 118
  scanning and discovery
    as a capability of WiFi-Pumpkin, 149
    Fern Wi-Fi Cracker for, 128
  slicing vulnerabilities, 448–449
  traffic monitoring as a capability of Snort, 323
  visibility

advanced monitoring tools for improving, 181
as a challenge of open Source Security (OSSEC) HIDS, 321
Wireshark for troubleshooting, 154
neural networks, 345
Newlin, Marc (researcher), 82
next-generation firewalls (NGFWs), 394
NIST Frameworks, 415–416
NIST Post-Quantum Cryptography Standardization, 469–470
nitrogen-vacancy (NV), 467
nonces, as a mitigation strategy for replay attacks, 201

O

OAuth 2.0, 376
onboarding, 377–379, 422–425
128-bit encryption, 56–57
192-bit encryption, 56–57
on-premised integration, as a capability of Palo Alto Networks Threat Prevention, 317
open ports, MITM attacks and, 166
Open Source Security (OSSEC) HIDS, 319–323
OpenID Connect, 376
open-source advantage, as a strength of Suricata, 329
open-source intelligence (OSINT), 255
open-source software, 498
operational continuity, 175, 179
operational disruption
  about, 479
  from DoS attacks, 213
  from man-in-the-middle (MITM) attacks, 164
  MITM attacks and, 168
operational impact, 335, 515
operational risks, as a risk of pacemakers, 241
Opportunistic Wireless Encryption (OWE), 54–55, 57, 105–107

organizational resilience, 508
Ossmann, Michael (developer), 94
out-of-band (OOB) management, 175, 377

P

pacemaker hacking case studies
  about, 229
  components of pacemakers, 231
  consequences of pacemaker hacking, 244–245
  ethical hacking demonstration, 236–241
  heart function, 230
  how it works, 231–232
  impact of pacemaker vulnerabilities, 241–242
  implanting pacemakers, 232
  mitigation strategies for pacemaker vulnerabilities, 242–244
  patient quality of life and pacemakers, 233
  replay attacks on, 200
  risks and limitations of pacemakers, 230, 233
  vulnerabilities in pacemakers, 233–235
packet analysis, 61
packet capture, as a capability of Wireshark, 154
packet injection, 60, 121
packet logging, as a capability of Snort, 324
packet sniffing, 147, 149
pairing, 70, 101, 171
Pairwise Master Key Identifier (PMKID) cracking, as a Wi-Fi security risk, 59
Palo Alto Networks Threat Prevention, 315–319
parallel processing, as a capability of Suricata, 327
Parrot Security OS, 84, 86
passive MITM attacks, 162
passive tags, 28
passkey entry, 378
passwords
  about, 398–401
  AI-powered password cracking, 478
  Aircrack-ng for cracking, 121
  Hashcat for policy evaluation, 133
PATCH Act, 170
patches
  best practices, 401–403
  ensuring regular, 176–179
  IDPS deployment and, 332
  for IoMT devices, 19
  lack of
    as a vulnerability of insulin pumps, 250
    as a vulnerability of pacemakers, 234–235
  as a mitigation strategy
    for Bluetooth vulnerabilities, 101
    for DoS attacks, 223
    for replay attacks, 201
    for spoofing attacks, 205–206
  as a mitigation strategy for pacemaker vulnerabilities, 243
  as a risk of wireless remote patient monitoring, 32
  for telemedicine, 34
  testing/validation, 177
patent protection, 497
patient advocacy, 508
patient autonomy, 498
patient consent, 495
patient flow, efficiency in, 15
patient safety
  about, 479–480
  advanced monitoring tools for protecting, 181
  as a benefit of device authentication, 174
  improved, as a benefit of update and patch management, 179
  of man-in-the-middle (MITM) attacks, 163, 167–168

RFID for, 28
as a risk of pacemakers, 239, 241
training and awareness programs for increased, 185
patients
  engagement, as a benefit of wearable devices, 283
  privacy, as a risk of pacemakers, 245
  protecting data during ethical hacking, 515
  trust improvements
    as a benefit of strong encryption, 171
    loss of, as a risk of pacemakers, 245
pattern matching, as a capability of Snort, 323
penetration testing
  about, 54
  Bettercap for, 122
  coWPAtty for, 126
  for DoS attacks, 223
  Fern Wi-Fi Cracker for, 129
  IOCs, IOAs and, 266
  Kismet for, 139
  as a mitigation strategy for DoS attacks, 224
  Reaver for, 143
  Wifite for, 136
Pentoo, 85, 86
perimeter security, best practices, 394–395
permission, obtaining for ethical hacking, 515
Persistent Control and Monitoring stage, in BLUFFS attacks, 78
personal health information (PHI), 167, 510
personal health tracking, using IoMT devices, 17
personalized medicine, 505
personalized security configurations, wearable devices and, 293
personalized treatment, as a benefit of wearable devices, 283

pestudio, 273
phishing
  AI-enhanced, 477, 482
  campaigns for, 256
  as a challenge for IoMT devices, 111, 114–115
  as a security risk in telemedicine, 34
  simulations for, 184
physical access, 235, 250
Physical protocol, of Bluetooth Low Energy (BLE), 50
physical security
  about, 254, 256, 257
  best practices, 425–427
  ethical hacking, 512–513
  as a mitigation strategy for insulin pumps, 260
  as a mitigation strategy for pacemaker vulnerabilities, 243
  testing, 255–256
Picture Archiving and Communication Systems (PACS), 199
platform exploits, as a security risk in telemedicine, 34
plugin support, as a capability of WiFi-Pumpkin, 149
policy enforcement, as a capability of Check Point IPS, 314
post-capture analysis, as a capability of Wireshark, 154
post-market approval, 496
post-quantum cryptography, 385
post-quantum Transport Layer Security, 468
post-test support, for ethical hacking, 518
power consumption, 52, 249
pre-auditing networks, coWPAtty for, 126
Pre-Cert Program (FDA), 506
predictive analytics, wearable devices and, 292
pre-market approval, 496

preparation, for malware analysis for digital forensics investigations, 272
preprocessing, 343
prescription fraud, man-in-the-middle (MITM) attacks and, 164
Pre-Shared Key (PSK) authentication, 54, 57, 105
pretexting, 256
principal component analysis (PCA), 344, 346
privacy
  with Bluetooth, 70–71
  breaches, as a security risk in telemedicine, 34
  considerations
    in data collection and sharing, 354
    for quantum computing, 470–472
  as a risk of wireless remote patient monitoring, 33
  public health compared with, 500
  regulations for 5G, 451–452
  violations
    man-in-the-middle (MITM) attacks and, 163–164
    MITM attacks and, 167
privacy by design, 502–503
proactive botnet mitigation, wearable devices and, 292
proactive threat mitigation, as a strength of Palo Alto Networks Threat Prevention, 317
proactive threat response, 299
proactive vendor partnerships, 177
processing power, as a vulnerability of insulin pumps, 251
professionalism, during ethical hacking, 516
profiles, Bluetooth Low Energy (BLE), 51
programmability, as a key feature of pacemakers, 232
proprietary rulesets, as a capability of Snort, 324

Protected Extensible Authentication Protocol (PEAP), 117–120
protected health information (PHI), 163–164, 392
Protected Management Frames (PMF), 107
protection services, as a mitigation strategy for DoS attacks, 219–222
protocols
  analysis
    as a capability of Snort, 323
    as a capability of Wireshark, 154
  awareness, as a strength of Suricata, 328
  detection, as a capability of Suricata, 328
Proximity Profile, 51
pseudonymization, 408–409
public health, privacy compared with, 500
Public Key Infrastructure (PKI), 171, 374
public networks, protection for, 57
purpose limitation, 496
PyBluez, 99–101

Q

QR code-based printing, 377–378
quality of life, pacemakers and, 233
Qualys VMDR, 481
quantum communications, 6G and, 444
quantum computing
  about, 459
  applications of, 461–462
  challenges of, 462–463
  ethical and privacy considerations, 470–472
  for ethical hacking, 521
  fundamentals of, 459–461
  future research directions, 472–473
  preparing healthcare industry for, 473–475
quantum attack on IoMT firmware, 463–466

quantum sensing and metrology, 467–468
quantum-resistant cryptography, 466–467
quantum-safe network protocols, 468–469
regulatory and standardization efforts, 469–470
threats, 450
Quantum Internet for Healthcare, 473
Quantum Key Distribution (QKD), 460, 461
Quantum Machine Learning (QML), 349–350, 461
quantum random number generation (QRNG), 461
quantum sensing, in medical devices, 467–468
quantum simulation, 462
quantum-enhanced anomaly detection, 472
quantum-resistant cryptography, 385, 466–467, 486
quantum-resistant lightweight cryptography, 472
quantum-resistant virtual private networks, 468–469
quantum-safe cryptography standards, 504–505
quantum-safe network protocols, for medical devices, 468–469
Quantum-Safe Secure Boot and Firmware Updates, 472–473
qubits, 460–461

R

Radio Frequency Communication (RFCOMM), 88–89
Radio-Frequency Identification (RFID), 24, 28, 35–36
ransomware
  about, 396
  AI-powered, 477
  on hospital networks impacting insulin pumps, 260
  increased sophistication of, 269–270
  man-in-the-middle (MITM) attacks and, 164
  as a risk of wireless remote patient monitoring, 32
  of surgical and imaging systems, 37–38
rate limiting, as a mitigation strategy for DoS attacks, 219
rate responsiveness, as a key feature of pacemakers, 232
reactive jamming, 210
real-time alerting, as a capability of Open Source Security (OSSEC) HIDS, 320
real-time analysis, 154, 342
real-time automated responses, 303
real-time communication, for ethical hacking, 518
real-time data transmission, impact of 5G on, 445–446
real-time detection
  about, 61, 298
  advanced monitoring tools for, 181
  as a capability of Check Point IPS, 312
  improving with machine learning, 360
  requirements for, 353
  as a strength of Snort, 324
real-time intelligence integration, as a capability of Palo Alto Networks Threat Prevention, 316
real-time mitigation, as a capability of Check Point IPS, 314
real-time monitoring
  for DoS attacks, 218
  as key function of IDPS in IoMT, 300
  as a mitigation strategy for spoofing attacks, 206
real-time progress tracking, as a capability of Wifite, 136

real-time protection, as a strength of Open Source Security (OSSEC) HIDS, 321
real-time threat intelligence, 308
real-time threat prevention, as a capability of Palo Alto Networks Threat Prevention, 316
real-time updates, as a capability of Suricata, 328
Reaver, 84, 86, 141–145
Received Signal Strength Indicator (RSSI), 343
recognition programs, 185
reconnaissance, 121, 266
Recorded Future, 481
recurrent neural networks (RNNs), 342, 347–348
redirecting traffic, 115
refresher training, 185
regulators, role of, 193–194
regulatory compliance
  about, 299
  advanced monitoring tools for, 181
  as a benefit of device authentication, 174
  as a best practice for wireless technology implementation, 44
  best practices, 414–417
  as a capability
    of Check Point IPS, 313
    of Palo Alto Networks Threat Prevention, 317
  as a challenge of ethical hacking, 519
  challenges with wearable devices and, 286–289
  improved, as a benefit of update and patch management, 179
  as key function of IDPS in IoMT, 300
  man-in-the-middle (MITM) attacks and, 164
  as a mitigation strategy
    for pacemaker vulnerabilities, 244
    for wearable devices, 291
  quantum computing and, 469–470
  standards and, 379–381
  as a strength of Cisco Secure IPS, 308
  training and awareness programs for, 185
regulatory considerations
  for 5G, 450–455
  for DoS attacks, 213
  for ethical hacking, 513–515
  as a risk of pacemakers, 241
regulatory frameworks
  about, 493
  benefits from regulation implementation, 505–507
  best practices for regulatory compliance, 502–504
  challenges in regulatory framework development, 500–502
  ethical considerations, 498–500
  future trends, 504–505
  key regulatory bodies and frameworks, 493–495
  legal considerations, 495–498
  stakeholder recommendations, 507–508
regulatory landscape, for wireless medical devices, 41–42
regulatory noncompliance, as a risk of wireless remote patient monitoring, 33
regulatory standards, compliance with, 57
reinforcement learning, 347, 405
Remote Authentication Dial-In User Service (RADIUS), 109, 376–377
remote medical support, using IoMT devices, 7–10
remote monitoring
  as a benefit of wearable devices, 283
  as a key feature of pacemakers, 232
  risks with, 31–33
  using IoMT devices, 16–17
remote reprogramming, as a risk of pacemakers, 240
replay attacks

about, 196–197
case study on infusion pumps, 199–200
examples of, 199–200
implications of in healthcare, 198–199
in IoTM systems, 197–198
mitigation strategies for, 200–201
reporting
during ethical hacking, 516
as key component of IoMT IDS, 300
for malware analysis for digital forensics investigations, 273
reputation damage, as a risk of pacemakers, 245
reputational, 479
research and development
Hashcat for, 133
as a risk of pacemakers, 241
resilience, against attacks, 57
resource capacity, limited, as a vulnerability enabling DoS attacks, 215
resource constraints
as a challenge
of Check Point IPS, 314
of ethical hacking, 520
of implementing secure communication protocols, 381–382
of open Source Security (OSSEC) HIDS, 321
of regulatory frameworks, 501–502
machine learning and, 354–355
in wireless devices, 353–354
resource demands, 325, 329
resource optimization, using IoMT devices for, 14–16
respiratory rate and oxygen saturation, IoMT devices for monitoring, 6
Responder, 116, 118
retail environment attack case study, 103
retention policies, best practices, 433–435

RFCOMM communications, with PyBluez, 100
risk assessment
conducting, 331
for ethical hacking, 517
quantum computing and, 474
risks
in application of wireless technologies in medical devices, 31–38
mitigating, as a key benefit of deception technology, 335
risk-based approach, 503
Rivest-Shamir-Adleman (RSA), 369
rogue access points
as a capability
of WiFi Pineapple, 147
of Wifiphisher, 151
of WiFi-Pumpkin, 149
as a challenge
for IoMT devices, 111, 112–113
in securing healthcare wireless networks, 157
detecting with machine learning, 351
as a Wi-Fi security risk, 59
role-based access control (RBAC), 19, 173, 370, 393, 398
routers, for Wi-Fi, 53
rule management complexity, as a challenge of Suricata, 329
rule-based attacks, Hashcat for, 132
rule-based detection, as a capability of Snort, 323

S

scalability
as a best practice for wireless technology implementation, 43
as a capability
of Open Source Security (OSSEC) HIDS, 320
of Palo Alto Networks Threat Prevention, 317

of Snort, 324
of Suricata, 327
of Trend Micro TippingPoint, 310
as a strength
of Check Point IPS, 314
of Cisco Secure IPS, 308
of Palo Alto Networks Threat Prevention, 318
scanning and reconnaissance, as a capability of WiFi Pineapple, 147
seamless integration
IDPS deployment and, 332
as a strength of Palo Alto Networks Threat Prevention, 317–318
using IoMT devices, 10–12
search and correlation, 277
secure boot, 383–384
secure remote access, as a benefit of MFA, 172
Secure Shell (SSH), 431
Secure Simple Pairing (SSP), 60, 70
Secure Sockets Layer (SSL), 163, 370–372
security
deploying solutions, 102
Reaver for training and research, 143
upgrades, as a challenge of implementing secure communication protocols, 382
security assessments
about, 383–384
as a best practice, 488
with vendors, 187
security by design
about, 507–508
as a best practice for wireless technology implementation, 43
for IoMT devices, 19
security information and event management (SIEM), 19, 180, 277, 358, 394
Security Manager (SM), for Bluetooth Low Energy (BLE), 50
security posture, as a benefit of device authentication, 173
security risks
of Bluetooth, 58–63
as a disadvantage of wireless devices, 24
for IoT devices, 57
of Wi-Fi, 58–63
segmentation
as a mitigation strategy for wearable devices, 291
with RFID technology, 36
for wireless remote patient monitoring, 33
semi-supervised learning, 346–347
sensitive data, capturing, 115
sensitive data environment (SDE), 156–157
sensors, 40–41, 300
SentinelOne Singularity XDR, 481, 483
sequence numbering, as a mitigation strategy for spoofing attacks, 205
service discovery, with PyBluez, 100
Service Discovery Protocol (SDP), 88–89
service level agreements (SLAs), 20, 188
ServiceNow, 484
services, Bluetooth Low Energy (BLE), 51
session hijacking
about, 163
in BLUFFS attacks, 77
Fern Wi-Fi Cracker for, 129
as a key feature of BLUFFS attacks, 76
session management, continuous validation and, 173
Session Manipulation and Data Injection stage, in BLUFFS attacks, 77
SHA-3 (Keccak), 369
SHA-256 (Secure Hash Algorithm 256-bit), 368–369

shared responsibility models, 497
Shor's algorithm, 462
signal replay attacks, as a risk of pacemakers, 240
Signal-to-Noise Ratio (SNR), 343
signature-based detection
　as a capability
　　of Palo Alto Networks Threat Prevention, 316
　　of Suricata, 328
　as a challenge of Trend Micro TippingPoint, 310
　as a key IDPS feature, 301
Silent Intrusions (Chirillo), 263
SIM swapping, 270–271
Simultaneous Authentication of Equals (SAE), 54–55, 57
6G, 20, 444
skill gap, as a challenge in implementing AI-driven defenses, 485
smart home device fingerprinting, for anomaly detection, 363–364
smart inhalers, 283
smart pill bottles/dispensers, 28, 36–37
smartphones, NFC for, 29
smartwatches, 283
sniffing, with BtleJack, 96
Snort, 180, 323–327
SOAR platforms, 483
social engineering attacks
　about, 254, 256, 257
　AI-assisted, 477–478
　ethical hacking, 513
　as a security risk in telemedicine, 34
software
　exploits, as a security risk in telemedicine, 34
　hardening, for DoS attacks, 223
　outdated, as a vulnerability enabling DoS attacks, 215–216
　unpatched, as a vulnerability of wearable medical devices, 284–285
　updates, as a mitigation strategy for wearable devices, 291
　as a vulnerability of insulin pumps, 251
Software as a Medical Device (SaMD), 506
something you are, 172
something you have, 172
something you know, 172
spatial features, 343
specialized certifications, for ethical hackers, 521–522
Spill, Dominic (developer), 94
Splink SOAR, 483
Splunk, 481
spoofing attacks
　about, 196–197
　in IoMT, 202
　mitigation strategies for, 205–206
　real-world implications of, 204
　with RFID technology, 36
Spooftooph, 84
spot jamming, 210
SQL injection, 255
SSL stripping, 149, 163
SSL/TLS decryption proxies, 355
staged approach, for ethical hacking, 517
stakeholders, recommendations for, 507–508
standards
　for 5G, 450–451
　as a challenge of regulatory frameworks, 501
　quantum computing and, 469–470
　regulatory compliance and, 379–381
　for Wi-Fi, 53
state laws, 514
static analysis, 272, 273
static application security testing (SAST), 19
Statista's IoMT and Connected Devices Statistics, 447
statistical analysis, with BlueMaho, 98
STORM, 145–146

streamlined workflows, as a benefit of wireless devices, 30
supervised learning, 344–345, 405
supply chain
  about, 188
  as a mitigation strategy for wearable devices, 291
  vendor attacks and, 270
  wearable devices and, 290, 293
supply management, RFID for, 28
support vector machines, 344
surgical systems, vulnerabilities of, 37–38
Suricata, 327–331
symmetric encryption, 373–374
SYN flood, 210
system control, 276
system downtime, man-in-the-middle (MITM) attacks and, 164, 168
system monitoring, as a capability of Open Source Security (OSSEC) HIDS, 319

T

tactics, techniques, and procedures (TTPs), 298, 517
tailgating, 255
tamper-evident seals, 426
targeted RFID, in hospital equipment management, 35–36
TCP handshake, 210
technical analysis, 275–280
technological advancement, as a challenge of regulatory frameworks, 501
telemedicine
  as a benefit of wireless devices, 30–31
  end-to-end encryption in, 386
  ethical hacking for, 521
  impact of 5G on, 446
  security risks in, 33–35
  using IoMT devices, 17
temperature levels, IoMT devices for monitoring, 6
temporal features, 343
Tenable.io with Nessus, 481
Terahertz (THz) communications, 444
Terminal Access Controller Access-Control System Plus (TACACS+), 376–377
3rd Generation Partnership Project (3GPP), 451
third-party apps, as a data privacy risk of wearable medical devices, 286
third-party audits, for telemedicine, 34
third-party integrations, as a risk of wireless remote patient monitoring, 33
third-party risk assessment, best practices, 411–414
third-party risk management, for IoMT devices, 20
threat detection
  AI-powered, 480
  as a capability of AI-driven threat detection, 181
  as key function of IDPS in IoMT, 300
  as a mitigation strategy for wearable devices, 291
  training and awareness programs for improved, 185
threat hunting, AI-enhanced, 487
threat intelligence
  about, 188
  as a capability of Check Point IPS, 313
  as a challenge of Snort, 325
  IDS and, 334
  integration with, 277
  as a key benefit of deception technology, 335
  monitoring, 178
threat landscape, as a challenge in securing healthcare wireless networks, 157
threat mitigation, artificial intelligence and, 62

Index ■ T–U

ThreatConnect, 481
timestamps, 201, 205
TLS 1.3 protocols, 19, 205, 242, 253
tools
  as a capability of Wifite, 136
  for malware analysis, 273–274
  vulnerabilities, 67–103
Toyota, 270
traffic
  Airdecap-ng for decrypting, 122
  filtering, as a capability of
    Wireshark, 154
  redirecting, 115
training and awareness
  about quantum computing, 474
  as a best practice, 488
  best practices, 420–422
  conducting, 182–185
  coWPAtty for, 126
  for ethical hackers, 521–522
  Fern Wi-Fi Cracker for, 129
  IDPS deployment and, 333
  for IoMT devices, 19
  Kismet for, 139
  as a mitigation strategy
    for DoS attacks, 223–224
    for pacemaker vulnerabilities, 244
    for spoofing attacks, 206
  for patients and healthcare
    providers, 261
  Wifite for, 137
  Wireshark for, 154
transfer learning, 348–349
transparency, 187–188, 499, 503–504
Transport Layer Security (TLS),
  370–372, 430
Trend Micro TippingPoint, 309–312
Trusted Platform Modules (TPMs), 374

U

Ubertooth One, 85, 94–95
UDP, 209–210
UL Cybersecurity Assurance Program
  (CAP), 454

Ultra-Reliable Low-Latency
  Communications (URLLC), 444
unauthorized access, 32, 285
unencrypted communication, as a risk
  of pacemakers, 240
unencrypted data transmission, as a
  challenge for IoMT devices,
  110, 111–112
unencrypted protocols, 255
unified data view, 278
Universal Asynchronous Receiver
  Transmitter (UART), 251–252
unsecured devices
  as a challenge in securing healthcare
    wireless networks, 157
  as a security risk in telemedicine, 34
  as a Wi-Fi security risk, 60
unsupervised learning, 345–346, 405
unused services, MITM attacks
  and, 166
updates
  best practices, 401–403
  as a challenge of Bluetooth
    security, 71
  continuous, 503
  ensuring regular, 176–179
  for IoMT devices, 19
  lack of
    as a vulnerability of insulin
      pumps, 250
    as a vulnerability of
      pacemakers, 234–235
  as a mitigation strategy
    for Bluetooth vulnerabilities, 101
    for DoS attacks, 223
    for insulin pumps, 260
    for replay attacks, 201
    for spoofing attacks, 205–206
  as a risk of wireless remote patient
    monitoring, 32
  for telemedicine, 34
usability, as a challenge of
  implementing secure
  communication protocols, 382

USB drops, 256
User and Entity Behavior Analytics (UEBA), 277, 278, 481
user awareness, 257
user education, as a mitigation strategy for wearable devices, 291
user feedback, 188
user permissions, 398
user spoofing, 202
user-centric design, as a best practice for wireless technology implementation, 43
user-controlled visibility, with Bluetooth, 71
usernames, 398–399

V

vendors
  accountability, as a mitigation strategy for pacemaker vulnerabilities, 244
  best practices, 411–414
  collaboration with, 186–190, 201
  communication with, 177
  role of, 192–194
virtual LANs (VLANs), 19, 54, 108, 175, 217
virtual private networks (VPNs), 33, 34
virtual reality (VR), IoMT and, 21
virtual wireless LANs (WLANs), 54
visualization, 122, 154
voice phishing (vishing), 256
Volatility, 273
Voltaire (author), 24
vulnerabilities
  AI-powered management, 482
  assessments of, 383–384
  Bluetooth, 67–103
  conducting scans, 178
  disclosure of, 388, 496
  DoS attacks and, 214–217
  enabling MITM attacks, 164–167
  in insulin pump communications, 387
  for insulin pumps, 248–249, 250–251
  of IoMT, 264–265
  mitigating Bluetooth, 100–103
  of network breaches, 264–265
  for pacemakers, 233–235, 248
  PEAP exchange, 117–119
  testing
    with BlueMaho, 98
    for insulin pumps, 251–258
    for wearable medical devices, 284–285

W

Wave Browser, 274–275
wearable ECG monitors, 24, 283
wearable medical devices
  about, 282
  artificial intelligence (AI) and, 291–294
  benefits of, 283
  data privacy risks, 285–286
  machine learning and, 350–351
  new trends and threats in, 289–290
  proactive measures for mitigating threats to, 290–291
  regulatory and compliance challenges, 286–289
  rise of, 282–283
  security challenges of, 283–289
  vulnerabilities in, 284–285
wearable sleep trackers, 283
Web Application Firewalls (WAFs), 394
web application testing, 255
WEP cracking, Fern Wi-Fi Cracker for, 128
WiFi Pineapple, 146–149
Wi-Fi Protected Access 3 (WPA3), 54–55, 58, 60, 105, 219
Wi-Fi Protected Setup (WPS) protocol, 128–129, 141
Wifiphisher, 116, 151–153

WiFi-Pumpkin, 115, 149–151
Wifite, 84, 134–138
Wired Equivalent Privacy (WEP), 165
wireless access points, 255
wireless audio streaming, as a primary use of Bluetooth Classic, 49
wireless communication
  insecure
    as a risk of pacemakers, 239
    as a vulnerability enabling DoS attacks, 214
    as a vulnerability of insulin pumps, 250
    as a vulnerability of pacemakers, 234
  securing, as a mitigation strategy for pacemaker vulnerabilities, 242
Wireless Fidelity (Wi-Fi)
  about, 23, 26, 46–47, 104–105
  best practices, 158
  hacking tools
    about, 120
    Aircrack-ng, 120–122
    Bettercap, 122–125
    coWPAtty, 125–127
    evolution of, 156
    Fern Wi-Fi Cracker, 128–131
    Hashcat, 131–133
    Kismet, 138–141
    Reaver, 141–145
    STORM, 145–146
    WiFi Pineapple, 146–149
    Wifiphisher, 151–153
    WiFi-Pumpkin, 149–151
    Wifite, 134–138
    Wireshark, 153–156
  Hashcat for penetration testing, 133
  in healthcare, 52–58
  operational guide for healthcare compliance, 156–159
  protected access weaknesses as a Wi-Fi security risk, 59
  security
    about, 105, 110

challenges for device management, 110–111
Opportunistic Wireless Encryption (OWE), 105–107
Protected Management Frames (PMF), 107
secure IoMT device management, 110
WPA3, 105
security risks of in healthcare, 58–63
sensitive data environment (SDE), 157
vulnerabilities
  about, 111
  captive portals, 115–117
  deauthentication attacks, 114
  disassociation attacks, 114
  evil twin attacks, 112–113
  insecure IoMT devices, 113–114
  lack of network segmentation, 113
  outdated firmware, 113–114
  phishing, 114–115
  Protected Extensible Authentication Protocol (PEAP), 117–120
  rogue access points, 112–113
  unencrypted data transmission, 111–112
  weak authentication protocols, 112
wireless infrastructure, as a mitigation strategy for DoS attacks, 219
wireless intrusion detection and prevention systems (WIDS/WIPS), 117
wireless networks
  encryption for, 169
  overloaded, as a vulnerability enabling DoS attacks, 216
  Wireshark for auditing, 154
wireless power transfer technology, 41
wireless remote patient monitoring, risks with, 31–33
wireless technologies
  about, 23–24
  benefits of in medical devices, 29–31

best practices for implementation of, 43–44
emerging trends, 40–41
future directions, 40–41
integration challenges and considerations, 38–40
in medical devices, 24–29
regulatory landscape for, 41–42
risks in applications of, in medical devices, 31–38
Wireshark, 83, 86, 118, 153–156, 273
workstations, unlocked, 256
World Health Organization (WHO), 288
WPA/WPA2 cracking, Fern Wi-Fi Cracker for, 128

Z
Zero Trust Architecture (ZTA), 217, 359, 405–407, 489
zero-day protection, as a capability of Check Point IPS, 313
zero-day threats, addressing, 178
ZeroSevenGroup, 270
zero-trust network architecture (ZTNA), 393
Zigbee, 23, 26–27, 214, 352, 372